A SYMPHONY OF LIFE

Triumph of Education Over Adversity

A Journey of a Persian-American Woman through War, Love, Revolution, and Freedom

Simin M. Redjali, Ph.D. FAAIDD

To order additional copies of this book, contact:
Xlibris LLC
1-888-795-4274
www.Xlibris.com
Orders@Xlibris.com
110319

Dedicated to my grandchildren,
Cameron and Sophia,
and to future generations.

CONTENTS

Fourth Movement: A New World

PREFACE AND ACKNOWLEDGEMENTS

This book, like a symphony, is composed of four 'movements.' With this 'movement' structure, I weave the notes of my life's story into a number of musical 'themes.' The story's 'melody' and 'development' are my transition from Iran's ruling class to my job-seeking struggles in the United States; the story's 'counterpoint'—social and historical changes I experienced: wars, revolutions and peace. My story reveals the shifts in 'tempo' and 'themes' in my life, with 'leitmotivs' of love and family, individual freedom, and unwavering hope for humanity. As a well-known public figure in Iran in the mid-twentieth century during the time of Iran's westernization and modernization, I was encouraged, motivated and obliged by my colleagues, former students, and friends to write this psycho-social and historical autobiography, which follows in parallel the social and historical events in the 20th and 21st century in Iran, Europe and the United States, for future generations. I have tried to be as objective as possible in illustrating the personal approach I adopted through my life in coping with and overcoming every adversity through using the power of education, which has been the cornerstone of my life.

I am indebted to and grateful for the efforts and support of the following friends, colleagues and families, who have helped me throughout the past 15 years of my journey of writing my autobiography for reviewing, editing, and verification of historical events: Mrs. Martha Goodman, Dr. William Goodman, Mrs. Soheila Hayek, Mrs. Christine Linton, Mrs.

Gita Khadiri Esq., Dr. Henry C. Meece, Dr. Duane Varble, Dr. Cyrus Azimi, Dr. David Rejali, Dr. Shahrawm Toumodge, Mrs. Elizabeth Tye, Mr. Mehdi Khadiri and Mrs. Brigitta Norton.

For verification of historical events, I'd like to thank: Her Majesty Queen Farah Pahlavi for granting me an interview, Prof. Dr. Hans Juergen Phistner, Mr. Mehdi Shamshiri, The Late Mrs. Sakineh Nazmi Ansari, Mrs. Vida Ghahremani, Dr. Farzaneh Khazrai, Mr. Abdollah Movahhed, The late Mr. Saifollah Tashakkori, Mrs. Saman Behbahani Esq., Heidelberg Alumni International, "Heidelberg Alumni U.S. (HAUS),The National University of Iran Alumni and Faculty(NUIAF), the International Society of Iranian Studies(ISIS) and the American Association of Intellectual and Developmental Disabilities (AAIDD)

I'd also like to thank the following persons and associations for providing me with the priceless ideas and pictures for my book: Dr. Zara De Saint Hilaire (Kafi), Mrs. Christine Linton, Dr. Duane Varble, Mr. Freidoon Behbahani, Dr. Mehdi Heravi and Mrs. Abby Heravi(Ansari), Mrs. Kathy Collins, Fairfax County Zonta Club and Zonta International., personal history groups at the Vienna Community Center, and all other friends and family members.

I am also grateful for the technical and publishing advice provided by Mrs. Soheila Hayek, Ms. Ann Hoffman the Vice President of the National Writers Union, Mr. Paul Heimer, Mrs. Brigitta Norton, Mrs. Charisse Veloso, and the XLIBRIS Publishing team members.

Finally, I am grateful for my family's continuous support: Dr. Said Khadiri, Mrs. Gita Khadiri, Esq., Mr. Reza Khadiri, Mr. Fred Khoroushi, Mr. Cameron Khoroushi, and Ms. Sophia Khoroushi.

With deepest gratitude to those people, including all the family members, teachers, professors, colleagues, students and friends who played any instrument in my symphony of life, I am donating the royalties of this book to the Drs. Redjali and Khadiri Scholarship Endowment at the George Mason University College of Education and Human Development.

FOREWORD
BY THE AUTHOR'S DAUGHTER
GITA KHADIRI

My Mother:
A Gardener in a Wasteland

It is a breezy and balmy summer night. Troubled by the chirping of a lonely bird, I glance outside my window before my cool sheets envelope my sweaty body and invite me to enter my dream world. "There is an evil feeling in the air," I think. However, as all my unfounded fears dissolve into the endless black ocean above where the moon smiles and the stars playfully wink without hesitation, I am assured that the calmness of the night is here to stay.

Suddenly, the clock strikes one, and I hear my mother scream. I jump out of bed, knowing that she is having a recurring nightmare. Once again, the gong of the grandfather clock explodes in her head, just like the bomb that had blown up near our house in Iran many years ago during the Islamic Revolution. I tiptoe into my mother's room to find her crying. I had never seen her cry before, for she had always presented herself as a strong, forceful, and ambitious woman. She clutches on to me and murmurs, "I can't believe that all my efforts to better Iran have gone to waste. I should have stayed and helped rebuild Iran after the revolution." Yes, once again, my mother felt ashamed for having deserted Iran in a time when Iran needed her most, even though her life was in danger. I quickly remind her of how proud I am to have a mother who had contributed so much to Iran and her family. To me, she is a heroine and a reformer, who, through her various careers, had succeeded in bettering women's rights and the Iranian educational system.

Being one of the few highly educated women of her generation, my mother knew that she would have to fight many battles when she returned to Iran from the University of Heidelberg, Germany, in 1961 with her doctorate in educational and clinical psychology. As a woman, she faced open resentment when she began teaching at the National University of Iran as the first female professor. However, her strong belief in bettering women's rights and her ambition earned her the position of secretary-general of the Women's Organization in Iran. When she accepted this job, she was like a gardener in a vast desert. No one could imagine that this wasteland would blossom into a garden one day. Through her careful supervision, my mother planted more than 150 family welfare centers in Iran, and soon, the fruits of her relentless efforts became ripe as she directed all 150 branches herself and became a leader of the women's movement in Iran.

In addition to being the secretary-general of the Women's Organization, my mother established her own college, Shemiran College, in 1973, in order to provide Iranians with the opportunity to enhance their understanding of the three needed fields of preschool education, family counseling, and welfare administration. Thus, my mother became the first woman in Iranian history to establish her own college for these new academic areas in Iran.

Then, in 1977-8, the government was eager to take advantage of my mother's knowledge and educational skills. In those days, Iran was like a wasteland that thirsted for my mother's innovative ideas. The government was quick to appoint her to the position of the queen's educational consultant. All this was done in an effort to convince my mother to accept the seat of the minister of education. However, she refused the offer, because she did not want to become involved with politics. I am very glad of this wise decision, for if she had accepted the position, she would have been another casualty of the Iranian revolution.

Here in the United States, my mother cultivated the wasteland of the underprivileged as the director of the Adult Training Center of the

Lynchburg Training School and Hospital, a center for the mentally disabled. She was responsible for the well-being of her 300 elderly residents and her 220 staff members. There, my mother planted the seeds of the Adult Training Center's fruit with her motto. Every day, my mother's presence reminded her patients and staff that "You are never too old to achieve a goal" and that "Your goal is never too old to achieve."

Now, when I look at my mother's tired face, I can see how her relentless efforts to better our society have buried themselves in the deep wrinkles of her forehead. I think about all her accomplishments and her struggles to fight for women's rights. I think about her amazing green thumb that has turned every wasteland within her sight into a garden that bears the fruit of her wisdom. I think about my mother's forceful, strong, and ambitious character. I think about my mother as a heroine and a reformer, and when she cries and holds me in her tired arms, I think of her as Mom.

Gita Khadiri, student essay at the University of Virginia, April 1985.

TRIUMPH OF EDUCATION OVER ADVERSITY

A JOURNEY OF A PERSIAN-AMERICAN WOMAN THROUGH WAR, LOVE, REVOLUTION, AND FREEDOM

Introduction

My life story begins in the time of Iran's Westernization and modernization spearheaded by Reza Shah Pahlavi, who ruled Persia (Iran) for about seventeen years at the beginning of the twentieth century, from 1925 to 1941. My life has been a symphony of experiences, places, and times, spanning from the early twentieth century to present—from Iran to Germany, and from Iran to England, finally to the United States. I have lived through wars, revolution, peace, and tranquility. I have been blessed with a loving, beautiful family; have faced family tragedies; and have gone from being part of the elite and the privileged in Iran to needing a job to get by in the United States. By writing about what I have experienced, I hope that even readers from diverse backgrounds may appreciate something about my Iranian and American homelands through the story of my life.

A powerful and unifying theme in the symphony of my life has been my education. Education has enabled my family and me to survive the challenges of revolution, immigration, cancer, and other unexpected events life has sent our way. I have come to realize with joy that some of us live longer than others, have happier lives than others, and have easier lives than others; yet despite our diversity, we share life as one. I feel surrounded by beauty and am heartened by the fact that life is so accommodating and forgiving despite our quirks, shortcomings, and faults. My musician husband and I share a love of music and sincerely believe that all people are unique, all singing and hearing different tunes, all as musicians playing our own symphony, yet all participating in the grand symphony of life.

As a background, I trace my ancestry to Prophet Mohammad's grandson, who was married to the daughter of the last king of Persia, Yazdegerd III, after the Arab invasion of Persia in the seventh century.

In the 1930s, under the reign of Reza Shah Pahlavi, the official name of the country changed from Persia to Iran. During this time, Iran went through many reforms and changes dealing with, among others, its educational system, military organization, communications, road construction, agriculture, and the status of women. There were also the economic and financial changes that led to upheaval in the country later on. I was fortunate to be born during the time when I could benefit from the educational opportunities that became available to young girls and women.

In terms of geography, Iran is a mountainous, high-plateau country populated by about 70 million people. Its 1,648,180 square kilometers (636,363 square miles) stretch from the Caspian Sea and the former Soviet Union (now Turkmenistan, Armenia and Azerbaijan) in the north, to the Persian Gulf in the south. It stretches from Turkey and Iraq in the west, to Afghanistan and Pakistan in the east. By virtue of its location, Iran forms a strategic land bridge between the Middle East and Asia. The country is rich in minerals and other natural resources—i.e., copper, oil, gas, and coal. Exportation of petroleum is the principal source of foreign currency. Iran controls about a tenth of the world's known oil reserves.

For thousands of years, Iran has been at the crossroads of cultures and strongly influenced by various civilizations. The country has been on the path of many conquerors, invading armies, and foreign influences. From Alexander and Genghis Khan, the Arabs, Mongols and Tartars in the early and middle ages, to the United Kingdom and the Soviet Union in the nineteenth and early twentieth centuries, to the United States after the Second World War—all have either by invasion or incursion, influenced Iran, its people, and its culture. Despite all these foreign influences, the Iranian cultural traditions and its language have shown remarkable resilience and continuity.[1]

Like all countries, and especially the United States, when in peace, Iran is a wonderful place to live. I have treasured memories of my life and the cultures of both Iran and the United States. My early years and early memories were some of my life's happiest moments—a great prelude to the symphony of my life.

FIRST MOVEMENT
EARLY YEARS, EARLY MEMORIES

CHAPTER 1

Early Years and Early Memories Through Kindergarten and Primary Education (1934-1946)

On the first day of summer 1934, I was born into an old family in Tehran, the Capital of Iran or Persia. Even though the Iranian society typically valued boys more highly than girls because they carried on the family name, my parents welcomed my birth with open arms. They had two sons already—Ali Akbar and Jafar—and definitely wanted to have a girl. As a late arrival in my family, I was about twenty years younger than my brothers. I grew up in a religious, open-minded environment filled with love and respect. My nanny, a godmother who lived nearby, and my parents gave me their full attention. I was the only one of the three children my mother nursed by herself. I spent all my time with her, with my nanny and my godmother, whom I called *ammeh* (aunt). My ammeh, a close friend of my mother, had lost her husband when she was quite young and had no children, so she treated me like her own daughter. She was modern and progressive and embraced the latest changes in Western lifestyle and fashion, an attitude I savored. My parents offered her one of our attached houses to live in, and I enjoyed spending part of every day with her.

Our house originally belonged to my grandfather, who held the title His Excellency the Honorable Haji Mirza Mohammed Taghi Dabir-al-Doleh. As an honorable member of Dar-al-Shora Kobra (Council of Ministers) and an able servant of his Majesty's Court of Nasser-al-Din Shah (circa 1847-1897), he served his country for forty years with honor and dignity, as *Sharafat Newspaper* confirmed in 1899 with his picture on the cover page.[2]

His Excellency the
Honourable
Haj-Dabir-al-Doleh
1899.

Keyholder Ceremony in giving
the Key of the shrine
of Imam Hossein to my
grandfather.

When my grandfather retired, he moved to the holy city of Iraq-Karbala, where he assumed the highly regarded position of the Key Holder of the shrine. As Key Holder (*Kiliddar*) of this holy shrine, he spent the remainder of his life in the service of Imam Hossein. Upon his death, officials allowed him to be entombed in the shrine, a rare privilege. I have been told that his lineage goes back to Hazrat Imam Seyed-al-Sajeddin Ali Ebne Hossein, the grandson of the Prophet Mohammad. His ancestors were related to the Saints, and for three generations, they were learned Mojtahed-Ozma (great religious leaders) who published many books, among which was the book titled *Rejal,* by Mir Mostafa, from the province of Tafresh, an expert in mathematics, accounting, calligraphy, and other arts and science related to government services.

My grandfather's mansion, which my parents inherited, had twelve columns—like the US White House—and a pool stocked with gold fish. When the façade reflected in this pool, I saw twelve columns, an observation that fascinated me. Pigeons nested on the columns and the ceiling niche, and I enjoyed watching them fly in and out. In the garden, there were fruit trees, especially peaches, pomegranate, and persimmon trees, and many flowers including roses. Inside the house, there were rooms with traditional mirror walls, and libraries full of old leather-bound books. The mansion was comprised of two houses: the Biruni with offices and social reception, where my grandfather had run his office, and the Andaruni for private life and family. Each house had apartments for the security guard and guests. Each building had about thirty rooms, with a private Turkish bath situated between the two buildings. We lived comfortably in the Biruni house, which had spacious rooms for reception, meetings, and entertaining. My parents gave one of the apartments to my godmother.

Aunt (Ammeh) Asadol Moluk or Godmother in our home with Mahin, my friend.

My parents made a lot of changes to the houses. They separated the Turkish bath and offered it for public use. They also converted a part of the house into a dental clinic for my brother, who was a dentist, and gave the security apartment to an immigrant couple from Russia. Even with all these changes, the compound was still very large, perhaps too large, because we needed a staff of five people to run the household—cleaning, cooking, gardening, helping us to perform our many social duties, meetings, and the volunteer services of my parents.

My mother Fatemeh, who was given the title *Sharafatdole* Honor of the government by the king, was in charge of our household. My father, Ali Reza, who was given also the title *Jalaelmolk* Honor of the government by the king, was an officer and lawyer with the rank of general in today's terms, went to work in the Ministry of Defense every day. He and my mother had a very active social life, and whenever they were too busy, I took walks or played with my godmother.

My Mother Fatemeh Sharafatdole.

My father: Jalo el Molk.

My father with my grandfather and uncles.

Three years old with my brothers.

My nanny was old and kind, but could not get around very well. Although she died when I was about three years old, I have never forgotten her. I vividly remember once she was sitting in front of a samovar pouring tea, but had forgotten the sugar cubes for her tea, so I ran to bring her some sugar; but in my eagerness to help, I fell down and cut my forehead and lip on the glass sugar bowl. Since I was bleeding profusely, a doctor came to our home and gave me several stitches. To this day, I have a scar from this accident. I had wanted to help to make my nanny happy, but I hurt myself badly instead. As I look back, amazingly this has been a pattern in my life to serve and help others, even if I harm myself.

One glorious memory of my early childhood is of the pilgrimage with my mother to Mecca. This pilgrimage is a duty for all Muslims who can afford it. I was old enough at the time to enjoy all the rituals and ceremonies of the Hajj. On the road to Mecca, we rode on camels and lived for quite some time in tents, where we would visit each other. We all dressed up in white cloths to go to Mecca and then performed the tawaf, a sevenfold "circling" of the Ka'aba stone shrine, circling around it counterclockwise. When it was time to circle the shrine (the Ka'aba), I was lifted on the shoulders of the leader of our group, taller than everyone else, and was protected by him from the crowd as we went around the shrine. Another ritual was gathering pebbles and stoning the pillars, which represented the devil. At my young age, these ceremonies seemed like a game which I followed with excitement and happiness.

Aged 3, sitting with my cousins.

Earlier, when I was two years old and too young to remember, Reza Shah had issued a most significant decree; on January 7, 1936, he ordered Iranian women to appear in public without veils and in Western attire. This is one of the most significant developments in Iran's modern history. Before that date, many Iranian women covered their hair in public by wearing a scarf or a Chador (a floor length scarf), but that day marked a revolutionary change. The Shah and the Queen, the members of the royal family, ministers, dignitaries, and celebrities and their wives attended a party organized by the minister of Education. All the women at the party appeared without veils and in Western attire for the first time. After that date, women in public were not allowed to wear veils in contradiction to the long-standing tradition and religion. This sudden change caused a serious conflict for some religious women, and they tried to modify the long veil concept by using a hat or a scarf. Many women welcomed the change, and it was a turning point for them, leading to increased opportunities in higher education for women, among many other things. Interesting to me, my mother modified her appearance with a hat and scarf, but my godmother welcomed the changes and always wore the latest fashions from Paris and had her hair done so that it looked fashionable, with or without a head scarf.

My mother's appearance with a long scarf during this time of change once led to a disturbing incident. One day after this decree, she and I were out walking, when suddenly, a policeman attacked my mother and removed her scarf with his sword. My mother was so shocked that she fell down in the *jube*—the drainage ditch at the side of the street—and her face turned ashen. I tried to help her and screamed for help. People recognized us immediately and argued with the policeman about her modified veil. When the policeman realized he had attacked a general's wife, he quickly ran away. I have always believed that my mother was close to having a heart attack at that moment, and to this day, I have not forgotten her pale face.

When I was about five years old, my family and I attended the wedding celebration of the Crown Prince Mohammed Reza to Princess Fawzieh, the sister of King Farough of Egypt. It was a great occasion with festivities and fireworks at the main square of Tehran. Although we had special seats on the second floor of a government building in the square, it was too crowded, and we left early, probably on my account.

Another wedding that I remember very well was the wedding of my first cousin Parvin. Parvin was very pretty, and since she was kinder to me than some of my other cousins, I gave her the title "pretty cousin." Two other older cousins were asked to hold the bridal train for the ceremony. They excluded me from this honor because of my tender age. I thought that I was treated unfairly as I wanted to be a part of the wedding. I became very upset and screamed that I wanted to join them in holding the train of my pretty cousin's dress. I repeated this wish several times and went to the front of the guests to try to be a part of the ceremony, but they wouldn't let me. Suddenly, my cousin Mehri slapped my face. I cried bitterly and felt very inferior to everyone. I was jealous, because my cousins were much taller and older than me. Maybe they were just trying to protect me from the crowd, but I still think it was because I had given the "pretty cousin" title to the bride and not to them. All that day, they mistreated me, and it seemed that they sought revenge. Later on, they treated me kindly, but I have never forgotten their rudeness that day. On the other hand, I have treasured Parvin's continuing kindness to me throughout my life, another aspect of the symphony theme.

My cousin Parvin and Dr. A.
Kafi wedding.

In my preschool years, I was lucky to attend two progressive kindergartens—the *Bersabeh* and *Shukufeh* schools, a result of one of the education reforms of Reza Shah. These were the first private kindergartens in Tehran, established during the education reform movement of Reza Shah. I was a member of the dancing group and participated in events at the school ceremony at the end of the year. These events were times for great celebration. There was a program with dancing and singing and an exhibition of our paintings, drawings, and crafts. Naturally, there was also much picture taking.

Graduation from Kindergarten 1940.

The preschool education I enjoyed was not available to everyone. Only the well-to-do families who accepted the modern reform of Reza Shah sent their children to kindergarten. The enjoyable time I had in these kindergartens may explain why I later pioneered the preschool education movement for all children in Iran.

My elementary school education started during World War II in the 1940s. The outbreak of the Second World War had an unfavorable effect on the development of education in Iran. By then, it had been half a century since Iran had adopted the constitutional monarchy. Under the new system of government, centralization in most fields of national endeavor took place. According to the new constitution, active support for the expansion of education in the country became the responsibility of the national government and according to the Third Article of the Educational Constitution, primary education was made compulsory. In 1932, another law was passed to make primary education free of charge too. World War II slowed this process.[3]

I was registered for primary education in *Maziar* School near our home. At the beginning of the term, Iran became involved in the war. First, Iran announced its neutrality in the war. However, Iran then received three ultimatums from the Allies to align the country behind them. The third ultimatum to Reza Shah came on August 6, 1941, from the Allies, especially from Russia in the north and England with interests in the south of Iran. They pressured Iran to align with the Allies. There were about 470 German professionals employed in Iran, most of them working on the railway between the Caspian Sea and the Persian Gulf, which was being built by Germany. England was concerned that Hitler's Germany might work its way through Iran for its oil and move on to occupy Afghanistan and India. To protect their interests, the Russian army from the north and the British army from the south occupied Iran. The United States later joined the Allies in this effort. Of course, the

Allies wanted to use the German-made railway between the south and north for transporting arms and the army from the Persian Gulf to the Caspian Sea and the Soviet Union.

Finally, after much pressure from the Allies, Reza Shah was forced to resign, and in September 1941, his son Mohammed Reza was sworn in as the king of Iran. Reza Shah and all his family were forced to leave Iran for Mauritius Island, near Johannesburg in South Africa.

The Allied occupation brought many changes in our lives. At the time of evening blackouts, we hid ourselves in the basement for fear of possible air attacks. There was a shortage of food and electricity, and the whole country was practically in a state of famine. The government rationed food and electricity and restricted travel by train. During the food shortage, we were fortunate that we had stored enough essential items from our farm and were able to help the needy families. Our house had storage rooms for water, oil, wheat, flour, rice, potatoes, onions, and even melons. Some of these storage rooms were very dark, and I didn't like to go into these rooms. I remember very well that on some religious days, our cook prepared food for about two hundred needy families. They came and ate in our home while listening to the mullahs praying for the end of the war. On all these occasions, I helped my parents to serve the needy families and their children. Both of my parents instilled in me the principle that we owe a responsibility first to others and then to ourselves. For me, this family motto remains unchanged.

Those days I was busy with feeding some chickens, which we kept in the corner of our gardens. We had hens and some other birds, and I also was responsible for finding their eggs, collecting them, and allowing some of them to remain there to hatch. The chickens were a great help in the famine, and they provided interesting work and even play for me.

When traveling, we were not allowed to use the passenger compartments on the train because those sections were reserved for the Allied soldiers. We could only use the baggage compartments, which did not have any seats. Generally speaking, the Allied soldiers treated the Iranian people with respect. I remember that on my trip to Qom, they gave candies to all the children in the train, including me, of course.

Gradually, the political difficulties with the Allies were resolved and finally, in October 1943, Iran officially and actively joined them in the war. On November 26, the heads of the Allied countries—Churchill, Roosevelt and Stalin—arrived for the Tehran Conference. A picture in this book was taken at my cousin's estates, which was also used for the meeting. The house was converted later to a museum. At this conference, Stalin was optimistic about winning the war, especially since the United States and England were supplying Russia with armaments. The Allies also publicly thanked Iran for its cooperation and the role it had played in the war. Iran was named "the Bridge of Victory" because the trains over bridges built by the Germans transported millions of arms from the south to the north to Russia.

At this conference, these leaders decided that after the war they would compensate Iran for its losses and for all the services rendered during the war. The members of the conference returned to their countries after December 2, 1943. Only Stalin, who knew some Persian traditions and customs, went in person to see the Shah before leaving Tehran, giving the Shah the "Stalingrad Sword" as a token of appreciation. The Shah went himself to see Churchill and Roosevelt at their headquarters at their own embassies, because they would not leave the embassy for security reasons. All three of them wrote a thank-you note to the Shah for Iran's contribution and assistance during hostilities. Later, on August 4, 1945, at the Potsdam conference, the Allies agreed that the Allied army should evacuate and leave Iran within six months.

**Tehran Conference—November 28-December 1, 1943
(photo original source Iran's government Museum).**

During this time, I was continuing my elementary education. Every day on the road to school, I saw the long lines of people waiting to get a loaf of bread from the government trucks for their families. I had very good teachers who understood how difficult it was to be a student during the war, and with their kind attitude, they tried to ease the war atmosphere. I loved my teachers, especially my fifth and sixth grade teachers, in a mystical way. It is important to know how our culture approaches education. To comprehend this teacher/student relationship, it is necessary to have an understanding of my religion and the Iranian culture.

In order to understand the development of education in Iran, a number of religious, cultural, linguistic, and historic considerations must be kept in mind. After the Arab invasion of AD 642, Islam spread rapidly through Persia. When Mohammad died, the Shi'a branch—which holds that the leadership of Islam was bequeathed to Ali, the cousin and son-in-law of the prophet—became the dominant sect in Iran. The influence of the Shi'a branch of Islam contributed to the development of the mysticism known as Sufism, which has profoundly influenced Persian literature. Sufism is derived from the word *suf,* meaning the woolen garment of the ascetic. Poets and teachers were disciples of this mystic belief.

On the relationship between teacher and pupil on the mystical path to God, the pedagogues are interested, and to me it was a part of the bond I had with my teachers. Accordingly, in the teacher/pupil relationship, the teacher becomes the master to whom the pupil opens his heart. The master, in turn, directs the inner life of the pupil until such time as the young person can find satisfaction and freedom in the Peace in God. This notion of the pupil's admiration for the teacher has lingered on in modern Iranian education. The connection between my teachers and I in the fifth and sixth grades was like a mystical path to God. Because of their devotion, I studied so hard that I became the top student. This bond also helped me later in life, when my brother Jafar died during the World War II.

Jafar was very sensitive and a fine writer, but during the war, he became very depressed. Under martial law, we had a curfew every evening in Tehran, and nobody was allowed out on streets after 10:00 p.m. One night, as was his custom, Jafar went walking outside, and did not come home before the curfew. We became very worried, and none of us slept all night long. My parents conducted a thorough search talking to other families, army, and the police.

The next morning, Jafar was still missing, so I wanted to stay with my parents, but they insisted that I go to school. I was in the sixth grade, the last year of elementary education in Iran. When I got to school, I shared my problem with my good teacher Mrs. Tabrizi. She was so caring and understanding that she gave me hope that my brother would be back and that everything would be all right. So I was able to concentrate and study. It was near final exam time, and in those days, the general final exams were very important. Three days passed, and still they could not find my dear brother Jafar. After the third day of searching everywhere, they finally found him dead in a military hospital. Apparently, he had been walking just a few minutes after 10:00 p.m. on the night he went missing, and he did not hear the soldiers' command to stop. He was shot three times and taken immediately to the military hospital where he died. My parents were very upset and angry. My father, as a military man, kept his sorrow inside, but my mother could not contain her grief and cried loudly. My father being a fatalist even dropped his charges against the soldier who had shot my brother and forgave him. My godmother was with me at this time and tried to take me to school while I wanted to stay with my mother who was suffering the most. I did not want to go to school, but then I saw my kind teacher at the memorial service for my brother. She had come with some of my school friends and sat next to me, expressing her sympathy, saying she missed me in class. She strongly urged me to return to school soon, stressing that I would otherwise lose the whole year. I promised her I would try. She also again added that she missed me in her class.

After my brother's death, my older brother, a dentist in Shiraz, came with his family to Tehran to stay with us for a while. Gradually, I started school again, but I continued to miss many days. The final exam was drawing near. However, Mrs. Tabrizi was so kind that I couldn't help but respond to her love and concern. I worked very hard to compensate for my absence from school, and amazed myself in the final exam by again becoming the valedictorian in the area schools. At first, I could not believe I had been awarded this honor, until I received a copy of the book *Ghabusnameh* from the Ministry of Education in a ceremony at the Ministry as a prize for being the valedictorian. When I received the book, I looked proudly with thanks at my good teacher Mrs. Tabrizi. I even wanted to give my prize to her. Although I was extremely proud of my achievement, and everybody was congratulating me, I still was not satisfied with myself, knowing my ignorance and lack of knowledge of the world. I was very eager to continue my education. This feeling was not shared by the majority of my school friends, who did not share my strong motivation for further education, because most of the their families were thinking that the elementary education for girls was enough, and they should get ready to enter into an arranged marriage.

---

1. Sakineh M. Redjali, "Education System in Iran," *The International Encyclopedia of Education*, Pergamon Press, Vol. 5, 2697-2702, 1985

2. *Sharafat* Newspaper 1899, Jumada 1.1317

3. Sakineh M. Redjali, "Education System of Iran," *The Encyclopedia of Comparative Education and National Systems of Education*, Pergamon Press, 1987, 369-374

CHAPTER 2

High School Years 1946-1952

It was not necessary for me to persuade my parents to let me continue my education, even though I was a girl. I was very fortunate for having parents who understood that for me, wanting to learn and continue my education was the topmost important facet of my life. My parents' understanding was a real blessing, considering the culture in which we lived. In September 1946, my parents registered me at the well-known girls' high school, Nurbakhsh, built and founded by Reza Shah Pahlavi. Later, its name was changed to Reza Shah School. It was a modern building with modern classrooms and labs with space enough for several sports and a gym. Each girl could take part in different games and be a part of several sporting teams. Usually each sports team was very active in competition with other high schools, and most of the time, our teams were number one.

Author's picture taken at the Reza Shah High School.

Author (from left 2nd from top) as part of the school sports team.

36

At age 13, in my first year of high school, which was the seventh grade, I had to study harder than in elementary school. We had different teachers for a variety of subjects, some requiring much more study, which I loved. For a change, I also signed up for two sports teams—cycling and table tennis, these took up less time in preparation for competition, and I won a medal for each. Other sports like volleyball and basketball required more time and dedication, and I didn't want to miss my studying. At the end of the year, I again achieved the honor of valedictorian among all the grade 7 students. Looking back, I realize that because of my dedication to study, I was often isolated from others and feeling lonely. At about this time, changes in my body added to my feeling of loneliness. As my breasts developed and my monthly period started, I tried to hide these changes as if I was ashamed, but since I also developed very bad migraine headaches during my period, I could not hide it easily. My mother and aunt discovered quickly what was wrong. They immediately gave me the right sex education and guided me as I adjusted to the changes. These were important times for me as a teenager.

During these years, music became a larger part of my life. My parents observed my love of music, and they encouraged me to take accordion lessons with my cousin who was already studying with a teacher, Mr. Sahakian, who came to their home for the lessons. Very soon my love of music replaced my loneliness, but it didn't take me long to discover that the accordion was a limited instrument, and so I asked my parents for a piano. When I did, they searched and finally found a German made piano, a Blütner, which had won several awards for excellence. Since we had plenty of space, a grand piano was no problem. I immediately began piano lessons, studying classical European music. Again, the teacher came to our house, and I had wonderful times with my instructor Mrs. Gregorian.

Playing the accordion.

Playing the piano.

Once World War II ended, Tehran experienced many social and political changes, which we noticed impacted even on our school activities. The major issue after the war was the control of Iranian oil—as all the superpowers wanted control. The American and English armies finally left Iran in 1945 and 1946, but the Red Army of the Soviet Union occupied the north of Iran and refused to leave Azerbaijan. Since the British controlled our petroleum in the south of Iran, so it was that the Soviet Union wanted to have the similar privilege for the oil in the north of Iran, near the Caspian Sea. The British had control of oil in the south through British Petroleum since before 1912. During the Ghajar Dynasty, before Pahlavis, Sir William Darcy, an Australian, had a contract signed with the government. The result was later the establishment of the Anglo-Iranian Oil Company, in reality, British Petroleum, which had power and authority to control our oil in Iran, with British Petroleum signs in every gas station. The Soviet Union wanted to have the same advantage in the north, so it was understandable that the Russian army would not leave Iran until it had the same oil privileges.

Because of this stalemate, Iran complained to the United Nations, asking that the Red Army be forced to evacuate. Harry Truman, president of the United States, sent a message to Stalin to have his troops leave. This blunt message was not well received by Stalin, but fortunately, the prime minister of Iran at that time, Ahmad Ghavam, was a very good diplomat. He went to the Soviet Union and, with great diplomacy, managed to have the Soviet government sign an agreement saying that the possibility existed for an agreement between Iran and the Soviet Union to have shared oil privileges in the north, just as the British had in the south, pending approval of the Iranian Parliament. As a result, and thanks to these efforts, the Red Army finally left Iran, beginning on March 25, 1946.

However, after the Soviet army left, the Iranian Parliament voted against the agreement that Prime Minister Ghavam had already made. Since World War II, there has always been a constant struggle between England, the Soviet Union, and the United States for influence in Iran because of the oil. This struggle led to the establishment of political parties and religious groups, which were used by each country to exercise influence. For example, the Tudeh Party (Tudeh meaning "people") was the Communist Party. At that time, their goal was to separate Azerbaijan from the rest of the country so that it could be controlled by the Soviets. The Tudeh Party became very active among workers in oil companies and factories and, surprisingly, even in high schools. Some of my school friends and even my brother's daughter Nahid, one year my junior, actually became active members of this party.

A photo of the author and other top students waiting to welcome the Princess Ashraf for an official visit.

Altogether there were three major political groups. In addition to the Tudeh (Communist Party), there was the Jebhe Melli (National Front Party), more aligned with the United States and Fadayan Islam (the Islamic front). These parties were influenced either by the Soviet Union, Great Britain, France, or the United States. Although my friends were active and attended group meetings, I did not. My reason was simple—I didn't want to join anything, which would take me away from my studies. I didn't have the time, even though the idea of democracy and equal roles in society for women did affect my thinking. I was concerned about social justice, but I realized I needed more education and needed to learn more about the whole world and about human beings. However, I did know that I didn't like the idea of one branch of the Tudeh Party, a separatist branch that very strongly favored the separation of Azerbaijan from Iran; and at that time, our country was strongly influenced by the Tudeh Party.

Eventually, fighting broke out over this separatist issue. On December 12, 1946, Mohammed Reza Shah ordered the army to fight in the north and troops entered Azerbaijan. In the conflict, Pishevari, head of the group supporting Azerbaijan's Independence, was defeated and escaped to the Soviet Union. This was a great victory for the Shah and the army. However, the Tudeh Party continued its activities for young people in the schools and with factory workers and permeated all other groups and activities. Some of the smart girls in the high schools became very active members of these parties. At the same time, some of my school friends dropped out of school because their families had arranged marriages for them. So my circle of school friends was rapidly changing. Since I was studying hard and was still excelling, my family did not dare to speak to me about marriage, although many people said I was beautiful and many families wanted to come to visit us and ask for me as a future bride for their sons. Although historically arranged marriages and *"khastegari"* have been our tradition, my parents fortunately honored my wishes to study and did not order me or trouble me with the subject of marriage. In the custom of arranged marriages in Iran—*"khastegari"*, parents with a daughter of marriageable age give permission for other families with a son of marriageable age to visit and observe the behavior of the young girl. They make an appointment for a *khastegari* and visit the girl's family. Often they have seen the girl and know her reputation and her appearance, but of course, they don't know what the girl really likes or how well educated she is. Usually a person, a facilitator, recommends the girl and makes the arrangements between the two families.

Taken at the wedding of the author's niece Nahid to Mohammed Reza Badii.

My parents, however, respected my wishes and didn't give permission to other families to visit us. Although there was much talk about my beauty, my mother always made excuses and said I was a dedicated student not interested in marriage. My mother had always told me that appearance is not important, and that what was inside a person was more important. Maybe that was also another reason why I wanted to enrich my inner self with study and knowledge. I am very thankful to my parents who did not force me into marriage and who honored my wishes, even though they were breaking with tradition. Perhaps they realized how much our world was changing and that women were to have a voice in the world.

As my parents were open-minded about studying and about my future, they were a strong influence about my understanding of religion. I learned my religious duties and followed the plan of daily praying. This daily prayer and meditation was relaxing for me and brought me very close to God in a mystical way. I began gradually to study our great poets and their poems and the mystical branch of Islam—Sufism. I was fascinated by Molana Rumi, a poet whose writing was an important factor in my parents' life and belief—they lived in harmony and believed it should be a part of every life. They never fought with each other, and I never heard them argue with each other. They supported each other in every way. They loved and respected each other.

During these high school years, I spent the summer holidays reading. I read works of Victor Hugo, Maxim Gorky, Dostoevsky, Hemingway, Stefan Sweig, and other famous writers. I read fast and finished books quickly.

Some personalities from these days remain in my memory. One in particular was an excellent principal, Mrs. Zahra Khanlari, who had a PhD in Persian literature. She was very kind toward all the girls and treated every student with respect and love. Everybody in our school admired her very much, because she was also an excellent manager of the school. One very good teacher was Dr. Farrokhru-Parsa, who later became the Minister of Education, the first woman minister. At the time she taught biology in our school and was also studying medicine at the University of Tehran. I respected her very much for continuing her education. Just having a BS in biology was not enough for her. Perhaps I learned from her example for my later studies.

Photo of the author and her teacher, the late
Dr Farrokhru-Parsa (later known as the first female minister
of Iran who was executed during the revolution).

Another good teacher was Dr. Hamidi-Shirazi, who also had a PhD in Persian literature. He was a poet and I still remember fondly the times when he read his poetry in class. It was a wonderful class, which we enjoyed very much. Yet another fine teacher was Mr. Ali Asgar Shamim, who made history classes very interesting. I liked history, knowing that we could learn much from that subject, because, as Hegel wrote, history repeats itself.

In class one day, we heard a rumor that Mohammed Reza Shah had separated from his wife Fawzieh. The rumor soon became fact, and it was announced officially by the court on November 18, 1948. Then other rumors started over who was going to be the next queen of Iran. My friends and I discussed several names, and everybody except me wanted to be chosen as the next queen. Finally, in October 1950, the Shah became engaged to Soraya, a very beautiful young lady, half German, half Iranian. The government said she was eighteen but she was really sixteen years old. After this announcement, gossip stopped, and my friends stopped wanting to be the next queen.

When I was in the ninth grade, the *Tudeh Party* became more influential in our school and since our wonderful principal's brother, Mr. Kianouri was a very active member of the *Tudeh* (Communist) *Party*, the Ministry of Education replaced her. This change ruined the pleasant atmosphere at school and led to student strikes. Students wanted to let the Ministry know how unpopular this decision was. The new principal, Dr. M., was the complete opposite of Dr. Zahra Khanlari. Although she too had a PhD in Persian literature, she could not communicate well with students and treated the school, its friends, and the girls poorly. Student strikes brought about more political pressure. Because Dr. M did not treat students with respect, students refused to attend class. Reluctantly, I too yielded to peer pressure and joined in the strike. The school became a battle zone between the new principal and the students, with the teachers caught in the middle.

Dr. M. acted like a spy. She ordered a triangle-shaped opening cut in the door of each classroom so that she could see into the classrooms when she was making her rounds. Often she hid behind the door of classrooms to see what each teacher was doing and to hear what the students said. In this way, Dr. M. tried to gain control of the school. (She later became a senator.) With all this strife going on, I became worried about our final exams and the impact on the learning environment; but fortunately, it didn't take long for the Ministry of Education to replace her.

In general, from 1949-1952, the school, and society itself, was very much involved politically, through different parties influenced by foreign countries. This situation was very disturbing to me as a young girl, and I attribute my illness at that time partly to my emotional state. I developed paratyphoid fever and couldn't go to school for three weeks (Soraya, the new queen, also had typhoid fever). Nevertheless, when I finished the ninth grade, I was awarded valedictorian again. However, I was unhappy because of all the unrest at the high school. The exams, which placed me at the top of the class every year, were not a national exam for all, and I worried that the lack of some knowledge would leave me behind at the twelfth grade final national exams. Each week, strikes kept us from several classes, and the school had become a political battleground. I shared my concern over this unrest at the school with my parents. My mother began to see what she could do, and after some research through her many friends, she found a less politically active private school in the south of Tehran. So in tenth grade, I changed from the best government school to a private school, Iran School, named after the country. It was also the name of the daughter of the owner of the school, Mrs. Shokatmalek Jahanbani. Here, the principal selected the best teachers for teaching. Dr. F. Parsa and several other teachers from my former school taught there part-time.

Most important was having an excellent literature teacher who was at the same time an excellent educator, Mr. Mohammed Sadigh Esfandiari. As we studied each story from our classic national literature, he analyzed it by comparing the story to the current political social situation of Iran. He was an excellent teacher, treating all the students with respect and love. These characteristics seem to me to be essential in all relationships, especially in education, and I have tried to treat people with the same ideals of service; respect and love, two elements closely aligned with my religious views and with the mystic sense, which comes from experiencing life in harmony. All the students loved him and his family in a mystical way, and we respected him very much. He tried to understand everybody. He invited the students to his home to meet his kind wife and children. Anyone who had any problem would discuss their problem with him. I was happy after leaving the political background of former school. Iran School was very quiet and conducive to learning. We had no sports teams, unlike the former school, activities were limited to academic subjects. There were no social or political activities. I spent two years in this school—the tenth and eleventh grade.

Photo of students and staff, including the principle at the time the late S. Jahanbani and her family, taken at an Iran High School's picnic.

One of my friends in this school was a talented poet. She would delight us during class breaks by reading and reciting her poems. She was determined to be a fine poet and wished to study literature and poetry, and I always encouraged her. During our weekends—Thursday and Friday—we would meet in our home where I played the piano and she recited her poems. At these gatherings, we often invited our dear literature teacher, Mr. Sadigh Esfandiari and his wife. This suited my protective parents who always preferred to have all the gatherings in our home, thus keeping me safe and close. I rarely visited the homes of my friends. Since my friends seemed to enjoy coming to our home, it became a center for social gatherings for my friends, which pleased me very much. All my adult life, I have entertained in my own home, a pleasure I still enjoy.

Playing piano at a weekend gathering of friends and teachers.

Another gathering of friends, including teachers Mr. and Mrs. Esfandiari.

Little by little, the atmosphere of Iran School became too narrow, i.e., not offering the wide selection of studies I wanted. At about the same time, my former school had settled down politically, with a good, new principal; so with the blessing of Iran School, to whom I was extremely grateful, I decided to return to my former school for the final high school year. This meant that I would graduate from the school whose name at this time had been changed to Reza Shah the Great School. On returning, I was pleased to see some students I knew and that some teachers were the same. I met one new teacher, Dr. Mehrangiz Manuchehrian, who was a lawyer, attorney, and teacher in philosophy and psychology. Dr. Manuchehrian was also a human rights activist fighting for the equality of women—and later received the Human Rights Medal from the Human Rights Committee of the United Nations. Her classes were always very interesting, because of her work as a defense lawyer she would tell us about her court cases. One valuable memory is the advice she gave us about the rights of women in our divorce laws. She said that since, in Islamic law, women do not have the same equal rights as men in divorce, it is better for us when we marry to get an unchangeable durable power of attorney from the groom as an addendum to our marriage certificates. This would allow us to have equal rights with men in the case of divorce or in other aspects of married life. In this way, we could also sue for divorce. Without this power of attorney, we would have to challenge the case in court for many years if the man contested the divorce. She explained all this by citing several cases as examples, and she convinced her students so well that later most of my friends, including me, followed her advice and added the unchangeable durable power of attorney addendum to our marriage certificates. Knowing that the power of attorney would be unchangeable gave us peace of mind for marriage. This knowledge also reassured me and lessened my fear of losing independence while I was married.

During this year, I read a three-volume book by M. A. Foroughi, *The History of Philosophy*, and also two books by Plato. I was very much fascinated by Plato's conversations with Socrates, and after I finished those books, I began to wonder about social justice, women's rights, the meaning of life and existence and what it meant to be human. Coupled with these questions, I contemplated where I should go to college after high school and what I should study. The vastness of study in science and literature raised many questions in my mind, which remained unanswered. The questions distilled into two—what should I study and where should I continue my education.

At the same time, I reflected on my high school years. During the breaks between classes, my friends would often come to me about personal or school problems, and I would always try to help them resolve their problems. Sometimes two or three students would come to me together after an argument and ask my judgment. Sometimes, I served as a mediator between them. Because of this experience, I thought perhaps I wanted to be a judge, but that was not possible for women in Iran because of Islamic law and government regulation, an issue that has always bothered me. So I could not study law with the idea of becoming a judge. I could be an attorney like Dr. Manuchehrian, who later became a senator, but I would never have the opportunity to be a judge; so I looked about for some other field. I was also getting myself ready for the final exams, the nationwide exams for male and female students held during the course of several days. Many unsettled political situations also were on my young mind, having to do with our oil and other resources. The superpowers were still influential in all three parties—the Tudeh

Party (the Communist Group), Jebhe Melli (National Front Group), and Fadayan Islam, which meant Islam Martyrs (Islamic Front).

Several incidents happened because of these political influences. An unsuccessful attempt on the life of the Shah occurred on February 1, 1949, while he was attending an anniversary celebration at the University of Tehran. However, two other assassination attempts on two prime ministers were successful. Former prime ministers Abol Hossein Hajir and Haj Ali Razmara were killed on November 5, 1949, and March 7, 1951, respectively, by members of the Islamic Front.

At the end of 1949, in November and December, the Shah visited the United States, and this visit seemed to offer interesting promises for the future. During his visit, the Shah worked to establish a better and closer relation with the United States, and as a result, several economic and social welfare projects were implemented with technical assistance from the US President Harry Truman, who supported all the projects, especially the project to strengthen the army so that Iran would be able to stand strong against the Red Army of our neighbor, the Soviet Union.

In addition to these political and economic happenings, there was a great movement to nationalize our oil, with many strikes and demonstrations. The people were adamant that the oil belonged to the people of Iran and not to the British government. The British resisted, and many riots occurred at the oil refinery in the city of Abadan. The Parliament (Majles) and the Shah appointed Dr. Mohammed Mossadegh as prime minister, the leader of *Jebhe Melli* (National Front Party). Both Britain and Iran lodged complaints against each other in the United Nations and the International Court in The Hague during 1951 and 1952. Finally, the British government agreed to the nationalization of Iranian oil. Immediately the name of British Petroleum, which was in all our gas stations, changed to National Iranian Oil Company—Sherkat Melli Nafte-Iran. I remember how delighted we were to see this change. No longer did we have the name British Petroleum on government buildings and on every gas station. All of us became very proud of the name change, but the British government continued to fight for rights to assets and interests for oil in the south of Iran. The British offered Iran rights to 50 percent of the oil, with 50 percent remaining British, but of course, Iran did not accept this proposal.

To end this stalemate, Truman sent Mr. Averill Harriman from the United States to find a solution. Mossadegh presented Iran's rights at the United Nations and the International Court of The Hague. The result was more riots and strikes, and fights between all parties—the *Tudeh* (Communist) *party* (which had gone underground but was still very active), the National Front, the government, and the Islamic Front. But Mossadegh was quite successful both with The Hague and in the United Nations. These caused a lot of excitement in Iran. Ultimately, Iran refused to accept the proposal to share 50 percent of our oil.

Meanwhile, in my last year of high school, my father, as an army general, became a judge. There had been many arrests over the nationalization of oil issue and the government tried to control everything. Newspapers reported the view depending on which party influenced them. The three main parties were still very active—the *Tudeh* (Communists), *the National Front Party* (which backed Prime Minister Mossadegh), and the *Islamic Front.* One case involved three journalists who were jailed for their stories, which the government had forbidden and did not want published. One night, about 3:00 a.m., an army military police car stood in front of our home and called for my father. My mother became very upset, and I began to cry. They took my father in the middle of the night back to the court and to his office, but at that time, we did not know where they had taken him. I learned later on that the judges were forced to change their ruling; they had ruled that the three journalists were not to be set free. Finally, all the judges, including my father, were forced to change this ruling. The next day my father came home. He was very quiet and upset, but he said nothing about what had happened. Very soon, after a few months, he asked to retire from the army. Apparently, he, as a religious man, wanted to be free in his conscience and avoid making other "wrong" rulings as a judge. Early retirement seemed the only way out.

Right after his retirement, my father became ill. The doctor said he had a heart problem and should rest and avoid excitement. But while he was in bed, he asked me to read the daily newspaper to him. He was very much interested in the news of oil nationalization for Iran and in social justice. I was fascinated with the activity of Mossadegh and enjoyed getting the news. It was a pleasure to read the newspaper to my father and discuss politics. The Shah and Mossadegh were involved in a power struggle, partly because of the oil nationalization issue, and this led to more political riots among different parties.

I had studied hard in the last year of high school, and when the time came, I worked to prepare for the national exam for the high school diploma, an exam centralized by the Ministry of Education and conducted on certain days at set places all around the country. The night before the first day of the exam, I studied late and set my alarm clock for 5:00 a.m. to get up early and have a quick review before leaving. The alarm clock sounded at the same time that I also heard a terrible scream from my mother. What followed was so horrible that to this day I cannot bear to hear an alarm clock. Apparently, my father had had a heart attack and died immediately. I began to cry and scream, not knowing what was happening. My mother's strength took over, and she did what she thought was best for me. She pretended that my father was just ill, and told me that she had called the doctor and that I should prepare to take the exam. She told me to go to my aunt's house and spend the night with my cousin so I could be rested for the next day and so I could be close to the exam site, near their house. Gradually, during the exam days, I learned the truth, which I had sensed all along. My mother was quite a powerful woman to control her feelings at this important time. It was not an easy thing for her to do. I sensed later that my father had died, but she pretended that he had just had a heart attack. She said, "Simin, after all your hard work, you must take the exam. You don't need to spend another year in high school."

There was no way out and no other choice. If a person could not take the exam on the days it was offered, then she had to wait for another year. However, I couldn't stop crying, and I was very upset. I really didn't know what I was going to do, but I went ahead with the exam. All the while I was answering the exam questions, I was crying bitterly. Every time I recall this time, I see it as one of the hardest times of my life. However, one of my teachers played a great role in giving me the strength to go on. Mr. Mohammed Sadigh Esfandiari, our literature teacher who knew every student very well, spoke to me, and his attention had a calming effect. Since the teachers moved about the room monitoring the tests during the three to four days of the exam, he could say kind words during breaks. Again, I felt a mystical connection to him because of his kind and fair attitude.

With the support of my mother and my teacher, I finished the final exam, although with sorrow and tears. Then I had thoughts that maybe I would fail. I couldn't remember anything I had written. All the time, my father's face was in front of me. I could not comprehend that he had died, and maybe unconsciously I was thinking I needed to do something to keep his name alive. I realized that I needed to continue my education and go on studying. Later on, when friends tried to express sympathy to me, I hated to hear that because to me my father was not dead, and I could not believe his death. So in this way, rather than attending my father's funeral, I went instead to the final exam.

Because of the exam, my mother, supported by the family, did not let me attend my father's funeral the next day. But I learned later that because of my father's popularity and service to the community, thousands of people walked behind his body, which was carried for three miles. Then his body was carried later on to the religious city of Qom, where my mother and my family had room in the shrine of Massumeh, the Holy Hazrate Massumeh, the sister of the Imam Reza, who was buried there as a child. Qom is a religious city and also a center for training clergy and religious men, or mullahs, at different levels.

After the ceremony of my father's funeral, which I still regret to this day not attending, I went with my mother and other family to his grave on the seventh day after his death. We hired several buses to accommodate all the family who wanted to attend the Seventh Day Ceremony. They were all invited to come with us, and they were all invited to have dinner or lunch there with my mother. My mother also, I noticed, arranged at the same time to have a similar grave next to my father of her own so that when she died she would have a place next to him. It was a very sad occasion, and on that day, I made a promise to my father that I would do my best to keep his name alive and promised him that, my love for him would never die.

After a couple of weeks, I began to be anxious about the results of my exam. I was still spending most of the days crying bitterly, and I began to worry too that maybe I had not been in control of myself in the exam and that I had given all the wrong answers to the questions. Since I really could not remember what I had written in that exam, my fears multiplied, but we had to wait for the results, which would be announced by the Ministry of Education, usually three to four weeks after the exam.

Then one night, my mother was reading the daily newspaper and saw news about the results of the national exam. She screamed out to me, "Simin, your name is in the newspaper under the article *Final Exam Report of High Schools*." I ran to the newspaper. I could not believe it was my name. I was listed as valedictorian of both males and females in Tehran. I could not believe it. I thought maybe it was a name similar to mine or belonging to someone else, but the next day, wearing my black dress and a scarf, I went to school, and when I arrived, everyone began to congratulate me. The list of scores of those who had passed was on the door of the principal's office. There at the top of the list was my name. The principal congratulated me, but still I could not believe how it happened that I received such a good grade in that situation. I had lost my dear father, and I was crying and deeply sad and in deep sorrow while I responded to all the questions. Looking back, I wonder if unconsciously I compensated for the sorrow and frustration by trying to respond positively and do well on the exam, but really, I still don't know how it happened, and this has been something I've wondered about all my life.

One night, not long after, my mother called my brother and me to read my father's will, and this night determined my future. My father had written, "It is my will that if Simin wants to continue her education, she should." He also wrote that my mother and brother should let me do this, and then came the big surprise. My father, a very religious man, knew Islamic law very well, but he chose instead to allow me, as a girl, to receive an equal share of the inheritance with my brother. Under Islamic law, a female would receive half of the male's share, and the wife would get one-eighth of the share. My father's last will shocked us all. He named my mother as executor and divided all of his belongings equally between my brother and me, this was a shock for both of us. My brother became angry at the decision, which was against Islamic law and regulations and against the law of the country, but I felt even more obligated to continue my education and maybe keep alive my dear father's name. I still had not fully accepted his death. Unconsciously, perhaps I wanted to make the effort to study to respond to the actions of my father's generosity, fairness, and good heart.

After our high school graduation, some of my school friends did not continue their education, because they were ready to marry and start a family. Two of my friends wanted to continue their education, but they could not get their first choice of subject in the university. There were entrance exams for each subject in higher education, but for me, because I was the valedictorian, I could choose any subject to concentrate on, even the most difficult entrance exams, which was medicine or engineering. All my family members, mainly men, or the few girls who had studied, had chosen either medicine or engineering. These two professions have special respect in our country. However, with all the privilege that I had, I wanted to be different, especially since the death of my younger brother and dear father. These events helped me in my mind to see if I could study further and find answers to important questions. I thought maybe if I chose psychology, I could find answers to my questions about human beings, and about my behavior and my mind. I thought long and hard about Hamlet's soliloquy, "To be or not to be," and that for me too was an important question. Fortunately, my father helped me in his will as my family didn't force marriage on me, and he paved the way for me to continue my education, which I was eager to do. Because of my mother and her sorrow over the death of my father, I did not choose immediately to go abroad to England, Germany, or the United States and leave my mother alone in Iran.

Finally, after much internal thinking and discussion with friends and teachers, I chose to study philosophy and psychology, one of the subjects in the curriculum at Tehran University. I then planned to go abroad for the graduate level. So I registered at the University of Tehran in Philosophy and Educational Science, which was the only subject that had the most credit hours in psychology. I thought, after all, philosophy is the mother of all sciences.

CHAPTER 3

The Undergraduate Years 1952-1955

The college I attended was the College of Science and Art, which was part of the University of Tehran, but not located on the main campus of the university. The college was near the Parliament, the *Majles*, and other political institutions, and within the earshot of all demonstrations. Each day, I passed in front of the *Majles*, where elected representatives of our country discussed and ruled on national issues. College had a mixed class of girls and boys, and there was a different atmosphere from the girls' high school. Most of the girls were literature majors, but in our classes of philosophy and psychology, there were more boys than girls. At this time, my circle of friends widened. In our neighborhood at home, there was a girl whose name was Mahin, who was related to my aunt, and she was studying English literature. Although she was one year older than I, we became friends. In the evening, we often visited each other and discussed different subjects, our social lives, and everything that happened at college. I also continued to gather on weekends with my girlfriends where we discussed new books, poetry, music, and the status of women and their activities. One of my friends was publishing her first book, and we all tried to help her in that venture.

Another friend was Homa, a poet, who developed a serious problem in this school because of the novelty of boys and girls being allowed to be together. Most of our schooling until this time had been segregated by sex. Between class breaks, girls and boys usually gathered in separate groups. But sometimes a mixed group of boys and girls would get together and discuss social science, social justice, politics, and of course different professors at the college and their ideas. One popular topic for us was Mossadegh, and his involvement in the national front movement and the nationalization of Iranian oil, a movement that Mossadegh handled well diplomatically, at least in my view. However, some of our students were members of the Tudeh (Communist) Party and a few were from the Islamic Front, studying just religious study and social science, and these students did not share the same view. Our discussions during these breaks were mainly social politics. I also joined a second group of students where the discussion was mainly about literature, philosophy, psychology, and the nature of mankind. I was fascinated to read and discuss different philosophers and compare the different ideas and schools of thought and approaches of different philosophers. All these debates and arguments, especially in a mixed group of boys and girls, led to more reading and more competition and deeper friendships. Sometimes, though a boy would display their attraction to a girl and this would occasionally cause problems, especially for the girl and her family. At that time, if a boy openly expressed love to a girl, the reputation of the girl could be tarnished, especially if the attraction is not mutual. My friend Homa (the poet) was studying literature and another male literature student, from southern Iran, fell in love with her and wrote poems openly about her and about his love for her. Every day we would find that he had distributed flyers throughout the school with a new poem about Homa, poems about how Homa was dressing and how she looked in that dress, and these poems were passed from hand to hand in every class. Poor Homa gradually became more and more upset at this because she wasn't even attracted to the boy. She was so embarrassed that sometimes she cried. She lost her self-confidence. Finally, after all this unwanted attention, she began to cry every day. To resolve the situation, she and her family filed a complaint with the dean of the College. All of Homa's friends, including me, rallied around her to try to help her, but it was no use. After the hearing, the college suspended him for one year, but he continued to harass Homa outside the college. Finally, after some time, she had to marry one of her suitors (in an arranged marriage) because he was leaving the country for Belgium and could take her out of the country with him. This was the only way to resolve this problem, and even though she had wanted to stay in college, she had to leave. The poet's life did not end happily. He, later, as a professor of literature was taken to prison where he was tortured and killed during Khomeini's time in the Islamic Republic of Iran.

After this incident, all the college students—male and female—including me, became very cautious in our relationships with each other. This incident also affected the way I approached philosophy and psychology. I became a more serious student and paid no attention to any boys' remarks to me. I was so serious in studying and in my advancement that the boys usually would not dare to come near me. Even though one of them began following me to my home every day, I tried so hard to avoid him that finally he gave up.

In the first year of studying, we had different professors for each subject, usually all with PhD's, who had studied abroad. Many of them had been sent abroad by Reza Shah to study in order to come back and teach at the university as professors. I remember my first paper in the college was about Aneximenes, the philosopher who thought everything originated from air and in the history of philosophy after Tales Maleti, who thought that everything originated from water. Every student had to prepare a paper on each philosopher and present an oral report. One of my professors was Dr. Sadighi, who was the minister of Interior in the Mossadegh government. He was a very serious person in the classroom and meticulous about details. I worked very hard for my first paper. When he returned my paper to me, I remember that in each paragraph of my presentation, he had written either "Very good" or "Excellent!" Later on I found out that apparently I had made the highest grade from him on the final exam—a B. We knew he never gave As. Everybody said I was very lucky because usually from him the highest grade was C or D.

In other subjects like psychology, ethics, and education, one the most popular of our professors and one whom I liked very much was Dr. Mohammed Bagher Hushiar. He had graduated from a German university and was a very serious thinker and writer. He was a real scholar who gave his opinions freely, and in his position did not have to do any administrative work, unlike another professor, Dr. Ali Akbar Siassi, who was professor of psychology, and later became the president and chancellor of the University of Tehran. Dr. Siassi must have been a very good diplomat to be the president of the University of Tehran at the time of nationalization of oil. Later on, he became the president of the Iranian Psychological Association (IPA).

The faculty represented many educational backgrounds. Another professor who had studied in both France and the USA was Dr. Sadighi-Alam. Dr. Jallali, professor of psychology, had studied in the USA. In sociology, Dr. Mahdavi was the instructor. My favorite professor was Dr. Hushiar who was a real scholar and could connect all subjects of education and philosophy and sociology together and discuss every subject from different viewpoints. Usually, his discussions and interpretations were continued after class, and they were so interesting that the students followed him after class and walked with him, talking all the way. Sometimes, there would be as many as fifty students accompanying him on his walk home, just to be near him and hear him talk.

Professor Dr M. H. Hushiar with the author and another student standing below the statue of the great poet A. Ferdowsi in Tehran.

Professor Dr M H Hushiar.

There were also two other professors whose thoughts influenced me. One was Fazel Toni, who taught ethics. He had a vast and deep knowledge of mysticism and Islam in our culture, especially in interpreting all my favorite poems. I even took extra private lessons from him to study his interesting and fascinating interpretation of poems of Molana Rumi, my favorite poet. The other professor, who taught literature, was Dr. Reza Zadeh Shafagh, who, like Dr. Hushiar, had studied in Germany. These two professors were instrumental in my decision to do graduate work. I had received an A+ from both of them. I continued to study very hard and did quite well in every subject. I was serious and eager to learn, unlike some of the male students who only tried to compete with me. Since they were active in politics, they often missed classes and fell behind because of their political activities. During the first year, I observed that many students were very active in three political groups—*Jebhe Melli* (National Front), *Tudeh* (Communist) *Party*, and *Fadian Islam* (Religious Front). Again, during this time—1952-1953—the political situation in Iran was very tense and caused people to strike and many businesses closed down.

Dr. Mossadegh, the head of the *Jebhe Melli* and also an appointed prime minister of the Shah, became very powerful, even gaining control of the army. He was given this extra power by the *Majles* (Parliament), for six months, in order to deal with the nationalization oil process and to settle with Britain and British Petroleum. He gradually wanted to extend his power by another year. It had been about one year that Iran had not exported any oil, and the Treasury of Iran had become empty. Government employees were not paid, and people were very worried. Still, Dr. Mossadegh wanted to extend the term of this special power that the Parliament had given him, a Parliament where some of his friends in the National Front Party, like Dr. Baghai and Ayatollah Kashani, disagreed with his views to extend full power to him. Nevertheless, finally, Mossadegh saw a way to extend his power, although with difficulty. The general public was of the opinion that he was the person who suggested that the Shah and queen leave the country for a "vacation." However, the news that the Shah might leave the country caused many religious groups, ayatollahs, and prominent politicians to go the Royal Court to prevent him from leaving. They were successful in their plea, and on February 28, 1953, the Shah announced in a radio message that because of the people's request, he would not leave the country. By then, the country was in a chaotic situation. Under pressure from Mossadegh, the Shah's twin sister, Princess Ashraf, went into exile in Europe and all the offices of the Royal family members were closed.

M. Mossadegh Prime Minister of Iran (1951-1953).

Another major shock, was the discovery of in a cave of the dead and uniformed body of General Afshar Tuss, head of the police department of Tehran. The chaos escalated. All three major parties were very active. Throughout this economic and political turmoil, people still loved Mossadegh and believed his claim that he could nationalize our oil and keep it out of the hands of a cartel. Every day, on my way to university, I remember passing the *Majles* and seeing people writing on the wall, "We are writing with our blood—death or Mossadegh!"

Meanwhile, in college, followers of all three parties often gathered for meetings, causing classes to close. Gradually, some members of the *Majles* (Parliament) began to oppose Mossadegh. So Mossadegh decided through a referendum from the people to close the Majles. Even today, some analysts are astounded at Mossadegh's sudden change because he had always reminded the Shah of our constitution, and he had respected the Parliament. The whole reason for the chaos was because of our oil and the great variety of foreign influence from many countries. Many books have been written about this time in our history and about Mossadegh, some favorable to him and some not. In short, on August 15, 1953, the Shah and queen left the country for Baghdad and Rome for three days. During that time General Zahedi with the support of the Shah led an uprising against Mossadegh. (Later on, Zahedi's son Ardashir married the daughter of the Shah from his first wife, Fawzieh; the couple later divorced.)

The public rallied around the Shah. By August 19, 1953, the uprising was over, and Mossadegh and his cabinet were arrested and jailed. People were proclaiming in the streets: "Long live the Shah!" The Shah, queen, and royal family came back to Iran. Apparently, the CIA had played a major role during these three days, and it seemed clear that the new president of the USA, Eisenhower, did not want to follow the same path former president Truman had followed.[1] President Eisenhower wanted Iran to include business with Britain and begin again to drill for oil and sell through a consortium signed by all the interested parties in a twenty-five-year contract. The consortium would act to control the oil, with fifty percent of the benefits of the oil belonging to Iran. The Iranian government would pay all the taxes of all member companies. So the oil share was to be divided with 40 percent going to the British Petroleum Company (Anglo-Iranian oil company), and forty percent to five American companies (Gulf Oil Corporation 8 percent, Soccony Vacuum Oil Company 8 percent, Standard Oil Company 8 percent, Standard Oil Company of California 8 percent and The Texas Company 8 percent). Bataafse Petroleum Maatschappij, registered in the Netherlands received 14 percent, and Compagnie Francaise Des Petroles, registered in France, received 6 percent. The days of this coup and events of August 15-18, 1953, are forever in my memory and probably in the memory of every Iranian living then. With Mossadegh and his cabinet arrested, the court hearings began. These hearings and the speeches that Mossadegh gave in his defense were very interesting, and we students followed them with interest. I was very fortunate to have the opportunity to experience one of these court sessions with Mossadegh, and I will never forget what it was like for as long as I live. At first he was sitting under a blanket, and then suddenly, he stood up in his own defense. It was an excellent performance. A great deal of research has been provided about this segment of our history, and many books have been published, with some still in the process of being published.[2] Historians have argued about who was truly considering the welfare of the country, the people and the development or improvement of Iran. Was it the Shah or Mossadegh or both of them in different ways? Their struggle has led to research, books, poems and art, about the three days of events from August 15-18, 1953.

Much remains to be studied about this time since many facets of the events are still not clear and need more enlightenment.

During the university summer vacation that year, I studied composition and music with Professor Hossein Nassehi from the School of Music. He taught me the subject of harmony in my home. I also attempted to find another house for my mother and I so as to distance ourselves from my father's memory, which was in every corner of our old house. Reminders of our love for him and our family life were everywhere. Moreover, the house was too large for my mother to handle, and the location was old and not fashionable anymore. So we bought a house on a street just off Avenue Pahlavi on Elahie Street, Number 12 plus 1. This number would have ordinarily been 13, but apparently, the former owners didn't like to use 13, so they used 12 plus 1. It was a very popular street and a new development toward the north of Tehran on the way to Shemiran. The move was very distressing for my mother, who was very sad about leaving our house. I think she suffered a lot because of this change, so much in fact that she became unwell once we moved into the new house. After a time, she recovered, but I learned from this experience how deeply change and moving can affect people, and that it is more difficult for old people to change than for young people, as change seems to come easier.

The author attending (with her brother Aliakbar) the celebration of the birthday of Shah M. R. Pahlavi.

The author (after the death of her father) with her mother in the family's new home.

The author (in remembrance of her father) with her nieces Nahid and Shahla
visiting the Persepolis (the old capital of Persia from 513 BC) and
the tomb of Saadi the great poet of Persia in Shiraz.

In the second year of college, some of my professors (such as Dr. Sadighi, the Minister of Interior in Dr. Mossadegh's government) were in jail. People generally seemed to think that behind every event in Iran there was a conspiracy made more complicated by the influence of foreign interests in Iranian resources, especially oil. The foreign interests—England, Russia, the United States, France, and Germany—had always tried to influence the three political parties in Iran and even important positions and personnel in the government. I tried to stay independent and keep myself out of political parties and focus on my studies, hoping in the future to try to see how I could later help my country and its people with some good service.

During the last year of college, we had to choose a subject to study and research for a thesis (which was mandatory). After some consideration, I followed my interest in music and psychology and chose the subject "The Effect of Music in the Treatment of Mental Illness and Efficiency in Workforce." I enjoyed writing about this subject. Also, in this year, there were a few male students in the class competing with me for the top grades. They mainly wanted to show themselves as achievers because they tried many times to get close to me and seemed to think maybe just because they were knowledgeable they could attract my attention. One of them, Hamid, who was about two years older than me, tried especially hard to show himself up as being very knowledgeable in philosophy. He was always staring at me, looking at me, and following me around. One day, in an indirect conversation, I tried to tell him that I was not interested in *any* kind of relationship with him because I wanted to continue my education and obtain a PhD. However, I was not sure that he would give up on his practice of following me. Since Iran had no graduate PhD program in psychology, I hoped to continue my education in another country. I was constantly considering which country I should go to for further study. I discussed this matter with my professors and friends, trying to get their advice, while at the same time I was studying hard to be the most successful student and get an academic scholarship. In high school and university, I had studied English as a foreign language, so I could choose either England or America. The United States was very far from Iran, and I hesitated to go there because it would leave my mother all alone, and I wanted to be able to see her during vacations. So, although I wanted to go to the United States, it seemed too far and not practical. Emotionally, I did not want to go to England because I considered that country had been involved in oil disputes and had treated Iran unfairly. Instead, because of the influence of my good professor, Dr. Hushiar and his recommendations, in my final exam and in my oral examination with him, I decided, perhaps wrongly, to go to Germany. I say "wrongly" because I did not know German, and English was a more international language. But Germany was closer, and on summer vacations, I could return to Iran to see my mother. This decision was not an easy one to make, as I would have to learn German.

As soon as I made the decision, I began to study German. One of our relatives, Keykavus Jahandari, was an excellent translator and writer of German, so I studied privately with him. Only a few of my friends knew of my plans because I only told very close friends. I tried very hard to finish all the exams early in the spring so I could have peace of mind to study German in the summer and pass the Ministry of Education exam, a requirement for leaving the country to study in Germany. I also learned that some of the college boys who were competing with me in order to attract me further, had also chosen Germany for further study. That year, 1955-'56, Germany, after World War II, had become a very popular place for the Iranians to go. Through my German language teacher, Mr. Jahandari, and my professor Dr. Hushiar, I selected the University of Heidelberg, the oldest university in Germany.

The author with her cousin K. K. Jahandari
(who was also her German teacher).

Accepting my decision to go to Germany as a girl alone was very hard for my family and especially for my mother. One day early in our new year, around March 21, the beginning of spring *and* our important holiday Nowruz, my mother, without telling me, invited people to a surprise party for me. She invited my favorite teacher from high school, Mr. Sadigh Esfandiari, whom I respected highly, and my closest friends and close family members. I did not know why they had come to our home, but I was very happy to see them because I loved them all very much. First, my kind teacher, with his powerful voice, started to speak, and then I began to wonder about why all these people were in my home, although I was anxious to hear what he had to say. Very soon I realized that the meeting was about my leaving to continue my education in Heidelberg. Mr. Esfandiari and my friends, like Mahin, and especially my mother, stressed that they would miss me and it would be better for me to stay in Iran. So I immediately had to justify to them my leaving, and more importantly to myself, I had to deal with my own conscience. I assured them that I loved them all deeply and that I would miss them too, but because of my father's will, my own motivation, and for later service to our country and people, it was necessary for me to study in Germany. I told them I would hold them in my heart and mind, and that by further study and increasing my knowledge, I would enlighten my mind, and I promised that when I came back from Germany with a PhD, I could serve my mother, my friends, my family, my community, and my country much better. It was difficult for me because all my life I have been unable to express my love and my emotions openly and freely to my friends, teachers, and relatives. I have suffered with this problem, but this inability to express love openly is a part of our culture. I remember that my mother also followed the message of our poets that a real love should be kept in the heart and mind and that if you express this real love to the object of the emotion you spoil the love. I used to have a private book in which I wrote to express my feelings, emotions and love, writing to the stars. So I had a problem with this meeting, saying that although I loved them all, I still needed to expand my knowledge in order to serve them better in the future.

The meeting went on for a very long while with arguments throughout the evening, but this only made me more determined. I was resolved to study harder for a scholarship and not to bother my mother much with my financial needs. I was very happy with the idea of attending the oldest university in Germany, and I studied German vigorously and even applied to enter the university in the summer semester in May 1956. The foreign language exam was in April, so I sent the application and got ready for the German foreign language exam. I received notice that I had been accepted before I took the exam, but the scholarship depended on my doing well in the German exam. I studied even harder, took the German examination, and made reservations and bought airline tickets for Heidelberg. My mother finally yielded to the inevitable decision and arranged for one of our cousins who was studying engineering in Germany to meet me at the airport and to help me get settled.

My uncle and his wife knew a friend whose daughter, Azizeh Hajizadeh, was studying dentistry in Heidelberg, and they gave me her address and wrote a letter to her. She later became my closest girl friend in Germany. I arranged to have the German test results sent to me in Germany. I was also praying that I had done well on the exam so that I could get an academic scholarship.

Of course, I felt somewhat guilty in my conscience for leaving my mother by herself, but she was not actually left alone. She was with my aunt, and she had two close servants from our old house. I promised to write her three or four times a week and asked my girlfriends to go to see her more often. One friend wrote a poem complaining about my decision to leave the country. In it she blamed me and said I did not love her and my other friends and that was why I was leaving. At that time it was not easy for a girl to go abroad for graduate studies, and I was determined to remember all the good advice of my mother and my aunt to protect myself as a girl traveling alone. At that time, a girl had to limit her relationship with boys and protect herself so that she would be pure and a virgin before marriage; otherwise, our society would reject the girl and see to it that she was punished. As I was preparing to leave, I heard through my friends that the boy, whom I will call Hamid and not his real name, who was competing against me at the University of Tehran, had already gone to Heidelberg. Sometimes I had the feeling that maybe he knew my intention and was following me to be near me. But I knew at the same time that I did not want to lose my independence and that I really did not love him either.

With some fear, guilt, much love from family and friends, and great hope for the future, I got ready to go to the airport. A large number of friends and family members (about fifty people) came to the airport to say good-bye to me. I was crying and they were crying as well. I did not like to use the word *good-bye*, and said instead, "I'll see you soon" or the German term, "Auf ein wiedersehen." I have always liked this German *good-bye* because it promises the hope of seeing you again. So I said "Auf ein wiedersehen" to my friends, family, my mother, and Iran at the end of April 1956.

[1.]   Kermit Roosevelt, *Counter Coup*, New York: McGraw-Hill, 1979.

[2.]   Stephen Kinzer, *All the Shah's Men*, New York: Wiley& Sons, July 18, 2003.

CHAPTER 4

On the Road to Germany and Heidelberg University for PhD 1956-1961

My first flight out of the country brought up many emotions at once: excitement, fear, hesitation, anxiety, deep affection, and massive guilt. I was leaving my mother, family, and friends. On the plane, I tried to control myself and keep from crying by thinking of my future. Reading one of the many books I was carrying in my hand luggage also helped, and I was able to take my mind off my sadness by reading. My hand luggage was heavy and filled with books and my own notes, which I thought I could not get in Germany. My flight on Scandinavian Airlines (SAS) made several stops, the common practice in those days. Since I was going to meet my cousin in Stuttgart first, before going to Heidelberg, I flew by way of Frankfurt, changing there for the shorter flight to Stuttgart.

I dreaded carrying my very heavy hand luggage, and I vividly remember the kindness and help of a passenger who was also making the same connections. He helped me to manage my bulky hand luggage as I boarded the very small connecting plane to Stuttgart. In Stuttgart, my cousin Massud and his girlfriend Iris welcomed me at the airport; and after an overnight stop in Stuttgart, they took me to Heidelberg. We arrived on May 6, 1956, and we went together to the Office of International Students (*Auslandsamt*) for official registration. Massud and Iris returned to Stuttgart the next day, leaving me to stay in a hotel until I could find a room to rent. The next day, I went to the *Auslandsamt* for a list of rental rooms and found that rental accommodations were scarce. There was still much war damage from World War II, and there were not many buildings and rooms available for rent in Germany, and especially not in Heidelberg. Because of the shortage of rooms, the university appealed to families to rent extra rooms to students. Finding a room was not easy, and even if you were successful, there were many limitations on cooking, bathing, individual self-care, and having visitors. I even wrote later an article, ***Zimmersuche ist ein Abenteuer*** (Finding a Room is an Adventure) on the difficulties of finding a room and sent a letter to the editor of the newspaper.

Heidelberg
- http://ww2.heidelberg.de/download/ bilder/300DPICM/02_SCHLO.TIF
- Source: Heidelberg Marketing GmbH

One day, while I was looking at the board that listed available rooms for rent, suddenly, to my surprise, I met Hamid, my former colleague at the University of Tehran, the student who had competed with me there. My heart started beating fast from surprise and astonishment. He greeted me with pride and acted as if he knew everything there was to know about Heidelberg. He said he had been there for a month. I wondered if he was following me or knew of my plans or if he was still competing with me. I had very mixed feelings, and I was skeptical of him. He eagerly offered to help me, and in spite of my skepticism, I allowed him to show me some rental rooms he knew of. Finally, I found a small (though not ideal) room in a large old building. Fortunately, there was no contract to sign, and the terms were on a monthly basis. You could cancel the rental room one month in advance. Because the university term and the classes had already started, a hotel would have been expensive for me as a student, so I took this room temporarily.

During this time of challenge and transition, I was very homesick. Every night I prayed alone, meditated, and cried for my mother. I wrote to her daily. I felt so guilty about leaving her alone. Then one day, I received a letter from my mother, giving me the good news of the results of my German exam, which made me eligible for an academic scholarship. This was wonderful news, lessening my guilt, because there would now be less financial pressure on my mother. My guilty conscience was relieved a little bit also when my girlfriends in Iran wrote that they visited my mother often and that my letters were helping my mother overcome her own empty nest feeling. My friends said my letters were a great help and told me to continue to write the long daily letters. In those days, telephone and international communication was not as advanced as today, so letters were very important.

It was significant for my goal that my studies in Heidelberg were going well. I called Azizeh Hajizadeh, my uncle's friend, who was studying dentistry in Heidelberg. She was very kind and immediately invited me to her room. When she came to visit me and saw my room she told me she would help me find a better place. She herself had a much better room. Very soon we both recognized we had much in common being in a foreign country. Little by little, through her, I met many Iranians who were studying medicine. Among them were Abbass Khalili, Darius Fahimi, and Sadegh Massarrat, who later became professors of medicine at universities in Germany—Heidelberg, Marburg, and others. In general, there was a larger group of medical students than philosophy and social science students. Very few Iranians (except for Hamid and me) were studying philosophy or psychology in the School of Arts and Science. In the beginning, Hamid was the only fellow Iranian in that faculty. We sometimes met each other, and he continued to follow me, trying to pretend to be close to me and understand me, but all the time his behavior looked insincere and I could not trust him.

Fortunately, Hamid studied philosophy as his major subject, not psychology or education, and not even sociology, which were my real interests, so we did not have classes together; and since I didn't see him at lectures, he didn't interrupt my studying. I had chosen a heavy schedule in the hope of finishing the PhD more quickly and returning home to my family and being of service to my country. Accordingly, I was determined not to waste time, and to diligently pursue my academic work. Above all, I decided to place my studies at the service of mankind. Understanding the classes in German language was not easy for me, since German was still a new second foreign language. I had to take many notes including words and terms that I couldn't understand, and I had to study independently. I took a small dictionary everywhere with me, and when I could, I would compare my notes with other German students. Gradually, I made friends with some German students and students from other countries. Since I was not allowed to cook in my room, I had to eat in restaurants or in the student dining room. I was not at all used to the food, especially dishes with ham and pork. In our culture and religion, eating pork was not permitted, so my choices were limited.

Hamid took advantage of my lack of knowledge about all the new food I was eating and always invited me to go to restaurants with him. After one or two invitations, I accepted his offer, on condition that I pay for my dinner. Azizeh told me that in my status as a single Persian girl, I should only go out if we were "going Dutch." I learned that this idiom meant that everybody would pay for himself or herself. If I followed this practice, she said I could go out with a boy without causing any expectations of a relationship, and I could maintain my independence. In our tradition, Persian girls were limited in their communications with members of the opposite sex. At that time (and still today in some families), Iranian girls are not allowed to have close relations with boys before marriage; otherwise, society and families, would reject them. It was important that a girl be pure and a virgin before marriage—that was practically a rule for all middle-class families and our society accepted these rules and regulations. In addition to following our traditions, for me, keeping my independence in relationships was also another issue. I always wanted to compete with boys. I wanted to be not only equal to males, but also to outshine them. I usually resisted any thought that considered women weak or inferior to men.

In this period of adjustment to my new environment, I gained about twenty pounds from eating Wiener Schnitzel, goulash, potatoes, and other rich German foods. In the *Menza* (the student dining room), I ate a great deal of the thick German soup called *Eintopf*. You could find everything in that bowl of soup—it was a very fattening dish. Soon, with the help of Azizeh, I found a larger room with limited permission to cook once a day. Since it was very far from the university campus, I bought a bicycle to ride when the weather was good. To keep to my demanding schedule, which required intensive language study, I stayed up until three or four in the morning, managing to stay awake by drinking the coffee I could make in the room. Thank goodness I was able to make coffee or tea in my room. Sometimes Azizeh would call me by whistling outside my window, and I would slip out quietly to walk with her to take a break from studying. Heidelberg was a very safe place to walk at night, and I noticed that most German people walked every day for about an hour.

Soon it was time for the first assignment to be turned in. My first assignment and paper was written for a colloquium, *Kolloquium for Graduate Students and PhD Candidates*. My professor was Professor Christian Caselman, professor of Education and Educational Psychology. There were only two women, including me, in this seminar. The professor gave us a list of topics to choose from, to study and research and present the results in a paper in class. During the first hour of the seminar, other students took many of the topics, but I didn't dare to choose immediately. I wanted to think about the subjects, but by the second hour, German students had taken the easiest paper topics requiring the least work. One or two difficult subjects were left. Professor Caselman noticed my hesitation to choose and said, "How are you, Ms. Redjali?" Then he said, "With your philosophy undergraduate background, maybe you could choose this subject: 'The Metaphysical Aspect of Punishment by Kant and Hegel.'" His suggestion put me in a state of shock. No German student had chosen that topic, and it would be difficult for me in a foreign language. But after a silence, I said that yes, I would choose that subject with only one condition—that my presentation would be scheduled at the end of the semester so that I would have more time for research and writing. Professor Caselman agreed and told me I would present the paper during the last week of the semester.

This demanding topic required intense study. As much as I liked the ideas of Kant and Hegel, their writing styles were not easy to follow. Sometimes, one sentence of Kant's would take two pages, finishing with the verb on the third page, and all the phrases being joined with many commas. Finally, after great effort, I finished the paper one week early, leaving sometime to develop my method of presentation. The hard work paid off; the grade was among the highest in the class, encouraging and motivating me toward a doctor of philosophy degree in educational and clinical psychology. I chose sociology as a minor subject. In writing this first paper, I became deeply involved with the philosophy of Immanuel Kant and especially his ethics, a system which I have, since then, followed almost all my life.

Along with my studies, I kept up with the news of Iran through newspapers. Mossadegh had finished his three-year jail term and was out. German newspapers published a lot of news about the Shah and especially about Queen Soraya, who was half German. Pictures of Soraya and her German mother were often in the newspapers. There was also news of her many trips with the Shah to India or America to seek traditional or modern medical treatment to become pregnant. Apparently, the Shah and queen wanted a son in order to continue the Pahlavi dynasty. According to the constitution of Iran, a girl could not ascend to the throne, although in earlier times in the Persian empire, it had been possible. In general, Iran was slow on the road to economic development and progress, but the country needed more development and an educated workforce.

In Heidelberg, I continued to study hard while at the same time Hamid was trying to get closer to me, claiming that he loved me. I told him I had cultural and personal barriers, which kept me from getting closer. In reality, I was also skeptical of his claim of love. I was not sure if his love was real. To me, real love means not only sex but also love of the existence of someone—love for the total life of another person. This love includes both mind and body, and a love of the existence of two people who have become one. This mystical love is a common belief in my culture. This love covers all time and all occasions, and one sees the other with him or her as mystical poets described in their poems. When two people see each other as one—one person rather than two—this is real love. Since I was not sure of Hamid's claim of love, and I didn't know how honest he was in his claims, I tried to avoid him. One day on the *Hauptstrasse* (main street) of Heidelberg, I noticed him walking and behind him was a blonde girl following. He would turn back from time to time to speak to her. This behavior was very strange to me, especially as in our culture it was usually that the boy followed the girl. He had a proud look on his face at having a girl following him. A few weeks later, I saw them again this time hand in hand, although again sometimes he would be walking in front, and she would be walking behind. Very soon the rumor among Iranian students was that Hamid had a girlfriend, so I was relieved and free in my mind of doubts about him and his claim of love for me. Still, I continued to try to avoid seeing him as much as possible and even attempted to find another room and change my address again. I realized what I had suspected—that physical attraction was more important to him than a relationship of the mind, and his claim of a real love was not real at all. While this experience was very painful for me, and I was disappointed in him, my concentration on studying became stronger, and I became more productive in all my classes, making good grades. At the same time, I believe he, on the other hand, was digressing in his path toward the PhD. German universities allow great academic freedom and they are designed only for students who are self-motivated and who do not abuse their academic freedom. Otherwise, one will be what Heidelberger's call "*ein ewige Student*," an eternal student. This term seemed to fit Hamid, since getting the *Magister* degree (a degree for those who didn't complete the dissertation) took him more than ten years. The German system is designed for elite scholars but gradually these universities are being made available for the masses.

This idea of academic freedom and other principles that shaped the purpose of a German university were laid out in the writings of Wilhelm von Humboldt from the design of the German University in Berlin in 1809. These principles cover

- relative independence of the university,
- the idea of academic freedom as the center of the university for both professors and students,
- the unity of research and teaching, and
- the political relevance of the idea of education.

Humboldt's principle of the unity of research and teaching and the idea of academic freedom attracted me as I read and studied deeply the idea of German University and the question of how German students could study with the consideration of the concept of academic freedom.

Another interesting fact of historical interest was that at this time foreign students, especially Americans, preferred the German University model above the traditional English and French University. In the decade after the war, Americans, followed by Iranians, were the largest international contingent of students in Germany. This preference did not extend to the study of either German history or the German language. Neither was well-known as a research subject nor were college libraries adequately stocked with writings of German authors. The sole explanation for this attraction was the fame and reputation of the German university system itself and the standing of German science, literature, and philosophy in the nineteenth century. Famous English universities like Oxford and Cambridge, on the other hand, were still marked by the thinking of the late Middle Ages, focusing on the study of classics. The French University concept seemed to develop as a vocational and trade-oriented type of institution. In the German university model, professors and students are not only teachers and students but are also research fellows at the same time. Famous and learned men, scholars and philosophers like Kant, Shilling, Hegel, and Schleiermacher emerged from this system—all academians and professors at universities. German universities were a home for most learned men in art and science.[1] In contrast, most of the learned men and women in France or England were based outside the university. In the Iranian's view of education at the university level, the courses were preset and the students just followed the curriculum, whereas in Germany there were many choices.

I became so fascinated with this concept of a university—the unity of research and teaching, and academic freedom for students and professors—that I started to read and study more about it, hoping the topic would help me in writing my PhD thesis. I became curious about the learning methods of students in German universities as they related to von Humboldt's principles. Every semester, I took the most credits possible to finish all the requirements in psychology, education, and sociology and have enough credits to apply for my thesis and work toward a dissertation for the doctor of philosophy degree. Between terms and midterms, I enjoyed the friendship of my good Iranian friends Azizeh, Abbass, Sadegh, and others. We sometimes hiked together from "Philosophy Road," *Philosophen Weg*, in Heidelberg, through beautiful Odenwald. Together we celebrated the Iranian New Year (*Nowruz*) and toured Europe together. I always cherished their friendship and treasured all the memories of my time as a student in Heidelberg.

Celebration of the author's birthday in Heidelberg with friends, including the late Azizeh (standing behind the author).

Azizeh and I chose Paris for our first study trip. For about a week, we enjoyed the rich experience of sightseeing in Paris and the surrounding areas. We loved the daily French habit of starting in the morning with croissants and coffee and finishing with French onion soup at night. In between, we enjoyed the excellent French cuisine. Whenever I think of Paris and France, I think of Azizeh. I still find it hard to believe how she died, much later. She just went to bed one night in Bonn and never woke up. She had been an excellent orthodontist in Bonn, and she remains in the heart and mind of all her friends. I will never forget all the help she gave me when I had first arrived to Heidelberg. After my first trip to Paris, I returned many times, and each time, I remembered my time in Paris with her. How I would love to repeat all my experiences there with her again. I think of her often.

I also enjoyed another trip arranged by the Education Department named *Pestalozzi's Tour to Switzerland*. This tour concentrated on the life history of the famous Swiss educator Johann Heinrich Pestalozzi (1746-1827), from his birth to his death in Switzerland. We spent one week with Professor Caselman, Professor Schorb, and members of the PhD seminar, visiting everywhere in Switzerland where Pestalozzi taught and wrote his theory of education and developed his idea of a training school for children. During the breaks we discussed his life, his relations with other educators like Froebel, Rosseau, John Dewey, and others. An added benefit of this tour was that, in addition to learning and studying Pestalozzi, the members of the PhD seminar came to know each other better, and our professors also learned more about us, which I'm sure helped them to guide us better. There is a proverb in Iran that says, "If you want to get to know someone, you need to travel with that person."

Professor Christian Caselmann during his lecture.

Welcoming Professor Caselmann at the Frankfort airport, on his return from a successful educational reform trip from Puerto Rico, the author, the professor's family, and his assistant, Dr A.O. Shorb.

A year later, this same group visited Holland with another theme: to study the Dutch educational system and to get to know the idea of the Dutch educator, Professor Longefeld. We also visited the International Court at The Hague and the World Exhibition in Belgium. On this trip, an Iranian medical student friend, Sadegh Massarrat, also joined our group. This trip helped us with international and cross-cultural studies, as we viewed the world exhibition in Belgium and saw the international court. Iran also had a pavilion in this World Expo, and I delighted in showing the Iran Pavilion to the members of the seminar. Our pavilion was one of the most interesting and beautiful exhibits, decorated with crafts and artifacts from all the different ethnic groups in Iran. Kurds, Ghashghai, Baluch, and other tribes of Iran were represented in the pavilion, and I tried to explain as much as I could about each tribe and its art. At that time, I really felt very proud of our pavilion and my country.

Meanwhile, my student-life was full of challenges. Each term I had about twenty to thirty hours, more than average, in psychology, education, and sociology. Usually, the average student would take no more than fifteen credits. But I was eager to learn and finish my studies as soon as I could, so I pushed myself to do more and work harder, not realizing that I was neglecting my health. Even when I became sick, I would wait as long as possible before going to the doctor, and on one occasion, I was so ill that I was hospitalized.

While I studied hard and always enjoyed my courses, I liked the various approaches to psychology. I soaked up the psychoanalytical approaches of Sigmund Freud, C. G. Jung, Alfred Adler, and the differences in their thinking. I became interested in developmental psychology, experimental psychology, and behavioral psychology, studying Piaget and B. F. Skinner. All these different approaches I found very interesting, and in our spare time, my colleagues in psychology, especially two of them Christa Meyer Quante and Hans Jürgen Phistner, and I spent hours discussing these scholars, their pathway, and their ideas. I met Hans in class and became friends with him and his family. His wife was a teacher and very artistic, and he had a very fine family. Later on, he became professor of psychology at the Teacher Training College in Heidelberg. His thoughts went very deep, and I cherished the strong friendship I had with his family. Christa Meyer Quante received her diploma in psychology—she was from East Germany and lived with her roommate Else Rabe, also from East Germany, who was a writer and author of many books. I was friends with both of them. They explained how they had escaped from East Germany and the Communist regime after the war. They had to leave all their belongings behind. Else Rabe was very upset about leaving her books, but she did choose to leave them for the sake of freedom. I have always respected them and learned much from them and their experiences. I gained knowledge from them, which has helped me all my life.

Because we were studying in the same field, I began to spend more and more time with my colleagues in psychology and education, especially with Christa Meyer Quante or with the family of Hans Phistner. I still kept time for Azizeh and my Iranian friends. My old friend Hamid would not join the Iranian group because he had apparently become very involved with his German girlfriend, who would not allow him to meet with others from his native land to speak Farsi. Strangely enough, I did not see him at the university either, only occasionally when he needed money. Then he would call me and borrow money from me.

Picture of author with the writer, Else Rabe, in Heidelberg.

Twice he came to me with his tape recorder and offered to sell it to me. I was surprised to see how he had changed. I was sure that he was getting money from his wealthy family, even more than I was, and I wondered how he could spend all his allowance and be so desperate. When I asked him about his PhD courses or philosophy courses, he gave me strange responses, which did not ring true. Since I was not involved with him anymore, and he had already hurt me badly, I did not ask further. But when he came the third time to borrow money, I told him that I was limited in what I had already and only had my scholarship money. I told him he could not keep asking me for money or trying to sell me something anymore. At these times, I would remember the poems and speeches about pure love and pure existence, written by Jean Paul Sartre, Kierkegaard, or Molana Rumi. With their truths in my mind, I sensed that Hamid was deceiving me. Anyway, I was making quite good progress in my university courses, and it was close to the time to choose the PhD topic. Hamid was still struggling in his courses, and I tried to avoid him completely. I think when he saw himself so far behind, he gradually tried to avoid me too. Maybe he was abusing academic freedom, which put more responsibility on the self-discipline of the students. I also wondered why he had become so strange and had changed so drastically.

Most of the foreign students, including those from Iran, tried to choose topics related to their own country for their theses and dissertations, but I chose various topics, always thinking of subjects that could help me serve my country and my people better. I made appointments with my professor to select a thesis for the dissertation, trying to relate the topics to Iran, the people, and their needs. My professor and I met for about two hours one afternoon, discussing my topic, but he completely rejected every topic I suggested about Iran, saying he did not have enough knowledge about Iran to supervise me. After exploring many subjects, I suggested studying the different systems of German universities and comparing them with those in Iran. The Iranian universities at that time seemed to me to follow the French university idea. After a silence in which he weighed this suggestion, he said, "How would it be to study and research the field of higher education reform in West Germany focusing on the time span when Germany was divided into West and East Germany?" He said that there was a need for research and study of the reformation of the German University model, and since he was very active in that reform process, he could supervise me as well. He caught my interest by saying that when I returned to Iran, I could help in the reform of the Iranian universities and higher education and could share the results of my studies. I thought that would be both a very ambitious plan and a difficult topic for me. I would need to know first in great detail more about the concept used by German universities, then I would need to know the present situation of the university model and conclude what reforms were needed and how these reforms could take place. I shared these concerns with him, and he said he admired my thinking and told me that he knew from the papers I had written that I could manage this topic. If I agreed to the topic, he said that he would provide me with the assistance of one of his associates, Dr. Alfons-Otto Schorb, who would work with me to determine the areas to be covered and to develop a study plan. A PhD dissertation requires an original research in the field, and Dr. Schorb would see that I was going in the right direction.

I left this meeting with my head reeling at the thought of what lay ahead, and the very next day, I made an appointment with Dr. Schorb to clarify everything. Fortunately, I already knew both him and his wife very well from the two education tours we had together. Dr. Schorb welcomed me warmly, and I began by telling him how in the beginning when a foreign student arrived at a class in a German University, the student could be completely lost, because there was no one to explain the system and how it worked. Students needed to understand the concept of the unity of research and teaching, academic freedom, and the need for self-discipline. Finally, after several meetings and working plans with Dr. Schorb, my topic became clear—"A Study of the Present Students of the College of Art and Science of the German University." In German, *"Wie gestalten die Studierenden der geisteswissenschaftlichen Fakutaeten der Gengewart ihr Studium."* The field was in educational psychology. The professors for the exam were Professor Rudert, head of the Psychology Department; Professor Caselman, head of the Education Department; and Professor Hermann Roehrs, who would examine the thesis. Dr. Shorb would help me with the draft of the plan, the testing, pretesting, posttesting, samples, evaluations, and the results, making comments and suggestions as I went along.

Planning how to do the dissertation was not easy, and I still needed to study hard for the courses I was taking. I also had to have excellent time management skills because I would still be taking courses in psychology and education. In sociology (my minor), I took courses with the well-known sociologist Alfred Weber, the brother of Max Weber. For a change, I also took a course in counterpoint in the Music Department. This made up for the loneliness I felt as I missed the music lessons I had in Iran. It was an interesting class, dwelling on the differences between harmony and counterpoint. I found counterpoint more interesting than harmony in modern music.

Unfortunately, I could not take any more music courses because of my heavy workload, but whenever I had time, I went to the opera in Heidelberg and Mannheim. I loved the operas of Richard Wagner, because his music seemed to mesh with my appreciation—it was as if his operas spoke to my mind and my emotions. Not many of my colleagues or friends were interested in either Wagner or opera, but I loved all his music. I tried to analyze his personal life and determine from the music where he was suffering a lot. Maybe without that pain, he could not have produced such deep and wonderful pieces.

Meanwhile, I prepared the draft of my research plan, changing it many times until it was approved. I had to learn the history of the German University, the idea behind it, and then prepare a test, a questionnaire, which covered the results for the present time. For the meetings with

Dr. Schorb, we sometimes chose a cafe near the university, where we discussed my thesis over coffee. Fortunately, in German coffee shops, you could have one cup of coffee and yet stay a long time, one or two or more hours, discussing and working. I was enduring my work, and he was persuasive and persistent in promoting it so far that after many meetings and work in my research plan and the subject, I became clear and sure in my methods, making progress step by step. The test I created, revised many times and pre-tested, had 100 questions, including the control questions. I planned to interview ten percent of students at the University of Heidelberg. I interviewed samples at three stages in their studies. One group at the beginning of their second semester, one group in the middle of their studies in the fourth semester, and one group at the end of their studies in the eighth semester. I was able to complete this time-consuming task, but it taxed all my communication skills. The participants were very cooperative, both during the interviews and later in the testing.

In the meantime, the news from Iran at this time kept us preoccupied. SAVAK had been established in Iran—the Center for National Information Service, similar to the CIA in the United States. With the influence of the Soviet Union and the tension between East and West, Iran established SAVAK in January 1957. The plan for SAVAK had been created during Mossadegh's time and approved by Parliament in 1953, but it was not until January 1957 that the Shah fully established SAVAK. The USA and several specialists from the FBI and CIA assisted in developing this organization.

The other news from Iran concerned the separation of Queen Soraya and the Shah, apparently because Soraya could not produce an heir. She suggested the separation herself and offered to divorce her beloved Shah so that he could find a wife who could provide a successor to the throne. On February 13, 1958, Queen Soraya left Iran for a skiing vacation in San Moritz, Switzerland, and did not return. Later on, in March, came the announcement of their separation, undertaken for the good of the throne, despite their continued love for each other. German newspapers carried pictures of her almost every day with her German mother, and these pictures revealed her great sadness over the separation. Much later, during the time when Princess Diana was so often in the news, I thought back to the rough times Queen Soraya experienced at that time and for the rest of her life.

Again, just as in my undergraduate days, Iranian students in Heidelberg became very active in different political groups *Jebhe Melli* (the National

Front), *Tudeh* party (the Communist party), and the *Islamic Front*. A few students, like me, remained aloof from this political involvement. I kept busy studying, and as always, my goal was to be a good student and not waste my time on politics. I kept focused on my goal. I wanted to return to Iran as soon as I could and to help people there. To achieve this long-term goal, I thought I could serve my country and humanity best by distancing myself from political groups in Heidelberg.

At the same time, I was extremely busy evaluating my research and testing. I had almost finished all the tests, and I was evaluating and counting using both qualitative and quantitative analyses when I received an interesting call.

It was the dean of International Students of University of Heidelberg, Mr. Helmut Zacker, and he asked me urgently to meet with him. I was busy with my dissertation and told him about my situation and time limit and stressed also how deeply I was involved with the evaluation of my research and didn't have much time. He insisted that it was important to meet with him concerning Iran and Iranian students in Heidelberg. He also said that since my field was psychology I would be just the person to discuss his concerns. After he mentioned the name of my country, Iran, I did not resist any longer and went to see him, to see what he expected from me. After all, my reason for study was to serve my country!

I met with him and his assistant Gert Schneider one morning about 10:00 am, and he began by saying that the number of Iranian and international students was increasing in Heidelberg. The greatest number of international students were Americans, followed next by Iranian. There was an urgent need for the people of Heidelberg and the community to have a better understanding of different cultures, he said, "especially your country and your culture". With better understanding and better communication, the community could treat the international students better. He provided examples of situations and problems which foreign students faced in Heidelberg. There was no doubt that something should be done. I admitted there was a problem because I had suffered myself, for example, in finding a room. I told him about my experiences trying to find a room in Heidelberg. Each time the landladies would ask many strange questions, and I could tell that when they heard the country I came from they didn't understand anything about my culture or my perspective. Mr. Zacker said excitedly that this was the very reason that the Office of International Students was trying to establish several programs for better understanding of different cultures. He had planned to develop programs through media, radio, newspaper, special presentations, and information evenings, so that each country's culture could be introduced and featured.

When I replied that I would like to help in this program and asked what he expected from me, he immediately said, "A lot—first, start to write your experiences in finding a room as an article for the Heidelberg daily newspaper". He also asked me to help him arrange a Persian evening to be held at City Hall—the *Rathaus*—for the public. This evening event would be focused on history, culture, and art from Iran. He asked me to involve other students he knew in different fields, who would be able to help with the art and handicraft exhibition so that we could show the variety of different parts of Iran. He also said he would like to end the evening with a program of music. Since I also studied music and composition, he asked me to include a new Persian music student, Sa'id Khadiri, in the program.

All these duties looked overwhelming to me, especially with my work on the dissertation. I explained to him my concerns about my studies, but I told him I would help as much as I could within some limitations. He understood and outlined three tasks for me: to participate in a radio interview and talk about all the problems foreign students face in Heidelberg, to write an article for the local newspaper, and finally, to give a speech on Persian music in coordination with Sa'id Khadiri, the Iranian music student in music education department. The dean said that Sa'id would play his own composition. These three tasks sounded manageable, and I could not say no, especially since my conscience made me feel obligated to help. Anything to encourage a better understanding of the diversity of culture, and especially my country and my culture.

After a few days, I had an interview at a local radio station, *Sud Deutsche Rundfunk*. This was my first radio interview, and fortunately, it went very well. My friends and professor were very positive in their comments. Next, I tried to write an article about my adventure in finding a room in Heidelberg. I titled it "Finding a Room Is an Adventure in Heidelberg," (*Zimmer Zuche ist ein Abenteuer*). I asked Mrs. Rabe, my friend the writer, to edit the article. She read it and said it was just fine. She thought that my realistic approach, including all of my conversations with landladies and their misunderstandings and inquiries of my country and me, and my answer would be interesting to readers. She helped me to add a little humor to the article. As a result, the daily newspaper welcomed the article and published it—my first published article in

German. I was happy that this article might help to improve life a little for foreign students in Germany.

We planned the cultural evening at a meeting at city hall. Iranian students attended, and we divided the tasks. One student assumed the job of speaking about Iranian culture and art. I was assigned to speak about the traditional and modern music of Iran. Then I was to introduce the pianist Sa'id Khadiri who would play his composition. Before the event, which was scheduled for Wednesday, July 31, 1959, the very last day of the summer semester, we had several meetings and rehearsals, all of which went well. We made a collection of handicrafts of different parts of Iran for this special evening. I still remember how wonderful the evening was. The foreign students, and especially Iranian students, invited their landladies, professors, friends, and prominent people of Heidelberg. The city hall was quite full and the local newspaper, *Rhein Neckar Zeitung*, published a report on the occasion. In the article, Sa'id's playing and his composition received a very good review, and the newspaper published his picture with the article.

Author with the professors and the people of Heidelberg at the Persian Cultural Evening at the City Hall of Heidelberg.

After the Persian evening celebration, our group of Iranian students bonded together much better, and new friendships were formed. During that time, I got to know Sa'id Khadiri and his music and was impressed by his compositions. He was very polite and a perfect gentleman. Little did I know that working with Sa'id on this project would change both of our lives forever. Since I was interested in music and opera, Sa'id started to invite me to operas and concerts. I was happy that finally I had found someone among the Iranian students who was interested in classical music and opera. The Mannheim opera always had a good program, especially for Richard Wagner, my favorite composer, and we went by train to Mannheim or sometimes to Darmstadt to experience a good opera.

Another result of the evening was that Sa'id was asked to give more concerts. After he spent a semester of wondering what his major would be, he decided to finish his studies with Professor Caselman in music education. I was very busy with finishing my dissertation and preparing myself for the doctoral exam. He was still busy with clarifying his major and minor and exploring a lot of topics for research in music education, which we discussed together. Little by little music brought us closer to each other, but I did not have much time to see him because of my exams and preparation of my dissertation. He was persuasive in inviting me to concerts and operas, which I always enjoyed. He would also play his own new compositions for me. I encouraged him and wanted to motivate him to use his talent. It was obvious that the Persian evening had been so successful because of his music. He had taken many bows and played several encores, which was reported in the newspaper.

Author's speech about Persian music and describing the concert pieces being performed by her colleague and friend Sa'id Khadiri at the University of Heidelberg.

Concert of Sa'id Khadiri.

My other Persian friends were also coming to the end of their own studies. Azizeh, Sadegh, and Abbass, who came to Germany many years before me, were at the end of their studies and had finished successfully at least the main part of their program and now were specializing in their fields, medicine and dentistry. Azizeh wanted a driving license, and I enrolled with her for the lessons. Both of us got our licenses. After that she went to Bonn to specialize in orthodontics. She passed all the exams with an A+. Abbass also went to another city not too far away to specialize. Sadegh, who had broken up with his pretty Spanish girlfriend Rosario, was upset, but he successfully finished his medical studies with an A+ and wanted first to go to Iran to visit his family in Tehran. He told me that maybe with his family's assistance he could go to different families for *khastegari* and meet their daughters and find a Persian girl to marry.

In the meantime, I had a letter from the same uncle who had introduced me to Azizeh. My uncle's letter said that the sister of his daughter-in-law, Shahin, a nurse, was coming to Heidelberg for further study in medicine. Soon after receiving the letter, Shahin knocked on my door. I immediately told my landlady that I had a guest for a few days while I was finding a room for her. Even though it was during the summer vacation, it was still not easy to immediately find a room. We tried many places, but we were not successful. After a few weeks, my landlady started to make comments to me about having another person in my room, and that I should find a solution. I remembered that Sadegh was going to Iran at least for two months, and I thought maybe we could arrange for Shahin to stay in his room, at least until she adjusted to Heidelberg and found her own place. One evening Shahin and I went to see his room, which was *a Dach Zimmer*, a room on the top floor, usually a small attic room. This type of room on the fourth floor under the roof was quite popular for students because they had more privacy and peace in that room. Shahin agreed to this arrangement, but at the same time, I thought also that Sadegh would be happy to meet a pretty Persian girl with long black hair like his former girlfriend from Spain. I was quite relieved and happy that Shahin had found good, safe accommodations, suitable for a Persian girl, and I introduced her to other Persian students so that she would have other friends and not be too homesick. I also tried to meet her periodically, as much as my heavy program permitted. Fortunately, Shahin was a goal-oriented girl and ambitious to be a medical doctor, and I thought Sadegh and Abbass could help her.

This story has a happy ending. Sadegh later came back from Iran without any success in marriage, and later on, Shahin became his girlfriend, and they went to another university in the north of Germany—I believe it was Kassel—and married there. He became a specialist in gastroenterology, and Shahin studied medicine, later becoming an anesthesiologist. They became my good friends whose friendship I have always cherished. Sadegh became professor at the University of Marburg and very well known through all his research, papers, and studies. He has read many papers at all national and international conferences.

During 1959-'60, many Iranian students, even those having scholarships from Iran, preferred to stay in Germany rather than return to Iran. Germany after the war provided great opportunities. Some of the Iranians who were under the influence of the *Tudeh* (Communist) party, or National Front, preferred to stay in Germany rather than go back to Iran. In the meantime, we had more news from Iran. The Shah was visiting Europe, especially Switzerland, Holland, England, Denmark, France, and Germany in order to meet with Iranian students and persuade them to return to Iran where their education and training was greatly needed in the development of the country. When he came to Germany, most of the students that I knew didn't go to meet with him. In Paris, the Shah was a very eligible single man, and he had a good relationship with General DeGaulle. On Saturday, May 26, 1960, DeGaulle honored the Shah with a ceremony for him. That afternoon the Shah received many Iranian students, among them Farah Diba, an architecture student. Apparently, the Shah stared at her for such a long while that she wrote to her mother about that meeting.

Farah was related to me through both my mother's and father's side, so I was interested in what was happening. That same year, in September, Farah went to the office of Ardeshir Zahedi, the son-in-law of the Shah, and also the advisor to all Iranian students abroad, in order to get a scholarship abroad. While she was there, he invited her to his home to meet his wife, Princess Shahnaz, who was the daughter of the Shah from the first marriage with Fawzieh. Princess Shahnaz liked Farah very much and invited her father to her home to meet Farah. Both Farah and the Shah liked each other from the beginning and were very soon in love. Shortly after, on November 22, 1959, they became officially engaged.

Their engagement—the romantic engagement of a twenty-one-year-old student to the Shah of Iran—was front-page news in every European newspaper, especially in French newspapers. The marriage took place on December 21, bringing great happiness to Iran. Our country again had a queen. We all hoped she would soon be providing a son, a crown prince, for the Shah. Many newspapers and magazines printed articles about this wedding and the promise for the future. It seemed like a fairy tale, or a story from *A Thousand and One Nights*.

In 1960, there were three important news events from Iran. The Shah modernized Iran, and part of this modernization was land reform. Up until that time landownership was limited. With this change, all the big landowners were required to divide their villages and land among the farmers. Another important piece of news was the establishment of OPEC (Organization of Petroleum Exporting Countries), an organization of a group of oil-producing countries like Iran, Kuwait, Saudi Arabia and Venezuela, to coordinate the price of oil and the quality of oil production, and other oil-related policies. The third news, a very happy piece of news, was the birth of the Shah's son. The Shah finally got his crown prince on October 31, 1960. Five days later, on Friday, he was officially named Prince Reza Pahlavi, the *Valiahd* (crown prince) named after of his grandfather, Reza Shah the Great. It was important that finally the Shah and the country had a crown prince for the continuation of the regime and the dynasty, and even more importantly, I would say, for the stability of Iran and the Middle East.

Meanwhile, writing of my dissertation was progressing. Some evenings during the week, whenever the Mannheim opera had a Wagner program, Sa'id and I would go to the opera. I never saw other Iranian students at the opera and always wondered why. During all these outings, Sa'id and I enjoyed our conversations and friendship. He told me about his work on a topic about music programs in high schools in Germany and designing a research plan. From my experience, I tried to help him as much as I could. He also continued to work on his compositions. After the Persian evening, many people, from students to professors, told him that his music and his performances were very good and encouraged him to pursue both music and composition. Sometimes he played some of his compositions for me, and they were beautiful, since his music captured the spirit of Iran, I remembered my beautiful country. I encouraged him to prepare another concert and asked him to discuss this concert and his dissertation with his piano professor. He would answer that his research topic was taking a lot of time but assured me he would continue to compose and would also work toward a concert.

Finally, the draft of my dissertation was finished, and I gave the final draft to Dr. Schorb for his review. After two or three reviews of my dissertation, each time suggesting changes, Dr. Schorb returned it to me with just a few comments and then it was approved by my professors, Professor Christian Caselman, and Professor Hermann Roehrs. After their approval, the dissertation had to be left open so that anyone in the university could review it. It also had to be checked for its original contribution of research in the field.

While I was waiting anxiously for this process to be completed, I tried to prepare an article on the educational system of Iran for a professional journal, in order to provide my colleagues in education and psychology with a better understanding of my country and its educational system and culture. Fortunately, I had access to the resources in the university's rich library, which contained enough literature and material to document the claims. I also had the support of the Office of International Students in this venture. At the same time, I was able to use my undergraduate studies in Iran for the article. It took me the whole summer vacation to prepare the article, which I then submitted to Dr. Schorb to review to see if the article was good enough to be published in the professional journal *Bildung und Erziehung*. He didn't take long to return the article with the recommendation that I send it to the journal. It was very exciting—my first article in German was accepted and published in the next volumes of the journal.[2]

After the article was finished and my written dissertation was approved, I had to prepare myself for the oral doctoral examination. The examination would last for one hour in the major subject and one hour for minor subjects, and I would be asked about every subject in the field, as well as defend my dissertation. It was very scary for me, and I knew I didn't have much free time anymore. I would have to stop going to the opera with Sa'id and stick to my studies for a while, with no time for my friends. I explained this to everyone, including Sa'id, who was usually very persuasive, but not until after the exam, could I take some time off, begin to attend events again, and maybe even have time for a vacation.

The good news came soon. When the Dean's Office notified me of the date for the oral exam, I knew that meant that my dissertation had been approved and had been accepted after the open time for university evaluation and critique for its originality. With great excitement, I bought a black suit, perfectly suited to wear to the oral doctoral exam. The oral exam covered three subjects: education, psychology, and sociology. The head of each department would be in a separate room, and I would meet each of them, one after the other. The first exam went very well, and I was sure that I had made an A+. But the psychology exam took much longer than usual. Although I answered every question correctly, apparently the professor became more and more interested in the subject and in my answers, and he did not pay any attention to time. I remember very well that after I responded to every question in psychology, he asked me a question that shocked me. He asked me if my parents or grandparents or great-grandparents had a German background, and this seemed to me a rather personal question. I answered respectfully, explaining about my origin and background traced to Mohammed or maybe the old king of Persia, Yazdegerd III. Then I told him that I believed I had answered all the questions correctly and asked him why he had asked the question. He then praised my responses. Later on, I understood that he was surprised that a foreign student would know all the answers to his questions. He analyzed my responses and questions, and he asked me almost twice as much as he asked the German students. So unfortunately, maybe he seemed to be still under the influence that Germans were a superior race. That was a sad feeling for me to know how he treated people according to their national origin. This experience is one of the most memorable of my life.

Anyway, I came out with honor from the exam room but with a sad feeling and unsure what grade he was going to give me. All of my friends were waiting outside the exam door and were worried about my delay. The last exam, the sociology exam, went very well. Most of the questions were about sociology of families, which was my favorite subject.

My concern about the outcome did not stop me from going with my friends for a celebration. I remember Sa'id, Ms. Rabe, Christa Meyer Quante, and Azizeh were among all the friends outside the exam door. We went to the *Shaffheutler coffee shop* to celebrate and had a wonderful evening.

A few days later, I went to the dean's office for the results and saw that my final average grade was A, magna cum laude. The dean told me that I was one of the few international students to receive the doctor of philosophy degree, with magna cum laude.

Apparently, even the professor of psychology gave me an A+ too, although he could not believe my background was not German. Always after that, when he saw me, he would say, "I still think that your background and your parents are German." Each time I would reply, "No, I am Persian, and I am proud to be Persian." Later, the university asked to publish a summary of my study in the professional journal *Ruperto-Corola*, "Wie gestalten die Studierenden der deutschen geisteswissenschaftlichen Fakultaten der Gegenwart Ihr Studium?"[3]

A brief summary of the article is provided below, translated by Dr. Ingrid Hester:

"How do Students at Contemporary German Humanities Faculties Organize Their Course of Studies?

The purpose of this study is to verify whether Wilhelm Humboldt's original conception of the German university's distinction being that of a close marriage of research and teaching to the academic freedom of professors and students is still valid. From her perspective as a foreign student from Iran, Dr. Redjali undertook the research to survey German as well as foreign students.

Dr. R developed a test and eighty-four-point questionnaire on the learning process and interviewed the representative sampling of students at the University of Heidelberg's Humanities Faculty (theology, philosophy, and law) in the winter semester of 1957-'58.

The main question was broken down into three categories:

1. How do male and female students differ in their approach to their studies?
2. What are the differences in approach at the beginning, the middle, and at the end of the program of studies?
3. How do the students of the three faculties differ in their approach?

Various additional factors were also included in the test questionnaire, e.g., family background, reason for choosing specialty, participation in student life, goal orientation, collaboration with fellow students, contact with faculty, free time activities, etc.

The first issue Dr. Redjali investigates is the motivation of foreign students to study in Germany and the following are found:

- Usual human need for new and previously unknown experiences.
- Search for knowledge not available in the home country.
- A desire for freedom from the authoritative dogma that may prevail at home.
- A need for unimpeded and pure research.
- To receive professional training that will secure an excellent career upon students' return to their home countries.

Next, Dr. Redjali contrasts the French and German university systems. In France the centralized study program leads to students graduating with professional training ready for the job market, whereas in Germany the pure research concept promoted by Humboldt leads to researchers and scientists cut off from the job market and with no professional training but producing the new approach and discovery in the field of science and art. Dr. Redjali sites that while Humboldt's ideas worked well for the eighteenth century, today's market (1958) requires not only researchers but also specialists in a large variety of fields.

On the question of how German students at the Humanities faculty organize their studies, Dr. Redjali found that a majority of the student population were in favor of receiving guidance from the school in choosing their courses as to maximize efficiency. About 90 percent cited using a plan of course sequences. Almost a third had changed their course of study due to inadequate orientation and counseling. They were not convinced of Humboldt's vision and were more interested in courses of study leading to a career; this was especially true among the male students.

In conclusion, Dr. R. returns to the question of whether German universities today have been able to retain their original (Humboldt) concept. Opinions are divided: on the one hand, students retain their academic freedom to pursue an independent education. On the other hand, the scientific and technological needs of a modern society require the formation of experts and specialists. Thus, the main problem of today's (1958) universities in Germany is that the vision of academic freedom cannot be realized without greater collaboration between the students and the university, in order to provide the students adequate guidance to achieve their goals.

Dr. Redjali makes the following proposals for improvement based on the result of the test questionnaire:

1. An orientation program for freshmen, both native and foreign.
2. Guidance in how to organize classes to achieve goals.
3. Continued guidance throughout a student's course of studies.
4. Greater contact between faculty and students.
5. Exams interspersed throughout the course of studies. For example, giving the magister degree to those students, who could not complete the PhD program.
6. A reform of the *Studium Generale* (general education).
7. Improvement of extracurricular and social activities, especially for female students.
8. Tutors to help students who are experiencing difficulties.
9. Modernization of the neo-humanities.
10. Better contact between German and foreign students.
11. More opportunities for German students to study abroad.
12. A club specifically designed to improve contact between German and foreign students. International dormitories would also be helpful.

For details, please refer to the article in: *Ruperto-Corola*, volume 29, pages 221-234 (University of Heidelberg Journal).

These were my thoughts, and I was happy to tie them into the life of scholars in Germany. With the completion of my dissertation and its acceptance and high praise, I was extremely happy and proud but not yet quite satisfied about my level of knowledge. There were still obstacles for me to overcome. I needed an internship and some practice in clinical psychology. John Dewey's theme was "Learning by Doing". I needed to put into practice what I had learned. I was also lacking communication with the broader world. Gradually, it became clear to me that the English language is an important language especially for global communication and it would be beneficial for me to learn to speak English. So I registered for English courses in London through the Office of International Students and made reservations to stay in a student dormitory for eight weeks during the summer vacation. I also registered for an English course in the Berlitz School. I planned to take two months of English studies before my internship and practicum began. I bought a train ticket for London by way of Belgium and obtained a visa, my first trip alone to England and the first experience of England. Many friends (including Azizeh, Abbass and Sa'id) came to the Heidelberg train station in September 1960—to say a temporary good-bye to me.

At the station, one of my friends asked a pretty girl if this was the train to London. She was an English girl, and she was going the same direction I was. My friends helped me with my luggage, and I sat facing this lovely girl in the same compartment. She was not only pretty, but also had a kind demeanor. After the train started, we started a conversation in German, and I learned that she had been in Heidelberg to learn German, and now she was returning to her home in London, exactly the same destination as I was going. I started to ask about London and particularly about the part of the trip, which required crossing the English Channel between England and Belgium. I worried that I would get seasick since I had never traveled by boat. She comforted me with her welcoming face and told me that I should not be worried and that she would look after me. Her name was Christine White. I relaxed and enjoyed the trip, and we exchanged information about each other. I gave her my telephone number in London and my London address. I never thought or predicted at that time that she, an English girl, would become one of my closest girlfriends and a lifelong friend. I enjoyed her company on the trip, and I learned a lot about England.

Christine provided me with my first impression of the English. I noticed that English people themselves were different from the government and English politicians. As we approached the train station, Christine was very excited. Apparently, her boyfriend was to be at the station, and she was very eager to see him. In the crowd at the London train station, I lost sight of her, as we were both involved in getting our luggage.

I took a taxi to my hostel in West London. When I arrived and showed my reservation, I learned that my roommate was a drama student at the Royal Academy of Dramatic Arts. During our time as roommates, it was interesting for me to notice how each night, and early morning, she would loudly repeat her lines from a play so that she could memorize them. Sometimes this would disturb my peace and sleep but it was great for me to learn English. I registered for an English class in the Berlitz School. Gradually, I figured out that English was quite different from German. It was an idiomatic language and did not follow rules and regulations as closely as German did. It was more flexible, which meant I had to learn more words and a variety of idioms. I learned that I could go often to the movies and usually see two movies for the price of one. I also listened to the radio just to hear English being spoken. I found listening to the radio and the movies helped me to learn the English language quicker.

A few days after I settled in, I received a message to call Christine. I was pleased to hear from her and immediately returned her call. She was very kind and asked how I was adjusting. She invited me to meet her and her boyfriend, David, who also spoke German, at Piccadilly Circus for dinner. It was very nice to meet both of them. David was a real gentleman, and Christine was a beautiful lady. We had a great evening.

Later on, she invited me to meet her family and parents for a weekend in High Barnet, north of London. Being alone in London without any friends and relatives, I was touched by her kind invitation. It was so sincere that I knew I had made a real friend. After meeting her kind parents, who asked me to call them Mom and Arthur, I was sure to my knowledge that I not only would have Christine and David as good friends, but also her whole family. Each time I saw her mother she would teach me some well-known English common proverbs, and Arthur, would combine these with English jokes, so I gained a strong knowledge of English idioms. He had a very good sense of humor like most English people I've met. His last name differed from Christine's, and I learned later that he was Christine's stepfather. Her own father died during the war. I sensed immediately how all of them were kind, deep, and sincere in the way they welcomed me. I cherished their friendship and invited them to come to Iran as our guests.

We kept in touch, communicating in German mostly, which both Christine and David knew. They had met each other at the University of Exeter in German class. Fortunately for me, there were no problems in communicating with them, and each time, if I could not express myself in English, I would switch to German and they also did the same.

After eight weeks, my summer course in English was finished, and I returned to Heidelberg to finish an internship in clinical psychology. My German psychology friend, Dr. Hans Jüerger Phistner, who finished his doctorate of philosophy one year before me, had become director of a clinic attached to a Christian church organization in Mannheim, and he offered me an internship. Since the clinic was in Mannheim, I had to drive there every day. I was also preparing to leave at the end of the internship to return to my beloved Iran, so I bought a new white Volkswagen to take home with me, taking advantage of the policy, allowing students to take one car tax-free to Iran when they returned.

Sometimes, Sa'id and I would go to Mannheim together, since I already had my driver's license and had begun to drive in Heidelberg and Mannheim. At first, I had a few small accidents, but then a major one in the snow and ice. One wintry day about 4:30 p.m., at the start of the rush hour, I left Mannheim for the return trip to Heidelberg. Snow had begun, but not heavy, and I was on the Autobahn (highway), going about forty to fifty kilometers when, suddenly, I noticed I was sliding. I put my foot on the brake and then I noticed the car was turning over. I didn't have any control, so I closed my eyes. When the car stopped, I opened my eyes and saw that the car was on the other side of the highway in the wrong lane. Very slowly I examined myself—my hands, my feet, my whole body. Fortunately, they were functioning, but I didn't know what to do. If I turned around, I might hit another car on the highway. However, that seemed to be the only choice, so cautiously I turned the car and got it going back in the right direction. I drove less than twenty kilometers to Heidelberg and went immediately to the police station to report the accident in case someone complained that I had hit a car. The police were quite surprised to see that both the car and I were safe. After I finished reporting to the police, I slowly drove to my home and called Sa'id to tell him about the accident. I really was scared. Everybody was shocked that I lived through this accident and more surprised that I was unharmed. Since that accident, I have been very careful when driving in the snow or ice, especially on ice.

Just before this incident, and before I began my internship, I had a very good driving record and enjoyed driving. I remember when Sa'id's mother from Iran was visiting him I was able to drive her around. This trip was her first trip out of Iran, unlike his father, who had been coming to Hamburg on business for thirty years. Sa'id told me his mother was alone and did not know German and that she was bored, since he was busy with his studies. His father invited me to come with his mother and Sa'id to Hamburg for a visit. Since the term was finished, and it was also vacation time, we would be able to tour Hamburg and the northern part of Germany—Hanover, Bremen, and other cities where I had never been. I was a new driver, and I did not know if I could drive that distance, but as a new driver, I also wanted to drive. Sa'id's mother was a simple, pretty, kind, very natural lady. She was blonde and used makeup, unlike me. She always had lipstick on, and Sa'id had told me she liked beauty products, jewelry, and fine clothes. I tried to take her shopping and help her buy what she needed while she was in Germany. I was now curious to meet Sa'id's father, so I accepted the invitation to meet him while in Hamburg. I knew I would have plenty of practice driving as I would be the sole driver.

We made the trip from Heidelberg to Hamburg in one day, starting early in the morning. As we got closer to Hamburg, I felt very tired and drank a lot of coffee, but I still felt my eyes closing, and I didn't think I could stay awake. Anyway, with difficulty, we arrived safely in Hamburg, and found the address to meet his father. It was a very nice flat on the Alster water, one of the best areas of Hamburg. Sa'id had told me that for the past thirty years his father had spent summers in the South of France and Hamburg and winters in Iran. He always chose the best places to live. It was strange as I hadn't met them before, but I tried to be friendly with both his father and mother for the week we stayed there and it worked out well for our relationship.

Every evening, Sa'id's father took us to the best restaurants with shows and entertainment. Since he was very fond of gaming and casinos, every year he spent time in Monte Carlo, he took us one day to Travemunde, which had a casino. I could only stay in Hamburg for one week, and then Sa'id and his mother returned with me to Heidelberg. Apparently, she was tired of Germany and wanted to go back to Iran. She didn't like Germany because she was not able to speak the language, and it was better for her to return to her familiar life in Iran. Summer ended pleasantly. My first trip from the south to the north of Germany had been successful with no accidents.

I enjoyed my internship and working in the clinic in Mannheim testing children, adults, and families. Dr. Phistner was very kind and eagerly explained all about the practical side of testing and therapy. His method was eclectic with an analytical approach in psychology, which he tested and analyzed on me too. He told me I could be a really good scholar at the university, a good teacher, or also an excellent administrator—whatever opportunity arose in my life. I learned a lot from the internship. Whatever I studied in theory in psychology, I learned how to implement in practice—from diagnostic tests of the patients to different techniques and approaches in psychotherapy. I was very thankful to Dr. Phistner for all these opportunities. He later became an associate professor at the Teacher's Training College at Heidelberg University and then was promoted to professor.

The winter semester finished; and on January 3, 1961, I received my official doctor of philosophy degree. I was relieved and proud of the work I had done and now I could actually see my achievements in writing, *PhD magna cum laude.* Still, I knew there were many things in my field that I did not know, and I needed to continue my education, working, gaining further knowledge, including attending seminars and workshops to expand my knowledge and continue my education. I received a good offer to work as assistant professor at the University of Heidelberg, but my conscience was calling me to return to Iran and give needed service to my country. My mother, other family members, and my friends often telephoned, urging me to return to Iran. While many of my Iranian friends in Heidelberg decided to stay in Germany and work there, I felt a responsibility to return to Iran and fulfill my promise to my country. That had also been my promise to my mother, friends, and relatives. Also, at the International Conference of Psychology, in Bonn, I met my former professor from Iran Dr. Ali Akbar Siassi, head of the Department of Psychology and Dr. M. Sanai, who came from England. Dr. Siassi mentioned the need for psychology professors at Iran's universities and persuaded me to return.

Author's participation at the International Association of Applied Psychology Conference in Bonn Germany sitting next to Dr. Ali Akbar Siassi, her former Professor of Psychology and the former chancellor of the University of Tehran, 1960.

Social gathering of author with Dr. A. A. Siassi and Dr. Mahmood Sanai and her friend Dr Azizeh Hadizadeh at the International Conference of Psychology in Bonn, 1960.

I began to prepare to return home, packing and sending my books to Iran. I sent home the whole collected works of Goethe, Schiller, and many books of philosophers, psychologists, and educators that I had collected. I was so attached to my books and my environment that it was as if I was leaving my second home or my second country alma mater. Because I did not dare drive back to Iran with my car, I had to find a company to ship it. Every student was allowed to bring back one car, free of import tax, when they returned to Iran, a benefit allowed by law to motivate students to return to Iran. The car would have been worth almost twice as much in Iran, so it was a good investment.

Last picture of author as a student in
Heidelberg after receiving her Doctorate.

As I prepared to leave, Sa'id kept expressing through his music and his words that he would miss me. But he was working very hard on his dissertation. As an artist, he was very sensitive. I told him we could keep in touch, and we could write to each other, but he said he was not very good at writing letters. Then he promised he would learn to write, and I promised to answer. With very mixed feelings, pain, and excitement, I bought a ticket and said *Auf Wiedersehen* to Heidelberg and my friends in Heidelberg, hoping sincerely that I would see all of them again.

---

1. Hermann Roehrs, *The Classical German Concept of the University and its Influence on Higher Education in the United States*, 1995-6

2. "Paedagogische probleme im Heutigen, Iran, Bildung and Erziehung" X.I. Bonn, Lippstatt, 1963.This article later was translated into English.

3. Redjali, S. M. "Wie Gestalten Die Studierenden der Deutsche Geisteswissenschaftlichen Fakultaeten der Gegenwart Ihr Studium, Eine Untersuchung an der Universitate Heidelberg, Ein Beitrag Zur Hochschulreform." Ruperto Carola Band 20/221/34, 1961 Heidelberg, Germany.

SECOND MOVEMENT

THE BEGINNING

CHAPTER 5

Returning to Homeland
1961-62

In the middle of March 1961, I arrived in Tehran, a few days before our New Year called *Nowruz,* which means new day and celebrates the reawakening of life on the first day of spring. *Nowruz* is an old Persian festival and is a celebration of life. This reawakening symbolizes the triumph of good (light) over the forces of evil (darkness), which are represented by the winter. *Nowruz* represents much of what our Persian character, history, politics, and religion are all about. For thousands of years, Persians have applied *Nowruz* to every dark challenge that they have encountered in their stormy history; and therefore, this spirit has made *Nowruz* far more meaningful than just an ordinary New Year festivity.

Returning with a PhD degree to my homeland after many years of study, I felt thankful and keener than ever to respect and celebrate *Nowruz* with my family and friends. This holiday season includes several symbolic and meaningful celebrations. It begins with *Char Shanbe Soori* on the last Tuesday evening before *Nowruz* and ends with *Seezdah Bedar* (which means avoiding the omen number 13) on the thirteenth day of the New Year. At the center of celebration of *Char Shanbe Soori* is the bonfire and jumping over fire, a practice which symbolizes giving thanks for the good fortune of having made it through another healthy year and exchanging sickness (paleness) with the life and warmth of the fire. This custom is deeply rooted in Zoroastrianism, an important religion before Islam.

To prepare for the bonfire, I went with my mother to buy several bundles of brush so we could light the fire shortly after sunset and jump over the fire at the right time. We also bought the special ceremonial items needed for the *Nowruz haftseen* table.

As a child, I had always liked *Char shanbe Soori* and reciting the words *Zardeeyeh man as toe; Sorkheeye toe as man,* which means "Let my pallor be yours and your glow, mine."

There is also another ritual for this night, *Ghashoghzani,* which is similar to the halloween custom of trick-or-treating. Children go door to door banging on a metal bowl with a spoon and asking for treats, such as money, chocolate, candy, or cookies.

After the bonfire, my ammeh and I arranged our special table for *Nowruz* called *Haft seen,* meaning seven items that start with the letter S. These items are *Serke* (vinegar), *Samanu* (a Persian snack made up of wheat sprouts juice, water, and flour), *Sib* (apple), *Seer* (garlic), *Sabzee* (sprouted seeds), *Sonbol* (the hyacinth flower), *Sekke* (coins). Candles, eggs, a mirror and a bowl of goldfish, and homemade cookies are also added to the table. Other items beginning with the letter S can also be added. All these items are symbolic objects for truth, justice, good thoughts, prosperity, virtue, immortality, generosity and good deeds. Looking at goldfish at the turn of New Year is believed to bring good luck and fortune. According to tradition, my mother had the house and the throw rugs cleaned and washed before my arrival. I had also bought new clothes from Germany to be worn at *Nowruz,* so we were ready for the New Year. At the very moment of the turning of the year, we all gathered around the *Haft Seen,* and while my mother read from the Koran, we prayed, thanking God and meditating on our deepest wishes for the coming year. On this occasion, I thanked God for being able to get my PhD and prayed that my friends in Germany would finish their studies and come back to Iran to be of service.

Immediately after the start of the New Year, the Shah and the queen spoke on the radio and television, giving their best wishes for the year. On this year, the Shah also gave his Queen Farah a new Persian title *Shahbanou,* instead of Arabic title of *Maleke.*

For the next twelve days, we received many family members and friends, who came to give special *Nowruz* greetings and to pay respect to my mother. They also came to congratulate me on my academic success, and it was strange for me to be addressed with the title of *doctor*, but that was the custom. Also, as an independent woman, I preferred to be taken seriously. Some of the visitors very kindly offered to help me readjust to the changes in Iran. But I did not accept their offers because I wanted to experience everything by myself.

As custom dictates, on the thirteenth day of the New Year, all the family and friends gathered in a big garden in Shemiran (north of Tehran) for an outdoor picnic to dine, play games, and end the holiday season in a relaxing atmosphere.

Spending the thirteenth day outside of the house, a day associated with bad luck, symbolizes our will and power to conquer evil in the coming year. All these festivities were beautiful and provided a great opportunity to see my family and friends once again and find out more about some of the changes in my homeland so that I might find an appropriate job and choose where my service was most needed. Understanding what had happened while I had been away was an important factor in reaching a decision for my future career. Immediately, after the holiday season, I began to search for possible teaching positions in my specialty field at the local universities and colleges.

While job searching, I also managed to get my white Volkswagen released from the customs office. For almost three weeks, I went daily to the customs office in the south of Tehran to try to get my tax-exempt car. All students who studied abroad and completed a degree were allowed to bring in one car when they returned after four years. I had to have many papers to prove that I had finished my studies and had returned for good. It didn't matter to the customs officials that I had eagerly returned to be of service to my country. All the officials wanted was to review the papers, which moved from table to table and office to office to be reviewed. If the right person of one office was off that particular day or if he asked for another document, that was enough reason to come back again another day. Although I was treated well and asked to sit in the office of the head of the custom office, and was even served tea, I still had to wait and be patient. A letter carrier would take my file from one table to the other for review and signature. Each time the head of the customs office would tell me that my entire file is correct, but still several times I had to leave and come back and wait again. There was no sense of urgency whatsoever, just the opposite of what I had become accustomed to in Germany.

I could have released my car sooner, probably within one week, if I had accepted the assistance of family members who knew people and the system, but I wanted to have a firsthand experience and to get to know the bureaucracy and procedure of the administration in Iran myself. I felt that the system definitely needed to be reformed, and I wanted to help to get rid of the red tape. Finally, after three weeks, I had my Volkswagen, and I was then able to drive around in Tehran. However, I still needed to learn the psychology of driving in Iran. Driving in Tehran was very different from driving in Germany. In Germany people drove more according to the rules and regulations of traffic and rigidly followed the laws. If, for example, they had the right-of-way, they did not give way, even if the other car hit them. On the contrary, in Iran, the people were driving haphazardly and driven by their own personal taste. My mother, who was very concerned about my driving in Tehran, asked one of my cousins, Mohammed, to show me how to drive in Tehran. It seemed to me that Iranian drivers were driving according to their own agenda and paid no attention to international traffic regulations. I learned immediately that if I wanted to avoid accidents, I would have to drive not only to avoid hitting the other cars, but also to drive defensively, even if I had the right-of-way. After a few days of driving with Mohammad, I learned a good combination of Iranian-style driving and combined them with the international rules and regulations, which I already knew. From then on, I tried to drive with a combination of the East/West style that I learned when I returned to Iran.

While I was trying hard to readjust and was being challenged to find a suitable job, Sa'id my friend was sending letters from Germany almost daily. He mentioned how he missed me, how hard he was working to finish his studies so that he could come to see me, and how we both would work together to serve our country. Since Sa'id had told me he was not good at letter writing, I was surprised to see that he could write so beautifully. His letters were like poetry. His first letters were one or two pages long, but gradually, he wrote nine, ten, and even twenty pages in even more beautiful writing. He was writing like he composed his music—smooth, melodic, and beautiful. I have kept all these letters, unfortunately, I cannot translate them well into English. His letters contained sentences like this: "Simin, since you left, you cannot imagine how I suffer from your absence here in Heidelberg" and "I do not think I have ever thought of someone like you in my life." Another one: "I really miss you very much. Now my mind and heart are with you one hundred percent. I see your beautiful face all the time . . . Yesterday I went to see our mutual writer friend Mrs. Rabe to read your letter and discuss with her whether your letters suggest that you are also thinking of me. Because of you, I am working days and nights on my dissertation to finish my study quicker to come to join you."

In another letter, he wrote, "Your picture is on my piano, and I am looking every day on your beautiful, kind face with its meaningful smile giving me hope for life." In addition, I was also receiving letters from his friends Heinrich Steidel and Mrs. Rabe indicating also how Sa'id missed me. In my letters, I focused on encouraging him in his studies and in finishing his dissertation. I told him how I was very busy in readjusting to life in Iran and in finding a job.

Every day I followed the same pattern. I would start with the Ministry of Education to check on the evaluation of my education and PhD so that I would be eligible for employment. There were three local universities that presented employment possibilities—the University of Tehran, National University of Iran, and the Teachers College (Daneshsarai Aali, later named the University of Teachers Training). I decided to visit each one and meet students, professors, department heads, and the president to decide which one offered the best possibility for good service to the country. I started with the University of Tehran, the oldest university, where I did my undergraduate studies. When I met with my former professors, they seemed delighted and wanted me to work with them. The president was Dr. Ahmad Farhad, my father's first cousin, who had also graduated from the University of Heidelberg, so he was both a relative and an alumnus. He was friendly, but seemed surprised at my achievement as a woman.

When he referred me to different departments, I sensed that he really didn't welcome my visit because I was both a relative and a woman. I also was so proud of myself that I hesitated to take advantage of my position as his relative. I didn't want anybody to think that I had been employed through nepotism.

Next, I went to see Dr. Ali Sheikholislam, president of the National University of Iran, a new private university near our home. After reviewing my degree and academic recommendations, he immediately offered me a position as an associate professor of psychology, with a salary four times higher than the salaries at the other two universities.

He criticized the University of Tehran, claiming that his university was reformed and free of red tape and other formalities. He explained that the method of teaching was patterned on American universities. He had graduated from New York University. When I asked him about his concept of the unity of research and teaching, he responded only about teaching, and there was no mention of research.

My next visit was to the Teachers Training College or University, where I made an appointment to see its president Dr. Khanbaba Bayani. He also referred me to different departments, and I was pleased to see that many heads of the departments were my former professors, like Dr. Sadigh-Alam. After they reviewed my papers, they welcomed me as their associate. However, I had to think about the salary. It was much, much less than the National University of Iran—in fact, four times less. My realistic advisors told me to accept the job with the highest salary, but those who knew my idealistic approach to service told me to accept the offer of the Teachers College.

Dr. Issa Sadigh Alam: Former Minister of Education and Professor of Education, University of Tehran and Teacher Training University. This professor chose the author (only) to teach while he took leave in 1962.

After much thought and consideration of each offer, I reasoned that if I got involved with teacher training, my students could then teach other students and be more effective in the early years of childhood education.

In this way, my own service would reach a wider group, and I would be able to better help expand the concept of democracy in education in Iran. So I accepted the offer of the Teachers College.

The college administration told me that since the government job had a great deal of red tape and formality before I could receive the government decree that all my papers were in order, they would give me a temporary contract with the same salary until I could have permanent status. I would have to take a written and an oral exam and give a sample lecture. However, I was very confident in my ability and I agreed to teach fifteen hours per week, lecturing in three subjects, and I began to prepare for the exams and the lectures.

On the examination panel, five professors were assigned to review my file and written papers and to attend my oral exam and sample lecture. I remember one of them very well because of the type of questions that he asked about psychology and sociology. His name was Dr.Amir-Hossein Aryanpour, a very familiar name to me from his own books and his translation of John Dewey's books. I enjoyed all the discussion of the oral examination because of him. After my sample lecture to about sixty graduate students, he was the only professor who came in front to congratulate me for my interesting lecture and to say that I was accepted. He told me that all the panel members were impressed with the quality of my teaching style and all agreed that I was by nature an excellent teacher. I thanked him for his creative questions and then asked how long he thought it would be until I received my decree from the government. He reiterated that with the bureaucracy and red tape, it might take weeks or months to complete the paperwork and told me that I should just be patient. Just as for the car, my file would travel from one desk to another.

So now I had to begin teaching with a temporary contract until I would receive the permanent decree. I began to prepare lectures and to translate Professor Caselman's German text "Psychology of Teacher" (part of educational psychology) into Farsi for Iranian teachers. His ideas would be considered a novel approach in Iran. I also tried to review all the publications in the field of psychology and education in Iran. I found several of John Dewey's works, including *Democracy and Education*, translated into Farsi by Dr. Amir-Hossein Aryanpour. These translations were clearer than the original books for my students, and

I chose his books as reference books for the course in philosophy and history of education. However, I would need to have permission from the author, so I arranged to meet him after his lecture. I had noticed that when he came out of the classroom, students followed him, as he kept the discussion going and argued passionately with them, just as my former professor at the undergraduate level, Dr. Hushiar, had done. Later, I learned that he had also been a student of Dr. Hushiar. I joined that group one day, but I did not want to interrupt him, especially since the discussion was very interesting to me. My first impression was that he was a good educator. After his discussion with students was finished, I asked his permission to use his books.

He immediately shook my hand and welcomed me as a friend. Of course, I could use his translations, he said. He also asked me if I could cope with the system and told me that if I had any questions about the college or the system I should feel free to ask him. He was polite, modest, and kind, and I thought immediately that I could trust him to answer my questions.

My first lecture was history of education, teaching the classes of Dr. Sadigh-Alam as a substitute while he was on sabbatical leave. He interviewed several people to teach for him while he was away, and he said that I was the only person he would choose to teach his course on history of education on his behalf. Although he was my former professor and knew me well, he still reviewed my educational file and interviewed me. His class was large, averaging about 180 students each, a large class because it was a required course for all teacher candidates. Most of the courses I taught, such as History of Education, Educational Psychology, and Philosophy of Education were required courses and were all large classes. There was no microphone, so I had to speak loudly and clearly and make the classes interesting for the students, many of them older than me. I also tried to establish a collegial relationship with students, and sometimes, we had field trips and went mountain climbing with other professors like Dr. Aryanpour on the weekends. All these trips were very interesting to me in helping me to get to know my students, their needs and their expectations. In addition, I started an open house one evening every week just as my father had done in the past. Every Tuesday, I welcomed my colleagues, students, and family members who came to an informal gathering and reception in our home.

Author (second from the right) with her colleagues at the Teacher Training University.

Author (standing in the middle of her students). Photo was taken in front of the building of the Teacher Training University.

These evenings were very interesting. Sometimes, there were poem recitations. At times, we held discussions on different philosophers, psychologists, and educators or other topics of human interest. Occasionally, we also argued in politics and social changes, usually when Dr. Aryanpour attended with his friend Mr. Abdollah Anwar. Mr. Anwar was a scholar who was in charge of the office for handwritten books at the National Library of Iran. One subject we discussed, which was very helpful to me, was the translation of special social science terminology into Farsi. Apparently, Dr. Aryanpour had worked for years in four languages; and each time we had a problem finding an equivalent word from English, German, French, and Spanish in Farsi, we would ask him for advice. This dear friend and scholar suffered from Parkinson's disease toward the end of his life and died in 2002. Many of his valuable works still remain unpublished. I hope his spouse, his son, or his students will finish his work and see that they get published. After one of the Tuesday evenings, when he called to thank me for the evening, he learned that I was sick. I still have the letter he sent me, along with some of his books. His sister, Mrs. Azar Aryanpour, very kindly translated it into English.

Dr. Aryanpour wrote to me on June 6, 1961:

> *I am sorry to hear that you are not feeling well. Your condition could be partly due to fatigue for being such a gracious hostess to friends. Your pain is felt by all your friends. I take this opportunity to express my special gratitude for your kind hospitality. My appreciation, like your kindness, is profound. I look forward to hearing from you in regard to your interesting view on "Man's*

Nature' and 'Existing Problems in Defending Science." You are an intelligent and dear person whom I respect. I hope that our country as well as others will benefit from your knowledge and humanity. The future belongs to people like you—free and insightful.

Please accept the enclosed insignificant books and articles written by me. Although my previous and present works are not as desirable as I would have wanted them to be, I look forward to a brighter future.

All his publications were very well written and still remain excellent resources for social science.

During this time, my days were quite full with teaching, reading, research, and some time for a social life. In addition to the day classes, I also taught an evening class for those administrators who worked during the day. This class was not so crowded and had about ninety students. It was therefore an easier class to teach, I got to know the students, and I didn't have to speak so loudly in the evening class. There were several poets in this class, and sometimes, they competed with each other to write about class subjects or the style of my teaching in their poems. Gradually, two of them and their families became friends of our family. These students were Nasser G. Mehdi Shamshiri and his wife, Puran, whose friendships I cherish.

From these poems, I concluded that the students accepted me as a female teacher, and that I could handle the large classes quite well, without a microphone. In addition to teaching responsibilities, I also had another assignment, dean of Women Students, a position that also brought me closer to the students, which allowed me to became more familiar with their problems and issues.

This year between 1961-1962, was not only an important year for me, it was also important in the recent history of Iran. Under the leadership of Mohammed Reza Shah, Iran had embarked on modernization and unprecedented economic development. He was following in his father's footsteps in making improvements to the army, the education system, improving the status of women and supporting economic development. He was also conducting land reform, elections reform, allowing women to vote and other similar measures. All these looked promising to me. However, I think that these top-down developments, coming as they did from the government down to the people, and not from the people themselves, led to resistance from several political groups under the influence of foreign interests or religious interests. *The Islamic Front* under Ruhollah Khomeini began its opposition at this time, and the underground *Tudeh* (Communist) *Party,* and even the *National Front* all resisted these developments.

In the area of foreign relations, Iran made progress through the visits of several world leaders. In March 1961, Queen Elizabeth II and Prince Philip visited Iran, and in May, the Shah and Shahbanou visited Sweden. This led to a visit to France to meet with General de Gaulle. In 1962, the Shah and Shahbanou attended the thirtieth anniversary of Queen Juliana in Holland. Even more importantly, on April 10, 1962, they visited the USA, and President John F. Kennedy welcomed them at the airport. He also reinforced the Shah's reforms and encouraged the Shah to intensify his reforms. Kennedy suggested that these reforms be directed through the Iranian peoples' participation.

I had to be very cautious in my lectures with all the reform ideas, the oppositions, and the different political groups. However, my independent personality and reliance on research in education and science helped me with successful lectures. Through my lectures, I tried to enlighten students of the influence of foreign countries, but in many cases the political forces were very strong, leading to student strikes. Usually, because of my good personal relationship with students, they would come to my office to notify me in advance of the days when there would be strikes. On those days, I did not park my car in front of the college. However, one day, I missed getting the information and parked in front of the university on a strike day. When students hurled stones at the soldiers, some inadvertently strayed and damaged my white VW.

In short, that year universities experienced many student riots and strikes. Even teachers went on strike for a salary increase. One result of these strikes was that during this year, there were three different changes in the presidency of the college. All this time, I continued to work hard and establish a good relationship with both colleagues and students, but I still did not have the official decree. Every time I asked about the decree's status, I was told that it takes a long time and that sometimes, some people making these decisions, delay the process by keeping a file on their desk. The strikes and change of presidents could also make the process take longer. Each time that the president changed, some of the university officers also changed and slowed down the process. When I started to teach, the president of the Teachers College was Dr. Khanbaba Bayani, who welcomed me. He was followed by Dr. Mahmood Sanai, and at the end of academic year, Dr. Filsufi took his place.

With increased uncertainty in my job environment, Sa'id's letter writing also increased. I did not tell him what I was going through so that he wouldn't worry. I wanted him to concentrate on his dissertation and concerts. He wrote that he had been accepted as a piano instructor at the College of Music in Heppenheim near Heidelberg, and so he was spending a lot of his time there. He also wrote that his music professor was planning a concert for him. He was thinking that he could use all his ideas in music education in Iran when he finished his PhD. He wanted to provide music opportunities for all Iranians. He also wanted to add music to the school curriculum in Iranian schools. He was very optimistic and highly motivated, as I was, to serve our country.

He wrote that he missed me very much and was saving his money to buy an airline ticket to come to Tehran during the university spring break to see me and his family. He said his brother did not recommend that he visit because of the political riots in Tehran. I was still frustrated because of the political and bureaucratic atmosphere of the Teachers College, and I did not think he should come, but I didn't think he would listen to us anyway.

Although I had committed myself to providing excellent lectures, and my students and colleagues were very supportive of my work, because of the political strikes and delay in receiving my official decree, I kept thinking that maybe I should return to Heidelberg and accept the open job offer I received from my German professor. In some ways it would be much easier. Colleagues and students, however, kept on supporting me, telling me that I should not give up fighting the system. They said I would have to fight to bring change.

One day, when I was thinking deeply about my inner conflict, I saw an announcement on the notice board of the Teachers College for a fellowship opportunity at the University of Leeds in the United Kingdom. Since my job and decree were still up in the air, I was not sure if I could apply and compete with those who were teaching on a permanent basis. But I thought—if I get this fellowship, it will be the best opportunity for me to improve my knowledge in the field of psychology and to learn the English educational system, since, during Hitler's regime, many prominent psychologists like Freud and his daughter Anna had moved to England. At that time, the president of the college was Dr. Mahmood Sanai who was always proudly telling us that he studied and had graduated from an English university. During those days, all the educated people who had studied abroad, in England, Germany, or the USA were competing for jobs and positions and claiming that the countries where they had studied were the best. They even formed associations and clubs where they could gather and sometimes invited the cultural attachés, who supported these alumni activities and cultural organizations. Since I had nothing to lose, I completed the application, which was long and detailed, and sent it to the the Ministry of Foreign Affairs. The fellowship was for the academic year of 1962-1963. I wrote to Sa'id about this application, just to let him know that rushing back to Iran might not be the most beneficial or easy thing for him to do. I also wrote to him that there was a lot of political resistance to Westernization and modernization movement and reform of the Shah's regime. Sometimes, I would think that maybe because I was a woman that was the reason I was not getting my official papers, and that was why the officers were consciously or unconsciously making it more difficult for me.

After some time, I was notified by letter to come to the Ministry of Foreign Affairs for an interview in response to my application for the fellowship. The interview lasted for about an hour and a half. There were many questions I had to answer, and I noticed that my educational background and my objective for the needed services in Iran seemed to interest them. After the interview, they told me I would hear from them within three or four weeks. I left the ministry with a good feeling that they recognized my educational qualifications and were impressed with my objective to serve where I was needed the most.

Meanwhile, Sa'id had not listened to the advice of his family or me, and he arrived for a one-month visit during his spring break. He was very eager and anxious to meet all my new friends, colleagues, and family. His love for me was so strong that he liked to follow my every move and enjoyed meeting my friends and colleagues. He was extremely curious and wanted to meet my family, including my mother and circle of friends. He was especially insistent on wanting to meet my mother. My mother already knew that he wrote to me daily, proclaiming his love for me; so in her conversation with him, she was very diplomatic. When he came to visit her, she praised him for his hard work and stressed that he must finish his PhD so that he could achieve the things he wanted to do in life. Sa'id, too, was very perceptive and understood her meaning. He told her he was planning to return to Heidelberg, finish his studies, and not waste anymore time.

At the same time, both of us knew that there were many obstacles in Iran, and we gave much thought as to whether we should stay and work to break down these barriers against the economic developments of the Shah's regime or whether we should consider job offers abroad. Many of the educated people who had studied in the West were also having the same conflict. Some chose the West, like my friends Azizeh, Sadegh, Abbass and—chose working in Germany, and some, like me, felt obligated to return and serve our country and do what we can to break down these barriers. In this situation, Sa'id decided to go back to finish his PhD as soon as possible. He came to recognize that it was better to have his education in order to be able to survive and succeed. Sa'id decided to return and finish his degree as soon as possible, but he wanted assurance from me, of my love for him. I assured him of my continued support of his work, hoping to motivate him to finish it.

Sa'id left after *Nowruz* in 1962, and I kept on teaching and wondering why I didn't have my official papers. Six months had passed since my successful exams and still I did not have the permanent decree that would allow my job status to change from temporary to permanent. My friends and colleagues became suspicious, especially Dr. Aryanpour, who went from desk to desk in the administration to see if he could see my file. He and the others concluded that my file was lost, but they said they would continue to search. In the meantime, I received a letter congratulating me that I was the top candidate for the fellowship for England. The next step was to go to the Ministry of Foreign Affairs and sign the acceptance papers. The letter said that if I didn't accept the fellowship, it would go to Mr. Razavi, who had been teaching for many years at the Teachers College. This news left me happy, proud, and surprised, but with mixed feelings. Mr. Razavi came to me and told me that he had been counting on this fellowship in order to finish his PhD. He already had completed much of the course work but had not finished his PhD because of family sickness. He also said his academic promotion depended on having the PhD. I was so proud that I had my PhD, but very sorry for his situation. I thought about this matter for a long while, and finally, I decided to help him. I called Mr. Akbar at the Ministry of Foreign Affairs, thanked him for his letter and good news, and told him that I was declining the offer and that he could offer the fellowship to the next candidate. He was surprised and shocked and immediately asked me why. I just told him I couldn't accept because of family reasons. He told me that I should go to the ministry to sign the appropriate papers. I called Mr. Razavi and told him the good news that I was going to decline the scholarship. He rushed to my office and thanked me sincerely. The next day, I went to the ministry. After I signed, Mr. Akbar said he would like to ask me a question and asked me if I would give him an honest answer. I said, "Yes, of course."

"Will you please tell me the real reason you have declined the fellowship?" He said this had never happened before, and he and the panel could not comprehend my decision, and they would like to know the real reason I had declined the fellowship. Since I promised him I would answer truthfully, I felt that I needed to explain the real reason. I said that I felt the promotion policy at the college was unfair to Mr. Razavi and that he needed the fellowship more than I did. I thought he might benefit more from the fellowship since I already had my PhD, and the only way for him to receive the fellowship would be for me to refuse it. I told him I thought Mr. Razavi might benefit more from the fellowship since I already had my PhD, and he needed his for a promotion. He thanked me for my honest answer. I got up to leave his office, and he asked me if I could wait there for a few minutes. He called some people and went to visit other offices. Soon, he came back and asked me, "What if we have another fellowship? Would you be interested if both of you could have the fellowship?" I was stunned but happy and immediately replied, "Yes, of course, especially if it is possible to attend the University of London where the most prominent psychologists are now teaching." I told him I could benefit more there and could also follow a postdoctoral program.

He answered, "Why not? If the University of London has an opening, I will send your application immediately." I answered yes without even thinking about the need for official recognition of my application.

When Mr. Razavi heard the news, he was so happy and thankful that I will never be able to forget his smile and his happy face. I was happy for him and happy for me as well. Being accepted at the University of London, would allow me to broaden my education and maybe find answers to some of the many questions I had. Fortunately, the process did not take long. Within two weeks, Mr. Akbar notified me that I had been accepted and asked me to come in to the ministry to sign the papers. He congratulated me warmly, and I asked him to explain how it had happened that one fellowship had become two. He explained that there were two reasons—one, I was qualified, and two, the panel was impressed because of my altruistic behavior in helping a colleague. I thanked him profusely. I reviewed the papers, signed them, and thanked the panel. Then I shared the news with my mother, Sa'id, and Christine in London. For my mother, I had to explain that I would be away for another year. I told her I felt a desperate need for something to compensate for my frustration with the bureaucracy in not granting me permanent status in my current position. I felt frustration because of the ongoing strikes, and the situation that was stumping my personal growth. I thought, at that time, that I had made the right decision—to accept the fellowship and resign my temporary position.

In the meantime student strikes had started again, and this caused another change of college president. My colleagues and friends were continuing their search for my file, and one day, Dr. Aryanpour excitedly came rushing into my office with the news that my file had been found on the desk of the departing president, Dr. Sanai, as his desk was being cleaned for the new president, Dr. Filsufi. Apparently, Dr. Sanai had had this file on his desk for two months, obviously never considering how his inaction might affect my life. I was told that he did not have any administrative experience and that he was replaced because of the student strikes. Dr. Aryanpur was so happy and told me that now the new president would sign and then my file would go to the Ministry of Education for final signature of the order/decree by the minister. Although Dr. Aryanpour knew I was thankful for his work, I looked at him and said, "It's too late. I have already signed to accept a fellowship to go to England for the next academic year." He replied, "That is a pity. Because, as a government employee with the permanent order signed, you could have also had both your salary and the fellowship money, just as Mr. Razavi will have."

I explained to him that it was still not clear how long the new president would take to sign the paper and how long it would take the minister to finish the process. There was still much political uncertainty all around. Again, I thanked him for his sincere efforts for searching for the employment file. So the news came too late for me to cancel my plan to go to England. I was so disappointed because I loved to train teachers, and I had been so successful in setting the exams and all the other university formalities. I have often thought how a simple neglect and delay of just one signature changed my destiny. However, I began to focus on going to London, and suddenly, the government job did not seem so important anymore. I still had offers to work at the University of Heidelberg and at the National University of Iran.

Preparations for this fellowship year were made through the British Council. They sent an organized package of information, including my ticket and the address where I would be staying in London, this included the names of my advisors. My room would be near the University of London. This information was so well organized that I noticed immediately the big difference between Heidelberg and London. Since I was allowed one stopover between Tehran and London, I stopped to see Sa'id and attend one of his concerts. So, although I left my beloved country with bitter feelings, in the summer of 1962, I was happy to see my friends in Heidelberg and London and to begin attendance at a new university which was a new challenge.

CHAPTER 6

On the Road to London
1962-1963

On my way to London, I stopped off at Frankfurt and then Heidelberg to attend Sa'id's concert and also to see my friends and professors again. My old landlady offered to let me to stay in my old room. My professors and friends were curious and anxious to know about the social and political situation in Iran, especially since some of them were trying to decide whether to go back to Iran after finishing their studies or to stay in Germany and take jobs there. It was common for Iranian students in Germany to feel conflicted at that time. My professor, who knew how frustrated I had been with my situation in Iran, told me that after I finished the fellowship in London, I would have a better opportunity to work at the University of Heidelberg if I chose to.

Sa'id asked me to introduce him at his concert again and to comment on his compositions. I accepted this task willingly, unlike the first time when I was so busy with my own graduate work that I didn't have much time to prepare and was so rushed in preparing the material. I also prepared an introduction to Persian music and explained the passion in Sa'id's music. The whole evening went very well, and Sa'id's music and his concert were successful and very well received. We celebrated afterwards with the friends, colleagues, and the university professors. After a few days staying in Heidelberg, I continued my journey to London and notified the British Council of my arrival time, as I had been instructed to do. I left Heidelberg with a good feeling about Sa'id. He was more mature and energetic about finishing his dissertation. He told me that he would try to finish his dissertation by Christmas, submit it to his professor to read, and come to London to visit me during the Christmas holidays. So with my best wishes for his success, in the hope of seeing him again soon, I said, "*Aufwiedersehen.*"

Meeting Sa'id in London.

A letter from the British Council had told me that a female guide from the council wearing all red would be looking for me when I arrived at London's Heathrow airport and she would help me get settled. Finding her was no problem at all. As soon as I cleared customs and entered the arrivals area, I saw her straight away as I had no trouble spotting a lady wearing a red suit, red hat, red shoes, red gloves, and carrying a red bag. In fact, she was wearing so much red that I have often laughed as I recalled this time. She was polite and friendly, and after our introductions, she took me by bus and taxi to my dormitory room, at 36 Bedford Way, London WC1. We left my luggage and went to the Barclay's Bank in Russell Square, which was very close by as this is where we deposited the first month's scholarship payment for me, and I received my checkbook, the experience gave me immediate peace of mind. After this pleasant experience, I called Christine, who was pleased to hear I had experienced a well-organized and easy transition on my arrival to London. She and her parents invited me to spend the weekend. Since everything had been so easy, I was immediately ready to begin the program at the Institute of Education, University of London. The weekend with Christine, David,

Mom, and Arthur went very well, and I was extremely happy and feeling secure and ready for the next challenge.

At the institute, I met many graduate international students. Next door to me in my dormotory was a student from North Carolina, USA, and next to her, a student from the West Indies. Over breakfast and dinner, we had the opportunity to meet representatives from all over the world.

The first Monday, I made the short block walk to the institute and went directly to see my advisor, Professor J. A. Lauwerys, a very dynamic international authority in comparative education. He welcomed me and introduced me to his associate Dr. Brian Holmes, who would act on his behalf when he was away. Since I was a postdoctoral student, they left me free to select my program and choose what visits I would make to educational sites. I wrote my plan and objectives for the year, giving myself quite a heavy load, but they did not mind and advised me on the best way to proceed and helped me fit in everything I wanted to do. All year long, in addition to the program at the institute, I visited approximately fifty public and private educational institutions in England, Wales, and Scotland. I also attended several seminars and conferences in other areas of the university and on different schools of thought in psychology. I took full advantage of many special courses in the areas of psychology, child development, testing, and assessment of personality and the work of psychological clinics and visited many schools for maladjusted children and other schools of handicapped children.

Although my program was intensive and full, it was well organized, and I didn't want to miss anything. In the evening, I often went with my colleagues to a play or a musical. Sometimes, Christine and David invited me to see a play with them. In short, that year was one of the richest mental and cultural challenges of my life. I welcomed all these experiences greedily and wanted more and more and didn't want it to end. Sometimes, I went without sleep just to cram in more of the learning and cultural smorgasbord that was on offer. All of us at the institute established diverse friendships with students from India, Pakistan, UK, Scotland, USA, Israel, Canada, Australia, South Africa, West Indies, and many other Commonwealth countries; I was the only Iranian.

Almost every day was filled with eight hours or more of lectures, seminars, and visits to educational sites. Once a week, I attended Anna Freud's seminar in Hampstead, one of the world's leading centers for child psychology. First, our group of graduate students observed about ten children in play and activities, and then we analyzed the children's behavior. Under Anna Freud's leadership, we discussed the children's behavior using the psychoanalytical approach. The sessions were interesting, and she led us kindly but firmly. I realized that Anna Freud herself was the founder of child psychoanalysis. Although she dedicated most of her life to her father Sigmund Freud and his work, she used a different technique with children from the technique that her father used with adults. Her father believed that symptoms give us our bearings for making our diagnosis. But Anna noted that children's symptoms were not the same as adults and that a child's symptoms were also related to their particular development stage.

Another interesting weekly seminar outside the institute was a group therapy program at the Tavistock Clinic. Tavistock training in psychotherapy is unique, since it is the only multidisciplinary training clinic for psychotherapy. Trainees in medicine, nursing and psychology all pursue same co-requirements and additional discipline requirement. In the evening, I attended a group therapy session conducted by Dr. Turkey. For these sessions, he would first explain the patients and their mental disorders. Then he would join these patients, who would sit in a circle for the session, while we observed from a one-way mirror. We could also hear everything. After his one-hour session, he would return to our group, and we would discuss the progress of the patients' therapy. I learned a lot from this program, which I later implemented in my teaching and practice as one of the first psychotherapists in Iran.

The third most interesting visit outside the Institute of Education was with the world reknowned psychologist, Professor Hans Eysenck, director of psychology of the Institute of Psychiatry, associated with Bethlehem Royal Hospital. A German, he had come to England at the age eighteen when the Nazis came to power, and his English training in psychology led to his PhD there. During World War II, his research into the reliability of psychiatry led to his lifelong antagonism toward mainstream clinical psychology. His more than seventy books and seven hundred articles develop his theories on physiology and genetics. Although he was a behaviorist who considered learned habits of great importance, he ultimately concluded that personality differences grow out of genetic inheritance. So he was interested in temperament. As an iconoclast, he enjoyed attacking established schools of psychological thought in psychology. I approached our meeting with some trepidation. When I began to tell him about my studies in Heidelberg, he immediately reacted very negatively, and sharply, asked, "Do psychology and psychologists exist in Heidelberg?"

He also criticized the scientific nature of many of the academic varieties of courses in Heidelberg. He questioned the effectiveness of psychotherapy, especially the Freudian variety. As a behaviorist, he told me that quantitative mathematical and physiological explanation were the only valid scientific methods he understood that could give us an accurate understanding of human beings. I listened carefully and did not argue back that many considered phenomenology and qualitative methods also scientific. He proudly showed us his laboratory animals that he used for experiments.

Professor Eysenck had first assumed that I was German and was surprised to learn that I was Iranian. He told me that one of his assistants, Jeffrey, was married to an Iranian girl. He said he thought her family name was similar to mine. She and Jeffrey were going to visit Iran in the coming year. I had no idea at that moment that the Persian girl was my second cousin Venus and that Jeffrey was Jeffrey Gray. When he went to Iran in 1964, he could not get an appropriate position, and so they returned to Oxford. As a university professor, he later became a well-known psychologist, succeeding Eysenck as head of the department at the Institute of Psychiatry, University of London. Jeffrey's research in the field of neuropsychology and then neurotransplantation attracted the attention of psychiatrists all over the world. Venus and Jeffrey (who passed away not long ago) remained dear and cherished friends.

With these wonderful experiences, the fellowship and well-organized program at the Institute of Education allowed me to make the fullest possible use of my time in England. I also visited several public, private, and special schools in England, Wales, and Scotland. I had a memorable visit to the old private high school Winchester College, which prides itself on more than six hundred years of broad liberal education, stimulating in its students a lifelong interest in intellectual and cultural matters. I cannot forget visiting a classroom for eleven—to twelve-year-old boys. The subject was the Middle East. The teacher and students were having a serious discussion about oil and the problems encountered by these countries—a serious university-level discussion. Many in top-level positions in England and from the best families in other countries are graduates from this school or other similar private schools such as Eton. Fieldwork like this strengthened my practical knowledge in education, mental health, normal, and special education.

By the Christmas holidays, Sa'id had finished the final draft of his dissertation, and as promised, he came to see me in London. Christine's family—Mom and Arthur—invited us to spend Christmas with them. Christmas 1962 was one of the coldest years in England, and we experienced a real white Christmas. It was an unforgettable Christmas for us. It was very cold, and it is the custom of many English people to sleep with the windows partially open. In addition to the bedcovers, Sa'id slept in his coat, hat, and scarf, with the snow coming in his window, and he still thought he would freeze. Everybody laughed at that in the morning. Despite the cold, we had a wonderful time, experiencing an English celebration of Christmas with a very kind family. We drank hot drinks in front of the fire beside a Christmas tree surrounded with gifts. We played many fun games with typical English humor and forgot about how cold it was. All four of us—David and Christine and Sa'id and I—were talking about David and Christine's upcoming wedding. David had finished university and was working in the family business assisting his father. They had several corset shops in London and surrounding towns. Christine's temporary job at the government home-office had become a permanent job, and they were ready to marry and settle down. They had met at Exeter University and had been in love for nearly four years. I was happy for them and enjoyed hearing their plans for the wedding and their hopes for their new home. As I compared Christine's situation with my experience in other European countries, it seemed to me that young people finished their studies earlier in England and entered the job market quickly and began their families earlier, especially earlier than in Germany. Maybe this is because of the educational system, which begins when children are five years old.

Christmas gathering with Christine
and David, friends and Christine's parents in front of their home.

After New Year's, Sa'id left to finish his oral exam and defend his dissertation. I continued my program at the institute. John F. Kennedy's 1963 State of the Union address brought hope to the entire world, especially Iran. The whole world seemed to welcome his idea of the Peace Corps. I think maybe it was because of Kennedy's tone of hope and his values and programs that the Shah of Iran announced his reforms, which came to be known as the White Revolution. The people of Iran felt the optimistic spirit too, and in a referendum on January 26, 1963, 99 percent of the people of Iran supported these reforms. People were demanding change and economic and political development.

The principles of the White Revolution were

- land reform,
- profit sharing for industrial workers in private sector enterprises,
- nationalization of forests and pastureland,
- sale of government factories to finance land reform,
- amendment of the electoral law to give more representation on supervisory councils to worker and farmers, and
- establishment of a Literacy Corps to allow young men to satisfy their military service requirement by working as village literacy teachers, and
- the right of women to vote.

I was fascinated by these principles of the White Revolution, especially the idea of an education corps, the status of women, and the right for women to vote. These same principles are important in a more progressive government, and it seemed that Iran was on the road toward economic and political development, so necessary for a democratic government. The education corps program was established in 1962-1963 to respond to the immediate needs of educated teachers in primary education, especially in rural areas.

When the revolutionary law of land reform was carried through, many old deep-seated traditions and institutions in Iranian life were subjected to change. Large landownership was abolished and peasants became, for the first time, owners of land and masters of their own lives. Consequently, they were also expected to play a full role in the social and economic development of the country. To play this role, a good education was necessary. Without it, the new social reforms could not take place. The idea was clear: the education movement had to be a part of rural and village life where the most uneducated people lived. The education corps was thus established to respond to complex needs and the new situation. This education corps tapped an existing source of manpower—males were required to complete twenty-four months of military service, according to law. Since the country was at peace, the education corps took these young people after graduation from high school and placed them in a teacher training program for rural areas. They were given four months training in basic military techniques and education. Then they were sent to the villages under supervision. For each fifteen education corpsmen, a trained supervisor was assigned to help them in teaching. These young people began to provide minimum educational opportunities and to help economically to provide a better standard of living and improvement of agricultural practices. This idea, together with voting rights for women had the potential to help the country educationally, socially, and economically.[1]

The news of the education corps made a great impression on me. It would be challenging to participate in the changes, especially since this news came at the same time I was offered a position as the associate professor at the National University of Iran for 1963-1964. The choices: should I return to Iran, be a part of the White Revolution, but perhaps face bureaucracy and red tape again, or should I accept the job offered by the University of Heidelberg, or should I take a job in England? I thought long and hard about which choice provided the greatest challenge and one which interested me. I still wanted to be of the greatest help to Iran and to mankind. Sa'id had a similar conflict, but with a difference. The type of music he had studied and the occupation of musicians traditionally was not respected in Iranian society. Music was not part of the school curriculum.

Life in England was organized and comfortable. I didn't have to decide until May, so I kept postponing the decision and concentrated on successfully finishing the program at the institute. A trip to Amsterdam to attend an international conference on comparative education with Professor Lauwerys provided a welcome distraction. It was a very informative and interesting conference, and many of the papers were about the educational system of different countries. These were later published as the Yearbook of Education (1965).[2]

Conference of the Comparative Education Society Group Photo, Amsterdam 1963. Author is first from the left in the fourth row.

Since no one represented Iran at the conference, and there was no information about my country in this yearbook, I promised the editors I would write about Iran and especially about the Education Corps of Iran. The theme of the next year's yearbook was "The Education Explosion."

After the conference, I joined a few colleagues visiting Luxemburg for one day before returning to London. I was fascinated by that small country with so many banks where so many countries and people from all over the world kept their money safe. This was a new experience for me since I had not given much thought to the role of money in everyday life. I asked many questions, just like a curious child. One colleague, Richard, patiently answered my endless questions. Since he was serving as Professor Lauwerys' assistant on this trip, I was glad for the opportunity to get to know him better and realized the truth in the Iranian proverb: "If you want to know someone well, travel with him." The trip brought all of us in the institute closer together.

Back in London, Richard helped me to get to know London and our surroundings better. Christine and David also took me to interesting places. We took weekend trips to Canterbury, Coventry, Stratford, Churchill's house Blenheim, and other interesting places. In the West End, we saw *The Mousetrap*, *My Fair Lady* and other musicals, concerts, opera, and movies. I remember seeing *The Sound of Music* with Christine. My friendship with Christine and her family grew stronger. Sometimes she and I had lunch together, and she shared her plans for the wedding and the ceremony, which would be very different from my experiences in Iran. One day, she said coyly, "Simin, keep Saturday, May 4, free," and I knew immediately this would be the wedding date. She helped me shop for appropriate clothes, and fortunately, I found a blue silk dress with a matching coat, hat, and gloves for the church ceremony. For the reception afterward, I removed the coat.

Author getting ready to attend Christine and David's wedding.

On that Saturday, I went to High Barnet in North London for the ceremony. More than a hundred family members and friends were gathered, and when Christine entered the church escorted by her stepfather Arthur, my heart beat so fast I thought it would stop, especially when she and David said "I do" to each other, a commitment of love for life. She was beautiful; David was handsome. After the ceremony, we congratulated them, and I wished them luck and happiness from the bottom of my heart for their life together. We all had a group picture with the bride and groom and then went to the reception area for dinner. Since I had been told that David and Christine were going directly on their honeymoon, I didn't hear from them for about three weeks. I knew they would return to their new home in Blackheath, southeast of London. Then one day she called and invited me to come and see the new house. Later, I learned that instead of taking the honeymoon, they had decided to save the money and spend it on their new home. What a sensible idea!

Christine and David's wedding photo. Author is in the first row.

Meanwhile, I was getting near to the end of my program at the institute and was quite busy. News from Iran was more promising. The White Revolution was making progress. In addition to giving women the right to vote, the family law in Iran was revised on April 16, 1963, allowing women a limited right in divorce for the first time. But the *Islamic Front* group under the leadership of Ruhollah Khomeini claimed that all these reforms and the White Revolution were contrary to the teachings of Islam. There were several riots in the religious cities of Qom and Mashhad. As a result, Khomeini was arrested by order of Prime Minister Assadollah Alam. Some high-ranking ayatollahs sought the title of *ayatollah* for Khomeini to prevent him from being killed, although he was not academically qualified for this rank, as he didn't have the knowledge or religious education. However, those with the rank of ayatollah were protected, and by this measure, he avoided being executed as a traitor. As a result, later, in an attempt to lessen his influence, the government sent Khomeini into exile. Conservative groups under the influence of foreign countries also opposed these reforms and the economic development of Iran. Sometimes, I think if our country had no oil, we could have had a better life.

I felt a strong urge to return to Iran to help educate young people and work toward democracy and freedom. Although I thought I would face barriers to these reforms, still I felt optimistic about the future. So I accepted the offer to return to Iran as an associate professor of psychology at the National University of Iran. Sa'id too chose to return, accepting a different challenge. He knew that the status of music educator was not a highly respected one in Iran, and, even among some conservatives, like Khomeini and his followers, music was forbidden. But he also felt the challenge to face this opposition and be a part of education reform. With these hopes in mind, I booked my return ticket to Tehran.

[1.] S. M. Redjali & M. A. Toussi, *The World Yearbook of Education*, 1965. Pp. 400-406.

[2.] *Yearbook of Education*, Professors J. S. Lauwerys and George G. F. Bereday, eds., Columbia University 1965.

CHAPTER 7

Life means Hope and Movement: Becoming the First woman Professor at the National University of Iran 1963-1964

"Life means hope and movement" was the motto of the National University of Iran. In Farsi, the transliteration is *Zendegi is Omid and Harekat* and that word *harekat* is difficult to translate to explain its rich meaning. *Harekat* carries with it the meaning of movement and progress and is a very positive word. With this motto, the university wanted to show its dynamic and progressive approach to higher education in contrast to the old University of Tehran and the Teacher Training University, which were more static and more similar to a government bureaucracy. I arrived in Tehran at the end of August, a few days before the start of the semester at the National University of Iran. I was pleased that the main temporary headquarters was only two blocks away from our home on Avenue Pahlavi. I made an appointment to see the president, Dr. Ali Sheikholislam, two days later.

I went early to observe the university environment and maybe to see some professors before my appointment with the president. While I was waiting, I noticed that an office next to the office of the president was open and a middle-aged man was sitting behind his desk. As soon as he saw me sitting outside his office, he smiled and came out, and politely introduced himself as Dr. Mohammad Hossein Farrokhpars, dean of the School of Economics and Political Science. We shook hands, I introduced myself, and he already knew that I was going to see the president. In the hall, he introduced me to another professor, his assistant, Dr. Bahman Amini. He immediately started to tell about this private university, and how different the atmosphere was in comparison with the State University of Tehran. They told me to come by after my meeting, and they would be glad to answer any questions. Then exactly on time, the secretary opened the door of the president's office, called my name, and very politely said, "The president is expecting you."

What a difference since the last time I had visited. His office was much larger than the one I had visited before, and his behavior was very different from our first meeting in 1961. He was both attentive and friendly, and this time he did not brag about his American-educated psychologists and professors. He asked me several questions about my postdoctoral course and seemed impressed with the recommendation of Professor Lauwerys and my university certificate. He immediately gave me a contract to complete and sign for the academic year 1963-1964 and return for his signature. I was happy and surprised by his behavior—happy not to have to go through the government bureaucracy and surprised at his extra friendly and welcoming gestures during the meeting. Apparently, during the academic year 1962-1963, he had not been satisfied with the two American-educated professors and had not renewed their contract for the academic year, 1963-1964. He was keen to hire me to replace the two former professors due to my successful teaching experience at the Teacher Training University in 1961-1962.

I took the contract, thanked him, and before I left, I dropped by to see Dr. Farrokhpars. While I was there, I took the opportunity to question him about the workload of teaching psychology. Bearing in mind I would be working alone in the department instead of both former professors who were gone and the number of students increased. I was going to teach more in his faculty and the faculty of medicine, but he told me that the university had another opening. The president was having difficulty in selecting a candidate, and he hoped that the university would make an appointment next year. He said they were very happy to have me as their colleague. I asked him several other questions about the university, and he responded fully and frankly. He also led me to believe that because the university was new, with modern ideas in higher education, the staff, faculty, and students were all highly motivated to work. He said that most did not mind carrying a heavier workload to help build the new university. He persuaded me to sign the contract quickly. The atmosphere of the new university impressed me. I thanked him and left his office, carrying my contract paperwork with me. In the meantime, my former friends, colleagues like Dr. Arianpur and students from the Teacher Training University, came to see me, happy about my return but trying to persuade me to pursue my career there as a government employee with less work and more security. They assured me that I would have job security, particularly since I had finished all the exams and completed all the formalities as an associate professor.

Remembering the frustration of the red tape I experienced previously, thinking about the independence I valued, and knowing that there was less political activity in a private university than in a government run university, I decided to sign the National University contract. I thought that I could handle the heavy workload and that they needed me more. After all, I felt that, as a woman professor, maybe I needed to be a workaholic to prove myself in a man's society. Moreover, what a challenge for a lone woman to take on a position previously occupied by two men—and with more students! So after a few days, I signed the contract on condition that, with the rapid growth rate of the student body, the university would hire another psychologist for the next academic year, so that I would have a colleague to share the psychology program workload. My terms were accepted, and I received my decree within one week, very different from my first experience.

Author, as the first woman professor at the National University, with the presidents of the University: Dr A Sheikholislam and the President of the University of Tehran Dr A Saleh at the Golestan Palace.

In the meantime, Sa'id finished his PhD and, in September, returned home. He was looking for a job, but he had two obstacles: one was the evaluation of his PhD by the Ministry of Education and the second and major one was military service for two years starting a year after the evaluation of his papers. Usually, for permanent employment, one needed both. For the first obstacle, with the experience I had had with my PhD in 1961, I tried to help him bypass unnecessary paperwork and bureaucracy, but for military service, nobody could help, if the country needed these services. There was only one possibility that may arise: if on the special military call-up day in the following year, the military met their quota with younger men and because of his age Sa'id might not be required. Sometimes this happened, and Sa'id was older than many recruits since he had been a university graduate student.

So while he waited to find out what would happen with military service, he searched for a temporary job. Very soon he received a job offer as a chief editor of the *Music Magazine* at the Ministry of Culture and Art and deputy director of the Schools of Arts and Music. This was temporary until the next year's military call-up date. By now it was the beginning of October, and he became impatient and insisted that his family should come for *Khastegari*, the traditional asking for the hand. He proposed marriage, saying that his studying was finished, and we were both working. Every day he pressed me to name the wedding date, but I remained silent. I was still torn between my independence and freedom and marriage. Finally, he persuaded my mother to give permission for his family to come for *Khastegari*. Getting permission from the family was still very important in our tradition. Although I was sure of his passionate love, sincere friendship, and deep understanding, I was still wavering and in conflict with myself. I was especially concerned about the divorce law which either gave little or no rights to the woman.

However, one afternoon, not long after, Sa'id and his parents came to visit my mother for *Khastegari*, I was very nervous and anxious. Usually, on these occasions, both families set out their own conditions for the marriage, which have to be acceptable to both sides. The first conditions come from the bride's side and are mainly financial requests. My mother, however, was more concerned about having the traditional religious ceremonies, with items like the Koran, the ring, a mirror, and other items as agreed by us, as bride and groom. Sa'id left all the conditions to me.

Since I was still thinking about my independence and freedom, I decided to follow the good advice of my high school teacher Dr. Mehrangiz Manuchehrian, who suggested that all girls should have an addendum to their marriage certificate. This addendum would be an unchangeable durable power attorney from groom to bride, allowing for divorce rights equal to the groom's. This durable power of attorney was the only way a wife could have the same rights in a divorce as her husband. With this power of attorney, Sa'id would have to agree to grant me an irrevocable right to divorce, should I request it. Sa'id and his family who were expecting *Mahrieh* from me (a monetary condition), were surprised, but agreed immediately. While I believed that marriage is a lifelong commitment of love, trust, and loyalty, I was also making the point that a woman is not an object for sale but a human being who should have equal rights with a man in everything, including the right for marriage and divorce.

After agreement was confirmed, we excitedly began to plan the wedding, both of us passionately in love. We chose November 28, which, according to my mother, was a good day religiously and was also on the Iranian weekend. My Ammeh (aunt) and my mother accepted the responsibility for organizing our traditional marriage ceremony in the afternoon. This ceremony would include a reception at home for about sixty of our oldest and closest relatives. The second part of the wedding would be dinner and dancing in the evening. Sa'id and I were assigned to find a large club to accommodate two hundred to three hundred guests for our younger family members and friends. After looking at many sites, we chose the Police Department Club. It was very near our home, and it also had the traditional Iranian mirror type of wall and old decorations like my old house. It was also large enough for the reception and dancing. For the music, we wanted an international band, which could play Iranian and German music. After some research, Sa'id found a band and signed a contract with them for the event.

My mother and aunt immediately started preparing the traditional low table—the "sofreh" for the private religious ceremony. Sa'id and I continued to plan for the large reception, and because our time was limited, we chose to have both parts of our wedding on the same day, although it was our custom sometimes to have the private ceremony on one day and the larger reception later. We invited our relatives, friends, colleagues, and as a gesture of thanks, our former favorite teachers and professors to the reception. The number of guests finally numbered around three hundred. Because we were very busy with our new jobs and my teaching schedule during the academic year, we did not have time for a vacation, so we postponed the honeymoon until the university summer vacation.

On November 22 (4 days before our wedding ceremony) we heard the news of the assassination of John F. Kennedy, the idealistic and powerful President of the United States. This news shocked the world. He was a strong advocate of human rights, democracy, and freedom in the world. This shocking news distracted me from my wedding preparations for a couple of days, but our plans were set, the guests were invited, so we rushed to complete the final preparations.

We chose 4:00 p.m. for the traditional Iranian wedding. We wanted to be as traditional as possible, and to include some of our wedding rituals in our ceremony. My cousin Eftekhar helped with my wedding dress, and she added a lot of beadwork for decoration, which was fashionable. My girlfriend Giti, who studied as a beautician in Germany came to our home and was responsible for my makeup. But despite all her kind efforts, I did not like how I looked. I looked feigning and not myself. So, at the very last minute before the ceremony, I wiped off all the makeup. I wanted to be my own natural self.

A wedding picture, standing in front of the traditional table Sofreh.

The *sofreh* prepared by my mother and my aunt was the focus of the room. Sa'id and I were each seated on a chair in front of the *sofreh*. On the *sofreh* were a copy of the Koran, a mirror in the middle of two candelabras, a bowl of hard-rock candy, a decorated loaf of long Iranian bread, all kinds of homemade Iranian cookies, honey, and other sweets. When the Muslim scholar who performed the religious ceremony began to read the prayers, some female members from both families stood behind us to start the ritual of *ghandsabidan*, which translates to "rubbing sugar." Over our heads, they rubbed two small cones of sugar against each other. The sugar did not actually fall on our heads because the female friends held white netting over our heads to catch the sugar dust. Rubbing the sugar symbolizes a collective wish and commitment from both us and those attending for a future marriage showered with sweetness and blessing. While the sugar rubbing continued, the scholar read special prayers, introduced us to the guests and asked each of us if we were committed to each other to marry and live as husband and wife together. We responded, "*Baaleh,*" which means "Yes, I do." Next, we exchanged rings, and we put sweets in each other's mouth, and finally, we were allowed to kiss and then sign the marriage documents. I went through all these ceremonies filled with anxiety, excitement, and fear of losing my independence. So before I signed the final marriage document, I looked carefully to be sure that the addendum was there for the power of attorney.

At the same time, I committed myself to Sa'id in love, trust, and loyalty for life. In the West, women have an equal right to divorce, but it is just the opposite in Iran, where women have no divorce right whatsoever. It was essential for me to have the power of attorney addendum to my marriage, and fortunately, Sa'id understood and respected my wish for freedom.

Cutting the wedding cake at the traditional wedding ceremony.

After the ceremony, we had the afternoon reception and cut the first wedding cake, which was large enough for the sixty people present. About 6:30 p.m., we got ready to go to the club for the larger celebration. I wanted to be there before 7:00 p.m. when the guests would arrive. Again, this differed from our tradition—that the bride should arrive last and find all the guests awaiting her arrival. I thought this was a strange custom, so I didn't follow it. I also wanted to be present at the beginning to welcome everybody myself because I thought that these guests were more important than my position as the bride. So I rushed to the club, throwing a white fur stole over my shoulders to go out in the snowy night.

When we arrived, I removed the long train of my wedding dress and with Sa'id stood in the front hall to welcome our friends and family, many of whom we had not had the chance to see while we were studying abroad. The guests were surprised to see us greeting them rather than making a grand entrance as was usually done at weddings. Some of my former professors and teachers, to whom I was eternally grateful, had been invited, and I thought I should be courteous and welcome and thank them personally. Dr. Sheikholislam, the president of the National University, and some colleagues also came to the reception. Our international band was playing just the music we wanted—music and songs from all over the world which included Iranian and German songs.

Welcoming friends, colleagues and relatives at the wedding reception.

After most of our guests had arrived, Sa'id and I started the dancing with the famous German song "Ich habe mein Hertz in Heildelberg verloren" (I lost my heart in Heidelberg). As soon as the band started playing this song, my former professor, Dr. Reza Zadeh Shafagh, who had graduated from German universities, began to sing the song in

German. Sa'id and I danced with as many guests as possible. We wanted to dance with everyone, and quite possibly, we did. Everyone seemed to have fun and enjoy the evening.

Dancing at the wedding while the international orchestra played the German Song.

Dinner was a combination of traditional Iranian and international dishes. Of course, we had the traditional *Shirin polo* (rice sweetened with pistachios, carrots, and orange peel), and almonds and chicken kebab. Finally, at the end of the evening, we both cut another cake. We were pleased with the evening and thought it was very successful. But I was so tired and very exhausted. My beautiful high-heeled shoes were hurting my feet, and I could hardly walk. That night and the day after, all we did was sleep. Because of my university commitments, I did not have any vacation or any day off and had to be at my lecture at 8:00 a.m. on Saturday, a day which is like the Western Monday. We looked forward to our honeymoon which was planned for the summer vacation.

Wedding photo: November 28, 1963.

My mother, who was extremely happy that we had decided to return to Iran and not stay in Europe like many of our friends, agreed with everything that we suggested and wanted to help us at the beginning of our life together. She furnished the second floor of my home with three bedrooms for us until we could build our own house. It did not occur to her that we might want to live separately from her, and we understood. We could not leave her to live alone after all the sacrifices she had made for me to study abroad for so many years. Sa'id understood, and because he cared about my mother too, we were fully in agreement on this choice.

Meanwhile, Sa'id worked in his temporary job until his military service could be clarified. We had heard rumors that he and other males over thirty years old might come under the "surplus" category and be excused from military service if the government had enough younger candidates. For the general call-up for service in 1964, all the candidates had to go to the sports stadium to see if they were called. Usually the military starts by selecting from the youngest candidates, moving up through the years. Once they have satisfied the quota, they would excuse the rest. Still, we had to live with this uncertainty until the following autumn.

While we were waiting, we were busy with our jobs. I worked to publish my research article, including an article about the education corps for the Yearbook of Education that I had promised my advisor in London. I also prepared several articles on psychology in Farsi for some of the best-known Persian academic journals such as *Sokhan*, *Mental Health*, and *The Journal of the Iranian Psychological Association*. I felt obliged to write in Farsi to inform my students and others in the newer aspects of psychology and education.

As Sa'id and I waited, we planned for another exciting part of our lives; our honeymoon. It would be a long wedding trip—two months. We contacted "Alitalia" and began planning, targeting countries around the Mediterranean. We were particularly interested in visiting Israel, a new country then, and to observe their progress, life, and educational and social system. We also wanted to visit Greece, Italy, France, and Spain, and of course London and Heidelberg.

Finally, the time arrived, and we set off on our two-month-delayed honeymoon. Again, we kept our focus on education, remembering what Ali, our Imam, had said: "*Seek knowledge from the cradle to the grave.*" As soon as I had finished giving exams and signed a new contract for the next academic year, 1964-65, we left for the first stop—Tel Aviv. Our first hotel had a balcony overlooking the Mediterranean with a beautiful view, but it was quite noisy. Under our balcony was a restaurant with music and dancing. We could look down on the passersby who did not seem to sleep in this dynamic society. The noise and dancing continued until 4:00 a.m. and started again two hours later! But we were young and didn't mind at all. We were enjoying our week in Israel and our vacation. My former advisor, Dr. Holmes at the Institute of Education, arranged for us to visit several special programs in education. We were very impressed with how progressive these programs were. They reminded us of what we had observed in Germany and England.

The scenery was interesting too—very green like Germany with no sign of the desert. Everybody we met—from taxi drivers to university professors—spoke several languages, especially German and English. We sometimes even heard Farsi spoken. We also visited a kibbutz and found the concept of this type of developed community living very fascinating. The country was on the road to fast political and economic development. I began to feel optimistic about Iran too, thinking that maybe with the White Revolution, we could be as proactive and successful as the Israelis.

After a week in Israel, we left for Greece. Our hotel was in the middle of downtown Athens. Here we enjoyed a complete contrast—learning more about ancient Greece and its history. Next, we visited Rome, Naples, Capri, and Sorrento, stopping to visit every interesting, historical place that we, a young curious couple, could enjoy. We had a full program and moved from one place to the next with practically no rest at all. One of the most interesting experiences we had was the performance by moonlight of Verdi's opera *Aida* in the open-air theater of the Baths of Caracalla in Rome, a truly unforgettable experience.

Three weeks passed quickly. Then we flew to Nice in the south France and visited Cannes, Monte Carlo, and Monaco. Sa'id was curious about Monte Carlo because his father usually spent two to three months each year in south of France because of the casino. That was a visit that I was not so keen to make. However, because of Sa'id's interest to know why this place was important to his father, we went to visit. It was interesting to see how some people spend money and time differently. In France, we had the best dinners of our trip. From there, we flew to Barcelona. We especially enjoyed life in the evening in this beautiful city. The people went out walking at 10:00 p.m. and then had a late dinner. Since Sa'id knew Spanish dancing, we went to see several performances of Spanish dances. But when we went to watch the Bullfight, we could not stay until the end because it was too rough for us. We also left early because I was beginning to feel sick during our trip.

Fortunately, our next stop was London to visit our dear friends David and Christine in their new home in Blackheath. I was happy to see them again and share our experiences with them. Here I could share with Christine my funny feelings, nausea, and changes in my body and especially with her kind mother, whom I still called Mum. We concluded that I was pregnant. The most important change was that I did not have my migraine headaches as often as before. That was the only positive change for me. One night, I remember Sa'id and I were coming back from London, we lost our way to David and Christine's home and walked so much that I felt pain in my lower back as if something was dragging me down. Several times I had to sit down on the ground. Fortunately, we finally found the house without any further trouble. Another afternoon Sa'id was in London alone and got lost on the way home. He was so late that David reported him missing to the police. We were all worried, but he eventually turned up, tired, and exhausted!

It seemed to us that the streets and houses in London were so similar that if you did not know the area well, you could easily get lost at night. We had another of our usual good times with them and with Mum and Arthur, and we have great memories of attending musical plays in London with them. I also visited the University of London to meet my former advisors, friends, and colleagues and went to the university bookshop to get the latest publications in my field to use in my teaching.

Our final stop was Heidelberg at the invitation of Sa'id's landlady. We met our former professors and friends who were happy to see us together as a married couple, and we received many invitations for dinner and lunch—and even breakfast!—where we enjoyed reminiscing about our student days together. Then the holiday came to an end and we needed to get back to Iran for the academic year and to clarify Sa'id's military status. So in the continuing movement of the symphony of our lives, we said "auf wiedersehen" to our friends and to Heidelberg and flew back to Tehran.

CHAPTER 8

Development and Services
1962-1966

Sa'id and I returned from our honeymoon with even more energy, knowledge, and motivation to serve our beloved country. I was happy, knowing that I was following the legacy of our family who had always helped those in need as much as possible. I was eager and anxious to begin the new academic year at the National University of Iran and any other institutions that might need my assistance. Strangely, my pregnancy improved my energy level and made me all the more ready to teach and serve. I was feeling very well, and more importantly, the migraine headaches from which I had suffered all my life disappeared while I was pregnant. With all these changes in my body, I needed a gynecologist. Our family physician, Dr. A. Kafi, who had married my pretty cousin Parvin, and other friends and relatives recommended Dr. Jafar Gharavi, professor of gynecology at the University of Tehran. When I went to see him, I found him to be a fine person with a good sense of humor. He assured me of my fine health and that the changes in my body were normal and told me I could assume my job and all other volunteer duties as much as I wanted to.

My husband, Sa'id, was getting ready for the announcement of the date of his military service. This was a national call-up, requiring all young men to go to the Amjadieh Sports Stadium. All those called up were to report to the stadium with their personal belongings, following a list of items sent to them by the government. Those selected would then be processed to go directly to their assignments. I wanted to go along with Sa'id, and we prepared all the recommended items to take with us. I went with him to the stadium to say good-bye to him in case he was called for service. I was probably the only woman in maternity clothes present among the audience in the stadium. Although we had heard a rumor that my husband might not be chosen because of his age, nobody could be sure of that. Sa'id was twenty-nine at the time and the preference was for those much younger. The main deciding factor was the date of birth. This moment of my life was an exciting time for me since I was carrying a baby. Soon, military personnel came to the microphone, gave a short introduction, and then began to call the names of the military candidates according to their birth dates, beginning with the youngest. As each name was called, that person would say good-bye to his family and line up in a group to be taken to the fields on a military bus. My heart began to beat faster and faster as I stared at the loudspeaker. As they got closer to the birth dates for 1937, the number of people present in the stadium kept dwindling, and my heart beat faster and faster. Then we heard the announcement that candidates who were born in and before 1937 were excused. I cannot express the complete happiness I felt at this moment and sat down to rest immediately, happy and relieved from anxiety.

Being excused from military service meant everything to us. Now Sa'id would not have a barrier to permanent employment. He received official papers exempting him from military service, and with the paper in hand, we hugged each other and rushed to give the news to our parents.

We now happily continued our jobs without the shadow of military service hanging over our lives. I was happy to see that the university was moving, progressing, and developing very fast, in both physical and human resources. The president of the National University, Dr. Ali Sheikholislam, had bought a large parcel of land from the government at a very low price for the campus in the village of Evin, a village near Tehran Mountain. He thought it was better to pay for the land in order to keep the university private and independent and free from government influence. The concept of a private university was a new one in Iran. Gradually others, especially the high-ranking employees of the National University, began to open other private nonprofit universities and colleges because there was great need for them. However, without permission and support from His Majesty the Shah or a member of the Royal family who understood the need for the expansion of higher education of Iran, establishing a college or university was difficult or near impossible.

During this year, 1964, our School of Medicine was preparing to open; but in the beginning, not all the classes were offered at the Evin campus, so most of my lectures were given in an old rented building near our home on Avenue Pahlavi. This was ideal for me while I was pregnant. Most of my classes began at 8:00 a.m. I always was very sensitive to being punctual. In order to set a good example, I always tried to be early for my classes and leave later in case the students had any questions. Fortunately, the university fulfilled its promise to me and hired another psychologist, and we could share the heavy workload; otherwise, I would have felt misused as a woman. My new colleague, who became a good friend was Dr. Cyrus Azimi. I offered him any assistance he needed as a newcomer from America.

National University of Iran. (Source: http://www.nuiaf.org/history)

Being a female, however, I sometimes noticed a lack of total support for women. Although the Shah was promoting the status of women in the society, in reality most people, even in the academic world, were not ready for equality. Consciously or unconsciously, they did not accept the idea of equal treatment for women or to take women seriously. Many examples illustrate this. One is the *salaam*, a special greeting and salutation to the Shah, which happened on important days—New Year, the birthday of the Prophet Mohammad, or the birthday of the Shah.

At these times, a certain number of representatives from each institution were chosen to go to this court event—*salaam*—to participate in the greeting ceremony to the Shah. On one occasion, when the Shah stopped in front of the representatives from the National University, after the president greeted the Shah and introduced the accompanying faculty members (all male), the Shah asked if the university had any female faculty members. The response was affirmative, and the president mentioned my name, as the first woman professor in that university.

When my colleagues and the president saw me the day after the *salaam*, they told me that I should prepare myself for the next salaam. So I obtained the proper academic regalia, which is what we wore. I have often wondered whether I would have ever been considered to participate in this honor if the president had not been questioned by His Majesty. However, at least the leader of the country wanted to promote this equal status.

The author (as the first and only female professor) along with the National University of Iran's president and colleagues attend Salaam (the greeting ceremony for the Shah of Iran) at the Golestan Palace.

Definitely, the White Revolution improved the status of Iranian women in a far-reaching way, but much education for both men and women was needed to aid understanding and to teach that there is no difference between men and women in their abilities except for physiological differences. We needed to teach that physical differences should never be a barrier for the advancement of women, and women should not be abused or ignored.

Therefore, I started to research the equality issue and included the results in all my lectures and writings. For example, most of the research and studies showed no difference in intelligence and IQ between women and men. I tried to show that all gender inequality can be traced to social and historical background and not to genetic causes.

I also noticed that even a newly established political group of young technocrats called the *Progressive Circle,* with the leadership of H. A. Mansur, weas really a *Men's Circle.* The group studied proposals and then presented them to the Shah; later, they became a political party.

At each of the succeeding *salaams*, I had to attend the ceremony, and each time when His Majesty stopped in front of our university, after the greeting of our president, he usually moved on to stop in front of me to inquire what I was teaching and to ask my position. It became clear to me that by showing this attention to a female professor, he was teaching a lesson to the presidents and all the academic audience and people present. The Shah's behavior at the Salaams gave me more courage to face and confront those colleagues who resented the equal status of women and to continue my objective toward education of people on this key issue.

The author attends Salaam along with her colleagues at the Golestan Palace.

In my lectures, in general psychology to medical and political economic students, I tried to relate psychology theories to their special fields of study by giving examples that were germane to their own fields. In this implementation, I would also bring out examples from my clients and current affairs of our society in order to make all my lectures interesting and relevant, according to the students' evaluations. Fortunately, some of my book and articles in professional journals attracted the attention of our new university press, which they published as the second edition and book.

Since my return from studies in Germany and England, I had received several offers from prominent psychiatrists to join them in their work in diagnosis and psychotherapy in various mental health clinics and hospitals. I visited the clinics of Dr. Chehrazi and Dr. H. Rezai. I accepted the offer of Dr. Rezai, whose hospital was in Niavaran, not very far from the new National University campus. His clinic was in Tehran near our home. I thought this work would benefit me professionally and also benefit our students, who did not yet have a place to get experience. Sometimes, I held my classes there in order to introduce them to all types of mental illness and to learn about the psychological tests for diagnosis.

The hospital had several psychiatrists, most of whom taught at the University of Tehran, but who referred their private patients to the hospital. The treatment at this hospital was limited to administering drugs, shock therapy, and sometimes physical restraints. Dr. Rezai and some of his colleagues had begun to believe in psychotherapy, and they referred several patients to me for the diagnostic tests and psychotherapy. Until this time, we did not have any standardized tests in Iran, and we had to begin to use these gradually. Therefore, I tried to use mostly the nonverbal tests like the Rorschach, Thematic Apperception Test (TAT), the Tree or the nonverbal part of the Wechseler test and other well-known nonverbal tests that psychologists of England, Germany, and America were using. At the beginning after diagnosis, I tried to design an individualized treatment plan and session for patients according to their needs. I had success in this area, and the number of referrals from physicians and the insurance company increased so much that I began to implement group therapy for some of them, using this method for the first time in Iran. Dr. Rezai was happy to give me this opportunity for the patients and students, and I was also happy and proud to be able to educate my students with practical experiences, while at the same time, I was giving my services to patients in need of treatment.

Sometimes, I had my lecture in the amphitheater of the hospital. Comparing our patients with those in other countries, I noticed that the number of patients who have paranoid reactions was much higher in Iran than in the West. I have often wondered if the uncertainty of political stability, the stress of reorganization changes, and the underground political activities of oil politics were not the important factors causing paranoia. For case presentation, I had more than enough client cases of paranoid schizophrenia in patients who showed unreasonable distrust and suspicion, or who saw themselves as very important. A typical patient that I remember well was a middle-aged man, whom I introduced to the students of my class. When I asked him to come to speak to the students, he welcomed the opportunity, but he kept complaining throughout the lecture. Even though it was the middle of summer, he wore a suit with a heavy winter coat. He dressed this way in the hospital and even wanted to sleep with his clothes on. When the students asked him why he was wearing so many layers of clothes and even a winter coat, he replied that it was because he had a very sensitive and important job and some people were following him to kill him and were poisoning the air in the hospital. Therefore, he was wearing many clothes so that the poison couldn't enter his body through his skin.

Another source for internship and practical experience for my students was in my volunteer work with orphaned disadvantaged children. Through my mother, I had been asked by Mme. Farideh Diba, the mother of Her Imperial Majesty (HIM) Empress Farah Pahlavi, if I could help and give some time and expertise to the problems of the children of the charity organization of Farah Pahlavi. Mme. Diba was the honorary deputy chairperson of the board of the charity. I agreed immediately to volunteer to help the children. My mother was very pleased that I wanted to do the charity work. The Shahbanu (the empress) was sensitive and did not want the children to be called orphans, even though that is what they were. She called their dormitories "boarding schools." The Charity Society of Farah Pahlavi had several boarding schools (orphanages). In addition, a group of women also volunteered to help the children as foster parents to provide individual needs of the children. Some of the children and young adults were disturbed and had developed mental disorders, a usual condition for children everywhere in the world who had a lack of love and education in their early childhood. HIM the empress was very much interested in the children and was herself the chairperson of the board.

I visited the boarding schools with some of my students and conducted a survey of the teachers and the caretakers. I noticed that the children and young adults had several problems and disorders that neither the teachers nor the caretakers were trained to treat. The number of some cases was so high that it was impossible to handle them even with help from my student assistants. I thought the only way to resolve the problem was to train the caretakers in behavior modification techniques and monitor the implementation of the technique in the children through my students. I believed this approach could be successful, and my guess was correct. After six months, we reduced the number of disorder cases by 60 percent, and after one year, the reduced number rose to 93 percent. The remaining 7 percent of the cases were the most difficult ones, and I handled each of these cases individually myself, since those children were suitable for another approach in psychotherapy. I was happy and satisfied with myself that I could help the children, and that their caretakers were learning their jobs better, while my students also were "learning by doing," as John Dewey proposed. In this achievement, everybody was happy and motivated because of the successful result. Following this service to the children, I received recognition, a letter, and a medal from the empress and His Majesty the Shahanshah, and I was appointed to the board of directors of the society.

After that, my students and I tried to improve the boarding school programs by monitoring them continually. My husband, Sa'id, also established a band and chorus for them. They even later performed on television and at City Theater, a new modern complex, with 150 other children from all over Iran.

A photo of the boarding school's choral group taken with Her Majesty Shahbanu Farah.

As the quality of my teaching improved, my service to people became more rewarding. The university was also continually developing and expanding its services, while at the same time, the country was reaping the benefits of the White Revolution. On March 7, 1964, the Shah appointed Hassan Ali Mansur as prime minister from the Iran Novin Party. He had already established the *Progressive Circle* (an exclusive club of senior civil servants and young technocrats) to study and make recommendations on economic and social issues. Later, he transformed the club to a political party named *Iran Novin,* which means "the new Iran." This party attracted a group from the educated class and technocratic elites. Membership in this party was limited. Although most of the members were men, they accepted a few women candidates in this party like my former teacher Dr. Farrokhrou-Parsa.

In support of the *White Revolution,* the Shah added more facets to it—a Health Corps, and Economic and Administrative reforms. To implement these additions, Mansur also added four ministries and appointed younger technocrats to senior officials as ministers. Since the majority of the Majles (parliament) were from the Iran Novin Party, he could pass several bills easily, including one bill on the status of foreign forces. This bill would allow American military personnel and their families who lived in Iran to have diplomatic immunity, and if they committed a crime in Iran, they would be tried in the USA and not in Iran. This point was a sensitive one for the Iranians because it reminded us of the humiliating capitulations to imperial powers in the nineteenth century. This bill, according to the Vienna Convention of 1961, had been under discussion for some time in the Majles and the government, even before Prime Minister Mansur. Also, this issue that the American military would be tried only by American courts was a standard procedure in many countries. However, Iranian media and newspapers did not explain this correctly to the people, and as a result, it was used by the opposition in a negative way. For example, Khomeini used this bill for his own purposes to undermine the Majles. However, this bill, based on the 1961 Vienna Convention, passed in the Majles by a small majority on October 27, 1964. Seventy voted in favor, 62 against.[1] Khomeini, who had just been released from house arrest, immediately denounced the bill in a public rally in the religious city of Qom. As a result of this protest, Khomeini was arrested again; and this time, on November 4, 1964, he was sent into exile in Turkey. Later, he settled in Iraq.

This date, November 4, in addition to being an important date in Khomeini's life, is a date memorable in the history of both Iran and the United States. When Khomeini later came to power after the 1979 Revolution, he took his revenge for being exiled for about 15 years on this same date—November 4, 1979. This is the day some Iranians entered the American Embassy and took American diplomats hostage for 444 days.

In October 1964, my colleagues and I at the new campus of the National University of Iran witnessed an unforgettable ceremony—the opening of the medical school by His Majesty the *Shahanshah* (King of Kings) and *Shahbanu* (the empress). The prime minister with several members of his cabinet and several dignities were also present. The president of our university gave an excellent speech on the history of higher education in Iran and his triumphs in establishing the university and the campus and its rapid development as a private university for the first time in Iran. This rapid development with our nondiplomatic president caused some resentment and resistance for the university; and in fact, while he was speaking about the progress of the university and offering the ring of the university to the Shah and Shahbanu who seemed satisfied and happy and full of praise, I noticed an expression of jealousy in the face of some people, among them the minister of health and education. The ceremony was very well organized, and it finished successfully. I told myself that I hoped politics will continue to keep itself out of our university and that the government would not interfere in the university.

The author (standing behind the president of the National University of Iran) at the opening ceremony of the new Medical School.
The president is offering the ring of the University to His Majesty, the Shah of Iran. October 1964.

In general, during the prime ministership of Mansur, although economically the country was progressing, politically in the country there was some unrest among people due to the increase of the price of oil and transportation and other social issues. The followers of Khomeini and radical Islamic groups were still active in opposition to the government. Shockingly, on January 21, 1965, Mansur was assassinated by one of these radical Islamic groups. Mansur was replaced immediately by Amir-Abbas Hoveyda, his friend and a high-ranking member of the Iran Novin party. With this appointment by the Shah, Iran enjoyed a decade of impressive economic development and growth with relative political stability. Most of the political parties like Tudeh, Jebhe Melli, or Nehzat Azadi (freedom movement) and the Islamic radical front, Mojahedin, were active mainly as underground movement opposing the government.

In the meantime, I was getting heavier. and my body was getting bigger and bigger. My doctors were concerned about me and recommended that I take a leave of absence. My gynecologist was worried that I might have the baby in the classroom. But I felt still energetic without any headaches. Finally, I took my leave on March 7. Fortunately, I did not need to wait a long time—the very next day on March 8, around 4:00 a.m., I felt pain in my back, and immediately, Sa'id drove me and my mother to the hospital.

Dr. Gharavi came in immediately, and also my cousin Mehry, who was the director of the lab. I had told my physician that I would like to have a natural birth and be aware of the whole process. I wanted to be with the baby from the first second in this world. Sa'id and my mother were waiting outside the door of the delivery room of the hospital. The pain was periodically excruciating, but I was not forceful enough to push, even though Dr. Gharavi even in this time, tried to use his sense of humor to relax me. Finally, he said that he needed to put me to sleep to have the baby; otherwise, the baby would be hurt. With this condition, I agreed and went to sleep. When I opened my eyes, Sa'id and my mother told me the good news. Sa'id and I had a healthy girl with all the classical standards of weight and height of a baby girl. According to one cultural belief, if the first child is a girl this brings good luck for the family. I think maybe this statement was created many years after Islam to protect baby girls. Before Islam, Arab communities did not welcome the birth of girls, but in Iran, girls were welcomed, and women had a better status than in Arab communities.

Anyway our baby daughter was welcomed by everyone in both families. We all took her birth as a lucky sign. And in fact, I noticed that most people who congratulated us referred to this statement and believed it. For the name of the baby, we were looking for a short syllable, meaningful name, and we studied names and shared possible names with friends and families, including Dr. Aryanpour, who was an expert in language, and arrived at the name of *Gita*, which in Old Persian means "the world." It is also interesting to note that March 8, Gita's birthday, is now called International Women's Day. So the meaning of her name fits.

In that time, I was pulled in many directions. I wanted to take care of Gita, my family's needs, my students, and my patients. While I was in the hospital, my migraine headaches began again with several severe attacks, and I had to take several strong medications for relief, all of which seemed harmful to the baby if I were to nurse her myself. While my physicians did not tell me not to breastfeed because of my medication, I had read the famous Dr. Spock's book during pregnancy, and he wrote that a substitute milk, which has all the required vitamins and minerals, might be better than the mother's milk mixed with prescription drugs. Considering this, we chose to use a bottle and special baby powdered milk formula. To compensate, I tried to hold her close in the same position as naturally nursing the baby. In the meantime because of my professional responsibilities, members of my family were looking for a good nanny. My mother and my Ammeh told me that they would monitor the nanny often during my absence and told me not to worry.

During the *Nowruz* vacation, which was about two to three weeks later, I had many interviews for a nanny. Finally, with several good references, we chose Aghdas, who could start to work a few days before the university began. I tried to describe every step and action that I wanted for Gita in front of my mother and Ammeh so that they would know how and when to monitor. I chose Dr. Mashayekhi, professor of pediatrics at the University of Tehran, as her physician. He promised to come to our home to see Gita and bring all the necessary vaccinations for her.

So for almost the whole first year of her life, especially in winter, Gita did not go outside the house, unless we took her in her cradle to the garden. We seldom took her outside because of germs. Despite all these cautions, it was not easy for me to adjust, and I was worried for her constantly. She cried most nights in my arms. My husband, Sa'id, with his sensitive ears, could not bear to hear her scream, and I had to keep her quiet. Most of the time, I had a migraine headache, and I took too many tablets to keep myself going. But I was fortunate to have my mother, Ammeh, and nanny for their assistance. Gradually Gita settled herself in her new environment, and as a result, we settled ourselves too.

The author with her baby girl Gita.

The author's baby daughter Gita.

My mother was so happy about the birth of Gita that she sold a part of her inherited farm to give us as a gift for Gita's birth. She wanted us to buy land to build our own house according to our need and taste. With deep appreciation, we decided to buy a piece of land near the National University of Iran and build our house near the university. This was a practical decision because I could come home during lunchtime to look after Gita and our home. After a little searching, we found the nearest land to the university. It was about two miles away from the university, and I would easily be able to walk to and from the university. The land location was on top of the hill in Velenjack in Shemiran, next to the campus of the university. This site had an excellent view of Tehran, especially at night, when Tehran looked beautiful with all the lights in the distance. We made a contract with an American-educated architect to build our house, choosing to have the living area of the house all on one floor, so that Gita and my mother could avoid steps and falls.

We had plenty of land. On the first floor, we planned a separate apartment for the gardener, cook, and housekeepers with three bedrooms and two baths. The rest of the house was on the second floor but leveled with street outside. Here we would build five bedrooms, four baths, two study rooms, one very large room for entertaining, connected to the study, dining and living rooms. The entertainment room had a very large half-circle window from which we could see the beautiful view of Tehran. It could accommodate about 150 to 200 people. Under this window was a labyrinth swimming pool so that one could feel, especially at night, that the house was built over water with the light of an underwater projector.

My Blütner grand piano would have a special place in the corner of the room for home concerts. Our kitchen had one of the largest spaces. It was divided in four sections: cooking, washing, breakfast, and a pantry—with the pantry connected to the bar in the entertainment room. The house design looked functional with enough bedrooms for everybody, including guests. Below the swimming pool on the left side of garden, we designed a green house, which would have perennial flowers. We also planned landscaping with several designs for different bushes and trees in garden. The contract we signed with the architect stated that the house would be completed in one year. The location of the land was so good that many friends and relatives bought land to build their homes there, even in the same lane, and very soon, the development that we started became occupied. I was especially happy that David and Sallie Rejali, one of my cousins, who had been educated in America, was going to be our neighbor. Later, his brother Amir and some of his friends also bought building sites nearby.

In the meantime, one night in a cocktail party given by the USIS and Fulbright Commission in Tehran, we met Dr. Manuchehr Afzal, who was the dean of the new School of Education at the University of Tehran. After we talked and he learned about our special field of study, his eyes began to shine excitedly, and he told us that the university had an opening for a PhD in music education, but that he had not yet been able to fill the vacancy. His expression indicated that he was happy to meet Sa'id, and he quickly invited Sa'id to apply for this teaching position. He seemed to value and understand the important role of music in education. He was unusual in this—not many people in Iran, even academicians, understood much about music at that time. Dr. Afzal himself had studied in the USA, and we were very happy to meet someone who understood the subject. Sa'id was excited about applying for the position as associate professor in music education. Since I had experience with the governmental bureaucracy in 1960-61, I tried to let him know in advance what to expect about the bureaucracy so that he wouldn't become frustrated and disappointed as I had been.

Fortunately, he was the only candidate for the position and passed all his oral, written, and practical teaching examinations with a very high rating. He was very happy that he might finally be able to reach his objective—to expand music education in the schools and make music part of the curriculum for children and young adults through teacher training. I was also happy for our family, since as a government employee, he would have more job security, rather than working in a private university like I was.

The construction of our home was gradually progressing. Each time, on the road to the university, I would look at our house to see the progress. But the progress of the building of our home seemed so slow that I doubted that it would be ready in one year according to our contract, while, just on the opposite side, our campus was developing and progressing very fast. Different schools, one after the other, were being erected and getting ready for the opening. With the leadership of Dr. Sheikholislam, the physical plant and the human resources of the university were expanding very fast. However, his style was an issue because he ran the university according to strict rules and regulations and lacked social skills. He stressed that our standard of quality must be higher than the state universities. For example, the minimum passing grade for students was 13 out of 20. In comparison, the minimum passing grade at the University of Tehran was 10 of 20. (In our tradition, the grades were based on points from 1-20, not 1-100, as in the US system). He was also very careful about the quality of our teaching. If the student evaluations of a professor were not good, he would fire the person, and he dismissed students who did not reach the minimum passing standard.

At the same time, political activities gradually increased in the country. Some of these parties like *Iran Novin* and *Mardom* operated openly. Some were underground groups like the *Tudeh* (Communist), which also had subgroups, groups of religious fronts, and several subgroups following Khomeini and *Jebeh Melli*, with subgroups like *Nehzat Azadi*. All these parties were influenced by foreign-interest groups because of our oil resources, resulting in great power plays. As always, the people of our country suffered the most in the middle of these political power struggles.

I liked the approach of the president of the university to these groups. He was not politically active and was trying extremely hard to keep the Shah's support. Therefore, he tried to keep political activity out of the university and keep the independence of the university. I was also trying to keep myself independent. However, with the increase of political activities in the country and the numbers of dismissed students, political unrest began at the university, especially in the School of Architecture. The ministry of the court of the Shah received several complaints, and our politically naïve president was not able to prevent a strike.

The strike expanded to the other schools, and suddenly, we heard that the president had received a message in December 1965 that he should resign without any explanation and should not re-enter the university, the university for which he had lifted the first shovel of dirt to build. I was very upset, and the situation seemed unjustified. Some colleagues joined in the complaints about what was happening to the president. But I went to his home as soon as I could to express my deep appreciation to him and his family for his untiring service to the university. I told him that maybe it was all a misunderstanding, and with time, he would be cleared. However, he had already been told by the Savak that he could not teach and would not be allowed to enter the university at all. This whole affair seemed so unfair to me that a person who had started the movement for private higher education should be dismissed so unfairly. Dr. Sheikholislam loved the university and placed the good of the university before family, friends, and faculty.

In the middle of the academic year of 1965-1966, we were waiting for the announcement of our new president. I told myself that maybe it would be one of the jealous faces I had noticed at the medical school ceremony. It had seemed to me then that members of the Iran Novin party were competing with each other to become president. My guess proved to be correct, and very soon, the announcement was made that the new president would be the former minister of Education, an active member of the *Progressive Circle* and the *Iran Novin party*, Dr. Abdolali Jahanshahi, educated in France. He was a very nice and kind person, but to me, not strong enough to run such an active, rapidly developing university. I predicted that he would not stay long at this position. However, he was very good at diplomacy, and because of that, he got money easily from the government for the continued construction of our school. As soon as he took over, I noticed that all the formerly expelled students and teaching personnel returned to the university. Their efforts against the former president had been effective, and they showed their victorious happiness openly. Dr. Jahanshahi had a different administrative style, not so strict and possessive of the university as Dr. Sheikholislam had been. But I can never forget how Dr. Sheikholislam had loved the university above all. One example of his style affected me. When Dr. Jahanshahi took office, he posted announcements for conferences, seminars, and fellowships on the bulletin board outside his office. These were for different subjects and the opportunities were national and international. Dr. Sheikholislam had apparently thrown all these announcements in the trash, fearing that his faculty might want to attend, or take advantage of the opportunities, or perhaps leave the university for a better position. He was protective of the university and the students, and he did not want them to fall behind in their learning.

I made it a habit to look at the notice board periodically, and I liked the method of the new president, who announced any information for the faculty members that he was receiving. Anyway, one day in early 1966, I saw an announcement for a summer program for psychology faculty in the United States offered by the National Science Foundation at the University of Michigan. The notice also stated that there would be one fellowship for a psychology faculty from another country to apply through the USIS. All interested people who taught psychology worldwide would be eligible to apply and compete for this one fellowship through the office of the USIS of their country. The application was attached to the announcement. I read and reread the announcement. I often read about the rapid progress of psychology in the USA and wanted an opportunity to visit the USA and see all this progress in person. But I thought competing with all the world for this fellowship looked very difficult; and for me, especially with the consideration of our family, it was even more difficult.

Out of curiosity, I made a copy of the announcement to show Sa'id and ask his opinion. This summer workshop would be composed of psychology teachers from each of the fifty United States with the addition of one international participant. I didn't think I had a chance. English was my third language, but Sa'id and my mother told me to apply and take a chance. They told me not to worry about Gita. If I was accepted, they would take care of her. Some good friends who knew me very well also persuaded me to apply, although I had little hope of being accepted. I filled out the application and went to the USIS office in Tehran for a written test and oral examination, which was more like an interview with a panel from the USIS office.

As soon as I finished the NSF exam, I saw another announcement on the board of the university from the Fulbright Commission for the next academic year. There was one fellowship for Iran and all academic personnel from all the universities in every field could apply for that. Since I did not have any hope for the National Science Foundation (NSF) grant, I applied for that too. The Fulbright application was completely different. I had to write out a research project and plan. In that time, 1966-1967, B. F. Skinner's behavior modification plan was popular in the United States. This Harvard professor had set forth very advanced and successful procedures in behavior therapy, behavior modification, teaching machines, and programmed learning; and I was eager to implement those in Iran for our illiteracy problems, especially for adult illiterates who did not want to go to school or were ashamed to go to school. With this method, they would have a programmed book or machine and could learn how to write and read without a teacher. So I made this my proposal and applied, again with nothing to lose, since I didn't think I could get the fellowship. To my surprise, I was asked to come for an interview with a panel from the Fulbright Commission in Tehran. They told me I would hear the final decision during the summer term.

I thought no more about these applications because I was very busy with my heavy workload at work and at home. I was also busy with the construction of the house. Between my teaching hours at the university, I would go by the site to see the progress and speak with the workers. Unfortunately, the building was proceeding very slowly. There was a great shortage of manpower for construction in Iran, especially in Tehran, because everything was developing fast. When our architect extended the contract for another year, we had no choice but to accept his suggestion. Along with my frustration at the slowing down of construction, I thought of the founder and former president of our university, Dr. Sheikholislam, and how hard he had worked to see that so many schools and buildings were finished on campus in a very short time. I continued to regret that he no longer was allowed any association with the university. Sometimes, as I drove on the road to the university, I would see an active person like him, just walking and wandering around the university. I wondered if he still would have thought that "life means hope and movement," our motto. I have continued to believe that motto, and for me, it definitely still means that our lives mean hope and movement. I find this in service to mankind, which I have given without any expectation of reward. I have kept to this motto through all the adversities in my life. Dr. Sheikholislam is still remembered as a first initiator of the concept of the private universities and colleges in higher education in Iran.

At the end of April 1966, I received a letter in the mail from the USIS. I thought probably it would say they "regretted to inform me," and my heart began to beat fast as I opened the envelope in a rush. I couldn't believe what I was reading and kept reading the letter over and over again. The letter congratulated me for being accepted to attend the NSF summer seminar in psychology at the University of Michigan and stated that with the next mail, I would receive a round-trip ticket. A daily allowance would be paid to me when I arrived in Ann Arbor. Professionally, I was very happy with this opportunity to learn the latest research and study in my field in one of the largest departments of psychology in the world. I would also be learning about the status of teaching psychology in different states in the United States since there would be fellow students from each of the states in the workshop. But I had a real conflict about leaving my baby daughter. I thought about canceling the offer and saying nothing to Sa'id or my mother. Now it was my turn to be in conflict. As a person who was used to helping others in their conflicts, I needed help myself. Full of doubt, I finally shared the news as objectively as I could, however showing more sadness than happiness with my husband. To my surprise, as soon as Sa'id read the news, he jumped in the air with happiness and hugged me. Then I told him I didn't want to leave Gita, but he immediately took the letter to share with my mother. He explained to her that this seminar was important professionally for me, but that I had conflicting feelings and didn't want to leave Gita. My mother looked at me, and with her typical kind smile, she promised me that she would care for Gita with the help of our nanny. Both she and Sa'id said that Gita was too young to notice my absence and both of them told me I should get ready to go. I told myself that I wished Gita herself could have given this permission to me. Anyway, with pain, I got ready to make the trip. Most of my friends were happy but some were jealous. Our president, Dr. Jahanshahi, congratulated me, and I thanked him for posting the announcement on his board for our information; otherwise, I would not have been aware of the fellowship. When he asked me if I had heard from the Fulbright Commission, I replied that they were going to notify the recipients in the summer. I never thought that I would have any chance for that fellowship among such competition with all the universities and professors in Iran.

After finishing the term exam and turning in my grades, Sa'id persuaded me to book my ticket to the USA. This would be the first time I had left my family, and it was very painful. However, I left with the hope that with more education in my field, I would be able to serve my country and my family even better.

---

1. Kenneth M. Pollack, *The Persian Puzzle*, New York: Random House, 2004.

CHAPTER 9

No Pain, No Gain
On the Road to the USA
as a Fulbright Scholar
1966-1968

At the end of May 1966, I booked my open NSF grant ticket to Michigan via London. As I made these arrangements, I felt more conflicting feelings of both pain and gain than ever before. Being separated from my family brought me pain, but my eagerness to learn the latest research and development in the field psychology in the USA would definitely be a gain. After a brief stopover in London to visit Christine and David, I was bound for Ann Arbor. Seeing Christine helped me put into perspective what lay ahead because she has always understood my position as a woman with dual responsibility to family and profession.

Ann Arbor, Michigan, is the home of the University of Michigan, and it was the site of the National Science Foundation Summer Institute for Psychology. Housing was also at the university, just opposite the Department of Psychology building, convenient and within an easy walking distance. Director of the program was Professor John Millholland, whose specialty was mathematical psychology. I warmed to him almost from the very beginning.

At our first session, we introduced ourselves, and I was a bit uneasy. As each of us told where we came from, giving our state, university, and teaching field, it became more noticeable that everyone but me was from a different state in the United States. When it was my turn, I gave my name, and my location, Tehran, National University of Iran. I expected some reaction to this, but strangely enough, my information caused no reaction at all. It looked like as if I were from the United States. Some of the people even asked if I was from a particular US state. Some asked me if Tehran was in the southern United States. This led to my showing a map and pointing out Iran. After that, I felt really accepted and even though I was the only foreigner in the group, I was never treated as an outsider, although some said my accent sounded Southern. This lack of curiosity was a little bit different from my experience in Europe, especially Germany, where I was constantly asked, "Where are you from?"

Next to me in class, I met Carol, a very kind woman who lived not far from Ann Arbor. One day, not long afterward, as we were walking from our residence to the seminar, she invited me to go home with her for a long weekend and visit her family. This spontaneous invitation seemed genuinely sincere so I accepted and postponed my plan to call a relative in Ypsilanti. This led to my first long weekend experience with a typical American family. As we drove, Carol told me about her family—her four children, two boys, and two girls. As we talked, I realized that she, like me, was a part of that generation of working mothers who were still seeking equal opportunity in working, and balancing everything they wanted to do, which is now a better possibility for women. Her husband was a professor of education at the university, but when their children came along, she had to stop working, and postpone her plans to finish her PhD. When her children were in high school, she wanted to re-enter the workforce and perhaps obtain her PhD. She was looking forward to the seminar to update her knowledge of psychology in preparation for teaching the next semester. I asked her if her husband agreed with her decision. She replied that he did, but only after much discussion. They still had arguments about whether this was the right thing to do.

Her home was a model of good organization. The house was large, with guest room, many bedrooms, and a study for her husband. The children were very pleasant and apparently excellent students, all of them making all As. There she was, managing this large household with no help, a full-time job in itself. When I met her husband, we enjoyed talking about education systems in Germany, Iran, and the United States. I told them about my work in Iran, and trying to help Carol, I said how lucky I was that my husband had always been as supportive of my work as a mother and a college professor. I sensed this line of discussion about the status of women might lead to an argument, so as a guest, I changed the topic of conversation. My first long weekend in the United States was a great experience. I remain thankful to Carol's family for their welcoming hospitality, and I wished that her husband would understand and accept the role of women in professions in addition to being housewives.

Since I did not have a car, I learned to use public transportation. On my first trip to Detroit, I was sitting in a middle row of the bus, and in front of me was a man with an empty seat beside him. At one of the stops, a black man entered the bus and sat down next to him. All of a sudden, the white man stood up, muttered something, walked to the back of the bus, and sat down there. The black man also began muttering something. I was surprised and stunned because I had never seen anything like this in all my life. I had read about segregation and racism in America, but I had never realized that it was so big of an issue. I could not understand that skin color would keep people apart, even on a public bus. In later visits to Detroit, I also witnessed several incidents of violence with young black men in conflict with police. I did not see any black police officers and wondered why. It occurred to me that young black teenagers would cooperate and abide by rules and regulations better if there were some black policemen. At least in Iran, I thought happily, racism was not one of our problems.

During my stay in Ann Arbor, Dr. Martin Luther King Jr., the black minister, was constantly in the news. He advocated following Ghandi's principle of nonviolence in the struggle for civil rights for all people. He spoke eloquently about freedom, equality, and dignity for all people. He made these speeches all over the country, and I was fascinated to read about them.

Sometimes, colleagues and friends invited me to join them in trips or gave me a ride somewhere. One friend, Mary, liked to take a drive to relax, and she would often invite me to join her. Just as German people like to go walking every day, it seemed that in America, the country of cars, people went for drives just for recreation. For whatever the reason, I enjoyed the outings with Mary. One day, as we drove and listened to the news on the radio, Mary told me how worried she was about her son who was fighting in Vietnam. As she was talking about her son and listening to the war news on the radio, all of a sudden, she lost control of the car and hit a tree. Thank God she wasn't speeding and only the front of her car was damaged. We went to her home, not far away, and she checked to see if we were hurt. Luckily, we were both OK. Mary showed me the picture of her handsome son who was in Vietnam and told me she was going to join a demonstration of students against war the following week. I found it interesting that people could demonstrate against war so openly and freely, something that we could not do in Iran. This incident made me think of my family in Iran, and I stopped going for drives with friends just for pleasure and began to spend more free time in the library and the psychology department. Then, everybody told me I should go back to the dormitory before dark and warned me not to walk alone. We could safely walk all night long in Germany. I was thankful that at least it was summer and the evenings stayed light till late.

During the weekdays, we had six to eight hours of classes. The department of psychology was one of the largest in the USA. When I was there, we learned that there were about 150 PhDs active in different teaching and research positions at the department and several institutes and clinics around the university campus. Whenever I had time, I visited these clinics and institutes. In every field of psychology, we learned of the latest developments—from developmental psychology to behavior modification, learning theories, emotions, and testing, to different schools in psychotherapy and even the mathematical psychology in which Dr. Millholland specialized. He had a strong desire to find a global language in psychology through mathematics, an ideal approach.

Finally, I was able to arrange a weekend visit to see my relative, Dr. Ahmad Kafi, and his family in Ypsilanti. He was a psychiatrist and director of Ypsilanti Mental Hospital near Ann Arbor. He was the brother-in-law of my pretty cousin Parvin, who had told him I would be in Ann Arbor. He and his wife, Joyce, were very gracious and hospitable in receiving me. The hospital was one of the largest hospitals in the state of Michigan. He was both the psychiatrist and administrator at this hospital. On a tour of the hospital, I was able to observe how they treated their patients. There were several differences between this hospital and those I knew in Europe and Iran. The main difference was that the gate of the hospital was either open or there was no gate, and patients were free to come and go. This practice had not caused many problems, and by US law and the Constitution, patients should have freedom. Another difference—in this hospital there seemed to be greater advances in psychotherapy and especially in behavior therapy. In those days, Dr. Joseph Wolpe (1915-1997), father of behavior therapy, was one of the leaders in this field in USA. During this weekend, I also attended a session of shock therapy using a new medication to reduce the side effects of shock therapy. Dr. Kafi claimed that patients tolerated the shock better with his method and referred me to research further on this topic. The experiences of this weekend were interesting and memorable.

Finally, I received my first letter from Sa'id, a letter that brought me great happiness in learning that all the family was well although they missed me. On the professional side, however, there was both good news and bad news. The surprising good news was that I had won the Fulbright fellowship from Iran for 1966. This stunning news meant that for the coming fall semester, I was to be in the United States. I could start the Fulbright immediately after the NSF seminar. As thrilled as I was to receive the Fulbright fellowship, I knew I could not begin the program in September. So I read on to the bad news—there was yet another new president of the National University. Even though my guess was correct that Dr. Jahanshahi would not last long as president, still it meant that I would have a new boss. The Shah had assigned Dr. A. A. Bina, who was already president of two other universities. Minister of Court, Mr. A. Alam, also supported this change. The faculty was upset at the change, especially since the new president was not honoring most of the decisions of the former presidents.

Now I had two problems—worrying about my family and my profession. I did not know whether the new president would agree to give me a leave to take the Fulbright fellowship. Manpower was short at the National University. In response to the letter of congratulation of from Fulbright Commission, I called the office in Washington DC and spoke with Mary, the program officer. I thanked her for the good news and explained about the new changes in the university and the situation in Iran. She made a great suggestion—that I postpone the fellowship for one year until September 1967. I replied that if most of the program could be completed during summer months, most probably I could accept, since during this time I had no obligation to the university in the summer. Then I would have no need to obtain permission to be away. Mary said, "Why not? You already have a round-trip ticket, and we can arrange the program from May to September."

Mary said she would officially notify me of the postponement for 1967 within a week. Next, I called home to talk to Sa'id and my mother, to hear news of my lovely daughter, Gita, I also asked their opinion. Sa'id said the postponement would be the wisest and best solution. He said many of the faculty members, especially those trained in the USA, were upset because the new president was oriented toward French universities and was hiring mostly graduates trained in France. He didn't think the new president would like to see me take leave to be a Fulbright scholar. Sa'id also said that for the good of the family, I should try for the postponement since Gita had started to ask about me and call for her mommy.

I remained grateful to the program officer of the Fulbright Commission for her understanding. Sure enough, in a week, I received an official letter saying that the Fellowship would be postponed until the next year. The letter suggested that I come to Washington DC to discuss the details after I had finished the seminar in Michigan. This lack of bureaucratic barriers made me very happy, and I continued the NSF summer seminar with great peace of mind. I met with Dr. Millholland to ask his advice on the best place in the United States to study programmed learning and teaching machines in order to combat illiteracy in Iran. He said he was happy to hear that I would return to the United States and invited me to come to Ann Arbor again. He said that summer institute had been his first experience with a foreign student, and since it had been a good experience, he was going to continue each year to include a fellow from another country. I congratulated him on the decision to provide for an exchange and the opportunity for greater global understanding for all members of the seminar. I didn't mention that some of the members still thought I was from the South of the United States. Since nobody gave me special treatment, I felt I had to work much harder than any member in the seminar. After all, America was new to me and I wanted to learn as much as possible about this land of opportunity and freedom. In Iran, we had social and cultural freedom, but not political freedom. I began to learn more about the Constitution of the United States.

I continued the NSF seminar with great contentment and left to return home by way of Washington DC to see the Capital, program officers of both programs—NSF and Fulbright—and my school friend who had settled in the USA. She was a poet in Iran, who had written a sentimental poem concerning why I was leaving everybody in Iran to study in Heidelberg. It was interesting to see how she herself had changed her position and left the country. She had kindly invited me to stay with her and her sister in Washington. She said she was working and studying part time and enjoying the freedom in America. She took me sightseeing, and we visited many government buildings, including the White House. I was fascinated that the door of the White House was open to the people. The house looked like a simple large house for a single family. I have seen greater houses in the world much nicer than the White House, but this is the country of "government of the people, for the people, and by the people." The White House seems just right for the USA.

I made appointments to see my two program officers, one with the National Science Foundation to thank her for the experience and give my report, and one with the Fulbright Commission to plan the program for 1967. The offices were not very far from each other, and I completed these visits in one day. A few days later, I was on my way back to Tehran. It was the end of August, the next academic year would soon begin, and I looked forward to seeing my family. Since my flight was from New York, I accepted the sincere invitation of my cousin Mehri Kalali, who was living in Norwalk, Connecticut, near New York. For years she had had a dental clinic in Norwalk. She always was happy to receive a relative from Iran. I met her and her new husband, Bill Cimikosky, an oral surgeon at Stamford. Their small daughter Mariana was just about the same age as our daughter, Gita. I have always admired her as a professional woman with dual responsibility. She arranged her clinic in a suite connected to her home, with a different entrance for clients. She had an inside door from her house to the clinic, so she could watch her baby and have easy access. I went shopping with her for souvenirs for all the family, especially presents for Gita. Gita liked everything related to Snoopy, so Mehri took me to the best toy stores and boutiques in Westport and the surrounding area. Then we went to New York City and visited the United Nations building and the Statue of Liberty, the symbol of the United States, before she took me to Kennedy Airport for the flight to Tehran. The visit was nice and short before my flight. She was so kind in helping me get ready to return home. I said "auf wiedersehen" to her and to the Statue of Liberty until the next year and boarded my Pan American flight.

The late Dr Mehri Kalali Cimikoski, the author's cousin, who welcomed the author in to her home and showed her New York City.

Postcard of New York and the Statue of Liberty, a symbol of freedom.

I had an easy flight through Frankfurt to Tehran, and I arrived at Mehrabad Airport in Tehran at 2:00 a.m. All the international flights arrive in the middle of the night, so Sa'id was the only one to meet me. We greeted each other passionately and eagerly, and I was laughing and crying at the same time with happiness and excitement. I had missed him and all my family so very much, and they had never been out of my mind. I thanked him for his tolerance, patience, and real love that allowed me to have this experience, an experience filled with pain and gain for both of us. As we drove home, we continued laughing and crying and sharing all our pains and gains during our first separation. He began by telling me all the good news. Gita and my mother were well and looking forward to seeing me. I wondered why he did not mention my dear Ammeh. Then he became quiet, and after a silence, I will never forget, he gave me some bad news. While I was away, she had become ill, and even with the good care of her physician nephew and other specialists, she had passed away. He did not want to let me know in the USA because of my love for her. He thought the news might distract me from my work. We drove the rest of the way home in silence. As soon as we arrived, I ran to see Gita in her bed. She was fast asleep and looked like an angel, so I just kissed her quietly and left all the Snoopy toys next to her bed. Then I went downstairs to see my mother, who was still up and waiting to see me. I hugged her and expressed my deep sorrow and regret at not being able to see my dear *Ammeh* before she died and at the time of her death.

I will always remember my Ammeh and remain always thankful for her deep love of me and our family and her care of me. My mother said that she had died peacefully, praying for me and thinking of me. I went to her room, empty of her bed and all her belongings, which had gone to her nephew. I missed her so much that I arranged for our family to visit her grave in Qom on the next Thursday (a day comparable to Saturday in the West). Now both she and my father were sleeping in Qom. As I sat by the flowers I had placed on her grave, I silently expressed my respect, love, and thanks for her sincere care and love to my family and me. In a subdued atmosphere, we returned to Tehran. Still keeping thoughts of her in mind, I began to plan how to continue my duty and service to humanity, especially people in need. These plans were some consolation in compensating for her loss.

At the beginning of the next week—on Saturday (equivalent to Mondays in the West), I went to my office at the National University of Iran for letters, messages and my schedule of teaching for the next term. On the way to the National University of Iran, I stopped to see how the construction of our house was progressing. To my delight, it would soon be ready to be moved into. All that remained was to complete the landscaping. In the autumn, we would plant everything. The architect wanted to add some large stones to finish his design, and these were put in place by a crane.

We wanted a wonderful and unique garden with seasonal plants and trees, which we bought from Sharifi Gardens in Karag. We chose more than five hundred trees, bushes, and plants for the different sections of the garden. We had a great variety of ornamental trees, pines, fruit trees, and other types. The roses were important because, after all, Iran is the land of roses and nightingales, and the soil is well suited for roses. I remember we bought almost one hundred different roses in the form of trees, bushes, shrub lets, and climber roses, all in different types and different colors for planting between stones, around walls, or near the swimming pool or as part of other areas of the garden.

With this extensive garden, we had to have a full-time gardener, but finding a full-time gardener was not easy because of the rapid development of the country and the need for manpower. I asked several family members who still had farms (mostly for grapes) to help us find someone. Fortunately, it did not take long, and we were lucky to find a husband and wife couple (Hajali and Molood). The husband would garden, and his wife would help the nanny and the cook in the house. We definitely needed a full-time gardener because just watering the grass in the dry climate took five hours a day. There was no sprinkler system available at that time. In addition to watering, the gardener would prepare flowers for each season, both outdoors and in the hothouse, do all the seeding and fertilizing, not to mention all the upkeep required for our beautiful, unique garden. So we hired the couple immediately and decided to get ready to move in before the winter. This was a good decision because the university had by now moved entirely to Evin near our home, and it was much easier for me to go to work from the new house.

When I returned to the National University, I found that most of my colleagues and many of the faculty members were upset with the new president, Dr. Bina, a real outsider who had reorganized the previous system, which had been modeled on the American college system, to a more French style, more like the old University of Tehran. At the same time, as he was president of our university, he was also serving as president of two other universities and continuing as professor of history at the University of Tehran. He had also upset the faculty by bringing in new personnel from France and promoting them immediately; directly to professorship, like Professor Safavian and Professor Puyan. This unequal treatment caused unhappiness and dissatisfaction among the faculty, but of course, nobody could express dissatisfaction because the minister of court was supporting him. Therefore, the faculty repressed their views as is usual in a dictatorial society. As always, however, I tried just to keep my mind on teaching and keep myself out of the political groups as much as possible. At this time, to bring to the attention of authorities that we needed a better system of higher education, I wrote an article about Higher Education in Germany, explaining their method of promotion and rotating administration among faculty. Of course, I could not state my motive directly, but I hoped that with this indirect presentation that we would one day have a fairer system.

I finally made an appointment to see the president Dr. A. Bina to introduce myself and report on the NSF work and tell him the good news from the Fulbright Commission. After a long time waiting for an appointment, I finally saw him and noticed immediately that he was totally indifferent to my subject and report and had no interest or understanding of the illiteracy problems in Iran or my Fulbright project to combat illiteracy with programmed learning. Seeing his indifferent reaction, I made the meeting short, only adding that the Fulbright Commission was allowing me to reschedule for the following summer and that I would use my summer vacation for the fellowship in order not to interrupt the teaching year. All the time I spoke, he was totally indifferent and kept looking out the window. That was just about my only meeting with him because I avoided him whenever I could. Many of my colleagues like Dr. Farroch-pars and Dr. Aryanpour had very negative interactions with him, with many disagreements. They were very impolite to each other and argued all the time and I wanted to avoid that. Because he was an outsider, he did not respect the opinion of the faculty, and the faculty had no respect for him as an authority.

At the same time that our university was reorganizing to a French-oriented system, the country also was expanding its relations with France from cultural to economical relations. In August 1966, for the first time, the National Iranian Oil Company signed an additional contract with the French Company Erap for discovery, refinery, and the use of oil technology, in addition to the oil consortium, which included several American companies. With this agreement, Erap would take 10 percent after the sale of oil. Gradually Iran had signed contracts for its oil with other East European companies, so as not to limit itself just to the consortium. As a result of this competition, the consortium's share also was increased, and Iran received more income from oil, and the Shah was happy to be able to fulfill his economic development plan for the country. He was even forecasting that the National Iranian Oil Company would become the largest oil company in the world, and at the same time, we had great hope in the Shahbanu, who was promoting improvements in social conditions, the arts and educational activities.

We began the move to our new house just before our wedding anniversary in November 1966. Moving is never easy, but we needed the space, especially for our many books. Each of us had a library and mine was full, with books in Farsi, German, and English. I had so many books that I had to use part of Sa'id's library to get all of them to fit. One of the more difficult tasks was finding a curtain to fit an extra large window. This window was the length of our large connected living room and dining room—the room for entertaining guests. The curtain company sent four people to carry the long curtain rod, because it was almost 14 feet long and was not possible to bring the rod by car. These men had to walk up the mountain carrying the rod and heavy curtain while I guided them slowly in my car. Even hanging the curtain was difficult. They had to work with two different kinds of curtains—the light sheer one and the heavy curtain.

The author with her daughter Gita in their new home.

The rest of the rooms did not present any problem, and all the other rods and curtains were carried by car. The architect had planned a bar, with several lighted arches and niches with recessed lighting to highlight our collection of old crystal bottles and other antiques. These bottles were orange and blue, with exquisite gold handwork and a picture of the old king of Persia. We finished our move smoothly with help from friends and family. From the new location, it was a short drive or an easy walk over the hill to the National University. When we had deep snow and couldn't drive even with chains, I just put on my boots and walked. I was on time at exactly eight o'clock every teaching day. If many students were unable to come to class because of the weather, I took advantage of this time to get to know the other students better, answering their questions and discussing their problems. I loved these students and cared deeply for them, especially as I sensed that they wanted to share their concerns and thoughts about their personal lives.

The author celebrating Gita's birthday with
other family members.

We gradually adjusted to our new home and our everyday routine
work and social life. At one of the cocktail parties given by the Fulbright
Commission, we met Dr. Brian Klitz, a Fulbright scholar from the United
States who was finishing his program in classical music and preparing to
return to the States. I was introduced to him as a Fulbright scholar for
the coming summer, and when I introduced Sa'id as a professor of music
education, he was very pleased and suggested that if Sa'id would come
with me, he would arrange lectures and recitals on Persian Music at the
University of Connecticut.

Just at that time, Dr. Richard Brown, director of the Fulbright
Commission in Iran, came by and joined our conversation. He added
that Sa'id could also be invited to give the lecture and recital at his
university, the University of Wisconsin. Moreover, he would ask other
US universities if they would like these lectures/recitals, and that, if
there was an interest, the Fulbright Commission might provide a travel
grant for Sa'id in 1967. My husband replied that this would be an ideal
time for him to study music education in the USA, where music is a
part of the curriculum from preschool to high school. Sa'id advocated
adding music to the curriculum of public schools in Iran, although he
knew there were religious and cultural barriers against this idea. Joining
in this same conversation, Dr. Afzal, dean of the School of Education,
added that he thought this type of cultural exchange through music
would be the best means of sharing our two cultures. Dr. Brown replied
that he was happy to hear this and said that he would do some research,
see which universities were interested, and let us know soon. Both Sa'id
and I were overjoyed at the possibility that he might be able to join me
in the USA.

Ironically, Sa'id had not initially wanted to come to this party with me. He said that although we were both invited, he knew that I was the one the invitation was really for. I was happy that I had insisted that he attend and now maybe we could go to the USA together thanks to the Fulbright grants. While we waited to hear from Dr. Brown, we said nothing to my mother and I thought about Gita and her place in our plans. At that same time, I heard some people say that 1967 would be the last year for the Fulbright Commission in Iran, since the country no longer needed any aid. If the country wanted to send scholars abroad, Iran could finance it, since the country had developed so well economically. I was the last Fulbright Scholar from Iran to the United States and the Fulbright Commission was replaced by other programs.

In the meantime, I received information about the scope of my program. For one part of it, I would be at the University of Illinois at Chicago Circle, under the supervision of Professor Susan Meyer Markle, who had been a colleague of B. F. Skinner at Harvard. She was a leader in the field of programmed learning and teaching machines. The second part would be at the University of Pittsburgh, supervised by Dr. Robert Glaser, another well-known educational psychologist in programmed learning. I would spend six to seven weeks with each of these areas, and for the rest of my time, I could visit any other research project and site they recommended.

Four weeks later, Sa'id received a congratulatory letter from Dr. Brown saying that seven universities were interested in having him give one or two lectures/recitals. Each would provide a small honorarium. These honorariums would help with his daily expenses. He had been invited by the universities of Connecticut, Wisconsin, and DePaul, the University of Michigan at Ann Arbor, and its Interlaken Music Camp, and by the University of Indiana, and the State University of Michigan at East Lansing. This was indeed wonderful news because all these universities had very large music departments, and finally, in each state, he would have a contact person at the Department of Education and would be able to visit the music programs in all the schools.

Sa'id and I were so happy that we could travel together to the USA and had thoughts of taking Gita with us. Words cannot describe our happiness. I inquired about day care for each place we would visit. Then we told my mother the news. She was extremely happy for us and happy that I would not have to travel alone, but the minute I told her we were taking Gita because there was good day care facilities for her, my mother's attitude changed. She was so angry she jumped up, her face red from anger. She said that under no circumstances could we take Gita. She would not allow it. I understood that she was thinking about how Gita would do in a strange environment. She also knew that Gita was very attached to her and stressed that Gita spent more time with her and with the nanny than she did with us. She emphasized that we would only be gone for a few months and keeping Gita would be no problem for her. She promised to take such good care of Gita and that she would not notice our absence at all. We thought about this matter for days, and finally, we agreed, on the condition that my mother invite an old friend of hers to come and stay with her. Since she liked having people around her, she was glad to hear our decision.

As we received information from the Fulbright Commission, we saw that the program officer in Washington DC was coordinating the two programs so that we could travel together as much as possible for the first two months. Sa'id would finish his program and return earlier because my program was for four months.

We bought several new toys for Gita and my mother's old friend Tuba came to stay with us. I took both Gita and my mother for a checkup with her physician Dr. Kafi, and he promised that he also would look after them. My cousin Parvin assured us that they would visit frequently and told us not to worry.

Our academic year was complete in May 1967, and we booked our ticket for New York to start our visit at the University of Connecticut. Again, we stayed with my cousin Mehri Kalali in Norwalk. She has always invited relatives to visit, and she even helps those who want to live permanently in the United States. We called Dr. B. Klitz who welcomed us and provided details of the times for Sa'id's Persian music lectures. He himself took us to Storrs, and Sa'id provided two interesting programs on traditional and modern Persian music, which he illustrated by playing samples.

We spent two days at the University of Connecticut. Sa'id's lectures in the Conference Hall were open to faculty and students, and as word spread, the second lecture was much better attended than the first, with many people standing in the hall. I was proud and elated to see that each time he went to the podium he was charming, professional, and completely at ease—just the way artists and actors should be. He seemed to develop instant rapport with an audience, and audiences were attracted to him and fascinated by his performances. After these lectures, we were scheduled to arrive in Wisconsin, the state where Dr. Brown resided, as the president of the University of Wisconsin. Both of these lectures also had large audiences, and I was pleased to see great interest in Persian music from the students.

Two days later, we traveled to Chicago, and from there, we were required to separate for a short time. I would remain in Chicago for about six weeks, while Sa'id would pursue his program at other Midwest universities, each with its own contact person for him. I went immediately to the University of Illinois at Chicago Circle, where Dr. Susan Meyer Markle was professor of Psychology and the director of Instructional Resources for the university. She was a very charming person, well oriented in her field, and she knew exactly what my project was. She had prepared studies for me and left them on my desk, near her office, and told me that any time I had questions I could go to her. Later, I heard that she was also the president of the Programmed Instruction Society, which I became a member of later.

From the beginning, Susan was very helpful. She recommended better accommodation than a dormitory—for a little more money we could have a furnished studio in a hotel type of setting. Students in Germany would not have had such good accommodation. Our studio apartment was very practical, and we could cook small dishes and make coffee and tea. The only drawback was the constant noise of the city because the apartment was located on a busy street. However, it was very near the metro station and only one stop to my office at the university. So for one month, we had a nice place with metro access all over the city. Being without a car was not a problem.

Sa'id made his contacts and arranged his visit to DePaul, the Education Office in Chicago, University of Indiana, and universities in Michigan and neighboring states. We experienced the twenty-four-hour liveliness of Chicago, a city that never seemed to sleep. We heard the sound of sirens all night and all day. The bars and restaurants never seemed to close, and we heard people walking outside at all hours.

Susan invited us to her home many times, and we met her husband. They seemed a nice couple. As soon as she heard about Sa'id as a music educator, she told us she loved jazz and invited us to an open-air concert when her friend Duke Ellington was playing. She thought that Sa'id should study jazz in addition to music education while he was in the USA, and we agreed. The concert was a memorable one in an open-air theater, which reminded us of the Baths of Caracalla in Rome. Duke Ellington played a variety of wind instruments, and we thought the sound was beautiful and unforgettable. After the concert, Susan went up to him, congratulated him, and then introduced us. He graciously signed some of his new recordings for Sa'id, which we valued as a dear souvenir from the USA.

For my project to use programmed learning and teaching machines to combat illiteracy, I was able to obtain the best project and program information. Of course, the key to the success of this project is a good program, and the machine is only an instrument. During my stay, Susan arranged several visits to a variety of research sites in Chicago.

These educational reforms in behaviorism and programmed instruction in the United States came about because of the Soviet Union's surpassing the United States in the space race. After October 4, 1957, when the Soviet Union successfully launched *Sputnik* into space, the United States began a race to catch up, with new political, military, technological, scientific developments—all of which hinged on a new focus on education reform. The United States government provided money for research in educational psychology to compete with the Soviet Union, and one focus was on Burrhus Frederick (BF) Skinner's theory. Elaboration of the theory of reinforcement and his advocacy of its application to learning helped to establish the behaviorism and programmed instruction movement in the USA. My interest in the theory of reinforcement and Skinner's advocacy of its application to learning led to a great interest at this time in the behaviorism and programmed instruction movement in education in the US programmed instruction is in fact a step-by-step individualized instruction, which replaces the teacher with systematic material. Individualized instruction was originally in book form, and then in order to prevent students from looking at the answers in the book ahead of time, program instruction became automated by inserting it into a teaching machine. Skinner in 1958 built a rote-and-drill teaching machine, and later on this basis, many sophisticated programs and machines were built.

An example of the 'talking typewriter' or
'teaching machine' from 1966-67.

One of these programs, the talking typewriter, was the well-funded research project of Dr. Omar Khayyam Moore, which focused on beginning reading and writing. (I also appreciated that his first name was the name of our well-known Persian poet, mathematician, and philosopher.) Dr. Moore's study was set in a poorer section of town, with black children aged three and four. Through programmed play, the children were learning to read and write with a positive reinforcement. I watched them demonstrate to me how they could write using the talking keyboard of a machine, and learning without a teacher. Dr. Moore's study showed that children from a disadvantaged area could learn quickly using this method, thus suggesting that other children could learn this way too. The US government had channeled millions of dollars for this type of educational research leading to improving education. There were many research projects like that for the purpose of improving education.

Following Susan's advice, I collected information on the most successful projects and sent these to Iran, where 50 percent of our population was illiterate. I hoped I could implement these projects when I returned. At the same time, Sa'id was also collecting many sample books on music education in schools in the USA after his visit to the office of education. One officer, Luis, helped him to gather information, and he and Sa'id became friends. He kindly invited us to celebrate the Fourth of July at his home. We joined him and his family for a cookout and fireworks. Our dealings with American people showed us that most Americans, like Iranians, are hospitable to guests. We found it to be a national characteristic. When our month's rental was up, Susan offered us her luxury apartment for the final two weeks in Chicago while she was away on vacation. So we had the use of this apartment with its lovely view of Chicago—another sample of American hospitality.

This summer of 1967, we witnessed riots and demonstrations in the United States, concerning the Six-Day War, June 5-11, between Israel and the Arab countries in the Middle East. We read the newspapers daily and observed free political demonstrations. Apparently, an ominous arms race developed early in the 1960s. Egypt and Syria were supplied with Soviet aid and military hardware, and Israel suddenly found European powers—the Federal Republic of Germany (West Germany), Britain, and especially France—to be willing suppliers of modern armaments. Jordan continued to receive arms from Britain and the United States.

Disagreements ultimately led to war, and the United States was unable to initiate any international action to prevent it. On the morning of June 5, Israel launched a devastating attack on Arab airpower, destroying almost three hundred Egyptian, fifty Syrian, and twenty Jordanian aircraft, mostly on the ground. This action, which virtually eliminated the Arab air forces, was immediately followed by ground invasions into Sinai and the Gaza Strip, Jordan, and finally Syria. Arab ground forces, lacking air support, were routed on all three fronts; by the time the UN-imposed cease-fire took effect on June 11, Israeli forces had seized the entire Sinai Peninsula to the east bank of the Suez Canal; the West Bank of Jordan, including East Jerusalem; and the Golan Heights of Syria. Since this was the age of television, the world could see, along with us, how both sides of this conflict could freely assemble, protest, and demonstrate—all in freedom. Finally, both parties agreed to a UN cease-fire, UN Resolution 242, which called for negotiation of a permanent peace between the parties and Israel's withdrawal from the land occupied in 1967. This conflict, which existed through the twentieth century, continues into the twenty-first century. Hopefully, the region may one day be at peace.

Sa'id finished his lectures, recitals, and visits at the Indiana University and DePaul successfully, according to the newspaper reviews. Unfortunately, I could not join him because of my intensive schedule and visits. He had nearly finished his program. Only three lecture recitals remained, one at the University of Michigan, the International Music Camp at Interlaken, and the State University of Michigan at East Lansing. Since I was eager to go back to the University of Michigan to visit the department of psychology and my friends in connection with my project, I went with him to Michigan. Dr. Millholland was happy to see me and said that because of his experience with me the year before, he now had someone from Thailand at his NSF Seminar that year. He told me that from then on, he would have someone from another country every year. I agreed with him that his decision was important to continue international exchange and understanding for all countries.

Dr. Millholland suggested that I visit several nearby research sites that would benefit my project. I also had a chance to visit a couple of colleagues from Tehran, Dr. Kafi and Dr. Vaziri, the latter from Dr. Rezai's hospital. Dr. Vaziri, a psychiatrist, had moved here with his family. From speaking with them, I began to see how welcome professional people are in the United States. They urged me to stay in the United States to work, explaining that the US values professional people for their qualifications, not because of their nepotism relationship to someone in the court or to someone with power. I learned that there was social and professional freedom in the United States.

As we talked, I thought about the atmosphere of the National University and could not agree with them. My point was that the need for service in Iran was greater, and that if everyone left for professional and financial success, who would then serve the needy in Iran? This same conflict was an argument I had had with myself in Germany and England and the conflict that faced many educated Iranian people. Anyway, Sa'id's program was very successful, especially at the Interlaken International Music Camp, and at the suggestion of some of the officers of the International Society of Music Education (ISME), Sa'id became a member of the Society.

From Michigan, Sa'id left the USA with plenty of souvenir books and material for Iranian children and students in music education, and I went to Pittsburgh to continue the rest of my program. I was pleased that Sa'id could leave earlier to take care of our dear Gita and my mother, although all the letters and telephone calls from my mother assured me that they were both well.

Pittsburgh offered another angle of study. In Pittsburgh, Dr. Robert Glaser, the director of Learning Research and Development Center, was conducting another multimillion-dollar project in programmed instruction in a school connected to the University of Pittsburgh. Pittsburgh was a different city from Chicago. It was a hilly city similar to

Stuttgart in Germany. Public transportation was not as well developed as Chicago, so I found housing near the university. At his center, Dr. Glaser and his large staff were developing all the programmed instruction for the experimental school and several of their programs had a high success rate. As a result, the center was expanding and had several openings and job offers for the position of research associate. Considering the unfair atmosphere of the National University of Iran, I was very tempted to apply for a job there, and for the third time, I ran into a conflict with myself. I called Sa'id in Tehran and asked him to go to the National University and see if he could find out the status of my promotion to professorship. I told myself that if I could not get a professorship after five years as associate professor, I would definitely apply for a position in Pittsburgh. I had published more material than my male colleagues, and the two recently appointed faculty members had been promoted directly from their studies in France without any experience because of their connections to the court. Fortunately, Sa'id found out that my decree for the professorship lacked only a signature and that it would be on my desk by September 1. That good news resolved my dilemma, and I turned my attention to collecting information from the center for beginning reading and writing. In Pittsburgh I saw Carol and her husband from Ann Arbor. Her husband had gotten a position with a promotion, and they had moved from the University of Michigan to the University of Pittsburgh. When I saw Horton at the university, he joked that they had moved to Pittsburgh because of my project in Pittsburgh.

But when Carol called and invited me to lunch, she told me that she had a lot to tell me. At lunch she explained that after the NSF Seminar, her husband had gotten a new job, they had moved to Pittsburgh, two of her four children were in college, and she had a good job as a school psychologist. But unfortunately, her husband did not want her to work, and they were planning to divorce and live separately. So even in America, an academic man was not ready for equal opportunity for his wife. She was very upset and sad, and I invited her to come to Iran to see us as our guest after she settled her divorce.

As the interesting program in Pittsburgh drew to a close, I made arrangements to go to the Johns Hopkins University in Baltimore, my next place of study. I would live in Baltimore with my friend. In Baltimore, I suddenly became very sick with flu and a high temperature. I rushed to the emergency room of Johns Hopkins in order to get well quickly so as not to miss any day from my program. I went there, thinking that going directly to that great hospital's emergency room would be the fastest way to get well and not miss any time. I couldn't believe how long I had to wait—three hours—until finally through a doctors' practice I saw a physician and got medication.

Because of the illness, I missed one of the scheduled visits. As the time drew to a close, in Washington DC, I met Mary, the program officer, thanked her for the rich, informative program the Fulbright Commission had provided, and told her I hoped to be able to conduct my own project in Iran. I very much wanted to provide programmed learning in the Persian language for illiterate Iranian people. With this hope, I finished the complete program and returned to Tehran.

THIRD MOVEMENT
EVOLUTION TO REVOLUTION

CHAPTER 10

A Young Family at Work
1967-1969

With great passion and high motivation to work hard for my beloved country, I returned to Tehran. I wanted to combat illiteracy in Iran by using the programmed learning method. I had missed my family very much. Sa'id, Gita, and her nanny were waiting for me at the Tehran Mehrabad airport. I hugged Sa'id first, and then opened my arms to pick up Gita. Her response was my punishment. She stared at me and asked, "Who are you?" When I answered, "Mommy," she jumped into my arms and did not want to let go. We walked to the car together, laughing and crying at the same time. Because of the guilt I felt, this remains a painful moment in my life, which I cannot forget. When we reached home, my mother was waiting for me. Her first words were "Thank God you are back because Gita has been looking for you incessantly." Although she looked older and tired, she was happy and seemed happy to be relieved from further responsibility. I hugged my mother and thanked her from the bottom of my heart for her care. Next, I gave Gita her presents. She was delighted with the Snoopy toys and all the storybooks. She held Snoopy, while I held her in my arms, and began to read a story about a princess. Before I could finish, she was fast asleep. Sa'id carried her to her bed, and we went to our room. I made a solemn vow to myself to spend more time with her and never leave her alone again.

One of the first things I did after coming home was to give Gita a developmental test, and the results showed that she was very creative. She enjoyed the sample programmed reading books I had brought with me from the USA for preschool education. I knew she was ready for preschool because she was alone at home, and there were not many children nearby. She needed a social life and playmates, so first I registered her in Golestaneh Bilingual Kindergarten, very near home and on the way to my work at the National University. This way I could easily monitor her program, her reactions, and her behavior. Within a month, I noticed that she had become very quiet and would not answer our questions about kindergarten. I decided then to make an unannounced visit to the school to observe her. I noticed that most of the time that she was not socializing with the other children and one time I saw her standing in a corner crying quietly. It was clear that she was not happy, so we finally took her out of the school and continued to search for a suitable educational preschool program. Fortunately, through Dr. M. Afzal, the dean of the School of Education, and his American wife, Martha, I found a good preschool program for the preschool age in Gholhak, which was a farther distance from our home. The school was founded by Mrs. Nelson, a South African. After visiting her progressive program, I learned that she also had arranged a car pool for parents living near each other. This meant that I would have the responsibility for the car pool for just one week per month. Without any hesitation, I enrolled Gita in this preschool program and joined the car pool.

Gita blossomed in the new environment. She was happy and eager to learn, and this showed in her face. Even when she was at home in the afternoons, she liked to use the sample book from the Science Research Associates Inc. (SRA), which for years prepared individualized beginner programs for reading, writing, and math. So gradually I had a peace of mind about her well-being and progress.

Author's daughter (Gita) and nephew (Parviz) in the author's new family home.

Author with her immediate family members celebrating Gita's birthday.

Meanwhile, at the National University of Iran, we witnessed another change of president. Apparently, Dr. Bina was removed because of several complaints from faculty and students, probably brought about by the weight of the responsibilities that carrying the presidency of three universities entailed. This time the Shah appointed Dr. Mojtahedi, a successful principal of a large, excellent high school for boys—the Alborz School in Tehran. Maybe it was reasoned that since he was an excellent high school administrator, he would also be an excellent administrator of a higher education institution, so he was given both to manage. I wondered, however, how he could juggle these two jobs, especially as each institution had a distinct set of goals and objectives quite different from the other.

In any case, I had to make an appointment to see him to report on my study in the USA and my project for combating illiteracy in Iran by using the latest method in educational psychology—programmed learning. During my meeting with him, he listened very carefully as a mathematician would. But while he seemed to be impressed with the study and the project, he surprised me by telling me that what he was really thinking about was having a college of home economics for women at the National University of Iran. This was his response to my project. I replied that in more developed countries, this type of curriculum is not considered an academic subject appropriate to college and university and that these types of colleges for women were changing their names and curricula so that women might have equal opportunity for academic education. However, my time with him was up, and I left his office hoping that he would forget about the home economics curriculum.

I came away thinking that I really needed to write some articles about programmed learning for the *Journal of Psychology* and that I should also speak on that subject at our Iranian Psychological Association (IPA). Dr. A. A. Siassi, the founder of the association and my former undergraduate professor, was always promoting new ideas in psychology and welcomed my suggestions. Finally, I made the presentation about programmed learning and published the article in the journal in 1973.[1]

Author as a member of the Iranian Psychological Association (IPA) panel which also included the president Dr. Aliakbar Siassi.

In the years 1967-69, we were able to see several favorable political changes in the country, but Iran still depended on more developed countries for its rapid economic development. The White Revolution, which was renamed the Revolution of the Shah and People, was making progress, and in this way, the state manipulated political life. The idea was that with the revolution of the Shah and People (White Revolution) there would be an aggressive reform program, and these reforms would strengthen the monarchy and the status of the Shah. As part of this plan, there was an official coronation of the Shah and also for the first time the coronation of an empress—the Shahbanou, his wife.

The ceremony took place on the forty-eight birthday of the Shah, October 26, 1967. A select group of people from all different classes and professions, including me—a university professor—were invited to participate in the coronation of the Shah and Shahbanou at Golestan Palace. The Shah had delayed his coronation for twenty-six years because he was waiting to ensure that Iran had progressed and had become a respected country among all the countries in the world.

Author attended, along with her colleagues from other universities, the Coronation ceremonies held at the Golestan Palace.

The coronation was a beautiful ceremony. There were two royal carriages, one with eight white horses and one with four black horses, carrying the Shah, the empress, and the seven-year-old Crown Prince Reza from the Marble Palace to Golestan Palace. The coronation ceremony was held in the Grand Hall, and Imam Djomeh, a spiritual leader of the country, began by reading some verses from the Koran. Then, after a special prayer, the Imam presented the Holy Book on a blue cushion to the Shah. The Shah kissed the Holy Book and placed it back on the cushion. Then the coronation ritual of His Imperial Majesty began. Just as Napoleon had done, the Shah was going to crown himself. Various high-ranking officers and members of the Imperial Household processed toward the Shah, one after the other. One carried the Emerald Belt, another the Royal Sword—the Shahi Sword—and another carried the Imperial Robe embroidered with precious stones. This robe was placed on the Shah, and then finally, the most important moment came. A general brought in the crown of the world's most ancient Empire, encrusted with diamonds and the *Sea of Light* diamond (Darya-e Noor), one of the largest diamonds of the world. This diamond had been brought from India in 1739 by Nader Shah. Including its setting, the diamond is 7.2 centimeters high and 5.3 centimeters wide (2.9 inches high and 2.1 inches). It is believed to weigh between 182-186 carats.

Coronation of Shahbanou Farah Pahlavi.

The Shah then took the crown and placed it on his head, the same crown that his father, Reza Shah, had used in his coronation in April 1926. Immediately, after the coronation, 101 canon shots sounded throughout Tehran, and the people began celebrating throughout the country. After his own coronation, the Shah crowned the Shahbanou empress of Iran, something new and unprecedented in our history. On the head of his wife, the empress, he placed a beautiful crown made of emeralds, the largest of which was located in the center of the crown, weighing 91.32 carats, pearls, rubies, two spinels, and about 1,500 diamonds, designed by a French jeweler, and presented on a green velvet pillow. Crowning his wife was an action also viewed as an important symbol of how the Shah saw the new role of women being important in Iranian society. Now, the first Iranian queen ever crowned, the empress, was also named Regent of the Empire, a title that would give her the reign of the empire in case of the Shah's demise before Prince Reza's eighteenth birthday and his maturity. The Constitution had to be changed before the coronation to allow her this high privilege.

In keeping with the desire to celebrate the whole nation and its customs and history, the design of the robe and crown was oriental and Persian, unique and beautiful, and the Shahbanou looked every inch an empress, a positive step toward the advancement of the status of women in Iran. The Empress Farah in her memoir is mindful of the importance of her coronation: "When he crowned me on 26 October 1967, the king made me feel that he was crowning all the women of Iran."[2] The star of the event was the seven-year-old Crown Prince Reza Cyrus Pahlavi, who entered after the empress. Resplendent in his blue uniform complete with military hat, he was surrounded by four saluting officers, and although he had a cold and was running a temperature, he played his role beautifully.

A few moments after the coronation, the prime minister, Mr. Hoveyda, congratulated His Majesty on behalf of the whole nation and praised all the work of the Shah during his reign. After his speech, the president of the Senate presented his compliments, and a professor from the University of Tehran spoke about the meaning of the coronation.

At this occasion, the Shah made a brief and important speech thanking God and asking God to give him the power to serve the country and its people well, proclaiming his hope for the independence and sovereignty of Iran and the progress of the people of Iran. He also said that he was ready, if necessary, to offer his life for the development of Iran. The speech was very moving to me and to all those gathered, and it was well received internationally. It was a confirmation of what the sovereign will do to modernize the country, stabilize the region, and create a powerful Iran. Shortly after the speech, the male members of the Imperial family came to bow and pay their respects to the Shah, and the impressive ceremony came to an end. Even though I was both fascinated and amazed by the ceremony and especially by the coronation of the Shahbanou for the first time in our history, I still wondered why only the male members of the Royal family should congratulate the Shah and Shahbanou and not the female members. There should have been at least a woman representative of the family or the country to congratulate both and participate in the closing of the ceremony. I thought again how far women had to go to receive equal treatment. Even the court ceremony demonstrated how much more education we needed in that area. Learning about equality of the sexes could not be done just through formal education. We needed the help of the media and other informal methods. I hoped we could take advantage of the Shah's support and play an important role in advancing the status of women.

Fortunately, I saw a way to work on this project. As a member of several councils and boards of organizations like Radio and Television, IPA (Iranian Psychological Association) and the Charity of the empress, I could observe and evaluate radio and television programs that related to the equal treatment of women. I also tried very hard to bring to the members' attention the stigma attached to women propagated by use of the term *zaife*, "the weak person, unequal in every aspect." So consciously and unconsciously, women were treated unequally. I urged every member of these organizations to become active in making people aware of the need to treat women as human beings equal to men.

But bringing about change was hard work. One day at the university, my colleague Dr. Cyrus Azimi and I were summoned to meet with the president, Dr. Mojtahedi. In that meeting, he spoke about the expansion of the department of psychology and of his plan for a new school for girls named the School of Home Economics. He gave each one of us two months to write a plan to develop these ideas and deliver them to him. It was obvious to Dr. Mojtahedi that, as a woman, I was responsible for planning for the School of Home Economics. I was ideologically opposed to this idea and had already told him my views on the subject. This School of Home Economics would mean a limited role for women and would continue to keep women at home. So again I made the point that more developed countries were changing their thinking regarding special schools for girls. I told him that even the Shah was working toward progress for the country and for women. My words carried no weight because his prejudice against women was much stronger than my argument.

My colleague was happy with his assignment; we left the president's office each with our individual tasks. I noticed that as we left, the president made a note in his notebook. During the next few days, I went to the United States Information Service (USIS) library for university catalogs, looking specifically for old catalogs. I also asked colleagues in Europe to send me information. In my plan, I included a rich, strong curriculum for the school so that if students wanted to continue their education, they could go on to law school or medical school, or become engineers. In this way, their comprehensive curriculum and all-round education would be some compensation for the lack of equal opportunity.

For some time, I had also been serving as the dean of women students and many of them brought their problems to my attention as a psychologist. When they came to me, I explored the idea of an all-girls school with them. Most of these young women, even those from religious traditional families, did not welcome the idea of separate education. I was sure I understood their feelings since I had gradually established a society of women students with regular meetings where I tried to address their general problems, all the while discussing what their role would be in a modern society. They were very close to me, and I was very close to them.

Meanwhile, the country was making progress in every aspect. At the Olympics, Iran placed second in the world in wrestling, with two gold and two silver medals. In a special ceremony at Harvard University, the Shah was awarded an honorary doctoral degree. More importantly, Dr. Farrokhru Parsa, my former favorite biology teacher for five years in high school, was introduced by Prime Minister A. A. Hoveyda as the first woman minister for the Ministry of Education. Another popular teacher of mine, Dr. Mehrangiz Manuchehrian, was appointed by the Shah as senator, and several other women became active in the *Majles*, the parliament. I was happy to see that women were gradually able to accept positions in the police department, air force, and other leadership positions in the government. Gradually, under the leadership of Dr. Manuchehrian and with the support of the Shah, there were several changes in the laws. The Family Protection Law was ratified. Divorce laws became more fair and balanced toward women, and laws against polygamy became more stringent, as polygamy was entirely discouraged and had become very rare. The marriage age was raised to eighteen in line with more advanced countries. Because of her efforts, Dr. Manuchehrian was awarded the human rights prize by the United Nations in 1968.

Dr. Farrokhrou Parsa the first female Minister of Education
for Iran and formerly the author's teacher for five years.
(Download original: http://www.iranian.com/
ArdavanBahrami/2005/May/Parsa/Images/p1.jpg)
Source: http://www.iranian.com/ArdavanBahrami/2005/
May/Parsa/index.html

At home, Gita was making excellent progress in reading and writing, using the programmed books, which she enjoyed. She was also happy in kindergarten. During this time, however, she had a series of accidents, some of which were very close calls. One incident in her bedroom was particularly scary. Her bed was surrounded by a long mosquito net, held in place by a round metal net holder. One day we heard her crying and screaming, and when we ran to her bed, we saw that her head and neck were caught in the middle of this round net holder and she could not get out. We couldn't figure out how to help her and couldn't understand how she had gotten into this situation. We tried every angle we could, but we were not successful. Finally, we called a metalworker to come and cut one side of the net holder, which was tightly wrapped around her neck. It was not an easy task. When he began to cut the metal attached to her neck, my heart beat faster and faster as I watched him close his hand and move nearer her neck. Very slowly, the poor man worked to free her. He was very skillful, and gradually made a fine cut, opening the metal circle without a single scratch to her neck. When she was free, Gita, who had been standing motionless, and in fear, on her bed for some hours jumped into my arms, and we thanked God she was not harmed. We gave a large tip to the metalworker, almost equal to his fee.

Other accidents were similarly unique with our inquisitive daughter who wanted to examine everything herself. Because of close observation by all of us, her nanny and my mother, who loved her very much, Sa'id and I, were able to keep her from many more serious accidents. Love and care should surround all children.

Because of Gita's accidents, we celebrated our anniversary very quietly at the Hilton Hotel, located very near to our home. In those days, the Hilton had a good, romantic atmosphere with a very nice dance band. Sa'id gave me a beautiful ring with a dark, double red ruby surrounded with diamonds, symbolizing our love and understanding. I loved that ring so much that from that night I replaced my wedding ring with it and wore the new one instead all the time.

Gradually around this time, Sa'id's specialty in music education came to be more understood and more in demand. He was also invited as an expert to be a member of the Council of the National Iranian Radio and Television (NIRT) for children's music programs. Gradually, his approach and plan to offer music education to children and young adults according to their developmental age was understood and attracted the attention of the members of the council and the progressive director, Mr. Reza Ghotbi, and his wife, Mrs. Shahrzad Afshar, who was the director of the Chamber Orchestra of the National Iranian Television. They even suggested that Sa'id should establish a music workshop for children and young adults and prepare the results of his study and research for all the children of the country as a scheduled television program designed especially for after school and Fridays (the day of rest in Iran).

Sa'id welcomed the chance to use the television in this way. He had been unsuccessful in bringing music education to the curriculum in public schools and was happy that he could expand music education though TV to reach the children. He liked the challenge. He also collaborated with the University of Tehran on this music workshop, which became a workshop for the university students and their practical teaching venue. With the financial support of the director of the NIRT, the workshop was very well equipped with educational instruments, tools, and methods including Carl Orff and Zoltan Kodaly, and other educational instruments and methods that Sa'id had brought from the USA. He became so motivated and busy in producing these television programs that he worked long hours day and night and even on Fridays and holidays.

He was very happy to be able to give this service to Iranian children and young adults for the first time. He selected and developed appropriate music for different developmental ages of children and young adults. He also selected children from all different classes for the workshop, and even reached children of needy families. I helped by suggesting that the children of the boarding schools (orphanages) of the charity of Empress Farah could benefit from the program.

Sa'id kept expanding the curriculum from the basic instrumental and vocal courses to include a diverse course for young beginners, using regional instruments from the various ethnic groups in Iran. He also used Western classical music. He focused on instrumental, vocal, and choral technique, research and education, and the actual production of the programs.

Sa'id began *The NIRT Workshop for Children and Young Adults* in Tehran with eighteen children and soon expanded it to close to three thousand students throughout—Isfahan, Mashad, Shiraz, Tabriz, and many more cities in Iran. He used regional instruments combining local instruction and augmented sometimes by teachers from Tehran. NIRT featured the talents of these students weekly. Student performances were common and popular, and every Friday many children eagerly watched these programs. As a result, Sa'id produced three books and over three hundred videos—for preschool, elementary, and high school age. The first book was published, and the last two were at the printer's just before the revolution. After the revolution, nobody knows what became of these manuscripts.

Our life was full of activities like teaching, research, and writing, but it still bothered me that I was not successful at implementing my project against illiteracy. On Fridays, we enjoyed mountain climbing around our home with academic friends such as Dr. A. A. Arianpour and A. Anwar and other colleagues and students. After the hours of mountain climbing, we usually invited them to our home for rest and a nice dinner prepared by our cook *Masht Hassan*. He was always happy when we had guests and enjoyed the opportunity to show his specialties and expertise as a cook.

During these gatherings with our friends, we discussed how best to serve our country, which, although it enjoyed social and cultural freedoms, still lacked political freedom. The Shah believed that first we should have economic freedom and then other freedoms would come. We agreed among ourselves that, because of the lack of political freedom and because of political influences and pressures from both the West and the East on several underground political groups, it would be more effective and better for us to keep our independence and to that end, we should not accept any administrative position in the government. We also unanimously agreed never to accept any position that involved handling money. In the meantime, in our lectures and writings, we would try to educate and promote independence for the younger generation. We would educate our students to fight against colonization by the superpowers and teach them to become independent thinkers, not just instruments to be played by superpowers. Our neighboring country, the Soviet Union's influence, was more organized in Iran through its longstanding *Tudeh* party, which was always active if most of the time underground. But other superpowers also were active in influencing several groups through religion. Gradually, some of my students and patients began to tell me privately of their bitter political experiences, and I was sorry for them that they were victims of the cold war, indirectly and unconsciously.

At the university, it was time for Dr. Azimi and I to present our two projects to Dr. Mojtahedi, the president. However, soon after, Dr. Mojtahedi resigned and returned to *Alborz,* his excellent high school. He was replaced by a professor of Surgery, A. Pouyan, dean of the School of Medicine, a man without much experience in the administration of higher education. His colleague, Professor Safavian, took his place as dean of the School of Medicine. We wondered what would happen to our plans. I was not sure if the new president, with his background, would follow the former president's plans and agenda. It was unusual for a new president to follow most of the ideas of the former one. We knew also that these two professors had political ambitions.

Professor Safavian was a well-known internist (he later became the Shah's personal physician), and I was still suffering from my migraine headaches, so many people suggested that I see him. I had suffered from these headaches for a long time and had tried specialists in Germany, England, and the USA. The best remedies doctors could suggest were a variety of tablets to take when the headaches started. None had been able to prevent the headaches. So I decided to try the French school too and went to see Professor Safavian in his private practice. He suggested that I needed to be hospitalized under observation so that he could try several medications for my headaches and see the results. When I told him that several well-known specialists in other countries had told me that I had inherited typical vascular migraine headaches, he did not accept this finding and wanted to examine me himself. Although it was difficult for me, I was hospitalized at the new university hospital. It was an interesting experience for me too. He first started with antidepressive and anti-anxiety drugs like valium and some other medications that were available in Iran even without prescription and very popular.

I tried valium, but my headaches became worse, and I began to vomit from pain. As a result, he switched to a new tablet—Deseril, but my head continued to bother me without improvement. So hospitalization did not help, and I went back to my former medication—Cafergot, because its side effect was much less than Deseril, and as a result, I discontinued my treatment with Dr. Safavian.

After a few months, I noticed that I had fewer headaches. I also experienced changes in my body similar to the time when I was pregnant. A few weeks later, I went to see Dr. Gharavi, my gynecologist. After the test, he told me that I was expecting a baby. I was surprised, but I had already been thinking that maybe it would be better for Gita and my family to have another child. I did not think that Sa'id and my mother would react negatively. My guess was correct, and everybody was happy. I personally was relieved from having more headaches, and because of the lack of pain, I took advantage of my well-being to become more active and energetic in writing several articles, working with Gita and beginning to read and think about the plan to combat illiteracy in Iran. Usually, my articles were published in the *Sokhan*, Iranian Psychological Association, and Mental Health journals.[3]

I was happy to learn from my physician that I was expecting a boy, and I thought this would complete the family—one child of each sex. The last months before the birth, I had summer vacation and peace of mind. This rest would have been beneficial for the child. This child was not moving much in my body—just the opposite of the first pregnancy with Gita. I sometimes even thought that there was something wrong. But the doctor confirmed that he was as alive, as a healthy boy should be, and was growing wonderfully well.

At the end of summer, our peaceful family life was shattered by a phone call from the office of her Royal Highness Princess Ashraf, the twin sister of the Shah. I was surprised and shocked to be told that I had to go to see the Princess's viceroy, Mr. Ansari. When I asked the reason, the caller said it was not possible to say and they could only give me an appointment. My mind reeled. Who dares not to go? My heart was beating wildly, especially since I did not know why I was being summoned.

Princess Ashraf was known to be a person to be taken seriously and to be disobeyed at one's peril. Fortunately, I had heard that her viceroy, who was a former minister of internal affairs, was an excellent administrator and more rational, and easier to work with. Anyway, on the day of my appointment, I drove to his office in downtown Tehran, not an easy task to drive such a distance when I was eight and a half months pregnant. At that time I really was looking very large, much bigger than the first pregnancy. It seemed to me that baby boys were heavier than baby girls. I arrived on time, and the secretary immediately led me to the office of Mr. Ansari. He was a very polite man, graying slightly, and he received me with a smile. My heart was beating hard as he stared at me and my appearance. I sat across from him, and he began by inquiring about one of my cousins—Kouros whom he knew very well because he used to work with him. After establishing this family connection, he began to explain to me that he had good news for me. He said that Princess Ashraf, as the honorary president of the Women's Organization, had ordered all university human resource departments in Iran to send all personnel files of women professors to her office for review. After reviewing these files, she had selected me for the position of secretary-general of the Women's Organization. She herself would serve as honorary president. I am sure that he expected to see an expression of happy acceptance from me, but I was quiet while I recovered my wits. Then I said, "May I ask what was the princess's criteria for selecting me?" He replied, "Your education, background, and achievement."

The princess wanted to reorganize the Women's Organization. She wanted the women of Iran to understand and value the rights that her brother the Shahanshah had given them. And since I had studied psychology, she thought that I could educate and change the behavior of women. It was a shock for me to think of taking on this enormous responsibility, especially in connection with my beliefs and my own situation within my family. In my ideal and independent life, I did not want to accept any administrative position. I was not involved or active in any women's organization—just the opposite. I was fighting for the social justice, for the equal role of women as human beings just like men, within a family setting or in society, and not in a separate setting. In addition, I had another issue to think of, my responsibility toward my new baby and my family. So I thanked Mr. Ansari for the honor of selecting me and requested that he kindly ask the Princess to excuse me from the job because of my pregnancy. I added that I would instead volunteer to help the Women's Organization as consultant, especially in combating illiteracy in women. I told him I already worked in the Charity Organization of the Shahbanou. After several arguments back and forth, Mr. Ansari, finally agreed to discuss the matter with the princess and maybe to excuse me from this position. It was a long meeting, and I became very tired, but I was relieved to think that hopefully Princess Ashraf would not press the appointment in view of my reluctance.

I drove slowly home to tell my husband and my mother who were anxiously waiting to hear about the meeting. They agreed with me and all of us hoped that Princess Ashraf would change her decision.

I continued my routine life in addition to preparing a room for the baby. In the meantime, I learned that Princess Ashraf was the honorary president of a center to combat illiteracy in Iran. We knew that usually a politician headed that center, and it had never produced any aggressive program in reading and writing to fight illiteracy. I wished I had been chosen for *that* job in which I believed I could excel by implementing the programmed reading and writing for men, women, and families in Iran. Through that program, I could have been more instrumental in advancing the status of women. About a week later, I had a call from Mr. Ansari who told me that he had discussed my appointment with Her Royal Highness Princess Ashraf, and he needed to meet with me again. This time driving was even more difficult for me. He smiled and asked, "How are you?" I replied, "Not so good, since I am becoming bigger every day."

I hoped that by complaining they would excuse me from the appointment. Then he began to tell me that he had spoken at length by phone with the princess at the United Nations. Her message was that we could wait until the baby was delivered and then I could assume the job.

In those days Princess Ashraf was very active as the head of the Iranian delegation to the United Nations. I saw that Mr. Ansari was telling me directly and indirectly that I could not make any excuse and that I should realize that this was both an honor and an order for me. He told me I should keep all this conversation strictly confidential.

Next, I began to tell him about my work as a Fulbright scholar in the United States and my project with programmed learning as a way to combat illiteracy in Iran. I asked if I could be active at the center of fighting against illiteracy rather than as part of Women's Organization. I told him I could serve much better in that capacity, creating programmed learning for every Iranian man and woman. I knew the present center was staffed by politicians, who I sometimes thought were more active in *preventing* literacy than in *fighting* illiteracy. Mr. Ansanri told me that he would try, but I should not hold out any hope. He told me instead to concentrate on the birth of my baby and get ready for the new job without discussing the matter with anyone else.

Distressed and feeling uncertain and under great pressure, I left the meeting and returned home. It was the middle of October, and I was becoming very heavy. My gynecologist had said that I could expect the baby any day now. Early in the morning of October 22, about 4:00 a.m., I felt pain in my back and immediately went with Sa'id and my mother to the hospital. Before long, our son arrived in the world, weighing almost eight pounds, and measuring fifty-two centimeters. The birth was easy and quick. Six days later, according to our customs, we named him. He was named Reza, after Sa'id's uncle, a very kind man with a great personality, who had recently died. Giving our son this name made everyone very happy, especially my father—and mother-in-law.

At first, I tried to nurse this lovely baby boy. But my headaches began again, and I had to stop after two weeks and change to bottle feeding. Fortunately, little Reza adjusted well, and in general, he was very calm and slept nearly five hours at night, even from the beginning. I began to realize that we would probably need another nanny if I were to take the new job, as Gita's nanny could not take care of them both. I had to accept the idea that I would probably have to take the position of secretary-general of the Women's Organization and would have a heavy administrative workload. In my heart though, I constantly hoped for the job of fighting illiteracy, and I hoped maybe some event would cause Princess Ashraf to change her mind!

[1.]   Sakineh Redjali. "Analysis of the Methods of Learning." *Journal of Psychology*, I.P.A. No. 6, 1973.

[2.]   Farah Pahlavi, *An Enduring Love: My Life with the Shah: A Memoir*, New York: Miramax, 2004. p. 145.

[3.]   Sakineh Redjali. "Some Theories of Learning," *Journal of Psychology*, Iranian Psychological Association, No. 5, 1972, I.P.A.

CHAPTER 11

Advancing the Status of Women and Becoming a Well-Known Public Figure As the Secretary-General of the Women's Organization of Iran 1969-1971

Soon after the birth of our son, Reza, in October 1969, I began to feel better and was able to pay more attention to my surroundings and catch up with the world news. Following Iran's notice to the consortium of oil-producing companies, Iran's share of oil and gas revenues increased substantially. The Shah welcomed the newly proposed doctrine of President Nixon. United States was at that time heavily involved with the Vietnam War and preferred to give other countries, including Iran, military aid to defend themselves. The three American astronauts Neil Armstrong, Edwin (Buzz) Aldrin Jr., and Michael Collins visited Iran and were warmly received by the Shah in his court. On the whole, the country's development, especially in the industrial sector, took off at a rapid rate. I felt strongly that women could play an important role in the development and revitalization of economics and politics of the country. Unfortunately, the rampant illiteracy was a great barrier to this development. At the end of November 1969, shortly after my recovery, and, incidentally exactly one month after Reza's birth, I received another call from Princess Ashraf's office summoning me to a meeting with Mr. Abdolreza Ansari, the viceroy of Her Royal Highness Princess Ashraf.

| Author's son Reza born October 22, 1969. | The author with her two children Reza and Gita. | The author's children, Gita and Reza, playing together in the garden of their new home. |

With a great trepidation, I drove to downtown Tehran to meet with Mr. Ansari. He was extremely friendly and congratulated me on the birth of my son, and then again brought up Princess Ashraf's command. I had no choice but to agree to be the secretary-general of the Women's Organization. When I started to speak about the areas of my expertise and the need for a campaign against adult illiteracy in Iran, using such methods as rapid programmed learning and instruction, he answered that as the secretary-general of the Women's Organization, I would have the best opportunity to help launch a campaign against illiteracy too. I would be able to restructure the Women's Organization and could develop and expand the multiple functions of the House of Women, and Center for Family Welfare. He wanted me to expand the multiple functions of these centers to include functional literacy, technical training, child care while women were being trained, family planning, and counseling. I particularly liked the name Center for Family Welfare because I have always desired to see women as equal partners in the family and not as objects. His suggestions, plus my love for the people of Iran, and to serve my country, placed me once again in a conflicting situation, between my family responsibilities and the needs of my country. What made this especially difficult was my deep-rooted education value and my family motto that, first and foremost, I should be responsible to others and then to myself. At last, I looked Mr. Ansari in the eye and said, "With due respect to Princess Ashraf's wishes, I'm driven to accept this position mostly as a soldier with a duty to Iranian people, women, and families. Moreover, I accept it under the following three conditions:

1. I would serve only one two-year term because I believe that opportunity should be given to others just like many International Women's Organizations. I would serve my tenure similar to an Education and Health Corps member and not like a member of the military. I also would plan a rotation system for the Office of Secretary-General so that women from different cities and provinces could receive and have hands-on experience since the needs of the provinces were equally important.
2. I wished not to be made responsible for any money management.
3. I would need an assistant to help with affairs of the cities and provinces where the needs were much greater than Tehran, the capital. This position would involve a lot of travel and knowledge of our multiethnic country."

Mr. Ansari acceded to my conditions and promised to change the organizational chart. So I acquired a new set of responsibilities, with a sinking feeling that I had sacrificed my family to a job requiring availability twenty-four hours a day, every day. Mr. Ansari then stood up, smiled happily, and congratulated me on my decision, and asked me to keep this confidential until he could arrange an audience with Her Royal Highness Princess Ashraf and members of the council. He told me that he would soon notify me of the date for the audience.

With a feeling of pressure and a heavy head and heart, I left his office. As I drove home, I thought of my new baby son, Reza, and realized he urgently needed his own nanny. As soon as I told my family the news of the appointment, I called several agencies to see if any suitable nannies were available. In those days of rapid economic development, it was very difficult to find workers for private homes because people preferred to work in offices or factories. For this reason, most of my friends and relatives preferred to get nannies from England, the Philippines, or a few other countries because they were more readily available, better educated, and ultimately less expensive. I still remember that night when I wrote to my dear friend Christine in England about my need for a nanny. The next day, I spent a great deal of time with my children and checked on their development and progress, and then I had calls from friends and agencies and arranged interviews with those who had good references. I really wanted to have someone in place before the announcement of my new job. Finally, Sa'id and I selected a Russian immigrant, Anna, for a six-month trial period, during which my mother could observe how she was with the children. If we were satisfied, she would be permanent. If not, we would hire an English nanny.

Not long after, I received a call regarding the time for the audience with the ten other members of the Central Council of the Women's Organization. I still remember this so clearly, the audience was held on a Wednesday afternoon in Saadabad Palace, the palace of Princess Ashraf, and that I wore one of the suits that I usually wore for my lectures at the university. Although I was on time, I was the last to arrive and the other women were already sitting in a circle. I knew most of them—Dr. Iran Aalam, Fakhri Amin, Dr. Zafar dokht Ardalan, Parvin Bouzari, Shamssy Hekmat, Dr. Kokab Moarefi, Heshmat Yussefi, Pavin Moeaid Sabetti, Dr. Mehry Rassekh, and Homa Ruhi (the former secretary). Soon after, Mr. Adib Mohammadi, head of public relations for the Princess, arrived, followed by Mr. Ansari, who checked to see if everyone was present. Then he left the room and soon after returned accompanied by the princess.

Mr. Ansari began by introducing everyone. Princess Ashraf then began to speak about the present status of women in Iran and the role her father and brother had in this movement; and after that statement, she addressed me directly and thanked me for all the sacrifices I was making to accept the position, considering all my other responsibilities. Everybody wondered and seemed surprised by her remarks. My colleague, the psychologist Dr. Rassekh, told me later that she had never before heard the princess speak in this manner and use the word *sacrifice*. She and everyone else congratulated me. After the announcement, there was a reception, and reporters took pictures. Mr. Adib Mohammadi told me that reporters would call me later. We stayed at the reception until Princess Ashraf left, and by then my head was spinning with my thoughts flying in every direction. I was anxious and felt the pressure of this new responsibility. As I drove home, I thought about the word *sacrifice*, and was happy that at least Princess Ashraf had shown some understanding of what she was asking of me.

As soon as I arrived home, I noticed that my poor mother had a long list of telephone messages for me from the news media. I took the list and glanced over it as I went to see my baby. Although the coming Thursday and Friday were the Iranian weekend, the telephone never stopped ringing. Even though I reminded the reporters that my first day of work would be Saturday, two aggressive reporters came to our home over the weekend, with a photographer. They never gave up. One of them from the *Kayhan* newspaper, Mrs. MP, came early the next morning on Thursday with a cameraman, using the excuse that she had to have the article about my appointment with information about my life in the paper on Saturday, the first day of the week and my first day of work. Since I knew that competition among journalists was very high, they would not leave me in peace throughout that weekend; I realized then that my sacrifice had already begun. I felt sorry that my time with my family was becoming so limited, so I tried to get by on less sleep and little rest to compensate and so spend more time with my family. Apparently, this was as the result of becoming a celebrity, and I had to adjust myself to this life accordingly.

Photo of the author when she was appointed
the Secretary General of the
Women's Organization of Iran from
1969 through 1971.

On December 3, 1969 (12/9/1348, in the Iranian calendar), my official two-year appointment, along with those of other council members began, this according to the official decree signed by Her Royal Highness Princess Ashraf, honorary president of the Women's Organization. Five members of this group had been elected by the General Assembly; six of us were appointed by Princess Ashraf. The honorary vice president was Her Excellency Mme. Farideh Diba, mother of Her Majesty Shahbanou Farah. The first question that came to my mind was this: why weren't all the members elected, as they were in other developed countries?

During the very first week of work, beginning on that Saturday when I arrived at my office as the new secretary-general of the Women's Organization, like all celebrities, I faced a line of reporters from all the media, and my name was on the front page of the daily newspapers. I was bombarded with requests for interviews, congratulatory letters, telephone calls and telegraphs from all over Iran, including the many messages from my large family and students and colleagues at the university. I spoke to all the media at once, with a message that I believed that the Women's Organization belonged to all the women and all the families of Iran. I asked all the people and all the groups to participate in our reorganization's efforts, stressing that my office door would always be open to everybody. I told them that all suggestions would be important and welcomed if we were to meet our varied needs and aspirations. With the help of the media, I wanted to change the organization from the bottom up and make it democratic since I believed that without the participation of the people and their respect, we could not achieve any progress and advancement in the status of women in Iran. So as I began my work, I spent time contacting people through the media and through personal contacts, stressing that the Women's Organization belonged to everyone. All the specialists—men and women alike—would for the first time, participate in several planning committees of the Organization. Women would not be segregated from men; everyone interested in the progress of women and families had a niche and a duty to serve. The idea to include men was new and was welcomed by colleagues and government employees, including the deputies and ministers of the government, many of whom expressed interest in becoming active and volunteered to be on the committees.

Gradually, several committees were established: Committee for Professional Women, Committee of Women Workers (laborers),

Committee of Education, Committee of Legal Issues, Committee of Women's Student Affairs, Committee of Women's Health and Welfare (chaired by Dr. Sardari, deputy minister for Health and Family Planning), and Committee for Public Relations (chaired by a deputy of the prime minister, Mr. Dawood Pirnia) to promote the status of women. Representatives from all newspapers and media also served on that committee. The Committee to Promote Women Artists and Poets was chaired by the poetess Simin Behbahani. The public responded well to the pledge in my message. Most of the specialists in the universities and ministries became involved to see in which areas of women's life they could assist in advancing equality for women and help in the planning. Even Dr. Farrokhru-Parsa, our first female minister of Education, volunteered to chair the education committee.

I was especially concerned about the Committee of Young Women Students, a committee aiding young women, which I had already established at the National University of Iran. I worried that since I was so busy that I might not be able to reach these students as often as they needed and wanted to be sure that they had the opportunity to be socially active and to have someone with whom to discuss their problems. At that time, there were no other female psychologists at the university. So I asked a colleague at the university, Mahnaz Afkhami, who taught English at the university and had spent many years in the USA, to cochair this committee with me. The experience was good for her, and in this way, she could also get to know many students from different parts of Iran and to learn of their problems and their hopes for their future. Since my availability was limited at the university, Mahnaz was a great help, and I told the students I would be available as a psychologist as needed.

My objective in setting up these committees was to provide a wide participation of educated people, specialists in the fields, and government representatives to study the organization democratically; their inputs and advice would be vital if we were to change the current laws or regulations. A large group of involved people would discuss the topic from different perspectives, and when they made a recommendation, they could defend it better, since they all had studied it in some detail. Moreover, it was my responsibility and duty to take these recommendations, studies, and suggestions through our council and see that they were approved. I wanted to be sure that we studied each issue objectively with the proper experts, since I hoped that personal opinions of the council members would not influence our objective study—a study aimed at removing barriers for women's progress.

Photo of the author introducing the members of the new study groups for the Women's Organization that she established for H.H. Princess Ashraf Pahlavi at the Saadabad Palace.

About two hundred specialists welcomed my suggestion, were interested, and volunteered to become members of a committee in advancing the status of women. However, the absence of a few activists and women's advocates who had already been struggling for years for women's rights was noticeable. Two people that I wanted to become involved were Dr. Mehrangiz Manucherian (a human and women's rights activist) and my friend Parvin Doulatabadi, a poet, who was related to Mrs. Sedigheh Doulatabadi, director of the Women's Cultural and Educational Center (Kanoon Banovan). I decided to visit them personally and ask for their participation. To my surprise, both women told me they couldn't participate directly because they had both had bad experiences before in the Women's Organization, but both said they would share their expertise with me. Since I was curious to find out more about their past experiences, I made an appointment to see Dr. Manucherian to discuss legal issues and women's rights. We had no one like her in Iran who worked as hard for equal rights for women. I had used her advice before I was married. In her classes, she had recommended to all her students that we add the clause granting us an equal right to divorce. I had added this clause in my marriage certificate and had been grateful for her advice. She had worked tirelessly for human rights and richly deserved the first United Nations Human Rights Award given to her and to Eleanor Roosevelt in 1968.

Dr. Mehrangiz Manuchrian, a Senator and the recipient of the first UN Human Rights Award for 1968 and the author's former teacher.

In the afternoon that I visited her in her home, she greeted me warmly, hugged me, and congratulated me. I began by speaking to her as her former student, asking her why, with her background as a women's rights activist in Iran, I had not seen her name among all the volunteer specialists in planning a revitalized Women's Organization. I stressed that her presence and her extensive knowledge of legal issues would be very valuable, and then asked her to chair the committee on legal issues. I told her she was the only person in Iran qualified to do this job. She smiled and thanked me for my words and began to tell the history of her activities in several women's associations, including the Women's Organization, under the presidency of Princess Ashraf. She provided valuable background and orientation for me in the work I had undertaken and I asked her many questions, which she readily answered.

The Women's Organization had evolved in three stages. Dr. Manucherian had been one of the fifty founding members of the Higher Women's Council, established in 1958-59, with Princess Ashraf as its honorary chair. These founding women subsequently became involved in other women's societies, clubs, associations, and committees, all working to advance the status of women.[1]

In the second phase, the name was changed to Association of Women's Higher Council and the membership changed. The bylaws were changed so that only an association could be part of the council. In the third phase, in 1964-65, in order to better coordinate and control the organization, the larger Women's Organization of Iran (WOI) was established, and both individuals and associations could be members, and membership was expanded to include all the associations and women's groups throughout Iran. Through all these changes Her Royal Highness Princess Ashraf remained as an honorary chair, with Her Excellency Mme. Farideh Diba as the deputy chair.

After providing this comprehensive history of the Women's Organization, Dr. Manucherian explained that she had been active from the inception, either directly or indirectly, but because of her bitter experience with Princess Ashraf, she said she would prefer to help me indirectly as I planned the legal committee. She even suggested who should chair this committee (Homa Afzal), but she added that she would not officially join the WOI. She added that she was still very busy with national and international lawyers' associations. She must have noticed that I was shocked and surprised to hear this. She looked me in the eyes and told me I need not worry as long as Mr. Ansari stood between the princess and me as a barrier and protector. She cautioned me to avoid direct contact with the princess as much as possible. If I followed her advice, she thought I could be successful in democratizing the Women's Organization, which was, after all, my goal. I kept wondering to myself why these two women, both activists for women's rights, one working from the top down (Princess Ashraf) and one working from the bottom up (Dr. Manucherian) could not get along. Dr. Manucherian had long been recognized for her 1949 book, *Critics of the Constitution of Iran from the Viewpoint of Women's Rights*. She had drafted several laws for family and children protection and even proposed a postgraduate training course for juvenile court workers at the National University of Iran in 1966. While I was disappointed in the overall results of my visit, she assured me that she would help me whenever I needed help or had a question. I began to wonder about the reason for the pain of my dear former teacher and to think of ways to heal it. I was pleased to see that the Shah had appointed her as senator, knowing that his recognition came because she was instrumental in drafting and defending laws for women's equality. With her advice ringing in my ears all the way home, I began to ask around about the reason she was avoiding cooperation with the WOI. I found out that most of the women who knew the background had already concluded that she would not join. Princess Ashraf had caused Dr. Manoutcherian great pain at the United Nations by refusing to support her when she received the human rights prize. I remember that when I was invited to the Hilton for the celebration to honor Dr. Manutchehrian on the occasion of her prize, it was Madame Diba, and not Princess Ashraf who was present.

My other friend Parvin Doulatabadi also excused herself from being a member of the committee on literature and arts. A minority of the intellectual women and men resented the work and did not want to participate in the planning of the Women's Organization because of their past experiences. But the majority welcomed my call, competing with each other for participation in the several committees for the planning. I began to understand the big picture—that some women who had worked with Princess Ashraf resented the women's institution. This organization, the WOI, had come into being through an amalgamation of all women's associations and individuals and was presided over by Her Royal Highness Princess Ashraf Pahlavi, with Her Excellency Mme. Farideh Diba as vice president. The Constitution of the Organization had four objectives.

1. To promote the status of women in Iran, to raise their educational, social, and economic status and acquaint them with their social rights and duties.

2. To assist Iranian women in fulfilling their social responsibilities as well as their duties as wives and mothers in progressive Iranian families.

3. To coordinate the group activities of Iranian women in different social and economic fields and encourage their participation in the general effort toward the achievement of social progress in Iran, especially by means of education, campaign against illiteracy and other educational efforts.

4. To establish mutual understanding and cordial relationship between Iranian women and women of other countries.[2]

To achieve the above objectives, I had invited, through the media and personal contacts, as many experts as I could muster to study and research the status of women in Iran.

Along with our research, we studied our needs, analyzed the data and obtained information about the identified problems, and subsequently proposed plans to eliminate unequal treatment of women. We devised short-term and long-term programs. In the short term, we established and expanded family welfare centers (houses of women) and provided services to support technical and vocational classes, literacy training, family planning and counseling, and child care services at these centers. Our long-term plan was to establish a school for training rural social workers and provide family counseling.

We began to implement the functional literacy program of UNESCO, which combined literacy and vocational training, and in the texts, I incorporated some material on programmed learning. One family welfare center, established in *Darvaze-ghar* in the south of Tehran, provided an example of how we broke down the barriers and resistance challenging us as we implemented services. *Darvaze-ghar* was a very poor area, and in order to help in the optimum way, we assigned the best professionals and volunteers to this center, among them a female medical doctor who could help in the family clinic and counseling. However, she would sit all day and few people would come to see her, sometimes as few as two clients per day. Obviously, we needed to do some advertising. However, I was told not to make a direct announcement because there was a very highly negative public religious sentiment against our work. As I sought a solution, I tried to find out what would appeal to women and decided to use some positive reinforcement techniques and noticed that people liked concerts by popular singers. So we planned a free concert just for women at a sports stadium, featuring two popular singers, *Sussan* and *Aghasee*.

The two singers volunteered their services, and we were offered to use the sports stadium for free. It was a good location, within walking distance of our center, and the concert was held as part of a holiday celebration. We advertised the concert, and to our astonishment, the six thousand tickets to the concert had all been taken within three days. On the day of the concert, the stadium filled so quickly with eager people that we actually started on time. After Sussan finished her concert, our physician came out dressed in white, welcomed the people, and said she hoped everybody was enjoying the program. She then described the family welfare center and its benefits and classes. She ended by saying that she hoped to welcome them to the free clinic, and finally distributed some flyers. Everyone then eagerly awaited the next singer, Aghasee.

At the end of the concert, the audience was singing along to the popular songs of the singers, while holding our flyers in their hands. The next morning, we had a line more than a mile long in front of the Family Planning Clinic and women registered for our different classes. Some of them were carrying their children too. I scrambled to provide staff and volunteers to handle the crowds and accommodate the interested. B. F. Skinner (the well-known Harvard psychologist) would have been proud to see how positive reinforcement and behavior modification were so well implemented in south Tehran.

With the success of this family welfare center, I welcomed the press and media who were usually standing outside my office every week, eager for a news story to be released. At this press conference, I did my best to explain that "men and women are equal, and that there is no difference between them, except physiologically and biologically." Both possess the same capacity for learning, have the same intelligence. I made the point that "all over the world women are now strongly objecting to the discrimination, which they have been subjected to throughout the ages. The roles of men and women are not inherent but determined by social norms. For example, femininity is in no sense an inherent characteristic of woman, making her different from man. The sole difference between men and women is biological. Femininity and masculinity were created by society, which gives little girls dolls to play with and little boys toy cars and guns. There is concrete evidence to support this."

I used the example of the famed American anthropologist Dr. Margaret Mead who had studied numerous tribes all over the world. She had found that norms differ drastically in various societies. In her book *Male and Female*, she explains how she had discovered that the roles of men and women are not the same everywhere. In one tribe, for example, she had found that the ideal type of woman was big, tough, and hard working—in fact, a common concept of the ideal man. Certainly there is no femininity in those women in the sense that the Westernized world knows.

I also told the press that since personality traits and the capacity for intelligence is the same in both men and women, women should undertake a greater role in all occupations and society as a whole. I also spoke about the role of the WOI and the family welfare centers such as *Darvaze-gar* in the south of Tehran. I stressed that placing centers such as this one throughout Iran was important to the country. Then I mentioned that the mass media can be a great help to us in changing the feelings of Iranians about women's rights and assist in women and families' participation in our country's rapid strides toward progress.

After this success and the news conference, I invited the WOI secretaries from other cities and provinces to come to Tehran to visit this functioning center. We trained them in fund-raising and in seeking matching funds from the government to establish their own centers. The volume of paperwork in our coordinating office was becoming very heavy, as mutual understanding increased between our offices and the Iranian society at large. My deputy, staff, and I were traveling all over the country, and we sensed a positive movement with a modicum of constructive competition among all the cities to attract our attention. We were beginning to operate as a group in a *we* atmosphere, rather than with an *I* attitude. Fifty single women's societies and associations had joined in this *we* movement, as active volunteers according to their expertise and experience.

Then suddenly, I received a telephone call from Mr. Ansari, summoning me to his office immediately. He told me that Princess Ashraf was very pleased with my work, and as she was head of the Iranian delegation to the United Nations, she wanted me to accompany her to the next session. I told Mr. Ansari that I was grateful that my twenty-four hours a day service was appreciated and acknowledged by the princess. However, since I was at the beginning of the work for a united Women's Organization and the princess was really serious about this united participation and the expansion of the family welfare centers throughout Iran, I would prefer to remain and continue my work. I went so far as to say that with the Princess's frequent absence in Iran, I thought that we could lose momentum and the motivation of women and families to participate in the activities of the WOI, that I believed that our progress would be hindered, and I really thought that my service was more needed in the country at that time than in the UN. After a long discussion, he finally accepted my argument and said he would talk to the princess and get back to me.

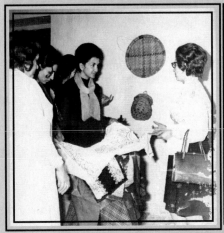
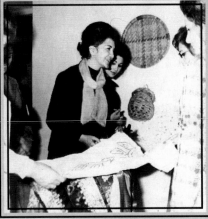

Author's visit to the House of Women (Family Welfare Centers) in different provinces throughout Iran for the openings or other functions or events.

Rapid coordination had begun among these multipurpose women's centers both in cities and provinces to establish family welfare centers (*Khaneh Zan*). The local council members of both cities and provinces were very active in fund-raising. While I was helping them, I was also active in obtaining the other half of the budget of the *Khaneh Zan* from Sazemane Barnameh (Office of Budgeting and Planning). In this way, Sazemane Barnameh created a competition in which secretaries and councils of the provinces all vied to be in the budget planning process and obtain funding. It would have been wrong to accept Princess Ashraf's command for my personal gain by going to the United Nations and leave the hard-working volunteers of the provinces without my support. I was hoping that Mr. Ansari would understand my serious commitment to WOI. After one week, in my weekly meeting with him, he mentioned that he had finally persuaded Princess Ashraf of my argument, and she accepted on condition that I select two other women, one who spoke English and one who spoke French, and could accompany her at the United Nations sessions in my place.

Immediately I made a search through all the files that had been sent to us through the human resource directors of the universities and the files of the members of our planning committees. I found a few names, and after checking with Mr. S. Tashakkori, the human resources director of the National University of Iran, he concurred with the two selections I had made. (He now lives near me in Washington DC and frequently reminds me of all the files of women professors and lecturers that he had to send to the office of Princess Ashraf for the selection of the secretary-general.)

For the English speaker, I chose Mrs. Mahnaz Afkhami, who was cochairing the women's student committee and had a master's degree in English from the USA. The other, Miss Soheila Shahkar, had studied French. I interviewed them, and they both welcomed the opportunity and were thrilled and excited at the idea of making the trip. I still remember when Mahnaz was giving me a ride home in her car, she mentioned how important this trip would be for her, since her mother was in the USA and she could see her too. I prepared a dossier with both of their files and gave it to Mr. Ansari and was very relieved for myself and happy for these two young women, who could learn to be active internationally.

In the meantime, while I had been so active at WOI, my husband, Sa'id, was busy with the music workshop activities and producing several weekly programs through National Iranian TV. Both children and families loved the programs because there was special music for the children for the first time according to their developmental stage and not made for adults. Sa'id also received great media coverage about his popular educational programs.

One day, he was called by the chancellor of the university telling him that Shahbanou Farah had seen his TV productions and liked them. She requested that Sa'id be assigned to the private school that she and the Ministry of Education had established in Niavaran Palace for the Crown Prince Reza. She wanted him to teach music there once a week. The follow-up to this call was a written decree for this assignment. We both hoped that music education would gradually become part of the curriculum in all the schools and for all the children. Again, a movement from the top.

Author with her children standing behind the King and Queen of Iran and their guests at the Niavaran palace watching the end-of-school celebration. The children of the Royal family's music program was under the direction of the author's husband Dr. Sa'id Khadiri.

At the home front, Sa'id and I faced a problem when we discovered that, for the first time, some liquor was missing from the bar where we usually kept alcohol for our guests. My mother who was monitoring the baby, guessed that Anna was the culprit, since alcohol did not go missing until after Anna joined us even though we did not mind that she might like to drink. But we were worried that if she drank too much, the baby's safety would be at risk when we were away from home since I felt responsible for Reza and my family.

We immediately began to limit the amount of the liquor at our open bar. When I asked her what type of liquor she liked, she showed me a bottle of vodka. I told her that she needed to limit her drinking, and I forbade drinking while she was on duty. I was worried that she could not control herself and would drink too much. My mother told me that she would monitor Anna more closely, but at the same time, I called Christine and asked her to search for an English nanny. We had only a six-month contract with Anna.

After we had observed the situation closely, we saw that each time Anna had time off and went to town, she would return with small bottles of vodka. So in reality, it was becoming very hard for all of us to cope with this unexpected situation, and we were moving more toward needing a more disciplined nanny from England. In response to my call, Christine had written us that she would try to select several from among the applicants and maybe I could join her for a few days for the final interviews and sign the contract if we found someone suitable.

At about the same time, I was invited to participate and speak at the International Women's Congress in Madrid, between June 7-14, 1970. I accepted the invitation and chose to present a paper on *The Role of Women in Education in Iran*, and also thought that if Christine had finished the search for a nanny by that time, I would fly to England after the Congress to interview candidates. I chose the subject—The Role Of Women In Education In Iran—because throughout the history of Iran (Persia) especially during the twentieth century, Iranian women were fortunate enough to have an equal opportunity for education, just as men, in all levels of education. Women had taken advantage of this opportunity and had responded eagerly and well. Statistical analyses supported my point.

Author speaking about the Role of Women
in Education in Iran at the International
Women's Congress held in Madrid, 1970.

In my paper presentation in Madrid, I showed that "since the White Revolution not only has the number of girls who had studied in the primary schools been steadily increasing, from 278,797 in the academic year 1951-8 to nearly a million in the academic year 1968-'69, the proportion has also changed in favor of girls. The number of male students in the corresponding years increased from 631,539 to 1,760,433. In other words, the increase in the attendance of girls was 3.5 times, whereas it was only 2.7 for boys. Considering this increase from another angle, it shows that the proportion of male to female, which was 2.26, had decreased to 1.77 for the corresponding years."[3]

It was also quite significant that the number of girls studying in Teachers' College in the corresponding years had increased from 347 to 5,388, an increase of 15.5 times. The figures, which were issued by the Ministry of Education, showed an enormous increase in the ratio of female teachers to male teachers too. During the two academic years of 1966-'67 and 1967-'68, a total number of 5,829 male teachers were employed by the ministry, whereas the corresponding figure for female teachers was 13,444. In the same way, the achievements in the fields of secondary schools were also very significant, and the proportion of male to female students changed from 3 to 1, to 2 to 1. The number of female teachers in secondary education increased 37 percent, whereas the number of male teachers increased 24 percent. Likewise, at the university level, even with a very competitive entrance examination, showed an increase in the female student population of 1.9 percent and the female teaching staff of the universities also increased to 12 percent. In short, I showed how women took advantage of equal opportunity in education in Iran and contributed significantly to the realization of the revolutionary objectives in education and how these were all signs of bright future prospects for improved cultural status and social standing for women in Iran.[4] In the presentation, I also described the programs and the educational role of the Women's Organization of Iran at the family welfare centers. On the whole, my paper was so well received that I was elected to chair the education committee of the International Women's Congress. The Congress was very well organized, and the receptions of the mayor of Madrid were very grand and sumptuous.

During the Congress, I received a call from Christine saying that she had arranged interviews for nanny candidates and asking me to come to London before returning to Tehran, so I flew from Madrid to join her. As soon as I arrived in London, Sa'id joined me from Tehran. Christine showed us the applications that she screened. The best one was from a girl who lived in Manchester who was just finishing nanny school. Her name was Elaine. Christine kindly arranged an interview with Elaine. She also came with us to Manchester. We went by train and had a good opportunity to visit and talk about our new jobs and family life. In Manchester, according to the agent's address, we went to Elaine's home. We met her and her family and were pleased. She was a nice-looking, tall, blond girl, who lived in a small home, and we liked her. She seemed anxious to leave home and accept the job. After the interview, Christine told them that she would notify them, and we returned to London the same day. It was a nice day, and as we traveled, we discussed the candidates and compared them. We finally agreed on Elaine; we signed the contract from the agent, and we notified Elaine the next day.

We were very grateful to Christine and David, and appreciated how they had always welcomed us in their home. And again, we invited them to visit us in Iran. Finally, they accepted our invitation to come to spend one of their vacations in Iran. We were happy that we were going to have them as guests in our new home. Christine also suggested that they would come in September, and they could bring the nanny with them, if she would like that. After a rather quick visit to Christine's parents, my dear Mom and Arthur, Sa'id and I rushed back to Tehran.

In Tehran, I had another press conference about the International Women Congress and the progress in expanding the family welfare centers in the cities and provinces. I also invited the council for our routine business meeting to give a report on the Madrid congress. In all our council meetings, I usually invited the honorary president, Princess Ashraf, and the honorary vice president Mme. Farideh Diba. Most of the time the princess was out of the country, but Mrs. Diba attended and seemed highly motivated, patient, and interested in our work. With her presence, she supported our efforts in a kind and diplomatic way, thus compensating for the absence of the president. In several center openings in several cities, women volunteers worked very hard to prepare for the opening and only to find at the last minute that the Princess had cancelled her visit. Fortunately, Madame Diba would step in to make up for the absence of the princess. Her respect and appreciation of the efforts people had made compensated them for the princess's last-minute cancellations. On the few occasions that Princess Ashraf was available for the opening of a center, she was surrounded by so many men, including of course Mr. A. Ansari, that sometimes I had difficulty in introducing these active volunteer women who had worked so hard in fund-raising for the center. We wondered why, on these trips, which were for and about women, she had so many political men surrounding her. Therefore, sometimes the women including myself, questioned the princess's interest and sincerity. We wondered how much she valued the hard work of these volunteers and whether she really cared about their efforts. The volunteers would ask me questions about their work, and I had to praise and reinforce them positively, and sometimes, I even had to praise them on behalf of the Princess. I was conflicted about how this was handled, but I had to praise them in order to prevent any reduction in their motivation and keep up their interest in the movement and campaigns. I took the services of the family welfare centers very seriously because they were valuable for the country, but I was also sacrificing my family life for them. Therefore, I wanted everybody at every level to promote and value these services that the women enthusiastically rendered voluntarily.

Later on, by reading the interesting memoir of the Princess Ashraf from exile, *Faces in a Mirror*, my above conflict about her attitude and behavior toward the women's activities and her preference for men was resolved. As an example, she wrote, "Since I identified so strongly with my brother, I suppose I became what Americans call a tomboy. Whenever I could, I joined him and his friends, at riding horses or playing tennis and other athletic games. In a society where there was very little free mingling of the sexes, those years gave me an unusual comfort and ease in the company of men. Even now, I still prefer the company of men to that of women."[5] There are several other examples that show even if the name of our organization was not Women's Organization, she would have preferred to give the job to a man, and of course, I then understood why I could not get the job for the campaign against illiteracy.

In September, we welcomed our dear guests Christine and David in our home. The new nanny arrived with them, and it was quite an adjustment for Reza, my son, who cried most of the time at first. I worried about my baby. Since I had to visit the family welfare centers in Isfahan and Qom, I took my guests with me. We visited the holy city of Qom and then the old historic capital of Isfahan. I recently asked Christine for some recollections of that visit, and this is part of what she wrote,

> Because we didn't speak any Farsi, we had to rely on you both and when you were at work [we relied] on Gita or on mimed actions. I remember the cooking was delicious, and we loved kharbozeh (the Persian melon). I also remember that there were always people at the door at about 6.00 a.m. waiting to see you and asking for your help as secretary of the Women's Organization. After a few days, you took us on a trip to the sacred city of Qom and to Isfahan. You had decided that you would not wear full chador but would have your wrists and ankles showing to encourage greater emancipation. We drove for hours in the desert, and when we arrived on the outskirts of Qom, I had to put on a Chador (veil) because it was still custom for women in Qom to be completely covered. When we got to the center of Qom, you told me I had to go into the sacred shrine, and I was very scared that someone would see that I was not a Muslim. David didn't manage to get past the guard, but I got in, hidden behind dark sunglasses. I just hoped no one would talk to me! After Qom, we went onto Isfahan, which was one of the most beautiful cities we had ever seen, and we stayed in the very luxurious Shah Abbas hotel. I particularly remember the paintings on the walls and the old man telling stories in the gardens. We were amazed that there was no water in the river. Although it was hot, we did not mind the heat because there were so many beautiful mosques to visit and look at. I think we also saw a Christian church.
>
> I vaguely remember that we went to lunch with the governor of Isfahan and that I was served first which was difficult for me because I did not know what was being offered. I do remember

some funny-tasting pickles! I think too that you bought some special sweets from Isfahan.

When we returned to Tehran, David and I went into town on our own but had trouble getting back because we could not find a taxi driver who could understand where we wanted to go. In Tehran, you also took us to see the Palace and the Crown Jewels. We were always conscious of the fact that when speaking about the Shah, people always said, "His Imperial Highness or Majesty." One day you took us to an open-air restaurant in Shemiran where we had chelow kebab and doogh. We thought it was a very strange drink.

One evening you took us to a club to hear the popular singer Suzanna. I am afraid we were not very impressed with the singing, but in hindsight, we should have realized that different cultures find different styles appealing.

Towards the end of our stay, we all went over the Alborz mountains and to the Caspian Sea. The difference in the climate and the vegetation on each side of the mountains was incredible. One side arid and the other green vegetation. The journey over the mountains was very scary because it was foggy, and the chauffeur had trouble seeing the edge of the road.

I think what we noticed more than anything else about our visit was the gap between the rich and the poor. It was our first experience of a middle-eastern country and we were very uncomfortable with people coming up to us and asking for money!

On the domestic front, we were thrilled to meet Gita and Reza. Gita was very difficult about eating up her food, and it was often a cause of conflict at mealtimes. Reza used to cry a lot for his previous nanny, Anna, and we felt very sorry for him. Our greatest regret was that we had not bothered to learn any Farsi, which was very rude of us, and so could not speak to your mother other than to say "salaam."

Their memories show the reaction of two friends to each other's home life. There was culture shock, I am sure, just as I had had to adjust to England. So it was interesting to see from these memories how two English friends from the West reacted.

We planned especially to visit with the women of the local center, who were so successful in fund-raising that they were able to build a center on the river (Zayendeh-rood). I also wanted to combine the workshop with the general assembly of the WOI, meeting for the first time in Isfahan rather Tehran. I thought the cities and provinces needed more attention than Tehran, and this way all these volunteers from all over the country would be encouraged and motivated by attending the workshops and visiting the old capital, while staying at the new beautiful Hotel Shah Abbass. These ideas were welcomed by all the women of the cities and provinces and by Mr. Ansari.

After Christine and David left, I concentrated on planning the General Assembly and preparing my report of WOI activities to the members. I also planned a workshop to the education program to follow the General Assembly. I had two months to plan and prepare. Fortunately, Elaine, the new nanny, was doing a good job in taking care of Gita and Reza. My mind was at peace for them, and I could concentrate on preparing the General Assembly of 1970, which I wanted to be very informative and helpful. The General Assembly itself would be one day dealing with general business and my report, but I added a conference with a weeklong workshop on the function of the family welfare centers and the functional literacy program of UNESCO. I invited specialists from all over the country to speak. Included in the workshop were visits to the successful center Darvze-gar in Tehran and a center in Isfahan. One of the Isfahan volunteers and a member volunteer at the council of Isfehan, the late Mrs. Sakineh Nazmi-Ansari, who later lived in the US state of Virginia, kindly provided her memories of the early work there as a volunteer.

She enthusiastically explained how busy she and the other members of the Isfahan Council were and how active their fund-raising efforts were. She was at that time the principal of a high school and in charge of the Girls Education Corps program. "At first, we did not have any special location for the center to meet, and we met first in a room in the *Chehelsetoon*, a historic building. Later, we met in a room in the governor's office building. According to our constitution, the wife of the governor of the province was the honorary chair of the council until the Women's Organization was well established and all the women's groups, clubs, and association became members of the organization.

"Then our membership increased to about two thousand. As a result, we had to meet in the city stadium to elect the new council. Usually, there were three representatives present from Tehran as observers, and sixteen members as active candidates. We elected seven of these candidates.

"As soon as we heard about the project of the family welfare center, we became more active in fund-raising. We were able to obtain a good piece of land by the river—the *Zayandeh-rood*—and then the great architect, *Saihoon,* chosen by the Tehran Center of the Women's Organization drew up the plans for the center. In our center, we could accommodate sixty children in child care center while the women attended class. We held our regular meetings there. We traveled in the areas around of Isfahan like Faridan, Nain, Ardestan, Shahreza, Najafabad and other places. Usually, by traveling to these areas, we helped them in their local fund-raising and preparation for their own centers. We would attend a branch meeting and get to know others."

Mrs. Nazmi-Ansari's account was typical of how the movement spread throughout Iran. I was amazed to see how, thirty-five years later, a volunteer still spoke with such real passion of her memories of this time. It was exciting that our plan and programs were welcomed by women members throughout the country and how my report was approved by the General Assembly, and especially women from the provinces. When I finished my report, the applause lasted for a very long time.

There was some concern about the hotel accommodation for the meeting. Some women from Tehran wondered why women from the provinces were assigned first to the Shah Abbass Hotel, a showplace and luxury hotel. I justified this decision by explaining that these women would rarely have an opportunity to visit Isfahan and that they deserved this extra treat since their work was so hard. Generally, women from the provinces had fewer opportunities than women in Tehran. Staying at the Shah Abbas hotel was a great way to encourage them to continue their hard work in more needy areas than Tehran.

The Shah Abbass Hotel had been beautifully renovated and was a unique hotel for Iran. It was originally a very old hotel called the *Caravanserai,* and had lovely Persian mosaic work. It dated from the time of caravans, which traveled long distances and needed a place to rest. After the week of workshops and visits, all the members returned to their cities and provinces, well motivated. They had learned how to build and develop their House of Women as a family welfare center for themselves in their local areas. I returned home with the satisfaction of knowing I had been helpful in serving women and families in Iran. However, I continued to worry about my own family and was concerned to keep a balance between my work and my wonderful home and family life.

Fortunately, with the supervision of my mother and cooperation and understanding of my husband, everything was going well at home. The children were satisfied with Elaine, the new nanny.

Now, I tried to work through the public relations committee members to distribute the news of the results of the General Assembly and the workshop, using the media as much as I could to publicize our work throughout the country and motivate the movement. It was important to recognize the participation of the women and especially the good volunteer services being done in some needy areas in the country. Gradually, I was getting information from the various branches that they were ready for the matching funds from the Sazemane Barnameh (Office of Planning and Budget), and because I maintained contact with the women, in this way, membership and numbers of Houses of Women were increasing rapidly. Just as I was very satisfied that my services were successful and beneficial to the women and families, I got a call from the office of Mr. Ansari. When I got there, while he was smiling and happy for the participation of the women and families, he had another task for me. He gave me a two-page list of the women who were candidates for Parliament (the Majles) throughout the country. He gave me the list to study and told me to add and modify the list and add names of other women, including mine. I was shocked to see a list like that.

I immediately rejected having my name on the list. I was even surprised that such a list existed because this meant that there really was no free election. In a free election, the candidates would be nominated by the people, and I even tried to follow a more democratic policy with elections of women in the provinces. I told him I could not add my name because, first, I was not interested in political activity and, secondly, because I felt there was no *free* election. However, I was given the list, which I had to review and modify, and then add the new names of active members from all of Iran. This was a private assignment for me. Since I had to do that, and this was not a free election, I tried to identify women who were giving sincere service to the people in their provinces and add their names if they had not been included in the list. I told myself that for them, just by being on the list would be a complimentary response for their sincere service, and because of that, they would be more popular, and people would tend to vote for them freely in recognition of their community services. After two weeks, I hand-delivered my list to Mr. Ansari. He looked at it as I described the criteria that I used for the selection. He was pleased and amazed by my selection. With each name, I described all the community services that the woman had provided for the community. I really tried hard to be as fair as possible, just as I graded my students at the university. In my teaching, no one had ever challenged a grade or complained, because they knew I was being fair. Even students who had not received good grades later became my friends, and even today, I receive notes and New Year's greeting cards from them. It was a pity that the monarchy, which provided the means to modernity and development, which meant economic, social, and even cultural modernity, was unable to provide political modernity and political development. As a result, the lack of individual and political freedom caused many problems and resistance in some areas as we established the family welfare centers. There were always underground opposition groups, but on the whole, the number of the centers was increasing rapidly. OPEC, under the leadership of the Shah, increased the oil price contrary to the wishes of the oil companies. That year there were no more English flags flying in the Persian Gulf. Instead, on the three islands of Tonbeh Bozorg, Tonbeh Kuchek, and Abu Mussa in the Persian Gulf, Iranian flags were flying.

The number of tourists visiting Iran was increasing, and we ourselves were receiving many visitors—friends and colleagues from universities in Germany, England, and the USA. Some of them wanted to visit the old capital of Persia, Isfahan, and even attend the yearly Shiraz Art Festival that our queen, Her Majesty Shahbanu Farah, was promoting. In her memoir, she wrote that in her opinion, there is no better stimulus for a democracy than a flourishing culture.[6] The whole feeling of the country was generally positive and upbeat.

Since Iran was gradually becoming a more developed country, their Majesties thought it was time to celebrate the country's independence and its 2,500 years glorious history. The queen herself assumed the chairmanship of the celebration, with planning for an entire year before the celebration. Heads of state from all countries were invited for the three-day event at Persepolis near Shiraz, the site of the first city of the Achaemenian (Hakhamaneshian) Persian empire during the time of Darius I and Cyrus the Great between 518 and 516 BC. The old city of Darius and Cyrus was looted and burnt by Alexander when he attacked in 330 BC, leaving only magnificent ruins that have lasted throughout the centuries. The Shah saw himself as heir to the kings of ancient Persia, and this celebration was to be a great event for all countries to observe the glorious history and richness of Persia and of the present-day Iran. However, at the same time, actions by the Shah seemed too arbitrary to many and provoked both religious leaders (like Khomeini) who feared losing their traditional authority, and students and intellectuals seeking democratic and political reforms. These groups opposed the Shah and criticized him for violating the constitutional monarchy and for the money spent on the celebration.

In any case, this huge, unique celebration at Persepolis did take place and brought to the whole world a glimpse of a great country and its 2,500 years of history. The celebration involved a united effort and was at great expense to show the Pahlavi era as a period of renaissance for the Iranian civilization. As a result, the whole country underwent a massive reconstruction. Two thousand five hundred elementary schools were built in the villages, and modern hotels and other buildings, monuments, new roads and highways were added. In addition, there were many art and historical exhibitions, and national and international conferences about Iran and the history of Persia during that year. For the site of the celebration at the ruins of Persepolis, appropriate accommodation, transportation, and security had to be arranged and provided for the heads of the countries and their staff. A tent city was built, which included tent headquarters for each head of state and a very large tent about 68 meters long and 24 meters wide (1,632 square meters) for the gala dinner and other events. I was notified that, as the secretary-general of the Women's Organization of Iran, I had been selected by the empress to serve as lady in waiting to the wife of the president of India, Mrs. V. V. Giri, during their stay for the celebration October 12-15, 1971, and General Massumi was assigned to be with the president himself. It turned out to be an interesting and memorable assignment.

I think because the Shahbanou (empress) was artistically talented, all the tents which would shelter the heads of countries and other dignitaries were designed beautifully. She wanted to showcase our famous Persian carpet weavers, so she arranged for each tent to have a small carpet hanging on the wall, with the picture of the leader of that country woven into the carpet. This carpet was also a souvenir to take home. In addition, all the guests also received a copy of the Edict of Cyrus the Great, which was found in Babylon and kept in the British Museum, the first Declaration of Human Rights. This declaration shows an amazing tolerance to all religions. It is no wonder that the name of Cyrus the Great appears more than ten times in the Old Testament, since following his Edict the Jews were permitted to return to Jerusalem and allowed to build their own temple. There were also several other books from our poets published beautifully for the celebration and each head of state received a copy.

The empress had thought about everything for this event. For each head of state and spouse, she had assigned a high-ranking person from our country to look after their needs, someone who also spoke the language of their country. One emperor, nine monarchs, three princesses, thirteen presidents, one sheikh and one sultan accepted the invitation and confirmed they would attend the celebration to pay homage to Iran's history. Because of security, The queen of England and President Richard Nixon did not attend, but were instead represented by Prince Philip and Princess Anne and Vice President Agnew, respectively. As hosts and hostesses to the world dignitaries, we tried our best to make sure that they were well taken care of, both for the three official days of the ceremony and, afterward, during their stay in Iran. October 12 to 15, 1971, were the three official days.

Just before the start of the official ceremony, I was notified that President and Mrs. Giri would arrive with their son and daughter—and their cook. The cook was a late notification, and we did not have permission from the security to allow anyone extra to come to the tent. All the food was prepared by the French restaurant Maxim's, and with the liability issues for so many dignitaries and heads of state, security was very important. Apparently, however, the food for President Giri and all his family was prepared with special spices and vegetables and they had brought all the necessary items from India with them.

Somehow, I had to get clearance for their cook; otherwise, our guests would not eat anything. I remember that I was in such a rush to escape the bureaucracy that I jumped a high step to reach the Empress directly to get clearance for the cook so that security would permit him to enter in the tent. The ceremony began at the tomb of Cyrus the Great on October 12 before the clergy and representatives of all the religions of the world, with a beautiful, meaningful, and moving homage by the Shahanshah, the king of kings, to show the immense gratitude and respect of the people of Iran for the great and oldest empire in the world and Cyrus the Great as a great liberator and the first human rights activist. Another interesting event was the Parade of Soldiers dressed in uniforms representing all the periods of the 2,500 years of Persian history. This was magnificent. Apparently, for some periods, the participants let their beards grow for the entire year proceeding so that they would look authentic. Again, it was a unique review of our history in a short time.

For the gala dinner, our empress had ordered identical white silk dresses for the ladies in waiting. These dresses by a French designer were very beautiful. I had two fittings for my dress, and it suited me very well, and I was looking forward to wearing it, but a set of circumstances kept me from attending the dinner. At the last minute, Mrs. Giri notified me that she wanted to miss the dinner. Instead, she wanted to visit the towns of Marvedasht and Shiraz to see how the people there were celebrating. She also wanted to go sightseeing in those cities. So we changed our plans; President Giri attended the official gala dinner with General Massumi, and I went with Mrs. Giri to follow her plan. It turned out to be interesting for me too. I missed the gala dinner, but I gained more by seeing the natural celebration of the people. We drove through many small towns that were all illuminated, and the people, especially local tribes' people, were playing music with their local instruments, and singing and dancing their regional songs and dances. We had to stop in several places because Mrs. Giri wanted to see more of these local celebrations, as they were very natural, original, and beautiful.

As we traveled along the road, she also saw our special melons—kharboze—displayed for sale on the side of the street. Mrs. Giri expressed her wish to have some of these melons to take back to India. For one moment, I hesitated and did not know what to do. I remembered that all the food was closely controlled by security, and I wondered if I should get the melons for her, but as we returned to the tent, I told the driver to stop. Then I jumped out of the car and bought a few kharbozeh for her as another souvenir from the trip. During this trip, I learned that she was a fine lady and a poet whose poetry had been published in Sanskrit. She translated some of them into English for me. Anyway, we had a wonderful evening, and I was careful to be back on time. I think our empress made the right selection for me to be with Mrs. Giri. The next day, we had more time for sightseeing. She immediately said to me that she wanted to go first to Pasargad to pay homage at the tomb of the Cyrus the Great. Then if we had time, she would like to go with her son and daughter to the Shiraz Bazaar to buy souvenirs for her children and grandchildren. She told me that she had a large family with, at that time, thirty-five grandchildren.

In the Shiraz Bazaar, I noticed that she was attracted by the complete set of melamine (thick plastic) dishes, which we made in Iran. They said these were strong and good and practical for their daily use. They bought several sets, and I was proud that our product attracted her and was surprised that they preferred the plastic to beautiful china. Since they had been planning to go to Tehran for a visit, and I would be accompanying them, I told them that they might find better dishes in Tehran. However, they happily bought several sets of melamine along with some other items. When we returned to the tent, I was quite tired.

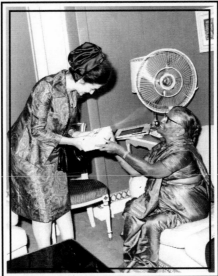

The author participated at the 2500-year celebration of the Persian Empire and was assigned to attend the President and Mrs. V.V. Giri from India.

On our return, General Massumi told me that President Giri was expecting to have a conference with the Shah, Vice President Agnew, and the president of Yugoslavia Marshal Tito. Heads of state took the opportunity of this gathering to meet together in small groups, so there were several conferences throughout the three days in different tents. They arrived very soon after, and one by one, they went into President Geri's office. They closed the door and had a long conversation. During this time, General Massumi and I had to stand in the hall. We could not hear the conversation, but I heard several times the word *Bangladesh*, a word new to me.

After the meeting was over, President Giri looked deep in thought and spoke first with Mrs. Giri. Then he came to General Massumi and me and told us that there was an emergency. They were changing their plans, they would not go to Tehran, and they would return to India the very next day. So we notified security officers of the change. I kept wondering why they would change their plans so suddenly. A few days later, we returned to Tehran, and I heard in the news of the establishment of the new country—Bangladesh—next to India. Then I understood why President Giri left Iran directly from Shiraz without visiting Tehran. We had a few pictures taken together, and they were very kind and invited me to visit India.

Part of the celebration was a magnificent sound and light show with fireworks at Persepolis, which was the work of French specialists. I was able to view this spectacular presentation, and I was finally able to attend at least part of the celebration—the informal dinner at the large tent to meet the heads of the countries and the dignitaries. It was interesting and unique. To me, Princess Grace of Monaco was outstandingly beautiful. She was in my direct line of vision, and I watched her bearing and gracious presence. She was one of the people whose face did not show jealousy and envy.

After the official farewell to President and Mrs. Giri, I returned to Tehran and back to work. In addition to the business reports, we had from our secretaries of the cities and provinces, we also received excellent reports of how they celebrated the 2,500 anniversary celebration in their areas. Most of them mentioned that they took advantage of the ceremony and found that it was the best occasion for fund-raising for the center and the family welfare center. As a result, I was getting from our provinces and cities additional names of other branches ready to receive matching funds. The number of our centers throughout the country was nearly reaching 180, and I was becoming concerned about the professional services in these centers, which were using only volunteer forces. I feared that the one school we had to train social workers for the rural areas was not adequate enough for these multifunctional service centers. Since I was aware of the great need for professional services in preschool education, family counseling, and welfare administration, the three main functions of the family welfare centers, I thought that maybe after my two years as a secretary-general were concluded, I would volunteer to establish and develop a college serving these three areas, where the most needed manpower in the country was lacking.

As November approached, I was getting ready to finish my two-year term in the Women's Organization and prepared my report to the General Assembly. Since I was getting ready to leave and would give my seat to another woman, I tried very hard to get the matching funds ready for all the cities who were ready for them. Finally, I remember exactly one week before the General Assembly and my last day at the Woman's Organization, that Dr. A. Majidi, head of the Office of Budgeting and Planning, called for a meeting for the family welfare center and all the interested parties who wished to receive matching funds. I reviewed the information and prepared the list so that if he mentioned the name of the area, I would be ready to announce it so the group would get the budget quickly. Quick response was a vital factor.

Sitting next to Dr. Majidi was Mrs. Sattareh Farmanfarmaian, who was also interested in centers affiliated with her school of social work. I sat opposite Dr. Majidi in order to read his lips better when he was pronouncing the names of the needy cities. I wanted to respond readily and quickly so they could get the funds. I had reviewed my list so many times that I knew the names by heart. Before the meeting, Mr. Ansari had told me if I received one-fourth of the budget, I would be lucky because everybody believed that Mrs. Farmanfarmaian was better connected and had a better chance for getting the money. After a short introduction about the needy areas, Dr. Majidi started announcing the names, and every party who was ready answered *yes*, if they were. I remember that I was saying yes very often. As a result, we were awarded three-quarters of the budget, and everybody in the meeting was surprised. After the meeting, Mrs. A. Nahvi, who was a director general (a high-ranking position) at the Sazemane Barnameh (OBP) said she could not believe that someone who would be leaving the organization in one week would be defending the budget of that organization so enthusiastically.

Everybody, including Mr. Ansari, was surprised by my efforts. But what they did not know was my feeling in response to the sincere efforts of the women of the provinces for their fund-raising for needy areas. I felt satisfied and had a clear conscience that during my two years of service, I had brought the budget of the Women's Organization from a 4-5 million *toman* budget to an availability of about 90 million *tomans,* for the development of about 180 family welfare centers throughout Iran. So I was ready to report proudly to my colleagues and members at the General Assembly our collective successful effort before saying good-bye to them. I included in my report the yearly reports of women's activities and services from the entire Women's associations, clubs, and provinces. I wanted to include all our efforts in my report to the General Assembly. I thought that every group had worked very hard for the advancement of the women of Iran and services to the families and mankind. I was thinking perhaps to continue my membership with one organization, which was more service oriented. Among about sixty associations and clubs, Zonta International attracted me. There were a few clubs in Iran, and the number was increasing. Zonta International was then and still is a worldwide service organization of professionals and executives in business working together to advance the status of women since 1919. As the day drew close for the General Assembly, I began clearing my desk of paperwork to leave proudly in the hope of passing on the opportunity to someone else to have the position. This method would provide opportunities to several generations from different provinces throughout Iran every two years. Many people, including Mr. Ansari, were insisting that I stay for another two-year term, because everybody from the top to the bottom wished it. This was the usual custom for all administrative and board positions—to keep a position as long as possible. For the progress of the country and education toward democracy, I thought this custom should be changed. The best way would be if Princess Ashraf would permit that change, beginning with myself. To explain my point, I used the example of Zonta International to illustrate how the president and the officers of the local and international branches rotated their positions, but I could tell from the expression on their faces that understanding this concept was very difficult. Most of the government or social officers from prime minister to minister to other professionals were very possessive and did everything they could to keep their positions. They did not want change. It seemed to me that this lack of change would keep people from participating and deter democracy and progress in Iran.

Then, just as I was getting ready for the General Assembly meeting—about two hours before the time—I suddenly had a call from Madame Diba, whom I highly respected. During the previous two years, I had been thankful for her kind attitude and respect for people. She had made my job bearable. I was now surprised by her call at that time. The fine lady told me that she had heard that I was determined to leave the job, and she wanted to know if it was in any way possible for me to continue in this position for another term. I first thanked her for her offer and request, and then I told her that from the beginning, I had made it clear that I had promised to serve for one term only. I explained to her that I could really be of better service to the country and the Women's Organization if I returned to my former position to educate the right personnel and manpower for the family welfare centers and, at the same time, give the opportunity to another woman to become active in the Women's Organization. The kind lady understood and respected my opinion, and I was very thankful as always for her understanding. Our telephone conversation took about forty-five minutes. My staff, who were first happy to hear about the telephone call because they thought maybe I would change my mind, were upset when they noticed that her call did not change my decision.

I took my report to the General Assembly. After the reading of the message of Her Royal Highness Princess Ashraf, I began my report. It was about fifty minutes long as I tried to thank everyone from the members of all the committees for planning, studying, and preparing all the necessary changes to be made in our legal system for family protection and equal rights for women. I also thanked everyone for the sincere services of all the members, especially in the provinces, for their efforts and their participation in the movement and rapid progress of the Women's Organization. I hoped they would continue to work and requested their continuous efforts with the new administration. After I finished the report, there was very long continuous applause, which I finally had to interrupt and bring to a conclusion because it was time for the election of the council members.

As I described before, according to the Constitution, of the eleven member council, six members were appointed and, unfortunately, only five members were elected. No more than five former members announced their candidacy and spoke about their services and activities. Suddenly, all the members in the hall began to call out that they would like me to be a candidate, and everybody began to shout "Dr. Redjali! Dr. Redjali is our candidate." They were so loud and continuously using my name that I went to the podium, and while I was thanking them, I also announced that I would not be a candidate for the council. I told them that I had responsibilities in the field of education, and that in this area, I could better serve the advancement of the status of women, and the status of the Women's Organization and the centers of the family welfare center for which they had worked so hard to raise the money. All this time, I was aware of the command of the Princess and of her dislike of change, and I knew already that my refusal to continue in my job could cause a problem for me. I definitely did not want to be a candidate for the council, either, but still the voices continued to call out my name.

Finally, a member from one of the provinces came to the podium and used the microphone to say that although Dr. Redjali does not want to be a candidate for the council, we would still like to vote for her to at least show our appreciation for her sincere hard work. They were all shouting my name, and finally, the chair of the General Assembly, Mrs. Hajar Tarbiateh, gave permission for my name to be added on the ballot, although she knew from my announcement that I would not be a candidate. Apparently, the chair of the General Assembly, Mrs. Hajar Tarbiat, and Mr. Adib Mohammadi, the director of public relations for Princess Ashraf, had been told that the princess did not want any change in the Women's Organization and that I would have to continue another two years. Princess Ashraf was satisfied with the way things were, and she did not want any change. When I think back, I understand why Madame Diba, the honorary vice president, spoke to me so long to try and convince me to continue for another term, and I understand the difficult position and conflict these two people had as the directors of the election. Anyway, the election went through. The women sent some representatives to monitor Mr. Adib Mohammedi in counting the ballots. The result was clear—I came out on top. In order to avoid the problem for the chair and the other responsible people I immediately went to the podium and microphone, thanked everybody for their appreciation and stressed that since I was not a candidate, the votes for me should not be counted. And amid the shouting and applause of the people, I left the General Assembly, with a kiss and a wave of my hand to everyone.

I was really shocked myself and surprised to see the reaction of the women, which I had never expected. As soon as I arrived home, I saw that many beautiful flower baskets and bouquets had arrived. The largest one was from Dr. Farrokhru-Parsa, our first woman minister of Education, with a personal handwritten letter congratulating me for my services and stating that at the meeting the women showed how the people understood and valued real service. It was Dr. Farrokhru-Parsa's opinion that people are not important and that people do not understand is wrong. Other flowers and a note of congratulation came from my colleague, psychologist Dr. Mehry Rassekh, with almost the same words. The next day, the newspapers and media reported about the meeting of the General Assembly, and especially the courageous reporter Mrs. Sima Dabir Ashtiani from the daily newspaper *Etelaat* described the meeting exactly as it happened.

In this way, the people and women of Iran showed that they understood what was going on, and that they wanted to be taken seriously as human beings by showing their resistance to the princess's unjustified command and pressure. Women needed freedom to deal with their own affairs. And this was the way I had accepted the job—not as a command—and this is how I left the job—also not as a command. I had accepted the job like a soldier, as a responsibility and duty to my country and society for two years, and I left the job as a responsibility and duty to other more needy areas for society and my family life. After I left, the only change in the Women's Organization was my absence there. Everybody else was following the command of the Princess Ashraf, whose representative Mr. Abdolreza Ansari had understood two years ago that I had accepted the job just for two years as a sacrifice, and fortunately, he honored his promise and I appreciate his understanding to help me to get out of this episode. She chose to ignore the need of the people for participation of women and myself later on. I was very thankful to Madame Diba, who had understanding for my position and valued the participation of women. I was hoping that gradually with all these movements where we exercised democracy in the provinces, the new secretary-general would be an elected position, rotated throughout Iran. However, I was wrong.

The new secretary-general was proposed and appointed in New York by Princess Ashraf, who chose Mahnaz Afkhami, the colleague I had selected to be with her at the United Nations instead of myself. According to Mahnaz's book and her interview in an oral history series, this choice was finalized while they were drinking martinis in a Chinese restaurant on Second Street in New York with the Princess Ashraf.[7] Since Mahnaz had lived in the United States for a very long time, even had attended high school there, I was hoping that she valued and respected democracy and would see the need for the participation of people and families in the Women's Organization and would work for rotating the position and for free elections. After the announcement of her position, I congratulated her and invited her for lunch to give her an orientation of the Women Organization of Iran and to share my experiences in establishing the family welfare centers. I offered my volunteer services for the planning and professional services that all the centers for the family welfare center needed, and I told her she could call me any time if she had any questions about the administration and professional services. She thanked me, and we went our separate ways. She never called me or invited me to any of the Women's Organization events or meetings. So she became the fourth and last secretary-general of the Women's Organization of Iran. She later became a consultant minister for women's affairs in the government cabinet, while she also was still holding the position of secretary-general of the Women's Organization, a position she kept from 1971 until the Iranian revolution in 1979 with almost the same council members. Gradually, and unfortunately during this time, the Women's Organization changed from a volunteer-, social-, educational-, and service-oriented organization to a more political institution and later even active in the political one-party movement of the country—the Rastakhiz—activity.

The result of suppression and repression of the rights and opinions of the people, especially in the provinces, was one of the unfortunate causes of the revolution. When the revolution came, the majority of the women again wore a veil and took part in welcoming Ruhollah Khomeini, even though he was against equal rights for women. Perhaps the women hoped eventually to obtain these rights. Alas, after the revolution, most of the rights given to women by the King of Kings (Shahanshah) or earned by themselves were taken away!

[1.] Badr ol-Moluk Bamdad, *From Darkness In to Light: Women's Emancipation In Iran*, Edited and Translated by F.R.C. Bagley, Exposition Press, Hicksville, New York, 1977, P. 112.

2. Publication of the Women's Organization of Iran, 1969.

Sakineh (Simin) Redjali, *The Role of Women in Education in Iran.* International Women's Congress in Madrid, June 1970.

3. All data, facts and figures adapted from the statistical reports of the Ministry of Education at the time.

4. Ashraf Pahlavi, *Faces in a Mirror*, Prentice-Hall, Engelwood Cliffs, N.J. 1980, p. 15.

5. *Enduring Love*, p. 227.

6. Gholam Reza Afkhami, editor, *Woman, State, and Society in Iran, 2003*, P. 45) in Persian.

CHAPTER 12

1972-1977

Establishing a College

While I was happy and proud of the essential services I had provided for women and families and appreciated the acknowledgement I received from many quarters, I recognized the great need for professional staff for the family welfare centers or Houses of Women (*Khaneye Zan*) with their multifunctional services. I was also concerned about my own family, especially my baby son. Already two years old, he called every woman "mommy," because so many women had surrounded me while I was with the Women's Organization. I felt guilty about not having paid enough attention to my family and especially my children, and I was determined to compensate for my two years' absence.

Celebrating Reza's birthday friends and
relatives and Elaine (English nanny).

Author with her children.

Author with her son Reza.

Author with her husband
Dr. Sa'id Khadiri.

Author with her family.

After spending a few days with the family, I returned to the university to teach my regular psychology courses. My students and clients were happy to see me back more often, but I kept hearing how the women, especially those from the provinces and cities, were unhappy that I had left the Women's Organization. Without my leadership, the provincial secretaries were about to quit their volunteer posts. I tried my best to motivate them to continue their sincere services and assured them that I would be arranging training programs for their centers. To persuade these women to keep their jobs, the new administration proposed changing the status of the provincial secretaries of the Women's Organization from voluntary to salaried. As a result, I was happy to see them remain active. But again, they too later became just like the other government employees who had worked with Prime Minister Hoveyda for thirteen years with minimum change in personnel or promotion. As a result, there were no opportunities for any new member participation or any fresh thoughts.

I thought that the experience of the women at the General Assembly of 1971 showed that people, and women in particular, understood the social issues, and that they were eager to participate, to vote and to share their knowledge about public concerns and make their own decisions. Alas, the people and the public opinion were not taken seriously at any level of the government. I often wondered why the Shah did not share his progressive plans and ideas for the country directly with the people through the mass media. Sometimes, I even thought that he liked Iran more than its people. For instance, the Shah was trying to increase Iran's power and independence and to minimize foreign influence, but he was not sharing any of these efforts with the people. His reforms seemed directed toward concentrating power without the participation of the people, or educating them, or considering their long-held traditions. I remember that on June 22, 1973, my birthday, he announced in a speech that he wanted to create a strong state to look after every Iranian from womb to tomb, as if the people of Iran were ignorant and needed a guardian. As a result, people did not appreciate his progressive programs and plans. Because of his failure to communicate, the people began to hear more of the underground voices and activities and less of the Shah's voice. In addition, Khomeini's lectures in Najaf were attracting anti-Shah Iranian students from all over the world, especially from Europe and the USA. I began to notice this unrest also through some of the questions asked by the students during my lectures. Also, The Islamic Center *Hosseine Ershad*, which was opened in 1964 under the leadership of Ali Shariati, became a popular center for the opposition to the regime. It was finally closed in November 1972 by the regime.

After the end of semester, Sa'id and I decided to have a summer vacation with the children in London, the place I liked the most because of its multi-cultural atmosphere. This was also a good choice because we could be near our dear friends Christine and David. It would also provide an opportunity through my contacts with the University of London and my former professors and friends to develop a proposal for establishing a new college to train professionals for family welfare centers. The new college would train professionals for early childhood education, family counseling, and welfare administration.

So we called Christine and David and told them about our plan, and as always, they managed to find us a furnished flat near the train station and near their home. Another bonus was a temporary nanny, who was in high school and offered to look after the children during the summer school holiday and on the evenings that we attended the theater and concerts. Gita and Reza's nanny, Elaine, chose to stay in Iran with her boy friend, who was employed by the Bell Helicopter Company in Iran, and she did not want to renew her contract.

Altogether we had a wonderful summer, as a family. Whenever I spend time in England, I always rest properly. This is an organized and culturally rich country, and I always enjoy my stays there and feel secure. At the Institute of Education of the University of London, I prepared my proposal for establishing the college with its undergraduate and graduate programs. Sa'id also contacted his colleagues from the International Society of Music Education (ISME) at the institute and, with their assistance, collected several children's music programs. Again, we returned to Iran with our hands full of new material and our minds full of new knowledge to serve our country.

When we returned to Iran, I noticed that my mother and her companion Tuba both looked pale and weak. My mother was complaining of shortness of breath. I immediately took both of them to our family heart specialist Dr. H. Kafi. He made several tests and told us that both, especially my mother, were suffering from enlargement of the heart and prescribed some medication. As my mother had always been an important part of our lives by helping us in many ways, we were very grateful to her and concerned and worried about her health. It was her custom to make a pilgrimage every month to the Shrine of Massumeh, sister of the Imam Reza, and to the tomb of my father in Qom. Now she could not go by herself and needed our assistance. Sa'id and I told her that we would take her and asked her to tell us in advance of the date so we could take a leave from our work and join her.

As the university term was starting, I prepared my lectures and began to pursue the plan for establishing the new college. The president of the university, Professor A. Pouyan, was a surgeon, and I wondered if he would understand the need of the country for new interdisciplinary professional subjects. But I still tried first to speak to him about my proposal for the new college. My guess that the previous president would not last was correct. During my meeting with him, I noticed that he was so politically involved in trying to become the minister of health that he did not even show the least bit of interest. Now that I was not anymore in the Women's Organization and no longer close to Princess Ashraf, who was influential in political appointments, he did not pay any attention to my proposal. As I had predicted based on the short meeting that I had with him, he rejected my proposal or any expansion for the National University of Iran, excluding the expansion of the medical school. So I had to find another approach to implement my plan.

Interestingly enough, several of my colleagues at the National University of Iran and other scholars in the country had already used this university as a model of a private university to establish other colleges and higher education establishments. Among these were the Higher Education School for Girls (*Madresse Aali Dokhtaran*). This name was later changed to Farah University (now Fatemeh University), Higher School of Accounting (*Madresseh Aali Hessabdari*), School of Business Administration, School for Insurance, Pars College, and Damavand College. Because of the rapid development of the country, there was such a great demand for higher education in Iran that even with tuition charges and a competitive entrance examination, all these colleges were successful. However, none of these schools offered the professional service-oriented subjects that I had in mind—subjects like preschool education, family counseling and welfare administration. These skills were vital, as the country was developing very fast, but there were several caveats for me to watch as I sought to develop my plan. The first was the need for start-up capital. Then, and more important for me, there was the financial handling aspect, which I dreaded. I simply did not want to be responsible for the financial management of a college. Moreover, we needed qualified human resources and a faculty at the national level. Finally, and most importantly, in order to move forward with our plan, we needed to meet bureaucratic requirements and obtain permits from the Ministry of Higher Education. I knew this task would be the most difficult one. The red tape associated with opening a new college usually required a connection to the court, and even then, it was difficult. But I pursued each issue step by step.

Some of my colleagues, among them Hushang, Parvaneh, and Hassan, became very interested in my project and encouraged me. Hassan, a journalist and very much involved with financial matters, completed my proposal with a financial plan and agreed to be the treasurer responsible for all the financial matters. His plan called for a start-up figure of 500,000 tumans or 5 million rials. My husband, Sa'id, was also interested in the project. We then needed to come up with 2 million rials. I discussed the project with my mother, and as soon as she heard about establishing a college, she became very happy and suggested that we sell our former house on Pahlavi Avenue, near the former location of the National University. From this sale, she would give us the 2 million rials and would use the rest for religious obligations. She made this sale without any hesitation, and her action resulted in establishment of a not-for-profit college specializing in three subject areas that were new in Iran.

For the name of the new college, we chose Shemiran, the name of a popular village in the north of Tehran where the college was located. By chance the building of the old American Club at Fereshteh Street off Pahlavi Avenue had become vacant and ready for rent. The owner even agreed to let us convert the building for college use. This building and the location were an excellent beginning for the new college.

One of the partners, Hassan, was doing well with the financial affairs. He was also working to prepare the building for use as a college. But I had the most difficult task because I had to get permission from the Ministry of Higher Education and to go through a lot of barriers and red tape. We made certain that our proposal was one of the most progressive plans for a college. We proposed the most forward-looking curricula for the new areas in preschool and early childhood education, family counseling, and welfare administration at the undergraduate and graduate levels. The major challenge was getting the bureaucrats at all levels of the ministry to understand the project.

Fortunately, both the Shah and the Empress had a keen understanding of this need. I began the statement of purpose by citing that in the first Ramsar Conference on Revolution in Education, the Shah had pointed out that education should begin at the kindergarten level. The proposal explained that research had also proved that early childhood were the most vulnerable years, and therefore, a good preschool program was essential in setting a sound and firm foundation for child personality development.

The government's Fifth Plan also emphasized the significance of preschool education and welfare programs. I justified the need for the new college by stressing that Shemiran College realized the importance of the role of education, especially in the areas of preschool education, family counseling, and welfare administration, in keeping pace with the country's growth. Therefore, Shemiran College would initiate these three fields of study for the first time in Iran in order to prepare qualified personnel to undertake these important responsibilities. I also described in some detail the objectives of establishing Shemiran College, which, as an educational institution, would contribute to development in specialized fields of services by offering a unique set of professional programs.

I described that the three fields of specialization each had their own objectives. Preschool education was to train specialized teachers for kindergartens and nurseries, as well as eligible personnel to administer preschool affairs in ministries, kindergartens and various other organizations, including the child care centers of all the family welfare centers throughout of the country. For family counseling, the objective was to train professional counselors for family affairs. The most important issue was to give proper guidance and counseling to families to enable them to cope with the rapid changes of a developing country. For welfare administration, the objective was to fulfill the need for trained administrators to work in welfare organization and centers.

As I finished the presentation at the ministry, I was faced with many unfriendly questions. For example, the minister himself stated, "I myself was raised by a badji [an uneducated nanny], and is there anything wrong with me?" He asked, "So why do we need a college for preschool or early childhood education?" I had to attend several meetings with officials at the ministry and educate them using data and research in psychology and education. I wanted to show that as we were about to change from a static to a dynamic society through rapid economic development and the White Revolution, we would need this education. In short, my battle sessions lasted all of 1972.

We also sent the proposal to Her Majesty, the Queen Shahbanou Farah, requesting her review of the project and asking if she would like to become the honorary chair of the board of trustees. She graciously received the request, but because she was chairing too many charities and educational organizations, she assigned Her Royal Highness Princess Farahnaz Pahlavi, her daughter, as the honorary chairperson and Her

Excellency Mme. Farideh Diba, her mother, as honorary co-chair. That support provided an important boost for the college and finally facilitated the approval of its establishment. Our first board of trustees meeting at Niavaran Palace was presided over by HIM Empress Farah, and I was appointed by the board of trustees as the first president of the college. Empress Farah acted as honorary chair of the board until Princess Farahnaz reached the legal age.

Shemiran College was finally founded in September 1973 as a private, not-for-profit institution operating under a board of trustees. The vice chair of the board was His Excellency Dr. Hossein Kazemzadeh, the former minister of higher education. The other ten members of the board included the minister of Education, the minister of Science and Higher Education and the director of National Radio and Television. The president of the college was to be appointed by the board of trustees and would be the executive head of the college. In this organization, I undertook another challenge. As president, I became responsible for planning, accreditation, program development, academic standards, recruiting and supervising staff, budgeting and fund-raising, international relations, and all other administrative duties. However, I accepted this challenge readily because it was a job I wanted to do. I had the opportunity to develop a topnotch accredited college, training professionals in new fields that did not exist before in Iran. I first tried to recruit the best teachers available in Iran, and next, through our international relations, from abroad. I was pleased to see that some faculty members from countries like the UK and the USA welcomed the opportunity to spend their sabbatical leaves for one-term or a year at our college.

Author working in her new role as President
of the Shemiran College.

To show how much Shemiran College was meeting the needs of the people and the country, I am adding two statements from graduates of the college, who I was lucky and happy to find by chance in USA. They continued their education in the United States and enjoy successful careers. Due to the revolution, they did not return to Iran. One of the first graduates is Dr. Farzane S. Khazrai, who, as the top student in family counseling, received a scholarship from the college to continue her education at Syracuse University, with which we had an exchange program. At present, Dr. Khazrai provides consulting and counseling services in USA. This is what she wrote about the college:

> *It was the summer of 1973 that I got the news that I was accepted to Shemiran College Family Counseling program. I was excited and looking forward to starting the program. I imagined continuing my studies to an as advanced level as was possible. I had been thinking about it for several years. Starting a family and being a full time mom for my two children seemed to have more priority at the time. So I postponed fulfilling my desire to go back to college until I started to seriously think and plan to go for it when my younger child was getting close to go to all day preschool.*

> *At the time I was looking for a program that was a good match with my interests and I could attend classes during the day and be able to be with my children during the evening. Shemiran College, a relatively new college established by the effort and directorship of Dr. Redjali in Shemiran, Iran was a perfect match. It was a college that planned its programs to meet the needs of the people and communities in Iran at the time. I was happy, excited and hungry for knowledge. Shemiran College and I being there changed my life. I have accomplished my educational and many other life goals. Dr. Redjali with her effort in establishing the college and her vision for its future played an important role in many students' lives. I am one of them.*

The other student, who is one of the last graduates of the college in the preschool education program is Vida Ghahremani. She also continued her education in the United States and is a successful actress, designer, author, and teacher, here she writes about herself and the college:

The year was 1955: I was expelled from high school and denied education for several years, merely because I had acted in a movie. Over twenty years later, in 1976, in the midst of separating from my husband and with three children, I participated in auxiliary high school final exams and received a diploma at the same time as my son. My high scores in the national university entry exams qualified me to register in several universities. A new field in a new college attracted me. Working with children and focusing on their physical and mental growth had always been my desire, so in 1976 I started my college education in the field of Early Childhood Education. Shemiran School of Higher Education was a new college with three innovative and needed fields of study: Family Consulting, Management, and Early Childhood Education.

The professors were mostly young graduates of American and European universities and the teaching system followed a liberal and modern style that was based on research, experience, and the study of professional articles. A kindergarten adjacent to my college allowed hands-on experimentation of theoretical lessons and enabled the implementation of new ideas in my field. In addition to my college education, because of my expertise in children's creative theater, I had the opportunity to work with children of diverse backgrounds and class at facilities such as the Health Department's modern orphanage and the Center for the Youth Development.

Now that I am in the US, I realize that valued opportunities which at the time existed for students in Iran come as a surprise to many in other countries, including the US. For example, not only did we not pay tuition, but also received a monthly stipend to help with expenses. In addition, the college buffet provided warm and healthy food, the recipe of which was provided by the resident nutritionist. More importantly, the Shemiran College and Syracuse

University had an exchange program which admitted Shemiran graduates to Syracuse University without an entry exam.

As one of the last graduates of Shemiran College, I easily received a four-year student visa to attend Norman College in Oklahoma. I hoped to return to Iran with a wealth of information and experience in the field of Education Technology to impart my knowledge to the children of my homeland! Alas . . . it was not meant to be.

In spite of all the underground opposition in the country (the religious front, the Communist, and National fronts and several other guerilla groups), during 1972-'73, Iran had excellent relations with the West, especially with the USA. Richard Nixon on his return trip from Moscow stopped in Tehran to meet with the Shah in 1972, and in 1973, both the Shah and the empress were received by Nixon in the USA. The Nixon Doctrine, i.e., to sell arms instead of providing an army, was welcomed by the Shah. Henry Kissinger, the security advisor, wrote a letter to the State Department and the Defense Department authorizing them to sell Iran any arms that the Shah required. The army budget increased fourfold. The Shah believed that peace belonged to those countries that were ready for war. Since we were in the middle of a cold war, the Shah ordered the most sophisticated arms and planes, such as F-14 fighters, and even F-16s and F-18s, which were under development. In accordance with the Nixon Doctrine, the Persian Gulf region was better policed by a regional sheriff. "Gendarme of the Persian Gulf" seemed the perfect role for the Shah of Iran. In order to keep the Arab countries from opposing this choice, the United States paired Saudi Arabia with Iran as the second, albeit weaker pillar of American policy. Even Henry Kissinger saw the Shah as "the rarest of leaders, an unconditional ally."[1] But in the war for the Sinai desert between Egypt and Israel, the Shah, while giving the spare plane parts to Israel, gave oil to Egypt and left the sky of Iran open for the Soviet Union to transport arms to Egypt, under President Anwar Sadat. In September 1973, due to OPEC's decision, oil-producing countries had to reduce their production by 5 percent, which meant that the price of oil doubled, and this price increase shook the whole world.

Most of the Arab OPEC members except Saudi Arabia boycotted the sale of oil to the USA and Holland because of their support for

Israel in the war with Egypt. Although Iran was not involved in this oil embargo, in January 1973, Iran revised its contract with the consortium, which had several US companies as members, and for the first time completed the nationalization of the oil company that was started by Mossadegh in 1953.

The nationalization of oil angered the United States because several American firms held a sizeable stake in the consortium. In addition, the Shah took advantage of the situation and started to sell part of the Iranian oil by auction, oil which was not included in the consortium contract. This was beneficial for Iran, and as a result, the income of the country increased significantly. At the same time, immediately after the nationalization of oil, the underground opposition groups like the *Mojahedin Khalgh* lifted their sanctions against the use of guns in their campaign against the Shah's regime and his friendship with the USA. This group even killed an American colonel near Fereshteh Street not very far from Shemiran College. In general, guerilla warfare became the norm for the opposition groups. So this was the political atmosphere in which the college was started. Being president of a college in this highly charged political situation was very challenging. Fortunately, Iran's economic growth was very high—10 percent per annum between 1963 and 1973, one of the highest in the world,[2] but without genuine social political growth, the Shah seemed to be acting as the Emperor of Oil.

My role in satisfying both the government demands and the young student population with opposition group members among them, as well as maintaining a calm, learning environment, became increasingly more challenging. To be admitted as a freshman required a high school diploma from an accredited institution, passing a computerized entrance examination (Concours), and an interview. Admission to the advanced degree, the master's, required a bachelor's degree or its equivalent from an accredited institution, a strong overall grade point average for the major field of study, the ability to read and write English, and passing an entrance examination given by Shemiran College, which consisted of a written paper and a personal interview.

For the first year of operation, we limited the enrollment to four hundred freshmen, selected from the top applicants from the entrance exam. The academic year consisted of two semesters, fall and spring. Each semester was four and a half months. The undergraduate curricula that

I prepared during 1972, which included an extensive comparative study, led to the degree of bachelor of arts (four years) in preschool education, welfare administration, and family counseling. Students could also minor in educational counseling by completing thirty required credits in that area. The college also conferred the degree of master of arts (two years) in these three fields. To concentrate on quality, we planned to maintain a student body of approximately one thousand. All undergraduate studies were conducted in Persian except for English language classes. But the graduate instruction was partly in English. We also planned to offer opportunities for juniors and graduate students to study in universities abroad. We had an official opening in 1973 and were visited in the first year by the Her Excellency Mme. Farideh Diba and the members of the board of trustees, including ministers of higher education, health and education.

In the meantime, Sa'id was very successful in teaching music education at the University of Tehran. Based on a sample of his teaching through National Iranian TV for all children and young adults, he was invited to the International Society of Music Education (ISME) Conference in Perth, Australia, for a presentation of his work and his production. Because it was during the summer break, he suggested that I should join him on this trip, especially as he was also due to visit several media music-educational programs in Japan, Thailand, and Singapore en route to Australia. This two-week program seemed to me to be very interesting and would also be of great interest to our college. We already had plenty of opportunities to observe teaching methods in the West, but this was our first experience of the East. As always, when I talked with my mother about the trip, she told us not to worry about the children as she would supervise their well-being while we were away. So we began getting ready for the trip to the Far East and Australia.

We started in Japan and noticed that the progressive media NHK had planned a constructive and organized program for Sa'id's visit. We were briefed on several successful programs, including the Suzuki method. It was also interesting to observe how nice and polite the people were in greeting and treating each other. Sitting in the lobby of the Intercontinental Hotel waiting for our guide was the best place to see these scenes in action. Sometimes, when two groups were meeting each other, they all bowed three or four times, a sign of greeting, before they stood or sat to speak with each other. We both had several good

The arrival of Her Majesty the Shahbanu and members of the royal family at the Tehran City Theatre for the performance of the Music Workshop for children under the directorship of Dr. Sa'id Khadiri, the author's husband.

A Music Workshop performance.

Japanese friends from our student time in Heidelberg and London, but never imagined that Japanese greeting would take such an interesting form. We did our best to learn quickly and follow their pattern. We soon saw how progressive the country was and how dynamic their music education programs were.

After our short visit to Japan, we went to Hong Kong and then Thailand for a day or two. There again, a very good program was arranged for us, including a tour of the local radio and television stations. In Hong Kong, at the Mandarin Hotel, we learned that a tailor could come and measure for a suit, which would be delivered, ready to wear, the next day. We had often heard this, but never believed it. I thought maybe it would be interesting to call them and see if we could have a new suit made for Sa'id to wear at his presentation at the conference and to see whether they could deliver it the day before our flight. A few minutes after we called, two people came to our room showed a large selection of very good English fabric, and they told us that they could deliver as many suits as we wished at the time we specified. They showed so many different fabrics that instead of one suit, Sa'id ordered five. After they measured him, I ordered one suit for myself as well. All this activity took place between 11-12:00 p.m. It was unbelievable that the next evening, between 9-10:00 p.m. our package of suits was ready. We tried them on, and they fit perfectly. Never before did we have so many new suits in such a short time so perfectly made and so reasonably priced. We asked them to send four suits by air to Tehran and kept one for the journey. This is one of the many ways we discovered that the Chinese people were quick and good business people.

The next day, in Bangkok, Thailand, we had quite a different experience. We paid three times more on our journey from the airport to the hotel as we paid on returning. I also lost my wedding ring, and the jeweler in the hotel showed us a catalog from which we ordered two rings that were delivered to us the next day and which were nicer than our original wedding rings. We also noticed this was the country for jewelry and silk. Sa'id bought me a few pieces of jewelry based on the recommendation of his colleagues. They also told us that we needed to be careful with our shopping and belongings. We enjoyed very much the cultural visit in addition to the music program. After these visits, we were ready to fly to Australia, first to Sydney and then to Melbourne before the conference in Perth. In both places again, we were very well received thanks to the radio and television companies. In addition to the introduction to their advanced music education programs, we were invited to the beautiful Sydney Opera House, which is designed like a magnolia. It is a unique building with excellent acoustics where wonderful performances are staged.

Next, we flew to Melbourne, and again, we were well received and saw an excellent pantomime performance by Marcel Marceau. We then went to Perth for the weeklong conference of the International Society of Music Education. This was a very well-organized conference. Although Sa'id and I had attended the ISME conferences before, this one was quite different. In addition to the lectures, recitals, and samples of music performances from various countries in the evening, the participants experienced the overwhelming hospitality of the friendly Australians. They even expected us to cancel our hotel reservations and stay with local families. Some people changed, but we stayed in the hotel. Sa'id's program included a video presentation with several samples of the music programs for children and young adults that he had produced at National Iranian Television. We were pleased that his program was extremely well received, especially by the board members. Some of them admitted that the presentation was the first music education program they had seen from the Middle East. Sa'id was proud to be able to represent our country with such a good program. Later on, some board members told him they would like to nominate him for the next board election to which he responded with a smile and heartfelt thanks. We made many contacts with people from several countries and every night enjoyed the live concerts by children and young musicians from around the world. The week passed very quickly, and soon the delegates began to leave to get back to their own country.

We prepared to return via Singapore and India. At the Perth Airport, we witnessed a scene that we still cannot forget. A prominent Russian violinist from the Soviet Union asked for political asylum and refused to board the plane. Suddenly, Perth Airport was full of government officials and the media, and all flights were delayed until the issue could be settled by the two countries. I thought the beautiful and democratic Australia, which combines British organization with the comfort of the USA, with outstanding hospitality of the people, attracted the young Russian violinist so much that he could not bear to return home. Finally, after hours of delay, the dispute was settled, and we could continue our journey on Singapore Airlines. We were happy that the young musician had been allowed to stay and enjoy the free world.

We stopped in Singapore and again were well received by Singapore Radio and Television. The Singapore Airlines as well as the country, even in the heat of August, was very clean, organized, and beautiful. This was a tax-free country, and most of the travelers were buying electronic goods, watches, and whatever they needed. While Sa'id had meetings with his colleagues at the radio and TV stations for music education programs for children, I had time to do some shopping. I bought an excellent small Sony Radio with shortwave, a Swiss watch, and a simple brooch at a very reasonable price. I liked the radio the most since I could receive BBC World News, and when I returned home I would listen to the BBC at 7:00 a.m. every morning while having breakfast before leaving for work. We continued our trip on Pan American Airline with a stop in New Delhi. I had the open invitation of President Giri to visit that country with me, but we were so exhausted by the trip, and I personally was so worried about my children and the college that we preferred to postpone our visit to India. Instead, we stayed in the plane, and after a short stop, the plane headed home to Tehran. For both of us, the journey had provided an invaluable and interesting educational experience.

Upon return, I found my children were having a good time, carefully planned by my mother to fit their summer vacation. Gita and Reza and their cousins were enjoying themselves in the swimming pool. In September I tried to prepare them for school. They attended the Community School, which was an international bilingual (English and Farsi) American independent school and had a good academic reputation.

The college was closed except for the administration. My deputy, Dr. Khalil Mossaed, a psychiatrist, was handling the college affairs very well. In general, I could trust him because I had known him as a colleague at Dr. Rezai's mental health hospital and clinic for a long time. Everything was organized, and the college was ready for the entrance exam. From the beginning, we recognized the importance of practical experience as the basis of theoretical understanding. Therefore, we were preparing another building attached to the college for the experimental kindergarten and counseling center, and work on this building had already started. My aspiration was that the students should have the best experimental and practical opportunities with the latest educational tools and methods. Again, "learning by doing" and internship was an important part of our programs. In addition, I tried to expand our international relations. I contacted the British Council and the cultural attaché of the United States in Iran for possible educational visits, exchange programs for our students, and later for our faculties, and we were in contact with them for matching exchanges with our college.

One night, in the middle of the semester, my mother suddenly complained that she could not move her feet and she could not walk from her bathroom to her room. I ran to the bathroom, and with her companion Tuba, we carried her to her room. I called our family physician Dr. A. Kafi (my cousin's husband) and my brother. Dr. Kafi came at once and, after checking her, immediately ordered her to be taken to the hospital. My mother had never been hospitalized before and had no faith in hospitals. She told me that from now on I needed to take care of my children, and she was leaving home for good. My mother bravely showed us all the burial items she had brought with her from Mecca and money for burial. I kept reassuring her that the hospital could help her, and she would soon be home, but she would not accept that. I told her that we would stay with her at the hospital. Dr. Kafi explained the advantages of going to the hospital with all the new medical instruments that would help her recover. We all accompanied her to the hospital. Dr. Kafi, who was an important partner of the hospital, had ordered a nice private room for her. When we arrived, all the medical staff were expecting us. My brother and I stood next to her bed. She was alert, but paralyzed from the waist down. She kept insisting that I "go home and take care of the children." I reassured her that they were not alone, since my husband, Sa'id, and their nannies and the housekeeper were with them. But she was still worried about them. After consultations with several specialists, prognoses indicated that her stay in the hospital would not be short, and she would need a long time for medical care. My brother and I took it in turns, day and night, to be with her all the time. I also divided my time with my husband so that he could be at home for those nights and days that I was at the hospital. At work, my deputy and I also took turns. I wanted to spend every minute with my mother because I was so worried about her. In the first week, many family members and friends visited her. Early one morning in the second week, I came to the hospital to take my shift and let my brother go home and to work at his dental clinic. As soon as I opened the door of my mother's room, I saw my brother weeping quietly, and my mother sleeping forever. My brother was with her as she passed away. I was so sorry that I was not with her in the last minutes of her life, and I even accused my brother of not being awake when she might have called for help. In this way, the most important person in the symphony of my life, my mother Fatemeh, or Mrs. Sharafatedoleh (the title given to her by the Qajar king) suffered a cardiac arrest and the symphony of my life was suddenly missing a key instrument. Her death was very painful for me, and I could not accept that she would never be a part of my life again. I tried to fulfill her every wish and follow her advice and keep it as a treasure in my heart and mind. I asked my husband to bring the necessary items for burial from the special cases that she had showed us before coming to the hospital. She had prepared everything. She had prepared her *Kafan* (shroud—the white cloth that the body would be wrapped in before being placed in the grave). She had bought the *Kafan* from holy Mecca when the two of us visited Mecca when I was a child. While the music of her life was playing and ringing in my ear and heart, I drove home alone to prepare myself for her funeral. She also had left the instruction document for her grave, saying that she would be buried in Qom, next to my father, in the plot nearest to the Massumeh Shrine. I also needed to look after my dear children, especially my daughter, Gita, who was very attached to my mother. Both children were already missing their grandmother a lot. My brother and cousins were busy preparing transportation—cars and buses for family and friends. According to the Islamic tradition, the body of the deceased should be buried as soon as possible.

The next day, everything was ready for the funeral procession. I cannot remember how many buses were behind the hearse as it was carrying her body. After the funeral, we had a reservation for lunch in a restaurant in Qom before returning to Tehran the same day. I was worried about getting back in time to meet the children as they left for school. In addition to losing my dear mother, our duties and responsibilities as parents were doubled as we did not have her to depend on. My mother's absence was noticeable for everyone. Gita, who had been accustomed to my mother repeatedly telling her "eat and finish your food" noticed that there was no one to tell her to eat, and suddenly, she started to eat independently, finishing all her courses as if she knew what her grandmom would like her to do. Even today, we still miss my mother dreadfully, never forgetting the care, love, and sacrifice she provided for all of us. She will forever be in our thoughts and in a special place in our hearts.

According to our culture, we held several memorial services with receptions on the third, seventh, fortieth days, and again on the first anniversary of her death. After the seventh-day ceremony, I asked my brother to open our mother's case to see her last will and testament. In it, we saw that it contained a savings book with more than 50,000 tumans, and a note instructing us to give that money to Ayatollah Najafi Marashi, whom we both knew. After the death of Grand Ayatollah Boroujerdi, my mother, among several grand ayatollahs, chose Grand Ayatollah Najafi Marashi, who was very knowledgeable and not much involved in politics, for his advice and her religious duties. With this money, mother wanted to buy fifty years of daily prayers and obligatory fasting that she might have missed because of illness or some other reason. Like my father, she was religious and respected all the rules and regulations of Islam. My brother immediately took the money and prepared to fulfill her wishes, and I asked to go along with him when he went to see the Ayatollah Najafi. He agreed. He did not pay any attention to the other item in the case, but I noticed an agate ring in her prayer clothes, the ones she wore daily when she was praying. On the agate was carved in Arabic *Ofazezo Amri Lel Lah*, a prayer phrase that means "I entrust my destiny to God." I took the ring, put it on my finger and ever since then I continually look at it and pray for the well-being of mankind, and for my family.

I thought that my brother would arrange a day to go together to give the 50,000 Tumans to Ayatollah Najafi before the fortieth-day memorial (*Shabe Chelleh*), but unfortunately, I did not hear anything from him. Finally, I asked him what he proposed to do about the money and our mother's wishes, about which she had often spoken. Strangely, he told me since he was going to remarry, he had spent the money on himself as he thought he was more entitled to it than the ayatollah. After the death of his wife, I had already noticed a complete change of behavior in him, which I attributed to his new girlfriend, who seemed to be encouraging this behavior and who was constantly pressing for marriage.

This behavior upset me so much that I discussed it with my husband, and we ourselves decided to carry out my mother's wishes. We were committed to honoring her wishes, and so one weekend, we went to Qom to visit Ayatollah Najafi Marashi. In this meeting with him, we gave him the money, and with that my conscience was clear and satisfied that I had fulfilled my kind mother's wishes. After that, I could concentrate on my work at the college.

At the college, I had a response from the British Council that they had arranged an educational tour for Summer 1975 for our students. This tour would enable students to gain insight into various educational aspects as well as the variety of educational materials in England. I reviewed the program and found that it was really an excellent program, reminding me of my own excellent experience with the program that I participated in 1963. I was extremely pleased for our students to have these experiences. At the same time, we could visit shops and buy educational materials and place an order for our experimental kindergarten at the college. We announced the registration for this program, giving students two months' notice.

Also, in the year 1975, we celebrated the International Year of the Woman. To celebrate, the Women's Organization of Iran invited three women from the West to visit Iran and to see our women's activities. Betty Friedan, the author of the *Feminine Mystique* and one of the founders of the Women's Organization in the United States, Germaine Greer, the British writer, and Helvi Sipila, the assistant secretary-general for Social Development and Humanitarian Affairs at the United Nations, originally from Finland visited the family welfare centers (House of Women) that I had worked so hard to establish and develop. They had an audience with the empress, and Betty Friedan also had an audience with the Shah. Dr. Mehry Rassekh and I Invited Betty Friedan to our board meeting of the Iranian Psychological Association, and I also invited her to visit our college and to speak and have discussions with students and faculty members. She accepted our invitation eagerly. She had very interesting meetings, especially the discussion with our family counseling students citing the rise of divorce in Iran due to women's rights and the important role the family counselor could play in the family welfare centers and the new family court for the mediation and prevention of divorce. She spent a few hours in our college, and we enjoyed having her with us. Later, she wrote about all the issues of discussion in an interesting article called "Coming Out of the Veil," published by *The Ladies Home Journal*, June 1975.[3]

Visit of the author visiting the Shemiran College's Family Counselling program with the American feminist Betty Friedan.

For the trip to England, many graduate and undergraduate students, including my deputy Dr. Mosaed, were keen to participate and registered for the tour. They would all have dorm rooms near the Institute of Education in central London, which was available in summer with minimal expenses. I also thought, since the great loss of my mother, to arrange a private trip to London for the whole family, including my sister-in-law, who joined us. Again, Christine kindly rented a house for us, and this time, Alison, David's niece, was willing to take care of our children. She joined our family in summer 1975 so that I could lead our educational tour and visits with peace of mind. I was also able to arrange an interview with two professors of early childhood education and psychology at the Institute of Education, University of London. They wanted to spend their upcoming sabbaticals at our college. One of the professors, Mary Waddington, was an authority in the field with her publications and was also an excellent teacher. Our visit was very successful, and we had several opportunities to talk with newspaper reporters. I remember well Mrs. Betty Jerman's interview with our students and me for *The Guardian*. Her interview was published later in a half-page article on Tuesday, October 21, 1975, titled "Everything in the Kindergarten."[4] On this trip, we also had an opportunity to visit factories for educational toys, and we were able to witness their application and use at several kindergartens. As a result, we received various samples and catalogs from which we could place orders for our experimental kindergarten at the college. So again, with hands full of material and information, we returned to Tehran to serve our country.

Author with students of the Shemiran College at an
educational tour of London and England.

The academic year (1975-'76) began smoothly. In Iran several rumors were going around, and the most important one was about the illness of the Shah and his treatment by my colleague and former physician, Abbass Safavian. He was still the professor and president of the National University. He was being assisted by some of his French professors. There was no official government news mentioning the Shah's illness and it was not until many years later it was clear he had cancer. Usually, this type of news or information was not shared officially by the government with the people. As a result, there were many rumors, and it was impossible to recognize what truth lay in the rumors. It was the same way with rumors about corruption in the Shah's circles.

The author introducing Professor Dr. Duanne Varble, who was visiting Shemrian College from the USA, to His Majesty the Shah of Iran during the Salaam Ceremony held at Golestan Palace.

On the birthday of the Shah, Shemiran College received several invitations for attending the Shah's birthday sa'alam. Several members of the faculty and I attended the court ceremony to congratulate him on his birthday. Usually, the audience and greeting ceremony was held at the Gholestan Palace, with each group given a different time. We attended with all the universities and colleges. Usually, the president and faculty members stood around the large hall, lined up according to the year of the institution's establishment. The Shah would walk around the hall, stopping in front of each group, and the president of each institution would speak and give birthday wishes on behalf of their group. So as the president of our college, I had the opportunity to express our birthday wishes. Because of the rumors I became curious, and included best wishes for his health in our wishes. In this way, I hoped to see for myself what his reaction would be. When he stopped in front of our group, I tried to look him directly in the eye to examine his expression and appearance in connection to his health. Unfortunately, I noticed that he had changed. He did not look as he had before, and to me, he looked as if he had lost a lot of weight. Although he responded positively to our college and to me, his expression showed a deep depression mixed with anxiety.

Later on, we learned that the Shah had cancer from 1973, and that the physicians and the French consultants tried very hard to hide the sickness, and even its treatment from him, his regent the empress, and of course the people of Iran. This knowledge was kept from them until 1979.[5] Several other documents were published later indicating that physicians did not speak to the Shah or the empress about the type of cancer he had and avoided using the word *cancer*, thus following questionable ethics in keeping the real diagnosis from the patient (the Shah), and his next of kin, not to mention the people of Iran. In addition, apparently, the Shah was taking some other anti-depression and anti-anxiety medication, and therefore, we understand now that the Shah was not taking his sickness and his treatment seriously or even taking the right medication in a timely manner, and this might have gradually affected his decision-making capability, his attitude, and his well-being as a leader of the country. In a later visit with the empress in Maryland (September 27, 2004), she confirmed again what she wrote in her memoir, that she did not know about the Shah's cancer for several years until finally the French professors notified her in Paris. According to several documents, it is not clear that the Shah himself was notified frankly and openly by the physicians about the correct diagnoses of his cancer until he left the country in 1979. The Shah was only told that he had "Waldenstroem's" disease, without anyone speaking frankly to him about cancer and the severity of his illness.

Meanwhile, in 1975, Iran was enjoying rapid development and prosperity. The finance minister Hushang Ansari announced through the media that the economic growth of Iran was expected to reach 41 percent, and the Shah announced in his interviews that Iran was about to cross the frontier and become a great civilization again. He even criticized the West and Britain for their economic system and their sociopolitical system and democracy. In this way, "the Shah finally laid to rest any hopes for political liberation, which might have permeated his thoughts in the early 1960s. Democracy had been definitely replaced by a paternalistic monarch who knew what was best for his people without sharing his decision with the people in advance."[6] In addition, the country received somewhat of a shock in this year 1975, when the Shah announced the establishment of a single governing party—the Rastakhiz (or Resurrection) Party, since he had formerly opposed the one-party system in his book *Mission for the Country*. Apparently, the proposal of the one-party system was prepared by some of my former colleagues at the National University of Iran—G. R. Afkhami, A. Alimard, M. Ganji, A. Ghoreishi, and some other political scientists.[7] This announcement of the Rastakhiz Party shocked many people, and it caused a great deal of resistance. The more the Shah and the members of central committee of the Rastakhiz party explained to people the party's intention and function, which they explained was political education and fostering democratic participation, the more people quietly resisted this type of democratic centralism and considered it as a political control under Pahlavism's umbrella. I remember well that the Shah stated in a televised speech, that those who do not join the party could be given passports to leave the country without any exit charge. In 1976, we also witnessed the change of our calendar, which the Shah suddenly imposed on the country without any preparation of the people. He changed the calendar from the Iranian Islamic calendar to an Iranian Imperial calendar based on the reign of the Cyrus the Great beginning March 21, 1976. This meant that the year 1976, 1355 in the Iranian Islamic calendar, suddenly became the year 2535. This news was announced on the fiftieth anniversary of the Pahlavi dynasty. As a result, the murmur of the opposition especially among the religious groups and people noticeably increased.

In this atmosphere, I was pleased that we were able to complete the experimental kindergarten and prepare for the official opening. Finally, on December 15, 1975, our experimental kindergarten, with a capacity for sixty children from the age of three to five, was inaugurated by Her Royal Highness Princess Farahnaz, assisted by Her Excellency Mme.

Farideh Diba, to enable students in the preschool education program to observe and work with children. At the same time, we also established a counseling center to expose students in the family counseling curriculum to various practical situations and problems. I was happy that we finally provided this opportunity of practical experiences for research and studies.

Meanwhile, the USIS and the cultural section of the US Embassy were preparing for us to visit several similar programs at colleges and universities in the USA, as part of their exchange programs for faculty, students, studies, and research. This educational and cultural exchange between United States' and Iran's universities and colleges was becoming very popular in Iran. For example, the University of Tehran had an academic exchange program with the University of Illinois for some time, and the National University of Iran had an agreement with the City University in New York. We definitely wanted to take advantage of this opportunity for our new Shemiran College. I thought that an exchange would be mutually beneficial. Therefore, after getting approval of the board of trustees, we started our visit that would take us throughout the USA.

We began our trip in Boston, visiting universities and colleges, including Boston University for our family counseling and Wheelock College for our preschool education program. I liked the mission of their college because it was similar to our college's mission: "To improve the quality of life for children and their families." We then went to New York and visited several universities and colleges, including Columbia, New York, and Syracuse University. In each state, a welcoming letter for me was waiting at our hotel from the coordinator assigned by the State Department, giving our schedule, maps, and meeting schedules with appropriate departments of the colleges and the contact persons. The dean of the College of Human Development of Syracuse University, Dr. Michael Marge, was very interested in our exchange program, as was the chancellor, Melvin A. Eggers. They provided a welcoming lunch at the office of the chancellor and discussed possible exchanges in their program in early childhood education and family studies. Later on, Dr. Kazemzadeh, vice chair of the board of trustees, joined us in discussing and preparing the draft of an agreement, and we invited them to visit our college and programs in Iran.

The author with the Minister of Higher Education of
Iran Dr. Hossein Kazemzadeh at the Syracuse University for
the establishment of an exchange program.

From New York, we went west. I skipped the midwest part of the trip
since I already knew their programs well through my former Fulbright
programs and contacts. In Los Angeles, we were welcomed at the airport
by a member of the women's association and transferred to our hotel
in the Bonaventura, where we were booked to stay. In the hotel, we
had under my name a welcome letter and all the appropriate contacts.
I visited the University of California at Los Angeles, the University
of Southern California, and then visited the University of California
at Santa Barbara Campus, where I was very happy to see one of our
graduate students, who had been accepted for the PhD program in early
childhood education under supervision of Dr. John Wilson. He and his
wife were very hospitable and invited us to their home. We then left for
San Francisco to visit the UC-Berkeley School of Social Welfare for our
subject on welfare administration. After visiting several other colleges,
we visited the Stanford University and the new department of Family
Medicine, which offered quite advanced and interesting programs. In
general, our visit was very useful and productive, mainly for two reasons.
First, I noticed that all these colleges and universities had heard and
knew about our college, and second, I noticed that because of the good
reputation of Iran and its development, how eager and anxious they were
to establish exchange programs. They even seemed to be competing with
each other on the conditions of an agreement, securing contracts and
type of connection with us. However, I also saw some posters at Berkeley
on gatherings of Iranian students about the repression and oppression of
the Shah's regime.

Throughout the trip, we noticed how welcoming Americans were of Iranians by the Americans and how strong and pleasant our relationship was. One college reception particularly illustrates how they valued this relation. The president of a college invited me to a dinner reception with other faculty. Before the dinner, there was a cocktail hour. When I was offered several alcoholic drinks, I asked the waiter for a nonalcoholic drink, a soft drink or water telling him I told him I did not drink alcohol. I had no idea that some of the faculty members overheard me. While I was holding my glass of water in my hand, we entered the dining room. As usual, similar to what we had at home, I saw on the table one glass for wine and one larger one with water. Suddenly, I noticed that the waiter was pouring water in the wine glasses and with the speech of the president everybody had a glass of water and toasted a possible exchange program with us. Then the wine bottle from the table disappeared quickly. Apparently, the waiter who was serving or the faculty member who heard me about my drink before the meal understood that I was not drinking alcohol. Therefore, to establish a better relationship with us, they avoided drinking wine with the meal.

I have never been so embarrassed in my life. After I understood the reason, I explained to them that I respected their customs, and I do not mind if they drink wine. I also told them that at home, if we have guests, we have wine on the table for them, and we definitely do not mind. The more I insisted that they could drink, the more they insisted they chose not to drink because I did not. I was so shocked by that evening that ever since I have never said I do not drink any alcoholic drink out of respect for the customs of others. This incident also showed me how important Iran was at that time. Everyone seemed to be competing for our attention, respecting us, and urging us to develop good working relations, and I was proud of that. I returned to Iran with more confidence about the quality of education in our college how progressive we were without any governmental assistance.

I prepared my report for the board of trustees, strongly urging that we establish an exchange program. The board agreed, and it was decided to start with Syracuse, since they were eager to come to visit us the following year, 1977. After their visit to our college, we would finalize the agreement with them. Actually, that year, we had a good number of visiting faculty with a contract with two professors from the USA who wanted to spend their sabbatical with us in teaching and research. One of these professor's was Dr. Duane Varble, professor of psychology and the head of the PhD programs at the University of Nevada, who wanted to teach in our Family Counseling Department and also conduct a research on families of Iran.

After we finished the academic year, I was so tired that we again thought of spending the summer vacation in London, which would be the best place to rest. The children knew English, and we could be near Christine and David and their families, and Sa'id and I could also develop and update our academic information, and we could also escape the hot summer of Tehran. So we chose London again. As always, we lived in southeast London near Christine and David in a furnished flat in Blackheath. I have always preferred Southeast London to Southwest London because of the opportunity to meet the original local middle-class English people, and I was able to learn more about their habits and customs. Most of my relatives preferred to live in Southwest London in Kensington or Hampstead when they visited the UK. All four of us were enjoying our visit and resting in Blackheath in the area near Greenwich. We had just started a good routine for a productive summer when we received a call from my brother-in-law Jamshid Khadiri from Tehran. We learned that Sa'id's father, Hassan Khadiri, had died in a hospital in Hamburg, Germany, on August 5, 1976. Jamshid asked us to handle the funeral and burial ceremony since we were in England and closer to Hamburg. Sa'id's father had specified in his will to be buried wherever he died. I became very worried since my husband, Sa'id, was crying and was too upset to be able to think, talk, or control himself once he heard the news.

As usual, I called Christine for advice. She had just had her first baby (Anna) at the time and was very much involved with taking care of her. However, she told me that she would check with her kind parents, Mom and Arthur, to see if they could come from High Barnet to Blackheath and stay with the children so that Sa'id and I could fly to Hamburg for the burial and funeral arrangement. We felt relieved and grateful that the children would be look after, especially since we knew that they would be in good hands and have a good time and that we would be able to concentrate on our responsibilities for the trip to Hamburg. I booked our flight and called our friend Dr. Massarrat, who was professor of medicine at the University of Marburg to inquire from the hospital the reason of my father-in-law's death. Mom and Arthur came immediately to take care of the children during our absence, and we went to the bank to gather cash in German marks and travelers' checks. We then flew to Hamburg. It was very helpful that we spoke German. As soon as we arrived in Hamburg, I called the Iranian Embassy, and spoke to staff who were already aware of the death of my father-in-law. He was known in Hamburg, and because of his business, he had spent a lot of time there for forty years. Sa'id was so upset that he could not handle the whole burial, and I had to arrange everything in the Islamic tradition. I also collected all his father's personal belongings from the hospital because Sa'id did not like to touch them or, for that matter, see them at all. It was really very hard for me, but I felt I had to at least search his pockets in case there were any important documents. After the search, I found only several credit cards and special cards for entry to the Monte Carlo Casino and other private clubs. There was a little change and nothing else. Sa'id told me to call the Red Cross and, without showing anything to him, give all the belongings to the charity. This was very painful for me. I asked the funeral home manager to arrange the funeral ceremony, invitations, and the date as soon as possible with a Muslim ceremony at the Muslim section of the Ohlsdorf Cemetery. I stressed that since we had our little children waiting for us in England, we needed to leave Hamburg as soon as possible. Ohlsdorf Cemetery in Hamburg, Germany, is the largest cemetery in Germany. Its 990 acres of land has been a cemetery since 1877, in continuous use with beautiful buildings and different sections for different religions. About 982,117 burials have taken place in a very beautiful garden full of all kinds of flowers. It is also a popular sightseeing destination for the tourists.

We waited in the hotel, counting the hours and days to hear the date and time of the funeral and hoping in a few days to finish the burial. Dr. Massarat called us about the cause of death. He indicated that the hospital thought it was liver cancer, but the hospital was not exactly clear as to the reason of his death. While we were waiting impatiently for the time and date of the funeral and I was worried about our Gita and Reza, I had a call from the funeral manager that we would have to wait about three weeks because there was a waiting list for burials. We were surprised and shocked at this news. In our culture, the burial of the body should be as soon as possible—either the same day or the next day, and I was amazed that Germany was so different. We thought we definitely could not wait for three weeks because I had promised Mom and Arthur that we would return to London in one week. Therefore, I appealed to our embassy. Fortunately, the Iranian ambassador in Germany knew both my father-in-law and me. When I told him that we traveled from London, and we needed to return quickly because of our little children, I asked him if he knew any way that we could speed up the funeral. He said that the Germans are very strict about rules and regulations, and unless the mayor of Hamburg would give an exceptional permission for exceptional circumstances, we could do nothing. I asked him to call the mayor and give him special greetings from two PhD alumni from the University of Heidelberg, now staying in England, who were in a difficult situation, trying to arrange a father's funeral and needing to return to their children. Maybe if he knew our circumstances, he would grant the special permission. In addition, I myself tried to call the mayor's office to explain these special circumstances. We decided that if after two days we did not have the permission, we would go to London and then return again in three weeks at the time of the funeral. Fortunately, in those days, Iranians with a valid passport did not need a visa in most European countries, including Germany. At that time, Iran enjoyed good relations with other countries, and Iranians were well received and respected.

Maybe all these factors plus the reality of the situation of not living in Germany or the love Germans have for children helped, and we received our special permission. The funeral director telephoned saying that although it would be difficult, he would arrange the ceremony in two days. He said he would call about the time on the following Saturday. In the meantime, we needed to go to the funeral home to choose the casket, the headstone, and proper inscription for it, and the type of flowers we wanted to plant. Knowing that we could return soon to the children gave us peace of mind to handle all these funeral duties, so that after the funeral, we could return to London.

I booked our return ticket to London and called Christine and the children about our arrival time. They were happy to hear the news because apparently they missed us a lot. It is interesting how in the middle of sorrow, one finds some happiness and life continues. So we chose a casket and a marble stone and appropriate writing in Persian and German to be surrounded by several pink rose bushes to be planted later around the gravestone. After all, Sa'id's father was coming from Iran, the land of roses and nightingales. It is one of the nice things about Germany that most of the cemeteries permit the planting real flowers.

As a result, the Muslim section of the Ohlsdorf Cemetery, because of Persian Muslims, looked like a rose garden.

Everything was arranged for Saturday at 11:00 a.m. The funeral director told us that he had received many calls from my father-in-law's friends who were inquiring about the funeral. He told us that he would notify them of the time and date if we had no objection. Unfortunately, we did not know any of them so we could not guess how many would attend the funeral. About 10:30 a.m., we began to see car after car arrive. All cars were the latest models of luxury cars such as Rolls-Royce, Mercedes, Ferrari, Cadillac, and others that I could not recognize. Most of the people who attended were the same age as my father-in-law and close friends of his, and they seemed very rich. All of them had sent floral arrangements in the shape of a very large crown. There were many other beautiful wreaths of flowers. Each of these friends came one after the other to Sa'id and me, and expressed their sorrow and sympathy. Most of them spoke highly of my father-in-law and with great respect. Most of them mentioned that he lived very well, and they wished they could be like him. It was known that Hassan Khadiri was very generous to his friends. He had lived very well and had a lavish lifestyle. This is when I found out why he did not have a penny in his pocket. He really was a big spender and spent all the money that he had in his life. He enjoyed his life so much that even some of his friends envied him for his good life even while at the funeral.

We were all standing in front of the funeral home when the special ceremony started. The coffin was covered with a beautiful crown of flowers and was carried by eight people dressed in black robes similar to academic robes. Behind the coffin was a carriage with several pink and white flowers in wreaths and crowns. We followed behind the carriage, with all the others following us. We never imagined there would be so many people. The carriage stopped near the grave, which had been prepared for us. In our culture, according to Islam, the body should be buried in a long white material and placed directly in the grave. The body should be in touch with the earth. Here I noticed that because of the German regulations the body was required to be buried in a coffin. To accommodate our religion, the funeral home in the Muslim section modified the regulation and placed some soil in the coffin. Just before the coffin was lowered, everyone placed flowers and soil on the coffin. Then following the Mullah's prayer from the Koran, we walked to the old historic building for the reception. At the reception again, all the friends spoke about him, and most of them invited us to lunch or dinner while we were in Hamburg. Since we were leaving the next day for London, we thanked them for coming to the funeral and for their hospitality and returned to our hotel to pack and return to London.

We called London and told Gita and Reza we would be with them the next day, Sunday. I told them if they continued being a good girl and a good boy we would take them to a movie in London. The next day at the airport, we bought gifts for Mom, Arthur, and the children. We arrived in London near noon and were met by a car and driver sent by Christine, and we rushed home. The children were watching for us from the window, so there was no need to ring the doorbell. They ran to the car, and after hugs and kisses, Mom and Arthur joined them, and we went inside the house. We did not know how to thank them for their endless kindness. We exchanged information, and it looked as if the children and they had had a good time together. Mom and Arthur then packed their things and left that afternoon to High Barnet where they lived, which was a long drive for them.

The children were expecting us to take them to a movie, as I had promised them. So after some rest, I saw in the paper that Walt Disney's *Bambi* was playing. Sa'id had dubbed that for the children of Iran too, so we were all interested in seeing this movie. It was playing near the Charing Cross Station, just one train line for us from Blackheath.

Since it was Sunday, most places in London except the cinemas were closed. Because we had been warned not to leave cash at home due to the frequent burglaries in the area, I was carrying my big handbag, which I had with me all the way from the trip to and from Germany. It contained the cash and traveler's checks that were left in my bag from the funeral. In the theater, I placed the bag on the floor in front of my seat. During the intermission, there are always in each aisle of the movie hall two young girls selling ice cream, chocolate, and snacks. Gita and Reza wanted ice cream. I took my small bag with change and ran quickly to buy that for them. As soon as I returned, it became dark and the second part started. I placed the small bag back in the large bag and suddenly noticed that my small wallet with the traveler's checks and paper cash was missing. Although it was dark, I searched around the front and back of my seats. And of course, I could not concentrate on the movie at all.

I also noticed that the two young men who had been sitting behind me were not there anymore.

When the movie finished, we rushed to see the manager to report the loss. After we told him, he said that he could not do anything. He directed us to the nearest police station. I was so tired, and I had a migraine headache by the time we reached the police station. This was the first time we were robbed in our life. As I excitedly described everything to the policeman, he listened with an English calmness and finished the report. Nine hundred English pounds in traveler's checks and six hundred pounds in cash had been stolen. He told us with a smile that this had become a new pattern of robbery. He immediately told us that we should not be optimistic about getting the cash back, but that we might get our traveler's checks by showing their numbers to Cook's Travel, who issued the checks. We returned home tired, and the children were so tired that they went to sleep on the train. That was a painful lesson for all of us: not to carry so much cash. Fortunately, our traveler's checks were replaced immediately. This was the only time in our life that we were robbed—and it was in central London!

We continued our next two weeks in London in beautiful surroundings. Christine and David were very upset about the robbery, but this could have happened anywhere. For example, two years ago, my father-in-law had been on a train in France when thieves injected him with a sedative in the back and took his wallet without him noticing it. To forget the whole incident and to thank Mom, Arthur, Christine, and David for their kindness, and their deep understanding of our situation and helping us, we invited them to a musical show in London. And then we prepared to return to Tehran for the new academic year, 1976-1977.

[1.] Henry Kissinger, *White House Years*, 1979, p.1261, and Kenneth M. Pollack, The Persian Puzzle, 2004, p.103.

[2.] Ali M. Anasari, *Modern Iran since 1921. Pearson Education Limited 2003, pp.166-167 and p.182*

3. Freidan, Betty. "Coming Out of The Veil," *The Ladies Home Journal,* June, 1975, pp. 71ff.

4. Betty Jerman, "Everything in the Kindergarten," *The Guardian* (Manchester), Tuesday, October 21, 1975.

5. *Enduring Love*, p.241-267, and also Houshang Nahavandi, *The Last Days, The End of a Reign and a Life*, Los Angeles, Ketab Corp. 2004, p.367.

6. A.M. Ansari, *Modern Iran since 1921: The Pahlavis and After*, p.184-5, 2003

7. Abbas Milani, *Persian Sphinx*, Washington, D. C. Mage Publisher, 2000, p.275.

CHAPTER 13

Between Two Revolutions
Academic Years 1976-1978

Our summer had been a sad one because of the death of my father-in-law in Germany. We returned to Tehran at the end of August 1976, wondering what had happened at Shemiran College during our absence. I found a great deal of correspondence waiting to be answered and met some of my colleagues who had returned from their vacation. Many of them had either attended an international conference in their field or had spent their vacation abroad. In those days, Iran had good relations with European countries, and we did not need any visas to travel. For this reason, many Iranian families escaped the summer heat by going to Europe.

At the college, I also met several students who wanted to arrange their schedules for the next semester. I noticed a great change in their appearance. Many of the male students had beards and mustaches and many of the female students were wearing scarves and were covering their hair. Since I always had good relations with the students and even considered them as my colleagues, I asked them how their summer had been. Some of them mentioned they were in training camps and had also traveled abroad. At first, I did not understand what they meant by training camps, but later through overhearing conversations among them, I noticed that they were talking about the guerilla training camps in Cuba, Lebanon, Libya, South Yemen, North Korea, China, and other places. Later on, through some of the students, I discovered that unfortunately in the Cold War, there was even an underground competition in guerrilla warfare between West and East and SAVAK. I was shocked and sensed that I would have a tense and challenging academic year ahead of me.

In general, I also noticed that the gap between the Shah and the people was becoming more intense and the one-party *Rastakhiz* (Resurgence), even with its two *Progressive* and *Constructive* wings, was not attracting people, especially the young, and did not benefit the country at all.[1] In contrast, the opposition groups had organized clandestine communication capabilities reinforced by foreign media such as the BBC. I started to listen more carefully and pay attention to the news about Iran through shortwave radio from different foreign countries, and I realized that their news stories were usually at odds with our official news. Unfortunately, the government was not sharing the real news with the people and kept them and even sometimes the Shah in the dark. Therefore, the people who had shortwave radios were listening to and trusting the foreign news more. I remember that every morning at 6:45, before going to the college, I used to listen to the BBC World News in order to understand what was going on around us. A lot of opposition groups were emerging against the regime. There was also a media war.

The poorer people were more religious and more influenced by religious leaders like Khomeini, who was opposed to the White Revolution, the *Resurgence* party, and the change of the solar Islamic calendar to the pre-Islamic Persian calendar from the time of Cyrus the Great. These opposition groups believed that the White Revolution was not providing progress as evidenced by the increasing gap between the rich and the poor. Even for the middle classes, who benefited from the Shah's Economic Development Plan, economic freedom was not enough, and they were demanding more political freedom and expecting the Shah to reign rather than rule, in accordance with the bylaws of the original constitutional monarchy act of 1906. The technocrats believed that a liberal economic system could not be run with an autocratic political system and the young people were more and more influenced by many leftist and religious leaders. Underground organizations like the Communist party, Tudeh, Tofan, Kurdish Democratic Party, Kumaleh, Fedayi, Mojahedin, Marxist Mojahid, Peykar, Rahe Kargar, Confederation of the Iranian Students, Hayats, and several others were growing stronger. All these organizations were under the influence of foreign countries from the West and East, and they increased in number, especially after the hike in oil prices under the leadership of the Shah. Some of these organizations had guerrilla-training camps in different countries. Unfortunately, neither the media nor the Shah were sharing with the people all the Shah's efforts in raising oil prices for the good of the country.

Furthermore, opposition groups were distorting facts about the Shah's programs. SAVAK utilized the recantation method notably with the guerrilla activists like Parviz Nik-khah in prison. After his public confession proved to be effective, the public recantation method was used on several other Confederation leaders using radio, television, and press interviews.[2] They were forced to share their experience and mistakes in misjudgments about the White Revolution and the progress of Iran after they returned to Iran and how they were misled by the foreign interest while they were studying abroad. I remember well the case of Mr. Nik-Khah, who was later employed, after his public confession, by the Iranian Radio and Television, where my husband was the director of *the Music Workshop for Children and Young Adults*. But the above method of the regime's public relations through recantation was not welcomed by the people, and it was nothing compared the underground public relations of the opposition parties. I deeply sympathized with the young and idealistic people whose passion for Iran, democracy, freedom, and justice could be abused by foreign interests. I therefore committed myself to enlighten them to the best of my ability.

It was the beginning of September 1976 when we turned our attention to a serious family matter. Our daughter, Gita, ran to me one day in her bathing suit, distressed and disturbed, and with a trembling voice, she said, "Mommy, it looks like my body is not straight anymore. Is this normal and is it part of my growing up?"

I took a look at her body carefully and noticed that the two sides of her waist were not even. One side had a little curve and her shoulder looked a little bit uneven. One side of her hips also appeared to be elevated in comparison with the other, and she was leaning to one side. This shocked me, but I quickly gained my composure to let her calm down. I hugged her and told her that it was nothing important and that we would go to see a physician soon. From that moment on, I was beside myself until several years later when her problem had been completely corrected. We were concerned for our sensitive daughter. She had artistic and creative talents like her father. Her poems in two languages had been published in the newsletter at her school, and she played the piano very well. I immediately made several appointments with our family doctors, Dr. Kafi and Dr. Mashayekhi, and an orthopedic specialist Dr. Shoja Sheikholislamzadeh, who was also the minister of health and social welfare and the husband of our friend Azar Aryanpour. Fortunately, these appointments were make quickly, and we found out that Gita had scoliosis, or curvature of the spine, which usually affects about 2 percent of the population during middle and late childhood, before puberty, and mostly in girls. I was shocked and upset and somehow felt guilty that maybe this was due to Gita carrying a lot of heavy books in her back pack. I was very careful not to use my business car or the driver for personal use, and I was professionally so involved that I did not have the time to drive the children to school. So Gita had to use the International Community School bus and carry the heavy books herself. When we asked the doctors about the cause of this illness, practically all of them told us that about 80 percent of scoliosis cases are idiopathic, meaning that the cause is unknown. They also told us that there were many theories for its cause. These included connective tissue disorders, hormonal imbalance and genetics—it could run in the family, although researchers had not identified the gene that may cause scoliosis. They assured us that scoliosis is definitely not related to carrying heavy books. They also told us that we were lucky to discover the problem early so that it could be treated more easily.

Then Gita had an x-ray of her spine and was referred to a new specialist who had just arrived from the USA and was probably the only specialist in Iran—Dr. Akbarnia. At the same time, Dr. Sheikholislamzadeh told us that his administration had invited several prominent orthopedists from around the world to conduct a seminar on scoliosis in two months' time. This topic was new to our physicians in Iran, and he told us that if we were interested, Gita could participate in the panel discussion as a case study, and we could benefit from the diagnosis of several specialists. He especially mentioned that Dr. Edward Riseborough, who had accepted the invitation, was a professor at Harvard and was very knowledgeable on the subject. We welcomed the suggestion, and Dr. Akbarnia prepared Gita's case for presentation at the seminar. In those days, scoliosis was not well known, and there was no screening test in schools for its diagnosis. All these physicians assured us that we had noticed the problem early enough to receive the best treatment. I especially reassured our dear lovely daughter who was eleven and a half years old that we would pursue the best treatment in the world. In the meantime, I did my own research on scoliosis and the best scoliosis orthopedic centers in the world, and we were preparing ourselves for the seminar. Both Sa'id and I did our best to be supportive of Gita and to keep her mind occupied including music performances directed by Sa'id.

At work, the fall term began, and we were very busy. As in the previous year, our students benefited from visiting professors from England. That year our students were also fortunate to have Dr. Duane Varble, a visiting professor from the USA in clinical psychology. He was on sabbatical from the University of Nevada where he was also the head of their PhD program. I was of the opinion that we should modify our traditional system of education to blend with the international system in a way to become global without losing our identity. I introduced Duane to our Iranian Psychological Association (IPA) members, and he presented an interesting speech on the development of psychology in the USA. My colleague and friend Dr. Cyrus Azimi, who knew him from his student days in the USA, also helped him and his lovely family in the adjustment to life in Iran. I also arranged for him to participate in the *Salaam*, the greeting ceremony on the birthday of the Shah.

At the *Salaam*, after the expression of our best wishes for the Shah's birthday, while I was introducing Duane to the Shah as our visiting professor, I tried to look at the Shah's expression to see if there were noticeable changes because of his illness. He seemed to be thinner and looked tired. The ceremony was very interesting to Duane. During his stay in Iran, I continued to familiarize Duane with our political atmosphere and the status of higher education in Iran. Later, when he was back in the USA, Duane kindly sent me a very perceptive statement about his memories of Iran, which I cite below.

Memories of Iran

In the fall of 1975 I applied for and was granted a year-long sabbatical leave from the University of Nevada, Reno, where I was a professor in the Psychology Department. My wife and I were looking for a place to expose our three children, ages 10, 13, and 15 to a country and culture that was very different from our own. We found it.

With the help of an Iranian friend, Dr. Cyrus Azimi, who had been a classmate with me in the Ph.D. program in Clinical Psychology at Michigan State University, East Lansing, Michigan, we arranged for our family to spend the 1976—1977 academic year in Teheran, Iran. I would be studying and also teaching at Shemiran College.

Dr. Simin Redjali, the president of Shemiran College and also a psychologist, was enthusiastic about having another psychologist to help teach in her new graduate counseling program.

In August 1976 we flew to Luxembourg and purchased a Volkswagen minibus in Germany. Over a period of several days we drove from there across many countries to Teheran. Even after having driven across Yugoslavia and Turkey we were only minimally prepared for the traffic and driving habits we found in Teheran. A mixture of taxies, buses, flocks of sheep, goats and camels and thousands of honking cars jammed all the major streets. In order to drive anywhere I went from being a courteous, careful driver to being an aggressive, horn honker in one day. I stayed that way until we drove back to Western Europe in June 1977.

The cost of housing in Teheran and our children's school tuition turned out to be much more expensive than we had originally budgeted. As a result my wife had to teach English at two colleges, which kept her very busy. Our children attended the International School of Teheran where English was the instructional language and enjoyed meeting other children from Iran and around the world. All three learned some Farsi with the youngest becoming the most proficient. They loved living in Iran and the oldest wanted to stay.

We made a deliberate decision to live in an Iranian neighborhood rather than an American enclave. We had many Iranian friends by the time our year was complete which included neighbors and colleagues. Dr. Redjali and Dr. Azimi included us in social gatherings, introduced us to their colleagues and families and invited us to holiday celebrations. For example, we were invited to attend the Shah's birthday celebration and at a later time I was personally introduced to the Shah and to the Queen. Colleagues and these true friends and their families hosted us in a genuine and generous way. Their friendships made our experience in Iran personal and very meaningful.

Teaching at Shemiran College was made easier by the superb leadership and organizational skills of Dr. Redjali. Through sheer determination, boundless energy and total commitment, Dr. Redjali developed Shemiran

College's undergraduate and graduate programs. She made the several foreign professors like myself feel welcome and supported.

We also traveled as a family at every opportunity. When there was a school holiday, we left Teheran in our VW bus to explore the rest of Iran. We visited all areas of Iran from the Caspian Sea on the north to Shiraz on the south and as far East as Herat in Afghanistan. We took in the mountains, the desert, the cities and small villages. Almost everywhere we went we were treated with curiosity and respect. We found that the Iranian people love children and our blond children always attracted the curious. We were invited by strangers to share tea and fruit with them. With the proper attire (chadors for the females) and attention to the local customs, we were welcomed into mosques as well as bazaars. We adjusted to the fact that males and females ate and often lived separately from each other, especially in the villages.

I am not saying that we did not experience culture shock. We did, particularly during the first few months. Both my wife and I found that our students ranged from the motivated and well prepared to learn from instruction in English to the poorly prepared and those who wanted to just get the grade with the least effort. That is not unusual for American college students either. However, my experience of teaching in Iran without a translator involved slowing the process down so that those students who had a good grasp of English could informally translate for their non-English speaking friends. There was also the shortage of appropriate textbooks, which resulted in photocopying of the available books for students. Iran has no copyright law.

But even more important was the message from college administration officials that we instructors had to be careful not to talk about problems in Iran—even not to use the word. We were told that there would likely be an informer in our classes. For me, that meant being careful to discuss family problems, psychological and social problems in an American Context not Iranian. As Americans we readily and openly discuss gender issues, intimate and sexual relationships, abuses, faults and failings. My perception was that not only were such topics forbidden but that generally the Iranian people do not trust any other person outside of their extended family member group. The possibility of betrayals by informers has made people cautious. The consequences were real. Our Iranian neighbor, a Harvard trained urban planner who was teaching at Teheran University would periodically be questioned by the authorities after having lectured about the urban planning problems he observed in the cities of Iran. He would sometimes be held for days.

There was also the quiet preparation for leaving Iran by some of the people we knew. There was some talk of buying apartments in London and Europe. We had no idea at the time what was coming. Nor did we ever suspect at that time that the government of Iran and the Government of America would become enemies a few short years after we left.

Near the end of our time in Iran I was invited to speak at a meeting of the Iranian Psychological Society. The topic was "Recent Developments in Psychology in America." Some of the audience understood English but many did not. Dr. Azimi served as a translator. The talk went well and was an interesting experience. When I told a joke, about half the audience would laugh and a short time later the other half would laugh after Dr. Azimi's translation. It was like having an echo and perhaps represents the difficulty of two very different cultures communicating with each other. Further, my memory of those echoes of laughter represent a mirror reflection of our common humanity.

In summary, our year in Iran fulfilled the desire for our family to live in another country and to experience a culture that differed from our own. Day to day living was difficult but we met many good people who are still friends after 30 years. We sought an adventure and found Iran to be an exciting adventure. It is a truly beautiful place with all its variety of terrain. And, indeed, it is a fascinating culture with its many facets reaching back to a long, complex history and moving forward as it was in the realm of education as Dr. Simin Redjali instituted the subject of psychology in Shemiran's course of study.

In fact, our experiences in Iran helped us to become world travelers. It was the first foreign country we came to know outside of North America. Since then we have visited and enjoyed many more countries and cultures but Iran remains unique.

Duane Varble, PhD

At this time, Iran had an autocratic and dynamic Shah, who not only reigned like a monarch in Britain or Sweden, but also ruled and made decisions about all the important aspects of the country. He was successful in making great strides in modernization, but not in human rights and political freedom for the country. In fact, these issues gave the opposition groups an excuse to criticize him. Each time that he was dealing with the oil companies or buying arms to shore up Iran's independence, we were hearing more about his neglect of human rights issues both in the opposition and the Western media and newspapers, without any counter public-relations attempt from the Shah explaining the rationale for his decisions. In the Shah's regime, three important factors were important in leading Iran to revolution. First, lack of an effective government public relations organization; secondly, lack of independent technical advisors who could provide the Shah with objective data, intelligence, and information; and thirdly, lack of attention to public opinion. Added to these factors was the Shah's cancer, which his physicians unethically hid from him, his relatives, the Iranian people, and the world. All these factors played an important role in the failure of the White Revolution and the victory of Iran's Islamic Revolution.

These factors are confirmed by several documents. The Shah himself in his books writes, "I do not employ any *advisors* in the usual sense of that term. To do [so], I think [is] dangerous for any head of state."[3] Instead, he used reports and information from various ministries and organizations. For example, on November 7, 1976, when he revived the Imperial Inspection Commission, he appointed his school friend Hossein Fardoust as its director, with its members from several organizations of his one-party system. This method seemed to him to be safer.[4] According to his twin sister Princess Ashraf in her memoir, she was convinced that Fardoust must have withheld vital information from the Shah, and that Fardoust was even actively negotiating with Khomeini.[5] Mr. Fardoust later became chief of SAVAMA, the secret service of the Khomeini regime after the revolution.[6] In the same vein, the Shah also confirmed in his own books that he did not much value the public opinions and the public relations programs. Even the United States ignored the need for public opinions in Iran.[7] President Jimmy Carter wrote in his memoir and diary journal of November 21, 1978, about a conversation he had in the Oval Office with the Iranian ambassador Ardeshir Zahedi that the Shah "had no public-relations program under way or in progress, that he had no advisers around him who could prepare such an effort."[8] During 1975, the Shah made several additions to the principles of the White Revolution. He proposed price stabilization and a campaign against profiteering, free education, and a daily meal for all children from kindergarten to eighth grade, free nutrition for infants to the age of two, extension of nationwide social security to the rural population, and fighting against corruption.[9] These additional principles were established because of the rampant social malaise. The sudden rise in oil prices during 1975-'77 led to a very high rate of inflation, much more than 25 percent. It was nearly impossible to tell the exact rate because of the difference of rates from the different government organizations.[10] In order to please the Shah, these different government agencies were not reporting the actual rate, and as a result, the government was not able to report the correct rate to the International Monetary Fund. The government's response to inflation was raising taxes, price control, price stabilization and campaigns against profiteering, by the inspections conducted by a cadre of inexperienced students and members of the *Rastakhiz Party*. This unprofessional method of fighting inflation angered many small businesses owners and *bazaaris* and led them gradually to contact and join the opposition and even send money to Khomeini's campaign against the Shah. Industries chose to employ skilled workers from other countries at higher wages rather than providing training to unskilled Iranian workers. As a result, the number of the unemployed increased and added to the opposition to the government. Students in higher education seemed to look for any excuse to go on strike—from the quality of food in the cafeteria to the behavior of an instructor or administrator. Fortunately, because of the sincere efforts of my colleagues and the immediate need of society and market for the graduates of our college, our environment was still peaceful, and we had fewer problems in comparison with other universities and colleges. We were even preparing for the visit of HIM the Empress Farah Pahlavi to celebrate the first commencement of the college. The atmosphere at Shemiran College was calm enough for me to concentrate on treatment of my lovely daughter.

In October of 1976, I was called by the office of the Ministry of Health about the date and time of the presentation of Gita's case at the scoliosis seminar. When I received the seminar program, I noticed that several prominent specialists from Austria, Germany, Switzerland, and the USA were scheduled to speak. Shortly before the panel discussion began, we met Dr. Akbarnia and prepared Gita. He introduced us to Harvard professor Dr. Edward J. Riseborough. Each panel member spoke about one aspect of scoliosis and their opinion about nature of its treatment. Then they showed Gita's x-ray and called her to go and stand in front of the panel. All the participants in the panel were specialists in diseases of the muscles and skeleton and were quite knowledgeable and qualified groups of physicians to diagnose, monitor, and treat this condition. They decided that since Gita's curve was small—about twenty-five degrees—an orthopedic brace might prevent the progress of the curve from getting worse. For her treatment, they chose the Boston brace, which, while less noticeable, allowed her more flexibility while doing physical and social activities.

At that time, bracing was used to prevent further progression of the curvature, and usually doctors recommended the use of braces for growing adolescent children with idiopathic scoliosis who had a curve of twenty-five to forty degrees. At this stage, she would be monitored closely by Dr. Akbarnia. I was so worried about Gita and I had so many questions for the panel participants that the one-hour appointment passed too quickly and some of my questions remained unanswered. Therefore, I invited all the panel members for dinner to our house. Soon, we found out that there were two other girls with the same condition and almost the same age whom we knew very well. Dr. Riseborough had already operated on one of the girls because she had a more serious curvature (over forty-five degrees). I invited all the doctors and the families of the children with scoliosis to show our sensitive daughter that she was not alone.

At the dinner party, Dr. Riseborough gave us his recently published book (1975), *Scoliosis and Other Deformities of the Axial Skeleton*.[11] With a kind smile, he told me that his book would answer all my questions that the time of the seminar did not permit him to respond. That book was really one of the best gifts that I have received in my life. I gave him the book to sign, and after the guests were gone, I stayed awake and read the book all night long, learning more about scoliosis, its treatments, and answers to my questions. This still remains an excellent book on scoliosis.

Later, I found out that Dr. Riseborough was one of the founding fellows of the Scoliosis Research Society (SRS) dedicated to the education, research, and treatment of spinal deformity. His kindness and expertise impressed us. Following his advice, we ordered a brace through Dr. Akbarnia from Boston Children's Hospital, affiliated with the Harvard Medical School where Dr. Riseborough was teaching and conducting his surgery. It took a couple months to receive the brace, and

Dr. Akbarnia adjusted it to Gita's body. This type of brace fits under the arms and around the rib cage, lower back and hips. The Boston brace is used primarily to stop the progression of curves that occur below the midpoint of the spine and is less visible than the other types of brace. To me it looked heavy, hard, and painful to wear. I felt very sorry for her, but she was brave and wore the brace without any complaint. This made me wish that I could have worn the brace instead of her. We had to change the size of her clothing due to the brace. After wearing it for almost a year, Gita told me she hated wearing the brace. It was uncomfortable and hot, making bending over virtually impossible. I always tried to help her by picking up her things. During her summer vacation in July 1977, I made several appointments with two orthopedic centers in Austria and Switzerland, to show her spine and brace and to see if they approved of her current course of treatment, because some centers in Europe had other methods of treatment. I knew about electrical stimulation of muscles, chiropractic manipulation, and exercise as other ways to treat scoliosis, although there was no evidence that any of these methods would prevent the spinal curvature from progressing. I knew well that Gita was suffering, but as always, she was keeping her feelings to herself and was quiet. She was more of an introvert, just the opposite of our son Reza who was more of an extrovert. As we had promised her, we just wanted her to receive the best treatment in the world, with the hope of preventing surgery.

Doctors usually recommend surgical treatment for people whose curvature is greater than forty to fifty degrees. The surgery is generally successful in improving posture and the function of the back, but is one of the longest and most complicated orthopedic surgical procedures performed on children. We were trying as much as possible to prevent the progress of the curve and the surgery, if possible. But this was related to the growth of the child too. We tried to keep her busy with her music. She was playing piano very well and singing in the choir of the music workshop. It is impossible for me to put into words how much Gita's sickness affected us all as we sought to make her painful life as pleasant as possible.

At the same time, the news of the US presidential campaigns of Gerald Ford and Jimmy Carter attracted the attention of the Iranian people, including the Shah. Jimmy Carter, in his primary campaign speeches, emphasized the importance of human rights throughout the world and criticized Iran's record on human rights. These words must have been very disturbing to the Shah, who, for years had depended on the support of the United States to balance the old colonial policies of both Russia and Great Britain toward Iran. Instead of depending on the people of Iran, he was counting on sophisticated arms and war machines, mainly from the USA. In October 1976, the Shah in a private audience with Amir Taheri, editor in chief of the Kayhan International, the largest daily newspaper in Iran, told Taheri, "Our people are not warriors like their ancestors, and we have to make sure that we have superiority in weapons in any war." When he asked whether that included a war with the USSR, the Shah replied in the affirmative, adding, "At least until our allies come to our help."[12] Perhaps he was consciously or unconsciously thinking on how we lost a great part of the Persian empire during the 1800s to Russia because Iran did not have a modern army. Perhaps he wanted to prevent further unfortunate losses in the future.

Once, the Shah noticed that Jimmy Carter had a better chance of winning the election, he announced a policy of "liberalization" in his political development plan, which was way behind the socioeconomic development of the country. This way allowed him to have good relations with Washington while maintaining access to American arms. Carter's election had definitely a great effect on the Shah's regime and the opposition groups, especially in connection to political liberties, and we witnessed many changes in 1977. For example, the regime amnestied 357 political prisoners, and later, the Shah gave permission to the Red Cross to visit prisons and to observe the inmates.[13] He also allowed foreign lawyers to observe the trial of dissidents and military tribunals, gave an audience to a representative of Amnesty International and the International Commission of Jurists, and promised to improve prison conditions and court practices. Some censorship was gradually relaxed, and the loosening of restrictions led to several campaigns and open letters from writers, lawyers, and university professors, including my colleagues for freedom of thought and academic freedom. Several opposition groups and parties were established like *Liberation Movement of Iran* (*Nehzate Azad-i Iran*) by Mehdi Bazargan, which joined the *National Front, the Society of Merchants, Traders,* and *Educational Society,* established by the theological students in Qom to overthrow the regime and support Khomeini for the creation of a theocratic state and to curtail the activities of the Shah's Resurgence Party. In addition, the underground Tudeh Party (Communist) and several Marxist groups became more active.

In May, in this atmosphere, we were preparing for our first commencement and the visit of HIM Empress Farah Pahlavi at Shemiran College. At the end of this academic year, while I was preoccupied with my dear daughter, not an easy task, I was also busy with the security details and permission from the SAVAK. I had to send SAVAK the list of all the students who were graduating, and all the professors and employees and guests who would be present at the time of the graduation. I had to do the same thing with the experimental kindergarten and the counseling center of the college. I worked with the National Iranian Television to have a direct broadcast of the whole graduation ceremony. I was very happy to learn that I was successful in my efforts so that family and relatives could watch the ceremony directly from their own homes.

Abdollah Movahhed the Olympic wrestling gold medalist and one of Shemiran College's top students.

At the last minute, our list was returned without any difficulty except for the names of a few people who were not allowed to attend, because of prior political activities. I was astonished to see the name of *Abdollah Movahhed* on the list of those banned. He was the top graduate student in welfare administration and a world wrestling champion who had received six championship medals, including Olympic gold medals. He was very popular among the people and students. Apparently, on one occasion in an international event, he had made some remarks about Iran. He and other top students were to be presented to the empress to receive their diplomas and prizes. My staff and I did our best to see if he could be allowed to attend, but we knew that it was difficult to change his political record. Nonetheless, we told him to be near the telephone in case we were successful.

I was sure that if there was enough time, the Shahbanou (the empress) herself would have intervened on his behalf, but SAVAK was controlling everything. I had to come up with a solution so that the students and the people watching the TV would not notice that his name was missing in case we were not successful with SAVAK. Therefore, in order to avoid attraction, we tried not to mention his name, in spite of it being in the printed program for the ceremony. After that incident, our staff helped him clarify his SAVAK file. As a result, he was able to leave the country, and eventually, he received his PhD in the United States. Later, I was fortunate enough to see him by chance in Northern Virginia, where he was running a successful business. In the end, the graduation ceremony went off well. The empress was pleased and our college received a strong international support. Our students were accepted in universities in the United States and Europe in master's and PhD's programs in schools with high standards of accreditation, even the Ivy League schools. We circulated our English brochure in every college and university, and I was very happy and proud of the results. We also planned to give as many scholarships as we could to our bright students so they could continue their education abroad and, after finishing, return to the college as teaching staff. In this way, we gradually became self-sufficient in our teaching personnel in the new areas that we were offering in our college. In fact, with this objective in mind, the agreement with the University of Syracuse was written and we were planning to sign the agreement in August when representatives from Syracuse would visit Shemiran College.

Visit by HIM Empress Farah Pahlavi to Shemiran College
in May 1976.

Author speaks at the opening of
Shemiran College. 1976.

Immediately after the celebration and the end of the academic year, our family went to Vienna and then to Zurich to the Children's Hospital of the University of Zurich where we had an appointment to see the specialists who would examine Gita with her brace. First, we went to Vienna. The meeting with the orthopedic specialist took a long time and both children became very tired, and we did not get any practical suggestions for her treatment. They recommended that we stay in Vienna for two to three months while they tried their rehabilitation method with physical therapy. She would continue wearing her brace, and we might get some success from the treatment. But they were not sure about the result. The advice was not promising, certain, or practical.

After the long, tiring day, we were near the Vienna Opera. Sa'id and I thought we could buy tickets for *The Magic Flute* by Mozart and take the children to the opera to forget about the doctors and to compensate for the tiring day. I remember that only the most expensive tickets were available in the first rows, but we were very tired and bought them. Even though we had the best seats in the best opera house in the world with the best performance, Reza quickly went to sleep in his seat, and I worried about the way he was sleeping. I had hoped that the opera would help Gita forget the horrible day at the hospital. The next day, without any positive result for Gita from Vienna, we flew to Zurich. At the airport, our Swiss friend Martin Gassmann met us and took us to a luxurious hotel near the University Children's Hospital. Both the hotel and the hospital were part of a beautiful location on a hill with a very nice, relaxing view. We were on time for our appointment, and again, several specialists examined Gita; and they reported that even with the brace, the degree of the curve had increased as Gita was growing. They agreed with and confirmed everything that Dr. Riseborough and Dr. Akbarnia were recommending for her treatment. She would continue to wear the brace and be monitored regularly to check her spine and the degree of the curve. If the curve increased to more than forty degrees, the brace would not be able to control the increase, and she would need to have surgery to straighten her spine. They confirmed that we were following the proper course of treatment. Also, rehabilitative methods and services to ease wearing the brace were recommended.

After our two-day visit at the hospital, based on the recommendation of both the hospital and Martin, we went to Leukerbad, a village and resort with natural hot water springs in the Alps, and to the Roma Clinic known for rehabilitation. Because it was vacation time for all of us, we took advantage of staying for a few weeks there near the spring and the clinic. Leukerbad is a nice place in the Alps on the border of German and French-speaking Switzerland, and its main attraction is the heated thermal waters, which flow from the ground at 51 °C (124 °F) into dozens of public and private baths. The village public baths were very impressive and equipped with several water pressure facilities. The resort had many lovely hiking trails in the summer, several cable cars for an easy mountain hike and good skiing in the winter. We promised Gita that we would spend time there after she got well and return for a winter or spring skiing vacation. Every day, we walked to the beautiful village for shopping, or went to the Gemmi Cableway Station for a ride to the high country, or hiked along several trails. When we returned, we had spa treatment, massage and bathing. Afterward, we prepared for dinner, and so we had a very restful and quiet time.

At the beginning of August 1977, we returned to Tehran and found that during, our absence, there had been many changes in our country, our college, and even to our destiny. The most important event was the arrival of the new United States ambassador, William H. Sullivan. He was replacing Richard Helms, who had resigned in December 1976. Ambassador Helms was an experienced diplomat and very knowledgeable about Iran and the Middle East. But the new ambassador, William H. Sullivan, according to his statement in the preface of his book *Mission to Iran* (1981), had been in the foreign service for thirty years, but had "no significant experience" in the Middle East and Iran. It was a critical time for our complicated country in the middle of a cold war with our next-door neighbor, the Soviet Union. What was promising for us at college was the appointment of Dr. Dorothy Robin Mowry as the new US cultural attaché. She was an educated person and the first woman cultural attaché to Iran. We had established some exchange programs with the USA through the former cultural attaché Bill Meyer, and we were going to have visitors from Syracuse University and the dean of the School for Human Development to finalize our agreement with that university in August. So I asked to meet the new attaché to discuss these current exchange programs with US universities and colleges. She immediately welcomed my suggestion, and with the president of Damavand College, Dr. Carolyn Spatta, we had a productive meeting about exchange programs. Later on, we had the occasional lunch or dinner together. They were both very kind, well-educated ladies, and we continued later to see each other in the United States. My main objective in the exchange programs with the American or European universities was to attract those on sabbatical because of the shortage of qualified scholars in higher education in Iran and especially in our service professional areas. There was a serious demand for professionals, and in our agreement, we emphasized sending our best graduates and undergraduate students to Syracuse for their master's and PhD degrees. Our goal was to have our best students trained at Syracuse and then have them return to enter our college workforce. I thought in this way we would become self-sufficient. In addition, the professors and teachers from both countries could benefit in joint teaching and research programs and update their knowledge in our new areas for the service to mankind. When Dr. Michael Marge, dean of the Syracuse College for Human Development, and Dr. Lowell E. Davis, associate for Academic Affairs in the Office of Chancellor Eggers, arrived, they were very impressed with our school, the experimental kindergarten and the labs, which were equipped with the latest educational tools from around the world. They also met with all the teaching personnel, and I believe they had an audience with HIM Empress Farah Pahlavi, in addition to an audience with Her Excellency Mme. Farideh Diba, the honorary chairperson, and Her Excellency Dr. Hossein Kazemzadeh and some members of the board of trustees. After getting approval from the board of trustees, I signed the contract on August 29, 1977. The contract was envisaged for implementation over a period of five years, and was going to start on September 1, 1978.

The author, as President of the Shemiran College, receiving the Pahlavi Medal at the Sa'dabad Palace from Her Excellency Mm Farideh Diba due to the accreditation and academic achievement of Shemiran College.

All faculty members and President (author) of the Shemiran College at the Sa'dabad Palace ceremony with Her Excellency Mm Farideh Diba.

Gradually, with the liberalization policy of the Shah, there was increased criticism about the different aspects of the government and the economy, attacking in open letters and accusing Prime Minister Amir-Abass Hoveyda, for example, of condoning the corruption of the government officials and the Royal family. During our absence from Iran in June, A. A. Hadj-Seyyed Djavadi wrote a letter and spoke about the necessity of trying Hoveyda for corruption.[14] Later on, documents of the US Embassy confirmed the corruption of the regime and stated that "they were aware of the serious charges of corruption against some members of the Shah's own family."[15] And further, "the Pahlavi Family with its 63 princes, princesses and cousins and about one thousand aristocratic families had turned their interests to urban ventures."[16] With all the pressure from outside and inside, finally Hoveyda, after twelve years of service, resigned his post as prime minister before he was ousted, and the Shah accepted his resignation on August 7, 1977. In the modern history of Iran, Hoveyda was the longest-serving prime minister (January 16, 1965—August 7, 1977).

On the day of Hoveyda's resignation, the Shah appointed Jamshid Amouzegar, the head of the *progressive* wing of the *Rastakhis* (Resurgence) party as prime minister. Also, on the same day, the Shah appointed Hoveyda as minister of court, replacing A. Alam, who was considered a close friend to the Shah and was on sick leave in Switzerland. Most members of the US Embassy, at first, wished Iran well and hoped that the modification and political evolution might have removed the threat of a revolution led by Muslim fundamentalists. They paid attention to every personal movement of the Shah, except "no attention was made to the serious reports, rumors that the Shah might have cancer and that the USA had built its entire strategy on one man who was suffering from a fatal disease."[17] In addition, the Shah was not aware of his serious sickness, so he could not start to think about his own mortality. If he had known his situation, he "might have abdicated in favor of his son, and the empress could have acted as regent. There is a lot of debate as to why physicians tried to hide his sickness."[18] Zbigniew Brzezinski writes in his memoirs as the national security adviser: "At this stage neither I nor anyone else in Washington, to my knowledge, was aware of the Shah's illness. Reports from Tehran did not give us any clues. If we had known earlier, it obviously would have made some difference in the kinds of assessments and policy options we formulated."[19] As mentioned before, the memoirs of the Empress Farah Pahlavi and Princess Ashraf, the twin sister of the Shah, also confirmed that they were not aware that the Shah was suffering from cancer. David Owen, the former British foreign secretary, as both a physician and a politician, also confirmed in a lecture before the Autumn Meeting of the Association of British Neurologists and British Neuropsychiatry (October 3, 2002) that the Shah had lymphocytic leukemia stage II, diagnosed by his French hematologist Professor Jean Bernard and his assistant Dr. Flandrin, but not revealed to the Shah because of the recommendations of the Shah's physicians, Dr. Ayadi and Professor Safavian. On the other side, the Shah, who was at the height of power and not aware of the seriousness of his sickness, gradually lost interest in national and domestic affairs and paid more attention to international matters. He was not traveling throughout the country and speaking with the people directly as he used to do, and he was depending more on his various administrative channels, like General Fardoust, the court minister, or prime ministers, the head of the plan organization, and General Nasiri, the head of SAVAK. Because they were afraid of losing their lucrative jobs, these people dared not give the Shah accurate and objective information in a timely manner. Therefore, he was spending more time with international and foreign visitors, dignitaries, foreign specialists, and journalists. And to assist him in meeting his newly formulated global responsibilities, he ordered the creation of a think tank, mainly with foreign members like Henry Kissinger; Edward Heath, the former prime minister of Britain; Rockefeller; and others, to hold a two-day conference at the Shah's seaside palace at Nowshahr at the Caspian. The second and last conference was held in September 1977.[20] Apparently, according to one note in the book, even the US Embassy was not aware of this conference and took it only as vague rumor and a seminar sponsored by the Aspen Institute.[21]

In the meantime, the opposition took this time to influence the people and to take advantage of every incident, even those not unfavorable to the Shah, SAVAK, and his regime. Several incidents happened to cause unrest. For example, I remember that in August, the mayor of Tehran, without warning, sent bulldozers to plough through some of the slums of south Tehran to build a highway. The people there opposed this and rose up against the authorities, and a number of people were killed. We also had student strikes regularly in the universities and colleges for no apparent reason. I always tried to have direct contact with the students with my open-door policy was available to them for their requests and demands and to solve together their problems and not give them an excuse for a strike. This method, although demanding, helped me prevent strikes through the year before the revolution. Early one morning, about 7:30 a.m., while I was walking in the college yard to a building, I saw a student wearing several veils and scarves. I was curious about her outfit, and when we both reached the building, I asked her if she had time to come to my office for a chat. She smiled, and we went together to my office. It was early morning before my secretary had arrived, so we were alone. She sat next to me, and we could speak freely with no one to hear us. I first complimented her for being Muslim and believing in God, and then I asked her about the rationale of covering herself in so many layers of veils. She looked at me and said, "Dr. Redjali, you yourself in two years will have to dress like me. This is our symbol of Islam." In a confidential manner, she added, "The different veils are the symbol of our group and a symbol of our opposition to the government because of injustice, and because of what happened in the south of Tehran with the mayor." I replied that I am also Muslim, and even a Seyyed—my family can be traced back to Mohammed. I told her that I think the veil recommended in Islam is an inside veil in our heart and mind and that the interpretation of religious leaders can be different. In the meantime, my secretary arrived and the student looked at her watch and told me it was time for her to leave for a lecture. I thanked the student, shook her hand, and then told her that whenever she had time, we could have another meeting and discussion about the veil in Islam. From this meeting, I learned a lot, and I noticed how politics play a part in our lives, even in the way women dress. I asked God that if I ever have to wear double or triple veils like that, to enable me to go somewhere so that I could be free in my choice of what to wear, what to think in my life, and to be able to remain free to choose at least my attire independently. I also noticed how women's clothing could become a symbol of opposition in different periods of time in the history of our country and realized that it could be abused for political purposes.

Another incident that built unrest and resistance came when the new prime minister, Amouzegar, cut off subsidies for mullahs and ulamas, because of budget cuts. They had received these subsidies for many years.[22] In addition, on October 23, 1977, Khomeini's son Mustafa died mysteriously in Iraq, and there were memorial services held by mullahs throughout Iran and many memorial services that turned into demonstrations against the government and SAVAK. Another event was the fatal heart attack of Ali Shariati, who was a radical and combined Marxism and Shi'a orthodoxy in a revolutionary movement. He died in London in Southampton Hospital in 1977.[23] But again, with strong PR efforts of the opposition, SAVAK was blamed for his death. Later on, after several years of research, it emerged that these rumors were purely false accusation by the opposition's PR machinery.

At about this time, a new book was published by the Shah concerning the future of Iran called *Toward the Great Civilization*. In this book, he stressed that the monarchy was central to the Iranian identity. He wrote about the concept of sacred monarchy and predicted that Iran would soon become like the countries of Western Europe in every aspect of life. In fact, in some areas like arts and culture, such as the Shiraz Art Festival, under the leadership of the Empress, we had progressed to that level already. But both the book and the festival were another detachment from social reality and both of these increased the opposition groups' appeal, and several antiestablishment groups were gaining more strength in London, Paris, Iraq, Turkey, and the USA.

The Shah had always used the opportunity to visit each new American president and had visited the White House several times, meeting with President Roosevelt and seven presidents after him, and he was generally "considered by Washington to be an enlightened monarch, a reliable ally, and congenial chief of state."[24] But when the Shah and the empress visited the White House on November 15, 1977, as we eagerly were watching on TV in Tehran, everything was different, from an inauspicious start. When president and Mrs. Carter, the Shah and the Shahbanou were formally standing in front of the White House, and immediately after the twenty-one gun salute and music, as they were getting ready to speak, a sudden eruption occurred on the Ellipse and the surrounding area. Apparently, anti-Shah demonstrators, under the direction of leaders like Ibrahim Yazdi, a pharmacy student from Texas, had broken through the fence and had begun to assault the pro-Shah demonstrators. To prevent further disturbance, the police unleashed tear gas to break up the demonstration. All of us watching the news in Tehran saw how President Carter and other dignitaries and guests, especially the Shah, were drying tears with their handkerchiefs. Demonstrators (in both Williamsburg and Washington) carried several banners: one group carried the hammer and sickle and the usual Communist slogan against President Carter, and the other group carried a banner depicting the Shah as a puppet of the United States and demanded "US hands off Iran."[25] This was the same religious group who had opposed all the progressive principles of the White Revolution for many years. But after this unhappy beginning, the visit went extremely well and the Shah and President Carter discussed issues on subjects interesting to both countries, mainly the sale of AWACS aircraft to Iran, the price of oil, and the development of nuclear capabilities in Iran. Apparently, "the Shah left Washington encouraged by his conversation with the President."[26] But at the same time, the tear gas incident encouraged opponents like Ibrahim Yazdi, president of the Muslim Student Association in the USA and advisor to Khomeini, to increase their contacts with the people who were demonstrating against the Shah.[27] The tear gas incident became known as *Washington Tears* and was considered a humiliation by the people and a victory by the opponents.

A few weeks later, on December 31, 1977, President Carter, in response to the invitation of the Shah, made a short visit to Iran in transit between Europe and India. We were very anxious about this visit, as we remembered how President Carter had toasted the Shah and called the Shah and Iran at a state dinner "an island of stability in a turbulent corner of the world." This toast had a very negative effect on the Iranian public opinion, especially on those from the National Front, Tudeh (Communist) party and the religious front under Khomeini. They now felt betrayed by President Carter, who did not mention the Shah's human rights abuses and this caused anti-American feeling among the people. People began to repeat in daily conversation the slogan presented in front of the White House that the Shah was the puppet of USA. I became very concerned for Shemiran College and our American professors and their families and constantly monitored their well-being.

There was a real inconsistency within the Carter administration in general and especially a conflict between the foreign service (*State Department*) and the *National Security* advisors in the policy and doctrine toward Iran. This inconsistency was becoming gradually more noticeable and intensified during 1978 and 1979 of the Carter administration. This was an important factor in the Iranian revolution, in the creation of an Islamic Republic (a theocratic regime for the first time in the history of Iran), in the hostage crisis, and in the defeat of President Carter in the following election. Several historical documents published later would show clearly these inconsistencies and conflicts. One is William Sullivan's *Mission to Iran*. In his book, the US ambassador to Iran wrote that "he did not realize it at the time," and characterized these inconsistencies as a "major internal weakness of the Carter administration." He wrote that subordinates in the Department of State and elsewhere did not respect the president's decisions concerning major policy matters, and that fact derived from the circumstance that they had been selected from members of political factions in the Democratic party who held no *personal loyalties* toward Carter and who felt that he, in turn, gave no particular loyalty to them. It was a curious situation."[28] In fact, Sullivan became like those members of the administration and played an important role in the defeat of the Shah and the creation of the Islamic Republic of Iran.

In another work, Zbigniew Brzezinski, National Security Advisor to President Carter, wrote in *Power And Principle* that "as the crisis unfolded, it became evident to me that lower echelons at State, notably the head of the Iran Desk, Henry Precht, were motivated by doctrinal dislike of the Shah and simply wanted him out of power altogether."[29] President Carter himself writes in his memoir, "I became even more disturbed at the apparent reluctance in the State Department to carry out my directives fully and with enthusiasm. Its proper role was to advise me freely when a decision was being made, but then to carry it out and give me complete support once I had issued my directive. Cy [Cyrus Vance] sent one of his deputies to Iran to straighten out Sullivan or remove him, and I asked the Iranian desk officers and a few others to come to the White House . . . I laid down the law to them as strongly as I knew how. I pointed out how difficult the Iranian questions had become, and described my procedure for making the decision; Sullivan had not been the only one who had caused me trouble. There had been a stream of news stories in Washington, seeming to originate with those who opposed my judgment that we should give our support to the Shah, to the military leaders and later to Bakhtiar. I told them that if they could not support what I decided, their only alternative was to resign—and that if there was another outbreak of misinformation, distortions, or self-serving news leaks, I would direct the secretary of state to discharge the official responsible for that particular desk, even if some innocent people be punished. I simply could not live with this situation any longer, and repeated that they would have to be loyal to me or resign."[30] Although this ultimatum came too late for Iran, it led later to the resignation of William Sullivan, the ambassador to Iran, and the Secretary of State Cyrus Vance, who also described these critical years in America's foreign policy in his book *Hard Choice*.[31]

While Washington was in conflict over policy toward Iran and there was much disagreement about Iran's future path, we were witnessing numerous demonstrations and media fights between the regime and its opponents throughout 1978. I had to concentrate fully on the news of both opposing sides in order to operate the college and keep the peace, in spite of daily increased student demands. In addition, the medical prognosis on my dear daughter was not promising. At her latest checkup in December, there were indications that the size of her upper and lower spine curves had increased to about thirty-five degrees, even with the heavy brace. So we had to monitor her growth more closely. We knew that if the curve increased to forty degrees or more, she would probably need to have surgery. Her spine was turning from straight into an S shape. My entire attention was practically consumed with her health. Fortunately, most of her school grades were A's in Farsi and English. I prayed continually to God for his help, and then suddenly, we heard that Dr. Riseborough was coming to Tehran in April. This news made us very happy, and I contacted him immediately in Boston to confirm an appointment for Gita when he came to Tehran.

In the meantime, a copy of an unusual handwritten letter with the title "A Fatwa from Imam Khomeini" was distributed to newspaper editors and to ulamas (religious leaders) in Qom, Najaf, and many other religious cities. (A fatwa is a published opinion or decision issued by a religious person [a Mufti] regarding religious doctrine or law.) Khomeini's fatwa was against the Shah and his policies and was full of spelling mistakes. My colleague Hassan, who was a journalist, showed me the letter, which was a kind of declaration of war by Khomeini. Amir Taheri, chief editor of Kayhan International at the time, provides details of the fatwa in his informative book *The Spirit of Allah*.[32] He writes that the letter contained new words, used in Iran for the first time. The title of *Imam* was used in the Iranian Islamic Schism for the first time, and the word *Taghut* was used to describe the Shah. Khomeini exercised his religious authority and announced that he had "deposed the Shah" and motivated his followers to have several strikes and disobediences against the "dethroned Taghut" with his policies of "Western corruption."

After a week's delay, the Shah learned about the Fatwa and expressed his extreme anger. In an audience with Mr. Taheri, he spoke of Khomeini and the mullahs only as instruments of colonial policy of Britain and the Soviet Union to interfere in Iranian politics. But the Shah miscalculated the power of the religious opposition among the people. Perhaps he should have appealed directly to the people and spent more time among them, but with his thoughts more engaged with global problems, he neglected the negative public opinion of the Rastakhiz Party and the people's anger at the change of the Islamic calendar. At the beginning of January 1978, we were surprised by an insidious article in the daily newspaper *Ettelaat* titled "Iran and Red and Black Imperialism," which attacked the Red and Black Colonialism and castigated and insulted the exiled Khomeini by connecting him with British Colonial centers in India using some false accusations. The article was written by an unknown Rashidi Motlagh, apparently a pen name used by two advisors to Mr. Hoveyda, minister of Court.[33] Mr. Hoveyda gave the letter directly to the minister of Information, Darioush Homayoon, to be published in a daily newspaper by order of the Shah. Unfortunately, Homayoon also, without reading the letter and carefully weighing the political atmosphere of the country, sent the letter to the daily newspapers. This letter became one of the key factors in the revolution and immediately caused a bloody demonstration when *Ettelaat* published it on January 7, 1978. In Q'om, religious leaders, seminary students, and bazaaris protested against these allegations. The army and security officers, not trained in dispersing demonstrations in the new liberal environment, killed two students and injured many others, according to the government report. However, according to the opposition's rumors, the number of deaths was much higher. Following that demonstration, Khomeini congratulated the demonstrators, and according to the BBC, in news which I heard myself, he called for more demonstrations against the regime and *Tagut*. Even the moderate Ayatollah Shari'atmadari in Qom complained in an interview about the government. This demonstration was the beginning of a chain of demonstrations in the country during 1978. According to Shi'a Islam, there is a mourning ceremony after the death of a Muslim. Therefore, on February 18, the fortieth day of the Qom massacre, we witnessed the mourning ceremonies and memorial services by the clergy in several cities in Iran. Most of the universities and bazaars closed and several peaceful demonstrations took place in Tehran, Mashad, Qom,

Isfehan, Shiraz, and Tabriz. But in Tabriz, the demonstration turned violent following the death of a student protestor. The demonstrators attacked the police stations, banks, the Resurgence Party offices, movies, banks, and other government offices. And again, in this battle, several people were killed, and the religious leaders called for the services on the fortieth day after the Tabriz riot. This date fell on March 29, when fortunately schools and colleges were still closed because of Norouz holidays, the Iranian New Year, and I was relieved that there would be no strike and demonstration in our college. But in fifty-five urban centers, large memorials were organized throughout the country.[34] And again, in some cities, especially in Yazd, the demonstrations turned violent with slogans like "Death to the Shah," "Long live Khomeini," and "Long live the martyrs of Qom and Tabriz." Again, a few protesters were killed.

Margaret Thatcher of England was one of the last Western political leaders to visit Iran before the revolution. She was received by the Shah on April 28, 1978, just one year before she became the first British woman prime minister. She described perceptively how "the Carter administration vacillated in its attitude to the Shah." She admired the Shah personally and believed that his "policy of modernization along Western lines was ultimately the right one." Apparently, in her audience with the Shah, she was very concerned about the new Communist-backed coup in Afghanistan and Iran being in the front line against communism. In general, she and the Shah probably discussed the uncertainty of the American government's commitment and the fact that the BBC Persian program was being used as a propaganda tool against the government. Many Iranians were concerned about these matters. Mrs. Thatcher seemed to be impressed by the Shah's grasp of world affairs, "But, of course, no amount of such wisdom is proof against the kind of subversion which he was facing at home."[35] While I had to pay attention and have full concentration on the daily political situation before the next fortieth-day memorial in May, we also had the appointment with Dr. Riseborough in April. During this time, I learned that several members of our family had sold their houses and had moved with their belongings to Europe or the USA. I wondered why, but didn't give it much further thought. With overarching concern for Gita, I could not pay much attention to the dangers these political conditions posed, dangers which could affect our family's future.

Dr. Riseborough examined Gita and told us that her spinal curvature had increased to forty-five degrees because of her growth, and therefore, he recommended a spinal fusion and surgery. Immediately, I checked with Gita, who was suffering so much because of her brace, and without hesitation, she welcomed the surgery just to get rid of the brace. At the same time, Sa'id had an invitation to attend the International Society Music-Education Conference (ISME) in Canada (London, Ontario) August 12-20, 1978. He was also preparing himself to present some of his work in the universities and the music workshops for children and young adults at the National Iranian Television during the summer vacation at the ISME conference. We thought since Ontario was not very far from Boston, it would be better to make an appointment with Dr. Riseborough at the Children's Hospital, Harvard Medical School, for Gita's back surgery in July. Dr. Akbarnia and Dr. Shaikholislam, the minister of Health, also approved of Dr. Riseborough's decision, especially since Iran, at that time, was not equipped for this kind of surgery.

The next fortieth day for the demonstration and memorial for martyrs of Yazd was in May, and there were strikes and shutdowns in most universities, colleges, and bazaars. Again, although we could manage classes even with few attendees and prevent any demonstration and clashes in our college, it was not an easy task for me with Gita's health and well-being constantly on my mind. My migraine headaches intensified, and I had to take many tablets for prevention and treatment. With the benefit of hindsight, my education in psychology helped me a lot in this time of social unrest and the tense atmosphere. There were many demonstrations and clashes between the protestors and the troops. Again, many people were killed and injured, and I recall that the army had followed the protestors to the home of Ayatollah Shahriatmadari, the religious leader in Qom. There was tension everywhere, and this intensified so much that the Shah cancelled his visit to Eastern Europe and later made a pilgrimage to the Imam Reza mosque in Mashad. Next, he replaced General Nasiri, the head of SAVAK for the past twelve years, with the more popular General Moqadam. The Shah also promised free elections for the Majles, ordered his families to end their business activities, and banned them from starting new ones, and welcomed a group of liberal intellectuals around the empress to establish a study group for the first time to examine the problems of Iran. In my opinion, this study should have started long before. I became a member of this group in 1977 as a consultant to the office of the empress, although I wondered how our studies at this late stage could have any effect on the immediate situation. Prime Minister Amouzegar also tried economic reforms to control inflation in order to reduce the discontent of the middle class. With these government strategies, our streets became calmer, and for the first time, in May, a fortieth-day memorial and demonstration was held without any bloody clashes. In June 1978, the government thought the crises were over.

With the newfound political stability and the permission of the board of trustees, I began to make plans for our trip in July and August for Gita's treatment and possible surgery. We needed visas for Canada and the USA. Fortunately, through the US cultural attaché, we received a multiple entry visa for both the USA and Canada. We knew we would have to stop over in Europe because of the doctors' orders to rest for Gita. My kind deputy at the college Dr. Khalil Mossaed would always agree to act for me, especially during summer vacations, since we did not have much activity during that time. So in July, we started our trip, going by way of London. On our flight to the United States from Iran, I was surprised to see that the majority of male passengers were Jewish, wearing yarmulkes. Later on I discovered in my reading that the French and Israeli governments were telling their people to leave Iran, although the American CIA was still saying Iran was stable and everything was fine. By the second week of July, we had settled into the Inn at Longwood Medical, which was located almost a block away from the Children's Hospital in Boston, on the edge of Boston's Back Bay. Longwood Medical Area is encompassed by the Children's Hospital. At that time, I did not know anyone personally in Boston, but my colleague and friend at the National University of Iran, the late Dr. M. H. Farrokhpars and his kind wife gave me the name and address of Doris May, an American lady from Boston, whose daughter had married Dr. Farrokhpars's brother. I had first met Doris with her daughter at a luncheon party in our home when she was visiting her daughter in Tehran. Dr. Farrokhpars had insisted several times that I call her when I arrived in Boston, and I promised that I would. Doris May became a very helpful friend to me. The day after we arrived in Boston, we all went to the hospital to see Professor Riseborough, who received us warmly. From the first time that we met him in Tehran, he communicated easily with Gita. He immediately ordered a new x-ray of her back and showed us how the curve had even increased to fifty-two degrees, which meant that the best treatment for her, without a doubt, was surgery. When he asked Gita about this, she smiled and said, "Definitely, yes." She hated the brace so much that she was happy to get rid of it. We had considered that she might not agree, and we wondered what we would do if she didn't; but following her courageous decision, we signed the consent form for the surgery without any hesitation. That was a big step in her life and ours.

Children's Hospital Boston was one of the largest hospitals in the country to offer all kinds of services for children from birth through the age of twenty-one. It was the primary teaching hospital of the Harvard Medical School, and usually, the physicians held faculty appointments. There were also many researchers and physician investigators conducting all kinds of projects from biomedical to clinical applications of new medications, and applications of new technological procedures. Dr. Riseborough was a professor in the orthopedic department, and known as one of the best surgeons and clinicians with a worldwide reputation.

We did not have any reservation or hesitation in choosing Dr. Riseborough as the surgeon for Gita's back. We received another appointment for the preparation and orientation before the surgery. I was so worried that finally I called Doris May in Boston and realized she was expecting our call. She kindly gathered a great deal of information about the surgery and newsletters showing the successful results for many families and teenagers after surgery. After the telephone call, she came to see us in our hotel with all this information. I remember how her presence relieved our anxiety and worries. She also found a nice summer camp for Reza, so that after the surgery while Gita was in the hospital, he could go to camp and not be bored. She asked me to report regularly on Gita's progress.

When we had our appointment to learn about the surgery, the nurse explained to us the whole process of her surgery, which was called spinal fusion with instrumentation. The doctor, with Gita fully anaesthetized, would make an incision down the length of her back. The fusion involved placing pieces of bone, taken from the pelvis, between two or more vertebrae. Eventually, the vertebrae and the pieces of bone would grow together. The surgery ended by placing a rod or instrument called the Harrington Rod lengthwise beside the vertebrae and putting screws in every vertebrae to hold the curve and keep it from moving for about six months or more so that the fusion would take hold. Instruments applied force to the spine to correct the deformity and make the curve smaller. She told us that the operation would take several hours, depending on the speed of the surgeon and the physical condition of the child. When I told her that I was impatient and would like to know about the progress as the surgery progressed, she said that we could wait with other parents whose children were having similar surgery. She told us a nurse would be assigned to communicate between the surgery room and the waiting room, and this nurse would come every half hour to report on the progress of each child. Depending on the child, hospitalization could last several days in intensive care, and activities would be restricted for several months to a year. She also mentioned that after surgery we should not be surprised by a sudden jump in Gita's height. But then her growth would slow down, and we should not expect her to grow much taller. When I asked about a private room for Gita, she said the Children's Hospital did not recommend that. They would usually allocate a group of children with the same surgery to one room, and that being in their same peer group would speed their recovery. After two hours responding to several more questions from Gita, who knew English better than we did, and telling us what to bring to the hospital, we were well prepared.

Gita was admitted to the hospital on July 13, 1978, and we had a meeting with the anesthesiologist. The surgery was performed early in the morning of July 14. We kissed her on the forehead, wished her the very best; and while I was praying, the nurses placed her on the bed for surgery and took her to the operating room. I really wished I could have been in surgery instead of her to prevent her suffering. My little girl's lips were shaking with fear as they were taking her to the operating room. I shall never forget this scene.

Then we were guided to the waiting room, where other parents were waiting to hear the result of the surgery every half hour. We received a code to protect our privacy. We sat in the waiting room gazing at the top floor where the nurse would be coming from the operating room. At about nine o'clock, a tall nurse in white uniform and cap came and stood behind the handrail in the top floor and called each number. She told us the operation had begun for Gita and was progressing smoothly, and Gita was tolerating it well. She was the tallest nurse that I have ever seen in my life. She was so tall that hardly anybody could have missed her. She was an excellent choice for this purpose. All day long, her duty was to go from one operating room to the next, monitor each patient's situation and report to parents every thirty minutes.

I seemed to keep my head, neck, and eyes focused on the top rail, and each time the nurse came out, my heart was beating faster and faster until she was gone and then I resumed waiting and staring at the top floor. At noon, Gita was still in surgery, but the progress report was good. Some parents went for lunch, but I could not move. Then Sa'id took Reza for lunch, but I remained staring at the ceiling. Sa'id brought me a sandwich with coffee. Because of my headache, I took two Cafergot tablets to prevent a migraine attack, while I continued to look to the upper floor for the appearance of the tall nurse. I was told that this nurse had been doing this job for many years. About 2:00 p.m., she announced that the surgery was nearly over. And finally, she announced the operation had concluded and that Gita would be transferred to the recovery room. She said she would notify us when we could see her. We were the luckiest—we were the first parents to hear this news. Later on, I heard that Dr. Riseborough was one of the fastest surgeons in the hospital. While the other parents were still waiting for the result, we were called finally to see Gita. We were led to her room, which was a very large hall with about twelve special convertible, turnover beds. We ran to her bed and kissed her. She was wrapped in the special bed, sleepy and tired. The nurse told us that the surgery was quite a success and that Gita could also move her feet easily in bed. She mentioned that in some cases the feet would be paralyzed and the child would have to have further surgery.

Gradually, the remaining beds also became occupied by the other girls who had undergone the same surgery, bringing them from the recovery room. The nurse told me that we could come and go at any time of the day or night and showed me the recliner for parents if they wanted to rest. So because of the location of the hotel, it was very easy for me to walk over to have a shower and come back quickly. Gradually, I got to know the other parents, and we arranged a kind of monitoring schedule between us, especially on the night shift, with lower coverage to assist the nurses. We monitored each IV, in case it needed attention and watched for any girls needing some help. It was a good arrangement. Gita saw that she was not alone and that there were many girls like her. When she saw one of the girls next to her who could not move her feet, she became anxious and concerned for her, and we thanked God for Gita's good fortune. The next day, she was happy to see the girl next to her, back safely after another surgery, able to move her feet. The treatment and handling of the patients was very special. Since the patients were wrapped in the bed for several days, they needed to turn the wrapped patient over so that the back of the patient would be up and the face would be down. I worried each time they turned her and tried to be present at this time. I spent most of my time with Gita because I did not want to leave her alone. Sometimes Sa'id and Reza came to see her, and I would rush to the hotel to have a shower and take my medication with some food. Dr. Riseborough reported that he performed a spine fusion from L4 to T9 using a Harrington Rod and bone graft. He said that he obtained a very satisfactory correction. Gita also made a satisfactory recovery. Doris came to see Gita, and she was very happy about the results. As soon as Gita could stand up, we were amazed to see her sudden increased height. Now she was much taller. She looked several inches taller than before the surgery. Sa'id and I stared at her and tried to get used to this sudden change. It was interesting to see the other parents' reactions. Some of them screamed when they saw the changes in their daughters and could not control themselves. A week later, on July 21, a Risser localizer jacket (i.e., a cast) was applied to Gita's back to maintain a proper posture.

The x-rays showed a satisfactory correction of the scoliosis, and Gita continued to make a normal recovery. She was discharged on July 25, 1978, but we had to be near the hospital for two to three weeks for weekly checkups. She was in a cast all the time for six months. With the help of Doris, we rented a furnished apartment near the hospital for three weeks. During that time, we bought several dresses for Gita's new size and in a style to cover her cast as well.

We also registered Reza for a summer camp. We were happy that Reza would go to the camp, and we could be free to help Gita and provide care after the hospital. As a little boy, Reza needed some change from the hospital environment and to have fun with other boys, but after one day in the camp, I had a call that he was ill. He returned with red eyes, a temperature and several rashes. Apparently, he showed a very strong allergic reaction to his campsite. I took him to a pediatrician, who prescribed two medications and referred him to an allergy specialist. After several tests on Reza's back, it became clear that he had many allergies—to dust, grass, pets, feathers, and several other things. That was the first time that we had discovered these allergies and this knowledge helped us later in keeping him away from those items as much as possible.

Doris was very kind. She invited us to her home and took us to several nice places, shopping areas, and restaurants in Boston and Cambridge. Through her, we became more familiar with the area around Boston. In her beautiful home, we saw many of her family pictures including pictures of her late husband, a professor at the Harvard Medical School, her daughters, sons, and her grandparents and ancestors. One of them, which attracted me a lot, was the picture of Pierre Curie, the husband of Madame Curie and their daughters. So it became clear to me that she had a French background. Her beautiful home was mostly furnished with old antique French furniture. Doris was a very kind, organized, and sensitive lady.

On one occasion, Dr. Riseborough invited Doris and our family to meet his family. He and his English wife Jennifer were very kind, and some of his children were close to Gita's age. That evening we learned that he had been born in South Africa, originally studied medicine in London and was awarded a fellowship from Harvard as an excellent orthopedic surgeon. Later, he became a professor at Harvard Medical School. He showed us his hobby—raising orchids. He took us to his nursery where he had a beautiful collection of orchids of every kind from all over the world. We continued to see him regularly in his office with Gita. At our last visit, August 8, 1978, he examined Gita and her cast and told us she was managing it well, and then he gave her permission to return to Tehran. He said she should have an x-ray in Tehran three months from the date of surgery and that this x-ray should be sent to him so that he could compare it with the post-operative films that he had at the Children's Hospital. He thought that the cast would probably not need to be changed. Gita could continue in the same cast for a period of six months. At that time, he would see her to remove the cast, to examine her and x-ray her back to confirm the solidity of the fusion. We made an appointment to see him again on January 3, 1979. In the meantime, Gita could return to full normal activities without any real limitation other than wearing the cast all the time for six months.

To express our sincere thanks to Dr. Riseborough and Doris before leaving Boston for Canada and London, Ontario, where Sa'id was to participate at the International Society of Music Education, we invited them and their family to the Colonnade Hotel French restaurant for dinner. It was one of the most authentic brasseries in Boston with a very nice music band and a good harpist. We all dressed up and Gita especially wore a new dress for her height. We cautioned her about her movements and went to the restaurant a little bit earlier to welcome our kind guests and friends. Very nice light music was provided by the restaurant's small band, and the sound of the harp was especially beautiful. Almost everybody ordered lobster, which was prepared very tastefully and was delicious. I remember when I expressed our concern about what activities Gita could do and what she could not. Suddenly, Dr.Riseborough (who we now knew as Ted) stood up and asked Gita to dance. It was one of the most beautiful and happy scenes of my life. I will never forget seeing my pretty daughter standing so tall and straight and dancing so easily. By this action, Ted wanted to eliminate our fear about Gita's movement and encourage her and us to have daily exercise. All of us at the table thanked him and wished God's blessings on him.

Then it was time to go to the conference. My cousin Mary (Mehri in Farsi) and Bell, her husband, expressed an interest in coming with us to Canada with their children Marianna and Billy, who were almost the same age as our children. So they were kind enough to come with their large station wagon to take us to the conference. Mary and Bill had been very concerned about Gita's surgery and had also stopped in Boston to see her in the hospital on the way from Norwalk, Connecticut, to their summer home in New Hampshire.

The theme of the conference was "Music Education: The Person First," which was interesting to me as a psychologist. There were several programs in connection with the developmental stage of children and music. I also tried to attend some of the programs when Mary took the children to the city. Otherwise, I spent most of my time with Gita and Reza. Sa'id was quite busy with the conference, especially after Egon Kraus from West Germany and some other members who knew about his challenges and his role in the movement of music education in Iran, nominated him to become a member of the board of directors of the International Society for Music Education. It was exciting for us to see if he would get enough votes. In the evenings, if Gita and Reza were not tired, I took them to concerts given by the children and young adults from several countries. This was interesting for them since they were active in music. Sometimes Mary and Bell and their children also attended the concerts. We were hearing the best performances and samples of music for children and young adults around the world. In the last days after the 1977-1978, the board gave their report, the meeting turned to voting for the year of 1978-'79. After counting the vote, Sa'id was elected to the board. He was the only one from the Middle East. We were happy and proud that for the first time a representative from Iran had became a member of the board of directors.

After the conference, we all left to return to New York, and on the way, I made a short visit to Syracuse to meet with Dean Michael Marge to confirm the program and placement of our graduate students for the academic year 1978-1979 as we had agreed to. Then Mary and Bell took us to their home to rest for the night, and the next day, we flew to New York Airport to fly back to Tehran via London. We had to stop a few days for Gita to rest in London according to the doctor's recommendation. Christine kindly booked a hotel in central London so we could do some shopping for Gita. I remember the hotel was located near Oxford Street and Oxford Circus where most of the department stores were located and we could do our shopping easily.

During this journey, I had little or no time to hear or watch the news to see what was going on in Iran. Therefore, as soon as I saw a television set in our hotel room, although my husband and children as usual did not like to watch the news, I turned the TV to the BBC channel for news. It was August 27, 1978, and suddenly, we noticed the program began with shocking news from Iran. The Shah had changed prime minister Dr. Amuzegar and appointed in his place Jaafar Sharif-Emami, a graduate from a German technical school and known as an engineer and head of the Pahlavi Foundation with no experience in government and one of the most unqualified and unpopular politicians in Iran. Immediately, after the announcement, the BBC interviewed several leaders of the opposition, including Mr. Hedayat Matin Daftari. In the next days, the London newspapers analyzed the reasons for the change of government. Apparently, the new prime minister was the son of a mullah and was also related to one of the grand ayatollahs called Golpayegani, who organized the opposition. While we had been busy during the summer in the United States with Gita's surgery, there had been several strikes, demonstrations, and changes in government policies, which hurt certain groups like the Bazaaries, who had already been hit once before in the anti-inflation campaign. This group was hit again by another new government measure in 1978. The ministry of Social Security and Health announced "that insurance scheme covering industrial and office workers would now be extended to all employees in the distributive trades as well." Also, in addition to the BBC, finally with the backing of the Tudeh (Communist) party, Radio Baku started regularly teaching the techniques of demonstration, the production of Molotov cocktails and plastic bombs.[36] But the most horrible event occurred on August 18, when a fire broke out in the Rex Cinema in Abadan, while the people were watching a documentary on the Shah's achievements and then a film by Kimiaa' I. All the exit doors were locked and almost a thousand people were killed or injured. This horrible event shocked the Iranian people, and Khomeini's strong public relations blamed SAVAK and the Shah for this cruel action, and spreading this message through the BBC. Later it became clear that the fire was set by Abul Reza Asshur, a twenty-two-year-old Iraqi who was following Khomeini's order.[37] After hearing the news and reading the newspapers in London, on our way home to Iran, I became concerned about the possible erratic tendencies among impressionable individuals in Iran. I was worried that Gita might be caught up in a similar situation, and she could not defend herself wearing a body cast that was flammable. In a fire, she would most probably be one of first persons to die. In my pocket, I still had some traveler's checks remaining after we had paid all the hospital expenses. We immediately went with Gita to open an account for her in Barclay's Bank near Oxford Circus and our hotel and deposited all the money into her account in case she might need to leave the country soon. She would have some money, which she could use immediately. Then after a short visit with Christine and David in London, we flew back to Tehran while I worried about Gita. There were many vacant seats on the plane and Gita could rest. It looked as though not many people were going to Tehran compared to the year before when the planes were full of children returning home from school. That was the end of August 1978.

1. Parvin Merat Amini, *A Single Party State in Iran*, 1975-'78, Middle Eastern Studies Journal, vol. 38 No. 1, January 2002, pp. 131-168.

2. Ervand Abrahamian, *Tortured Confessions: Prisons and Public Recantations in Modern Iran*, Berkeley, Los Angeles, London: U. California Press, 1999, p. 114.

3. Mohammad Reza Shah Pahlavi, *Mission for My Country*, 1961, pages 321-325. No publisher given.

4. M.R.Pahlavi, *Answer to History,* New York: Stein & Day, 1980, p. 125.

5. HRH Ashraf Pahlavi, *Faces in a Mirror,* Englewood Cliffs: Prentice-Hall,1980. p. 195.

6. General Robert E. Huyser, *Mission To Tehran,* New York: Bessie/Harper, 1987. 1986 P. 64-75.

7. Amir Taheri, *Nest of Spies,* New York: Barnes & Noble, 1988, p. 75.

8. Jimmy Carter*: Keeping Faith: Memoirs of A President,* New York: Bantam Books. Inc. 1982, p. 441.

9. *Answer to History,* pp. 119-120.

10. Kenneth M. Pollack, *The Persian Puzzle,* P. 111.

11. Edward J. Riseborough, *Scoliosis and Other Deformities of the Axial Skeleton.* Boston: 1975.

12. Amir Taheri, *Nest of Spies,* 1988, p. 284 note 6.

13. Ervand Abrahamian, *Iran Between Two Revolutions,* 1982, p. 500-501.

14. Abbass Milani *The Persian Sphinx,* P. 281, 2000.

15. Amir Taheri, *Nest of Spies,* P. 80, 1988.

16. Ervand Abrahamian, *Iran Between two Revolutions,* 1982, P. 432.

17. *Nest of Spies,* 1988, p. 80.

18. Amir Taheri, *The Unknown Life of the Shah,* 1991, Hutchinson, p. 285-287.

19. Zbigniew Brzezinski, *Power and Principle,* New York: Farrar, Strauss, Giroux, 1983, p. 363.

20. *Nest of Spies*, p. 76.

21. *Nest of Spies*, p. 284.

22. Nikki R. Keddie, *Roots Of Revolution,* 1981, p. 241.

23. J. Matini, The Journal of Iranshenassi, 1993, No. 4, and 1994, No.2

24. William H. Sullivan, *Mission to Iran,* 1981, p. 121.

25. *Mission to Iran*, p. 126

26. *Mission to Iran*, p. 128 and Cyrus Vance, *Hard Choice*, 1983, pp. 322-323.

27. Amir Taheri, *The Spirit of Allah*. Bethesda, MD, Adler & Adler, 1979 pp. 215-216.

28. "William H. Sullivan. *Mission To Iran*, 1981, p. 23.

29. *Power And Principle*, p. 355.

30. Jimmy Carter, *Keeping Faith*, p. 449-450

31. Cyrus Vance, *Hard Choice,* 1983, P. 314-333.

32. *The Spirit of Allah*, 1985, pp. 170-174.

33. Abbas Milani, *Persian Sphinx*, 2000, p. 285/6.

34. Ervand Abrahimian, *Between Two Revolutions,* 1982, p. 507)

35. Margaret Thatcher, *The Path to Power*, pp. 380-2.

36. *The Spirit of Allah*, p. 218.

37. *The Spirit of Allah*, p. 225.

CHAPTER 14

Sliding into the
Middle of Iran's Revolution
1978-1979

With some trepidation, we arrived in Tehran and as usual in the middle of the night. I could not sleep the rest of the night. I took some Cafergot for my headache, with strong coffee, and drove to my office in the college early that morning to see what was going on at the college and to find out more about the current politics of the country and to find out what had happened during the summer holidays. I noticed a change at the school. The executive director of the office of Empress Farah, Dr. Hushang Nahavandi, had become the minister of Science and Higher Education in the new government of Prime Minister Sharif-Emami. In my position as the advisor to the office of the empress, I had known him as the former executive director of the Office of the Empress. In fact, in the previous year, he had established a large group, made up of specialists, to study the problems facing the country—the *Barressi Massael Iran Group* (Iranian Problems Study Group). Now, in his new position, he had become an important member of the board of trustees of our college. I called his office immediately and made an appointment to see him and brief him on our college, our activities, and our international exchange programs, which he may not have been familiar with. Fortunately, he was able to see me quite quickly, so I met with him in his old office, and not at the ministry. I told him about my trip during the summer vacation, my daughter's surgery, and my visit to Syracuse University. I also told him about my husband's election as a member of the board of directors of the International Society of Music Education, the first time an Iranian had been elected to this position. I then asked him about the political events of the summer. I wanted to gather this information so that I could take it into account as I made decisions for the new academic year. Staring at me with a strange expression, he told me that the academic year might start with some delay. Then he said regretfully that it is a pity that I, as a woman, would have to be ready for many changes. I asked him if these changes were preventable. With the same stare, he replied, "I hope it is not too late." To be absolutely sure of the situation, I asked him if it was now too late to prevent changes in the status of women. He replied, "It might be too late." So I realized that with my responsibilities, I was trapped in a difficult situation for the coming year. I would need to be very alert at the college, and I needed to pay particular attention to our daughter, Gita, both at home and at her school. While I was driving home, this warning and the conversation kept playing over and over in my mind. I thought back to the student who had sat in my office and who had predicted that I would soon lose the freedom to choose what to wear and what to think.

A week later, we received an official letter from the ministry that all the universities and colleges would start the academic year two weeks later than usual. In a way, I was happy that I had enough time to prepare for any unrest or strike by the students, who usually reacted to any social and political issues quickly before other groups could respond. In the meantime, I met with all the recipients of scholarships to Syracuse University. They were very excited and happy about this opportunity to continue their education. I told them that I went to Syracuse before leaving the USA to check on their housing arrangements as well as their academic program. I assured them that everything was in order and Syracuse University was looking forward to welcoming them. I wished them a happy and successful journey. So they left Iran in the hope of finishing their programs and then returning to the college to teach. The country had a shortage of educated manpower, especially in our areas of study at Shemiran College.

I also noticed that several members of my family, friends, and colleagues had sold their houses and left the country due to the unrest experienced over the summer. In fact, a real estate friend came to our house and offered to sell our house for 3 million US dollars. I told him that it had taken us about three years to build the house for our personal use and did not wish to sell it at this time. He looked at us and said, "I thought you are coming from the USA, and you would be better informed about the situation in Iran." Of course, he did not know about our anxiety and preoccupation with Gita's surgery and that we had been so consumed with caring for her that we did not have any time left to follow the news and the politics while we were in the US. We told him that we were not interested in selling our house. So we continued our routine work every day with increased tension. The new government of Sharif-Emami had taken a conciliatory approach, which was considered as a sign of the Shah's weakness by the opposition.

Examples of this weakness became patently clear when the yearly Shiraz Art Festival, under the leadership of the empress, was cancelled and the Islamic calendar year of 1357 replaced the Royal calendar of 2537, a concession to the Khomeini forces. The government closed all casinos, censored some films, and prohibited nightclubs and restaurants from serving alcohol. Guerilla fighters that were trained in different camps such as the camps of Al Fatah in Lebanon or others in Cuba, South Yemen, Libya, and Algeria were allowed to return to Tehran. After the revolution, several of these fighters became key officers in the oil ministry, the military and other important facets of the Khomeini's regime. Furthermore, in the name of "national reconciliation" the government released political prisoners like Ayatollah Hussein-Ali Montazeri, who joined the opposition. We became eye witnesses to many events and unrests throughout September, which negatively affected our daily life, especially while driving my two children in heavy traffic, with Gita carrying a flammable cast on half of her body.

In September 1978, the president of China was in Iran for an official state visit. I remember seeing this on TV. At the official dinner, he spoke in support of our country and praised its independence. I believe that was the last official visit to Iran by a head of a state before the revolution. This visit was during a short break of unrest in the country. Those days were at the end of the fasting month of Ramezan (Ramadan). Usually people would celebrate at the end of the month and at the beginning of the new month. On Thursday, September 7, the Eid of Fitr, after the early-morning group prayers, several ayatollahs and the leaders of the National Front and the non-religious groups like Tudeh Party (Communist or Marxist groups) called for a demonstration on the main streets of Tehran. I heard this as I was listening, as usual, to the BBC early-morning news. Because of this, we did not go out, and since it was a holiday, we all stayed home. It was estimated that there were between one hundred and two hundred thousand participants in the demonstration. The pictures of Khomeini were carried in the streets, and people kept chanting against corruption and denouncing the Shah. We heard all this on the radio, particularly through the foreign stations. I constantly held a shortwave radio in my hands and searched the channels for details of the demonstration. The details varied quite substantially. Some demonstrators decided to have another demonstration the next day, which was a Friday, and a regular holiday weekend. This demonstration took place at Jaleh Square, near the Community School my children attended. After this demonstration, the government imposed martial law in Tehran and twenty-three other cities. Martial law was to begin at midnight of September 7 and was announced by radio and television, interrupting their regular programming, and repeating the message several times about the imposition of martial law. All gatherings of more than five people were banned, but at the same time, the army was told not to make any arrests should there be any violations of this law. The next day, on Friday, September 8, early in the morning near Jaleh Square, a small group began to gather for a meeting and a demonstration. Obviously, they had not heard the news of the suddenly imposed martial law. I remember that when I heard the news, I was happy that the schools and colleges were closed on Friday as usual, but also worried in case there would be a clash between the army and the people, especially since the army was most likely not trained in negotiation or equipped to handle opposition or unrest of the local people. The troops were guarding the Parliament buildings and the surrounding streets including Jaleh Street about a mile away from the people. Through their bullhorns, the troops ordered the crowd to disperse and reminded them of the martial law, but most of the people in the crowd were unaware that martial law had been imposed. Gradually, the soldiers came face-to-face with the crowd. Apparently, first, they smiled and were friendly to the crowd who listened and began to scatter when suddenly some motorcyclists drove into the troop's formation while shouting "Allah is the greatest." The inexperienced troops reacted nervously and began to fire, killing several riders. Then, the demonstrators returned and charged the troops. Suddenly, someone shouted over a bullhorn that the troops facing the people were Israelis. The soldiers were in fact Kurdish, but because of their dialect, they were mistaken for Israelis. "Massacre the Jews!" thundered the bullhorn, and some snipers began firing from the water department building on the square."[1] By the time the crowd had been dispersed; several people from both sides were dead. According to the government, the number of the dead was 191; 70 from the army and 121 demonstrators, among whom were some Palestinians. But the opposition spread rumors that the number was much higher, ranging from 200 to 4,000. However, Ervand Abrahamian writes that, "Whatever the true figures, September 8 became known as Black Friday and left a permanent mark on Iran's reputation. It placed a sea of blood between the Shah and the people. It inflamed public emotions, radicalized the population . . . Undermined moderation . . . in short, Black Friday ended the possibility of gradual reform and left the country with two simple choices: a drastic revolution or a military counter revolution."[2] After Black Friday, we were anxious about sending our children, especially Gita, because of her flammable cast, to the Community School near Jaleh. We were also expecting several strikes throughout the country. From this point on, the school was often closed because of the uncertainty of the situation. We heard about the strikes from the BBC and other news agencies. Therefore, we decided to send Gita to a private boarding school in the United States for the next school year. We chose Boston because Gita's surgeon was also in Boston. Since her grades were good at the International Community School, I was optimistic that she would be accepted to Phillips Academy in Andover, which was very competitive and had a very good reputation in all aspects of education, since many of its students eventually assumed leadership positions. In fact, many members of the Kennedy and Bush families graduated from that high school. But I also applied to other private independent schools like Exeter and Concord just in case she did not get accepted by Phillips Academy. All these schools required personal interviews. Since Gita and I had an appointment with Dr. Riseborough the first week of January 1979, I arranged her interviews during that time. We were hoping that despite the political atmosphere that we were experiencing, she could finish eighth grade in Tehran and start high school in the United States.

Immediately, after September 8, Black Friday, a wave of strikes began by the oil refinery workers throughout several cities, demanding higher wages. Sharif Emami and his government, following his national reconciliation policy and for the sake of changing public opinion that had turned against the government and the Shah, asked for the resignations of several ministers and other government officials. He even sent some to jail on charges of corruption. Later, he continued to ask the Shah for the resignation of the minister of Court, Mr. Hoveyda (the former prime minister for thirteen years), and the director of the National Iranian Radio and Television, Mr. Reza Ghotbi, the first cousin of the empress.

These must have been very confusing times for the Shah. He met every other day with the American ambassador Sullivan and the British ambassador Anthony Parsons for long, discursive discussions, during which the Shah would go over the options he saw for his regime.[3] In the meantime, it seemed that the United States was not paying much attention to Iran. President Carter was very busy with the process of his Camp David Summit and actively involved with the Arab-Israeli relations. Apparently, the news of September 8 came to the immediate attention of President Anwar Sadat of Egypt who was a close friend of the Shah. Sadat called the Shah to express his sympathy and offer his support. President Carter also called on Sunday, September 10 (between 7:56 and 8:02 a.m.) and expressed his friendship, support, and concern about the events of September 8, wishing him success in resolving these problems and success in the implementation of reform, and even supporting his military action.[4] The news about President Carter's telephone call was not welcomed by the people of Iran, who wanted to have an independent country and an independent Shah; and again the opposition groups, especially the Communist groups, used this action of President Carter as an excuse to oppose the Shah on the grounds that he was an agent of the USA, publicizing this message widely. In addition, rumors about the Shah's medical problems were now circulating, especially because of his erratic behavior and decision making during recent years. But nobody, including himself, knew that he was suffering from an aggressive and serious disease. As I described and documented previously, from 1973 on, the Shah's private physicians, for unknown reasons, were hiding his illness from everyone, including himself. As Dr. David Owen describes in his lecture and article, "it may be that the Shah was diseased, demented, and depressed because he was suffering from

Lymphocytic Leukaemia."[5] Because of the uncertainty and insecurity surrounding the political situation, a number of people began to transfer their money out of the country. On September 18, the Central Bank published a long list of prominent people, including Sharif Emami himself, and the director of the National Iranian Oil Company, who had transferred millions of dollars to other countries. A natural disaster on September 16—an earthquake in Tabas, added to the political unrest, although the immediate visit of the Shah to the disaster site was well received by the people, but later, Mr. Sharif Emami made a very strange decision without notifying the Shah. He announced that the opposition and the religious groups (mullahs) would take responsibility for handling the affairs of the earthquake victims.[6] I also remember well that when many of the volunteers of the charity of the Empress Farah, of which I was a member, came to the site of the earthquake to help orphaned children, they were surprised to see how well organized the mullahs were. The mullahs were much more organized than the Red Cross and the government. At that time, we could not believe that the prime minister gave this responsibility to the mullahs and religious groups of the opposition. This issue again influenced public opinion against the Shah. The Shah still had several good opportunities to influence public opinion in his favor on September 20 and 21. He could have spoken at the opening of the Parliament or the commencement of the military school and universities to restore calm and order, but he kept quiet. Later on, we followed his speeches eagerly in the hope that something good would happen.

We also learned later that after Black Friday, an Iraqi Airline on an unscheduled flight landed at Mehrabad airport with one passenger, Barzan Takriti, half-brother of Saddam Hussein and the chief of secret police of Iraq. He had brought a message from his brother Saadam for the Shah, indicating his support and offering to eliminate Khomeini in Najaf. "The Shah, expressing his gratitude for President Hussein's concern and offer of help, ruled out any suggestion of organizing an 'unfortunate accident' for Khomeini. Instead, he asked the Iraqis to force the ayatollah to leave their country. Barzan instantly agreed."[7] So Khomeini was ordered to leave Iraq immediately. Khomeini's followers like Ibrahim Yazdi, Ghotbzadeh, and Bani Sadar first approached the Muslim countries near Iraq, like Kuwait, to secure a visa for Khomeini, but they were not successful. Then, in October, they learned they could accommodate him in France, near Paris, in the village of Neauphle-le-Chateau. As a result of being in France, Khomeini had a greater exposure to the international media and newspapers and Paris was better suited for the public relations of the opposition. From the Parisian suburb, the ayatollah gave 132 radio, television and press interviews during his four-month stay. He issued some fifty declarations, which were quickly published and distributed (as cassette tapes) in Tehran. He also addressed a total of one hundred thousand Iranians who came at an average rate of over a thousand each day to pray with him, hear him speak, or kiss his hands. Many brought with them cash gifts.[8] So the Shah's decision to have Khomeini leave Iraq proved to be a fatal mistake. In the last days of September and beginning of October, there was an increasing wave of strikes among workers who were demanding economic and political concessions according to the call of Khomeini, not only through the BBC but also through several other media outlets. We heard messages from him hourly, and some of his messages and interviews were recorded and reproduced by the thousands in a studio in Tehran, by order of his friends Ayatollah Motaharry and Ayotollah Montazeri. Ayatollah Motahari was also teaching at the University of Tehran, in the School of Religious Studies, where our friend Dr. Arianpour was teaching philosophy and sociology. They were in constant disagreement according to several statements made by Dr. Arianpour and his students during our mountain climbing trips on Fridays. Another friend of Ayatollah Khomeini, M. H. Beheshti and some of the National Front movement leaders like Bazargan and Sanjabi collected more than 230 million rials in donations for Khomeini from the Bazaar, the backbone of Tehran economy and the people. Others like Yazdi and Chamran provided security in Khomeini's home.

On October 26, the Shah's birthday, several of our faculty members and I received the usual invitation to attend the Salaam ceremony of the Shah's fifty-ninth birthday at the Golestan Palace. This was something we did not want to miss, especially since we were all curious and anxious to see and hear what was going on throughout the country. In this Salaam, which turned out to be the Shah's last Salaam, many high-ranking government personnel were absent. But among academic groups, there were few absentees and almost all the university and college presidents were present. First, Dr. Abbollah Shaibani, the president of the University of Tehran's oldest higher learning institution, started with a long congratulatory statement and then the Shah made his round, and as usual, he stopped in front of each university or college representatives. When he came in front of our college group, he looked more tired and bitter than at any time I had ever seen him. After I expressed my best wishes on behalf of the college, he left the hall with a bitter smile, as if he knew that it was the last time he would see an audience on his birthday. This turned out to be the only ceremony on his birthday for that year, as the annual afternoon ceremony at the large stadium was canceled due to security reasons.

While Khomeini's campaign was picking up strength and the ongoing crisis was deepening, the Shah was mired in internal and external conflicts, and his position was changing back and forth, due either to his sickness or the deep division in US policy toward Iran or both. On one hand, he was wearing his iron glove and extending martial law to other cities, even ordering the army to take over the major newspapers; but on the other hand, he was continuing his *liberalization* policy and the *national reconciliation* through the government of Sharif Emami. He freed more than a thousand political prisoners, including Ayatollah Taleghani and leaders of the Tudeh party (Communist). He ended the censorship of the press and dissolved the Resurgence Party, which had caused so much discontent. The people of Iran, including my colleagues, friends, relatives, and I were quite perplexed and quietly and carefully were watching the news to see which way the country is going so we could make our short-term decisions as we were unable to make plans for the long-term future. For the short term, every morning before sending my children to school and going to the college, I listened to the BBC and other media very closely to help me make decisions concerning my personal and college responsibilities. It was not an easy task. Some days, the school was closed, because of the demonstrations and the school buses were not running. We were worried more for Gita because she was wearing her flammable cast. On and off, we had irregular closings at the college and the university. Sa'id still gave music lessons at the palace school, although Prince Reza was out of the country. Mme. Diba still held her board meeting of the empress's charity at her palace in Saadabad, although she kept the radio nearby for the news. I remember our last meeting because we discussed the situation of the orphaned children after the Tabas earthquake. Nobody would ever think that in this battle, Iran, with its well-equipped army, rated sixth in the world, could not handle the riots and the street disturbances. The fact was that the army did not have proper training in handling street riots by the Iranian people who were not their enemies. At the end of October and beginning of November, the BBC kept announcing that Khomeini had called for a general demonstration. As a result, on November 4 and 5, we had demonstrations, riots, and violence everywhere: in universities, banks, and movie theaters. The British embassy was briefly overrun, the schools and colleges were closed, and students joined the rest of the demonstrators on the street on that day. I immediately got permission to take two-weeks leave for Gita's January 4 appointment at the Children's Hospital in Boston. It was difficult, but we managed to book our departure air tickets for the end of December. Interestingly enough, Gita was more worried about missing school and falling behind in her studies.

On November 2, 1978, apparently, the US ambassador Sullivan secretly warned the United States that the Shah's regime might be in jeopardy. Sullivan reported on a meeting with the Shah on November 1, during which the Shah shared his thoughts and conflicts about changing his ineffective civilian government to a military one. He even spoke about "abdication" and asked for guidance from Washington. Brzezinski immediately took the issue to the Special Coordinating Committee (the SCC) for crisis management. Considering the long-standing deep divisions in the policy issues with the US State Department and Iran, Brezinski sent the following message:

1. The United States supports the Shah without reservation in the present crisis.
2. We have confidence in the Shah's judgment regarding the specific decision that may be needed concerning the form and composition of his government; we also recognize the need for decisive action and leadership to restore order.
3. That once order and authority have been restored, we hope that he will resume prudent efforts to promote liberalization and to eradicate corruption.[9]

Since Brezinski had no faith that Ambassador Sullivan would accurately communicate the message to the Shah, he made a phone call to the Shah to give the president's message. At that time, a rumor was already circulating about a change of the civilian government to a military government, and that the Shah would appoint a hard-liner military officer, General Oveyssi, to establish the government and to settle the unrest throughout the country.

Finally, on November 6, after a long silence and absence from public appearance, the Shah spoke on television and radio in an address to the people of Iran. We eagerly and anxiously heard and watched his message. His statement was surprising. He was extremely apologetic to the people, and he even said that he had heard their voice of revolution. In order to settle the unrest and restore peace and order in the country, he announced the appointment of the mild-mannered, unmotivated, and retiring General Gholam Reza Azhari (instead of the hard-liner General Oveyssi) to establish a temporary government. This message was very surprising to me and my colleagues, especially with his selection of a passive and aging general. The Shah read his message from a text with little direct eye contact with the people, using the word *revolution* in his text. : "I heard your voice of revolution." In this speech, we heard for the first time the word of revolution from our king. Up to then, the people were speaking about unrest, and not revolution. But after this message, the people spoke with ease about the revolution and the opposition groups considered the Shah's apologetic speech as a weakness. While the Shah was reading his message, he looked as if he was not himself, as if he had never even seen the text of his speech before.

After the Shah's speech, with the announcement of the military government, we had a few quiet days in Tehran. Dr. Dorothy Robin Mowry, the US cultural attaché, and Dr. Carolyn Spatta, the president of Damavand College, gathered in our home a day or two after the speech. It was an interesting gathering and a day to remember. Dr. Mowry wanted to know my reaction to the speech, and I eagerly wanted to know how they evaluated our situation from the US point of view, especially as I was taking Gita to Boston. When I told them that throughout our history, Britain had been influencing religious groups for their own interests in oil and other resources in Iran and how, in reality the BBC was working for Khomeini and his followers, they laughed. That was our last meeting together in Iran until sometime after the revolution. The next time we saw each other was at the International Club in Washington DC in 1979.

On November 8, Hoveyda, the former prime minister for thirteen years, and many former government officials, including Nasiri, the former chief of SAVAK were arrested as scapegoats for their past policies and actions.

On November 9, 1978, the US ambassador William Sullivan sent his famous cable entitled "Thinking the Unthinkable,"[10] in which, "he cautiously but seriously indicated that the United States had best begin preparing contingency plans in case the Shah did not survive politically."[11] In his very interesting book, James Bill analyzes how deeply the State Department, the National Security Advisor, Department of Defense, Central Intelligence Agency, and Department of Energy with several advisors of the Carter administration were involved in the formation of Iran policy and how deeply they were in conflict within themselves and with each other.[12] As a result, President Carter's task became complicated by the sheer amount of conflicting advice he was receiving, causing frustration for him and the Shah who himself was receiving conflicting advice, and was looking to the USA for support but in return was receiving conflicting messages. These unresolved and conflicting advice caused frustration and hastened the collapse of the political system of Iran. As a consequence, the people of Iran, including myself, became entangled within the chain of conflicting messages and vacillating actions of the government at all levels of the country.

In this tense and unsettled atmosphere, the presidents of all universities and colleges received an important invitation through the ministry of Higher Education to attend a meeting to hear the Prime Minister Azhari's speech. This was the first time that we had received a message from the prime minister. So I eagerly attended this meeting to see what was going on in the country, where we were, and the direction in which the country was heading. At this meeting, there were many university and college presidents and vice presidents. I sat in the front row next to Dr. Abdullah Sheibani, the president of the University of Tehran, the oldest and the largest university of Iran. Historically, the bulk of the student unrests and strikes started at that university. Before the meeting, I asked Dr. Sheibani about the rumors of the unrest in that university, including the incident of November 4, when the students wanted to pull down the Shah's statue. It was a serious clash between the army and students, which he confirmed. Certainly in this political climate, I had sympathy for his position, and I did not ask him any further questions. As soon as General Azhari started to speak, everybody became extremely quiet and attentive.

He began by speaking about a variety of issues; his temporary position, a media war, the interest of the oil companies of the West and East, the issue of the Cold War, and their collective competition to influence the several opposition groups, their success through strong public relations, and a psychological warfare through the media against Iran. He then said that if it were not too late, he hoped that with the army's help, he would be able to open the road for an elected government. As soon as he mentioned that, he hoped his efforts were not late, Dr. Sheibani whispered in my ear, "In that case, you should not be worried because of your ancestral lineage to both Prophet Mohammad and an old Persian king." I smiled and wondered how he knew about my ancestry. We kept listening attentively to the prime minister and wondered how he could bring order to the country. He looked too mild and unmotivated for a person in his position. The meeting, which was held in the evening, finished after several questions from the audience to which the general responded cautiously, and the meeting had to conclude to allow us to reach home before 9:00 p.m. because of the curfew. This was a memorable and important and multifaceted event in my life. It provided information about the political issues the country was grappling with, it affected the running of the college as well as impacting on my personal life and family responsibilities. In the next few days, I was very careful of reactions within the college, watched the news continually, and listened to BBC.

In the meantime, Sanjabi and Bazargan, leaders of the National Front and the Liberation Movement, went to Paris to visit Khomeini there, and when they returned to Tehran, they changed their former position for the implementation of the original constitutional monarchy. Instead, they called for a referendum for a regime change to an Islamic government and advocated and prepared their followers for the eventual regime change. As a result, Sanjabi was arrested, and from November 12 onward, the bazaaris, and the university and college students went on strike. On November 16, the oil workers also joined the strike, which hampered the oil production. Violent demonstrations and strikes spread throughout November in Iran.[13] In this politically charged atmosphere, I had to respond constantly to the questions posed by the students and the faculty in our meetings. The most frequently asked question from both groups was whether or not we were going to have classes. In general, my advice was that the classes should continue and we as administrators should be available at all time. Both groups were also in deep conflict. With respect to academic freedom, I told students in the school council and my colleagues that it would be better to be available in classes and, to use their own judgment, in their teaching, review the previously covered subjects, or respond to student's questions. As a result during all the unrests, all college staff were available and our college was one of the last to join the strikes. This was so conspicuous that on a day when there were strikes everywhere, the daily morning newspaper *Ayandegan* used the following as its headline: EVEN SHEMIRAN COLLEGE JOINED THE STRIKES. I was worried that the students might not be able to finish the term in December.

Muharram, the Muslim religious month, especially for the Shi'a sect of Islam, fell in the month of December in 1978, and the demonstrations became more violent and intense. This month always reminds me how every year my father, who was in charge of a trust for his aunt Mrs. Afifedoleh, would arrange a religious gathering in our home with dinner for the needy families, in memory of the martyrdom of Imam Hossein, according to the trust. Later, when my father died, my brother was in charge, and after his death, his son Massud. Due to the increased red tape and bureaucracy, Massud transferred the trust to the government to be free of the responsibility. So during this time, my family did not have this responsibility anymore, and the country was commemorating the martyrdom of Imam Hussein, the prophet Muhammad's grandson, who was killed brutally in the seventh century in Karbala. The opposition took advantage of the time, and in the beginning of December for three days, during the day, they had demonstrations; and during the night, because of the curfew, people went on the roof of their homes and shouted *Allah'o Akbar* "God is Great," and the opposition leaders called for a general strike. Every night from our home in Velenjack, we heard the chant of *Allah'o Akbar, Allah'o Akbbar* repeatedly, loud like a large chorus. Later, I was told that the oraganizers used simultaneous tape recordings of the same chant, which made the chorus much more impressive. Even when the windows were closed, we still could hear this repeated and forceful chant, like a cannon, the eerie and fearful sound of the people's voices in unison. At the same time, thousands of people wearing white shrouds to show their readiness for death would break the curfew and march in the streets. Undoubtedly, there were several clashes with the army and several hundreds were killed.

For the final days of the mourning period on the observance of *Tassua and Ashura* (religious holidays) on the December 11 and 12 of 1978, Khomeini announced through the BBC that people should ignore the curfew set by the military government and march on the streets.

As a result, the government was forced to lift the ban and even freed more than four hundred political prisoners as a gesture of reconciliation. During *Ashura and Tassua*, very large rallies of peasants marched down the streets of Tehran led by Ayatollah Taleghani and Ayatollah Montazeri, leaders of the opposition. Although the leaders of the rallies tried not to authorize chants against the Shah, the radical groups like Fedaian, Mojahedin, and pro-Communists (Tudeh) carried anti-Shah banners like "Death to the Shah, the American Puppet" and similar slogans. The rally ended in the Shahyad Aryamehr Square and the crowd ratified the change of the regime from a monarchy to an Islamic government by endorsing the leadership of Khomeini. The two days of incessant rallies demonstrated the military government's weakness. The students of the college told me that many soldiers were defecting and leaving the army and later reports showed that this was indeed true. Practically every day, we had demonstrations, unrest, and strikes. The Shah noticed that his choice of a military government was not a good one and wanted to replace it with an opposition leader that the people would accept and who would be able to establish a unity government. There were several candidates for the position of prime minister, among them Dr. Gholam-Hossein Sadighi from the National Front, a former minister of the Interior under Dr. Mossadegh, who incidentally was my former professor of sociology at the University of Tehran. While at college, Dr. Gholam-Hossein Sadighi had given me one of highest grades with a complimentary note that had made me very proud. I mused that since he was a very serious, detail-oriented person and popular among the people he might be able to help Iran if his requests were met. Apparently, after pondering the matter for a week, he accepted the assignment with only one condition—that the Shah should not leave the country—and because this condition was against the recommendations of both the ambassadors of the United States and Britain, it fell through. So here again the Shah did not value a nationalist's opinion and instead followed the suggestion of foreign ambassadors. Subsequently, Mr. Mozaffar Baghai was unsuccessful for the same reason.

During these uncertain times, off and on, both Gita and Reza were still going to school. It was quite interesting to see their homework. I remember well that Reza wrote in one of his papers that the Shah and Khomeini were both good. The poor child, who was seeing and hearing two different views and chantings on the street, wanted to come up with a compromise in his mind to satisfy the unknown opinion of the people of his school and surroundings in order to protect himself.

Fortunately, we did finish the first term of the college, although with difficulty. My daughter and I had to leave the country at the end of December to be in Boston for Gita's appointment with her surgeon in January. Reza and Sa'id stayed in Iran. Since it was rumored that due to the unrest, her school might be closed in 1979 and also because of uncertainty about her back problem, I took Gita's report cards with us and decided to travel by way of Los Angeles where Gita's twin cousins Mona and Neda were going to school.

So in the last week of December, we flew to Los Angeles. The plane was packed—without a single vacant seat. It was a strange atmosphere. Most of the passengers were showing anxiety and uncertainty in their expressions and most probably were thinking about their destiny and what would happen to the country and the regime. I remember well that, because of the fog, the plane could not land in Los Angeles, and we landed in San Francisco instead where we stayed one night at a Holiday Inn. The next day, we flew to Los Angeles. At the airport, we were met by Mona and Neda and the aunt they were living with. They arranged for us to visit Disneyland, Universal Studios and some private boarding schools. All these visits were interesting for Gita, and for a few days, she could forget her pains of her body and her soul. We kept watching the news anxiously.

Throughout 1978, President Carter was receiving conflicting advice from his secretary of state, Cyrus Vance; his ambassador to Iran, William Sullivan; his National Security advisor, Zbigniew Brzezinski; his secretary of defense, Harold Brown; and the head of CIA, Stanfield Turner about what to do about Iran. Finally, after long discussions, President Carter sent a cable to the Shah, which reflected his indecisive, conflicting mind. This cable sent on December 28, 1978, was the last one he sent to the Shah.[14] The cable recommended strongly that "(1) the Shah should end his vacillation and act; (2) a civilian government that could restore stability was preferable; but (3) if that was impossible, the Shah should appoint a firm military government that would end the disorder and violence; and (4) if none of these options was feasible, the Shah should consider establishing a Regency Council (i.e., stepping down from the throne in favor of his son) to supervise the current military government."[15] The Shah, who did not want to show his iron fist and order a crackdown on the opposition, ended martial law, and I heard on the news that he appointed Shapour Bakhtiar also from the National Front as prime minister to form a government and this time with the condition that the Shah would leave the country. He also appointed the Regency Council members. In this way, he wanted to avoid the bloodshed and civil war.

On New Year's Eve 1979, we flew from Los Angeles to Boston, and with the disturbing news about our country, we went straight to our room in the Boston Sheraton Hotel and sat in our beds watching the news on TV until we fell asleep; this ended up being a terrible night for us. Because of the New Year's Eve celebration, the hotel was extremely noisy, and we were awakened several times during the night, with the sound of the fire alarm, which young people were setting off as a joke. Because of the flammable cast that Gita was wearing, each time the alarm rang, we jumped up and ran out of the room; we did that many times that night. That was really an unforgettably awful and unnerving New Year for us. The next day, New Year's day, we rested in the morning and talked about Gita's upcoming hospital visit and her interview at the Phillips Academy in Andover, Concord, and other schools planned for the coming days. In the afternoon, our kind friend, Doris May, came to pick us up for dinner at her home.

The first week of January 1979, we had several appointments for Gita. First, we went to the Children's Hospital to meet her surgeon, Dr. Riseborough "Ted," with the hope that if everything was ok with her spine, the horrible cast she had worn for six months could be taken off. This would be an important moment in her life and for our family. On that day, after the x-ray, Ted came to us with the good news that her back was in good shape and the cast could be taken off. I cannot begin to describe the extent of our happiness at hearing that news. Gita was beside herself with joy as they took off her cast. We thanked God for the wonderful work Ted had done on Gita's back. After his office visit, we met his wife, Jennifer, who also worked at the hospital, and we had lunch together and celebrated the removal of the cast and Gita's good health. At lunch, Ted brought up the issue of political unrest in Iran, saying he was sorry to learn that his colleague, our former minister of health, Dr. SheikholIslamzadeh, was in jail. Dr. Sheikholislamzadeh had introduced him to us and that is how we had come to Boston in the first place. He was happy to hear that Gita was interviewing for high schools in Boston because this allowed him to follow up on her progress. At that point, we had no intention of letting Gita stay for the current school year in Boston. The school interviews were for the following year—ninth grade—and we were hoping that she could finish eighth grade at the International Community School in Tehran.

After lunch, I took Gita who was very happy not to have the cast anymore to a department store to buy some clothes. It was interesting to see how she eagerly wanted to have some trousers and slacks, which she had not been able to wear with the cast or the Boston corset. In fact, she did not want to wear a dress for her interviews either, choosing to wear trousers instead. Then, we returned to our hotel to rest and prepare for the following days of interviews at Phillips Academy in Andover, Concord, and other schools. These schools already had her report card and recommendations from her teachers, which I had sent from Tehran. The interview was the last requirement to complete her application. All these interviews went very well due to her enthusiasm and happy mood. Because of the successful surgery, she was radiant in her interviews. After each interview, school authorities showed us the campus of the school. Gita liked Phillips Academy campus the best. All said we would be notified in a month or two, before the school year finished, whether she was accepted.

Every day I read the *Boston Globe* and followed closely the international news where Iran was always the top news story, and it was not promising. One day, just by chance, in the Boston Sheraton, I peeked through an open door to a conference room where former president Gerald Ford was speaking at the podium. I entered the room quietly and heard him talk about the Guadeloupe Economic Summit. He was criticizing their decisions and the Carter administration's policy on Iran and the Shah. Not knowing what was happening throughout the country, I stood and listened to him. His speech and all the news showed how extremely unsettled conditions inside Iran were, and of course, I was worried for my daughter, my family, the college, the students, and the people of Iran. I left the conference hall, bought several newspapers and, in this worried state, went to the hotel room to join Gita, who was watching TV. I eagerly read the newspapers, which were full of bad news about Iran.

During the time that we had been away from Iran, the end of December 1978 and beginning of January 1979, the news showed that since there was little confidence in the legitimacy of the government of Iran, the new prime minister, Dr. Bakhtiar, had to struggle to even form a cabinet. However, according to the memoir of President Carter, behind the scenes, Ambassador Sullivan "insisted that we [America] should give support to Khomeini, even if it meant weakening Bakhtiar and the coalition government he was trying to form"[16] In his book, Carter states that Ambassador Sullivan was recommending opposing the plan to support the Shah and insisting instead on the immediate departure of the Shah and promoting establishment of friendly alliance with Khomeini. During that time, Carter was very interested in an assessment of the Shah's military strength, and because Sullivan seemed unable to provide that, the President ordered General Robert Huyser, deputy commander of the United States Forces in Europe, to carry out this assignment in Iran. Then on January 4, 1979, President Carter went to Guadeloupe, a French possession since the seventeenth century (1635) in the Caribbean Sea, to attend the G-7 Economic Summit.

This economic summit of the seven major industrial democracies, which meets in a different location each year, was originally intended to deal with economic issues, but political issues always have also been discussed, first informally and gradually formally as well. Apparently on January 4, President Carter went to Guadeloupe to meet with the leaders of France (Giscard D'Estaing), Great Britain (James Callaghan) and Germany (Helmuth Schmidt). These leaders, especially Giscard D'Estaing, had little support for the Shah, but all agreed that the military should be kept strong and united.[17] Unfortunately, documents of the meeting are still not available for the public to access. It is still not known who supported the Shah and who supported Khomeini at this summit. Hopefully, this will become clear in the near future. However, the decision in this summit played a crucial role in the destiny of Iran, its people, and the world. What began as a breeze in 1979 has now, after thirty years, become a raging storm that they all have to deal with.

While following the news daily, we prepared to return to Iran. Then one day, I read a report in the *Boston Globe* that, amid the unrest and strikes in Tehran, the American schools were closed, including the International Community School. We were both shocked to read this news. Gita, who, until that moment, was enjoying herself and still on the high of a cast-free holiday, started to cry loudly and said that she would lose one year of school because she could not finish her eighth grade. She said she would be one year behind even if she were accepted for the next year to the Phillips Academy. Since she was not going to be able to complete her eighth grade, she would not be able to start her high school. While I was trying to calm her down, I made several calls to Tehran, to Doris, and to the schools where she had interviewed, seeking advice to find a solution to prevent her from losing a year of school. Most of the schools we had interviewed had no openings or vacancies in their boarding school at that time. They recommended that I find another school for her for the rest of that academic year. So, after a long search, we found a boarding school near the home of our friend Doris May in Boston, which had an opening. Walnut Hill School was a private day and boarding school for girls ages thirteen to eighteen, which also offered intensive training in writing, music, ballet, theater, and visual arts. (Later on, the school became coeducational.) The school was near Wellesley and, in fact, had been founded in 1893 by Wellesley College graduates Florence Bigelow and Charlotte Conant and was at the forefront of education for young women. Considering the increasing riots and strikes in Iran, I called Sa'id, who was experiencing the chaotic environment in Tehran firsthand, and he and I decided that Gita should stay and attend that school. This was a very painful decision. Gita was going to be separated from us for the first time, and we were all very upset, but kind-hearted Doris told me that I should not be worried and assured me that she would check on Gita and see to the follow-up visits with Dr. Riseborough. I promised Gita that as soon as I could, I would return to her. I explained that while this was very painful for me to do, as the president of a college, I had my own responsibilities to the college, and to an international teaching staff, including several Americans. Fortunately, Gita was a very mature girl for her age, and since she understood my position and my responsibilities toward the family and the society, she endorsed my return to Tehran to resign from my position and subsequently then return to Boston. Iran was the top international news story every day, and I was certain that the frustration and uncertainty that I felt was also frustration and uncertainty felt by the people in my homeland. In a strange way, however, I had some peace of mind for Gita, who would be in a safe place in America.

It was easy to get a reservation to return to Iran. Uncertain about my country, my people, the rest of my family and myself, I left Boston on January 14 and arrived in Tehran on January 15, 1979. For the first time in my air travels to and from Iran, I was aware of so many vacant seats. No one wanted to travel to a troubled country. I had a whole row of seats for myself, so I tried to lie down and sleep. I laid down, but I could not get some shut-eye even for a minute. I was worried about Gita, separated from us for the first time, and I searched all the available newspapers on the plane for news and commentary about Iran, hoping to find some promising and positive news. Alas, I could not find any. Tired and anxious, I arrived in Tehran and found Mehrabad airport so crowded that I did not recognize it. It looked as if the entire population of the country was leaving. A royal court newspaper correspondent, who happened to know me, came toward me and asked, "Where are you going, Dr. Redjali?" I told him immediately that I was not leaving, but arriving from Boston. He replied, "How strange, everybody else is leaving," and then he continued, naming many people who had already left or were leaving, among them many who had administrative positions like me. He said even the Shah and Shahbanou might leave, although many people did not want them to go and were working to keep them in the country. While I was waiting for my luggage, he continued to inform me about what had transpired during weeks of my absence. What he told me was scary and difficult to understand, which made me realize that I was sliding into a very difficult situation. Because the airport workers were on strike, soldiers from the army were working at the airport instead. With difficulty, I finally located my rolling luggage and said good-bye to the reporter who was staring at me and following me with his eyes in disbelief even as I rolled my case to the exit, where my husband, Sa'id, and my son Reza were anxiously awaiting me. We hugged each other. They both looked much thinner, as if during my absence they had not had enough food to eat. Reza asked me about Gita: "Where is she? What is she doing?" I told him that she is going to school to study and told him that education is the best resource for everyone. I told him I hoped that he was studying well too. But he answered that the school was closed, and he was playing in the snow with his cousins Hossein and Mehdi most of the time. Then Sa'id started to tell me what was going on around them. He cautioned me that everything would look confusing and told me I needed to be very careful and cautious when I spoke with anyone because people had changed in the chaotic political situation. Sa'id told me that during my absence many people and representatives of many groups went to see the Shah to request that he stay in Iran and not leave the country, but he did not know if the Shah would heed these requests.

We went straight to bed when we got home (flights from Europe always arrive at a very late hour) and when we all woke up the next day, January 16, 1979, we suddenly heard on the radio and television that the Shah and Shahbanou (the empress) were leaving the country and going to Egypt at the invitation of President Anwar Sadat. They were at the airport. It appeared that they had not announced their departure earlier because they were frightened that many people would rush to the airport to prevent them from leaving the country. However, some representatives of the people were present at the airport for ceremonial purposes. These were the speaker of the Majles (Parliament) Javad Saeed, the minister of Court Alighoˈli Ardalan, many generals from the army, and later, the Prime Minister Shapour Bakhtiar, who, in an effort to distance his fortunes from the Shah's, kept them waiting. Their majesties seemed to want their trip to look like a temporary visit away, although they took some Iranian soil with them, something they had never done before on their departures from Iran. Some people were crying, and many people seemed to believe that this was the last departure of the Shah and Shahbanou from Iran.

In deciding to leave Iran, the Shah once again followed the recommendation of the US ambassador Sullivan and not the recommendation of the people who had his best interest and the best interest of the country at heart and were urging him to stay. President Carter himself was facing rebellion and dissension from the state department for his policy of backing the Shah while he struggled to establish a successor government.[18] At the request of the Iranian ambassador Zahedi, Carter offered the Walter Annenberg estate in California to the Shah and his family for their use.

The Shah however decided to accept the invitation of President Sadat and go first to Egypt. In this way, the captain abandoned the ship and its passengers in a stormy ocean, hoping that his prime minister, Dr. Bakhtiar, could navigate the ship. Ironically, the Shah himself became the captain of his own destiny and piloted the plane to Egypt. It seems that he had become so paranoid that he preferred to direct the plane himself to be sure where he was going. He was officially welcomed in Aswan, Egypt.

Immediately after the departure of the Shah, unrest accelerated and all the opposition groups began to celebrate and have demonstrations for his departure, shouting "Shah raft" (the Shah left) and bringing down his statues, not knowing what would happen to them and the country in the future. The same day, with difficulty, I was able to contact our daughter, Gita, and Doris in Boston to assure them of my safe arrival in Tehran and promised a speedy return to Boston as soon as possible. Doris told me that Gita had adjusted very well and was happy not to be losing a year of study. Assured of Gita's safety, I now turned my attention to my work and cautiously went to Shemiran College. Everybody I saw, from students of different parties and groups to my colleagues and employees, expressed surprise, wonder, and shock to see me, asking me why I had returned. As they stared at me, some of them said, "How strange that you are back, Dr. Redjali, while everybody else is leaving!" I told them that I had been away for three weeks on a family sick leave for my daughter and had returned on time to be with them in this difficult time. Nobody had expected that I would return to my troubled country and that I would still be willing to serve our country and its people. I felt responsible toward the students, colleagues and people and my country, although I also felt responsible toward my family and their safety too and toward my daughter whom I had left behind in the United States. Gradually, after they got over their surprise, they started to tell me what had happened during my absence. I learned that some of our teaching staff had already left the country, and that there had been continuous unrest, strikes, demonstrations and classes were not held regularly. Some of their expressions showed happiness that the Shah had left, and they hoped that Mr. Bakhtiar would be able to offer political freedom and that we would have a democratic government. Others showed more fear and anxiety and were frightened to lose what they had, and still some others had changed their attire to the Islamic garb and were citing Khomeini. For the first time, I noticed large pictures of Ayatollah Khomeini and Ayatollah Taleghani being distributed for free throughout the college. My husband was right; there was a gargantuan change in people's attitude and behavior.

My first task was to assist our foreign professors and the teaching staff, who, following the recommendation of their governments in USA and Europe, were trying to leave Iran. I noticed that they were very hesitant and concerned about their belongings, and I told them that they need not worry and promised to help them as much as I could. I did my best to appear calm and collected, hopeful for the future of the government and the governing body of the college, although I knew that several members of the board of trustees had already left the country. Rumors were rife about the possibility of a military coup, maybe because of the presence of General Huyser, who was assigned by President Carter "as the President's personal representative" to show the support of the United States and to work as advisor to the military to keep them united in backing the Bakhtiar government.[19]

In the news we heard that the Shah and the empress left Egypt on January 22 and traveled not to the USA but to Morocco where they were welcomed by King Hassan II. Every day we faced demonstrations by the opposition and heard the sound of gunshots. Only one of these demonstrations was surprising, and that was the gathering of followers and supporters of the Shah. They demonstrated in support of the Shah and wanted him back although they were upset and angry at the Shah's departure and leaving the country in such a chaos and turmoil. They had been gathering in Amjadieh Stadium to establish a platform against the revolutionary groups and using the name of National Rescue Team, and demonstrating in support of the Shah. They had limited or no support from the government and had no idea about public relations. After many meetings, they finally arranged a demonstration and gathering in the Baharestan Square on Friday, January 25, in front of the parliament of Iran. It was estimated that there were 150,000-300,000 people in this gathering, shouting, "Long live the Shah."[20] I heard more about these gatherings from our students at college, who told me that while they attended these meetings at the stadium, the opposition slashed their car's tires in order to handicap their activities. In general these groups could not succeed and continue with their activities in the absence of the Shah because they lacked support and resources from the government, and the silent majority who supported Bakhtiar was not actively supporting them. As I mentioned, they had no active PR in place, and as a result, there was no communication among these pro-Shah groups, with the masses, with the media or between these groups and the Shah in Morocco. It was just the opposite with Khomeini and his followers, who had well-established communications between the opposition groups and the people of Iran using a very simple language easily understood by the masses.

During the bitter cold months of January and February, even after the Shah had left Iran, the policy conflict within the Carter administration toward Iran continued. On the one hand, General Huyser was in direct contact with the president and Defense Secretary Brown, backing the army and Bakhtiar. On the other hand, Ambassador Sullivan who viewed the Iranian military as a "paper tiger" was in contact only with the under secretary and assistant secretary of the US State Department and was trying to establish relations with the opposition—with Bazargan and other members of the National Front who were following Khomeini. Both Huyser and Sullivan wrote in their memoirs of their disagreements with each other on many issues. As a result, each acted differently, and reported every day to different US departments, as if, Sullivan writes, "they were reporting to two different cities."[21] This conflict was adding to the confusion within the Carter administration and the crisis that the country was facing. In one incident, Ambassador Sullivan sent a message saying that for the interest of the United States, it would be better to accommodate to the revolution effectively. For saying this, he received "an unacceptable aspersion upon his loyalty" response that nearly caused him to resign in the middle of the revolution.[22] General Huyser meanwhile met regularly with the five highest-ranking Iranian Generals: Gharebaghi, Toufanian, Rabii, Badraie, and Habiballahi. Some of these meetings were in the presence of General Moghaddam, the chief of Savak, in the office of General Gharebaghi, who was chief of the Supreme Commander's Staff. They discussed the unrest and strikes in the country, "tackling three areas: breaking strikes; cementing relations between Mr. Bakhtiar and the military: and taking precautions against a collapse of the civil government."[23] Almost all the generals volunteered themselves and their staff to help with different tasks. They volunteered to help with transportation, customs, oilfields, and the other needs during strikes if needed, and they were making progress in planning toward these goals. However, all five generals were skeptical about the US support and wanted to be sure that US policy supported them. They also were against the Shah leaving the country. They thought it would have been better if he had stayed in Bandar Abbass, Kish, or another area in Iran. Sometimes, they were surprised that their confidential conversations were seen in international newspapers like *Pravda* with misinterpretation, which affected their planning in the middle of a Cold War. General Huyser believed later that the leaked information came from the office of General Fardoust, who was in an adjoining room to General Gharebaghi.[24] General Fardoust later became the chief of

SAVAMA, the secret police of Khomeini's regime. Also, at another time, articles about the US activist and former attorney general Ramsey Clark's meetings with Khomeini in the front pages of newspapers became counterproductive and damaging to their planning and work as it portrayed the United States seeking to establish relationship with Khomeini, while they were trying to support the current government of Bakhtiar. In fact, I recall seeing in the television news at that time Ramsey Clark sitting in the waiting room of the Ghasr Prison to see antigovernment political prisoners in clear support of them. This again looked like US support for the opposition.

Another important American who came to Iran during this time was Ross Perot, chairman of the board, Electronic Data Systems Corporation (EDS), which had been contracted to develop the social security system for Iran. He arrived after his unsuccessful bureaucratic efforts in the USA to secure the release of two EDS employees: Paul Chiapparone and Bill Gaylord, who were unjustifiably being held in prison, charged with bribing authorities of the Ministry of Health and Social Welfare. Perot directed a successful rescue mission composed of EDS employees and led by retired Green Beret Colonel Arthur "Bull" Simons. They were freed when the mob opened the Ghasr prison and Perot and his team entered the prison where his men were held. The rescue team subsequently brought them to Turkey and then to the United States. Ken Follett wrote a best-selling novel *On Wings of Eagles* where he described the rescue in detail.[25] This real-life incident was later made into a film, directed by Andrew Mclaglen with a leading role by Burt Lancaster. I saw this film on NBC Television Network, originally aired on May 18 and 19, 1986.

During the last week of January, we were living a day-to-day existence and sometimes on an hourly basis with uncertainty and anxiety about what would happen around us. Because of the strikes, periodically, we did not have electricity and sometimes not even telephone. The airport had been closed for some time too. I was worried about not being able to contact our dear Gita in Boston. For an urgent call, one could go to the central office of the Post Telephone and Telegram. I remember well that I had to stand for a long time in line to be able to call or to send a telegram to Gita, telling her that we were well and thinking of her and trying to come to see her as soon as possible. That was not an easy task in those days. We heard news reports and rumors about the return of Khomeini from Paris and the people were waiting for him and some even reported seeing his face in the moon. One night, our gardener, Haj Ali called us to come to the garden with him. At first, we were surprised and then we rushed to follow him. He took us to the middle of the garden, carrying his gardening shovel in his hand. There was a full moon, and he began to tell us that he saw the picture of Agha (Khomeini) in the moon. He pointed the shovel toward the moon and asked, "Do you see his picture in the moon yourself?" Sa'id replied that he didn't see anything, but before he could say more, I took his hand and said, "Your eyes are not seeing well. We will have your glasses changed." I told Haj Ali that he was right and said, "I am seeing Agha in the moon." I realized in that instant that our peace and security might be in jeopardy living next to Haj Ali in that chaotic environment. For a moment, I even thought that he might have been so angry at our denial that he could have hit Sa'id on the head with his shovel. I thanked Haj Ali for showing us the sight, and we returned to the house. Seeing Khomeini's face in the moon was a typical belief in those days and reflected the changes in thinking, belief, and behavior of the masses at that time.

At the college, I continued to hear a lot of news and rumors. Daily newspapers and the radio were full of various stories. One story was that Bazargan went to Paris to see Khomeini and brought back a message or a declaration from him that, when he returned, he was going to live in Qom like the other grand ayatollahs and that he would devote his life there to teaching, studying, and guiding his followers and that he would avoid politics. After that, some people began comparing him to the pope. Bakhtiar also decided to get an audience with Khomeini in Paris. However, Khomeini would not grant an audience unless Bakhtiar resigned from his premiership as it was a post appointed by the Shah. According to Khomeini, that appointment was an illegal act, so therefore, Bakhtiar did not go to Paris, and he did not resign either. Later on, when Mr. Tehrani, head of the Regency Council, went to Paris to see Khomeini, he did resign. Khomeini, with his charismatic authority, established an Islamic Revolutionary Council with advisers like Bani Sadar, Yazdi, and Ghotbzadeh, and even developed a shadow government while he pretended that he was going to be only a religious leader and not a political leader. He also asked the people to be kind to the military.

At the end of January, Khomeini decided to return to Tehran as soon as possible. However, on his arrival, the government closed Tehran airport because of security reasons. Another time Air France cancelled all its flights to Tehran. His followers in Tehran, like Beheshti and Motahhari, were trying to arrange this "arrival." *Pravda* blamed the US interference in Iran, mentioning the name of General Huyser who directed the army. Demonstrations in Tehran were becoming routine. One of them showed a picture of marchers carrying placards and banners with No Imperialism (USA) and No Communism (USSR) and called for the return of Khomeini. Practically every day, the demonstrators were anxiously awaiting for Khomeini's arrival.

Finally, on February 1, 1979, with the effort of the air force to open the airport, Khomeini left Paris for Tehran on an Air France 747. The plane was full of his close allies, followers, and representatives of the important media and newspapers. Most of the activities in the plane were shown on television. We saw that for most of the trip Khomeini was asleep. Once, when he awoke, the ABC correspondent Peter Jennings and a French reporter asked him, "How do you feel to be returning to Iran after being in exile for fifteen years?" He responded with an indifferent expression, "Nothing!" This response was the first shock to many people in the world, including some of his followers, about the emotional status of Khomeini as a religious leader. For three days, Bakhtiar lifted martial law for the arrival of Khomeini. The crowd began arrive at the airport as early as 5:00 a.m.

At the National Security Council, it was decided to withdraw the troops, which had been mobilized in the streets for some time. The ayatollah was received by the air force staff and escorted to Shahyad Square where his followers were gathering. The crowd on the street was estimated at more than a million, and all the newspapers had headlines like WELCOME HOME, or HOMECOMING. Live television and radio coverage showed the whole arrival and we watched eagerly to see the arrival ceremony. At Shahyad Square he gave a short bitter speech about the illegality of the Bakhtiar government, using common and crude language like "I will punch the government in the mouth," a surprising use of the language unbefitting the status of an ayatollah. Of course, that type of coarse speech appealed to the masses. After the Shahyad Square he proceeded to Behesht e Zahra cemetery, where he gave his first major speech, in which he praised the martyrs of the revolution and attacked with bitter simple language the Pahlavi regime that "expanded the cemeteries and destroyed the universities." Khomeini promised free housing, electricity, and water for all people, up until this day this has never happened. Here he also made his first political mistake by claiming the illegality of the Bakhtiar government and announcing that he would convene a government. With the prompting of the Ayatollah Motahhari, he immediately modified and corrected this statement by adding "*as the representative of the people.*" I think this immediate change was not noticed by the masses. But many of my colleagues and even his close followers from Paris noticed it and were surprised, shocked, and disappointed as they realized that he had not come to Iran to perform religious duties and studies as he had said in Paris. Before his return, he had also assured women that they would be treated as equals to men and had pledged full freedom of the press. Here on his return, he changed his position; he immediately began to perform as a political leader, and gradually, we noticed that in our history for the first time, we had a political ayatollah who would rule above all.

Khomeini and his followers achieved success in Paris and Iran by using all the traditional tactics mentioned in some narrations (Hadiths) about Mohammed and his followers. They used *Khod-eh* (trickery—deception by tricks and strategems), which means tricking one's enemy into a misjudgment of one's true position, *Tanfih (to defang)*, which means taking the sting out of one's potential rivals or enemies or tricking one from understanding the truth, *Taqiyyeh* (obfuscation), which means creating confusion and misleading everyone about one's true beliefs in a hostile environment, and *Ketman* (dissimulation)—withholding crucial and useful information. Later, Khomeini, in 1984, admitted having used *Khod-eh* in order to "trick" the enemies of Islam.[26] The strategy of using these tactics has been implemented and used throughout the last thirty years, from Khomeini to his present followers. Khomeini's followers have used these tactics in their worldwide politics, leading to a drastic adverse reaction to our religion and country in the world. To the best of my knowledge, none of the ayatollahs my family knew or followed used these tactics, and they all had a different interpretation of Islam.

After the speech, the helicopter, which was arranged by the Air Force Commander General Rabiee and his crew, took the ayatollah to the Tehran Hospital, a change from the route originally planned. He then stayed for two nights at a friend's house and did not go to Qom as he had said in Paris he would do. Finally, he settled in the Refah Girls School near the parliament. Of course, no girls were there.

As a result of the change of plans, General Rabiee and his crew were worried about his security for two days.[27] Refah School served as the residence of Khomeini and his family, as well as the headquarters of the Imam. Ayatollah Motahhari had taken care of the security details, and the Refah School was heavily guarded by Lebanese and Iraqi armed guerrillas. As a result, the Refah School became the headquarters and political center for Mullahs, journalists, the followers of Khomeini, and a revolutionary court for high-ranking government officials. In the meantime on February 2 and 3, the army was still backing Bakhtiar. But the presence of General Huyser in Tehran as well as the American presence became questionable, and Huyser himself feared for his own life because of the increasing resentment of Khomeini's followers and also because of frequent negative comments in *Pravda* and *Tass* (Russian news agencies). Following the recommendation of Ambassador Sullivan to the State Department, to prevent acute hostility toward him and other Americans in Iran, the White House asked for the departure of General Huyser, especially since Bakhtiar's government with the support of the military had survived, although General Huyser was apprehensive about General Gharebaghi, who, after his departure, would be charged with defending the government.[28] During 1978, there were about fifty-four thousand Americans who worked or lived in Iran, and their evacuation had begun on December 8.[29] On February 3 and 4, Khomeini held several meetings to plan for his future government. Then on February 5, he made an official announcement: Mehdi Bazargan, a seventy-three-year-old engineer and close friend of Bakhtiar was appointed prime minister and asked to form a provisional government, arrange a referendum, and then hold a general election. Bakhtiar considered Bazargan's appointment a sham and a joke. He announced courageously that he was not going to tolerate any infraction of the laws. In retaliation, the Imam ordered civil servants to prevent Bakhtiar's ministers from entering their ministries. As a result, some of them worked from home. In this way, the country during that time had two governments, and the people of Iran were faced with two governments, each vying for their loyalty and support. Bakhtiar still had the army behind him, and Bazargan had the masses following Khomeini and the trained guerillas. At Shemiran College, the students, instead of going to class were gathering in the cafeteria in groups to discuss the news and rumors in the city and to decide which government they should follow, and which one would eventually win. One of these critical days, when I was standing in the yard of the college, one of the women students came to me very excited. She showed me a package containing a black veil, which she had been given on the street near her home in the south of Tehran. She told me that a van was distributing these to the women as a gift from the Imam and that the women were rushing and competing to get the gifts. I became curious and asked her, "Can you show me what is inside?" She opened a very nicely packed black silk veil (Chaddor), and suddenly, a fifty Tuman bill (Iranian money worth about seven dollars at that time) fell out. We both were shocked. I was very sorry to see how in the middle of a revolution for freedom, with a small gift, they were trying to take away freedom from the women. After this, the student asked me, "What do you think will happen to our country, Dr. Redjali?" I looked at her and replied that at that moment I did not think that anybody could know, and I thought to myself that even Khomeini, President Carter, the Shah, and his Prime Minister Bakhtiar did not know what would happen in this conflicting chaotic situation. However, I looked at her innocent fearful expression and advised her, "Be yourself, think before you take any action, and be careful not to be influenced by any gift or by the people whom you do not know much about or their ideas."

In these fearful and fateful days in which we were caught in a web of conflict, the leftists and Communists (Tudeh Party) guerrillas gathered in Tehran from all over Iran and from outside the country and took advantage of Khomeini's permission to force the pace of the revolution. In addition, Khomeini called on people to defy the martial law and called on soldiers to desert the army and to either join the revolutionary forces or return to their villages. In this confusion, almost from February 6 on, the Imam became a hero even to the leftist guerrillas who began to kill in the name of Imam, although they were atheists. They seized the opportunity to be active and strengthen their position. For the whole week, the guerrillas attacked and raided banks, police stations, and other institutions. Some army officers joined them with tanks, and they became more powerful. Day and night, we heard the sounds of gunfire and shooting. The fight between the forces of the two governments continued. We were very cautious about going out because of gunfire from both sides. Bullets were coming from our right and left, even when we were in our home. I remember sitting in my mother-in-law's home in Jami Street, when suddenly a bullet passed from the street through the yard, entered the dining room and pierced the table leg. This hole in the table leg remained for some time as a vivid reminder of the revolution. Every step we wanted to take was becoming dangerous and risky. You could easily find bullets scattered on the streets, and in people's houses and gardens. However, amid all this struggle, I was able to go to the central telecommunication center to send a telegram to Gita in Boston to tell her not to be worried about us. Unfortunately, telephone calls could not go through any longer.

On February 10 and 11, the fighting and the sound of gunfire became at first very furious and then gradually subsided. It was about 4:00 p.m. on February 11 that the radio announced with a military march playing in the background that the revolution was triumphant and congratulated the people. Apparently, when on the morning of February 11 the chief and high command General Gharebaghi, had not been able to have a meeting with the five generals and announced the army's neutrality, this announcement was taken by the people to mean there had been an armed insurrection in Tehran and with that Prime Minister Bakhtiar had gone into hiding in the afternoon. The sound of gunfire was replaced with the sound of car horns and revolutionary songs played on the radio and television, while General Rahimi, who was still loyal to the Shah and was the administrator of Tehran's martial law, kept urging people to go home, reminding them that they were still under martial law. We were watching the television and witnessing how this loyal general, even after hearing the news on television, was still faithful to his oath as an army officer. This loyal gentleman, General Rahimi, was one of the first to be executed by the Islamic Revolutionary Court. While we were proud to see him expressing his loyalty to the rule of the army on television, we became disappointed at the statement of General Gharebaghi on behalf of the army. It was because Gharebaghi that the armories were opened to the masses, and guns fell in the hands of the people on the street. General Gharebaghi was one of the few Shah's generals who was never arrested and was allowed to live his life after the revolution. All the other military leaders were either taken into custody or executed immediately by Leninist leftist guerillas. They were held in custody in the Refah School, and the revolutionary court was held within twenty-four hours in a classroom by the order of Khomeini through special prosecutor Ibrahim Yazdi, with Khalkhali as judge and a firing squad led by Mostafa Chamran. Khomeini didn't want to be outshone by the leftist Communist guerillas who were killing government officials and attacking the armed forces. From February 12 throughout the month, we witnessed these shocking, horrible scenes of hastily arranged executions with no appropriate legal defense. The Shah's action, seeking to avoid bloodshed by not giving orders to the army to use force even in the last days and minutes, had led to the death of his generals. On the street and even at home, we had to be very cautious. The mob opened the armories and prisons so that both criminal and political prisoners (this is the time when EDS employees were rescued) were on the street with all kinds of sophisticated guns. Some of the Shah's officials who were in prison fled the country, but Prime Minister Hoveyda and some of the ministers like Dr. Sheikholislamzadeh who were also in prison, thought that Khomeini would have mercy on them as an ayatollah, presuming that "when the devil departs, the angel shall then return." With difficulty, they went on their own, from their prison to the Headquarters of the Revolution at Refah School to introduce themselves and were all summarily executed.[30]

On February 14, Valentine's Day, I was not feeling well and went to see my physician, Dr. Jafar Gharavi, on Iranshahr Street near the American Embassy. Since there were few traffic police officers on the street, at the traffic lights near Shemiran College, some of our students were directing traffic. I did not recognize one of them who had grown a beard, although he recognized me and said, "Look, Dr. Redjali, I have a new job." I told him that we should all help to bring order to our country. He opened the road for me, and I drove cautiously to the doctor's office. There, I finally found a parking place on the opposite side of the doctor's office, so I had to cross the street. While I was hearing the sound of the gunfire, and cautiously looking to the right and left as I walked, suddenly a military jeep full of militants and guerillas stopped in front of me in the middle of the street. They jumped out of the jeep with their machine guns and called out, "Dr. Redjali, where are you going? Do you hear the gunfire? This is from the American Embassy which the revolutionaries are trying to take over. The situation is changing!"

I looked at them and saw some of my former and present students. My heart began to beat faster because I had heard that the students had already arrested Mrs. Farmanfarmaian, the president of the School of Social Work, and taken her to the Imam's Committee and the revolutionary court at Refah School.[31] I said to myself maybe this is my turn. I suppressed my emotions and tried to be calm and listen to what they were telling me and watch what they were doing. They said, "Do you know that we opened the armory doors and that we all have guns?" Then, for a few seconds, they talked among themselves, almost like a jury discussion, while they blocked the traffic, and then they came toward me. I could feel my heart beating. They repeated, "Dr. Redjali, the situation is changed, and you need to protect yourself. Don't you know Mrs. Farmanfarmaian is arrested?" Then they said that they would like to help me and asked me to go to the back of the jeep where they opened the trunk. I saw various kinds of guns in the trunk and then they told me that I could take any gun that I chose. I was enormously relieved to find that they were being friendly and did not mean to harm or arrest me. I saw friendship and loyalty in their actions, and I thanked them and told them that I was frightened to even look at those guns. I said, "The only help you can give me is to close the trunk, stop blocking the traffic, and let me rush to my doctor's appointment." Although I had not accepted their offer, they clearly were happy that they had been able to show me that they were in power. As we were still hearing the sound of the gunfire from the US Embassy, they warned me again to be careful and drove toward the US Embassy. That episode was a real and shocking warning about my political environment. I realized at that moment that I needed to think about my own symphony of life and what I should do to take care of myself and my family. When I finally saw my physician that day, I noticed he was terribly worried about his life and was thinking about his family and his children who were students in United States. He wrote a three-month prescription for medications that I needed badly for my headaches in case I could not see him again.

When I left his office, I could still hear gunfire in the streets. Apparently, at around 10:00 a.m., the embassy was attacked by leftist guerrillas (Fadaian) who later managed to enter the embassy grounds. As I drove north toward my home, I passed close to the embassy; it was very loud, and I could barely make out the words of someone with a megaphone standing on the hood of a car commanding the crowd. With fear and caution, I slowly drove home, where it was much quieter. Later, I learned on the news that the person standing on the hood of the car speaking through the megaphone was Ibrahim Yazdi, the newly appointed foreign minister of the New Government of Bazargan. He was heading a rescue team of guerrillas to free the American Embassy and its staff. He apologized for what had happened and said that it was due to the undisciplined revolution. It is interesting to note that this incident took place in the morning of the same day that "the US government decided to continue diplomatic relations with Iran despite the change in government."[32] This was definitely not a good start for American-Iranian relations. The new regime continued this anti-Americanism throughout the revolution until November 4, 1979, with the hostage crisis and the breaking of diplomatic relations with the United States. In his *book, The Eagle and the Lion,* James A. Bill holds President Jimmy Carter as the *engineer responsible* for his "confusing policy that contributed to the disastrous American foreign policy loss in Iran."[33]

Throughout the time of the revolution, the people and the country lived in anarchy. More than a hundred thousand weapons were in the hands of the people of different political groups, who were seeking rewards for their struggles against the Pahlavi regime. Workers and students took over the factories and universities. Peasants rose against their landlords, and in some cases, they even killed them. They took advantage of the confusion to settle personal grudges and to take revenge. Soldiers shot their commanders, and mobs destroyed banks, stores, movie theaters and hotels. Sometimes, they attacked private homes and, with weapons in hand, entered and took whatever they wanted. There was a lot of vandalism. Gradually, I began to understand why the students in the jeep wanted me to take a gun from them. They knew I might need it. I was happy about one thing only at that time. I was happy that our daughter was not with us; she was safe in Boston recovering from a most difficult surgery on her back. However, I was worried because the revolutionary government, in a move to block the flight of people involved in the Shah's regime, had closed the airport. We had no idea when the airport would open and no knowledge of when we could leave the country. I had promised Gita we would return to her soon.

For our home security, as had become common in many neighborhoods, we employed a group, who, in exchange for a weekly fee, patrolled our neighborhood. They made rounds every night and checked everywhere and, in general, took the place of the police. Every night, we heard on the news that the new revolutionary authority was arresting high-level government officials of the Pahlavi regime, jailing them and executing them without any proper legal defense, all in the name of justice. Most of the judgments were made by Sadegh Khalkhali, known as the Hanging Judge, and Asadollah Lajevardi. At the same time, violence was deepening throughout the country, as the new regime, acting against humanity and human rights, and in the name of Islam, continued its misinterpretation of Islam. The number of people wearing black increased every day—some to show mourning because of the daily increase in killings and executions, and some because they were religious leaders and relatives of Mohammad or Imam Hossein.

At the National University of Iran, the student revolutionary committee began holding sessions to judge which professor could keep their job or life. Some of the professors, who were teaching part time in our college, were describing the whole scene, which showed how some of them changed their political views to please the governing body of students. I was very sorry to see how some of them did not remain true to themselves and were opportunists by changing their colors. Perhaps they had no other choice in order to keep their jobs and even their lives. Later on, I heard that one of Sa'id's colleagues, psychologist Dr. Khossro Mohandessi, who had a PhD from the USA and was a professor at the University of Tehran, was killed because he was Ba'hai. Subsequently, at an APA (American Psychological Association) conference in Washington DC, he was remembered by Professor Hunt from the University of Illinois who had a joint research program with him in Iran. In this situation, I gradually became worried and consumed by my own inner conflict, deciding whether if it was safe and wise to stay and serve in Iran or to go to my daughter, who was alone in a boarding school and continue what I could do for Iran from there. In order to resolve my conflict, we went to see our friend, Dr. Amir-Hossein Aryanpour, for advice. He knew that our families were religious, and he suggested we go to see Ayatollah Najafi Marashi for advice because he thought he might be in a better position to know about the political and social/religious environment of the country and where it might be heading, Most ordinary people were gradually surprised and then very disappointed at the outcome of the revolution. Not only had they not gotten their political freedom, they were gradually losing even their social and economic freedom and the security that they had enjoyed for years. So a few days later, we went to Qom to see this ayatollah. The city did not have its usual familiar faces. It was decorated heavily with numerous new green flags on both sides of the streets for the arrival of Khomeini. There was a rumor that Khomeini would like to change our flag to green. I became very emotional when I saw these drastic changes. This really saddened me as I felt that my identity was changing. First, we visited the graves of my parents, which were very near to the shrine of the holy Massumeh. Then, after praying for the souls of my parents, we went to see Ayatollah Najafi Marashi, who knew our family very well. He received us immediately, and as usual, he started first to speak in praise of the book *Naghdol Rejal* (critics of hadith) of my great grandfather Mostafa Tafreshi. It is necessary to mention that most of the ayatollahs know about his book and admit that the book was scholarly written. After the usual greetings, I told him about our daughter, her surgery, the unrest and revolution, leaving her in Boston, and my responsibility and my conflict in making a decision. I asked him what he knew about the future extent of the violence and the political direction of the revolution and what he would advise me to do at this time. He immediately replied that since he was not involved with politics, it was better to ask Ayatollah Taleghani, who was more knowledgeable about politics. However, about my family and conflict of the job and service to my country, he would recommend that it was better and more advisable to go as soon as possible to my daughter and to take care of her in Boston. Indirectly, he recommended that it was better and wiser to leave the country as soon as possible, although he was clear to remind me that he was not involved in politics. We thanked the ayatollah, and in great emotional pain, we left the green ornamented Qom for what was the last time. At least three generations of my family were resting forever in the holy city of Qom, and I did not know if I would ever see that city and their tombs again.

During this fateful February, from the eleventh of the month onward, every night, we witnessed the cruel continuation of executions of high-ranking government officials who were tried, judged, and summarily executed without any legal recourse, all in the name of being *mufsed fel-ardth* (corrupter of the earth) and accused of being corrupt by virtue of having been associated with the Shah's regime. In fact, we knew some of them who were innocent and served the people well. In the meantime, Imam Khomeini issued daily directives through radio and television and among those directives, what affected our life drastically was the one about music. He thought that music corrupted the mind of the youth, similar to opium, and he even thought that foreigners were, through music, trying to influence our youth to deviate from a righteous path in their lives. This was contrary to what education and psychology and other sciences had taught the rest of the world; even our old Imam Mohammed Ghazali had promoted Persian classical music and recommended music for transcending the mind. So in this chaotic situation, we had to hide and cover with blankets and tableclothes Sa'id's huge grand concert piano, in case the revolutionaries would attack our home. In addition, Sa'id was being questioned by the revolutionaries about all the songs and music that he had produced on television, to see if any of those educational songs were against the revolution. Although they did not find anything, he was constantly under questioning, especially since they found in his file at the university that he was assigned to teach music to the crown prince and princesses in the palace school. Every day he returned home, tired and depressed, and when the invitation from the University of Michigan arrived requesting him to teach *Music in World Culture* for the academic year 1979-'80 arrived, he immediately accepted it. And after thirteen years of teaching, he applied for a sabbatical leave from the University of Tehran. His application was approved quickly since his colleague and friend Dr. Hormoz Farhat agreed to teach in his place in his absence, although they did not think that the course would be offered in the new academic year under this regime. In fact, very soon, Dr. Farhat himself left the country for Ireland.

At Shemiran College and other universities and colleges, it became the fashion to be a follower of Khomeini, and encouraged by the pressure from the revolutionary regime, prayer groups for students and teachers were established. I remember very well that, one day soon, after the revolution in February, I was standing with several professors looking from the window at the students in the yard, when several of the revolutionary students ran to my office and called me to go to the courtyard of the college to pray with them. It would have been quite dangerous for me to refuse. Suddenly, I remembered that by chance, I had my monthly period, a time when women in Islam are excused from prayers. So I told them that I was excused that day, but added that my colleagues who were standing with me were ready to join them. I have always preferred and believed in private individual praying. Fortunately, the students accepted my excuse. The next day, the students invited a revolutionary named Garmarudi to speak to them in the college cafeteria, which was near Fereshteh Street. I chose to sit at the end of the cafeteria near the street. I listened to his speech against the Pahlavi regime, in which he asserted that the true name of the famous epic *Shahnameh* (Book of kings) by our national poet Abolghassem Ferdossi was in fact *Mardom nameh* (Book of the people). He continued in a similar way, making confusing and distorting statements to these poor students. Once I heard his distorted and false arguments and assertions, I realized that I was not in a position to argue with him in that hostile environment. However, to show my opposition, I left from the back door of the college cafeteria to the street without going to my office. That was the last time I left the college I had worked so hard to establish. His speech was so out of touch with reality and so full of nonsense that it triggered in me the clarity to resolve my conflicting issues, and I decided to go directly to Prime Minister Bazargan to resign as soon as possible from my post, get ready to leave Iran as soon as the airport was open, and go to my daughter who was waiting for me in Boston. I had been in conflict for quite some time. I wanted to stay and help my country and my people, but was disappointed and dismayed by the results and actions of the revolution; a revolution which increasingly did not look it would achieve anything promising or to benefit Iran's people.

In general, this revolution did not look genuine or original to me and to a silent majority. I had been observing the nasty conspiracies and competitions between the superpowers, from guerrilla training to the organized media campaigns from the West and East and their actions. Later, it became clear how the foreign oil companies, who were very angry about the resistance of the Shah to sign a new contract, were against the interests of Iran and Iranians and were influencing the students and the revolution. With deep sadness, I realized that the future government would be a religious government, and we would not be able to support the people in that atmosphere where we could not be ourselves anymore. I was reminded of what I had learned of the Middle Ages in Europe, and how the rule of the religious leaders made the life of the ordinary people miserable and intolerable for a thousand years. It was shocking to see that we were losing our progressive secular constitution and instead were getting a religious government for the first time in our history, a government interfering in politics, our personal religion and even our private daily life, telling us what to wear, what to eat, what to drink, and so on. The main slogan of the revolution was Freedom, Independence and Islamic Republic. We, not only were *not* going toward getting the political freedom and independence that Khomeini had promised, but our situation was just the opposite. We were beginning to lose the cultural, social, and economic freedom that we already had. In this way, we resembled the Middle

Ages of Europe, and the regime was changing from autocracy to theocracy. I was awakening to the fact that the competition of the superpowers and their decisions in the world including those for my country were not based on humanity and democracy, but solely based on their own interests. Their interest in Iran was only in Iran's rich resources of oil, gas, gold, uranium, and other minerals, and not its people. In fact, these foreign interests had created many obstacles on the road toward democracy and freedom for the people of Iran.

With a firm decision, without telling anyone, I drove to the prime minister's office to resign. Since he had not yet assigned a minister for Science and Higher Education, Prime Minister Bazargan was the only official at that time who could accept my resignation. I remember well that I stopped on the way and took a sheet of paper from my briefcase, wrote my resignation letter, put it in an envelope, and then proceeded to the office of the prime minister. At that time, the Imam and the provisional government were hosting Yasser Arafat, the leader of the Palestine Liberation Organization, as an official guest. He had brought with him his ambassador Hani al-Hassan, who declared that the PLO had trained more than ten thousand anti-Shah guerrillas. Therefore, he considered the PLO as a partner in the victory of the revolution. Also, from February 18 onward, the PLO "provided about 800 Palestinians to help train the Pasdaran (new army) in Tehran, Qom and Ahwaz."[34] When I arrived at the prime minister's office, I noticed extremely tight security, which I had not seen when I had been there before. This was a new scene. When I asked someone at the door what was going on, they told me that *Yasser Arafat* was visiting. But it was not clear where and with whom he was meeting. Therefore, I parked a little further away and walked to the building and the office of the prime minister, which I was familiar with from my last unsuccessful visit with Prime Minister Amouzegar when I had gone there seeking a government grant for the college. I was stopped and warned several times by the security, but I continued assertively to go toward the prime minister's office, saying that I needed to see him urgently in connection with Shemiran College. I emphasized the urgency, and when they asked what the emergency was, I told them that it was highly classified and confidential. While one of the guerrilla's was following me closely, I stopped in front of the prime minister's office door to open it. The security guard suddenly pushed my hand from the door handle and said that I could not go in because he was meeting with Yasser Arafat. As soon as I heard this, I pushed him back, and this time aggressively opened the door and very loudly said, "I need to go in" and opened the door and found myself in the middle of the room. I noticed immediately that Mr. Bazargan, who was sitting with Yasser Arafat, jumped from his seat and came quickly to me. He stood in front of me and sent away the guerrilla who was following me. I first apologized for interrupting his conversation and meeting with his guest, and then I said, "I am the president of Shemiran College and my daughter had spine surgery in Boston. I left her there in this situation and returned to Tehran to resign from my post and responsibility. Now there is no one to resign to, although the college is not a governmental institution and is a private nonprofit college without any governmental assistance, I could not find any member of the board of trustees to offer my resignation to, and since you have not yet assigned anyone as the minister of higher education, you are the only one that I can resign to." I offered him my handwritten resignation letter and gave him the names of the two vice presidents of the college. I told him that both of them, especially Dr. Mosaaed, the psychiatrist, could lead the college very well at this time, and said that I would appreciate his acceptance of my resignation. He immediately said okay, but I was so determined to have proof that I added, "I need your acceptance in writing." He opened the envelope I had given him, took out the letter, and wrote his acceptance on the back of the envelope, returned the envelope to me, and gave my letter of resignation to his office manager, who had come in because of the noise I was making and my aggressive entry into the office. Never in my life I have ever seen myself as aggressive. yet defensive, as I was at that moment. I still do not know how I took that risk and how I got that courage. Maybe it was because I believed in and wanted to fight for human rights in Iran and maybe it was because of my motherly instinct that wanted to protect my daughter. Anyway, as soon as I got the envelope with his signature, I was relieved, and my heart, which was beating very fast, became calm. I thanked him, apologized again to him and his guest Yasser Arafat, and left his room relieved and happy. My conflict was resolved, and I was painfully relieved from the responsibility of the college in that chaotic and uncontrollable revolution. I was in pain because I worked, fought, and challenged so much for the establishment of the college and worked so hard and fought for my country and my people.

With peace of mind about my responsibilities being resolved at the college, I drove home. On the way, I began to analyze my behavior and that of Prime Minister Bazargan, when suddenly I remembered that the name Bazargan was familiar to me in our college and at least on paper. After I verified this with a colleague, I found out that Feresteh Bazargan, one of our students, who had received the highest score in our college entrance examination while Mr. Bazargan was still in prison, was his daughter. So in that case maybe Mr. Bazargan knew about our college and about his daughter having received top marks in our fair computerized college entrance examination at a time when college entrance exam results were usually rigged to benefit the children of those in power. Maybe that was a factor in his acceptance of my resignation so quickly. Anyway, as soon as I arrived home, I told Sa'id, who did not know anything about my drastic action on that day, about my resignation, and I asked him not to tell anybody, because, as a result of the revolution and changing times, people's attitudes toward us had changed. Because of our status in the former regime, when Sa'id taught music at the palace school and I was the secretary-general of the Women's Organization and a member of the Queen's Charity, some friends and relatives were avoiding us and even pretending that they did not know us. On the other hand, some people and former students that we were not very close to came to our home or called and, knowing of our daughter's situation, offered their assistance to help us. Of course, some friends and relatives who had strong personalities did not change their relation to us. At any rate, I decided it was better that I would not tell anybody about my upcoming trip to the United States. I called British Airways and asked for a return ticket to Boston as soon as they resumed flying and quietly began preparations to leave the country as soon as the airport opened. Since the people were changing, and we did not know at that time who our true friends and foes were, I told friends and relatives that since the universities and colleges were closed, I was planning a pilgrimage to Mashhad and made a small suitcase ready for travel. I remember very well the moment when I read in the newspaper that the airport was going to open for travel for women only. I jumped up and screamed with joy at being a woman and being able to travel—the first and only time that I was happy to be a woman, and I felt I was not being discriminated against because, normally, women were facing discrimination in every other aspect of their lives. Or maybe we were being discriminated against by being considered unimportant enough to be allowed to leave the country.

The announcement said that every woman who wished to leave the country should submit a valid passport and her ticket to the office of the prime minister forty-eight hours before the flight, and these would be returned to them at the airport. Since its establishment, this has been the only regulation from this regime that by chance benefited women. So in this way they could control who could leave the country. There was a ban already in place forbidding all top-level officers of the government from leaving the country. I got my ticket for the beginning of March from British Airways. I went the night before to the home of Mehri, my sister-in-law, who lived near the prime minister's office in Tehran. In the early morning, we went together standing in the long line of women with passports and tickets. It looked as if many women were rushing to leave the country. I did not know if I could leave the country with the administrative position that I had held. Therefore, I did not call Gita in case I could not to leave, although I had full intentions if possible to be with her on her birthday, March 8, the same date as the International Women's Day. After submitting my passport and ticket, I went home and packed a small suitcase for travel. I did not take any jewels or anything valuable, not even my diamond wedding ring, in case it attracted someone's attention at the airport. I just took my mother's prayer ring, which, after her death, I always wore on my finger; and by looking at it, I called on God for protection. Before the departure, I called our good friends Pouran and Mehdi to thank them for their friendship and say good-bye and asked them to watch over Reza and Sa'id who were staying in Tehran and reminding them that I did not want anybody else to know about my trip.

I did not make the flight for March 8, but on the morning of March 11, 1979, I wore my old black coat with black scarf, and Sa'id took me to the airport. I remember that the radio in the car announced that Kate Millett, the American feminist, was in Iran to participate in the women's march to demand equal rights for women. Khomeini's promise of equal rights in Paris had been forgotten. Later, another news indicated that the marching women, including Millett, were attacked by the regime, and even Kate Millett was detained for three days before being deported to the United States.

At the airport, the passengers, all women, lined up to receive their passport. I noticed in my line that a few women did not receive their passport and had to return with their luggage. I was very anxious, and my heart was beating fast to learn if my passport was there. Finally, I was standing before the person behind the desk. I stated my name and he began to look through the list, while my eyes were staring at him and following his movements eagerly. Fortunately, he found my passport. I then went through a search of my handbag and stated that I did not have more than the equivalent of $5,000 in foreign currency, the limit a person could leave the country with. Both my suitcase and my body were searched, and of course, they could not find anything. I tried to be as simple as possible to avoid attracting any attention. I didn't want to do anything that could have prevented my departure and to reach Gita. In the waiting room of the airport, the airport employees were complaining that their March salaries had not yet been paid. I tried to tell them that they needed to be patient in the revolution. After one hour of waiting, the airline authority called for boarding. I was happy to get on the plane. After everyone had boarded and fastened the seat belts, suddenly, some security officers came on the plane and called out the names of three passengers who needed to leave the plane. I watched anxiously and was happy that they did not call my name. The plane did not wait and began to move. Again, I was relieved that finally I could leave. Gradually, the women who had veils or scarves took them off to be free. The plane made a stop in Kuwait, but we had to stay in the plane. However, everybody was happy that we were completely out of Iran's air space and free to face our destiny. I never thought that that would be my last departure from my homeland. After a short stop in Kuwait, the British Airways plane had a direct flight to London, and then after three hours wait in London, I would be on another flight to Boston. Once at the London airport, I called Gita, and fortunately, I was able to reach her. I wished her a belated happy birthday and told her how happy I was that, in a few hours, I would be with her. In response to my question as how she was doing, she began to cry for some time. It was a long time before I could learn whether her tears and cries were from happiness or sadness. Finally, I knew she was crying to show how deeply she had suffered from the absence of her family and knowing they were living in a troubled country. After what seemed like quite a long time, finally, she said she was fine and her back was better with the physiotherapy, but she was worried that we would not be able to get out of Iran. She immediately asked about Sa'id and Reza. I told her that hopefully they would come to the United States in the summer. Sa'id would be teaching music in world culture at the University of Michigan. After I finished talking to her, I called Doris with my flight details. She was very happy that I could leave Iran and so gracious and understanding about our situation that she insisted on picking me up with Gita at the airport. I also called Christine and David in London, who were much concerned about us. Then, very quickly, I bought something for Gita and Doris from the airport and went to the gate to meet my destiny.

Revolution of Iran of 1979: Iran_revolution_ap_543.jpg
Source: http://www.sott.net/image/image/s5/102689/full/Iran_revolution_ap_543.jpg

Revolution of Iran of 1979: iran-706135.jpg
Source: http://www.cinestatic.com/different_maps/uploaded_images/iran-706135.jpg

1. Amir Taheri, *The Spirit of Allah*, 1985, p. 223.

2. Ervand Abrahamian, *Iran Between Two Revolutions*, Princeton University Press, p. 516

3. William H Sullivan, *Mission To Iran*, W.W. Norton & Company, 1981, p. 165, and Anthony Parsons, *The Pride and the Fall of Iran: 1974-1979*, London, Jonathan Cape, 1984

4. Zibgniew Brezezinski, *Power and Principle*, New York: Farrar, Straus, Giroux, 1983, p. 361, and Cyrus Vance, *Hard Choice*, New York: Simon and Schuster, New York, p. 326)

5. *Autumn Scientific Meeting of the Association of British Neurologists and the British Neuropsychiatry Association, October 3, 2002.*

6. Houshang Nahavandi, *The Last Days*, page 196, 2003.

7. Amir Taheri, *The Spirit of Allah*, Adler and Adler, 1985, p. 225.

8. Amir Taheri, *The Spirit of Allah*, P. 228

9. David Harris, *The Crisis*, New York and Boston: Little, Brown and Company 1979, pp. 97, 98,99

10. William Sullivan, *Mission to Iran*, New York: W.W. Norton & Company,1981, pp. 199-213.

11. James A. Bill, *The Eagle and The Lion*, New Haven: Yale University Press, 1988, p. 248).

12. ibid. pp. 233-260.

13. Ervand Abrahamian, *Iran between Two Revolutions*, Princeton University Press, chapter 11, "The Islamic Revolution," 1982, P. 496-510.

14. Vance, *Hard Choice* pp. 332-334.

15. Kenneth M. Pollack, *The Persian Puzzle*, New York: Random House, 2002, p. 134.

16. Jimmy Carter, *Keeping Faith*, Bantam Brooks, p. 444.

17. ibid. p. 445

18. ibid. p 443.

19. General Robert E. Huyser, *Mission to Tehran*, New York: Harper & Row, 1986, P. 16

20. Nahavandi, p. 349.

21. Sullivan, p. 230.

22. Sullivan, *Mission to Iran*, p. 240.

23. Huyser, *Mission to Tehran*, Harper & Row, New York, 1986, p. 283.

24. Huyser, p. 283.

25. Ken Follett, *On Wings of Eagles*, New York: William Morrow and Company, Inc. NewYork, 1983, p. 284.

26. Taheri, Pp. 229,230.

27. Huyser, p. 252.

28. Huyser, pp. 255-272.

29. John D. Stempel, *Inside the Iranian Revolution*, Bloomington: Indiana University Press, 1981, p. 74

30. Abbass Milani, *Persian Sphinx: Amir Abbas Hoveyda and The Riddle of the Iranian Revolution*, Washington, D. C. Mage Publishers, 2000, pp. 306-307) and Azar Aryanpour, *Behind the Tall Walls*, Danbury, CT. Rutledge Books, 1998, pp. 137-9).

31. Sattareh Farmanfarmaian, *Daughter of Persia*, New York: Crown Publishers Inc., 1992 pp, 356-60.

32. Sullivan, p. 257.

33. *The Eagle And the Lion: The Tragedy of American- Iranian Relations*, New Haven: Yale University Press, p. 988.

34. Stempel, p. 200.

FOURTH MOVEMENT
A NEW WORLD

CHAPTER 15

Wandering in a New Country
March-December 1979

On the plane between London and Boston, I tried to close my eyes and rest, but all the macabre scenes I had witnessed of Iran's revolution kept whirling in my mind. I kept worrying about the fate of the millions of defenseless people, my country, my family, my religion, and my identity—my symphony of life. We were definitely experiencing a unique revolution, unlike any of the past revolutions—the French or the Russian revolutions. The Iranian revolution mimicked a major political earthquake, with its landscape completely different from any other revolution in history. The landscape was our country, religion and identity of the people; and unfortunately, the earthquake did not look like that it was going to settle soon. Unfortunately, after thirty years, it is still not clear when and if it will ever settle enough for the people to regain a modicum of their freedom and independence.

At the Boston airport, I passed through immigration and customs quickly with my multi-entrance visa and received six months permission to stay in the USA. I took my small case and ran excitedly to the exit looking for my dear Gita and Doris who were anxiously waiting for me. I hugged them and was overjoyed to see them healthy and happy. Doris kindly took us to her beautiful home for dinner. There, we exchanged our experiences and news from our two completely different environments. Unforgettably, Doris told me that Gita had studied so hard, and with such good grades on her midterm exams that she had been accepted by all the prep schools she had applied to, including the Phillips Academy in Andover, which she liked the most. Of course, the acceptance depended on finishing the school year successfully. In the middle of dinner, I jumped up and hugged both and felt that my fatigue and weariness from the long, tiring travel had disappeared. In a happy mood, after dinner, we took Gita back to the Walnut Hill School, her boarding school, which was near Doris's home. Doris and I returned to her home, furnished with very nice antique French furniture, including three old clocks, which chimed every hour, telling the number of hours and the passage of time. After watching the news, which was mainly about Iran's ongoing political turmoil, the continuing execution of the defenseless people and ruin of our nation and religion, we were ready to go to our rooms to sleep. I was very tired and exhausted and went to sleep quickly. However, I could not sleep for long because, as the clocks struck on the hour, I jumped from my bed as if I was hearing the sound of gunfire that I had experienced every night in Tehran. It took me a few nights until I gradually became accustomed to the presence of those clocks.

During the next few days, I called several cousins and friends who were scattered throughout Europe and different states in the USA before the revolution. All were happy to hear that I had been able to leave the country. My cousin Mehri and her husband, Bill, who lived in Connecticut and had always been very hospitable, invited Gita and me to go to Florida with them during Gita's school spring break. Since their daughter Marianna was the same age as Gita. I thought, with all the uncertainty and trouble in our life, this trip would be restful for her and allow me to think about what to do next with our life while waiting and hoping for Sa'id and Reza to join us in the United States. Gita welcomed Mehri's invitation, and we went to Norwalk, Connecticut, where her dental clinic and home were located.

Dr. Mehri Kalali (Cimikoski) with her children in front of her home in Norwalk, Connecticut, where family and friends, including the author, were always welcome.

In their large station wagon, we all then went to their vacation home in St. Cloud, Florida. It was a long trip driving through several states. On our way, we stopped in a hotel to rest for the night, and the next day, we arrived in St. Cloud. It was the beginning of spring and the weather was very pleasant, but I was not accustomed to the warm and humid climate. On the first days, Mehri and Bill took us to Disney World, Cypress Park, and other popular sightseeing areas. Gita and Marianna were often joined by Mehri and Bill in cycling, swimming, and other sports activities.

The author's daughter Gita Khadiri relaxing by the pool at Dr. Kalali's home in Florida 1979 during the spring break holidays.

I was especially pleased to see that Gita looked very beautiful, straight, and tall. I preferred to sit at the lakefront and think about our uncertain future because of the revolution. I had been permitted to take only $5,000 from Iran when I left, and I had already spent some part of the money. I needed to find work soon. Mehri suggested that I see a lawyer to change my visa status from a six months' tourist visa to permanent residency; otherwise, I would be unable to work. She knew a lawyer who specialized in real estate law, but was not sure if he could be of help. This was a good suggestion since my six-month permit to stay was about to expire. Considering all the continuing horrible news from Iran, I thought it was a good idea to go along with the suggestion until Sa'id and Reza arrived. Gradually, the weather in Florida was becoming warmer, and I was finding it harder to cope because of my frequent migraine headaches. Since the school spring break was nearly over and Gita would have to return to school, I bought two air tickets to Boston, thanked Mehri and Bill sincerely for the lovely vacation and their deep understanding of my uncertain situation. We left the next day for Boston, Gita went to her boarding school, and I again stayed a few days with Doris.

Then, one day, my cousin and a neighbor in Iran, David Rejali, surprised me by calling from Fairfax, Virginia, near Washington DC, where he had settled. Just before the revolution, he and his American wife, Sallie, and his family had left Iran, but I had lost contact with him for some time because of the revolution. However, he had made inquiries from another cousin and found my telephone number through Mehri. I was very happy to hear from him. He said that he had rented a house in Fairfax temporarily to see if the revolution would settle. After he heard my story, he invited me to his home. Since I was wondering where to settle temporarily, and bearing in mind my frequent migraines in Boston, I asked him about the weather in Fairfax. His answer was that Northern Virginia had about one or two months of summer and winter, longer autumn and spring, and was definitely warmer than Boston. When I told him about my plan to have a lawyer change my visa status and to look for a job, he concurred with my plan. Accordingly, I called Mehri and on the way to Washington DC. I stopped in Norwalk to see the lawyer accompanied by Mehri.

Author standing next to her late cousin Dr. Kalali
and Dr. Virginia Park in Norwalk.

First, the lawyer told me that he was not an immigration lawyer. Moreover, since I did not have an immediate family member who was a a US citizen, it would be difficult to proceed. After I persisted and showed him my résumé with the PhD in psychology from the University of Heidelberg, professor of Psychology at the National University of Iran, Fulbright scholar, National Science Foundation fellow, secretary-general of the Women's Organization of Iran, president of Shemiran College, exchange programs with Syracuse University and other universities, he consulted a law book. After a few minutes, he told me that he might be able to prove my eligibility for a third-preference status, provided that he had enough materials and supporting documents to prove that I was an internationally known scholar with exceptional ability whose special ability the country needed. He made me a copy of the law and instructed how to provide all the necessary documents. After reviewing my documents, he would then decide whether to take up my case. At first, collecting all the documents seemed to be a formidable task, since I had left Iran in the middle of a revolution with only hand luggage and with no documents other than my passport. But since this task was essential for me and my family and our well-being, especially if the revolution continued and did not settle soon, I decided to work hard to obtain the documents as soon as possible. After all, my German professors characterized me as "Ich liebe die Schwierigkeiten" (I love difficulties), so I accepted this challenge. Soon, I left Mehri's house and headed south to visit my cousin David in Fairfax, Virginia.

In Fairfax, it was very nice to be reunited with Sallie and David after the revolution. Each of us exchanged our experiences after leaving Iran. They had left just in time before the revolution. I told them about my situation. They thought that if I could gather documents of my educational background and experiences and find a copy of my publications, with the consideration that I had been a top-class student throughout my education, I might be successful in getting a permanent visa and work permit according to the criteria written in the immigration law. With this in mind, all three of us went daily to the local library and the student union of George Mason University and the community college, which had the office machines for writing letters and preparing our résumés. Sallie and David, who, as Americans, did not have any visa and residency problems, were searching for jobs. This was a difficult time to find a job since the unemployment rate in the United States was very high, between 8 percent and 9 percent.

The news of Iran was mostly about a controlled referendum to be conducted under the watchful eyes of the "Guardians of Revolution" (Pasdaran) in which, by casting green (yes) or red (no) ballots, the people were to accept green for the Islamic Republic form of government for Iran. The news also featured a number of executions and a great amount of bloodshed on a daily basis. After the revolution, the Revolutionary Justice Court was responsible for the execution of many former army, internal security, and high-ranking government officers. On TV, every day we witnessed these gruesome executions without trials. Among those was the shocking and painful execution of Prime Minister Hoveyda, who, after the rebels opened the prison doors, turned himself in voluntarily to the revolutionary court in the hope of defending himself in a fair and just court. For years to come, we had an endless number of summary executions. One of these was the execution of my dear biology teacher and Iran's first woman Education minister, Dr. Farrokhru-Parsa. This was especially cruel because she had returned to Iran from Paris after being given assurance of her safety if she were to return. This dear lady, who had provided years of excellent educational service to the people of Iran, was executed upon her return to Iran. May God bless her soul and may she rest in peace. Evin Prison, not very far from our home in Iran and Shemiran College, became known for the numerous executions there and after it became full, the government used other buildings in Tehran to execute people without trial. Violence was replacing ethics, law, regulations, and security. Khomeini responded to the pleas and protests of the temporary prime minister Mr. Bazargan and many others for moderation and respect for human rights by declaring that criminals should be summarily executed and not tried. In foreign relations, the United States was struggling with no success to find a replacement for Ambassador Sullivan, who, surrounded by the various security groups of revolutionary forces, barely made it out of Iran on March of 1979.

All of these shocking daily reports of Iran motivated me to work very hard in preparing my résumé and getting a copy of all my educational and professional background and publications for immigration and employment. I called and wrote letters to the University of Heidelberg, University of London, US National Science Foundation, the Fulbright Commission advisors, and the dean and the chancellor of Syracuse University with which we had exchange programs, and the other professors who had come to Iran and witnessed my professional activities. As expected, I could not obtain any information from my troubled country about my undergraduate studies. At the same time, since I was near Washington DC, I called the US Department of State and USIS to find the address and telephone number of the former US cultural attachés to Iran whom I knew. Fortunately, I found the two of them, one was Dr. Dorothy Robin Mowry, who immediately returned my call. She was happy that I could get out safely from Iran and immediately invited me for lunch at the International Club. Later, the former cultural attaché Bill Meyer, who was retired, invited me to his condo in DC. At the lunch at the International Club, I was also happy to see Dr. Carolyn Spatta, the former president of the Damavand College in Iran. We exchanged our experiences in leaving Iran. Carolyn and Dorothy had both left Iran before the revolution, and since I came immediately after the revolution, they were very anxious to hear more about it. Carolyn, like me, was looking for a job but without my problem of residency and work permit. Anyway, the lunch meeting was very informative and helpful. Very soon after that, Carolyn came to see me at David's house. In our informal conversation, she told us that one of her former professors at Damavand College, Dr. William Goodman, was at Lynchburg College in Virginia and suggested that I send him my résumé, and using the records I had already obtained, including documents from Heidelberg and London, to inquire if they had any job openings. So every day, I placed several phone calls, mailed job applications, and sent letters of support on my professional and educational background to prospective employers, including Dr. Goodman at the Lynchburg College.

Gradually, I received positive responses to most of my letters and telephone calls. However, some people that I contacted now treated me differently, perhaps because of the change in the political climate and the revolution, and acted strangely. Some friends of mine in Iran did not bother to respond to my calls and letters. After all, I must have looked like a jobless immigrant from a troubled country and not like a college president of a strong and prosperous country. Fortunately, as a psychologist, I understood their position. People react differently to change and especially to a sudden change like our unique revolution. In fact, I was very surprised by the behavior of one particular person that I still vividly remember. He used to be dean of a US college, and as an international colleague and friend, we visited each other in Iran and the USA. He answered that he had bad news because he was no longer the dean and, as a result, was very sick and depressed. I asked him, "Are you still teaching as a tenure track professor?" He said, "Yes, of course." I could tell from his voice how depressed and sad he was, and I tried to cheer him up by pointing out that, in Germany, most professors were happy not to have any administrative responsibilities to devote more time to their research and that he too should look at this as a positive stage of his career. From that point on, I was calling him to extend help, rather than asking him for any assistance. I thought about the irony of the situation. Here I had no job, home, country, and identity, and was wandering in the United States, yet I was the one to help this American friend emotionally. I was surprised to see how people's tolerance levels could be so different to the failures and barriers in their lives.

Very soon, I received a positive response from Dr. Goodman at Lynchburg College telling me that there was no opening at Lynchburg College in my field, but that he had sent my résumé to the director of the Training School, Dr. Ray Nelson. At the time, the Lynchburg Training School and Hospital was being reorganized and had openings for new programs for psychologists as program or center directors. I went to the library to learn about the Lynchburg Training School and

Hospital (later the name changed to Central Virginia Training Center), and I learned that it was one of the largest and oldest institutions in the United States, established in 1910 as Virginia State Epileptic Colony. It began with almost twenty residents and, in 1979, had about three thousand clients mostly suffering from mental retardation and mental deficiency. Coming from a country and society where families resisted placing their relatives in institutions, I became curious and interested in seeing their programs, functions, and levels of care, especially since I had not visited these types of large institutions in my former visits to the United States. Anyway, I thought I might like to visit an institution like this someday.

I continued writing to several universities and colleges, excluding those with which our college in Iran had exchange programs. I found that openings for the next academic year were mostly for assistant professors and that the closing date to apply had passed. Some of my colleagues advised me to change my résumé. They thought if institutions read that I had been a full professor with a PhD and president of Shemiran College in the past, they might reject me because I was overqualified. This was one of the problems for many of my colleagues who had left Iran. Highly qualified and valuing freedom and democracy, they had left Iran because of the revolution, hoping to get full-time academic jobs in their own ranks in the United States. In fact, one of these was a professor with a PhD and a dean of a school, who, after several rejections because he was overqualified, changed his résumé and wrote graduate studies instead of PhD, and with the first application, he became a full-time assistant professor. Later on, he was promoted to associate and then full professorship in a very well-known university. There was another group, whom I had employed in Iran, who left Iran for the United States before the revolution and had already obtained good jobs, but I definitely did not like to ask them for any assistance, unless they would offer and insist. However, I did not change my résumé, as I wanted to be myself, like always in my life, and I was not giving up. I wanted to be sure if I could stay in the United States longer than six months, or whether I should go to Germany at the invitation and affidavit of one of my former Heidelberg professors, or to go to London, at the suggestion of my friend Christine, who also worked at the Home Office. As a wanderer, it was certainly a challenging time for me and my family. In the meantime, I got some positive response for the next academic year 1980-'81 from some colleges and universities, but this time frame could not meet my immediate need of employment for the residency permit since these jobs would begin after my six months' residency permit had expired.

At about the same time, Sa'id called me to say that his sabbatical leave from the University of Tehran was approved, and he and Reza would soon join us. I immediately called Gita, who was busy with final exams, and when I told her that her father and Reza were coming soon and we all could go together to the University of Michigan, she screamed with delight. For my lawyer, I was gathering all the affidavits, documents with a few copies of some of my own articles, which I could find in the libraries of Fairfax County and the rest I thought I could find at the library of the University of Michigan, which is one of the largest in the USA. I received almost twenty-five national and international affidavits from colleagues and friends who knew me. All of them were very concerned and supportive. A letter of support from Chancellor Eggers of the Syracuse University is typical of many I received.

Syracuse University

Syracuse, New York 13210

Office of the Chancellor   5 July 1979

To Whom It May Concern:

Dr. Sakineh Mostafavi Redjali, formerly President of Shemiran College, Tehran, Iran, is known to me personally. She was instrumental in initiating in 1977 a formal agreement for academic cooperation between Shemiran College and Syracuse University in the fields of Early Childhood Education and of Family Counseling. Dr. Redjali worked directly with Dr. Michael Marge, dean of our College for Human Development, and with Dr. Lowell E. Davis, Associate in our Office of Academic Affairs. The initial contract with Shemiran College covered the period 1 September 1973 to 30 August 1981, but it has recently been abrogated unilaterally by the

Office of Cultural and Educational Affairs of the Embassy of the Islamic Republic of Iran, Washington DC.

Dr. Redjali is an extremely well educated and productive scholar and administrator. Her professional experience has been wide-ranging from family guidance work, clinical psychology, and teaching in psychology to founding and administering Shemiran College. Her linguistic skills are impressive and include fluency in English, German, Persian and Arabic.

Dr. Redjali is a widely known and respected administrator, teacher and researcher. She is deemed to be well-qualified to undertake professional work in the fields of Child Development, Social Psychology, Clinical Psychology and related fields. Her organizational and administrative skills are considered to be of the highest order by professional personnel from Syracuse University who have worked directly with her in a professional context.

(signature)

Melvin A. Eggers

Chancellor

State of New York

S. S.

County of Onondaga

On 5 July 1979, before me, the undersigned, a Notary Public in and for said State, personally appeared MELVIN A. EGGERS, known to me to be the person whose name is subscriber to the within instrument and acknowledge that he executed the same.

M. Helen Wigler

Notary Public in the State of New York

I am still grateful to all of them for their immediate understanding and response in this wandering time of the symphony of my life.

I also received two important telephone calls during that spring, which played a crucial role in our life. One was from Iran and one from America. The first one was from Dr. Khalil Mossaed, my former colleague and the vice president of Shemiran College, who became president after my resignation, appointed by the revolutionary government. He said the government was in the process of nationalizing private colleges, including Shemiran College, and he wanted to know what to do with the share of capital that Sa'id and I had contributed for the establishment of the college or where to send the proceeds. I was in such a state of shock and disappointment and pain that I told him that he could make the decision how to spend the money to benefit the students and improve the college. So in this way, all the years of our mental, physical, financial resources and efforts spent for establishing Shemiran College for the people of Iran and their well-being were disappearing in the revolution. I thanked him for continuing to work in the college. Later on, I heard that he was killed in a road accident during the Iran-Iraq war. May God let his soul rest in peace. This was the first memorable call.

The next telephone call, which was almost in the same time period, came from the office of Dr. Henry Meece. His secretary, Mrs. Kathy Collins, called to set up an interview with Dr. Meece and his team of center directors and then to visit the Lynchburg Training School and Hospital and its different centers. I was surprised by his call, because of my interest and curiosity about the function of large institutions, I accepted the opportunity for an interview immediately, and we set a date for the next week. The hospital campus was located in Amherst in the middle of the Blue Ridge Mountain Range in Central Virginia, near the city of Lynchburg. The 350-acre facility overlooked the James River. I had never been in this part of the United States before. David and Sallie told me that it should be a beautiful area. Alas, because of the big loss I was going through, my eyes were closed for some years to the natural beauty around me, and I could not see it. I called Dr. Goodman to thank him for sending my résumé to the Training School, and I told him about the telephone call and the date for the interview and visit. He was very kind and immediately invited me to meet him and his wife, Martha, at the Howard Johnson Restaurant in Madison Heights after my visit to the Lynchburg Training School and Hospital.

A week later, I traveled from Fairfax to Lynchburg by a Trailways bus and arrived very early in the morning for my appointment at 1:00 p.m. At that time, the Trailways Bus Company had a good connection between Fairfax and Lynchburg. There was no interstate highway to that city and the best direct road to Lynchburg was Route 29. On the road, we passed through several towns, including Charlottesville, where the University of Virginia and the house of Thomas Jefferson are located. Jefferson, the principal author of the *Declaration of Independence* (1776), is my favorite former president of the United States. From Charlottesville to Lynchburg, the route became hilly and seemed like a labyrinth climbing up and down hills. When I got near Lynchburg, after three and a half hours of travel, passing the James River Bridge and entering Lynchburg, the city of seven hills, it reminded me a little of the City of Heidelberg, Germany, and my alma mater, the University of Heidelberg. I took a taxi from the bus station to the address in Madison Heights where the hospital was located next to the administration building.

Lynchburg Training School and Hospital, later known as the Central Virginia Training Center, a State institution from 1910, the location of the author's job interview held in 1979.

There, I went to the office of Dr. Henry C. Meece, the assistant director, who was chairing the interview panel. Mrs. Kathy Collins, the kind young lady who had called me, was expecting me. She immediately guided me to another building where the interviews for all the candidates were being conducted. I entered the room and saw four men and one woman sitting around a table. One of the gentlemen stood and came forward to introduce himself as Dr. Meece and, after shaking my hand, introduced me to the members of the panel. Then he gave a short introduction about the institution and its reorganization plan. The center was going to be divided into eight centers, according to the medical, developmental, and functional levels of the clients. All the center directors were required to have a PhD or graduate studies in psychology or education. The institution was changing from the medical model to the educational model to train and prepare clients with skills to facilitate their adjustment to the outside community, leading eventually to deinstitutionalization. I understood their objective immediately, and I was happy to see that the country was going in that direction. They asked several questions about educational programming. I tried to respond extensively to the questions and continued the response for each question until each time they stopped me to ask the next question. I tried to give them samples and examples from other countries in Europe and the Middle East, including the new country of Israel. They seemed interested in hearing all this. I asked Dr. Meece to write what he remembered from that time and from the interview, and he replied kindly:

> In the U.S., the field of Mental Retardation/Developmental Disabilities (MR/DD) was changing from a significantly under-funded model of minimal care (custodial) in large institutions to individually-based training model (developmental). The developmental model was used both in large institutions and in newly created homes in the communities around the institutions, and it was significantly different from the custodial, both in funding and training mandate. The increase in funding for the Developmental Model came from a partnership between the Federal Government and each state that wished to participate. One of the conditions of state participation was an agreement to meet or exceed the standards set by the Federal Government in the newly created designation of Intermediate Care Facilities/Mental Retardation (ICF/MR). Training mandate_standards defined and focused on Active Treatment as the primary responsibility of the State through its ICF/MR certified facilities. Active Treatment includes an individualized training plan designed for each individual living in an ICF facility and is based on the various interdisciplinary evaluations and subsequent training plans and therapies developed from those assessments.
>
> It was during this period of time that I was interviewing professionally trained leaders to act as agents of change for each of the centers located at the Lynchburg Training School and Hospital. I hired Dr. Redjali whose remarkable resume included experience in *Leadership* as the Secretary General

of the Women's Organization of Iran and as President of Shemiran College in Iran. Both of these leadership experiences required her to influence others as an agent of change. Also impressive were her knowledge and education in *Human Learning and Special Education from* a Post Doctoral Fellowship at the University of London Institute of Education (focusing on comparative and special education) and as a Fulbright Scholar with focus on Research Programs in Psychology and Programmed Learning. These were important in implementing the training mandate. Dr. Redjali, as Center Director for the Child Development Center and later as Center Director for the Adult Training Center was responsible for "Planning the conceptual development and structure process of Resident's Care and Habilitative and Program Services for about 300 developmentally disabled persons according to intermediate care mental retardation, accreditation and certification standards.

The interview took about two hours. Then, when I asked about my interest in research possibilities and in visiting the campus, they immediately responded that there was a good connection among all the universities and LTSH and many students and professors conducted their studies and research there. As for my visit, they had already arranged for me to visit the two centers, which had openings for center director. These were the Child Development Center (CDC) and the Community Adjustment Center (CAC). Both centers each had approximately 250 to 300 residents. The other centers, whose directors were members of the interview team, were the Educational Development Center (EDC), the Multi Handicapped Center (MHC), Adult Training Center (ATC) for geriatric patients and the Social Skills Center (SSC) for the clients with maladaptive behavior, and the need for behavior modification and therapy. Each of these centers also had between 200 to 300 beds or residents. In addition, there was a hospital for residents who needed a higher level of medical care and which also accommodated residents from other centers who needed temporary acute care or skilled nursing care. There was also an Independent Living Center, which was a transitional housing for placement in the community. When I got the map of the campus, I noticed that there was no way I could visit all of them in one afternoon. That would take days, and I had to meet Dr. and Mrs. Goodman at the Howard Johnson at 6:00 p.m. and then return to Fairfax. Scott, one of the center directors who had been at my interview, seemed fascinated by my account of programs in other countries, and he volunteered to drive me around the campus. Therefore, I thanked Dr. Meece and the other center directors and continued the tour and visit with Scott. We visited the CDC and CAC, the two centers that were without center directors, and Scott's new center, the Social Skills Center, with a new program of behavior modification and therapy. At each center, a person was waiting to show me around. At CDC, an anxious teacher showed me around and spoke of his concerns about the immediate implementation of the new Public Law PL 94.142 requiring five and a half hours of active programs per day for each child under twenty-one. At the CAC, a young lady with a pencil behind her ear was the program manager, and she explained the vocational training of residents. She seemed to have a curious expression. Finally, I visited the new social skills center. Scott gave me several brochures and programs to take with me. To me, the institution seemed extremely large and a wonderful place with opportunity and challenges for different research projects in the field of mental disability and the facilities to help the residents with appropriate training and services. However, the time was fast running out, and I had to be on time at Howard Johnson to meet the Goodmans. When I told Scott about my meeting at 6:00 p.m., he generously offered to drive me to the Howard Johnson. I thanked him for all his kindness.

At Howard Johnson's, I met a very friendly couple who shook my hand and smiled so sincerely I felt we had known each other for years. They started to speak about their time in Iran as visiting professors at Damavand College. During dinner, they told me that they had returned from three years of teaching at Damavand College in Iran in 1975, having led a wonderful life there with friends they still treasured and great memories of that fine country they loved dearly. Then they continued to say that as soon as they got settled again at Lynchburg College, they began to hear about the Ayatollah Khomeini and the unrest in Iran. However, they stayed busy, as Lynchburg College welcomed many Iranian students—male and female—and Dr. Goodman served as director of International Students, in addition to teaching religious studies and ancient history. He had also taught world history and world religions at Damavand College in Tehran and had enjoyed travel in the country and independent study of archaeological sites in Iran. In Lynchburg, they kept in touch with Iran through his travels for Lynchburg College and followed the news with interest. Iranian students in their classes (Martha taught at Central Virginia Community College, which had about twenty Iranian students—all male) seemed to support Khomeini's efforts. They remained convinced that the students didn't realize what they would be getting with a theocracy but tried to remain objective throughout all the uncertainty of 1978 and 1979. When they asked about the revolution and my life and departure from Iran, I gave them a short description. They were sorry about what was happening in Iran, and Bill said that when they received Dr. Spatta's letter in May, they were also sorry that the Lynchburg College had no faculty vacancies. The only positions that he thought might possibly interest me were at the Lynchburg Training School and Hospital, and so he had sent my résumé to them. They asked me about my interview and visit, and I told them it had been an interesting one and that a job as center director would be challenging and demanding with twenty-four-hour individualized programming, services, and responsibility for nearly three hundred mentally disabled. We went on talking long into the evening, but I had to leave to catch the last departure of the Trailways Bus to Fairfax, so we had to end our conversation. They kindly took me to the bus station. Although our meeting was short, it was a starting point of a lifelong friendship, which my family, and I cherish and treasure.

Meeting Dr. Willam and Mrs. Martha Goodman,
in Lynchburg Virginia.

It was very late when I arrived in Fairfax, and David, whose home was near the Trailways station, was waiting there to meet me. He was very interested to hear about my trip and interview and wanted to know all the details. He told me that if the organization selected me, they would contact me. During the next few days, on our daily walks—David, Sally, and I—we went to the local drugstore to buy some things and one day we had our blood pressure checked on the instruments at the drugstore. David and Sallie had normal blood pressure, but when I put my arm in the machine, it showed that my blood pressure was extremely high—between 120 for diastolic and 200 for systolic. I took my blood pressure several times just in case the other readings had been a mistake. Every time it was abnormally high and it was no wonder that I had frequent migraine headaches. I even tried to take my blood pressure with other different blood pressure instruments, but the result was the same. I had no physician, so I called another cousin, Dr. Abbass Rejali, who was a professor of medicine at the Cleveland Clinic and Case Western Reserve University, and he advised me to go to George Washington University Emergency. He always recommended the University Hospitals for treatment. Since I did not know any other physician in Fairfax, I went to the George Washington University emergency room. All I had was a foreign passport, no social security, no private health insurance, and at first, I wasn't sure I would be accepted but with the assurance of cash payment by traveler's check, I was admitted to the internal medicine department immediately. Fortunately, a nice lady professor with a Greek background saw me. After examining my blood pressure, she ordered a comprehensive blood test. She told me that I needed immediate assistance and possible hospitalization for observation for a few days. When I explained my situation and the need for me to attend my daughter's graduation in Boston, she grew quiet. She was thinking, I could tell, and then wrote a prescription for immediate use for my blood pressure problem and told me to come back to see her in three days. Then she said, when she could view the results of the blood test and the effect of the medicine, she would make the final decision about my hospitalization. I thanked her and bought the medication at the university pharmacy and took it immediately, and with David, who was waiting for me, went home. In three days, I returned to the hospital for the appointment. The doctor had the result of my blood test and took my blood pressure, and I noticed her expression was much better than the first time. This time too she noticed the unusual size of my goiter and told me that my blood pressure was better and that wherever I settled, I would need to have detailed tests and attention to my thyroid function. She told me to continue the medicine until my blood pressure was under control. I thanked her sincerely, and after the payment in the hospital, we went to David's house.

Very soon I had to go to Boston because of Gita's end of term and to attend the end-of-school celebration and to vacate her room. This time in Boston, I stayed with one of my cousins, Mohammed Yamin Afshar (sadly now deceased), who, after the revolution, settled in Newton, near Boston to be near his two sons who were studying engineering as he had. Doris continued to be so very helpful to Gita and me by showing us around. As a native Bostonian, she showed us all the historical places, and we did a lot of sightseeing with her. I remember well that Doris and I went together to Gita's graduation from Walnut Hill School. In cleaning her room afterward, I was happy to find a Shemiran College brochure that I copied and which also helped me for my international exchange and activities for support when I met the lawyer to discuss immigration. Before leaving Boston, I went with Gita to the immigration office to change her passport from tourist visa to student visa. She had her acceptance letter to the Phillips Academy. The officer in Boston told us we were one day too late to change the visa status. Finally, she approved the change, but told us we needed to be very careful to meet the time and day deadline next time. She issued Gita a one-year student visa, so for Gita, at least we had peace of mind.

Then, Gita and I went to see my other cousin Mehri in Norwalk, Connecticut, near New York to await the arrival of my husband, Sa'id, and my son, Reza, from Iran for the summer program and workshops in June. Sa'id would be teaching Music in World Culture at the University of Michigan. When we heard that they had departed from Tehran, we were very happy and all of us went to John F. Kennedy airport for their arrival. At the airport, we welcomed them with hugs and kisses. Both of them had lost a lot of weight and looked much thinner. We stayed for a few days in Norwalk to let them rest. While they rested, I went to the lawyer's office with all the documents and affidavits I had collected to see if I had missed anything. The lawyer told me that the local congressman John Stewart McKinney was impressed with my résumé and would write a letter in support of my application for permanent residency in the United States. He said he would notify me when everything was ready and to tell me when to file the petition. While we were in Norwalk, my cousin David called me from Fairfax to tell me that I had a call from the Lynchburg Training School and Hospital (LTSH) and he had given them Mehri's telephone number in Connecticut. The next day Mrs. Kathy Collins called me with a message from Dr. Meece to ask me which center I preferred from my visit—CDC or CAC. Without knowing just what she meant, I asked where the immediate need was. I remembered the anxious expression on the face of the male teacher who spoke about implementing the law. I replied, "the CDC," if there is an immediate need. Then she said that I would hear from the director of the LTSH soon. Just before leaving Norwalk, I had a call from Dr. Nelson, indicating that he was happy that I had been selected as the center director of the Child Development Center (CDC). He said he was going to mail the appropriate papers for my acceptance or rejection and signature and that I would have one week to respond to Dr. Meece, the assistant director. I thanked him and told him that when I received the package, I would consider the offer and would respond on time. After this call, I was so shocked that I called David and my lawyer and told them about the phone call, as both of them had experience in the employment procedure. They were both happy to hear the news and told me to discuss the package with them when I received it.

Then we had to go to Ann Arbor, Michigan, for Sa'id's university program. At the University of Michigan, when Sa'id was going to be teaching his classes, I was with Gita and Reza, and we spent time at the library finding my articles in English and German, articles that I could not find at the Fairfax library. I knew from my past experiences that the university was very rich, especially in reference books. I remember well that a kind and friendly lady librarian had helped me to find my articles and as I had several difficult names this was not easy so she had helped me to have the copies notarized as genuine and true to the original. I was especially very happy to find my article in the *World Yearbook of Education*, which was published by the University of London and Columbia University.[1] That was one of the best examples to justify my claim and prove that I was internationally known in the field of education and psychology. I made a copy for the lawyer and asked what else he would need. He told me if Dr. Meece would write the process of my selection to add to the package of the Training School employment that would help too. I remember calling Dr. Meece from a telephone booth in Ann

Arbor to ask if he would write a letter supporting my selection for the job. I told him this was an important document in getting a work permit and a visa for permanent residency. He was very kind and understanding and agreed to send a letter to my cousin Mehri's address in Connecticut. In Ann Arbor, I shared my situation with Dr. Millholland, my former advisor in the National Science Foundation program, who also wrote a letter of support for me. He asked why I hadn't approached him at the University of Michigan for a similar job. He scanned the job openings in Ann Arbor, and when he saw there were no immediate openings, he advised that maybe it would be best to accept this job offer, pending the immigration work permit and residency. Soon, I left Michigan with the children and went to Connecticut to my cousin Mehri to pursue my immigration and work status while Sa'id continued his program for the summer term in Michigan. In Norwalk, I saw the lawyer and gave him what I had prepared in Michigan to add to my file. My file was becoming quite thick, and he said he was ready now to go with me to file my petition in Hartford where the immigration office was located.

We left very early in the morning from Norwalk to Hartford to be early for our case. We arrived at the immigration office at 8.30 in the morning and delivered our thick file with all the publications in three languages—English, German, and Persian. I was one of the first applicants. We were expected to sit and wait until we were called by the immigration officer who would determine if everything in the file with the application was complete. We sat and waited. I was very impatient and looked constantly at the face and mouth of the officer to see if he would take my file and call me. My lawyer's behavior was just the opposite. He was reading the newspaper, while I was observing the officer's action. The officer was calling many people, even those who came after us, and each time, he would take a new file and put it above my thick file. This scene continued. After 1:00 pm, I was still not called. Finally, I asked my lawyer these questions: Why are we not called after more than four hours of waiting, and why are all the people who arrived after us were called and not us? What is the procedure and why are they not paying any attention to whose turn it is? Can we ask when it will be our turn? He replied indifferently and calmly told me we needed to be very patient in the United States, especially in court, and said we should not interrupt the officers or judges. Another two hours passed, and it was almost three p.m. I finally decided not to listen to my lawyer and went to the desk of the officer and said, "I have been here since 8:30 a.m., and I would like to know when it will be my turn."

He looked at me and said, "What is your name? Which one is your file?" I pointed to the thick file. He looked at the file and then at me, and said, "You have to be patient with this file and wait longer." He said he would call me. I came back to my seat, and my lawyer was still reading newspapers. He said, "You see, I told you, we need to be patient." Gradually my headache began, and I immediately took two pain tablets to be able to wait longer. The time was passing fast, and I remember that it was a few minutes after 4:00 p.m. and nearly close to the office closing time. I became very impatient for my file and my destiny. I did not want to wait another day to come back from Norwalk to Hartford, so before the officer called another person who arrived about 3:00 p.m. I went in front of his desk and my lawyer jumped up to join me. I said, "Sir, I have been here since 8:30 a.m. I ask for your attention because my destiny depends on your acceptance of my petition. I need to know where I belong, and if it is not here, then I have to go to another country." At this moment, my lawyer began to speak on my behalf. The officer suddenly asked, "Who is the lawyer? I am confused. Are you the lawyer, or is he your lawyer?" At this time, my lawyer finally started to speak and introduced himself as representing me as a international figure. He explained that he was filing the petition for immigration based on the third-preference clause and read each item on my résumé and referred also to the international and national documents and letters of support, including the letter of Congressman McKinney and the letter from the agency, which wanted to employ me. He said that all these documents proved that I was internationally known, and that the publications and copies of newspapers and journals in many languages and all the affidavits proved my exceptional ability and the job offer proved the need of these skills in our country. While he was speaking, the officer was looking at the documents, and then in the middle of perusing the document, he asked me, "Do you have any immediate family like mother, father, brother, or sister in the United States? I replied, "Unfortunately, no, but I have cousins in many states and around the world, and I can give their addresses. I am staying in Norwalk with my cousin Dr. Mehri Kalali. However, I have all these notarized documents that are in front of you." Then he replied, "You have too many documents. I need to have time to study them to make a decision about your permanent residency." I replied, "If your study takes a long time, I might lose my employment, because I have to accept or reject the offer in one week." He immediately said that he could authorize employment with six months' extension of residency immediately, and that he would make a decision later for permanent residency. Then he stamped my passport Employment Authorized and then separated all the Persian books and articles in my file, returned them to me, and said he could not read Persian, but he would keep the English and German publications. I took the Persian books and publications and asked his name. He said, "Sherwood." I replied, "Mr. Sherwood, I will never forget you as long as I live," and I have not ever forgotten him or this day either. He really changed my life. My lawyer also thanked him, and we left the office at about 4:50 p.m. near closing time. I was in a way a little bit relieved, and my lawyer was happy, and he told me that Officer Sherwood would probably approve the petition. It was rush-hour traffic; we had not had any lunch, and I was supposed to take my blood pressure tablet with a meal. So I invited my lawyer for dinner near the immigration office. He welcomed my offer, and I thought probably he was going to add the dinner time to his hourly rate, which he did. At dinner, I called my cousin Mehri, who was very anxious to know about our trip and our delay in returning home. She was worried, but when I called her, she was pleased to hear the outcome. During dinner, my lawyer explained that he was a real estate lawyer and that he had had no experience in immigration law. He said that my file was the first and probably would be the last immigration case he would do. He accepted because of my cousin Mehri and Bill and their friendship, and he said that what I prepared for the petition was very good and complete. Through this first legal experience in America, and also later, I learned that the signature of a lawyer is very important even if they do not specialize in any field and that in every case, one should know and prepare everything oneself if she or he has a legal case.

The next day, I called Dr. Meece to explain about the day I had spent at the Hartford immigration office. I told him that since my employment had been authorized, I could legally accept the job as the center director of CDC. He told me that I should return all the documents with my signature and welcomed me and said that when he received the documents he would notify me which day I would start to work. Also, at this time, I called Dr. and Mrs. Goodman and told them that it looked as though I would be their neighbor in Lynchburg and explained the whole procedure at the immigration office to them. They were very happy to see that I was offered the job and congratulated me. I remember well that I thought it would be better to go first by myself to Lynchburg. Gita and Reza could stay with Mehri and Bill since they were almost the same age as their children Marianna and Billy, and they could play together. Sa'id, after finishing his workshop and summer term, could join them until I was settled and sure of the job and had appropriate housing for them. Then, when everything was ready, they could come to Lynchburg.

The news from Iran continued to show the violence and executions in the name of Islam. The people, especially women, were treated with harshness and rudeness, and the situation in Iran was at the top of the international news on the radio and television and in newspapers. Day by day, I was hearing about the exit from Iran of family members, academic colleagues and friends of my family. It looked as if the revolution was hijacking our religion too. I had grown up in a religious family where moderation, kindness, service, and respect for people, others, and ethics were the top values in our family life. It seemed that the message "Moderation is the best action of a Muslim" *(Khairolomoor osateha)* that I heard from my parents and teachers in our daily life was forgotten. Therefore, watching the daily news was depressing because it showed the Iranian people wandering as strangers in the world, including in our own country Iran, losing their country and religion. Most people, including even our king and queen, were also wandering from one country or location to another. So in this way, we all became wanderers—wanderers in pain. I went with my cousin Mehri to New York to buy a few suits and some clothing for my new professional position, as the center director. However, first, we needed to wait in a long line for gas. Mehri said, because of the Iranian revolution, there was a shortage of gas with a gas price hike. We could see this problem in gas stations everywhere. Apparently, about 10 percent of the US oil was coming from Iran.

In the meantime, my cousin David in Fairfax told me that I had received responses from all my writing and had offers for several interviews from different colleges and universities for the next 1980-'81 academic year. With the uncertainty of my permanent residency, I had to thank them all and take the immediate job offer.

On the second week of July, I had a call from Dr. Meece that I could start my job on July 16, 1979. I bought an air ticket to fly from New York on a small commuter plane on July 14 and told Dr. Meece my plans. He kindly arranged transportation for me to his home, and I was welcomed by his kind family, his wife, Beth, and their three sons. His oldest boy, Jeff, was the same age as my son Reza. Dr. Meece told me they wanted me to stay with them for the first days and then I could look for my own place. During dinner, I understood what a generous and kind family they were and how much they knew about the Middle East, the oil companies, their political influences in the world, and even the history of our troubled country. Apparently, Dr Meece undergraduate major was history, and his father-in-law worked for an oil company. What I needed immediately was a car because, without a car, I would have been handicapped. Lynchburg, like the other small cities in the United States, was not like London or New York and Washington DC, which have public transportation.

The next day, Scott, Dr. Meece's colleague (and later mine), came to show me around and help me look at a few cars. Since Sa'id and Reza could each bring with them $5,000, I would have to buy a new car with cash because I did not have a credit background. I just had one American Express card with good credit and an international account at the Chase Manhattan Bank in New York, which I opened when Gita had her spine surgery in 1978. At that time, Chase had a branch in Tehran, just as American Express did. With Scott's assistance, and without knowing anything about consumer reports then, I bought a station wagon from the Chrysler dealer, a well-established dealer in Lynchburg. American cars in Iran used to be very popular, and we ourselves had had both a Chevrolet and a Buick at some time. In addition, I was thinking I had to take Gita and her belongings to Phillips Academy in Andover near Boston, and the station wagon was roomy enough. Looking at a few hotels, I chose a suite at the Holiday Inn, which had a swimming pool, thinking that until I find a rental place, the best place for our children during the summer holiday would be a place with a swimming pool, which they would enjoy. This would keep them busy and give me some peace of mind. Thanking the Meece family, I moved to the Holiday Inn and called Sa'id in Connecticut to fly down with the children. They came immediately and joined me in the search for a furnished rental house. I also shared my information with Martha and Bill Goodman, who were very kind and interested to know how we were beginning to adjust to the new country, and they immediately started looking for a furnished rental flat or house, which was not easy to find in Lynchburg. Finally, we found a rental house in Boonsboro, the home of a new retiree who wanted to travel for a year.

As a center director of CDC, my job description was to plan programs and services for over 250 developmentally disabled residents up to twenty-two years of age, supervise approximately 250 staff, plan the budget, assume responsibility for maintaining accreditation, intermediate care, mental retardation (ICF/MR) certification standards, training staff, and to develop an overall plan and support for training and evaluation of training according to the rules and regulations of the federal, state, and LTSH policy and procedures. On my first day of work, when Dr. Meece introduced me to the excited and curious staff, I told them that I considered all of them at every level as my colleagues, and that I would value and respect their opinions. I also mentioned that, like my college administration, I would have an open-door policy, and they could have access to see me any time if they had a need. In addition, I would make rounds in all three shifts to all living areas. I thought to myself, that if I treat them with respect and dignity, I could expect them to treat our residents and clients with dignity and respect as well. That day, I noticed not only the expression of the staff became much calmer, and they seemed to look forward to working with me, but also that Dr. Meece supported my style of management.

Appointed Center Director

Dr. Sakineh Redjali, a native of Tehran, Iran, was appointed center director of the Child Development Center at Lynchburg Training School and Hospital on July 16, 1979.

Dr. Redjali did her undergraduate work at the University of Tehran. Master's and Doctoral Degrees in Educational and Clinical Psychology, were awarded at the University of Heidelberg, Germany. She did post-doctoral work in special education at the Institute of Education at the university of London. She founded and was president of Shemiran College in Tehran from 1973-1979. Prior to 1973, she was associated with a number of universities and colleges in Iran as associate professor, professor of Psychology and dean of women.

Dr. Redjali holds membership in professional associations in Iran, England, Germany and the United States. She has been published extensively in professional journals in all of these countries. One honor bestowed upon Dr. Redjali was the Tadj Medal in 1978, for services rendered to Shemiran College and for excellence in academic contributions.

Dr. Redjali is married and the mother of two children. The family lives in Lynchburg, Virginia.

Dr. Sakineh Redjali

The author's biography and photo when appointed Center Director as published in the Lynchburg Newspapers and local Newsletters in 1979.

The Germans say *Aller Anfang ist Schwer*, which means "every beginning is difficult." However, my first days and weeks of work went very well, and in comparing this time to my former jobs, it was not very difficult. My knowledge and years of experience in the field helped my family and me to adjust to this big change and other adversities in my life. For the Individualized Program plan, we arranged schedules to meet with interdisciplinary teams to plan the five and a half hours of training for our residents. Each team had a team leader, our program coordinator, psychologist, physician, teacher, social worker, speech pathologist, and other disciplines according to the policy and procedures; and I wrote in my daily calendar about each meeting and followed up the implementation of their programs.

In the personnel area, there were a few strange disciplinary administrative problems, which I had to deal with in the first days on the job, following the disciplinary action policy and procedures. This was the paperwork for the disciplinary actions for firing three night-shift employees who slept on duty. All the paperwork was ready on my desk for my signature. I found it shocking and strange that on my first days of employment that I had to sign off on these firings without any investigation of the reasons or knowing the strong justification for the action. When I asked my secretary and program coordinator, I noticed that the procedure was routine. Other center directors fired employees, and I heard praise about one center director who had fired five people for the same reason. Then I was told that the employees could file a grievance if they wanted, and they would have a hearing in a panel and that they might win their case. I made up my mind that no matter what, I would not sign the paperwork before studying the reason of action. I needed time to study the reason for this routine behavior and to see if the firing could be prevented. All my life, I have believed more in prevention over treatment in my profession.

I called Dr. Meece and asked him how much time I could have before making this decision. He was surprised that I questioned what was waiting on my desk and said the maximum time that I could have according to personnel policy and procedure was three days. I reviewed the job description of the night-shift staff and the personnel file of all three employees and noticed that the two of them had been seen sleeping in the living area in a rocking chair but had never had any disciplinary action before. Since I was planning anyway to visit the living areas and meet the night-shift staff I made an unannounced visit to meet the night-shift staff and the shift supervisor. I remember that it was 2:00 a.m. in the morning when I arrived at the CDC. I called the shift supervisor, introduced myself, and with her, I made rounds and asked her opinion about the activities and duties of the staff from 11:00 p.m. to 7:00 a.m. I noticed that, in reality, the third shift was not engaged in much work with residents until early morning, and since the residents were usually asleep at this time, they had much more free time than the employees in the first and second shifts. I made a note of this information for myself. After speaking about my open-door policy and how I was available twenty-four hours a day, which was part of my job description, I saw a big difference in their tense expressions; and when I told them that I would make rounds periodically to come to see them, they looked relieved.

I also noticed that the rocking chairs in the living areas were probably designed for the use of our clients and residents, and not the staff. The next day, I reviewed the job descriptions for the second and third shifts and tried to change some of the duties. For instance, I assigned washing, drying, and putting away clothing to the third shift. When I randomly asked the opinion of the staff, I noticed all of them were happy and satisfied and welcomed the changes. The first and second shifts were pleased to have this duty reassigned, leaving them happy to have less work and more time to communicate with the residents. Third-shift employees were also happy to have something to do so as not to get bored and possibly fall asleep. I tried also to speak with the three employees individually, the three who were supposed to be fired, and I found out that each one was in different circumstances and had different work habits. I prepared a package with revised job descriptions of all three shifts with a draft memorandum, indicating that since the rocking chairs were there only for the use of our residents, the staff should not use them at all. I took the personnel files of all three employees to Dr. Meece and the director of personnel and discussed with them that because of the job environment and the job description of all the shifts, these employees should not be fired, but instead given a lower disciplinary action, such as suspension from one to three days if the policy and procedure and their practice at the Training School would permit. Dr. Meece and the director of personnel liked my changes and even suggested they would share that idea at the weekly center directors meeting. He also sent a memorandum to all center directors indicating that all center director should ensure that the job description of the first-shift aids be more program related, second shift program related and some maintenance, and for the third shift be primarily maintenance related.

In a way, I was happy to see that my first recommendation for disciplinary action was accepted by everyone including the employees. I did not have any grievances filed against me, and even began to establish greater authority and a trustworthy relationship among our clients, employees, and the top management and myself. The most important result was that our clients were enjoying far more interaction and learning with staff because they were available to them for more time in the first and the second shifts.

While I was extremely busy at devising programming at CDC center and its twenty-four hours management, Sa'id spent time with Reza and Gita, who were at home because of August vacation, showing them around and registering Reza in the fifth grade of Paul Munroe Elementary School near our rented home. We were also getting ready to take Gita to her new school, Phillips Academy at Andover, Massachussets. Fortunately, we later learned that both of them would not have any problem with the language, and in math, reading and writing; and in some other areas, they were more advanced than their classmates. They had really had an excellent bilingual education at the International Community School in Tehran. This issue was very important for us. However, there were cultural problems. Both had a strong British accent, and their different social and cultural habits from Iran influenced how they viewed the United States. For example, every day Reza was accustomed to asking, "Who is coming today as our guests?" If we replied, "Nobody," he asked, "Where are we going today?" All of us were accustomed to our big family and a large circle of friends in Iran. After several days of his surprise and disappointment, we explained to him that the pattern of our social life had changed because of the move to another country, and we had to behave according to the new country's customs. As for the accents, Gita's very soon sounded like her Massachusetts friends and Reza developed a Southern Central Virginia accent to fit in. We learned how important peer pressure was in the United States, and that in some areas peer groups played a more important role than the family.

At the end of August, we took Gita with all her belongings in our new car to Andover for the start of the school year. Of course, this time she was in a better position than her first time of separation from family, especially since we were all in a new country together and that was good support for her, although the news from Iran was not promising at all and was still as distressing. Our travel to Boston and Andover went well. Arrangements to welcome new students for orientation were very well organized. Because of my work, we could not stay long in Boston, and we saw Doris very briefly. On the return trip, we also stopped in Norwalk to greet Mehri and to see my lawyer to follow up with my petition for permanent residency. He said he was going to write a follow-up in connection to that. Then we rushed to return to Lynchburg.

Unfortunately, on the road, on the New Jersey Turnpike, our new car broke down. We had no idea why; and after a temporary repair, we drove cautiously back to Lynchburg. Since the new car was under warranty, I returned it to the Chrysler dealer who, after checking it, noticed that the car was defective and would take a long time to repair and supplied us with a courtesy car. However, we continued to have great problems with that car. Finally, we had to sell it back to the dealer when the engine was burning and boiling right on the same street as the dealership. Our first experience with a car in the United States was not a good one. Later, we learned that the dealer should have done more to help us and should have even given us a better car in exchange.

This is just one example of how hard it was to live in a new country. So many rules, regulations, and business practices have to be mastered. That experience caused me to be very careful in any shopping and dealing in the United States, and I learned the rules and regulations before buying anything. Now I first read the consumer reports about the product, something that I did not think about doing in other countries, including my home country. The United States is fortunately a country of laws and regulations. However, one has to have the opportunity to learn those rules and regulations in order to protect one's rights in case of facing people who fail to follow the laws, rules and regulations and try to violate one's rights. In general, I learned quickly that in this new country, in order to survive, I would either have to be defensive or offensive. My education helped me to be more defensive in my life, my profession, and my job, a job that required a knowledge of numerous federal and state laws, rules and regulations as they related to clients and staff. I collected all the policy and procedures manuals and all the laws and rules and regulations, and whenever I had time, I read them and learned, although sometimes, I would notice conflicts in the documents, so I wrote these down in case I needed them.

Gradually, I was thinking that we could get settled in Lynchburg; however, watching the evening local news every night was casting doubt in my mind. The local news would start with the Training School and all its problems, which was interpreted to me as internal political issues within the department of Mental Health and Mental Retardation of the government. The world news would start with my troubled country Iran. Executions continued, and the country began to polarize. There was disagreement and fighting between the different political groups like left links and national front groups for the draft of the new Islamic constitution within the temporary government of Bazargan and even later between Bazargan and Khomeini, and a new concept of *velayate-e faghih* (Guardianship of the Islamic Jurist or supreme leader) was emerging. Velayet-e-Faqih monopolized and institutionalized the power of the clerical power and *ulama*. *Vali-e Faghih* (the Supreme Leader) was to be selected as the leader among the highly qualified ayatollahs (Shiite clergy) by the Assembly of Experts (*Majles-e-Khobregan*), an institution composed of *Ulama*. Within this system, *Vali-e-Fagih*, as the leader of the nation, gained extensive powers, much greater than the Shah's. He gained the power to set the general direction of the country, with no limit on his term, with powers to declare war as the commander in chief, appoint senior officers of the military and Revolutionary Guards, as well as the members of the judiciary and clerical members of the Council of Guardians (*Shura-ye Negahban*). The first such leader was of course Khomeini, the leader of the initial revolution (*Rahbar-e-Engelab*). In this way, gradually one by one, all the other active groups, excluding the radical religious front, were separated from the new regime during the first two years after the revolution.

With this continuous frustrating news, I became concerned about my residency and called my lawyer in Norwalk, asking him to call the government for a follow-up response to my petition. He told me again that I needed to be patient and told me that my response was not late considering the government bureaucracy. However, he said he would go through the office of Congressman McKinney in Norwalk. My cousin Mehri told me that since I worked in Virginia in the field of mental health, maybe it would be beneficial to speak with my favorite actress Elizabeth Taylor, who was at that time Mrs. John Warner, wife of the senator from Virginia and an advocate for mental health, about my petition for permanent residency. I asked some friends in Virginia as to how I could do this, and they recommended that I make an appointment to see Senator Warner. I called the office of Senator Warner and got an appointment for the end of October 1979.

At work, I was making progress in communicating with my clients and staff and in the daily programming of our clients, whom I always tried to see every day and monitor their progress. One day, I finally got a call from my lawyer saying that he had heard from the office of Congressman McKinney that my petition was approved, and I would receive a written confirmation soon. After that, every day I anxiously checked the mailbox for the written letter, and finally, toward the end of October 1979, just two days before my appointment with Senator Warner, I received a formal approval of my application from Hartford with the indication that because I lived in Lynchburg, they were sending my files to the Immigration office in Washington DC and then I would receive my permanent residency card, known as the green card.

I was happy, relieved, and grateful to all the people who were instrumental in getting this petition approved and grateful to the United States for its progressive laws, rules, and regulations. Some colleagues and friends told me maybe it was no longer necessary to see Senator Warner because I did not have anything to ask him. However, I thought this would be a good occasion to go and see him to express my situation, thank him, and learn what he, as the representative of the people of Virginia and United States, expected from me. I wanted him to know that I was serving the country and the people who needed special attention relating to their developmental disability and mental deficiency. So I took one-day annual leave and went to Washington DC to the Senate. That was my first visit to the Senate. First, I met his office manager, with whom I had spoken many times on the phone. After a few minutes, he guided me to the office of Senator Warner, a very charming man, who listened as I talked about my life and the revolution. He expressed sympathy and even regret that the Shah had left Iran. With regard to Gita and her school Phillips Academy, he mentioned that it was a good school and that his daughter, Sarah, was enrolled there and then he asked about my residency status, which was the reason of my visit. When I told him about the very recent letter from Congressman McKinney and approval of my petition, he became relieved, happy, and admired the congressman's activities and his knowledge. When I was going to ask him about his expectation and recommendation in my service, he received a telephone call from London, with a woman's voice, and immediately, I understood that was a private call from his wife, so I left the room and went to the waiting room until his conversation was finished. Then he called me in again, and when I saw him again, his expression was changed, and he was in a different mood, clearly the result of the telephone call. I made my remarks short, and I asked him about his expectation. He responded that he was always happy to have information about what was going on in the state and that he was always interested to hear about the professional activities and progress in Virginia. He asked me to send him a copy of any of my professional presentations or papers from state or national conventions. Since the person after me was waiting to see him, I thanked him for his valuable time, and I promised to fulfill that expectation and left his room. Later, any time I had made a presentation at a state or national conference, I sent a copy to his office, and I always had a nice response from him. So this was my first memorable experience with a representative of the legislature in the United States, which I will always remember.

Iran continued to be the leading news while the Shah and his family were wandering from one place to the next, and Khomeini's regime grew and increased anti-American and anti-Israeli slogans. I was happy and relieved that, although I did not have money, at least my family and I had found this permanent residency through my education, and I could serve a needy group with intellectual and mental disability, while our children could go to school until the revolution settled in Iran. The Shah and his family, wandered from Egypt to Morocco to the Bahamas before finally settling in Mexico, where they became aware of the seriousness of the Shah's cancer. He needed surgery and treatment, and finally, President Carter issued a permission for the Shah to go to New York to get his treatment. The Islamic regime of Iran did not believe this story and thought instead that the United States was once again preparing Shah's return to Iran as they had done in 1953. On October 21, the Shah and the empress departed from Mexico to New York for treatment.[2] On November 1, 1979, Khomeini urged his people to demonstrate against the United States and Israel. Khomeini denounced the American government as the "Great Satan" and "Enemy of Islam." The television news reported that thousands of people had gathered around the US

Embassy, protesting in a similar scene as I had witnessed during the revolution. The embassy grounds had been briefly occupied before, during the revolution; however, it looked as if this time the police were not helpful and protesting crowds outside the US Embassy walls became a common sight, until November 4, when a mob of students called "the Group following the line of the Imam" again occupied the grounds of the embassy and militant Islamic students—clearly contrary to the international law—took almost sixty-five people at the embassy hostage. This time the revolutionary guards and police did practically nothing to stop the students, and even the Iranian TV praised their actions and broadcasted the situation live, also against international law. Ayatollah Khomeini, who exactly fifteen years before to the date, on November 4, had gone into exile in Paris, supported the students and their actions. The students demanded that the Shah, who was undergoing cancer treatment in the United States should be extradited to Iran to stand trial. ABC News established a special program from November 4 called *Nightline* at 11:30 p.m. hosted by Ted Koppel. In addition to daily coverage of the Iran story and the hostage crisis during news programs, this program focused on the hostage crisis specifically. The storming of the embassy followed months of serious political and religious tension in Iran and political tension in the United States and the world. The hostage crisis affected especially deeply the lives of Iranians living in the United States, Iranians who had left Iran because of their opposition to the revolution. Strong feeling against Iranians in the United States delayed their adjustment and integration. Every night I monitored the news and went to bed after *Nightline*. Watching *Nightline* became a habit, which still continues today. I was addicted to the news to see if I could find a road or a way that Iran and its people would be free, but sadly, this revolution continues up to this day and still there is no way to free the people of Iran. Within two weeks, the militants freed thirteen hostages (mainly female) and members of the minority groups. One of the hostage takers spoke by telephone from inside the embassy and assured the world that the hostages were safe, and they were in no immediate danger.

Since the hostage crisis, many unfortunate incidents have happened to Iranian Americans. Attacks on their homes, families, and hardship in their daily lives and clashes of cultures. Some of these incidents have been revealed in stories, dramas, and films. *House of Sand and Fog*, from the novel by Andre Dubus III, starred Oscar winner Ben Kingsley and an Iranian actress, Shohreh Aghdashloo, who was nominated for an Oscar, is a good example. The hostage crisis did not affect me personally at the beginning, because between July 15 to November 4, I had established good relationship among my colleagues, staff, and my clients. However, immediately after the hostage crisis, I had a call from Paul Munroe Elementary School that our son, Reza, had been attacked by his classmates who knew nothing about the deep political background behind the hostage crisis, and just because he was an Iranian boy. I drove quickly to the emergency room of the hospital, and fortunately, his injuries were not serious. This incident affected him greatly in his relation with the schoolchildren throughout his school years, even in high school. We began to monitor his school life more closely and registered him for karate classes to learn self-defense. I noticed again in our new country, we needed to be either offensive or defensive. We chose to be defensive in our daily life. I also called Gita at Phillips Academy to see how she was doing, and fortunately in her older, international atmosphere, nobody had attempted to harm her. The news from Iran was getting worse, and the universities and colleges of Iran were closed by the revolutionary government in order to make changes for the cultural revolution in curriculum, subjects, and personnel. Consequently, many Iranians who had come temporarily to the United States, planning to return to Iran after the revolution, could not return home, and were stuck here with the American physical attacks and their harsh reaction to Iranians. Stones were hurled at their homes, windows were broken, and other acts of vandalism, such as driving a car over the lawn of a home where Iranians lived were routinely perpetrated against the Iranians. These Iranian Americans were practically strangers in both their old and new countries. (The Iranian proverb *"Randeh az Iran and Mandeh dar Emrika,"* which means "Not wanted in Iran and not welcome in the US" This prejudice was not felt so strongly against those Iranians who went to England, Germany, France or other European countries. Therefore, the level of frustration and stress for Iranian Americans in the United States was much higher than in other countries. The hostage crisis affected their life, their identity, and their personality. Even the response to the question, "Where are you from?" had to change. They learned to respond "Persia," Iran's ancient name, or "Egypt," or to give no response; whereas, two or three years before the revolution, everybody was proud to say they were from Iran. Now we faced a big change and some fear. Some people even changed their names. However, our family insisted on being ourselves, even with our difficult names, to keep at least some of our identity, especially with all the hardship that we were going through.

Ever since November 4, 1979, each year, the Islamic government has celebrated annually the November 4 takeover of the embassy, when fifty-two American diplomats were taken hostage for 444 days by militant students, chanting anti-US and anti-Israel slogan and even burning the flags of the two countries. Each year the radical leadership celebrates the event to frustrate and antagonize the government and people of the United States.

So in this way, the hostage crisis became part of the history for both Iran and America, and immediately after that diplomatic relations between the two countries broke up, a rift lasting to the present time. Approximately 5 million Iranians who thought they were leaving Iran temporarily had to settle around the world permanently, especially in the United States. Gradually, I was finding out that most of our family and friends had scattered around the world, and gradually, we found each other again and even now are still discovering each other.

At work, my main focus was in curriculum development, which consisted of units of instruction in four broad developmental areas: sensory, motor, self-care, and language. Each instructional unit consisted of instructional objective, readiness, procedure, task evaluation and material and equipment. In this step-by-step curriculum development and procedure, I could use the programmed instruction material that I was unable to use in the literacy program in Iran, so the detailed study during my Fulbright program in the USA was very helpful in developing curriculum for these developmentally and intellectually disabled children and in implementing the new federal law 94-142 in Virginia. In reorganizing and redesigning programs to adhere to public law and to meet the need of our residents, we noticed that about 60 percent of our educational programs should be in the area of self-help and the other 40 percent would be in the area of preacademics, prevocational, and academic areas. To be defensive in my management style and ready to respond to justify any positive change to benefit the clients according to the rules and regulations of the federal, state and educational mandate, I gathered all the operational policy and procedure manuals with their latest updates to study and review frequently with the staff. Thanks to my good memory, whenever the inspectors or auditors from the state or federal government came to review our center, I could respond to their questions by citing title number—Code of Federal Regulation and parts in the Federal Register, Health Care Financing Administration Interpretative Guidelines number. As a result of my methodology, most of the time, the result of the inspection of our center was either deficiency free or with little citation. However, although because of the good result of our audits, I always received congratulatory letters; ironically, my budget would not be increased for the following year. Sometimes, I thought that we were being punished for the good work we were doing, and whenever I asked why our budget had not changed, I was told that it was because we did not have deficiencies in our center. I did not think this was fair, and I even noticed that some centers with deficiencies such as "lack of communication with residents" would receive more staff. We also definitely needed more staff and budget increases, but we were being ourselves and sincere with residents and following the law and regulation and not playing games. I tried to establish a family-type atmosphere with my open-door policy. As a result, each time when the Medicaid inspector would visit our unit unannounced, the staff performed very well. I heard later that in other centers, as soon as the staff noticed that an inspector was visiting, the staff would often show their anger with less communication with the residents and unsatisfactory performance as if they were taking revenge on the management. Anyway, although I was denied budget increases and punished because we lacked deficiencies, while other departments received the budget increases and more staff because of their deficiencies, we still continued to be ourselves.

I worked at the CVTC for almost fifteen years, and this practice continued the whole time. I had the least turnover of staff in our center, which again was beneficial for the progress and mental improvement of the clients, who emotionally were dependent on the staff because the staff knew their residents and their needs better. I also had less need for taking disciplinary action and fewer grievances and court visits. I remember, for example, one case in the second shift. The second-shift supervisor told me that he had an alcoholic employee under his supervision who drank on the job, which was forbidden. The former center director and the supervisor tried very hard to catch the employee drinking, but they were not successful. One day, near Christmas 1979, he asked if I could suggest a solution. I replied that if the employee was an alcoholic, he might show some violence in his behavior, either when he could not drink or when his drinking got delayed. So I suggested we had to establish a team of staff to monitor the behavior of that employee and his actions closely, and then we might be able to observe a behavior to which we could assign disciplinary action. Otherwise, he would hide his drinking while he was working, and we would never catch him for drinking or discover he might be under the influence of alcohol. As I had guessed and predicted, because of close observation of his behavior, he gradually showed violent behavior to his colleagues, until one day, he became aggressive and violent with a coworker and used abusive language, which was observed by several people. The shift supervisor prepared a disciplinary action paper, with his background on tardiness, but the highest written notice that he could give was a three-day suspension, and we definitely could not fire him this first time. After that, as I always did for the difficult cases, I established a counseling session to find out the reason for his behavior, interest, and motivation at work. Fortunately, at that time, the job market near Christmas was good. In the counseling session with him, I found out that he was working just for the money and the paycheck and that he really wasn't interested in providing special services to special people. Therefore, with his background of several disciplinary actions in his file, which showed that with the next incident, there was the possibility he could be fired after the three-day suspension, I showed him a list of job openings in the city and surroundings and told him that with the possibility of being fired, perhaps he should look for another job that he liked more and which would suit him better. I suggested that it would be better for him if he would find a new job before he was fired. After his suspension, he returned, with his resignation in hand for the shift supervisor, saying he had found another job. Our supervisor was so happy that he immediately ran to my room, smiling and said, "I don't know what you said to the employee, but I have his resignation." I also was happy that I could help the employee and the supervisor and, more importantly, relieve our clients from being possibly harmed or abused because of his use of alcohol.

After that incident, I noticed that directly or indirectly, in our center, we had achieved a family-type atmosphere and work environment. We had the least turnover and the least number of disciplinary actions compared to other centers. Everybody was happy, and all the residents and staff united together, like a large family, to celebrate Christmas. Before the celebration and Christmas night, we prepared a Christmas float to participate in the City of Lynchburg's Christmas parade. There was competition among the centers for the most decorated floats, and our staff and resident were motivated to work hard. We wanted the CDC to win first place. That was my first year to participate in this happy occasion, and I also wanted our float to win. Some of the decorations required a small person to go under the float to secure them. My son, Reza, who worked as a volunteer after school on the float volunteered to go under the float just minutes before it entered the city parade. This decoration made our float exceptionally beautiful, but just as Reza finished and was coming out from under the float, he lacerated his head. I drove him quickly to the emergency room where he received eight stitches, all the while praying that our float would win. Afterward, I took him straight home to rest, and when we arrived home, we had a message from our program coordinator that our CDC float had won first place, in large part due to Reza's work. The program coordinator thanked Reza for his fantastic job. I remember that he listened to the message twice before he took his pain medication and went to bed happy. I was proud of his volunteer work. This turned out to be his second experience in the emergency room that year.

The author participating in the annual Christmas Parade.

For Christmas, all the units and centers were decorated. More importantly, our Christmas present was that we had had finished all the programming for the five and a half hours required by law. I was happy to notify Dr. Meece of this good news, and fortunately, the auditor did not find any deficiencies or errors. Another good news for Christmas was that I finally received my Green Card and our family could live in the USA permanently. However, at the same time that I was relieved by the adjustment to my new country, new job, excellent family environment for education and residence, I received an official letter from Dr. Meece congratulating me on the achievements of the CDC (Child Development Center) and assigning me as center director to the ATC (Adult Training Center). This was a lateral transfer to a Geriatric Center with about three hundred residents living in twelve living areas in three buildings. It was a swap with the position of the center director of ATC effective February 4, 1980. I was surprised and shocked at this administrative decision, especially since I did not know the rationale behind it. I kept the letter in my hand without sharing it with anyone and asked for an immediate appointment with Dr. Meece. I hoped this change would be a positive change for residents. In my meeting with Dr. Meece, I found out vaguely that because of the positive and the successful changes in the management of CDC and some problems in ATC, he thought it would be better for the LTSH that we swap our positions and centers. With mixed feelings, I left his office and walked to my center, thinking how to inform my staff and residents. I had come to love them, and it would be hard to tell them that I was being transferred. Finally, I decided to tell them the news as soon as possible before the rumors went around. The next day was the center Christmas party, and we all celebrated Christmas together. At the party, we exchanged our gifts. I opened mine and saw that it was a tray with a thank-you note from the staff. I thanked them and hugged them in appreciation for their wonderful service to the residents. Then I told them that I had news, which out of respect for them I wanted to share with them first before they heard from someone else. I told them I trusted their understanding and their cooperation. Now they became quiet and looked expectantly at me. I said, "The management of LTSH needs my service in another center, and I have to report to ATC effective February first. However, I am not leaving LTSH and I will be available if you need me."

I noticed they became quiet, and some of the staff even cried a little. I tried to control myself, and I told them again that I was not leaving them, but that always in my life I preferred to work wherever I was needed the most for my services, and it looked as if there was a greater need for my service at the ATC than at the CDC. I continued to thank them for their wonderful job and cooperation in the successful programming and wished them a merry Christmas. I thought that they could get used to the idea of change through the Christmas holidays and would have less resistance toward the changes of the new center director, but I myself did not know where and why I was going to the ATC and what type of problems were awaiting me. I felt that I was taking a step into the dark. It looked as if they had hired me to be an agent for change.

Our family was invited to celebrate Christmas with David and Sallie and their family. They had bought a house in Fairfax and both had gotten part-time teaching positions at the Northern Virginia Community College. So we were happy, thanking God that we were together again with all the children after we had left Iran as neighbors and family.

The author and her family attending a Christmas gathering held at
Dr. David Rejali's house in Fairfax, Virginia.

Author with her family in
Lynchburg, Virginia.

1. The Education Corps in Iran: *A New Experiment in the Expansion of Education*, published in *The Yearbook of Education of Teachers' College*, Columbia University, New York, by Evans Brothers, Ltd., London, 1965.

2. (For details please see Farah Pahlavi's memoir, *An Enduring Love*, Miramax, 2004. p. 330-430)

CHAPTER 16

Never Too Old to Achieve a Goal: New Job, New Home, and New Country

January 1980-1987

On January 14, 1980, I received a congratulatory letter from Dr. Meece for my efforts, achievements, and successes for the implementation of the new public laws and the necessary rules and regulations that the Child Development Center required. However, that month, I had to prepare myself for another position. Difficult and painful as it was, I had to acknowledge that I had been hired as an agent for change. With sadness, I attended the farewell meeting with the CDC staff and colleagues and thanked them for their service and cooperation and ended with the German word *aufeinwiedersehen* instead of *good-bye*. The next week, on February 4, I started as director of the Adult Training Center. The center's motto was *"Never too old to achieve a goal,"* which matched my own outlook toward life.

The Adult Training Center (ATC) comprised of three buildings (numbers 18, 19, and 20) and 12 living areas, which housed nearly 340 ambulatory and nonambulatory residents over the age of forty-five. The residents were grouped into six developmentally sequential levels, each with its entrance and exit criteria. This grouping afforded the opportunity to move to a higher level when requisite abilities were developed, with the potential for eventual placement in the community group homes. Education and training emphasis was placed on language, socialization, recreation, prevocation, speech and hearing, preacademics, and personal hygiene.

At the Adult Training Center, I felt quite welcomed, but I again needed to establish a new relationship with the residents and staff and to let them get to know my style of management and open-door policy. My office was in the basement of Building 20, with two clerical staff members. Daily, I had to sign anywhere from fifty to one hundred documents for the clients and staff.

Very soon, I became acutely aware that our geriatric services were woefully inadequate, and unlike Iran, where old people were treated with respect, the aged in the United States were mostly neglected. This was especially noticeable with old patients with mental disability, which made my job very challenging. In order to provide the best services, I had to learn about the center in some detail and evaluate its needs from the point of view of its clients, staff, and environment before I could do any planning. We were providing services to people with mental deficiency, intellectual, and developmental disability exacerbated by years of neglect.

Historically, persons with mental retardation were kept hidden away either at home or in institutions, isolated from the mainstream society. Fortunately, during the twentieth century, the Western world gradually recognized the importance of the rights and abilities of these people, and the keyword *normalization* became in vogue, providing the persons with mental retardation the necessary skills and opportunities for a normal life within the society. Since 1876, the American Association on Mental Retardation (AAMR), later renamed as the American Association on Intellectual and Developmental Disabilities (AAIDD), had defined mental retardation as "A disability characterized by significant limitations both in intellectual functioning and in adaptive behavior as expressed in conceptual, social, and practical adaptive skill."[1] In this context, *normalization* connotes providing similar life to that of children in our communities and society.

To my surprise again, I soon found out that my first task was to handle and resolve an important matter at hand. This was an Equal Opportunity lawsuit from a black social worker (Gary) against the ATC and the LTSH Center management. I also had to read several reports pertaining to abuse throughout the ATC and study behavior modification plans and psychotropic medication reduction programs. I later learned that this was also one of the reasons why I was moved to the ATC, to handle these difficult cases. I immediately applied for membership to several professional associations for mental retardation and aging such as the American Association on Mental Retardation (AAMR), the Gerontological Society of America (GSA), American Association of Homes and Services for the Aging (AAHSA), Virginia Association of Non-Profit Homes For the Aging (VANHA), and attended a workshop on the clinical psychology of aging at the Center for the Study of Aging and Human Development at Duke University, as recommended by the American Psychological Association (APA). I wanted to gain as much knowledge and information and especially the latest research on aging and retardation to help me make the right decisions for my new job, believing that *"Education and information is power."*

I also reestablished my connections with Zonta International, a global service organization for women executives and professionals, which I had belonged to while living in Iran. Through my international directory, it was easy to contact Dorothy Rancourt, its local governor of the area. I had a chance to become acquainted with Louise Volker, the past president of the Fairfax Club, and Edith Nalls, who became president of the Fairfax club from 1979-1981. This was the nearest club to Lynchburg, and I became a member of the Fairfax County Zonta Club in 1980. The mission of Zonta International is to advance the status of women worldwide (presently in sixty-eight countries) through comprehensive programs.[2] Zonta Club differs from other service clubs because it provides an environment where women of diverse professions and age, through fund-raising, networking and hands-on service projects, can help the local, regional, and international community.

Author with friends from the Zonta Club of Fairfax County and Zonta International.

At work, I realized immediately the need for staff to attend intensive training and workshops on aging and retardation, especially those working directly with clients. This required funding, but there was no budget for training workshops at the Training School. I found out that the Gerontology Department of the University of Michigan had an excellent training package with a group of experts on aging and retardation. I discussed the needs with Dr. Meece and asked if I could prepare a budget justification proposal for these training needs to the department of Mental Health/Mental Retardation of the Commonwealth of Virginia. He discussed this proposal with Dr. Nelson, and I was told that the Central Office had never provided this type of help before and most likely would not support the budget request. However, they encouraged me to pursue the project. I wrote a strong justification showing how this training workshop would promote the education and knowledge of the staff in treating our clients. I explained how such training workshops could reduce and even prevent the incidents of abuse, stemming from lack of education. I sent the funding request to the geriatric department of the central office in Richmond. Surprisingly, after a visit by its director and the deputy director to our center, the budget item was approved. This made me very happy and proud, and needless to say, I gained respect and clout among the top management as well as my staff. We immediately contacted the University of Michigan and arranged the workshop in the basement next to my office. It was a very informative and interesting workshop. That was my first achievement for the staff, especially for the direct care staff of all three shifts in the ATC. The workshop was so successful that LTSH later established a larger department for staff development and training.

Gradually, I had more time to work on other issues such as abuse and the EEOC lawsuit. The social worker in question was very frustrated that I was the new ATC director. I noticed his anger and confusion and tried to be careful in communicating with this very sensitive man. Apparently, he was hoping to be successful with his suit before I came to ATC, and of course, I could not give him any excuse to complain. Since I believed in equal treatment for all people, he could not find any excuse to complain about. Finally, one day, he stood at my open office door (placed his hands on the doorframe) and said angrily, "Why don't you return to your country?" I told him I don't plan to return because I strongly supported the civil rights movement in the USA. I told him that, unlike women in United States, Iranian women did not enjoy equal rights, and with the new regime in power, they had lost more rights and were practically hostages, just like the American hostages being held in Iran. After that, he quieted down. A short while later, in a meeting with Dr. Meece, when I was following up about this man's complaint, Dr. Meece told me that fortunately he had dropped his charges, and as a result, LTSH management was free from this serious EEOC lawsuit. I was happy to hear this news. However, later, unfortunately, the worker kept complaining about our program manager and other staff, as if he enjoyed criticizing others.

Another hot issue covered extensively in the newspapers and media all over the United States concerned the past practice at the Lynchburg Training School of sterilizing the mentally retarded, a practice also carried out in other institutions around the country. The records of sterilizations, finally halted by the State of Virginia in 1972, were brought to light and unearthed by the current director of the institution, Dr. Ray Nelson, who had traced this practice back over fifty years previously. While disclosing the Lynchburg records, he said that the rights of the retarded were now very much protected and that sterilization as a "treatment" would not happen again, and the law that was still on the books was in the process of being repealed. The greatest number of operations were carried out in the 1930s and 1940s, when thousands of people all over the country were sterilized under the now discredited theory of eugenics, which held that preventing the mentally incompetent from reproducing would improve the human species. Dr. Albert S. Priddy, the physician who started the program, wrote in a 1924 letter that he considered the hospital a "cleaning house to give these young women education, life and moral training, sterilize them and send them out to earn their own living."[3] This issue became widely publicized when, on February 23, 1980, in a *New York Times* article. Robert Reinhold covered the subject, and the NBC headline that night was about VIRGINIA'S INVOLUNTARY STERILIZATION: "Over 50 years, more than 4000 men, women and children diagnosed as mentally retarded were rolled into the operating room of the state mental hospitals weekly and sterilized to 'raise the intelligence of the people of the state' in the words of the of the Virginia Supreme Court." One case really attracted the attention of people—the case of Carrie Buck. Carrie Buck and her sister Doris had been sterilized at the training center, but Doris did not learn about this until she was sixty-seven years old. She thought she had had an appendectomy. She and her husband had wanted badly to have a child, but she was not aware of her situation. Carrie herself had been raped by the nephew of her adoptive mother, who then committed Carrie to the training center as a mentally disabled person and denied her custody of the child resulting from the rape. Later, she was persuaded to take her case through the courts and even to the Supreme Court. In 1994, her story was made into a television court drama *Against Her Will* with the role of Carrie played by the Oscar winner Marlee Matlin. The *Roanoke Times and World News* published on Sunday June 26, 1994, a detailed historical article by Mary Bishop, which showed "how historical social judgment of the day forced sterilization" and publicized the Lynchburg story several times when it appeared on the Discovery Channel in June and July.

Very soon I learned that some of the elderly women in our center at ATC were among those who were involuntarily sterilized, a fact we tried to consider in their treatment. This sterilization was an unjustifiably painful experience in their life. These events influenced other political issues surrounding the LTSH and raised questions about the management of such places in the Commonwealth of Virginia. As a result, the name of our hospital was continuously in the local news.

Meanwhile, the international news continued to focus on the American hostage situation in Iran, my troubled country, and the defenseless silent majority in Iran, who were also hostages but in their own country. The hostage crisis dominated the news as well as the American and Western policy toward Iran. Khomeini's theocratic ideology with mob power was expanding, and the clerical dominance under Khomeini became a standing challenge to secular governments. Iran, a country with the old Western trend of separation of church and state, had become a theocratic government. Khomeini, at first, in his position as *Veli-e Faghih*, had allowed a non-Mullah, like Bani Sadar, who served him well in Paris, to be the first president of the Islamic Republic of Iran, but later, just as he forgot his other promises and statements, replaced him with a mullah as president. However, the real power stayed with Khomeini, and in reality, the president and the prime minister did not wield much power. Execution of the opposition continued without any trial. Amnesty International strongly criticized the regime for its revolutionary executions. President Carter's freezing of Iranian assets and imposition of arms embargo and economic sanctions gave the hostage crisis a high priority, which was the daily focus of his and the country's attention.

Many homes in the United States displayed yellow ribbons to show support for the safe return of the hostages, and ABC's nightly program, *Nightline*, kept a count of the days the hostages were in captivity and covered the news of the day. The Iranian government benefited a lot from this high level of publicity, but constant attention to the hostage crisis took time and attention away from other important problems, like the Soviet invasion of Afghanistan and the 1980 US elections. Then a top-secret hostage rescue mission failed on April 23, 1980. The mission was an attempt to free the American hostages held in Tehran, but it collapsed right at the beginning, with the death of eight soldiers. President Carter announced the disastrous mission in a broadcast to the nation and took full responsibility for its failure. While the whole world was shocked and saddened, in Tehran, there were raucous celebrations over the failure of the rescue mission with demonstrators shouting "Death to America" and "Death to Israel." The Iranian foreign minister Sadegh Qotbzadeh announced that the mission was an act of war. Every night, throughout 1980, we watched similar news. Even though the death of the Shah on July 27, 1980, in Cairo, left no more excuses for the students to demand the Shah's extradition to Iran, the hostage crisis and its news continued until President Carter lost the election to Ronald Reagan. The hostages, who were held for 444 days, were released on January 20, 1981, right after Ronald Reagan's inauguration.

Because of the horrible news from Iran—closure of universities, and no prospect or hope of an immediate ending of violence in Iran—we made the painful decision to sell our house in Iran. When our one-year rental lease expired, we also decided to buy a small house in Lynchburg. This was a very painful decision because it had taken us more than three years to build the house with a great deal of love and passion. We knew that there would be a drastic drop in real estate prices in Iran because of the revolution. We also were told that if we did not sell our house, the government and the revolutionary court would expropriate it because we were not living in it. It was also rumored that the Communist groups in the country were becoming stronger, and it was predicted that the whole country could become Communist like the Soviet Union.

We decided to buy a small house near my work with a minimum down payment, hoping that when we sold our house in Iran, we could pay off the mortgage. It was interesting that we had issues with establishing credit when buying the house because we had not had any loans or mortgages in the past. For the first time, we understood that if you do not owe money or have no previous loans, obtaining credit can be a problem. Fortunately, our American Express and Diners Club cards at that time helped us to secure a loan. Otherwise, we wouldn't have known where to turn to achieve our goal of buying a home in America. We soon found out that the more loan history and punctual repayments you establish, the better your credit rating will be. In The *Wall Street Journal* (January 31, 2007, Section D2), I read the article, "Credit Problems: What to Do When You Have Been Too Good. You have zero debt, a hefty salary, a fat portfolio—and no credit score."[4] I read further that "yes, it could happen, some 50 million Americans don't have enough credit activity to qualify for the most commonly used credit cards." The article gave the advice that for financial self-defense, it is best to borrow and use credit cards. At first, this experience with credit was very strange, but I accepted it gradually. From the article, I saw that we were not alone with low credit at the beginning of our life in America. My monthly income from the State of Virginia was also an important factor favoring the loan. We found a house on Krise Circle, which we liked. Because it was the summer break, Gita and Reza could help us with the move, especially since we did not have much furniture as the house we had rented before was furnished. We therefore bought only essential furniture for the bedrooms and a dining table until we received money from the sale of our house in Tehran.

We shopped after my work and on weekends. We were told that we should check newspaper ads for auction sales since we might get a better deal than from a local store. Sadie, one of my colleagues, was an expert shopper who collected antique furniture. She kindly showed us her lovely home and her collection and directed us where to look for auctions for what we needed. We all enjoyed visiting her home where much of her china and other pieces reminded us of what we had in Iran and what we had inherited from our grandparents. We also enjoyed going to auctions in the hope of finding something to remind us of what we lost and missed from Iran, especially since we were not sure if we would ever again have our old family antique furniture and belongings that we had collected and had to leave behind.

We moved into our new house at the end of July. This house was located behind Virginia Baptist Hospital and had been built by an administrator of the hospital, who had retired and was leaving the city to tour the United States in his motor home. Krise Circle was down the hill from one of the major streets of Lynchburg, Rivermont Avenue. The house had four bedrooms and three baths on two floors. Behind the house was a creek, and on the property, beautiful azalea bushes and trees provided natural wild beauty and privacy. In many respects, the new house was different from our house in Tehran. Our previous house was built at the top of a hill in the middle of roses and fruit trees, with a grand view of the city of Tehran. Our new house was at the bottom of a hill, and the flowing of the creek suggested the flow of our lives. This new setting helped us evaluate, think, and contemplate on how to cope with the new challenges in our completely new and altered lifestyle, culture, and particularly hostile environment because of the American hostage crisis.

A photo of the author's new house in Lynchburg Virginia during a visit by the late Dr. Abbass Rejali and his family during Thanksgiving.

The author's son Reza playing his trumpet in preparation for playing at a local political rally.

A photo of the author's new house during a gathering of friends and colleagues in 1980.

At about this time, we had a call from Sa'id's nephew, Hossein, from San Diego, California, where he was a college freshman. He was very upset, homesick, and angry enough to leave the United States and return to Iran. He had suffered from prejudice against Iranians in the United

States because of the hostage crisis. His brother, who had been with him in San Diego, had already returned to Iran, even though he would have to serve in the military there. Their poor mother had worked very hard to send both sons to study in the United States, but now he was telling us with an angry voice that he too wanted to return to Iran and was calling to say good-bye. He was so determined to leave the United States that I could not argue with him over the phone. I noticed how scared he was immediately, just like many Iranians. There was a pervasive rumor that the United States would attack Iran to free the hostages, and the American government would deport all the Iranian students or separate all Iranians and put them in a camp, as they had done to Japanese Americans during World War II. Hossein was so upset that his voice was trembling. I tried to calm him down and told him that he could come to visit us in Lynchburg before he left the United States. I added that if he liked it here, he would be most welcome to stay with us. I told him his uncle Sa'id, Reza, Gita, and I would love to see him before he left for Iran. After several more telephone calls, he finally promised that he would come to see us before making his final decision. It was already a shock for us to find out that his brother had left America for Iran without calling us. We could imagine the grief his mother must have gone through to send him back to the United States to study during the chaotic revolutionary times in Iran.

We were elated that Hossein accepted our offer, drove all the way from California with his American sports car, and arrived safely in Lynchburg. It was summer, and after a few weeks, we discussed his education with our dear good friends Bill and Martha Goodman, who always have been of great help. Dr. Goodman at that time was director of International Studies at Lynchburg College, and after he studied his transcript, he suggested that Hossein register there for preengineering, and after two years, he could transfer to an engineering school since Hossein wanted to study electrical engineering. We were all relieved that he accepted Dr. Goodman's good advice and stayed with us. We turned over the first floor to him and Reza to share, which turned out to be a good arrangement. He was a successful student and, later, transferred to Florida Tech. He is now a competent electrical engineer in the medical field.

While we were settling down, my husband, Sa'id, was trying to find a job in the area of music education. He had offers, but none of these were for full-time employment in Lynchburg or colleges nearby.

The job offers came from the West and the Midwest. The head of the music education department of the University of Michigan came to visit us with an offer for Sa'id to teach in Michigan. To be separated so far at this particular time would have been extremely difficult for our family. For one semester, one of the professors at Lynchburg College, who trained music teachers, was going on sabbatical, and she asked him to teach as acting professor in her place. He accepted the job, hoping that by the semester's end, we would have received the money from selling our house in Tehran. We were learning to cope with uncertainty of day-to-day living and managing only short-term plans for our life after Iran's dark revolution. This seemed to be a pattern of life for many Iranians scattered throughout the world by the revolution. Many were either highly educated professionals or well-to-do businessmen who had been able to transfer money prior to the revolution. Most of them, like us, were in a continuous waiting mode, constantly watching the news about Iran, and wondering if at any time soon, this heavy darkness would be lifted by the forces of freedom. Alas, since 1979, this has been just wishful thinking and a dream for both the Iranians in exile and those who are still in Iran.

Finally, we had a call that the revolutionary court had given us permission to sell our house. Since many people with outstanding debts were selling their houses before leaving the country, every sale had to go through this court. Our wonderful house that we could have sold in 1978 for 3 million dollars before the revolution was sold for 300 thousand dollars, one-tenth of the original price. We were very happy that we were able to sell the house and hoped we would receive our money soon. However, hope very soon changed to despair with the news that Khomeini officially banned any transfer of money from the country, and the law-breakers would stand before the revolutionary court. So our money remained in the bank in Iran. We definitely could not ask our friend who undertook this transaction on our behalf to send over the money, especially since the money was being held in the bank along with his own money and under his name. He told us that he needed to go to court periodically and show the bank statement to the court. In the meantime, the value of our money in dollars was dropping fast, and life was becoming very difficult and expensive. The only way to send money abroad would be through a known illegal and trusted source at a great risk and should be done clandestinely. Our trusted friend who went through the house sale and was aware of our needs, without telling us, sent the equivalent amount of ten thousand dollars in Iranian money. He sent it as a test amount through a Greek man named Paraskis who had a highway contract in Iran. Our friend called us and asked us to let him know when we received the money. He said that if this method worked, he would risk sending the rest of the money. We were very anxious and curious to learn if we would receive the money. Our good friend said he would replace our money with his own money to show the court that our money had not been sent out of country. We were thrilled to receive the money, and since the test of this transfer had succeeded, we were hoping to receive the rest soon. From that money, we bought a secondhand piano, which somewhat relieved the depression of Sa'id, who had suffered, having been without a piano. We waited anxiously for the rest of the money to arrive, but weeks went by without a word from Mr. Paraskis. Every week, we called our friend to ask if he knew anything about what had happened to the money.

While we were waiting for the rest of the money from the sale of our house in Iran, another conflict and horrible war between Iran and Iraq began in September 1980. It arose from the old conflict between Iran and Iraq over the Shatt-al-Arab waterway, which empties into the Persian Gulf and is the boundary between Iran and Iraq. In 1975, during the reign of the Shah, when Iraq was militarily weaker than Iran, Saddam Hussein signed a treaty giving Iran partial control of this waterway. Then after the 1979 revolution, Saddam Hussein, believing that the Iranian military was weaker, attacked Iran on the territorial dispute over the Shatt al Arab, seized the western region of the oil fields in Khuzestan province, and even succeeded in capturing the port city of Khorramshahr by the end of 1980. The Iranian resistance, however remained strong and with the old well-trained army of the Shah still in place. The Iraqi troops were forced to withdraw from the occupied areas in early 1982. However, Khomeini did not cease fighting and now wanted to topple the Saddam regime. In reality, he wanted to consolidate support of the Iranian people behind the Islamic regime. This war continued for eight years, with Saddam's indiscriminate and infamous use of chemical weapons. I remember well that after a few years of war, I was reading an article in the *Zuriche Zeitung* analyzing the war and predicting that this war would be a long one, since more than forty countries, including the USA, were covertly selling arms to both countries in exchange for oil. The prediction was correct. The war unfortunately became one of the longest and deadliest in modern times. It took about eight years and left more than 2 million Iranians dead or disabled before Iran was forced to accept a cease-fire mandated by the United Nations in July 1988.

With all this horrible, distressing news, we waited and waited for the rest of our money. Then one day, our friend in Iran called to give us Mr. Paraskis's telephone number in Greece. He had not been able to reach him there and wanted us to try. After several attempts, I reached him and learned what he had done with our money. I will never forget this telephone call. He said, "Your country had a revolution. I lost all my money, and I am bankrupt. You are now in the United States, and you know what bankrupt means. You should stop waiting for any money from me." With this phone call, we learned that all our entire capital accumulated over several generations was lost, along with the twenty years of work we had put into our house and its contents. This news was such a shock that, for some time, we were incapable of doing anything. Our minds were simply numb.

After a while, we partially recovered and started listening to more news on the bloody Iran-Iraq war with its violence and the unjustified executions by the regime. We simply could not believe our ears. There was a chain of murders, in Iran and abroad, of the opposition activists by the new government in Iran. This began in 1980 in the United States when Ali-Akbar Tabatabai, who actively opposed the regime, was assassinated in the Washington DC area. On a hot summer morning, he was killed by someone who was recruited by the Iranian regime and pretending to be a postal worker. Later, in Germany, the popular singer F. Farouhkzad was murdered, and in France, the former prime minister Bakhtiar was assassinated in his flat in Paris. In Iran, a member of the opposition, Dariush Frouhar who was a leader of the Mellat Party, along with his wife, and several poets and writers like Saidi Sirjani, and Mokhtari, were assassinated. Several political Kurdish oppositionists were killed in an attack in Berlin's Mykonos restaurant. Still, many others faced political assassination by the new regime. Putting the loss of our money in proper perspective, we thanked God the Almighty for being healthy and out of harm's way in a free country.

Mr. Paraskis was well aware of the fact that we could not pursue him legally because our friend had been involved in an illegal money transfer. Furthermore, our friend had taken a great risk for himself, his own family, and us for which we would have suffered if he had been caught. He and his family could have been sentenced to death by the revolutionary court for disobeying Khomeini's command.

I told our children the shocking news and urged them to study hard because education would be the only means to success, the best and safest capital in their life that nobody could take away from them. Fortunately, the regular letters from Gita and Doris indicated the good news that Gita was really doing well and making good progress. In addition to receiving good grades at Phillips Academy, she was participating in rowing—which was very good for her back—drama and choir, and continuing the piano lessons she had started in Iran. Reza also had finished Paul Munroe Elementary School successfully and was making progress in Middle School. He played trumpet in the school band and also participated in soccer and wrestling. Hossein too was studying hard at Lynchburg College and was on the college soccer team while also holding a part-time job. Our financial situation had changed drastically, and everybody had to work to survive and study hard to succeed. As for my husband, who could not find full-time employment near Lynchburg in music, some of his former students in Northern Virginia helped him with a loan to open a music studio to teach classical music on piano in Alexandria. He began teaching at his own studio after he finished his semester at Lynchburg College.

His new job was challenging, but required driving more than a 140 miles each way, a three-hour drive from Lynchburg to Northern Virginia. This was difficult, but was better than working in two different states.

Sa'id decided to stay in Northern Virginia, and we used to take more long weekends to visit each other in order to keep our family unified, especially for our teenage son, Reza. This pattern continued for many years—one weekend Sa'id would come to Lynchburg and the next weekend Reza and I would go Alexandria.

At my work, LTSH was trying to become accredited for the first time. All the centers were working very hard to meet all the standards and requirements for accreditation, and that was very challenging. Being accredited would be prestigious and raise acceptance for the level of services that the federal and state regulations expected. Of course, the University of Michigan's workshop on aging and retardation, with its focused educational program helped and prepared our professional and direct care staff to meet the requirements of accreditation, even with shortage of staff. But despite the lack of manpower, the staff was motivated and the quality of our services was excellent. However, the Board and the Central Office were more involved with the sterilization issue in the news and were very unhappy with the publicity that Dr. Nelson's publications and interviews were bringing to the center. As a result, they did not pay any attention to the LTSH accreditation issue, while at the same time our center was growing happy and proud of our achievement and possible accreditation. Then we were surprised to hear that the Board of Mental Health and Mental Retardation did not renew the contract for Dr. Nelson after eight years of service.

Establishing a workshop for staff development on aging and intellectual and developmental disability with the cooperation of the University of Michigan and central office in 1980 and later in recognition of her service at the Adult Training Center.

I remember well that at the end of June 1981, everyone was asked to gather in the Davis Building, the largest auditorium we had, to hear the result of the accreditation application. We were very anxious to learn the results. At the beginning, Dr. Nelson announced that he had two items of news to share with us. Then he called the accreditation director to give his report, and the good news was that we were now accredited, with a few citations of ACMRED Accrediting Council. When he finished his congratulatory speech, we applauded with pride and happiness. Next, he announced that since the board had not renewed his contract, he had accepted a job offer as the commissioner of mental health and mental retardation for the State of Arkansas. He wished us well and told us to keep up the good work. I was especially shocked and saddened, and when I asked my colleagues about the reason, I was just told that the decision was politically motivated. I was sorry to learn how politics affected public services, with decisions taken with no bearing on professional expertise. This was the way LTSH became accredited for the first and last time. Unfortunately, because of the lack of communication and cooperation of the professional staff with the new management, the accreditation was not sustained, and LTSH lost its accreditation with the new administration. Since I was already a political victim and motivated merely to give the right professional services to clients, I made up my mind that I would never apply for any position that might be construed as political.

During the accreditation process, the ATC was one of the largest facilities at the LTSH and designed primarily to serve older persons with mental retardation. Our problem and major thrust was twofold. The staff had to cope with the problem of training persons with mental retardation in addition to the psychological, sociological, and other aspects of aging and its accompanying medical complications. We were all very motivated and proud of the accreditation. However, everybody was disappointed that Dr. Nelson was leaving. We wondered who would replace him and were anxious and curious. It was ironic that no professional administrator applied for the job. No one from the LTSH, or the State of Virginia or members of the American Association on Mental Retardation (AAMR) applied, because everyone in our field knew that Dr. Nelson had been treated unfairly in Virginia. There was an atmosphere akin to a boycott. There were many center directors with PhDs and experience in LTSH or in other centers in Virginia and through the country among the members of the professional associations who knew Dr. Nelson, his efforts and did not wish to be involved with this political environment. As a political victim in all this, I learned also that it was not safe to have a very high position. It seemed that political influence could prevent anyone in the high level of management, who wanted to provide the right and appropriate services to the clients. Therefore, in my new country, I decided not to apply for a highly political position.

Dr. Nelson's post was advertised nationally for a long time. It was rumored that if no one with a PhD applied, the position would be opened to people with a master's degree as well. We were told to keep the issue confidential and quiet. Then one Saturday morning, when I was working overtime to finish my massive paperwork, I noticed that the LTSH assistant director was accompanying a visitor on a tour of our center. They were surprised to see me working on a Saturday, and I wondered who the visitor was. The assistant director introduced me to a sharp, short, and anxious lady from New York, who was visiting the LTSH. I explained about the ATC, and she listened quietly. I went back to my office and wondered who she could have been. A few days later, the Lynchburg *News and Advance* announced her as the new director of LTSH, and I was one of the first people who had seen and spoken with her. So for the first time, in this resistant atmosphere, LTSH was to be led by a woman as the director with a master's degree, but not a PhD or MD. Apparently, because of the boycott, this lady was the best or perhaps the only qualified candidate among the applicants for the position. Everybody was curious and asked about my impression of her. As an advocate of women's rights, I was happy that a woman was getting an executive management position, and I was wondering how most of the male assistant directors with PhDs or MDs would tolerate this or could work with her. I wondered if they would not accept her, this could bring some changes and turnover in the top management team. My guess was correct. Gradually, the LTSH management team began to lose most of its PhD members. These people left the LTSH for higher positions in or out of the State of Virginia.

At first, I was happy that Dr. Meece would stay on, and I could work directly with him. However, it was not long before he came to my office and, while kindly asking how settled my family felt in the USA, told me he had accepted a job in Nevada as superintendent. He was especially concerned to know whether I was satisfied with my position and if I was ready for another job change. I immediately understood his kind concern and assured him that I could handle the current job atmosphere with my diverse educational background. I felt that any further change, even with a promotion, would impede the adjustment of our family life, and I needed to stay in Lynchburg for some time in order to adjust to our adopted country, which, with the ongoing hostage crisis, was not easy for us. So I was sorry to see that he was leaving Virginia. Later on, some of the center directors and management team member also left, one by one. My education and professionalism through several membership in professional organizations in the field of mental health, developmental disabilities, and aging was a way of protecting myself, and I did not leave nor applied for any other position, preferring instead to concentrate on the quality of my work and the adjustment of my family in the new country.

After Dr. Nelson and Dr. Meece left, the Lynchburg Training School and Hospital entered a long period of change, insecurity, and turmoil. At ATC, we continued to maintain the high quality of our work. I had drawn up a short—and long-term planning program according to the needs of both the residents and the state for the appropriate community placement and for deinstitutionalization of our clients. The important issues facing us were the promotion of vocational training, and the participation of residents in art and music and the Special Olympics in the area, state, and the country. I always tried to join our excellent special activity aides when they were working with the residents to evaluate and motivate them directly for their participation and readiness for community placement, which was not easy for this age-group. I have very dear memories of this participation, from singing patriotic and religious songs with the residents or supporting and helping them in drawing and participating in the art festivals, to dancing with them and pretending to learn from the client Edna. Edna was good at tap dancing, and she worked to teach the other residents, including myself. This always gave her self-confidence and brought her out from her depression.

One person I remember well was Luther Grant, who often brought his drawings to my office to show me. Sometimes, he gave them to me to put on my office board. One day, he came in, very excited, to show me his drawing of the White House after his field trip to Washington DC. Drawing was the best way he had to show how impressed he was by the White House. Later, he entered that drawing in the special state and national art festival and was fortunate to be selected as a Virginia State winner for which he received a congratulatory letter from President Reagan, along with a picture of him with the First Lady.

Both Luther and his social worker came to my office, very excited about the letter, and again, he wanted me to keep the letter with me in my office. Apparently, we had established a trust between us. We immediately arranged an exhibition of his drawings and invited the daily newspaper reporter to view his exhibition near my office and the opportunity to interview him. That was a good booster for his confidence and excellent preparation for his community placement—not to mention good news for the training center. Strangely, later, when we were placing him in the community, I tried to return the framed congratulatory letter from the president to him, but he insisted that I should keep the letter with me because he thought that was the best way of keeping it safe. He wanted me to promise to keep the letter in my possession at all times. So he left us for his new home and left his letter with me. We tried to visit him and follow up to see how he was adjusting in the group home, where his drawing and painting was the best tool to help him express himself and adjust to life in the community.

Because of the change of management, my job environment changed, and again LTSH was in the news. This time, it was the problem of abuse of employees and patients, but my center was not involved in this charge. I always tried to foresee needs and develop strategies to meet them. For example, I remember one severe ice storm on January 22, 1982. As a matter of habit, when bad weather was forecast, I always preferred to go to work much earlier than usual, taking with me everything I would need for forty-eight hours so that I could be at the center with the residents and staff, supervise the shift, which would be operating with minimum coverage and be available through the storm. This was much better than monitoring them by phone from home. That day, a state of emergency was declared, and because freezing rain and sleet had made driving hazardous, each center director was responsible for ensuring that staffing was covered for a twenty-four-hour period. We began usually by determining who could come to work the next shift, and in case we were short of staff, we asked for volunteers to stay and work overtime. My presence with the staff and residents always stood me in good stead so that most of the time I had the required staffing levels that allowed me minimum coverage for client care. Sometimes, we even sent staff to other centers when they could not reach their minimum staffing levels, and I never had any problem with this issue. In snow and ice storms, I always arrived early and stayed overnight and we had enough volunteers.

Our center had fewer employees calling in sick, less turnover, and good cooperation of staff. There was a sense of togetherness in our center. Apparently, however, on that day in 1982 and the day after, the staff from other centers were forced to stay over the next shift and some were even threatened with the loss of their job if they refused. One person was forced to resign. (*The News and Daily Advance*, January 30, 1982)

Another topic in the news in February and March 1982 was about the injuries to staff and patients. On page 1 of the February 28, 1982, *The News and Advance*, had an article titled LTSH WORKERS SAY INJURIES GO UNREPORTED.[5] Several articles had titles such as INVESTIGATIONS: TRAINING SCHOOL EMPLOYEES TAUGHT TO LOOK INTO CHARGES" and TRAINING SCHOOL DIRECTOR VOWS ACTION TO CURB WORKER'S FEARS (March 1, 1982, vol. 117, no. 41) or WORKERS AT TRAINING SCHOOL FEEL ABUSED BY SUPERVISORS (March 2), and again another article about the moral issue on March 3 and so on. I was happy to see that the name of our center was not included in any of these complaints, and again, we owed this to our knowledge of and compliance with the rules and regulations and the latest treatments for residents in our care.

An issue in the training and treatment of residents that I was working to change was behavior modification of the client programs. Sometimes a reward given to clients as a token reinforcements was a free package of cigarettes provided by the tobacco companies. Ironically, the training school had been promoting the use of the tobacco as a positive reinforcement for our clients for years. I did not think that smoking was the right choice for our residents without their knowing or understanding its side effects. Changing and challenging this custom and habit in a state that grew tobacco as a main crop was not easy. Most of the managers and staff were smokers themselves and some, like the director of the agency or my kind secretaries whose cigarette smoke permeated my office, were even chain smokers. I began to study research about the side effects of smoking and to disseminate this information among the staff and employees. Gradually, through information and knowledge, I noticed that the Interdisciplinary Team (ID) and Behavior Management Review Committee (BMRC) stopped choosing cigarettes for use in behavior modification.

Then in later years, the guidelines of the state helped us prohibit smoking in all living areas. For the resident smokers, we provided a smoking area and established programs through the ID team and behavior modification through BMRC to help residents stop smoking. The BMRC found other positive ways to reward good behavior, according to the needs of residents. Our staff could smoke only outside the living areas and buildings and some of them were trying to quit. My two generous and hardworking secretaries were chain smokers whose smoke I had to endure with my open-door policy. I later found out that I had developed COPD (chronic obstructive pulmonary disease) through the passive smoking I experienced during those years. As a result of this education, and changes in the smoking policies, the number of smokers was reduced to a minimum. Later, I was pleased that we could make changes in the smoking policies and had educated our residents.

Next, we revised and finished the assessment of our all twelve living areas with the authorized bed capacity of the residents according to the level of their function. I have many memories of this time at the training school, several of which are noteworthy. One troubling memory that bothered and worried me for some time was the frequent fires in one of our living areas. A resident was setting fire to various mattresses in the living area, but we did not know who the arsonist was. Since could not accuse anybody, we kept guessing who it might be. Finally, we thought we had the answer, but we could never catch him red-handed. Fortunately, our staff were trained well in evacuating the living area during the frequent fires so that nobody was injured and that, at least, was a blessing. However, each time there was a fire, we all went through a lot of anxiety and fear for our clients. With the assistance of our interdisciplinary team, I studied the files of residents of the living area in detail and found that one resident had lived through a house fire in his childhood. However, it was not clear that he was setting the fires now. After this discovery, we decided to observe his behavior on a one-on-one basis, day and night. It was interesting to discover that he was collecting matches and that most of the time his pocket was full of matches, although no one was able to see how or when he came by these matches. He was smart enough to obtain matches without being discovered, but each time he changed his clothing, whoever was observing him would find matches in his pocket. He was very fond of those matches. Before too long, one night on August 28, 1984, we again had a fire in the same living area, but nobody saw him in action. The sheriff and local law enforcement of Amherst County arrived while the staff were evacuating the residents. Then two officers conducted the arson investigation. I also explained to the officer our observations and our experiences, and finally, the officer suggested a temporary transfer of this resident to a restricted center, the Social Skills Center for six months to see if the fires would stop in our center. I was happy that they supported the observations of our professional staff and their suggestion. I had noticed that most of the time the criminal justice and mental health institutions did not cooperate with each other closely in my new country. Thank God that the suggestion was accepted by the sheriff and the authority of the training center and the fires stopped. As a result, even after the six months, one of our residents continued to live in the restricted areas, and the rest of our residents and staff lived in peace, free of the fear of further fires at ATC.

The author, as the Adult Training Center Director, participating in the Christmas celebration for residents and staff.

Other memorable experiences happened on Christmas days when most of the management team members wanted to have time off with their families. I usually volunteered to be on call, and I always tried to make rounds at LTSH and ATC and participate in gift-unwrapping ceremonies of the residents in different living area. It was rewarding to see the happy faces of our residents as they opened their presents and to share in their pleasure. All of them wanted to show their gifts and share their happiness with me. These scenes were unique notes and memorable melodies in the symphony of my life. Gradually, under the new administration, the Lynchburg Training School (LTSH) lost its accreditation and its name changed to Central Virginia Training Center (CVTC) effective in July 1983.

In addition, gradually from 1983 to 1987, CVTC as a large institution became a major target for the federal government with several audits for possible decertification and even closing because of the federal deficit during the presidency of Ronald Reagan and the deinstitutionalization and community placement of the ICFMR clients facilities. Then secretary of Human Services, Margaret Heckler, in an effort to economize, sent several auditors to large institutions in the country to determine how to downsize or close down in order to cut the federal budget deficit. Federal money would be cut if institutions did not meet the standards, and the auditors could either decertify them or downsize them. This audit especially targeted the programs in Intermediate Care Mental Retardation (ICFMR) facilities. Several large institutions in the country were closed, and we had to defend our center and go through five plans of correction for ICFMR. The final plan involved a major change: conversion of the level of care of ATC to a workable plan called intermediate care general (ICF). This action rescued the CVTC from decertification and closing by a drastic downsizing of about three hundred of the number of clients in ICFMR level at ATC. Of course, there were a lot of changes and challenges for me in the conversion of level of care in the Adult Training Center, which I describe in the next chapter in detail.[6] As a result, and because of the uncertainty, the working atmosphere at this time was very apprehensive, and it was difficult to work in peace. I had to pay close attention to staff morale and to relieve them from the anxiety of the possibility of decertification and job loss.

In order to manage my job effectively, I worked with a number of interested professional staff such as psychologists, speech therapists, social workers, teachers, and a few others to form a committee to research and study the interdisciplinary areas of aging and developmental disability. This work led us to progress in this field and motivated some of us to pursue our ideas and findings for publication in professional journals. Some members were motivated to continue their education to a higher degree. For example, our psychologist Nancy applied to the PhD program at Virginia Tech University and was accepted. That was rewarding for the staff and for me. Although these studies were in addition to our job responsibilities, we tried with difficulty and hardship to fit them in, and still our findings were rewarding especially when later we could change our level of care and help to maintain the certification of CVTC and keep it from being closed.

In the meantime, I received two invitations from my international academic friends. One of them was from the University of London and the Teachers College, Columbia University, who were instrumental in publishing the World Yearbook of Education in 1965 by Evans Brothers Ltd., London, to which I had contributed a section on Iran. During the 1980s, a group of these colleagues wanted to publish for the first time *The International Encyclopedia of Education* through Pergamon Press. They invited me to join them to write about the "Education System of Iran." This was not an easy task because of Iran's revolution, during which the goal of education was in the process of changing from a secular, modern educational model similar to the French system to a more Islamic religious education. In spite of the difficulty, as my teachers always reminded me that I loved a difficult task, I accepted the challenge to write an objective and up-to-date history of the educational system in Iran, which was published in 1985.[6] I was happy and proud to accomplish this for my country in the middle of a horrible political and economic war. Later on, I updated the same article for another reference book and published in the *Encyclopedia of Comparative Education and National Systems of Education*.[7] The second invitation, dated on March 15, 1984, was from Dr. Gerhard Hess, the executive director of the College Consortium for International Studies, New York, to attend an all expenses paid seminar in Heidelberg, Germany.

I was very happy to receive this invitation for two reasons. First because I would get to visit my alma mater and see my former professor Dr. Hermann Roehrs, who was still active in international education in Heidelberg. Secondly, during the week of seminars, I would have the opportunity to update my knowledge in education, mental health and disability, which would help me at work as I was implementing change at the institution. Members of the faculty seminars were from several universities in different states of America like Texas, New York, New Jersey, Florida, and some from Europe like England, Spain, and

Germany. Since I did not expect any payment, I contacted the director of the CVTC requesting the leave to be able to attend, and I got immediate approval. Participation in the faculty seminar provided me with substantial-international expertise in my field, and I returned well equipped with the latest information and knowledge, enabling me to face the political administrative "games" at work. In fact, education, especially in psychology, has always been the cornerstone in my life and has enabled me to fight against so many adversities in the world and to be triumphant.

At the beginning of the 1980s, my husband and I had to face another new experience, and that was the yearly income tax preparation and tax return. We had never filed or paid income taxes in the United States, and we were not familiar with this system. We were accustomed to the Iranian flat-rate tax system, which was uncomplicated and easy. However, I quickly realized that we might need the assistance of a tax preparer in the United States. Some of the employees were using the services of local accountant (referred to as Mrs. L) and suggested that we let her handle ours as well. So for the first three years, she prepared our taxes. The third year, we received a letter from the district director of the IRS stating the following:

"We selected your Federal Income Tax Return for the year shown below (1981) to examine the item at the end of this letter. (Utility and Schedule C)."

The letter stated an appointment time at the IRS office in Lynchburg. Of course, we were very nervous. I was told that periodically, and on a random basis, the IRS chose some clients for auditing. I was not aware of the system, and since we had been accustomed to a flat tax, we were not used to keeping all our receipts. I obtained copies of our credit card and bank statements for the year in question, as much as I remembered from two years before, in case these were needed and went to the address given at the appointed time.

We were anxious to find out what they wanted to review in our tax file. The tax officer (referred to as Mr. S) was a friendly and polite young man who immediately noticed that we were new in the country and listened with patience to the story of our losses because of the revolution, which of course could not be documented. Then he went over each page of the tax form that we had submitted for that year. In fact, we were very grateful for his review with us, and we really learned from him how complicated the system was. Mr. S asked for several documents for Sa'id's music studio—the price of the piano and the amount of the utility bills, an amount included in the condo fee. Fortunately, we had all the supporting documentation. He then explained that the tax law for small business had been changed by President Reagan, and according to the new tax law, Sa'id could have used the new aggressive method of depreciation for business. Apparently, our tax preparer Mrs. L either did not know about this or preferred to use the old system. He said that if she used the new system, in future, we would have more money returned to us. We could use that rule when we filed for the next year, but for that year, he accepted our method. When he finished his recommendations, he stood up and shook our hand and said, "Congratulations," and added that we would hear in writing from Richmond confirming his audit and that there would be no changes on our tax reporting. We were happy at how helpful Mr. S had been, thanked him, and left his office, very much relieved.

I immediately called our tax preparer, who had been unable to come along with us. When I told her about the result and the auditor's suggestions for the following year, she was happy for us, but told me that she preferred to be more conservative and not to show too much loss in the new business. She also wondered why Mr. S had not followed his own suggestion and changed our filing so that we would have received more money in our federal return for that year. She said she wished she had been with us to ask that question. Of course, in that case, our return would have changed. However, for the following year, she said she would consider Mr. S's recommendation in preparing our tax. Two weeks later, in a letter dated on May 16, 1982, we received a letter from the district director of the IRS stating that our returns "are accepted as filed."

That, however, was not the last we heard from the IRS. That year and the next few years, it seemed, brought a different auditing system and judgment and the whole thing became more confused because of the subjective influence and whim of the auditors. The next year, when we received a letter from the district director, we went along confidently with our file because Mrs. L had prepared our tax return and Schedule C in line with Mr. S's suggestions. We were even looking forward to meeting him again. However, when we arrived, we were met by a woman instead (referred to here as Mrs. W). We asked about Mr. S, and she said he had been promoted to audit the corporations and did not do personal audits anymore; she said she would conduct our audit and began to ask us questions about the new president of Iran. "What do you think about Mr. Rafsanjani, the new president of Iran?" she asked. This question startled and surprised us because she also pronounced Rafsanjani's name correctly. Wondering why she was interested in our national origin, I just told her that "I do not know" and I hoped that she would not be prejudiced against Iranian Americans because of the backlash of the hostage crisis. After my answer, she asked several personal questions followed by questions about our tax return. Her first concern was why we chose to depreciate aggressively. I became upset and asked, "May we speak to Mr. S who suggested this method?" She became defensive, her face turned red, and said, "No, you may not," and told us that he was not in the office. I told her that she could ask him herself because the year before he had suggested we file this way, and therefore our tax preparer followed his suggestion. She then said that she did not agree with his suggestion. She had another interpretation and asked us for more documentation about Sa'id's studio and also about my administrative leave without pay to attend the AAMR convention. Since this documentation was not needed the first time, I did not have it with me. She gave us another appointment and a question in a handwritten note to give to our tax preparer.

We began to wish that Mrs. L had been with us from the beginning. Tax issues and tax filing in the USA are so complicated. For newcomers, it is extremely difficult to keep up with federal, state, county, social security, Medicare, city, real estate, car, sales, and other taxes and the whole experience is quite overwhelming. Nearly half of my salary every month was deducted for tax and insurance, which I needed to file for return later, and every deduction every year was dependent on the tax year and changes of tax law for that year. So I gave the auditor's note to Mrs. L and prepared a copy of my unpaid administrative leave paper from the State of Virginia, a copy of registration fee, hotel and travel expenses payment with my own credit card and personal check and all the other documents for my husband for the new auditor Mrs. W.

This time we went with Mrs. L. I also heard that the new auditor had been employed after Mr. S was promoted and that we were one of the first clients she audited. I was told I should be quiet and let Mrs. L handle all the questions. The meeting was long and my migraine headache started. My expenses for the professional meeting were accepted, but the argument over the depreciation issue between the two took a long time and finally we needed to pay about 200 hundred dollars more, with interest, for the different interpretation requested by Mrs. W. I immediately wrote a check and gave it to Mrs. W., the new auditor, who was smiling at her victory. It was an interesting expression, which I will never forget. I tried many times to find Mr. S but I was not successful and could not tell him about my story. After the meeting, I thanked Mrs. L who had come with us and a few months later, she wrote a nice letter, telling us that she was not working in the tax business anymore. She suggested an old CPA firm in Lynchburg to handle our taxes. Therefore, we took her advice and gave our tax business to that company, signing a statement that they would handle any auditing issue on our behalf.

For a couple of years, we had questions from the IRS until Sa'id's new business for the music studio showed a net profit. With this experience, we learned to use a Certified Public Accountant for our tax filing and bear its expenses and let them handle our taxes, keeping in mind the different personalities of the tax auditors and their interpretation and judgment and the yearly change of the tax law.

During this time, Gita and Reza were going through different phases of mental and physical development. I followed this closely, especially with regard to the effect of the horrible news from Iran and its impact on their physical growth and mental health in a new culture. For Gita, who was going through adolescence and living away from home at Phillips Academy, we were worried and tried either to write or call her as frequently as we could so that she would not feel isolated from her family. She was encouraged to call us any time she wanted to, and we suggested that she not forget her faith and urged her to write in her diary whenever she felt upset or depressed. She took my advice and started to write whenever she needed spiritual relief. I hope that one day, she will publish her beautifully and skillfully written diary and poems. In her diary, she writes that she had a gift of telepathy because she knew exactly when we were calling her and we knew when she was upset. However, this was not easy for me to accept, even as a clinical psychologist. I also was in contact with her kind school counselor, Zandra. We tried not to miss the parents' days, and I tried most of the time to have a private meeting with Zandra. I thought it was necessary to tell her about our culture and the status of women and girls, in which girls are more openly protected in comparison to the West, especially the United States. Zandra needed to consider that Gita might be stuck between the values of two very dissimilar cultures.

Later, I heard that Zandra and Gita formed the Women's International Organization at Phillips Academy, which enjoyed the membership of a lot of foreign girls from different cultures. They established regular meetings to speak about themselves and their cultures. Apparently, this helped Gita immensely. Another positive aspect of her life was her keen interest in piano, and through regular practice, she was making progress in playing the three movements of Beethoven's *Pathetique* Sonata and other pieces that she had played for years in Iran. However, she chose Chopin's "Nocturne" in E major for her school concert because she imagined that Chopin would love to hear her play, and she herself loved to share her personal interpretation with other music lovers. She, like my husband, played Chopin beautifully. In addition, Gita was also active in the Cantata choir as a soprano. Another activity that kept her going successfully was her involvement in the school theater. She played the role of Mrs. Plumb, the house counselor, in the play *Uncommon Women, and Others*, and she loved it.

Another of Gita's chosen activities, which I found to be surprising, was her choice to visit a nursing home as an "Andover Friendly Visitor," instead of participating in a sport for the winter months. When I asked her for the reasons, her response was that the physical fitness that she gained in the fall from being on the rowing team was not satisfactory, and that she needed to grow mentally, and the only way she could achieve that was through daily interaction with older people. It was her chance to love and respect them as is the custom in Persian culture. She was feeling good because she was making daily visits to Elsie, a ninety-year-old lady, whose relatives had practically abandoned her. Their visits were enjoyable and rewarding for both Gita and Elsie; and each time I called Gita, I made sure to ask about Elsie too.

Later, I understood that because of the horrible news about the revolution and the war in Iran, she chose the topic of death for an essay she wrote, and she was learning a lot through Elsie's views about old age and death. Gita read many books about death, including a book about death and society, and all the while dreaming and thinking a lot about war, revolution, death, and faith. She was also observing the difference in people's attitude toward the elderly in various societies; she wondered why Elsie, who had forty living family members, was placed in a nursing home and why none of them would cherish the joy of taking care of Elsie personally. Gita thought it was an honor to have an elderly person in one's house. She was reminiscing how we all valued my mother's presence in our home. Gita remembered how her grandmother taught her the essentials of love, justice, and personal faith in Islam.

I remember well that Gita wrote poems in both English and Farsi. One of her poems was entitled "Darkness." Her poems contained horrifying images of black crows killing the innocent pigeons that live in the mosque's courtyard and, with a sudden sound of "Allah o Akbar" (God is great), showed the image of crying black crows who tore their own hearts out in the process of killing the pigeons. Then the black crows covered the gold dome of the prophet like a black silk and then Gita thought she would one day walk with bare feet on the flat and nameless graves of the Persian martyrs and scare the crows with the burning fire of her soul. Only then would she be able to sit by the Saint Massoumeh's pool in the courtyard and pray like a Moslem so that she could enter her house with true love and a calmed spirit. Only then could she kiss the shrines and see God's beauty and justice. Then she wrote that she would wash her hands and feet with the dirty green holy water and would pray continuously, until she would finally feel that her soft spirit and God would take her to the skies and set her spirit free.

My dear Gita, like many other young people from Iran, was in deep conflict between two cultures, especially since our religion and country was taken hostage by the dark forces of revolution, and this darkness was showing beautifully in her poems. This conflict was made obvious again in her resistance in her history classes in school. She wanted clearly first to learn the history of Iran and then the history of America. Fortunately, her good school and counselor understood her needs for that and arranged for her to have private Iranian history lessons by a known prominent scholar, Dr. Hossein Nassr, who was professor and president of a university in Iran, who, like us, had left Iran because of the revolution and lived in Boston. I knew him, and I was happy that my daughter had the opportunity to study both American as well as the Persian history, the old and modern history together. In general, we were very thankful to the school management and their understanding of her emotional, financial, and academic need.

In Gita's junior year, we visited several universities with her. She liked the University of Virginia, which was near our home in Lynchburg. In her senior year of high school, she felt uncomfortable with the university application process; therefore, I visited her more often with a list of suggestions, in the hope of reducing her stress and ensuring her success. After reviewing her school choices, we both decided that she should apply as an early decision applicant to University of Virginia (UVA). We hoped to reduce the waiting period and stress as Gita was a Virginia resident and had an impressive academic record.

On October 25, 1982, Gita sent her application to UVA. On November 17, 1982, I had the flu and was in bed when the telephone rang and Gita was on the phone. Gita usually called us with good news. It was when I was not hearing from her when I usually had to call her to find out how she was doing and whether she was either sick or depressed. I jumped from bed, and Sa'id took the other phone and heard her unforgettable happy voice, telling us that "Mom, Dad, I made it! I've been accepted!" Then she read her acceptance letter from the University of Virginia while I was crying quietly from a deep happiness for her success. Unfortunately, I cannot explain and describe how happy we were. Gita kept asking, "Is this real?" Gita said that at no time ever was she so happy. She kept thanking God, her teachers, and counselor. She was feeling strong, secure, and wholesome, and we were all very happy. She was relieved and relaxed, while her friends and classmates were applying for regular admission to universities and colleges, waiting for a response. Gita was now giving them advice and trying to relieve their anxiety and stress. She was working with peace of mind to finish her senior year with even advanced placement credits.

Gita was also involved and active in her graduation ceremony. We will never forget her graduation ceremony. Our family and Doris May went to the combined church and auditorium of the school and sat in the first left side front row near the podium in the section for international parents. Gita's name was in three different places in the program. She was going to play her favorite Chopin's "Nocturne," and her name was listed in the school choir and in the graduation list. The ceremony started with the national anthem, and then the priest read a special thanksgiving prayer according to the Christian religion. After that, the rabbi of the school read a thanksgiving prayer, and then suddenly, we were shocked and surprised to see Gita come to the podium. She said that all Iranian people thanked God daily according to Islam, and then she started to sing "Hamdo Sur-e," which includes the phrases of thanksgiving in

Arabic from the Koran. She sang so beautifully with all the appropriate nuances that we and most of the people were surprised, impressed, and some, including us, cried and the hall was completely silent for minutes. While I was crying, I was observing that the audience was in a deep silent mood and some were even wiping their eyes. We were very proud of her and wondered how she had mastered the prayer in song without any assistance from a family member. Everybody was telling us that her performance was unique, and we were very proud of that and her excellent performance of Chopin. This was the result of our passionate family life and the influence of my passionate and religious mother who read the Koran to Gita and recounted the adventures of Mohammed as Gita sat on her lap. After the moving graduation ceremony, the graduates said their farewell, and we returned home with our treasured daughter, whom we had missed for so long. We thanked God for Gita's excellent educational experience at Phillips Academy and her beautiful graduation performance.

For Reza, who just finished Paul Monroe Elementary School and was going next to Linkhorne Middle School in Lynchburg, the situation was different. There were no international schools and not even another international student in his school. He was the only one in his class from outside the United States. Therefore, although he was at home with us, he was under more pressure than Gita from the community backlash to the hostage crisis.

The location of Lynchburg, the lack of understanding of other cultures, his impressionable age, his peer group and classmates led to great stress for Reza. I remember that in the first year of middle school, one day, I had a call from school notifying me of his absence from school and asking me to write a letter explaining the reason for his absence. In shock, we wondered and worried where he could have been, while he was not in school. About 4:00 p.m. the regular hour of his return, we were happy to see him return safely. When I asked him where he had been, he denied his absence from school. After I asked him about his homework for the day, he realized that we knew about his absence. He became very quiet and told us that he had had a warning from a group of students—a gang—the day before, saying that they would attack him because he was Iranian, and that if he told his parents, they would beat him even more. Therefore, in order to avoid a fight, he hid himself in the woods to prevent a fight and cause problems for us. Apparently, he had a flashback of his first experience with the primary schoolchildren assaulting him right after the hostage crisis at the American Embassy in Tehran, which landed him in the emergency room of Lynchburg General Hospital. Reza told us that most of his classmates knew karate very well, and he was frightened that he could not defend himself. While we were happy that he had returned safely, we told him that he should have shared his concern with us. We then immediately enrolled him in karate classes for self-defense. The next day, without telling him, I went to the school and spoke to the principal and the counselor privately and asked them to watch his situation and relation with the peer groups.

After this incident, in order to avoid a similar problem for the next year, I spoke to Beth Meece and made inquiries about her children, to see in which school they were enrolled. They were going to Holy Cross, a private Catholic school not very far from our home, and she was satisfied with the school. Her son, Jeff Meece, was the same age as Reza. My main desire was to find a school where he would not face hostility as he had in the public school, and leave both him and myself to study and work in peace without fear and anxiety. So in this way, Reza continued his studies and finished middle school and part of his high school at Holy Cross School. We did not mind his daily Bible study class in his new environment. He was on both the soccer and the wrestling teams and active in community volunteer work, helping with fund-raising in our neighborhood. He also played the trumpet in the school band.

One day, Mrs. Louise Breeding, one of our next-door neighbors, called me to ask if I would give permission for Reza to volunteer with two other boys to play the trumpet at political rallies in the state political convention. She herself was volunteering to prepare lemonade for the participants and could pick him up. Since Reza liked Mrs. Breeding for her generosity in his school fund-raising in our neighborhood, he wanted to accept her request to play the trumpet. I thought if they would accept me as a legal alien in the convention, I would not mind to attend myself as a volunteer and help her to prepare lemonade. Reza would not be alone, and it would be interesting to observe the political election process in America for the first time. When I offered to help, she welcomed me, and we went together to Waynesboro, where the state convention was taking place in a stadium. We arrived a little bit early to prepare our lemonade. Gradually, the people began to arrive. Reza was curious and anxious to meet the other boys who were to play the trumpet with him at the beginning of the rally. I was assisting Louise by pouring lemonade in the paper cups, and she, who knew many people, was greeting them as they arrived, giving each one a cup of lemonade and a program. The stadium was getting full, but there was no news from the other musicians. Finally, the parent of one of them rushed up to tell Louise that his son was too scared to play in front of such a large crowd and decided at the last minute not to come. He was supposed to play the clarinet. There was no news from the third boy either. So Reza was left to be the only one. When he realized that he was the only one to play before the large crowd, his face became pale, and he looked at me. I was happy that I came with him. Louise and I told him that we were very proud of him. As he was standing at the front getting ready to play, we said, "Aren't you proud to start the state convention by yourself?" Just then, he saw the hand signal to begin, and as he marched and played the trumpet, the flags of America and the Commonwealth of Virginia followed behind him. They marched around the stadium and took their seats. The stadium became quiet, and after a moment of silence, the program started. I was happy that he played and acted very well, and I really was proud of him.

Reza was gradually adjusting to the life in America and handling the backlash to the hostage crisis better. He knew many people, and in the evening after school, our telephone would ring nonstop and most of the time it was for Reza, sometimes with invitations to visit friends in their homes. He was making progress in karate and moved up the belt levels,—from green, to red, to brown. His self-confidence level was growing too, and he was no longer afraid of his peers. He knew many people in Lynchburg and got his driver's license on the very day of his sixteenth birthday so he would not lose a single day of driving. He also found a part-time job.

Since Holy Cross was not challenging enough for him anymore, and Jeff Meece had moved away, after making several inquiries, we registered Reza in EC Glass High School where several of his school friends had gone and was an excellent public school with more activities. Now, our telephone in the evening was constantly ringing, and he and his friends were visiting back and forth, and we became worried about his academic work and grades because of this busy social life. I tried indirectly to get to know his friends, but this was not easy. He seemed to know everybody in town. You can imagine our surprise when we saw the letter of commendation from the National Merit Scholarship program. His PSAT Index score placed him among the upper 50,000 of more than 1 million students who entered the 1987 Merit Program, and his name was in the Lynchburg newspaper with the other honor students in an article headlined AREA HIGH SCHOOL SENIORS HONORED. His report cards were an A average most of the time.

On the whole, the peer pressure in America are much stronger than the family values, and keeping a proper balance between fun and academic work for teenagers is not easy. Fortunately, Reza made the honor roll and received many academic awards, athletic honor awards in soccer, wrestling, karate, and a band award for playing the trumpet. He was also a member of the French Club, Ski Club, and Math Honor Club, and helped in Special Olympics. He liked the honor system, which is based on one's own honor and self-respect and being judged by his own peers. He also thought that the student run system of American high schools created an atmosphere of mutual trust and respect among fellow students where any violation would be judged accordingly. Reza followed his peer groups more for fun than for academic work. He wanted to be like them as much as possible and maybe even wanted to prove that he was not an outsider and so protecting himself from any attack. I began to notice that, on a few occasions when he was faced with violence, he could defend himself, and overall was very good in the practical aspects of life to the point that each time we or any of his friends had any problem, he was the problem solver.

He applied to four public universities, and he was accepted at George Mason, Virginia Tech, and University of North Carolina. We thought maybe George Mason in Northern Virginia would be more suitable with honors admission and a diverse community, which included many Iranian families who had settled in the area. Since there were many Iranian students at the university, they even had a Persian Club. So overall, we thought that Reza would feel more comfortable there as an Iranian, especially since his father's music studio was also in Northern Virginia and close by.

Reza graduated from EC Glass in June 1987, and on the day of his graduation, we experienced an event that we will not forget. On the day of graduation, he asked us not to take a camera to the ceremony because he did not want us to take a picture of him in the graduation cap and gown. We honored his wish, although I was eager to have a souvenir of his graduation. He was very excited, and he told us that after the graduation, he would not be coming home since he would be celebrating with his schoolmates. So we gave him permission, although from the bottom of my heart, I was worried since there were a lot of car accidents among the young people who get permission to drive at the early age of sixteen, much younger than in other countries, and especially since they would be highly emotional on that occasion. He was driving his car with friends that night, heading to Wintergreen, a resort area near Lynchburg. I could not sleep that night until he came home very late and, thank God, was safe. He looked very tired and exhausted, and we immediately went to bed. The next day, the daily newspaper published the report of the graduation on the cover page with only one picture, a picture of Reza and his friend Will Pitt in their graduation robes, holding up their hands together and exclaiming that they had made it! We were happy to have at least one picture of his graduation, a picture that he did not oppose, and it was a nice picture.

High school graduation of the author's son Reza Khadiri with Will Pitt published on the front page of the local newspaper.

While we were happy to finally have one graduation picture, when we asked him about his celebration with his friends at Wintergreen and what they did, he said that the party was good. However, he was sorry to notify us that he had received a traffic ticket in Amherst because of the possession of a radar detector. He had gotten the radar detector for the times he drove to West Virginia to visit the parents of his friend Will Pitt where its use was legal, and he had forgotten to hide it. He told us he would work to pay the fine and do whatever the judge decided. We were shocked and upset and were concerned about our insurance, but he was working to save money for the court date.

On the court day, he filled his pocket with nearly one hundred dollars in cash for the payment since he had found out how much the charge would be—$96. He knew he would be charged for owning and using the radar detector, and he was relieved that he had enough money for that. Because he was under eighteen, we as parents were required to go with him to court, so in the morning of the court date, my husband and I went with him. I took the newspaper with his picture, which proved that the ticket was issued on the same date of his graduation. At the Amherst Courthouse, several cases were called before Reza's. Then, the judge called him, and first, the police officer who wrote the ticket explained how he had followed Reza's car had thought that he had a radar detector and stopped him even though he wasn't speeding. The judge asked Reza if he had any comments or questions. Reza explained that he had used the instrument only when he was in West Virginia and Maryland, where it was legal and wondered why it was not legal in Virginia. After Reza's comment, I raised my hand for permission to speak and said, "Your Honor, I would like to bring to your attention that the date of offense was on the evening of his high school graduation, and the students were very emotionally excited." I showed him a copy of the newspaper with the picture of Reza for proof. Then, everyone in the courtroom became quiet as we waited for the pronouncement of the judge. While Reza was preparing his money in his pocket, we all were staring at the judge, who was studying the file. After a few minutes, he looked at Reza and said, "In the State of Virginia, the possession of a radar detector is illegal even if you do not use it." The judge ruled that Reza should write a detailed account, free of grammar and spelling mistakes of his research into why radar detectors were forbidden in the State of Virginia to be handed in three weeks' time to the charging officer, who was present in the court room. If Reza did that, and the paper was satisfactory, the judge would dismiss the charges.

That ruling surprised us and everybody in the courtroom, especially Reza, who was ready to pay the fine. As an educator, I was deeply thankful and impressed with such an educational judgment. We thanked the judge and left the court. The next day, we noticed that Reza went to the law library of the city to prepare his assignment, and we were happy that he was going to learn and be prepared for his college work too. As a result of his paper, the judge dismissed the charge. Just recently in 2006, I heard that a member of Virginia House of Delegate was pushing for a repeal of the state ban on the possession and use of the radar detector because, although it has been shown that these devices prevent accidents and save lives, Virginia is the only state that still bans the sale and use of them.

In 1986, the city of Lynchburg celebrated its bicentennial and Central Virginia Training Center celebrated its seventy-fifth birthday with great relief that we had done well in a federal government audit. The governor of Virginia visited our center on May 15, and we provided a time capsule for him to place in the ground in front of the administration building. The visit to the museum of the facility and to review services at the facility from 1911 to 1986 was fascinating. It showed how in May 1911, a farm on the James River was claimed by the Amherst County proudly as an institution for the special people called feebleminded and epileptic. From the four corners of the State of Virginia, these special people were sent to live here. During seventy-five years, the institution had about ten directors, and its name was changed five times. In 1970, the institution became one of the largest institutions in the country for the mentally retarded with 3,694 residents, and then due to the deinstitutionalization movement, the new facilities in the state and the number of the residents reduced to less than half.

Meanwhile, the news of the repressive and regressive revolution of Iran was very painful to us, and the continuation of the Iran-Iraq war was not encouraging. It became obvious to us that there would be no returning home anytime soon, and so the whole family began adjusting to the new country, and even though this meant losing all our retirement money in Iran for our years of service and sacrificing all our belongings in Iran, we made the painful decision to apply for citizenship in the United States. We completed the application forms and were honored with citizenship during the country's bicentennial year.

For Sa'id, his citizenship was celebrated on July 4, 1986, at historic Monticello, the home of Thomas Jefferson. A day of perfect weather, Monticello was beautiful, and some of our neighbors came to join us for the celebration. This was an important moment in our life, and we felt almost as if we were getting a second birthday. Members of the Daughters of the American Revolution welcomed us, guided us around, and gave us a flag of our new country and an excellent Manual for Citizenship. We valued and honored this manual, which included all the necessary information for a new citizen—from the early history of America to the Declaration of Independence, the Constitution of the United States, Bill of Rights, and the Pledge of Allegiance and other useful information that even today I still refer to.

The author and her family attending their Citizenship Ceremony on July 4, 1987 and receiving their Citizenship certificate at the Thomas Jefferson's *Monticello*.

The author with her family; Dr. Sa'id, Gita and Reza Khadiri.

After this ceremony, we left Monticello with a happy feeling and returned to our home in our new country and celebrated our citizenship with all our friends and colleagues in Lynchburg. We celebrated on Sunday with the typical food of our two countries and finished with a cake made by one of my friends in the shape of a map of the United States, which they asked us to cut while singing the national anthem. One of my colleagues, who was a member of the Daughters of the American Revolution, Mrs. Celia Vandegrift, invited me to address her chapter in Brookneal on the subject "What it means to me and my family to be citizens." I accepted with pleasure and was honored by the invitation, and on April 6, 1987, the two-hundredth-year anniversary of the Constitution, which was very important to me, I spoke at the regular meeting of the chapter. I think the speech was good enough that the Brookneal *Union Star* published my speech on Wednesday, April 29, 1987, with the headline NEW AMERICAN DESCRIBES WHAT IT MEANS TO HER AND FAMILY TO BE CITIZENS.

First of all, I would like to thank you for the honor of inviting me tonight as your guest speaker. I have been looking forward to speaking on this occasion since it is a great opportunity for me to express my gratitude to be a citizen this year on the 200th anniversary of the American Constitution, whose principles have come to mean so much to me and my family in the past few years. However, I would like to first describe the developments that led to my decision to become an American citizen.

Many years ago, I was first exposed to America through my textbooks in school. My first feelings toward America were those of awe and admiration, for my textbooks painted a picture of a trouble free land where freedom and equality were as native to its people as was my quest to establish these American ideals in my previous country. Iran. As a young woman, I was very aware of the many inequalities and lack of rights that existed in Iran, and in particular, I was greatly saddened by the inequality and prejudice Iranian women were faced with. Therefore, I based my life goals on promoting the image of women in Iran and to crush the image of women as helpless, weak and uneducated human beings. Now, when I reflect upon my younger days, I realize that my dreams were not different from those of our founding father whose main concern was for all Americans to reap the benefits of freedom and equality. I wanted every Iranian woman to have the opportunity to excel because of her merit and to never be denied the opportunity to fulfill her dreams because she was not a man.

Since I was a true believer of merit, I found that the best weapon to fight injustice was a good education and hard work. Therefore, I concentrated on excelling in my studies and my persistence and hard work finally resulted in earning my PhD with high honors from the University of Heidelberg, West Germany, one of the oldest universities in Europe.

I first realized my dream of promoting women's rights in Iran as a Professor of Psychology at the National University of Iran, where I served as one of the few women professors on the faculty. My husband, a Professor of Music Education at the Tehran University was also an ardent supporter of my efforts.

Then in the summer of 1966, the United States National Science Foundation offered me a fellowship at the University of Michigan which I readily accepted, for it was not only a great honor to be selected as the only representative from Iran and all foreign countries, but it was also a chance for me to finally visit the country I had read so much about since my youth. But, as you well know, 1967/8 was a time of great unrest for America as the Civil Rights movement was surging ahead with great strength and controversy. As a foreigner, I was shocked to find that the America I had idealized for so long, was in a state of upheaval because of the discrimination and prejudice that seemed to question the principles of equality and freedom which had been so firmly expressed in the Constitution and the Declaration of Independence.

I returned to the United States the next year as a Fulbright Scholar visiting professor and researched psychology and programmed learning in several U. S. universities and was impressed to find that the American people were ardently supportive of the Civil Rights movement with even more vigor than the previous year.

Inspired and impressed by the magnitude of reforms that were taking place in the United States to promote quality, I returned to Iran with a deep conviction that Iranians could also overcome their prejudice against working and educated women. Thus, I became very involved with the women's rights movement in Iran and was finally elected as the Secretary-General of the Women's Organization of Iran in 1969. From 1969 to 1971 I established and supervised 180 Family Welfare Centers (House of Women) throughout Iran.

Although I was proud of the family welfare systems, I felt that the country needed a firm education base geared toward strengthening these special centers. Therefore, I established Shemiran College in order to offer all specialized programs of pre-school education, family counseling, welfare administration and special education. There I served as the president of the College until 1979 when the Islamic Revolution broke out and the government shut down all educational institutions. The Islamic government proclaimed that it was no longer interested in what the universities and colleges had to offer since they believed that the Islamic teachings of the Koran are sufficient for Iran's educational needs.

After the arrival of Khomeini in Iran, it became evident the government was there to oppress its people in the name of God, freedom and equality for all. Betrayed by my own government's abuse of these sacred principles, I saw no other choice for my family and me but to leave the country while it was still possible.

We left Iran with 20 pounds of luggage, thinking that we would return when the hype had died down. We left with our dreams but with little to show for them, but we left with the warm feeling that there is a better world.

We climbed over the walls of terrorism, forsaking all that we had created and given to Iran in the past 20 years. We left unthanked and unwanted, but we left with faith in our souls. We left Iran with many doubts but willingly accepted what was to be our new country, America.

And when I reflected upon the bygone years and remembered the good and the bad, I remembered a place I had visited not too long ago where the hearts were warm and the spirits more free, a place where freedom and equality were the underlying principles of its government and a place whose people had chosen to replace discrimination with love and understanding, and I knew America was the only place in the world where I would want to live and raise my children. Among other things, the American Constitution guaranteed its citizens that their rights to vote "shall not be denied or abridged by the United or by any state on account of race, color or previous condition of servitude." In fact the Constitution and the Declaration of Independence guaranteed my family and me the many rights that the Iranian government did not even consider important.

However, my problems did not end once I knew I wanted to move to America. Having left everything behind, I knew that my family found great strength in God and in ourselves as we knew that we could rebuild our lives through hard work, experience and our good education.

Fortunately my faith in the values of having a good education paid off in the summer of 1979 when the United States government granted me permission to permanently reside in the United States through the third preference clause of the Immigration Laws which requires that the applicant for permanent residency posses exceptional ability and be internationally well known. I accepted the first job offer to serve the mentally retarded as Center Director of Lynchburg Training School and Hospital (now known as Central Virginia Training Center). After one year my whole family became permanent residents of the United States. As Center Director of ATC at the Central Virginia Training Center, under supervision of Assistant Director of Health Services, I have the good fortune to work with a dedicated staff of approximately 220 people who work with 267 developmentally disabled persons and so throughout the past eight years I have been responsible for the implementation of appropriate policy and procedures of the Center in addition to organizing and managing the financial, physical and human resources of the staff in realization of center's goals and objectives.

During these years I have always considered the option of becoming a US citizen and the decision was a difficult one. To become a citizen, I had to not only believe and accept the American way of life, but I also had to renounce my Iranian citizenship. The first part of my decision was simple because accepting the United States as a new home had already taken place in 1979. However, the test of being a US citizen was not in loving this new country but in renouncing the one that had been a part of my life for so long. I had to come to terms with myself and when I did, I realized that this truly was my one and only home as it was for my children and husband.

But becoming a citizen does not just mean a new home. It also means all the principles that our founding fathers brought two centuries ago. To me it means accepting the founding principles of this country that are so similar to the principles I fought for in Iran for many years. It means living in a country where my son can realize his dream of becoming an engineer and my daughter of being a lawyer.

When I asked my daughter how she would summarize why she wanted to become a US citizen, she spoke from my family's heart when she said "good citizenship does not mean a passive acceptance of laws and rights our founding fathers gave us two centuries ago, but rather demands an active acceptance of these endearing values by taking the responsibility to uphold principles as stated in the Declaration of independence and Constitution of the United States.

Delivered on the April 6, 1987, meeting of the Red Hill Chapter, Daughters of the American Revolution.

---

1. AAIDD website.

2. Zonta International website.

3. *New York Times*, February 23, 1980.

4. The *Wall Street Journal*, January 31, 2007, Section D2.

5. *The News and Advance* covers most incidents at the Center. Sample articles: "Investigations: Training school employees taught to look into charges" and "Training school director vows action to curb worker's fears" *The News and Advance*, Lynchburg, VA March 1, 1982, vol. 117, no. 41) or "Workers at training school feel abused by supervisors," (March 2) and again another article about the moral issue on March 3, and so on.

6. Redjali, Sakineh M., "Education System of Iran". The International Encyclopedia of Education, by Torsten Husen; T. Postlethwaite Pergamon Press, vol. 5, pg. 2697-2702, 1985.

7. T. Postlethwaite, Pergamon Press, Oxford, New York, 1988.

CHAPTER 17

Deinstitutionalization, Research, and Relocation

1987-1996

In my position as the center director of the Adult Training Center (ATC), again, I became an agent for change and responsible for the conversion of the care level of our geriatric clients from Intermediate Care Facility Mental Retardation (ICFMR) to Immediate Care Facilities General (ICF/G). This change was in accordance with CVTC's fifth plan of correction that was submitted to the Health Care Financing Administration (HCFA) of the federal government and finally accepted by that agency. Fortunately, this plan was beneficial for the geriatric clients as well as for the state. For the conversion, we needed to change the certification and the standards of service. My membership in professional organizations of aging and mental health and mental retardation helped me tremendously in the successful implementation of this conversion and all the related tasks. I had regularly presented papers and shared any changes we went through at national conventions and annual meetings. It was important to have the input and support of professionals from other states, and sometimes, they published these papers in their own professional journals.

During the 1980s, despite the trend toward deinstitutionalization, a significant number of older persons with mental retardation and physical disabilities continued to reside in institutional settings like the Adult Training Center of the Central Virginia Training Center. Our mission was to serve this group. Because of the characteristics of the residents and the difficulties inherent with continued use of the ICF/MR standards and placing the clients in community nursing care, the management decided in the fifth plan of correction to seek an alternative certification to be called ICF/General. ICF/MR clients could no longer participate in or benefit from a full-time program of active treatment due to their medical status and required twenty-four-hour nursing supervision and care. The focus for ICF/General clients had been in habilitation needs and return to self-care. The conversion started in 1985 and was completed in 1988. Consequently, the Medicaid program had in place a funding mechanism for ICF/General to pay for services to the majority of our clients who were qualified for long-term care.

After six months of planning, communication, and close coordination with appropriate Medicaid representatives, the application to convert our operations from ICF/MR to ICF/General was approved. The approval for this change and the actual conversion process was unique because this was the first time anywhere that such a significant number of residents with intellectual and developmental disabilities in a public institutional setting would be served under ICF/General long-term care regulations. Also, few resources were available to guide the development and implementation of such long-term care for persons with the intellectual and developmental disabilities with geriatric care needs. For the certification of the long-term care facility, we needed to go through a lot of alterations in the physical plant as well as staffing requirements. We had three two-story brick buildings, which were constructed during the late 1950s. These buildings were connected through separate front and back stairs without elevators. Within the framework of the formal requirement of Medicaid for our residents, we justified the budget for three elevators, and although we had to go through the hard and painful process of temporarily moving our residents to another center while the elevators were installed, we were happy that the budget was approved. Fortunately, we successfully finished this challenging task in a year and met most other building requirements like safety, fire, sanitation, and a central call system and created a home like atmosphere including basic needs like privacy curtains in showers.

Staffing adjustments however posed significant problems. We were involved with shifting the educational staff, which included teachers and special activity aides to rehabilitative staff of nurses, physical therapy aides, and occupational therapy aids. We also had to establish a new resident problem-oriented record (POR) containing new forms to accommodate the assessment and monthly/quarterly report on residents' condition. Our efforts to meet ICF/General documents were successful, and we continually evaluated documentation and reporting forms for clarity and function. To meet Medicaid requirements that each resident be served by a full interdisciplinary team made up of designated professional and direct care staff member, we had to only slightly modify the interdisciplinary team in our practice. We also added quarterly meetings. From our experience and studies, we concluded that the new programs and standards were necessary for service delivery to older persons with developmental and intellectual disability who also had geriatric care needs, particularly because there were conflicting interpretations of long-term care standards for both ICF/MR and ICF/General. This group was not seen as highly desirable by geriatric programs, which generally served the nonretarded elderly population, or by mental retardation programs, which primarily served younger individuals with mental retardation and ignored the problems of aging in their standards and interpretations of active treatment.[1] While we were very busy and deeply involved with the conversion process in 1986, a new director of the Central Virginia Training Center (CVTC) was hired. The new director, Dr. B. R. Walker, was from Texas and also the former president of the American Association of Mental Retardation (AAMR). I had heard him speak in an earlier annual meeting of AAMR in Philadelphia. I was not sure if he would be familiar with our center's conversion, which was then unique in the nation. I was hoping that I would not have to go through a struggle to get him to understand and approve of what had now become our routine work. Fortunately, as soon as he saw that a paper, a colleague and I had written, about the center and its conversion process was accepted for presentation at the 112th Annual Meeting of the AAMR in Washington DC, he was convinced. Program manager John R. Radick and I titled the paper "A New Residential Service Model: ICF/General: An Alternative for Older ICF/MR Residents with Geriatric Care Needs." (1988) As the former president of AAMR himself, Dr. Walker was very happy, and I thought even proud, that we were presenting our paper. Also, when our travel request with expenses for both of us was approved, he signed it immediately, and he himself added in my hotel expenses. I had planned to economize by staying with relatives in DC, but he wanted us to be in the location of the conference at the Washington Hilton to have more access to the meetings with the other professionals.

Dr. Walker's suggestion turned out to be practical. Our presentation was scheduled at 8:00 a.m. on June 2, 1988. At first, I thought that was too early, and we would not have much of an audience. At about 7:30, we went to the designated room to get the tables and overhead projector ready for the presentation. It was a large room, and I was surprised to see that it was already half full. Dr. Walker was standing in the front of the hall. Gradually, the room became almost full, and promptly, at 8:00 a.m., the moderator introduced us. As soon as I started to speak, the fire drill began and the sound of the alarm caused the evacuation of all the rooms at the Hilton. While we were waiting for the second signal to mark the end of the fire drill, I thought to myself that maybe the majority of the audience would not return, but when we returned to the room, we noticed that the room was even more filled this time. I started my speech again, and then my colleague John Radick concluded with the presentation of the slides. I never thought that this topic was of so much interest to the other states, but we had so many questions that we had to stay after our time to respond to all them. I was happy that we had brought enough copies of the paper we were presenting, as all of them were taken away by the attendees. Finally, because the next program scheduled in that room was about to begin, I suggested that for any questions left unanswered, they could call or write to us. Dr. Walker was very proud to see the interest and the curiosity about our conversion program. This interest continued even after we returned to our center in Virginia. A week later, we were still receiving letters and requests for the packets of our conversion program from other states by people interested in following our plan in their states. These requests and letters were a kind and firm confirmation of our success. We had more than twenty letters and requests from other states, and I sent a copy of all these that supported our good work to the central management and Dr. Walker. The *Mental Retardation Journal* of AAMR also published our paper.[2] The conversion to ICF/ General also facilitated the deinstitutionalization of our residents with the ICF level of care and their future relocation into the community and into the long-term facilities and nursing homes near their families and relatives.

So in this way, following the deinstitutionalization movement, we could participate in the reduction of the number of residents through our unique innovative methodology, which made it easier for us to discharge our clients and relocate them to the community facilities and nursing homes that had the same level of care (ICF). As a result, during 1998-1992, we gradually reduced our residents and could close our twelve residences one by one.

It was encouraging to see that our director Dr. Walker supported us at the national convention. I have always wanted to have the latest information in my field and to receive the professional support and input of my work at the convention. In this way I was prepared to defend our clients' position and their well-being against any barriers that might have risen to hurt them. Also, while relocating our clients, I was very careful to consider the relocation of our staff to the other centers too so they would not lose their jobs. At the same time, we wanted to have their cooperation so that the transition would go smoothly. One day, after we had been successful in discharging several clients and employees in the community, Dr. Walker asked me to his office for a meeting. There was no one else in the room. After I sat down, he praised our successful relocation of our clients and staff and then he said, "I just wonder how it is that you are thinking so much of others and not of yourself. Aren't you afraid with all the discharges and closure of one living area after another that you will gradually abolish your own position?" I was surprised by his question and then explained to him about my culture and the cultural modesty of the Iranians. I told him about my family values that were deeply rooted in my mind and heart, stressing that in my life, I should first think of others and then of myself. Consciously or unconsciously, this value had influenced my decision-making process in all stages of my life. Then I told him that I also always wanted to be involved with research for the good of mankind and that perhaps I would apply for a position requiring more opportunity for clinical research than clinical administration. I said that with the rapid deinstitutionalization, maybe CVTC should be moving to have a collaborative program with the community for training and collaborative research with the universities and colleges. With that perspective, I asked him for a letter of recommendation in case I needed this in my search for a new job. I thought maybe it would be better to conduct my search in Northern Virginia, especially since all my family and relatives had settled in Northern Virginia. A few days later, I received his letter of recommendation on the letterhead of the COMMONWEALTH OF VIRGINIA and the department with the title and content as follows:

December 6, 1991

TO WHOM IT MAY CONCERN

Dr. Sakineh M. Redjali has been an employee of the Central Virginia Training Center since July 1979. During her tenure here, she has served in several managerial positions. Currently, she is the Director of the Adult Training Center. This is a residential unit consisting of 230 employees and 184 clients who have mental retardation.

Dr. Redjali is a very conscientious employee who thoroughly researches the regulations relating to her operation and vigorously operationalizes them. Dr. Redjali has presented papers at professional meetings and published them in scholarly journals. She takes an active role in professional activities in job related areas.

She is very loyal and supportive of the facility. Her dedication to serving clients is of the highest degree, and she is very supportive of staff.

Dr. Redjali is a person who cares about others. She possesses the highest ethical, professional, and moral Standards.

Sincerely,

B. R. Walker, PhD

During this same time, I also tried to present the result of our discharge program in a symposium at the Forty-Fifth Annual Scientific Meeting of the Gerontological Society of America, Washington DC, on November 21, 1992. It was interesting and exciting that when we wanted to start our symposium, suddenly, we heard in the loudspeaker of hotel that all the programs scheduled at 11:00 a.m. would be postponed for one hour due to an unforeseen event and that we were all invited to the large ballroom of the hotel. Of course, we were curious and rushed to the ballroom and faced with a surprise visit from President Clinton, who was campaigning heavily on the need for universal health care during the 1992 election campaign. He spoke about the need of the universal health care for seniors and also he received an award on behalf of Mrs. Clinton for her efforts toward universal health.

Another challenge, which I assumed after conversion, without any requirement from the government, was to volunteer to get my license as a nursing home administrator. Later, John, our program manager, also pursued his license. I thought that by having these licenses it would establish a strong position for us when we discharged our clients to the community nursing home, although there was no requirement for government employees like the community nursing home, in which the administrator had to have a license. We needed to pass the board, a four-hour multiple choice exam, of all the rules and regulations that we followed daily after the center's conversion. I did not know why everybody at CVTC was saying that the test was difficult, and that a few years before, many people had tried to get the license, but they had not been successful and had given up. However, this became a challenge for me testing myself. I thought I would have more confidence in communicating with other professionals as a licensed administrator. Although studying for the test was boring, I decided to pursue that, and one morning, without telling anyone, at 5:30 a.m., I drove to Richmond to take the test at 8:00 a.m. I was the last person to turn in my paper at twelve noon. Two weeks later, I received a temporary congratulatory letter of my success in the test, with the notice that I would receive the official certificate of the Board of Nursing Home Administrators later. I received the formal license signed and dated on November 4, 1991, an ironic date for my country and me. On November 4, 1964, Khomeini was sent into exile, and later after his return and Iran's revolution, he took revenge by establishing his command; and on November 4, he took the Americans hostage in their own embassy in Tehran for 444 days. This date changed the destiny of many Iranians, including myself. This license did not help me financially, but I received some respect and some jealous reactions, especially among my nursing staff and supervisors in the new conversion for ICF. More importantly, I gained self-confidence. At the same time, I was pleased and proud of our successful discharge work of our residents to be closer to their families—a triumph in America, especially that the Health Care Financing Administration (HCFA) was moving ahead with the challenge of meeting the Omnibus Budget Reconciliation Act of 1987 (OBRA). Since August 1986, HCFA has required all the nursing surveyors to focus on evaluating resident care outcomes. The new resident assessment should be comprehensive and all care provided by the facility should flow from the resident's comprehensive assessment and subsequent care plan with the emphasis of residents rights and quality of life not much different from the active treatment issue that we used to practice with our mentally retarded, the ICFMR.[3]

In the meantime, I continued to hear the shocking news from Iran. During these times, I consciously or unconsciously followed the news of Iran. For example, I heard again a major news story that on July 16, 1988, Khomeini finally accepted a cease-fire in the eight-year war with Iraq, describing it as drinking the chalice of poison. However, during the Reagan administration in 1987, the Iran Contra Affair (or Irangate) was developing into a political scandal. Members of the executive branch sold weapons to Iran and illegally used the profits to continue funding an army of rebels in Nicaragua. So again, every night, we witnessed in the news about the investigation of this deal. In addition, Khomeini, in a shocking *fatwa* (religious decree), ordered the execution of thousands of political prisoners throughout Iran. This *fatwa*, a crime against humanity, was carried out by several high-ranking members of the government called the Death Commission. September 1 was recognized by Amnesty International as an International Day of Remembrance of the massacre of political prisoners. The mass execution was followed by burial in a mass grave in a location called Khavaran. With the 1988 massacre, the theocratic government sought to extinguish the flames of resistance against the regime. Although they did not succeed, their reign of terror has continued, even after the death of Khomeini on June 1989. Every year the victims' families and relatives have a memorial on September 1 and gather in Khavaran cemetery even when the government bans the gathering and sometimes closes the main road to the mass graves of their relatives as they did in 2007. They carry pictures of their relatives in a quiet march along with prayers.

While I worked hard to place our clients in the community near their families, gradually transfer our staff to other centers, and ultimately close the Adult Training Center, I began a job search in Northern Virginia in the hope of finding a job and finally settle near my family. This was challenging for several reasons. First, since I was in a high-level to mid-level management position, there were not many job openings at my level or higher in Northern Virginia. When I did apply for lower-level positions with lower salaries, so I could be with my family, the interview teams told me I was overqualified. In some cases, they even perceived me negatively and commented on my lack of ambition, so it was difficult for me tofind a position. With this experience, I learned that America is not like Iran, and the family reason could not be considered a reason to take a position with a lower salary. I learned that a person should normally apply for a higher position and more money, even though these jobs were not readily available in Northern Virginia. I found also that life in Northern Virginia was quite different than in Central Virginia. In addition, Dr. Walker's letter of recommendation saying that I first think of others rather than myself was also interpreted negatively too. Of course, in addition, there was also the effect of the politicization of the delivery of service to the mentally ill, and the backlash of the hostage crisis in my case. As a result, getting a new job in Northern Virginia was a great challenge requiring more time and networking. It was just the opposite in Central Virginia, which had quite a different atmosphere and environment.

One day, in the spring of 1992, I was engaged in discharging clients from the last living areas of the Adult Training Center when Dr. Walker called me into his office. I had no idea what he wanted to see me about, and I was curious. He was very polite, and after some compliments about our efforts at the ATC, he referred to our meeting in 1991 when I had suggested that Central VA Training Center (CVTC) should have a research department with a collaborative program with local universities and colleges. He said that he had been thinking for quite some time to establish a research department at CVTC in the middle of 1992. He then asked me if I would be interested in being transferred as research director to establish the research department when my present position was closed. Since research had always been my desire, and I never had enough time for research, I responded enthusiastically, "Yes, with pleasure." He replied that the timing was good because the commissioner of Mental Health and Mental Retardation and Substance Abuse, Dr. King Davis, was advocating, promoting, and supporting research; and with his political support, the job looked promising, at least for a few years. Usually money for research in a state budget is the first to be cut, and the least important factor for management, which thinks for the short-term rather the long-term solution in any decision process. So I stopped my job search in Northern Virginia and committed myself to the change—establishing a research department with a minimum staff of two, in the hope of facilitating the use of the students of the universities of Virginia and our local colleges in internships and collaborative research projects and studies. Dr. Walker was happy that I accepted his offer, especially since the commissioner, who himself was a professor at Virginia Commonwealth University, had liked the idea of the collaborative projects. My job was to plan, develop, organize, and direct research programs to improve the lives and service delivery system for persons with intellectual and developmental disabilities. The location of my office was moved so I could be near the Staff Development and Training Programs. An immediate need was to plan a short—and long-term program for the first time to prove the importance of research for Central Virginia Training Center and to gather the forty community service boards that provided services to individuals with intellectual and mental disabilities. After the CVTC placed a large number of residents in the community in 1992, CVTC met only the training and programming needs of those persons who could not be served in a community program. CVTC was moving rapidly toward the future through collaborative initiatives with community-based services that included residential and employment programs, training, and research. In addition, technical assistance, consultation and resource development services were available to providers and families.

The Research Department at CVTC was established in mid-1992, and we communicated with all the colleges and universities, encouraging research projects and welcomed collaboration with them on joint studies. The facility also supported the dissemination and application of research findings and adhered to established departmental regulations, instructions, and ethical guidelines, as outlined by the Department of Mental Health, Mental Retardation, and Substance Abuse Services (DMHMRSAS) pertaining to the protection of the subjects of human research. We established the Research Review Committee consisting of experts from the departments of universities and colleges and different professional disciplines. The Research Review Committee reviewed all the proposals, involving research and studies regarding clients and staff initiated by CVTC staff, department staff, and for staff outside the agency prior to initiation of any project.

Very soon, after the announcement of the Research Department, university professors and colleges welcomed our approach to give them and their students the opportunity for research studies, internships, and joint research. I remembered well the time in Iran when I was a university professor and president of a college, I was constantly searching for internship and research possibilities for students and professors. I was happy that we were providing this possibility at our Research Department at CVTC, which could be beneficial for both. My résumé was examined and discussed at the board of the universities and departments, and I was honored as a clinical faculty member in the psychiatry department of the Medical College of Virginia and Research Associate at the University of Virginia. We even had a grant from the University of Virginia for one of our studies. In the meantime, Dr. Walker took another job in Texas and left the CVTC. His successor Dr. Stan Butkus, the new director of CVTC, continued to support our research department and became interested to join in some of our studies. Sample topics of our research projects with which our department became involved were either presented at national professional meetings or published in professional journals.

Relationship of Health Attitudes in Employee Risk for Injury and Rehabilitation Outcome

Institutionalization, Involuntary Sterilization and Mental Retardation

Profiles from the History of Practice; Deinstitutionlization and Community Placement: Profile from the Process.

Validation of the Depression Checklist for Individuals with Mental Retardation with the Psychiatry Department of Medical College of Virginia (MCV)

The Effects of Sertraline on Depression in Adults with Mental Retardation. Again with MCV

Validation of Facilitated Communication in a Group of Nonverbal Mentally Retarded Individuals.

Relocation of Geriatric Clients with Mental Retardation from Institution to community Residential Facilities with Collaboration of Piedmont Geriatric Hospital

This study was presented at the 117th Annual Meeting of the American of Mental Retardation and at the Forty-Fifth Scientific Association of the Gerontological Society of America in 1992 and later published as Redjali, S. M. and Lewis, R. E.

From Institution to Community-Base Care: What Happens to Elderly Clients with Mental and Illnesses or Mental Retardation? The Digest, vol. 14, no. 21 Journal of Association of Public Developmental Disabilities, July 1995.

Family Perception of Services to Persons with Mental Retardation—A survey study with our Director Dr. Butkus was presented at the 119 Annual Meeting of the American Association on Mental Retardation, San Francisco, California, June 1.1995.

The last project was a pilot project carried out in conjunction with Community Services Boards (CSB). The primary purpose of our survey research was to assess family perception of services to persons with retardation. In addition, we expected the data analysis to help identify support services offered and the perceived adequacy of support. This research project was performed in several phases and explored issues of deinstitutionalization, such as transition, community inclusion, available services, and needed support services and programs for the consumers.

We were making quite good progress and the Research Review committee was reviewing all the research projects quarterly for approval, and the progress reports and the minutes were signed by members and sent to the Central Office.

Graduation ceremony of Gita Khadiri (the author's daughter) from Law school, the ceremony was held at Constitution Hall in Washington DC, 1990.

Meanwhile, in my family, during this period, both Gita and Reza graduated from college and found jobs, which was a great relief for us. Gita assumed a position in the legal section of the Treasury Department in the Internal Revenue Service (IRS) and lived in Washington DC. Reza, who was more under the influence of his peer group, wanted to first work in Hawaii after graduation, as his friends were doing and as was becoming fashionable among young people. Reza later gave us a surprise for our anniversary. He invited us to visit him in Hawaii for the week of our anniversary, which usually falls during Thanksgiving. We were a little concerned about his choice and had never been to Hawaii, but we accepted his invitation to visit him on the island of Maui. We spent Thanksgiving 1992 and our anniversary with him. This was an unforgettable experience, unique and beautiful. Maui is really the land of rainbows and smiles with a mild climate throughout the year. I did not get any migraine headaches that I was suffering in Virginia because of the change of weather. Reza drove us all over the island in his Honda to show us the beautiful sights and his scuba-diving activities. It was no wonder that the young people liked so much to live in these islands. They definitely had excellent taste in choosing Hawaii.

A Thanksgiving trip to Hawaii at the invitation of her son Reza Khadiri.

During this period, we also had another piece of good news. Our daughter, Gita, became engaged to Fred Khoroushi. One weekend, when I was visiting Sa'id in Northern Virginia, Gita called from DC to say she and Fred had a surprise. Fred had proposed to her. He was a young man we had known for some time. He had proposed to her in a very typical American style and not a Persian style, which would have involved his parents asking us for Gita's hand. We were very happy that both of them, who had spent more than half of their life in America, had decided themselves to be engaged and then marry. We congratulated them with our best wishes and invited them to celebrate and to find out what their plans were for the wedding. We were very happy for Gita and Fred, and we wanted to fulfill their wish, and we offered our help. They both wanted a garden ceremony. Since I was in Lynchburg and we trusted the maturity and the good taste of Gita, we left them to make their own decisions. In Lynchburg, I shared the good news with everybody and, of course, with our best friends Martha and Bill Goodman. I had witnessed the wedding ceremony of their daughter Jessica, and I knew that Bill conducted a very nice church wedding, and I now wondered if he could conduct a similar garden wedding for Gita and Fred. Bill, who was a licensed, ordained Presbyterian minister kindly agreed to officiate, if Gita and Fred would like that. Fred and Gita, after a long search, finally found a place, the Newton White Mansion in Maryland that was available for Friday, August 20.

The Mansion, according to its website, was built in 1939 by the architect W. E. Bottomly for Captain and Mrs. Newton H. White and was located in a picturesque setting in Mitchellville, Maryland. With its Neo-Georgian-style brick building, it sat on 586 acres of lush, green land that included a golf club, a beautiful garden, and an outdoor brick patio with a central waterfall fountain. This site appealed to us because it was similar to many gardens in Iran with their typical fountains. Views of the surrounding golf course and gardens from the atrium were spectacular, and weather permitting, it was the best choice for a garden wedding celebration around a fountain near Washington DC.

After a long search, Gita finally found a wedding dress, which had to be altered exactly to her dress size, in a special wedding shop in Bethesda. During this time, we were fortunate that my mother-in-law with my sister in-law, Sarieh, were visiting us from Iran, and they helped us in the preparation for the wedding. It was a pity that they could not stay for the wedding. Reza offered to send beautiful flowers from Hawaii for decorations, and invitations were sent to our friends and relatives, who were scattered all over the globe. One could see the pervasive result of the revolution from the number of countries represented by guests attending the wedding.

Gita and Fred chose one of the best caterers in the DC area—Susan Gage, who provided international food, including American and Persian gourmet food. For the ceremony, Sa'id asked a quartet of his friends and colleagues to play classical music and the wedding march in the garden, and Fred chose a very popular band with a famous singer, Aref, who came from California to perform a mixture of Iranian and international music for the reception.

Many things about an American garden wedding were unclear to us. However, Martha and Bill came the day before, and there was a rehearsal that cleared up all the details. Bill had been a part of many wedding ceremonies, but he probably never had a Persian-American ceremony like this. We arranged two rows of white chairs in front of the fountain. The right and the left sides of the fountain were reserved for the bride's and groom's relatives and friends respectively. In front of the five steps leading up to the terrace patio, we placed two large baskets of the beautiful Hawaiian flowers, with a podium in the middle for Bill to conduct the ceremony. On the left side, the quartet would be playing classical music and the wedding march while the people waited for the arrival of the bride. My husband would escort Gita, who would come from the second floor, accompanied by her close friend from childhood, Padideh Alai, who fortunately lived in the DC area. Padideh would help with the veil and the train of the dress.

The groom and his three brothers would wait for the bride and bridesmaid on the first floor. Sa'id would then take Gita's arm, and they would walk from the house to the garden, coming through the garden with the music of the Pachelbel *Canon*. They would walk around and enter through an aisle formed between the rows of seats and arrive at the fountain. The music would stop, and the ceremony would begin. After the conclusion of the ceremony, members of both families would make short speeches, and Gita and Fred would greet all the guests from behind the fountain. Some of the guests would have come from long distances, and some we wouldn't have seen for years. Waiters would serve drinks and hors d'oeuvres. Afterward, the Persian band, with Aref, would begin playing and people would take their seats at tables arranged with beautiful Hawaiian flowers. These were the details we discussed at the rehearsal, and everything went smoothly, and we were relieved.

After the rehearsal, we planned to invite our guests to dinner at Fred and Gita's new home in Great Falls. The dinner reception was to be prepared by the best and the oldest Iranian caterer in the DC area, the late Susan Kassrai. We had invited close relatives from both sides who had come from very long distances. Everything seemed to be in great order except for two things. One was the weather. A possible thunderstorm was forecast for the wedding day, Friday. The other was Sa'id's back as he was suffering from a slipped disc. The pain had started two days before the wedding and was so great that sometimes he could not move at all. We looked for a neurologist or orthopedist for treatment so that he could perform as father of the bride, but I was not sure he would be able to walk the long distance in the garden. We finally found a neurologist and got strong medication for his pain. However, he was suffering with back pain the whole wedding day and was under the influence of the pain killers. I myself was suffering from a nagging headache because of the storm and worries about the ceremony in case the storm would disrupt everything. On August 20, we all went early to the Mansion to watch over everyone's work and to help where needed. The flower lady was arranging the Hawaiian flowers for twenty-five nice round dinner tables, each of which would accommodate ten people. Fortunately, all the tables were arranged under a large waterproof tent covered from the top and open from the side. The weather was cloudy, hot, and humid. However, the main ceremony was arranged in the garden with the quartet situated on the corner near the steps.

From six o'clock on, the guests began to arrive and take their seats, either on the bride or the groom side. It was very exciting for us to see our relatives and friends, especially those we had not seen from childhood. One was the cousin I called "pretty cousin." She came from Michigan with her son, Dr. Ali Kafi, her daughter-in-law, and Sera, one of her granddaughters. We were also very happy and thankful to see our friend from Boston, Doris May, who, even in sickness, still came to be a part of Gita's wedding. When the majority of the guests had arrived, and it looked as if it was about to rain at any minute, we began the ceremony. The quartet was playing the "Four Seasons" of Antonio Vivaldi when we started at 7:00 p.m. The music then moved to the Pachelbel "Canon," which Gita had chosen. I was sitting next to my cousin Parvin in the first row. My heart was beating very fast, and as I looked to the left, I saw my husband, Sa'id, holding Gita's arm, walking toward the fountain with difficulty, most likely from pain, followed by Gita's friend holding the train of Gita's dress behind her. Then she changed position to walk in front of her. As soon as they started to walk up the aisle, all the guests stood and watched them as they walked up the steps where Dr. Goodman, in his Duke University gown, waited with Fred and his oldest brother Fariborz. At this moment, my eyes were wet, and I tried not to let this show. Bill began and Sa'id, after giving away his daughter's hand in marriage, came to sit with me.

The ceremony was very simple and beautiful. One amusing thing happened. When Bill asked Fred these words

> Fred, will you have this woman to be your wife,
> and will you pledge yourself to her
> in all love and honor
> in all duty and service
> in all faith and tenderness
> to live with her and cherish her,
> as long as you both shall live?

Fred said in a strong voice, "Definitely yes." Everybody laughed. At the conclusion, Bill said, "You may kiss the bride," and he presented them to the guests as Mr. and Mr. Khoroushi. After this, Dr. David Rejali, my cousin, spoke on behalf of our family to congratulate the young couple. Then, Faribourz, Fred's oldest brother, who had come with his family from England, spoke on behalf of Fred's family. After that, my husband went up the steps again to read a poem that we had prepared together with the help of our close poet friend in Iran. He read in Persian, then thanked our dear guests for coming and gave congratulations to the young couple. Our dear Gita, who was talented in poetry, was expecting to have poetry recited in her wedding, and we tried our best to fulfill her wishes. My son, Reza, gave its rough translation in English as below:

> *Tonight, with merriment, joy and delight.*
> *We shall put the grimness and sulks of daily life to flight*
>
> *The angels, too, it seems are with us,*
> *Elated and in joyous frolicking,*
> *Flutter their wings, prance and feast tonight.*
>
> *Gita Khadiri and Fred Khoroushi,*
> *With profound love, join hands in holy wedlock,*
> *And their happy and joyful life will start.*
>
> *This whole assembly wishes this loving pair,*
> *Happiness galore, and union sweet and fair*
>
> *Simin and Sa'id proud and joyful with all their hearts*
> *Are thankful to the Lord Omnipotent,*
> *That the young loving couple,*
> *Are thus united in body and soul.*
>
> *Gita the blossom of SIMIN and SA'ID's garden.*
> *Is now a jolly companion of the adoring love bird.*

Reza, the loving brother, too, offers his
Felicitations with joy and cheer.
Along with a hundred kisses,
To his sister so beautiful and dear.

Our thanks go to our amiable friends, who
Brought happiness and joy
With their kind presence to this blessed ceremony.

And favored us with their sincere jubilation,
And lightened and adorned this holy celebration.
By their jovial dancing, frisking, singing, and mirth.

Exhilarated are all present here that,
GITA and FRED have attained their desired goal
In life, through this happy union
SIMIN and SAID KHADIRI
August 20, 1993

Wedding photos of Gita Khadiri and Fred Khoroushi on
August 20, 1993 with family and friends.

After this ceremony, the bride and groom went behind the fountain, and the guests went one by one to congratulate them either by shaking hands or hugging. As the quartet was playing "The Four Seasons" of Vivaldi, suddenly, a thunderstorm began so suddenly that everybody ran to get under cover. Unfortunately, the musicians and their instruments got wet. However, the whole ceremony went well, and the thunderstorm at least waited until the marriage ceremony was completed. In the house, drinks and appetizers were being served, and very soon, Aref with his band started to sing the Iranian wedding song and, after a while, called the bride and groom to start dancing. Soon after, the guests joined them in dancing while they were in between finding their seats around their dinner table. Dinner was served at 9:00 p.m., and tables were filled with several popular American and Persian gourmet dishes of fish, beef, chicken, and other delicacies. The dancing continued with Persian and American popular songs with a short interval for cutting the wedding cake and coffee at 11:00 p.m. At 2:00 a.m., the bride and groom left for their honeymoon. We were all tired and left with a relieved feeling, thanking Martha and Bill and all the friends who helped Gita and Fred for a uniquely successful wedding, a great combination of Persian and American. It was a memorable evening for everybody. It looked like everybody had a good time. In a way also, I was happy that Gita and Fred chose the Mansion with its similarity to the home that we lost in Iran, where I had always wished to celebrate Gita's wedding.

After the wedding, and a week away from work, I needed to return to my job. From my colleagues at work, only Mrs. Celia Vandegrift with her husband could attend the wedding. I think they had a good time, and when I returned, she had spread the news and description of the wedding. Apparently, she enjoyed the occasion very much, and many people in our small town knew all about the wedding because of her description.

At the end of 1993, and beginning of 1994, the governor of Virginia and his political appointees changed and the Department of Mental Health / Mental Retardation and substance abuse experienced drastic changes as a result. The charismatic and experienced commissioner Dr. King Davis left to work in another state and was replaced with an inexperienced person who had just received his PhD. This political appointment damaged the integrity of the experienced professional staff and professional services. As a result, we were often receiving news of the resignations of the most competent professionals leaving either for work in other states or going to private industry. Immediately, I anticipated this politicization of the department would cause a lot of problems and possibly a chaotic situation. My prediction soon turned out to be correct that the lack of competent and experienced professional staff gradually adversely affected the services to the mentally ill clients, and complaints by them and their families began to mount. Thanks to our good country and its respect for the law and regulations, the Justice Department interfered in the services delivery to patients in the several agencies in the State of Virginia, including the two agencies in Northern Virginia.[4] Later, the legislators of the State of Virginia modified and revised the budget to restore most of cuts by the governor. Another issue was that the new governor offered a five-year buyout of additional service to the employees who met a few requirements to have the opportunity to retire early. This was also another avenue for some competent and experienced people to leave the state.

In the meantime, Sa'id's back problem continued, and he was not allowed to drive the long distance back and forth to Lynchburg, and I had to drive to see him instead. In addition, one day, he called me from Alexandria to tell me that his doctor had called to say that a lesion on his left finger indicated an aggressive cancer, and he needed to go to a specialist. He was so distraught and upset that he couldn't even speak clearly. I also became quite distraught since his hands and fingers were essential to his career as a pianist and music teacher. I immediately took a few days off to go with him to the dermatologist in Northern Virginia, the specialist who had conducted several tests and had suggested surgery, radiation, and amputating the finger to prevent the recurrence of cancer. The last two suggestions for radiation and amputation disturbed us extremely, and I made an appointment with a specialist at Johns Hopkins to get a second opinion, as my cousin in Cleveland had suggested. At Johns Hopkins, after several tests, the specialist suggested just surgery but not radiation or amputation because of the side effects of radiation on the hand and Sa'id's career. They thought that with the recurrences, we should have surgery each time. This suggestion relieved us a little bit, and we thought that always it is better to have a second opinion in any medical treatment, although he had periodically had some lesions on his hand and elsewhere. As time went by, he continued to have these lesions removed surgically, and more importantly, he could continue to work. However, with each occurrence, we went through a lot of stress so that our daily long-distance calls between Lynchburg and Alexandria sometimes lasted hours.

During my frequent visits to Northern Virginia, I noticed that just as much as our family stress intensified because of the separation of the family, the news of the investigation of the Department of Justice (DOJ) in the two state agencies in Northern Virginia intensified. Therefore, I thought maybe it would be beneficial both for the state and our family if I shared my family situation with the associate commissioner, who was still in the central office and knew my work background. I planned to request a transfer to Northern Virginia in case there was a need to help in the requirement of DOJ. I also planned to put our Lynchburg house up for sale to be ready in case the transfer made it possible for me to move. Even if I couldn't get a transfer, I could take advantage of the five-year buyout offered by the state and take the bonus and early retirement, although this would not have been so beneficial for us since we both had lost our other retirement benefits in Iran because of the revolution. When I shared these thoughts with Sa'id, he became happy and greatly relieved with all the anxiety and stress that he was facing. So as soon as I returned to Lynchburg, I made an appointment to go to see the associate commissioner to explain my concerns and discuss the needs and job openings in the two state agencies in Northern Virginia.

On July 13, 1994, the day of my appointment, I drove to the central office in Richmond, arriving about fifteen minutes earlier than my appointment, and the secretary notified the associate commissioner of my arrival. Exactly at 11:00 a.m., she received me by entering her room where another lady was in her office standing and ready to leave. She introduced me as the research director of the CVTC to the other lady, who was the director of the Northern Virginia Mental Health Institute (NVMHI). She asked me about my work and the position I held in Lynchburg, and she seemed to be impressed. She then invited me to visit her institute. I thanked her for her invitation, and I told her my husband had a music studio in Alexandria near the institute. She left the room and I sat in front of the friendly associate commissioner. She immediately said that she would discuss with the two directors of the Northern Virginia state agencies to see if they needed someone with my qualifications or if they had any openings and then she would notify me. I thanked her and left her office, driving back to Lynchburg. On the road, I thought I needed to share my request and my family situation with the director of CVTC, who was supportive of research, and even he himself joined in one of our studies. The same day, I wrote a formal letter to the acting associate commissioner, and I met our director of CVTC the next day with a copy of the letter and explained my situation. Following is a copy of the letter explaining my situation:

July 13, 1994

Dear Ms. G.

Thank you very much for meeting with me today. As I mentioned to you I started working at the Central Virginia Training Center (CVTC) in Lynchburg, Virginia in 1979. Initially, I was the Center Director of Child Development at the CVTC. I subsequently became the Center Director of the Adult Training Center and as of May 1992 I am working as the Research Director of the Research Department at CVTC. As the Research Director I have had the good fortune to work on projects of utmost importance to the welfare of the community. I have always found my work at CVTC to both personally and professionally rewarding. I find my work as the Research Director particularly rewarding.

While I have been employed by CVTC my husband has been forced to move to northern Virginia (Alexandria) for employment reasons. Currently, both of my children as well as my husband and other family members live in northern Virginia. In the past several years, my husband's health problems have made it difficult for him to drive to Lynchburg. Particularly in the past three years he has been suffering from disc herniation and other ailments which has made it difficult for him to drive. Consequently, I have been forced to come to Alexandria almost every weekend to take care of him. During the past year I have had two accidents while driving between Alexandria and Lynchburg and I am concerned that a part of these accidents is the strain that such a regular commute puts on someone in my condition (I also suffer from an upper back injury on the job).

Therefore, although I am very satisfied with my present position professionally I request that you give consideration to my transfer to either of the Agencies in northern Virginia: Mental Health Institute or the Northern Virginia Training Center.

I appreciate your consideration and thank you in advance. I trust that you understand the pressures which have necessitated this request on my part. For your convenience another copy of my resume is attached. If you have any question about my request, or otherwise, please feel free to contact me at the following address and phone numbers.

Very truly yours,

Sakineh M. Redjali

In this way, by giving a copy of this letter to the director of CVTC, I had already prepared him before he could hear any news from the central office or another place. He seemed to understand my conflict and pressure of my family life. While I was waiting for the response of the central office, we listed our home with a popular real estate agent. In the meantime, I also made an appointment to visit the Northern Virginia Mental Health Institute, the institute the director of which had invited me to visit. The visit to the institute turned out to be informative and productive. The lack of a comprehensive staff development and research program was obvious. The director, DOJ, and staff needed such a program to continue their training for their license, and the director was very eager to have a director for staff development and research. This was a position that with the cooperation of my colleagues at the psychiatry department at the Medical College of Virginia was not difficult for me to handle, although it involved more work than my current job, if I should I have been involved with both implementation and research. In fact, one of my colleagues at the Medical College of Virginia was a DOJ investigator himself for another state and could have helped the staff with training sessions in connection with the DOJ citations. At the suggestion of the director, I prepared a comprehensive draft for the position of Staff Development and Research and mailed it to her. In Lynchburg, while I was waiting for the response to my letter and visit to the associate commissioner, I continued pushing the real estate agent to advertise more and hold more open houses to sell the house quickly. We had many visitors, but no offers. Most of the buyers were looking for a colonial house, and as a result, even when we reduced the price to the assessment provided by the city and bank, we did not get any offers. We had to change the real estate company, but still we did not get any offers, and the house stayed on the market for over a year.

In the meantime, the associate commissioner was contacting all the directors of Northern Virginia and Central Virginia centers to find out if there were any positions available and a possible solution, especially now with the news about complaints surrounding the death of patients who had been restrained for long periods of time. The media's coverage of the DOJ investigation intensified; deficiencies cited by the DOJ were in mental health treatment, quality and quantity of staffing, medication practices, protection of patients from harm, and many other constitutional violations. Inadequate mental health care demonstrated a need for a comprehensive plan for staff development and research and warranted to correct all the deficiencies through education. Finally, after about six months of waiting, I was called in February and told by the associate commissioner that, unfortunately, there were no positions available in Northern Virginia. The associate commissioner said that he had spoken with the director of the CVTC, and that he agreed that my position would be transferred to Northern Virginia for the fiscal year of 1995-'96, and that, apparently, the director of the Mental Health Institute would carry the position for the year after. From this call, I was moved by the understanding of three administrators to the urgent need of responding to the DOJ investigation and their citation while at the same time they understood the importance of our family union. I wished that they would stick to their decision in the central office. Next, I had to prepare myself for the move. At this point, because I was so eager to move, I failed to ask for written assurance of the transfer and my position, something we always do in working for the state. Unfortunately, I did not receive a written copy of the transfer and its content, although I found a copy of it in my file a year later. Since I was so excited about helping the State of Virginia with its deficiencies in mental health, to be responsive to its needs, and to be very active in selling the house, I was not too concerned with the content of the transfer letter. Either by mistake or intentionally, I did not receive the copy of the transfer and was unaware of its content. Unfortunately, I would need the letter later in the 1995-'96. This letter, dated on March 2, 1995, from the associate commissioner to the director of the Northern Virginia Mental health institute stated,

> . . . *As we discussed, this will confirm that the director of CVTC agreed to the transfer of Sakineh M, Redjali, PhD from CVTC to NVMHI and that he will fund the position through June 30, 1996. As we discussed, by that time if not before, you should be able to carry the position. I believe Dr. Redjali will be a real benefit and asset to you in the areas of training and research . . . We would like the transfer to occur as soon as soon possible." Signed by the Associate Commissioner/Community/Facility Services.*

(I found this letter in my file after I had retired in 1996.)

I was also extremely frustrated in our efforts to sell the Lynchburg house. The house had been off the market for a while, although three different realty companies had tried to sell it. I really did not know what to do. Then, one day, as I was reading the daily newspaper, one small advertisement caught my attention. The ad stated that an investment company was looking to buy several pieces of real estate for investment and urged interested people seeking a quick sale to call the telephone number. No address was given. I cut out that page of the newspaper immediately and called many people for advice. Everybody said it looked suspicious, and I needed to be very careful. However, I was so desperate to sell the house that I took the risk and called the number. A young man's voice answered. He immediately made an appointment and said that he would bring a contract with him in case he decided to buy for his investment company. Since everybody was telling me to be careful, I called a friend to come over when the investor visited our home. The investor came on time. He examined the house throughout and its title deed and gave me a contract within the price range of the city's assessment and the bank's appraisal of the house and asked for an immediate answer. I told him I needed three days since my husband was in Northern Virginia. He agreed and left the contract with me for my signature. I immediately made an appointment with our attorney in town to show him the contract and ask his advice. He added a line to the contract and agreed to be present at the settlement with us. Sa'id was happy that finally someone was going to buy the house, and he began to look for a house in the Northern Virginia with a floor for his studio and near my workplace. The investor accepted the contract, and we were happy to close on the house within a month. We sold the house for only seven thousand dollars more than we had paid nearly fifteen years before. We probably paid twice as much in interest, but thank God, at least we could sell without losing the money, as we had experienced in the painful loss of our former house in Iran. Sa'id found a house near Tyson's Corner, which had a basement with a separate door for his music studio. We applied for a mortgage with the same bank Crestar where we had had a mortgage in Lynchburg. This time we had established a good credit score, our mortgage was approved, and we bought the house easily, a new model home near the busy area of Tyson's Corner.

At the same time, finally, I received a transfer letter that I could start to work as the director of Staff Development and Research in Northern Virginia. I was so happy that finally after fourteen years, I would join my family and friends, most of whom had settled in the Northern Virginia area, Washington DC and Maryland after Iran's revolution. I immediately called to give the good news to our good friends Martha and Bill Goodman, who knew our family and understood well how we suffered with anxiety because of family separation in the new country. They were happy to learn we were going to finally be together. Martha offered to arrange a farewell party for friends to come to say good-bye on April 22, 1995. Although saying good-bye to my friends and colleagues in Lynchburg emotionally was not easy for me, I accepted their offer. It was springtime and the Goodmans's azaleas and rhododendrons were in bloom, and it was a very pleasant time. It looked as if the house was built in a flower bed. Martha sent invitations to all the colleagues and friends in Lynchburg. She arranged a very nice reception with all kind of lovely food. In one room, people could watch the video of Gita's wedding, and everybody was listening to classical and Persian music. Several friends brought souvenirs from Lynchburg and the surrounding areas. The guests seemed sorry that I was leaving Lynchburg but happy that our family would be united. I too was sorry that I was leaving my friends and colleagues in Lynchburg. The farewell was a mixture of sadness and happiness. I wished that Sa'id could have been there to observe the kindness and love of friends and colleagues, which I have missed since I left Lynchburg.

Farewell party with colleagues and friends in Lynchburg held at the beautiful
home of the author's good friends Dr. and Mrs. William Goodman.

After a day or so, I contracted a moving company and started to pack and get ready for the move by myself. This was not easy for me alone without Sa'id, who could not drive to Lynchburg because of his back. However, in April 1995, I began working day and night to get ready for the move. The closing went smoothly with a power of attorney from Sa'id, so I could handle it alone with the assistance of our lawyer. His presence was very helpful for me since it became apparent that we were not selling our house directly to the investor, who was now acting as a middleman, selling our house with $10,000 profit. In this way, the investor, within one month, found a buyer for our house that we could not find ourselves within two years with three realtors, and he even made a profit of ten thousand dollars. He didn't even have a real estate license, just a small ad in the newspaper. He said at the closing that he had many other similar contracts with other sellers. I was happy that our lawyer was present in this unusual closing; otherwise, I probably could not have handled it by myself. I took one week of annual leave for the move. When the moving van was ready, I drove off by myself in front of them to the house where we live now. So in this way, after I placed the clients of the ATC in the community near their families, finally I placed myself in the community near my own family.

Our physical move and change to a new home went well, with the help of my friends and our children. My daughter was so happy that she prepared and had printed a pretty card with a picture of roses on her favorite purplish paper notifying all the family and friends scattered around the world because of the revolution. She wrote, "We finally moved to Northern Virginia as of May 1, 1995. Please contact us at our new home," including our new address and telephone number. However, although the physical move had gone smoothly, I faced a sudden and unusual shock in my job transfer. Just as we finished the closing of our new home, I read in *The Washington Post* on March 18, 1995, this headline: DIRECTOR OF N. VA. PSYCHIATRIC HOSPITAL OUSTED. This was a very unusual practice and might have been the first time a director had been fired in that department in this way. I was sorry for the director of the agency who became a political victim in the State of Virginia because of the lack of leadership, politics, and mismanagement of the Department of Mental Health and Substance Abuse. I myself was in shock. The firing was a heavy blow and struck many people with great surprise and agitation, so sudden and unusual that many employees became concerned about their own uncertain future. Apparently, according to the newspapers, the director had been an outspoken advocate of mental health services and against the budget cuts and the privatization in the state agencies that the governor and central office were planning.[5] However, the commissioner stated that this was an internal management issue and not a political issue as most people perceived. So in this way again, I was going to slide in the middle of a political fight and chaotic environment, although the commissioner had appointed the director of another state geriatric facility near Petersburg, Virginia, as the mental hospital interim director.

I started the new job, wondering to whom I should report. On my first day, at the main entrance, fortunately, a nice receptionist was on duty, and when I entered and introduced myself and asked if she knew where my office was, she smiled and said that since the librarian had resigned, her office was temporarily available, and that I could use that office until the new director or acting director arrived. In this uncertain atmosphere, I did not mind being near a library, and in fact, in that chaotic situation this was the best solution for me. I preferred to be near books than near other agitated employees who were concerned about what would happen to them, who would be the director, would they be a good director, and finally, what would happen to their jobs. Could the governor privatize with the opposition of the General Assembly? I just wondered how the staff, who were suffering from uncertainty and anxiety could treat the mentally ill patients, and in a way, I wondered if it would be better to first prepare a training program to help themselves. Fortunately, it looked as if the experience of the dark revolution of Iran had made me stronger to face this sudden unusual changes at the beginning of my new job in a new environment with so many of anxious people. I was happy that I did not apply and did not have a director's position, which is so affected by politics.

After a few days, I made an appointment to meet with the interim director, who was now acting as director of two centers. He was not very familiar with the institute's organization and the community politics of Northern Virginia in relation to the mental health activities and advocacies, which were completely different from Central or Southern Virginia, where he had become very involved with the DOJ investigation and the budget cuts of the central office. It was clear that he did not much know about my transfer and my job description and duties, which had been agreed on and approved by the former director. The library was without a librarian, but this position was not included in my job description. My responsibility was to establish a new department for staff development and research, and the library with a licensed librarian could have been part of that. He probably saw my temporary usage of the office of the librarian who resigned recently and thought being a librarian was part of my job. Anyway, because of the time shortage, he appointed me to work with the director of Quality Improvement / Risk Management of the hospital, who had worked closely with the former director. First, I was relieved and thought that he would know better the environment and needs of the community and the institute, the staff, and the issue of the citation of the department of Justice. Alas, my prediction was wrong, and each time I saw him, because he was upset at the firing of the director, he was complaining and criticizing the system and central office and the governor. I had to listen to him as a clinical psychologist and try to make him calm down from his angry voice and attitude. In fact, he and all the staff were more or less upset and confused like him. As a result, he could not be of any help to me. Therefore, I started to plan to work according to the job description, acting prudently by writing, especially since there was no one to talk to due to the high level of anxiety all of us felt. I tried to clarify that there was a need to fill the position of a librarian and, because of the budget cuts, to have at least a temporary position for the library. The need was immediate, because hundreds of journals, books, and correspondence had piled up in the library because of the absence of a librarian for some time. As a member of AAIDD, the Mental Health Association, and the Zonta Club, I attended all the meetings and advocacy groups to get to know the characteristics of the Northern Virginia Community and its needs. I also contacted my colleagues in the psychiatry department of the Medical College of Virginia (MCV) to have their advice and cooperation in establishing weekly educational programs called Ground Rounds, like the MCV Ground Rounds program, plus all the requirements for continuing education for all the professional staff from physicians, psychologists, social workers, speech, physical, and occupational therapists, nurses, nurse assistant, and custodians, to a wide variety of the multiprofessionals. In addition, I contacted the local universities for internships and their cooperation in training and research.

While I was planning and starting the Ground Rounds program for NVMHI, on July 25, I suddenly saw several DOJ inspectors and the attorney general standing in front of my door, which was also near the main arrival entrance to the institute. They were expecting the arrival of some members of DOJ, who were probably a little late because of the morning traffic. They were making a surprise inspection visit. Apparently, the commonwealth had originally denied DOJ access to inspection to NVMHI after July 1, 1994, and now after about one year of extensive negotiations, the Commonwealth had allowed the department attorney and experts of DOJ to inspect NVMHI from July 25-27, 1995. This group identified deficiencies that violated rights of residents in seven areas: mental health treatment, staffing, medical care and medication practices; use of restraint and seclusion; appropriateness of placement and evaluation and planning for discharge. In my comprehensive plan of staff development and research, the subjects of the above deficiencies were included automatically. The plan was prepared and examined and implemented gradually as much as the limited personnel and the disturbing political environment of the institute permitted. This was accomplished with the cooperation of my colleagues at the universities and other training centers, and it was a comprehensive plan based on studies and surveys of other agencies in the State of Virginia, the existing system at the institute, all related departmental instructions for staff development and training, JCAHO requirements, and other established rules and regulations during almost a year. The mission of the department was to provide learning opportunity to understanding persons with mental disability, professional development and training for better performance of the employees, mandated training required by law, regulations to meet the agency certification, management and supervisory training, documentation of all training and attendees and opportunities for experience and internship for students of colleges and universities. I described in detail what staff development would accomplish in its mission through fifteen programs and services, such as curriculum development according to the guidelines of the DMHMRSAS and the identified needs of NVMHI, new employee orientation, preservice and mandatory training, ground rounds in service for continuing education, CME for the multidisciplinary continuing education programs for professional staff, research support to encourage the research projects designed to improve the lives, services and treatment for persons with mental illness with or without collaboration with the higher education institution, colleges and universities several other action programs including the library services by the medical library under the direction of a qualified librarian who would provide basic reference, online searches, interlibrary loan services. I also provided in three appendices in detail generic curricula, mental health curricula and the template of the contract with universities and colleges. All together this work became like a book with more than one hundred pages, which I was happy to be able to deliver, after much hard work, to the acting director in April 1996 for his review and signature.

During the whole year of 1995-'96, and even for a few years after that, the department of DMHMRSAS continued to face frequent turnover in the higher level of management and professional staff and a major drop of quantity and quality of staffing while dealing with the DOJ demands and requirements. It looked like a political battleground. Many letters and news were exchanged for years between the United States of America, plaintiff, and the Commonwealth of Virginia. I attended several farewell gatherings, including one for the associate commissioner who resigned and became a vice president of a managed healthcare company.

In the meantime, I was notified on January 26, 1996, with a congratulation letter from the American Association on Intellectual and Developmental Disability (AAIDD former; AAMR) that I was nominated to be a fellow for meritorious contributions to the field of mental retardation. The letter stated that I would receive this status and certificate during a ceremony at the annual meeting in San Antonio, Texas. Actually, three of my colleagues from New York, Texas, and Wisconsin who were aware of the challenge I met in services, effort, and success nominated me to receive the status of fellow. I was in a way happy to see that the recognition came from the professional association. I was the only one from the State of Virginia to receive that status of fellow. Twelve others from other states also were named fellows. I sent a copy of the congratulation letter to the acting director and commissioner, who were deeply engaged in the politics and the Department of Justice. As I predicted, I received a formality response. However, immediately I noticed that in the next newsletter of the Department of Psychiatry, was written the following:

> *Dr. Sakineh M. Redjali, Clinical Faculty and the Director of Staff Development and Research, Northern Virginia Mental Health Institute, has been honored by being awarded the status of Fellow within the American Association on Mental Retardation in recognition of 16 years of continuous active membership and meritorious contribution to the field of mental retardation. The award presentation will be held at the 120th Annual Meeting of AAMR in San Antonio, Texas. There are 13 active members of AAMR in 1996 who are receiving the Fellow status, Dr. Redjali is the only one from Virginia. Congratulations to Dr. Redjali on achieving such an honored status with AAMR.*[6]

I was proud and happy that my hard work and services were recognized by the professional association in my new country, which was important for me. My husband was happy at the news and joined me for the first time to come with me to the conference and be present in the ceremony. In order to be away from the political and chaotic situation away at work, I took four days of annual leave (not administrative leave) for the end of May to attend the meeting. I noticed that the majority of the members, especially those who had been named fellows, had administrative leave with all the travel expenses and registration paid by their agencies. It was promising for me to see at least that the other states value and promote the professional services. San Antonio is the second largest city in the state of Texas and is famous for its River Walk and the Alamo. I did not have much time at the annual meeting to see much of the city; however, it looked like an interesting and unique city because of the River Walk. The ceremony went well, and I received a certificate as part of the official ceremony on the afternoon of the May 29, 1996:

> *American Association on Mental Retardation*
> *Be it known to all, that upon recommendation of the Awards and Fellowship Committee*
> *And approval of the Board of Directors,*
> *This Association has selected*
>
> *Sakineh M. Redjali, PhD as a Fellow*

in recognition of meritorious contribution to the field of mental retardation and is hereby authorized to use the signature FAAMR.

In witness thereof, we have set our hand and seal This 29th day of May 1996.

Signed and sealed by the chair, Award and Fellowship Committee and the President

The author participating at the Annual Conference of the AAMR or AAIDD and receiving her certificate in a ceremony on May 29 1996. The author is pictured between the president Dr. William Kiernan and the Executive Director Dr. Doreen Croser.

The author participating at the Annual Conference of the AAMR or AAIDD, along with other fellows from other states.

While I was happy and full of hope, living with my family after so many years of separation, at the beginning of June 1996, I received a call from the new human resource director that she needed to speak with me about my position as soon as possible. I went immediately to see her. She said that during my four-day leave, the institute had received approval of the biannual budget for the next year, which would begin July 1, and that my position was not included. This position was supposed to be created by the director of the agency according to the letter of the associate commissioner to the director of agency on March 2, 1995. She showed me the letter mentioned above from the associate commissioner to the director of agency—I had never seen the letter before, and I had not received the copy before moving from Lynchburg.

It seemed that due to the change of directors, with first an acting director and then a new director and a new human service director, nobody paid any attention to establish and include my new position. According to the letter of my transfer from Lynchburg, the budget of CVTC was for one-year 1995-'96, and for 1996-'97 the director of the institute should have included this position for the following years, but this was forgotten due to the changes of directors and the agency being busy with the Department of Justice charges. Of course, since I also did not receive a copy of letter at the time of my transfer and so was not aware of the content, I was not able to remind the administration to follow up the funding of my position. I was shocked, looking at the astounded face and expression of the human service director who was curiously observing my reaction. For a few minutes, I became so quiet that I could not say anything. I was just speechless. When she saw my silence, she began to say that she was prepared to see what other vacant position in the State of Virginia were available and where I could be transferred to, but of course, there was nothing available in Northern Virginia. All the vacant positions were again in the south, in Richmond and Lynchburg. This was a shock as I felt that after one year of being settled in Northern Virginia with family and friends, after fifteen years' separation and struggle and a move, and more importantly because of my husband's back problem, it was not feasible for me to move again to another location. The other option was to use the five years' service bonus of the governor to retire early. The third possibility that many people urged me to pursue was to sue the Central Office for misstatement and neglect. However, if I had done that, the names of the three kind people who understood my position and need of the department would have become involved. These were the ousted director of the institute, the associate commissioner, who went out of state as the vice president of a health organization, and the third one, the director of CVTC, like many other qualified people, was promoted and left to work in another state. Although an administrative lawyer in Richmond, after reviewing my case, told me the possibility of wining was very high, I did not think it was fair to involve these three service-oriented people who themselves left the DMHMRSAS due to its mismanagement. As a result, I chose early retirement with five years' service bonus. So in this way, within one month, I finished my work and revised the comprehensive plan of the staff development for DOJ. Without any preparation, I preferred to be retired from the State of Virginia and to be left as a political victim. Many of the state employees wanted to join me or suggested that I joined them for a class action lawsuit against the commissioner and were surprised that I did not want to join them or to complain. Of course, none of them had the experience of the loss of job and their belongings as I and millions of Iranian people had experienced due to the dark revolution.

In the meantime, the health of my husband, Sa'id, had begun to improve; and to help change my mood after the loss of my job, he accepted the invitation of the University of Heidelberg for us to go together to establish the Heidelberg Alumni International Association. So we would return to our alma mater and see our friends and colleagues from our graduate studies at Heidelberg in the years 1956-1963. With an acceptance of the invitation, he, my husband, was so kind, and in this way, wanted to help me overcome the hurt I felt for the loss of my job. Most of my colleagues and friends who knew me very well suggested that I start a consulting service, which I started to think about. However, before that, I felt in a way, in my conscience, that I had a duty as an advocate for mental health in my new country to inform the legislators about the status of mental health services, which already, according to the National Mental Health Institute, was on the lowest rating, and there was a great need for improvement with a strong management. I felt a duty to the patients, their families, the state, and my country. So I prepared an objective report about the history, function, and need of the mental health service and the effect of the politicization of the department and agencies in the professional services and treatment of the patients and went to meet our local delegate, who was a newly elected delegate from the Republican Party and also our senator from the Democratic party, who had been for years in her position and fortunately was aware of the DMHMRSAS management situation. In my conversations, I also told them that sometimes in my former country, if due to political reasons, the government could not fire an unqualified and unsuitable person holding a high-level position, usually they tried to find another lateral or higher job for him to relieve him and the staff under him. Every week, there was a report on a managerial problem of the institute in *The Washington Post*—anything from the frequent turnovers and changes of directors to resignations and protests of the medical staff and others. I was happy with my decision to be retired and free, and not being in the middle of this battle zone. Then fortunately, I finally heard and read again in the news that the Mental Health commissioner resigned after harsh criticism of DOJ of patient abuse and deaths; however, he claimed that his resignation was unrelated to the Justice Department report, and said, "A wonderful opportunity has come up for me to join the national gambling impact study commission . . . I wish I could stay through the end of the term of the governor, but to get this job, I've got to go now."[7]

I was happy to hear this news in the hope and wish that now patients and staff and the needy would be treated by competent mental health professionals and managers and not politicians, despite deep damages to the many communities involved. I hoped that with the attention of government to a comprehensive mental health program, it would not take many years for damages to the mental health system to be corrected. If that were to happen, the people of Virginia and America would be able to live more in peace and reject more the violence and tragedies such as the massacre at Virginia Tech in 2007 which I'm sure, could have been avoided.

[1.]   M. P. Janicki and M. Wisniewski, "Aging and Developmental Disabilities: Issues and Approaches, Baltimore: Brookes, 1985. and
Seltzer, M. M. & G. G. Selzer, 1985; *The Elder Mentally Retarded: A Group in Need of Service*, G. Betzel Mellor, ed. Gerontological Social Worker Practice in the Community, New York: Haworth, 1985. and

M. P. Janicke, M. M. Selzer & and M. W. Krauss, Contemporary Issues in the Aging of Persons with Mental Retardation and Other Developmental Disabilities, Catholic University of America, Data Institute, 1987.

2. S. Redjali, & J. Radick, ICF/General: *A New Service Model; An Alternative for Older ICF/MR Residents With Geriatric Care Needs,* Journal of Mental Retardation, Vol.26, No.4, August 1988.

3. provider guide line, April 1990 Page 14-19.

4. *The News and Advance,* February 6,1995 vol. No. 37; *Washington Post* 2-3, 1995, or Eric Lipton, *Washington Post* Staff writer: "US. Blames Poor Care for 4 Deaths in VA Mental Hospitals," and "Poor Care Endangers Hundreds in VA. Mental hospitals, U.S. Says" *Washington Post,* May 27,1995.

5. Rajiv Chandrassekaran, *Washington Post,* March 18,1995, Section B.03.

6. Medical College of Virginia Bulletin, vol.7, No. 2, 1996.

7. The Norfolk Virginian-Pilot, Associated Press, September 5, 1997.

CHAPTER 18

Reunion with the Family and Friends and Becoming a Cancer Patient From July 1996-2005

We had already experienced unexpectedly the loss all our retirement money in Iran, and now it was very difficult to adjust to another early-forced retirement. My monthly pension was only one-sixth of my working salary, and now we were concerned with the mortgage repayments for our new home. However, moving to Northern Virginia and living in this very expensive area, was rewarding too. It gave us an excellent opportunity to reunite with our immediate family and also gradually to find our other relatives, old friends, former students and colleagues from Iran, the majority of whom had left after the revolution and had settled in the Washington DC area which, after California, hosted the greatest number of Iranians in the USA who were escaping revolution and war. My niece Nahid and her family who lived in London moved to America and, by choosing a house in our locality, added to our happiness and reunion.

Each time we attended a cultural event or passed by on the street, we found familiar faces. Seeing them and making contact with them again after more than seventeen years was always a cause for celebration and a source of happiness. Since our home is near Tyson's Corner, a commercial center, most of the time after a walk in the two malls near our home, I returned home with the contact details of a newly discovered old friend or relative, who had recognized me. Reunion was becoming a constant process due to the continuing revolution in Iran and the eight years of war with Iraq. It was not, and still is not, clear when this dark revolution would end and light would finally conquer darkness for the people of Iran and set them free. As a result, there were continuous waves of Iranian immigrants moving to all parts of the world and especially to the United States. Even some revolutionary people such as Azar Nafisi, the author of *Reading Lolita in Tehran,* who became disillusioned by the revolution and its dark outcome, could not stay in Iran any longer and returned to, or immigrated to, the USA or other countries. So we were facing a perpetual revolution, an ongoing immigration and reunion with friends and relatives. Many radio and cable television stations as well as Persian language newspapers in Northern Virginia and California were connecting the Iranians in exile; this opportunity had not existed in central Virginia. This aspect of our new environment made the loss of my job a lot easier to bear.

My husband fortunately was feeling better, and because of the increasing number of Iranian immigrants, his reputation in Iran and recommendations by his past successful students in America, he was getting more piano students. Soon, the number of his students doubled, and it got to a point where we had to start a waiting list for future students even though there was a low turnover among his students. So that was a blessing, and as always, our education at least helped us overcome the financial adversities we were facing.

There were many cultural events and shows in our area that we always attended. One of these was a show of two prominent and popular Iranian comedians and writers Haadi Khorsandi and Parviz Sayyad in the auditorium of a high school near our home. They had both relocated to London and Los Angeles after the revolution, and their shows were renowned for their examination and critique of the new regime. The auditorium was full of Iranian Americans, and we were sitting in the middle. Suddenly, during the intermission, somebody from the back row called my husband, and when I turned, I noticed that my husband was hugging his friends Nazi and Khosrow Youssefzadeh from the music school in Iran. Sa'id was excited and delighted to see them. He introduced me and spent the whole time during the intermission speaking about old times. Apparently, Nazi and Khosrow were visiting their daughter

Soheila and their grandchildren in Arlington, Virginia, for a few days. At the end of the successful show, their talented grandchildren Gisèle and Daniel were selected from the Iranian school to give flowers to the two actors. Of course, there was not enough time during the intermission, and we needed to celebrate our reunion.

Since Sunday was the only day that Sa'id was not working, we invited them and all the members of their family to come to our home to get together again, to celebrate and exchange our experiences after the revolution. Khosrow and Nazi were musicians and artists, and we discovered their two daughters were educated and artistically talented as well, and what's more, their grandchildren Gisèle and Daniel by their daughter Soheila Hayek showed talent in poetry, music, and acting. Daniel, who was about nine or ten years old at the time, was mimicking the action of those renowned actors very well. I am happy to learn that Gisèle is now a successful lawyer in London, where she is still writing her poetry and Daniel is an actor in Hollywood and also has his own band. After a few days Nazi and Khosrow left, but Soheila and her children stayed longer in Northern Virginia, and we were fortunate to be able to continue our friendship with Soheila and her family, which we cherish dearly. Soheila, with her Iranian family background, immediately understood our situation, and it felt as if we had known each other for years. Her husband who was Lebanese American was always traveling because of his job, so we had a lot of opportunities to spend time together and to discuss ideas about a new job or business. On the Fourth of July 1996, she invited us to the Capital Hill celebration and provided a picnic of delicacies that we enjoyed while listening to music and watching fireworks in nice weather—an unforgettable occasion for us. She, like my old students that I was in contact with at that time, was very interested in my experiences in Iran. Retelling those stories motivated and convinced me that it would be illuminating to write about the modernization in Iran and that I was obligated to the new generation to write about my experiences that covered time periods before during and after the revolution. There were already several valuable memoirs and biographies published by Iranians in exile, more by women than men, because they suffered more after the revolution, and mainly depicted a picture of the time of the dark revolution. So I felt compelled and obligated, in addition to finding a job, to start collecting research notes about my challenging symphony of life, which I was unable to do sooner because I had to work hard and adjust to the American way of life. One day, in the middle of exploring all these ideas with my friends, including Soheila, who had kindly and urgently encouraged me to write my autobiography, she told me that her husband Alex had taken a job in New York, which required them to move to New York. With this news, I was happy for her and her talented children, although we were going to miss her being near us. However, Soheila, with her warm personality and excellent communication skills, has kept our relationship alive and active to the present time, even after she left Arlington, and living in several other countries. She has never given up inspiring me to write my life story, and it was she who found the resemblance between life and a musical symphony. Over the years, we have visited each other many times, and we continue to cherish our friendship. It was a shock to learn that she had been diagnosed with breast cancer at a young age. She handled the mastectomy and the process of her treatment so well and wrote so beautifully about the whole process that those notes about her sickness could be an excellent introduction and guidance for patients who are diagnosed with breast cancer. As a matter of fact, those notes helped me tremendously when I faced my own cancer later in 2002. I wish she would publish her beautiful written notes for the benefit of everyone.

Soheila Hayek, who questioned the author about her life in Iran and who motivated the author to write a Symphony of Life.

As I mentioned before, after my painful and hasty retirement, Sa'id accepted the invitation of the University of Heidelberg in August 1996 to attend the first reunion of the Heidelberg Alumni International. This was an unforgettable, unique, and beautiful gathering in our alma mater after the fall of the Berlin Wall between East and West Germany in 1989 and German reunification in 1990. The first night at the City Hall of Heidelberg, we saw our old friends from around the world, and there was a lot of kissing and hugging as they expressed their surprise that we had survived the dark revolution and could be present there. This occasion was a unique experience for all of us due to the fact that the University of Heidelberg had decided for the first time to establish the Heidelberg Alumni International and to provide an opportunity for all former international students to get together. We had an intensive and well-organized cultural program at all the memorable places of Heidelberg—from the old historical auditorium (Alte Ula) to the castle (Schloss), which we did not want to miss. Even in the middle of a downpour, we were able to watch the opera in the castle courtyard under the protective covering of a white umbrella with the logo of the Heidelberg Alumni International. We brought these home with us as souvenirs and in memory of that time and we still use them. During the week, all the alumni had a choice of several programs to attend according to their interest and expertise, and every day, the local newspaper, the *Rhein Neckar Zeitung*, reported on the events and interviews with the participants. My husband and I were among those being interviewed. Our interview was published on Tuesday, August 13, 1996, with our picture and the headline STUDIERENDEN ZWISCHEN TRADITION AND GEGENWART (studying between tradition and present).[1] Since our pictures appeared in the local paper, everywhere in the beautiful University of Heidelberg, we were welcomed by people who had seen the article.

During our stay, we visited our old friend, Professor Hans Jüergen Phistner, and his family in Mannheim. I was surprised when I saw that he had kept all our correspondence and pictures since we met them in 1958 during our studies and the years after. We also met the children of our old landladies who themselves had died. The meeting with one of our professors who lived and was still active in Heidelberg was also memorable. He was Professor Hermann Roehrs who was finishing his own memoir. He too motivated me and urged me as a duty to write my autobiography for the next generations and for the freedom for the people of Iran. He had been both my and Sai'd's professor during our studies in Heidelberg and was an expert in international and comparative education whose view and recommendations I valued. In fact, he knew us very well. He also mentioned that he wrote about our stories in his books while he was visiting us as a guest in our home in Tehran in 1973 and in Alexandria, Virginia, our job in USA, and my participation in the seminar in Heidelberg through the College Consortium for International Studies, New York, in 1984.[2] Again, we said *aufwiedersehen* to Heidelberg and our friends, and filled with memories, we returned to the USA. The Heidelberg Alumni International gradually expanded to other parts of the world, including USA in New York City in 2007, and in each country, the alumni have gatherings in connection to their alma mater.

During our absence from home, we heard the good news from our dear daughter, Gita, that she was pregnant and was expecting a son at the beginning of December. We were very happy for her and Fred and excited to know that we were soon going to be grandparents. I also received several invitations to take part in several committees and research projects, which required my response. The most interesting one was an invitation to become a member of the National Institute of Mental Health Grant Review committee for states mental health projects, being responsible for a research team for a project on the Telecommunication Management of Depression and several volunteer services in the field of Mental Health.

Then I received an important call from Iran that delayed all my projects. During the administration of the fourth president of the Islamic Republic, Akbar Rafsanjani, some time in September 1996, our friend Mehdi and his wife, Pouran, who had been very helpful to us during the dark revolution, called us from Iran. Mehdi said they were ready to leave Iran for the USA in order to publish his books that he could not publish in Iran due to the lack of freedom and heavy censorship. They therefore wanted to return to us some of our personal belongings that we had left with them in our hasty departure from Iran. I had always wanted to revisit my former homeland since leaving in 1979, but for two reasons, I had not dared to do that—first because of responsibility to my job, community, and family in America; and second due to news from Iran and lack of minimum security and freedom. I had been especially

The author and her husband participated at the opening of the first University Heidelberg Alumnae International in August 1996 which was a reunion of old friends and colleagues, including Gert-Schneider (Dean of International Students) Dr. and Mrs. Shibuya, Professor Hermann Roehrs the pioneer of International Education, Dr. and Mrs. Massarrat and Dr. and Mrs. Phistner.

concerned because, some years before, the revolutionary court, through an announcement in the newspaper, had wanted me to give myself up to the court. The rulings of this court had always been unjustified, especially in the case of Dr. Farrokhru-Parsa, my former teacher and the first woman minister of Education. She was executed because of her dedication and advocacy to Western-style education for young people, including me. So after this call from Tehran, being completely free of all professional and family ties, I thought maybe at this time I could risk making a short visit to Iran to relieve our friend of the responsibility we had given him. This trip would also fulfill my desire to see Iran and my friends and relatives, whom I had not been able to say good-bye to before. Gita's baby was due at the end of November, and I wanted to be with her at that time. Nevertheless, I decided to take a risk, and in October, I arranged a very low profile, short visit to Iran. I did not tell anybody there or in the USA about my trip to Iran especially since some of my relatives were frightened for their own security because of our similar family name. They continued to write, call, and tell me that it was still too dangerous for me to return and had the court's announcement sent again. So I just told everybody that I was going to Germany and England for a visit and to help in the establishment of the Heidelberg Alumni International. In fact, I may have made the right decision to make a low-key trip to my beloved country, thus avoiding the fate of many Iranians with dual citizenship, like Haleh Esfandiari (the author of *My Prison My Home*, 2009), the Canadian and American journalists Zahra Kazemi and Roxana Saberi, who either landed in jail, disappeared, or were killed. My husband and children, who knew I was going to Iran were worried. Because of my ankle and knee problems and years of pain, I needed assistance in travelling, and in addition, they worried that if the authorities recognized me upon arrival, I might disappear like many other people with similar history. However, I thought that after seventeen years of absence, I had aged and would not be recognized, particularly as I would be wearing a long black coat and a black scarf and would enter the country in a wheelchair, so I should not attract anybody's attention.

I was proved right, and when the person who was assisting me in a very old rusted wheelchair, which was not running smoothly, came near the pass-control desk, the authorities were more concerned that the wheelchair might disintegrate in the middle of the crowd. To avoid this, they let us pass through all the control sections of the airport very quickly. During all this time, my heart was beating so fast that I thought it might stop or I might have a heart attack, but the old rusty wheelchair proved to be my salvation.

When I found myself outside the exit door, with our friends Mehdi and Pouran, waiting for me, I was so relieved that I gave a large tip to the person who had escorted me safely with the broken wheelchair to my friends' car. As usual, the weather at that early morning hour of 2:00 a.m. was beautiful and dry, and the sky was shining with stars. In the car, we exchanged all the news about each other and the truth about the political atmosphere and its effect on the daily life of the people. It appeared that the people in Iran had developed a dual lifestyle because of the theocratic regime: one for life outside and one for inside their homes. As a result, they could not be themselves, and when I communicated with them, I had to be very careful. Once again, my education, especially in psychology, helped me in understanding how they were placed themselves. It upset me to see how the majority of the people could not be themselves because of lack of freedom and fear of the cruelty of the regime. I understood our friends who had spent seventeen years living in Iran after the dark revolution could not bear to live there anymore and wanted to leave. I could understand that Mehdi wanted to live and publish his book in a free society without censorship. In my short stay in Tehran, I had to be cautious and selective about how I spent my time. Tehran had completely changed with many incongruous high-rise buildings. I saw a lot of cultural changes in Iran by watching the TV and listening to the radio. For example, I noticed how the traditionally beautiful wedding ceremony had changed. On television, I watched hundreds of young couples getting married in a collective wedding ceremony in a stadium. We never had weddings like this before.

The first thing I wanted to do in Iran was to visit the holy city of Qom, where the graves of my parents, aunts, grandmother, uncles, and other family members were located, to pay my respects and pray. On the road to Qom, I planned to stop at the old grave of the Reza Shah the Great and pay my respects, but when I got there, I was told that there was not even a ruin left, and it was just land without any sign. I was shocked that the tomb, with its magnificent art work that we always proudly showed to our international visitors, had been obliterated. In hindsight, it proved to be an inspired decision of Mohammed Reza Shah, before leaving Iran, to send the body of his father to Egypt to prevent people like Sadegh Khalkhali, a representative of Khomeini, from burning it.

Instead of that tomb, it was suggested that I visit the new building nearby, which was the grave of Khomeini. So the regime destroyed one tomb and built another. While I was shocked that the regime could so wantonly destroy such a historical monument, I was impressed by the tomb of Khomeini with its magnificent sanctuary. There were many elementary school buses arriving at the shrine and the courtyard was full of schoolchildren with their teachers. They were wearing uniforms, the girls sporting a scarf, and following their teacher into the sanctuary. In the shrine, as in the shrines of other Imams, you could see large amounts of cash that the people, including children, threw to the inside next to the tomb. At the yard of the sanctuary, I noticed that someone was giving cookies and food to the children after their visit to the shrine. So after a short visit and after taking several side trips on the road, we continued our trip to Qom. On the way, we had to stop to ask an old man, who was walking, for directions. When we asked him, "Sir, could you please let us know how we could get to Qom?" He stared at us and said he would tell us on one condition. Asked what this condition was, he told us that as soon as we saw the golden dome of the shrine of holy Massumeh, the sister of the eighth Imam Emam Reza, we should pray that God bless the soul of Reza Shah who did so much for the country. Of course, we said we would and continued our trip to Qom.

In Qom, we faced another shocking scene. Most of the graves of our family members, old kings of the Ghajar dynasty, and prime ministers had been destroyed and flattened. The government had taken every belonging, even the stone on the graves, some of which were beautiful works of art. So with this pointless action, it looked like the regime was opposed to any signs of the past. I still cannot understand how they could destroy over 2,500 years of history. Our family tomb where my father, uncle, and mother lay with several other members was right next to where they had built the shrine. The authorities had divided the gravesite in two, and on the side closest to the shrine, the graves were abolished in order to create the grounds around the shrine. I saw that my father and mother's gravestones on the wall were still in place with their names but without any pictures or light. However, work was still in progress in the shrine, and I could not be certain whether or not their graves were designated for abolition too. At least I was happy to be able to pay my respects to them in this depressing location, and I could keep in my mind and heart the memory of this place as it was before they destroy it. After taking a look in the shrine, we returned downcast and heavy-hearted to Tehran.

After my visit to Qom, I chose to pay a surprise visit to a few close friends and relatives. I thought if I had let them know in advance, they might notify other friends and relatives, and the news might get around, and I might face problems. I saw two of my brother's children, Shahla and Massud, who could not leave Iran, and my brother in-law Jamshid, my sister-in-law, my dear friends Mahin and Kawuss, Amir Hossein and Homa Aryanpour and Abdollah Anwar. Interestingly enough, most of them, at first, did not recognize me, but after staring at me for some time, they recognized me, and we hugged and kissed each other. One of them even said, "You look like Dr. Redjali" before they realized that Dr. Redjali was me! During one of my visits, I noticed that one of our dearest friends, the now late Dr. Aryanpour, had developed Parkinson's disease when I saw him struggling to write his new mailing address, although he did not mention it to me. I felt deeply sorry for him, and as soon as I returned to America, I became a member of the Parkinson's Society in order to send his wife all the journals and information about the latest treatments, for as long as he lived, which fortunately was for many more years. God bless his soul!

I also went by the Shemiran College, which I had struggled so hard to establish so many years before. I already knew that after the revolution the college had been nationalized and renamed a university after one of the religious persons, one Allaameh Tabatabai, but I couldn't figure out (did not know) what had happened to the building. Therefore, I stopped nearby and inquired where it was from the locals. A sad and shocking story emerged. Apparently, immediately after nationalization of the college, the building was evacuated by the student bodies and was given by the revolutionary government to a number of Arab assassins and their families, who did not speak Farsi, and who were recruited to kill the supporters of the Shah in the Evin Prison because the government could not trust Iranians to kill their Iranian prisoners. Every night they were going to Evin to kill prisoners. After some time, the neighborhood noticed a foul smell coming from the building and complained about it. The investigation revealed an overflow of human waste in the septic tank, of which these people were ignorant, as they did not have any knowledge of the existence or the location of it in the building. The waste just built up, overflowed, and caused impurity to the ground around it and a terrible smell for the neighborhood. As a result the government moved all these assassins with their families to another college, the "School of Social Work," which was also nationalized. The owner of the Shemiran College building could finally repossess the ruined structure, which was first initially the American Country Club and then was converted to a college for learning and finally became the house for assassins and a ruin full of waste.

The author on visiting friends and relatives in Iran and observing the drastic change in the educational system and the changes due to political and religious values, including brain washing children even from early childhood with slogans such as "Death to America and Israel".

Finally, at the end of November, with a few painted pictures of my grandfather hidden between my clothing in the luggage, like my arrival, I left my beloved old country quietly, with a sad memory and a lot of pain. I realized, without a doubt, that as long as religion and government were intertwined so deeply, this beautiful land with its people could not be free. I had to accept that I could no longer hope to return there to serve my people and as my daughter, Gita, characterized my life in her university essay assignment. I could not continue anymore as a "Gardener in a Wasteland."

As I am writing these lines, I have heard that my dear friend Soheila Hayek visited our homeland Iran after thirty-two years. When I asked her about her impressions, I saw in her e-mail the following citation, which shows, twelve years after my visit, her perception of Iran was not much different from mine, and she described the experience so beautifully that with her permission I cite her words here:

> I have wanted to write about my trip to Iran but the words have been hard to come by. It has very much been like revisiting a favourite colour picture only to find it has turned brown!
>
> To say that I returned to a much more advanced country technologically speaking is the most I can say on the positive side but then that is not such a positive thing to say. After all, Iran, being the rich country it is, having all the natural resources that it has, from oil and gas, to gold and silver, to chromium and copper, to saffron and pistachios, not to mention rugs and caviar, is expected to have made advances in the span of 32 years. What was very sad and heart breaking however, was the condition of the people.
>
> I had prepared myself to see women dressed in long coats with their hair covered under a scarf. What I was not ready for was to see men and women so exhausted psychologically. I wasn't ready to see so much stress, so much anguish, to hear so much complaint and to read so much desperation and hopelessness in people's eyes. I wasn't ready to have to search for the noble faces I used to see everywhere. I wasn't ready to face the rudeness and the total loss of courtesy and

civility. The Iran I remember was filled with *joi de vivre,* and prided itself for being the cradle of civilization, but now I saw the face of savagery barely disguised under the cover of fake civility. Even that thin layer of civility though completely disappeared once confronted with anyone in an official capacity. The staff at the airport, bank and security were all extremely rude and oppressive from the get go. This, I had not expected.

The really dangerous thing was how unaware the people were of the extent of government intrusion into their lives. They saw themselves free! The fact that they had to cover up head to toe in 40 °C in the heat of summer (this included men who were not allowed to wear short sleeve shirts and shorts which are not seen anywhere) was just how things were. The fact that girls would get stopped for having a strand of their hair hanging outside their head cover while driving and could be taken to the police station and all the troubles the family had to go through to get them released, all of that was to them just a bit of a nuisance! The fact that they had to dial a special number every day to see what was on offer and where, in exchange for their coupons, was not an intrusion, but an advantage, as the government was offering coupons for people to buy sugar, oil, rice and tea at a "good" price. What they did not say was that otherwise they couldn't afford to buy anything at supermarket prices! The fact that they could not watch anything on TV other than the Iranian channels or Turkish channels with a dish, was not strange at all. They had no need of other channels. The news would be the same everywhere, so why listen to it in French or English when there was a Farsi version. The exception was, that during my visit (Oct 29-Nov 12, 2008) after the Israeli advance on Gaza, everyone in Iran was shown footage of Hezbollah rockets hitting Tel Aviv in revenge. As is well known, no such event ever took place. As far as the Iranians were concerned though, it did, and that would probably justify the amount of help (close to a billion dollars annually, according to what the people I came across believed) given to Lebanon to support Hezbollah and make paupers out of Iranians in the process. No one seemed to wonder why everyone was in such an economic tight spot when their country had the second largest gas, and the fifth largest oil reserves in the world. As far as they knew it was a worldwide problem! Well, since a few months ago it is, but they have been suffering the same fate for the past thirty years!

Soheila continued in her email "I can summarise my impression of Iran today by saying that I will go back with Alex (her husband) to show him all the natural beauty and the cultural riches of the past, but I will visit it no longer as my country, but rather as a very interesting tourist destination, a foreign country where I understand the language and can read the sign posts.

Sadly, I no longer belong there and more sadly Iran no longer belongs to me.

Love,
Soheila

Upon my own return to America, I immediately responded to those invitations and opportunities that I had received earlier to serve as a member or volunteer in the grant review committee of the National Mental Health Institute, Telecommunication Management of Depression Project, Alzheimer Association, Zonta Club, AARP and several other volunteer organizations either for advocacy or training for my new country. At the same time, I was awaiting eagerly the good news of the arrival of a baby boy for Gita and Fred. I was a little worried that Gita might need a C-section because of the Harrington Rod in her back.

My waiting and worrying did not last long. On December 2, 1996, Fred called us early in the morning from Fairfax Hospital to say that Cameron John Khoroushi was born at 3:53 a.m. through natural birth weighing six pounds and thirteen and a half ounces and measuring twenty and a half inches in length. They had not wanted to bother us when Gita had gone into labor. Immediately, Sa'id and I rushed to the hospital to see them all. Some people don't like to be called grandparents as they think it makes them appear older than they are, but Sa'id and

I both welcomed the titles and were thrilled to have a grandchild. Ever since then, we have celebrated Cameron's birthday and Christmas for a whole month with the added excuse to have a family reunion. For the first six months, Gita had maternity leave from work and did not need much assistance, but whenever she needed me, I was delighted to be available for her and her baby. In the meantime, Sa'id and I were looking for a full-time nanny for her which we were lucky to find from among our friends. A lady named Jaleh, whose two sons had left for college, took on the job and was pleased to go to Gita's home daily to take care of Cameron so that Gita could return to work, and I became the substitute nanny for my dear Cameron John.

The author during a Persian New Year holding her grandson Cameron on her lap and sitting next to her son Reza, teaching them the traditional value of the celebration of Nowruz.

During this time, I gradually became more active in my consulting services. I felt more free to express my opinion in my new country even if it was without any financial reward but rather as a volunteer or an advocate. After all, I chose this country because of liberty and being able to give myself in service to others. As a new American, I have always utilized and valued my freedom of expression to humanity to make my new country a better place to live in. As a member of the grant review committee of the National Institute of Mental Health, we reviewed mental health research projects of different states. Members normally reviewed the grant projects of a state other than their own because of a conflict of interest. So I could not review the grant proposals of the State of Virginia, although I was told that the State of Virginia was rarely sending any grant projects from the federal government. By reviewing the mental health projects of several states from the west, midwest, and southern states, I became familiar with the status of mental health systems of many states, and by comparing them with my state, I was sorry to see how our state was among those (states) ranking at the bottom of the scale. It came as no surprise that, in the end, I had to advocate and fight for the promotion of the status of mental health in Virginia. Usually, the other states were competing for federal grants, and we as members of the committee were rating each project and the highest-rated project would get a grant according to the budget of the federal grant for NIMH. I continued as a member of the committee for a few years until my time and health required me to stop. I regret that I got this membership only around the time of my retirement in the state and not earlier when I could have pursued a grant for our state myself.

To compensate for the insufficient attention given to mental health at the state level, I became motivated to join a group that carried out research projects on the use of Tele-Practice in health. During the 1990s, with the change in the Health Care Financing system and emphasis on cost reduction through managed care techniques (HMO) and the advancement of the telecommunication systems, a few research projects using telecommunication and computer-assisted programs in the health management system looked promising. One of the first Tele-Practice projects was called Tele-Practice Inc., promoted by Dr. F. Alemi, which was a telephone system created with $3 million funding from a grant from the National Institute of Drug Abuse and other investors in Jacksonville, Florida. Tele-Practice focused on providing systems for online medical care management of HMOs. In particular, Tele-Practice provided direct voice response systems for health education, social support, and counseling for participating members. Tele-Practice products were the subject of a series of clinical studies, showing potential in reducing cost of care.[3] I thought this could be a new approach for bringing a better quality of health care to a wider group of patients, especially in the mental health field, which needed the most attention. Dr. Alemi conducted or participated in many research projects, and some of them had positive results. So I joined him on a research project called Telecommunication Management of Depression. The purpose of this study was to use telecommunication systems Tele-Practice to organize computer-assisted treatment of depressed patients and monitor their use of antidepressant drugs. By telecommunication systems, we referred to computer services that could be accessed through a standard touch-tone telephone. A voice-interactive, or talking computer, enabled one to call a computer, to manipulate the computer by pressing keys on the telephone, and to exchange messages in a public forum. Clients did not need to have or borrow a computer in order to use this electronic bulletin board. The only equipment clients needed was a standard touch-tone telephone, and the service was delivered to the client's home, not to a community station. Should clients become homeless or lose their access to a telephone, they could call the computer from any public phone through a toll-free number.

This study included conducting a randomized clinical experiment comparing the computer-assisted care to current care. Patients in both the experimental and the control groups received a free voice mail system, through which the study collected information from the patients concerning the outcome of their care. In addition, the experimental group also received weekly *home monitoring*, monthly *reminders*, biweekly *motivational interviews*, participation in *electronic support groups*, and biweekly *electronic group therapy*. Neither the experimental nor the control patients were asked to alter their regular visits to the clinics. Then the impact of the proposed changes was examined in the areas of satisfaction with care, mental health status, utilization of services and compliance with care. This was an add-on aspect of care to help clinicians—managed care and not a replacement of contact with clinicians.

This intervention would have provided an innovative treatment and needed monitoring system of patients' quality care, while at the same time it was cost effective for the managed care organization. Tele-Practice system was already being sold to managed care organizations and the content that we developed could be an added value and sold along with the Tele-Practice system. Unfortunately, the Tele-Practice company later closed operations several years after marketing its products, mostly because the systems sold went unused as many HMOs failed to make the necessary process changes to take advantage of virtual managed care possibilities.

As Dr. Alemi wrote in one of his articles: "Technology succeeds when management innovates." Management innovations make the difference between the success and failure of a new technology. Technology is important, but it is not enough. Without new practices, we can buy the technology but will fail to use it effectively. Unless management modifies the very nature of its business, technology's promise to the healthcare industry will go unfulfilled."[4] However, from the year 2000, the movement to use technology with some modification improved and continued and became an ongoing process, several Tele-Practices were created and interactive voice media and interactive video presentation, Internet and even text messages have become an important tool in the research and treatment of mental health patients.

While I was settling in and adjusting to life in our new home and enjoying reunions with my family and friends after so many years of suffering separation and isolation, I had a call from the office of the new governor of Virginia, Jim Gilmore, asking that I have an interview with Dr. Cloud Allen, the secretary of Health and Human Services, for the position of inspector general for the state mental health and mental retardation agencies. I was surprised since I had not applied for any position, and I had had early retirement from the state for some time. I inquired immediately about the position, and I learned that it was prompted by the crisis in Virginia's mental health system during the 1900s and that the new governor had established the position in Richmond. I was given a few options of time and location for an interview. I did not like the name and function of the position as inspector general, and I did not think that appointing just one person would be a solution to correcting the mental health system. Professionals in the department of mental health and community service were needed more. However, my curiosity was piqued, and I accepted the invitation for the interview, wondering how they had got my name, why they had nominated me as a candidate for the appointment, and how I could serve as a watchdog and detective. Before the interview, I sent a résumé including my education, experiences, and the commendations for my work to Dr. Allen's secretary. My interview with Dr. Allen took place on an early afternoon at in his office, and I noticed my package on his desk. He was polite and curious and appeared impressed with my résumé and services. He seemed especially surprised about the progressive function and development of the family welfare centers in Iran in the past, my commendations from the state authorities for running and directing two centers in Virginia with no deficiencies, and maybe he had also heard within the department about my unfair and unjustified early retirement due to the bureaucratic mistakes of the former administration. Not many people could imagine the time of modernization and our progressive programs in Iran before the dark revolution. I could tell from his expression the interview had been successful, and when I asked about the location of the position, he said it would definitely be near the governor's office in Richmond. It seemed that the governor had been involved so intensely in his former position as attorney general with the Department of Justice that he now wanted to oversee all the agencies himself to vet their plan to correct their deficiencies and improve their quality. He also wanted immediate access to the duties of the Department of Mental Health Mental Retardation and Substance Abuses (DMHMRSAS). Thinking of my family, I asked whether the location of the office could be located elsewhere with the use of the Internet and technology, but he replied, "Definitely not." I understood, knowing that the State of Virginia was years behind in implementing new technology. The interview finished pleasantly, and I left the office and hurried to return to Northern Virginia on Interstate 95 before the rush hour. This road between Richmond and Northern Virginia is one of the busiest roads and has one of the highest records of traffic accidents. On the road, I was thinking about the position, which would involve a lot of travelling to the various agencies in the state and possibly another move and further separation of the family and friends. I also had to take into account the reaction of my husband whose cancer was in the process of being controlled and my daughter who was counting on my availability for her son, Cameron. All these were more important than my thought of how one person, as inspector, could change the system merely by writing reports but without any implementation authority.

After one week, I received a thank-you note from the office of the secretary detailing the job description, which required the use of the office next to the governor's office in Richmond and thereby my immediate availability to the governor and my acceptance of the position. After a long review of the job description as a watchdog and considering the hardship that I had gone through to bring about a reunion with my family and the hard adjustment that had taken, I recognized that this job was just not suitable for me. I couldn't move, I couldn't make the daily 150-mile trip, and I didn't want to have to drive on Interstate 95 so often.

Ironically, today, my son-in-law who now lives in California can run his office in Fairfax, Virginia, and his factory in Dallas, Texas, using the Internet, but then I was not permitted to work for the governor of Virginia from Northern Virginia by using the Internet. So I notified the office of the secretary, thanking him for the nomination, and informed him I had to decline the position for family reasons. As I predicted, the inspector general, Dr. Anita Everett, who occupied this position after four years, in an interview later with Jean Archart-Treichel described the demands of the job in an article in *Psychiatric News*.[5] She described making several visits to the fifteen state mental health facilities, questioning staff and patients and then writing seventy-eight reports. These reports contained some seven hundred recommendations to the governor, for which the department of mental health should have devised a plan of correction similar to other plans of correction to the federal government or DOJ or state. She also mentioned how in her inspection the staff felt threatened by her, which was one of the reasons that I did not like the name and function of the position, since if members of the staff felt threatened they might refuse to respond openly. In fact, if the governor's selection for the department staff were based on professional expertise and experience rather than political affiliation, this position would not have been necessary. Rather, it would have been a burden and increased bureaucracy and expenses. A bureaucracy that could not prevent incidents such as the Virginia Tech massacre of 2007, whose perpetrator was mentally ill and whose needs were overlooked.

As our family reunited in Northern Virginia, surprise visits of friends, family, colleagues, and former students became an ongoing process with several get-togethers with each group. In addition, ever since we had settled in our new country, we had celebrated and honored two holidays—Thanksgiving Day for America and the Persian New Year on the vernal equinox (spring).

A continuous reunion and gathering of family and friends during Persian New Year and American Thanksgiving celebrations.

These two days became fixed days for reception, meeting and gathering and celebration for our families and friends and reuniting with former friends and relatives. At these gatherings, I tried to motivate my former colleagues and students from the National University of Iran to establish an alumni association similar to the Heidelberg Alumni International. I thought, with starting a new life in America, this would be the best way for them to network and find each other throughout the world. Fortunately, after several meetings in our home and in cafés around our home, the association was established with the name of National University of Iran Alumni and Faculty (NUIAF). The work of this association is ongoing with several social, cultural, and academic programs each year. Their board of directors have graduated from different faculties of the university, e.g., economics, political science, medicine, literature, architecture, and dentistry. Currently serving, as I write this book, are Saeed Alagheband, Kianush Alem, Freidoon Behbahani, Shirin Hadian, Homa Hutan, Faramarz Pezeshkpour, Ramin Riahi, Shahla Sarfaraz, and Susan Shekarian. Since psychology was a general subject for all the faculties, the majority of them were my former students and friends, I knew them well, and in the event of disagreement, I tried indirectly to mediate. I am so happy that they now work together in harmony, and their programs have continued to improve and become more organized. I told the president of the club that if sometime in the future they could get my retirement money from the university, they could have that to improve their cultural activities, especially since this alumni association, unlike other alumni associations, was not supported by the university itself.

On November 13, 1998, at one of our reunions, we were honored and happy with a surprise visit of his imperial highness Crown Prince Reza Pahlavi and his wife Princess Jasmine. When the crown prince met our son at a party and discovered that Sa'id (was his former music teacher in Iran, he came to our reception. This was a great moment for all of us, especially for my husband who had always admired him and his behavior in his class and remembered his kindness and modesty. For example, when Sa'id directed the musical play *Cinderella* for their school, the crown prince chose to play a soldier, not a prince, and he played his role beautifully. At the reception, everybody was impressed by his modest and humble personality. Some people had tears of happiness in their eyes, seeing themselves in the presence of such a charming prince. He has

Author with the board members of the National University
of Iran Alumni and faculty at the Iranian traditional Yalda (the
beginning of winter, the longest night of the year on the 21st of
December) reunion and celebration.

been leading a democracy and freedom movement for Iran since Iran's revolution, and through his efforts, Americans gradually understand how the people of Iran are different from the present government of Iran and its political and religious leaders.

A few months later, we were honored to receive an invitation for dinner with the crown prince and his family. He and his family received us in their home with charm and modesty. He said that he would have a surprise for us later, so we wondered what that could be. About an hour later, a very charming young woman arrived—Princess Laila, to whom Sa'id had also taught piano lessons in the Niavaran Palace. She had just arrived from California, and she seemed delighted to see her former piano teacher. She hugged my husband, greeted us warmly, and they had their picture taken together. She also had a small picture album with her of her friends, and she wanted to add her piano teacher to the album. She showed me the picture of her friends. She went through several memories with my son, who was the same age, and they shared several memories of their childhood. It was clear that, like us, and millions of Iranians who had lost their beloved country and home, she was trying to collect and keep what was lost, at least through pictures and meetings

November 13, 1998 when the author and her family were honored by a
visit from His Highness Crown Prince Reza Pahlavi and his wife
Princess Jasmine, they were photographed along the author's family including
her husband Dr. Sa'id Khadiri, the Prince's former teacher.

and sharing some part of her lovely memories. She had graduated from
Brown University, and when I asked her what she was planning to do,
she said she would like to write a children's book of stories from the
famous Persian epic the *Shahnameh* written by our famous poet Firdausi.
These two evenings and our reunion were unique and unforgettable
for our family. This dearest princess, like millions of Iranians (due to
the dark revolution), suffered from depression as she wandered among
the countries of Europe and America, and unfortunately, because of an
overdose of medication, she died in a hotel room in London on June
10, 2001. Millions of people were shocked and mourned the death *of
the youngest child of the Shah's family.* As soon as we heard the news, we
and especially my husband went through deep sorrow and grief. Sa'id
has always liked his students and has been close to them. This was the
first time one of his dear students had died, and he was very sad and
depressed for some time and frequently recalled her elegant entrance
into her brother's house that one evening and having his picture taken
with her, a picture she kept personally with her.

During this time, many Iranians who had voted for Mohammed Khatami in 1997 as the fifth president, with his platform of reform and liberalization, were disappointed and felt betrayed that he, like Khomeini, did not fulfill his promises, and he was not successful in his promise to make Iran a free and democratic country. Many young people and students who voted for him were betrayed and killed by the regime or, like Ahmed Batebi, landed for years in jail and suffered various kinds of tortures. Batebi was arrested after *The Economist*, in their July 17 issue, published his picture on the cover page (1999) while he was carrying the bloody T-shirt of his friend who was killed in the student demonstration for reform on July 9, 1999. He was to be sentenced to death because of that picture, but after a global outcry, the sentence was reduced to fifteen years in jail. However, during the presidency of Khatami and Ahmadinejad, he was tortured so badly that he became very sick and suffered a stroke. The government did not want him to die in prison so gave him three months' sick leave from jail for medical treatment. During that time, with the help of the United States, he escaped through Iraq and arrived in DC. With the use of his cell phone, he recorded his trip, complete with pictures. During 2008, he gave several radio and television interviews including one with *The Economist* (July 10, 2008) about his trip and the torture he suffered while in jail. I watched his interview on CBS when he appeared on the television program *Sixty Minutes* on Sunday April 5, 2009, with the pictures that he took from his escape route by his telephone. He and his attorney, the human rights activist Ms. Lili Mazaheri, described his life in jail in detail.

It seems that, as long as the government of Iran does not separate itself from religion and remains an Islamic republic, the people and even the religion suffer under this repressive and regressive regime and day by day, the number of Iranians who become atheists, Christians, or Zoroastrians (an old Iranian faith) increases as people try to achieve their freedom in other ways.

In August of 1999, our good friends Christine and David who travelled extensively around the world, usually on cruises, invited us to England and suggested that we take, for a the first time, a week-long cruise to Italy and the Greek Islands on the Mediterranean Sea. We had always hesitated to travel by ship with my previous experience of getting seasick and so usually avoided this type of travel, but they mentioned that they had taken this route before and found the Mediterranean Sea to be very calm, and there would not be any problems on the recommended cruise; on a new ship called *Mistral*. This trip was fantastic, memorable and relaxing, everything on the ship was comfortable. Visiting the Greek islands, especially the beautiful Santorini with its combination of modern convenience and ancient ruins similar to Persia, like a painted city, enhanced our knowledge of this beautiful country. The only problem that we faced was the heat and the sun, which was harmful for Sa'id's skin cancer. Therefore, we had to minimize our outside tours and avoid the sun. This was practically our last trip to Europe together, because after the return flight to Washington, Sa'id's back problems, like our last two trips to Europe, started, and he had again to be under treatment in America. However, thanks to David and Christine, this was a new, unique, and memorable experience for both of us while at the same time it was also a warning for Sa'id to reduce his air travel.

At the beginning of the twenty-first century, we were blessed to become grandparents again when Fred notified us of the good news of the birth of Sophia-Lily. On March 29, 2000, Sophia-Lily Khoroushi was born at 1:19 p.m., weighing seven pounds, thirteen and a half ounces, and nineteen and a half inches long. We raced to the Fairfax hospital to welcome her and congratulate Fred and Gita. We were happy that Cameron now had a lovely sister and would not be an only child.

Since 2000, I have turned most of my attention and time to face the challenges to my own health. Fortunately, with much recent progress in the medical field, and the care of family, friends and colleagues, I have survived and continue to work and write about this ongoing symphony to dedicate it to them and to my readers. When I moved to Northern Virginia, through former colleagues, friends and reunion, we were lucky to meet Dr. Sedigheh Feisee and chose her as our family physician.

I knew her mother from Iran, Mrs. Nazmi Ansari, as an active lady at the Women's Organization in Isfahan, when I was the secretary-general of the Women's Organization.[6] Dr. Feisee had been the most trusted and well-respected physician (internist) in Iran and the DC area in the USA. She studied in France and has two clinics near our home in Fairfax. She is a dedicated, knowledgeable, and experienced internist and has a teaching appointment at the Georgetown School of Medicine.

The birth of the author's second grandchild Sophia-Lily, who along with the first grandchild Cameron brought much joy to the author's family life.

After we moved to Northern Virginia, my migraine headaches from which I have been suffering most of my life intensified. This was perhaps due to the higher humidity and frequent changes of weather in this area in comparison to Central Virginia. Because of the frequency of these headaches, I participated in a clinical research team supported by NIH for migraine headaches, and I kept a diary of my headaches to find out whether they correlated with the storms and changes of weather in this area. For the treatment of my headache, there was a new medication in the form of a nasal spray called Imitrex. The nasal spray provided fast action relief. However, on August 8, 2000, when we had frequent thunderstorms, I had to use the nasal spray much more than normal, and it became an overdose. With no pain relief, I drank a lot of water, but the pain did not abate. I also felt sick in my stomach. We called 911 for an emergency hospital admission for the first time in my life, and

Dr. Seddigheh Feisee, the author's physician.

of course, we notified Dr. Feisee who fortunately was a member of the Fairfax Hospital. At the emergency section of the hospital, after waiting a long time for the registration and bureaucracy of admission procedure, I was transferred to a bedroom and connected to many tubes, and it was noticed how dangerously low the sodium level of my body was. It was well below the normal range, which is between 135-147. I have always been a little bit low in sodium and potassium due to the diuretic medication that I take for blood pressure control, but never was I so low as it was with this blood test. Immediately, I went through several x-rays scans. I was diagnosed first with severe headache, due to low sodium (hyponatremia), which might have several causes. My supportive physician Dr. Feisee asked several specialists, e.g., neurologist, infectious disease specialist, rheumatologist, and others to see me and each one ordered several tests to be sure of the correct diagnosis. Therefore, I went every day through many tests including an MRI, lumbar puncture, or spinal tab, carotid cerebral bilateral, several chest x-rays, etc. I was in the critical care section and every day, I had several doctors visiting and a full program of diverse tests, many of which ruled out several serious diseases like herpes encephalitis or meningitis. At the same time, due to the circulation of the news of my hospitalization among friends and relatives, I received lots of flowers and goodwill wishes. In addition, some of them insisted on coming to see me to express their good wishes. Many looked as though they had come to see me for the last time. Apparently, I looked so bad that many people had given up on me. I received many long-distance and international telephone calls in the hospital. However, I gradually became rehydrated, and my headache and my sodium level improved; and after about two weeks of hospitalization, I was discharged on August 21, 2000, thanks to good coordination and treatment by Dr. Sedigheh Feisee. In fact, after being discharged, the frequency of my headaches gradually reduced, and I continued my treatment as outpatient at Johns Hopkins. I am thankful to Dr. Carol M. Ziminski for treating my arthritis, and to Dr. Stephen Stephen C. Achuff for taking care of my hypertensive heart, which was beating abnormally fast. Thanks to their attention and care, my arthritis and blood pressure came under control.

The experience of my first hospitalization was a blessing in disguise since I learned many lessons relating to my treatment. The most important lesson was that since there is no correlation between salt and blood pressure, I no longer needed to be on a low-salt diet. The next lesson was about the harmful side effect of pain medications such as Tylenol on liver function. Also, my sickness and its difficulty in diagnosis was a wakeup call for me to work as much as possible on this book to fulfill my obligation to the next generations. As a result, I limited my consulting work, and with as much as my time and health permitted, I concentrated on the research and writing of this book.

On September 11, 2001, in the morning I went for a follow-up x-ray of my chest and lung.

As soon as I arrived home at about 9:40 a.m., we had a call from one of Sa'id's students. He said his school was closed, and he wondered if his music class was being held. I answered, "Why should we close his studios?' In response, he said, "Please turn on your TV, and you will see why." While I was speaking with him, I turned the television on and was shocked to see a plane crashing into the Pentagon. The TV report was about the four attacks and crashes of commercial planes—two into the Twin Towers of the Trade Center in New York, one into the Pentagon, and one in Pennsylvania. These attacks were the work of nineteen Arab Islamist terrorists linked with Al-Qaeda. My first thought was, "Thank God none of the nineteen terrorists were from Iran." The reporter said that all airports, schools, and public places were closing or had already closed. In a state of shock, I told the student if he did not want to attend his lesson, then he was excused and could rest with his family. I called my husband in his studio in Alexandria and told him about the attacks seen on the news. Shaken, he told me that if anyone called and did not want to come, he would be excused. However, if anyone came, he would be welcome and maybe he could reduce their fear and anxiety through music. As an educator, he would need to give this choice and chance to his students, and if they came, he would be available for them. So after that, we were glued to our seats to watch the stream of news. How these organized terrible attacks happened is still an open question, even after so many books, films, and studies. These attacks have affected the social, political, and economic life of the United States and the rest of the world tremendously, and the investigation of their root cause is still ongoing. Since then, we have been faced with *a unique kind of war, namely* the War on Terror. So after bitter experiences of *the unique revolution of Iran* in my former country, we now needed to adjust ourselves to *a different war* situation in our new country, although hopefully, nothing would be as dreadful as Iran's revolution.

In those critical days, we were waiting to receive our dearest friends David, Christine, and their daughter Anna from England to visit us on September 23, and we did not know if the airports would be open or if they would have to cancel their trip. They had booked their tickets in advance for Washington DC and Florida to spend their vacation partially with us, but many passengers had cancelled their trip out of fear. I called them the same day about the news and inquired about their intentions, but they knew already about the horrible attack and the closure of the airports. As usual, Christine had control of her emotions and said that they were not changing their plans, and if the airports opened, they would still travel. She said that they were accustomed to these types of terrorist attacks in London. So they kept their reservation and arrived on September 23, 2001. We went to the Dulles Airport to welcome them. We had never seen the Dulles airport so deserted and empty of people. They arrived from the customs very quickly looking very calm and collected, and since the plane was not full, they had the opportunity to sleep and rest using the empty seats. As usual, we had a wonderful time together. At that time, we heard the good news that their son Philip and his friend Kevin who were finishing law school in England were accepted as interns in the office of two US congressmen in the Capitol. However, the Capitol Building was closed for sometime due to security concerns, and they ended up spending more time in the office of Mark

Warner in Alexandria, who was a gubernatorial candidate from the State of Virginia. I am sure they both had a good experience and learned a lot about the political system of the United States.

Before leaving the United States, Christine and David kindly invited us to join them the following year to spend a week at the English sea side in a very nice house, which belonged to David's niece in Folkestone. During 2002, we were still suffering not only mentally and socially but also economically from the shock of September 11, 2001; and as a result, Sa'id needed to work over that summer. In addition, he was concerned for his back and feared a repeat of loss of ambulation similar to his last visit to Europe, so he declined their invitation, but suggested that I should accept, particularly as I always enjoyed visiting England. Health-wise that year, I was on a diet of 1,200 calories per day to lose weight and was feeling better, and after some time, the results of my checkup and blood test were excellent. My migraine headaches, hypertension, hypothyroidism, and arthritis were all well under control. I was also happy losing weight, and therefore, I accepted their invitation and spent nearly two weeks with them in Folkestone, Calais, and London. Before that, I visited our friend Dr. Sadegh and Shahin Massarrat in Germany for two days. Since I was traveling without my husband, I missed him a lot, but in general, I enjoyed the trip because I was visiting our longstanding dear friends. I was well rested and returned on August 22, in time to have my yearly mammogram test on August 26, which I could not schedule before the journey.

On August 26, I went to my appointment at 10:40 a.m., for a mammogram at the Fairfax Radiology Consultants. Afterward, I went shopping in an excellent mood. Three days later, I called about the results. I was surprised to hear, that for the first time, the results were incomplete, and I needed to go for further tests and that they had faxed the results to Dr. John Maddox, my gynecologist. I rushed to the doctor's office where I had been just before my trip and had had my yearly exam and checkup, the result of which was that everything was fine. I just had to have my mammogram after the trip. At the office, I received the copy of the result of my mammogram, and with shaking hands, I read that "a small mass has developed in the infer medial aspect of the right breast, when compared with the prior study from 08/15/01. The lesion is deep against the chest wall. The patient will be recalled for further characterization." So the assessment of my mammogram was incomplete, and was signed by Dr. R. J. Butch. I was feeling so well, and throughout my breast exams by my doctors and myself nothing was noticeable.

Since I had heard and read that some mammogram test results may be false, I became skeptical about the result, and I could not believe it. In an anxious and assertive mood, I asked to see Dr. Maddox immediately. With the help of the office personnel and his kind concern, I was able to see him quickly. He calmly told me that many times regular checkups could not detect the lesions when they were too small. Therefore, he always thought that a yearly mammogram was necessary. He ordered other tests, an ultrasound and possibly biopsy to verify the characteristic of the lesion. I became a little calmer and hurried home to call for another appointment and test. Still, I could not trust or believe my mammogram result, and I called the nearest university Breast Cancer Hospital, in Georgetown, to speak with the director of the radiology department, who, at that time, was Dr. Rebecca Zuurbier. She was kind enough to return my call promptly. After discussing concerns about the results of my mammogram, she gave me an immediate appointment for September 12.

In an uncertain and anxious mood, I counted the days and hours to the date of my appointment. On September 12, I arrived in Georgetown Medical Center at 1:30 p.m., half an hour before my appointment time. I was guided to the Lombardi section. I was familiar with the medical center because of my professional meetings, but I noticed a lot of changes and unusual traffic everywhere. In the elevator, I heard that several prominent surgeons and physicians were leaving Georgetown because of the medical center transfer to a managed care company. So the center had a transitional atmosphere. Finally, I registered and waited impatiently for my turn, until I was called to the office of Dr. Zuurbieh. I first thanked her for seeing me so quickly and placed all my mammogram files in front of her. I told her that neither my doctors nor I had not felt a lesion and that I was hoping maybe my mammogram was not read correctly and that it was a mistake. She was very charming and, after seeing the picture, guided me to the ultrasound room and showed me the suspicious area on my right breast. After the test was finished, she directed me to her office to wait for the result. While waiting in her office, my heart was racing. She came into her office and told me that she thought that the finding of the sonogram was consistent with the mammogram and that she was highly suspicious it was malignant. Putting her hand on my shoulder, she kindly assured me that I was not going to die because of that small lesion of five to six millimeter, and when I died, it would most likely be from other causes. She added that I needed to consult with a surgeon for a surgical evaluation as soon as possible. She added that she would be glad to perform an ultrasound-guided core breast biopsy as needed to facilitate the diagnosis for the surgical consultation, and even if she were not there, she would be able to do it in the Sibley Hospital, where she was going to be the director of the Breast Center. So she too was leaving Georgetown. I asked her for recommendations for surgeons. She mentioned a few names, including the name of Dr. Theodore Tsangaris whose name I knew due to his expertise in breast surgery, but she also mentioned that Dr. Tsangaris had recently left Georgetown and moved to Johns Hopkins Hospital. It looked as though the rumor was true that many good physicians were leaving Georgetown due to the new managed care changes.

With the cancer diagnosis, I faced another shock and more uncertainty. Who was going to do my surgery? It looked like everybody that I knew was in a state of transition. I thanked Dr. Zuurbieh for the advice, and she said it was better that I first choose the surgeon and then have the biopsy where the surgeon was working. I left Georgetown anxious and confused, driving home slowly to think what I should do and how I should tell the news to my family, especially my husband who himself has been fighting skin cancer for some time and is scared to hear the term *cancer*. So I started by telling my daughter, Gita, who needed to know because of the genetic aspect of the disease and also because she usually reacted wisely. While I was disturbed and agitated, I explained to her that I had the yearly mammogram as I have done every year, but this year they found a small lesion about five to six millimeters in my right breast, for which I needed to follow up with a surgeon. Since Johns Hopkins had helped my husband in the treatment of his skin cancer and had prevented him losing his hand, I told her that I might approach their breast center and the new director Dr. Tsangaris who had moved recently from Georgetown to Johns Hopkins. She was first surprised and then concurred with me. Then I told my husband in a casual way that I have a small lesion similar to his but with the difference that my lesion was in my breast and not external, and I was thinking, like him, to go to Johns Hopkins for surgery. He was first quiet or maybe too shocked to comprehend what I told him and asked me to explain what I meant. I told him I might have a case like Diane, our neighbor, who had courageously informed the neighbors about her breast cancer a few years ago before. We were all amazed to observe how openly she talked about her cancer to everybody in our neighborhood without any reservation. This showed too the cultural differences between my new and old country. As I described in previous chapters, one factor in the revolution of Iran was the cancer the Shah had that nobody, not even his physician had told him about. At that time, the people of Iran would not have spoken about cancer openly. Anyway, my husband finally took on board what I was telling him and slowly understood that I might have cancer. My son heard the bad news from my daughter. After telling my family, I called Johns Hopkins and a few surgeons in Georgetown and northern Virginia who had been recommended. I felt the urge to clarify the diagnosis as soon as possible. Fortunately, I received the first response from Johns Hopkins to have an appointment with Dr. Theodore Tsangaris, on Monday, September 24 at 9:00 a.m. I thought the earlier I clarified my situation, the better, for my physical and mental well-being, especially since Dr. Ted Tsangaris had established an excellent reputation in breast surgery like his father. Also, my cardiologist Dr. Steffen Achuff was at the cardiology department of Johns Hopkins if his presence was needed during surgery.

On September 24, 2002, my daughter volunteered to come with me to my Johns Hopkins appointment. Due to the revolution and other adversities in my life, I have missed out on being with her enough and I always look forward to being with her. So she was kind enough to come at 7:00 a.m. to pick me up. Her presence was definitely reducing my anxiety as I was uncertain of what was going to happen. On the way to the hospital, I talked, and she simply listened. I told her how I was surprised to have cancer especially because no one in our family had had cancer, although the recent research had shown that stress was one possible factor that weakened the immune system, leaving our bodies defenseless against cancer. Of course, we had plenty of stress in our rocky life. As she listened, I explored my feelings and mused on what was again shattering my life. We arrived half an hour ahead of time. In the hall, several women, some with hats or scarves covering their heads were sitting and waiting. We registered and sat next to them. I told myself that maybe I also needed to look for a hat and in a way I was mentally preparing myself for the cancer treatment and loss of hair.

We did not have to wait long before I was called in to the clinic. First, I met a nurse with a questionnaire about my health. One of the first questions was if my parents or my relatives had had breast cancer to which I replied no and told her I wondered why I did. She responded that more than 75 percent of breast cancer cases were not genetically related, and in the USA, one out of every eight women had breast cancer. we discussed that the number in England was one in every nine women, and in some countries, in Asia, the ratio was one in every twelve. So it looked like the environment and other factors in life like stress might have caused cancer too. Hopefully, future research would clarify and show the road to prevention because the progress in the methods of treatment was already more promising. After a few minutes, Dr. Tsangaris entered and, in a charming manner, reviewed my mammogram, read the result of the ultrasound, and examined me. Despite being a competent breast surgeon, and according to his own clinical notes, he was not able to detect any mass, tenderness, discharge, and maxillary adenopathy on either side. So he immediately ordered an ultrasound guided core biopsy, and fortunately, there was one slot available at the department of radiology and the cardiovascular diagnostic laboratory. And after one hour, I was able to have the biopsy. It was fortunate that I had my daughter with me because it was essential to have someone with the patient for this test so that they could drive back home after the use of the anesthetic medication. In a way, I was happy that in my situation, I was going to have a quick clarification of my hidden lump and cancer, which had not shown up in a regular checkup. Although this was the least-invasive exam, it was very painful for me. Under ultrasound guidance and anesthesia, according to the clinical notes: "Five passes were made into the 7×7 mm hypo echoic mass in the lower right breast 5 cm away from nipple. Needle position was optimal. Specimens obtained were sent for surgical pathologic evaluation." I was sorry for Gita that she had to witness my suffering while she was standing in the hall of the examination area. After this painful test, my daughter called her home to check on her children Cameron and Sophia, their nanny, and my husband, letting them know that she was on her way home. I was exhausted, tired, drowsy, and sleepy when Gita drove me; and as soon as we arrived home, I went straight to bed.

I had to wait at least two days for the results of the pathologist. During this unbearable waiting period, I busied myself with reading about cancer in general, breast cancer and different methods of treatment. I wanted to be educated in this field and to know the latest research and their results, which were overwhelming and promising. On September 26, early morning, I called to hear about the histopathology results of my right breast biopsy. With my heart pounding, I waited beside the phone while the secretary of the radiology department was looking for the results. These revealed infiltrating mammary cells with predominantly lobular feature. This corroborated the first imaging findings and recommended surgical consultation. So now that I was sure that I was facing another adversity, I needed to start to fight with that in mind as soon as possible because cancer cells are different from the normal cells and continue to grow and divide instead of dying off like normal cells do. Cancer cells travel to other parts of the body, where they begin to grow and replace normal tissues and cause metastasis. As a result, I needed to get rid of the cancer as soon as possible. I immediately called Dr. Tsangaris' office and arranged with his senior clinical office coordinator Mrs. Joan Woodall to have an appointment for presurgery and surgery with him as soon as possible. She said she was sorry, but he was booked up for three months, and if I were in a rush, I could choose another surgeon. I definitely did not want another surgeon, so I took the appointment and requested that she inform me of any cancellation. She kindly promised to do so. Again, I tried to adjust myself to wait out this horrible time until I could get rid of this hidden cancer in my body. In my professional experience, when I had patients in similar cases like myself, I recommended that they write their feelings to help deal with their anxiety and the healing process. So I thought again I had to continue my autobiography. I was in the middle of chapter four when I was interrupted with the horrible news that I had cancer, and it occurred to me that I might not have much time to finish the book. So I planned to continue writing my book and do research about my cancer, the recent treatment methods, searching to choose an oncologist and fulfill obligations in my daily life and to my family. I arranged a busy program for myself so that I wouldn't notice the passage of time for the coming weeks. However, as soon as had I organized a program for the coming weeks, Joan Woodall called on a Friday, "Dr. Redjali, I just had a cancellation for next week. This is short notice, but do you think you can come on Monday morning for presurgery procedures and tests?" She suggested that she would arrange a telephone conference call with Dr. Tsangaris with the results, and presurgery consultation on the following, Wednesday, October 2, instead of an office visit so that way he could operate on me on Thursday, October 3, early morning at 6:30 a.m. I was very surprised, shocked, and at the same time happy. I said, "Yes, of course I can," and thanked her for remembering my request. That weekend, everybody in my family was excited, supportive, and happy that the surgery was scheduled for the following week. Since my husband was teaching, my son volunteered to take me that early Monday morning for preoperative tests, and my daughter volunteered to be with me for Thursday, October 3, the surgery day. I am grateful to all of them.

My preoperation exams went very well; then when I returned home, I prepared myself to speak about my surgery with Dr. Tsangaris. I read a lot about the different kinds of surgical procedures and their differences. I am very thankful to the American Cancer Society for all the materials and publications that they sent me and the Internet sites they referred me to. As a result, I found out that I actually preferred to have the radical mastectomy that for years was the standard treatment for breast cancer. I wanted to have peace of my mind and be free from further cancer development or recurrence, especially after two of my close friends had, within the last twenty years had a mastectomy and were feeling well and free of recurrence. Although the recent studies were showing that for stage I, the survival rate of lumpectomy surgery or breast conserving surgery with radiation and chemotherapy was equal to the traditional mastectomy surgery, I wondered which one my surgeon would choose for my case. This was also going to be my first major surgery.

While I was thinking and reading about surgery, Joan Woodall called me on Wednesday and put me through to Dr. Tsangaris for a telephone conference the day before my surgery. He firmly told me that he would conduct a lumpectomy with a needle-guided localization since my lump was small and not palpable. When I asked him why not mastectomy, which I preferred, he again very firmly said that in my case, he thought it was better to perform only a lumpectomy and that professionally and ethically, it was not possible for him to conduct a mastectomy on me. This left me in a conflict whether or not to go for surgery the next day or look for another surgeon to have a mastectomy or to have a lumpectomy and then, in case of recurrence, to go for a mastectomy. In any case, it looked wiser to take the cancerous lump out of my body as soon as possible and not to lose this important opportunity to be in a good hospital with a competent and well-known surgeon. In fact, I liked his professionalism and firm attitude as a surgeon. Of course, my education and information about the recent research result in connection with lumpectomy also helped me reach a quick decision. So I thanked Dr. Tsangaris and said I would see him the next morning in the hope that I would not need to have any further surgery or a mastectomy in the future.

On Wednesday evening, my daughter, Gita, was kind enough to stay overnight at our home so as to be ready to drive me the next morning. My appointment was at 6:30 a.m. in the lower level of the outpatient center; the surgery department. On Thursday, October 3, we got up at 4:00 a.m. to get ready, and we left our home at 5:00 a.m. At this early morning hour, there was not much traffic on drive to Baltimore, and we arrived early and had to wait for the surgery department to open. Gradually, few other patients joined us, until the staff arrived one after another. Then I was registered and admitted to the room to be prepared for surgery. My daughter was given a phone number to be called during the surgery, or after, if it was needed. After getting ready for a needle-guided lumpectomy, I was taken in a wheelchair to the radiology department, the same place that I had my painful biopsy a week earlier. After a local anesthetic, the radiologist used first an ultrasound to guide a needle into the area of concern and then placed a wire in my breast to help pinpoint the specific area to be removed. The wire was then covered with a dressing to hold it in place. They then returned me to the lower level near to the operating room, where I received a needle in my arm to make me sleep during the surgery procedure. First, the nurses tried my left arm but could not find my vein. Next, they tried my right arm, and this time were successful. As I was getting ready for surgery, Dr. Tsangaris dressed, in his scrubs, came to check me with all the needle locations in my right arm. He was not happy with the use of my right arms for the needle since my surgery was going to be conducted on my right breast, and he wanted my right side to be free for the surgery. Therefore, he said to the head nurse that she needed to change the needle location to my left arm. When she said, they tried; it was not possible, he commanded and stated very firmly that they needed to try again, and he was not going to conduct my surgery in that position. So again, they needed to change the location of the IV. This was not an easy task, but after many attempts, the head nurse finally succeeded, and everything was ready for the anesthetic medication. Although I felt very cold in the surgery room, I eventually went to sleep while I was watching Dr. Tsangaris and several assistants. Usually, the surgeon uses a wire as a guide to locate the lump precisely and, through an incision, removes the abnormal tissues and its surroundings, along with the wire. When the surgery was complete, I was taken to the post-anesthetic care unit or recovery unit. I was told the operation would last about three hours. They then called my daughter to come and see me, and we waited together for Dr. Tsangaris who came to see us. He told me that I could go home and prescribed some pain tablets if I needed them and told us that he had done his best with the margin, and we needed to wait for the results of the pathologists. He also suggested that I choose an oncologist and a radiation oncologist for follow-up treatment and that he would see me at our postsurgery appointment. About 3:30 p.m., my daughter was asked to bring her car to the front door of the hospital, and one of the nurse assistants helped me dress and took me in the wheelchair to the car. I was tired, drowsy, and felt heavy headed; and in the car, I went to sleep while my daughter drove me home. My husband, who had been in constant contact with my daughter even during his teaching, was waiting impatiently for our arrival and had a light meal ready for me on the table. We arrived home at 5:00 p.m. right in the middle of rush hour. Gita, who was worried about her children and their nanny, left immediately to go home, and I ate a small portion of the meal, took my pain tablets, and went straight to bed. The healing was bearable, and its pain was less than my migraine headaches. I also was very careful with the wound, and fortunately, I did not develop any infection. I also researched my choice of oncologist and chose Dr. John Fetting who was also an internist.

On October 17, I went for my postsurgery appointment. Dr. Tsangaris was satisfied with the healing process of the surgery, and the results of pathology were promising too. He explained my pathology results in a seven-page report, which fortunately indicated that my right two sentinel 1 lymph nodes showed negative for tumor, but the tumor of my right breast was "infiltrating mammary and in Situ Ductal Carcinoma with size of 0.9 cm microscopically," which had so quickly increased from 0.7 after the biopsy a few days before. It was an Elston grade III lesion, vascular invasion was identified, ER and PR positive, HER 2 was negative. As a result, he told me that I would benefit from additional adjuvant therapy cancer treatment given after the primary treatment to lower the risk of cancer coming back. He referred me to Dr. John Fetting at John Hopkins and Dr. Susan Pierce at Fairfax hospital near our home for oncology and radiation oncology, respectively. So my postoperative course had been uneventful at the beginning.

I immediately made an appointment with Drs. Fetting and Pierce for the end of October. As usual, I started to study about my follow-up treatment in view of the pathology report and my own physical condition to learn more about the different treatment methods, used in adjuvant therapy, any medications they might use, and their side effects and try to understand better which one might be more beneficial in my case. I always believed that patients, especially in the United States with its legal system for the clinical profession, should be well informed about their condition and the different courses of treatment available to them and their side effects before seeing any physician to be able to better participate in the decision-making process regarding their treatment.

On October 29, I went to see Dr. Fetting at Johns Hopkins. I also prepared copies of my recent tests and clinical notes on my health history. However, I did not need to use them since most of my clinical notes were in the Johns Hopkins' computer system, and any physician had access to all of them. This is an excellent system, and I noticed straightaway that Dr. Fetting already knew about my health history and even knew about visits or tests that were not done at Johns Hopkins, due to the excellent coordination of my own physician Dr. Carol Ziminiski from the rheumatology division in her clinical notes. As a result, after a few questions about my health, he examined me thoroughly and mentioned that the incision of my breast was nicely healed. He then showed me the statistics on the results of research for the treatment of breast cancer, which I had already studied and concluded that I needed to have a seven-week radiation therapy course. For this first stage of cancer treatment, he recommended adjuvant hormonal therapy, which was estimated to reduce the risk of recurrence of cancer from 18 percent to about 12 percent. He said that chemotherapy would only add two more points, and that he believed that its benefit was too small to warrant risk of its side effects. Therefore, he recommended that hormonal therapy alone would be potentially more helpful (for me). In regard to the hormonal therapy, since I was already taking raloxifene hydrochloride (Evista), which was similar to Tamaxifen, which might have made my lesion resistant to the medication, he suggested Arimidex, which would be a good alternative for postmenopausal women like me. Since I had read about a five-year study of the efficacy and safety data in the primary adjuvant therapy after surgery for postmenopausal women with hormone receptor-positive, I agreed with his suggestion, especially because I thought the side effects of Arimidex for me would be less harmful than the side effects of the alternative medication, particularly those related to the risk of blood clots. Of course, these side effects vary in each individual; for example, for me, the main side effect of taking Arimidex was joint pain, weight gain, and hot flashes and the disappearance of migraine headaches, from which I had suffered all my life. Dr. Fetting also recommended that my medical oncologist be a local doctor and, therefore, referred me to Dr. Nickolas Robert near my home and my radiation therapist at Fairfax Hospital.

After this visit, I saw Dr. Susan Pierce at the Fairfax Hospital radiation therapy center. She first made a physical exam, reviewed my medical history, and then scheduled my treatment plan. First, I started with the *stimulation* process. I was asked to lie still on an examination table while she and her assistants used a special x-ray machine to define my treatment field or areas, which is the exact place on my body where in my right breast the radiation would be aimed and marked the treatment areas on my skin with tattoos or a tiny dots of colored permanent ink. It is very important that the radiation be targeted at the same affected area each time to kill any remaining cancer cells. This process took about one hour. Then after a team meeting with the radiation physicist and the dosimetrist and a review of the result of my x-rays and my lab tests, she decided on the dose of radiation and the particular machine to be used. I had to attend these sessions for seven weeks, five days a week, except weekends, which allowed normal cells to recover. In the treatment room, the radiation therapist used the marks on my skin to locate the treatment area and position me correctly on a table. I was covered with a special shield to protect my healthy tissues and organs. So every day, at a certain time, I would spend fifteen to thirteen minutes depending on the schedule in the treatment room, but I was getting radiation for only about two to three minutes. The machine was noisy, we were watched from the control room, but the treatment session was not painful. However, my doctor was monitoring me weekly because of my sensitive and dry skin, which needed close watching during treatment as sometimes I had a side affect similar to that of sunburn, which with a special cream was healed. So I was quite busy with this daily program during the month of November and December of 2002.

I also had my appointment with my medical oncologist Dr. Robert and started my hormonal therapy with Arimidex. I must confess that the whole experience was overwhelming. There was fear, anxiety, and once again uncertainty in my life, but my education once again helped me to overcome these obstacles—this time as a psychologist and also as a writer. As a psychologist, I had always recommended to my patients who were dealing with cancer to write. Writing this memoir and also meeting with friends who were cancer survivors like Soheila and Martha gave me the courage to continue my research and writing and were of great help to me. Especially as I kept thinking about the recurrence of cancer, I thought I had better write and finish my obligation to the next generations, and this I found was the best tool to fight my cancer even as I was adjusting to the reaction of skin rashes and burns and the side effects from the oral chemo Arimidex. I experienced all the side effects—weight gain, dry mouth, sore mouth and throat, dental and gum problems, nausea, lactose intolerance, constipation, joint pain, fatigue, and water retention or edema. Since then I have been trying hard through dieting and following the advice of the nutritionist to cope with the side effects.

While I was gradually adjusting my life in handling the breast cancer and its side effects, participating in a support group at Fairfax Hospital in the program life with cancer and my writing had again started to progress, in January 2003, I noticed the presence of a new small lesion on my left thigh, which was growing but was not painful. I began to worry that I had a *second cancer*. First, I went to see my family physician. She said I should not worry since the lesion didn't look cancerous, but I needed to keep an eye on it. Then after I noticed that the lesion was growing, I went to my dermatologist at Johns Hopkins. He too, after examination, said he didn't think that was a cancerous lesion, and I should not worry. However, I asked him to take a sample to send for pathology. Again, in an uncertain mood, I left the hospital. To fight this new anxiety and uncertainly, I continued writing my memoir while counting the days.

Finally, after ten days, as I had not heard from my dermatologist, I called him for the result. He said that he was planning to call me about the pathology report, which showed that the lesion was a squamous cell carcinoma, which had extended to the deep margin, and I needed to find a surgeon. When I asked him for a recommendation, he mentioned a name at his department, saying that his schedule might be full for some time. I was shocked and surprised because a squamous cell carcinoma is usually the result of a long-term sun exposure and the damage to the skin, a condition that I did not meet as I never in my life exposed myself to sunshine. The other possibility I thought might have been that I was exposed to radiation during radiation therapy for my breast cancer, but this seemed unlikely since my thigh was covered and protected during all my radiation therapy.

Anyway, no matter what the cause, I knew from my own research that squamous cell carcinoma was an aggressive cancer, enlarged slowly and steadily and could invade the neighboring tissues, and spread to distant parts and organs of the body (metastasize) if not treated early. I had to act quickly, especially since the location of the lesion in my left thigh was very near to the vulva, womb, or uterus and other organs. So first I called the surgeon that my dermatologist mentioned and received an appointment in three months' time. I took that appointment, but started the search for a specialist surgeon to fight this new adversary. Most of my physicians were also surprised to see that I had developed squamous cell carcinoma and wanted me to remove this lesion as soon as possible. Because of the location of the lesion, I consulted with my gynecologist Dr. Maddox in the hope that I could have surgery with him. While he also was amazed and surprised, he said that he was not doing that type surgery, and I needed to see a gynecology oncology pelvic surgeon. He referred me to two surgeons. One, in Northern Virginia, and one, at Johns Hopkins Hospital, the Kelly Gynecology Oncology Service. I immediately made appointments with both of them for a consultation. First, I saw a doctor in Northern Virginia near my home on April 11, 2003. After the examination and reviewing the pathology report and its slide, he advised me that I should undergo a wide local excision, which might be done under local anesthesia in his office. The scar tissue should be excised with a margin of 1.5-2.0 centimeter in each direction. If residual invasive carcinoma were found again at that time, it might then be necessary to perform a lymphadenectomy and additional biopsies and surgery under anesthesia in the hospital.

After this evaluation and visit on April 17, I went to see Dr. Robert Edward Bristow at Johns Hopkins. He examined the file, most of which was on the computer system of Johns Hopkins. Then as a breast cancer victim and considering the risk factor, he first ordered for me on the same day a pelvic ultrasound to better assess the uterus and adnexa and an abdominal and pelvic CT to check for any intra abdominal or pelvic mass, as well as lymphadenopathy. He mentioned that he would perform two surgeries. The first procedure would be to take several biopsies around the lesion to clarify the extent of the cancer in the area for surgery, and the second surgery, would require a radical cut of the affected area. He gave me the name and telephone number of the surgical coordinator, who was to call me to set up appointments for the preoperative tests. I finished most of those tests on that day and returned home.

On the way back, I was thinking about the two surgeons and their different methodologies It seemed to me that the procedure and method of surgery of Dr. Bristow was just the opposite of the other method and the difference between the two methods was quite significant. So I began to consider which method was more suitable for me. I had several questions. I wanted to know which method was going to be better for me long term. With one method, I had to go through two surgeries under anesthesia. With the other, I would do one procedure under local anesthesia in the doctor's office and perhaps not need a second procedure under full anesthesia. The next day, I receive the call for the preoperative and first surgery appointments on May 7, 2003. I made another appointment to see Dr. Bristow to ask my questions about the surgery. Initially, however, when I went to Johns Hopkins, he was not available, and I saw his colleague Dr. Taylor. I asked her several questions, which she could not answer, and she referred me back to him and gave me his e-mail address, saying that he would call me too. So after finishing my presurgery tests, I returned home with a number of unanswered questions while I was waiting eagerly for Dr Bristow's call. The next day, I sent an e-mail to Dr. Bristow, and I wrote, "*that I had questions to ask of him*" I wanted to be sure who was conducting my surgery and to ask him if he would consider proceeding as the other doctor had recommended.

He replied directly by email and provided me with justification why he suggested proceeding with two surgeries. He wanted to know first the extent of the cancer to be sure of the margin and prevent further surgeries.

The difference between the two methods of surgery of the two surgeons was so wide that I consulted with my oncologist to make the final decision. In the meantime, as I was nearing my first appointment with the surgeon that my dermatologist had earlier recommended, I told him that because he had not had an opening for me, I had consulted two other surgeons and was now in a dilemma over which of two courses of treatment to pursue. He and my oncologist both recommended that for the long term and to have more peace of mind of the fear and anxiety of recurrence, Dr. Bristow's procedure was the preferred one. As a result, I had to go through all the procedures twice. First, on May 7, I went for the several biopsies, and then after the pathology report, on May 19, I went through a wide radical excision of the left posterior vulva operation for the clinical stage I squamous cell carcinoma of the vulva. Both times my daughter, Gita, volunteered to drive me and be with me and waited patiently and kindly with me all the time. The surgery procedure went well except I had an allergic reaction to the ointment, which was applied to the incision site and had to change the ointment several times. This delayed my healing compared with my breast cancer surgery. My sensation of irritation and pruritus became worse even with changing the creams and ointment until I consulted two dermatologists, and finally, one of them introduced a new cream called Elidel, which, for the first time, relieved the burning and pain. Then I threw away almost three thousand dollars worth of creams and continued with Elidel. During these months, I missed attending my breast cancer group meeting, but reunion with our friends and families and writing this autobiography has been a great support for me. Finally, after nearly three months, I felt better again and could sit and walk. In this journey of my life, this is one part I would have much rather skipped, but I had no choice in having two forms of cancer. This was not my choice. Usually, cancer chooses and unfortunately, cancer chose me, and this is worrisome. Anxiety will be part of your life if you have cancer. However, I had a choice as to how to fight my cancer. I tried to revise my diet and exercise pattern according to the nutritionist, American Institute for Cancer Research, American Cancer Society, rehab specialist, and also improve my information and education on cancer. As I always suggested to my clients to write about their pain, experiences, to help them be survivors, so it was I took my own advice and continued to write my symphony of life in addition to gather for reunions with friends and relatives, this continuously helped me to be connected with their support and in turn become a survivor. There is an excellent book that I recommend to everyone who has had cancer—*After Cancer Treatment*, by Dr. Julie K. Silver, who is herself a cancer survivor.

In the meantime, in the middle of my battle with cancer, we received a kind invitation from our dear friend Christine in London to go to London and join her for a week on a cruise to Norway's fjords. She had always a deep understanding during my life whenever I faced adversity. She was thinking, after so many months of suffering from two cancers, it would be beneficial for us to accept her advice, and it would be a good peaceful change for me. I discussed the suggestion with my husband, who, because of his work and his back, could not travel, and he immediately said it was a wonderful idea and that I should accept the invitation. So in the last weeks of August, I went to London and joined Christine for the cruise to Norway. Before that, I had a the opportunity to join Christine and David to visit the garden and flower show at Mottingham and to meet with our dear friends Soheila and her mother Nazi. They were kind enough to drive all the way from the west side of England, through central London to the south east where I was staying. I was appreciative of their visit, as always, as they had brought some herbal drops to boost my immune system against virus and bacteria. Soheila, who studied herbal products, was always offering me kindly advice. I was happy too that they got to know two of our old and dear friends, Christine and David.

The idea of a cruise to visit West Norway was just what I needed, as it was one of the few areas that I had not seen in Europe, and I had always wanted to visit this area. David was still working and could not join us. Christine chose a family-owned Fred Olsen Cruise, with the Black Watch ship, to visit Bergen and fjords in west Norway. David drove us to Dover to join the ship. The weather was beautiful or the whole trip with unique scenery of mountains and fjords. One of our main stops was Bergen, located on the southwestern coast of Norway, in the county of Hordaland, in between a group of mountains known as De syv fjell ("the Seven Mountains"). Unofficially, Bergen is considered the capital of this region of West Norway, and also recognized as the gateway city to the world famous fjords of Norway. We visited the old part of the city and its old wooden houses from the eighth century, and then stopped at the popular tourist attraction of the open-air food and fish market on the harbor and tried smoked salmon and prawns. Further, we found the main shopping area that was rebuilt after a fire in 1916. As the cruise continued, we also saw several villages and farms near the fjord like the Geirangerfjord and the Nærøyfjord's area. After experiencing my three painful cancer surgeries, I found this trip very peaceful and relaxing, and it soothed my anxiety level.

The author visiting with her friend Christine Linton on a holiday to Norway.

During this peaceful trip, I kept thinking that due to the recent battle with cancer, I needed to plan a new normal life and revise my lifestyle. When I returned home, I tried to plan a short-term and a long-term goal for myself. Since I had had experience in helping others in similar situations, I knew that nobody else could help me do this. I was thinking that I did not have much time left, and time alone could not be a healer for me, as I was a fighter and an impatient person. At present, all the cancer treatment from surgery to radiation and chemotherapy involve cancer cells as well as healthy ones, but in the future, there is hope that the treatment will affect only the cancer cells. Also, many studies suggest that by boosting the immune system, which consists of certain types of cells, this could help to reduce the risk of cancer and its recurrence. Several factors could play a role in fostering the immune system, which I have tried to consider as much as possible in my short—and long-term plan for my healing process: I have tried to include more vegetables and fruit in my diet, to have a daily meditation session and exercise on my stationary bike, and stretch according to the recommendation of my physiotherapist, especially since my oral chemo (Arimidex) has caused me serious joint and muscle pain. I cannot take pain relievers, and the only way that I could fight with my pain was exercise. I also tried to have regular sleep and to keep in touch with several professional associations, support groups and family, colleagues, and friends. To reduce my stress and anxiety of recurrence, I was continuing to finish my historical autobiography. So in this way, I have fought these two cancers. My daily schedule was full, and as a result, I reduced my consulting services hours and added my volunteer services to support programs.

In addition, I help my husband by doing the administrative work for his music studios. Fortunately, his method of teaching has been quite successful, and he has been very busy and has had a waiting list to take on new students. Many of his students have continued music as a major or minor in the colleges and universities. Every Christmas, Thanksgiving, or New Year we are happy to hear from his former students' successful life history and the thank-you notes from them about what they learned from him and hearing about their lives have all been a rewarding testimonial for us. Every year, he arranges a home concert for his students and their immediate relatives to attend and observe the yearly result of their progress. To see the results of working and learning is an important factor of motivation as part of the learning process, and his students have always worked hard for the home concert. In fact, the reputation of his home concerts led him to have interviews with several newspapers.[7] When the Voice of America showed video footage of his home concert, this attracted some of his former student in Tehran. They were happy to find him and to learn that he was still active. They contacted us, and some of them wrote and sent their books or articles about his activities in Iran.[8] One of them, even on the cover of his book, had thanked Dr. Khadiri as the pioneer of music education in Iran and credited him for being the first to implement the Karl Orff method in Iran. We were happy to see that, after twenty-five years, he was not forgotten in Iran. We received several similar calls from Iran from his former students. It is amazing how education both in learning or teaching has helped us in all our life.

All the while, Iran was in the news, and this time, about its nuclear program. This news focused on its uranium enrichment and on its plutonium, both of which could be used for civilian uses and for nuclear weapon development. In any case, the sites of this work were spread around the country to avoid the risk of attack and detection. Because of Iran's work in this area, many meetings are held in Europe and many countries to ask Iran to give up this work in the nuclear area. If Iran acquired atomic bombs, other Arab countries in the Middle East like Saudi Arabia and Egypt would pursue their own nuclear options and this would lead to a nuclear arms race in the region. All these meetings and discussions have been ongoing for many years, with Iran never giving a definite answer. Even with the UN sanctions, Iran has continued to claim that the country has pursued only a civilian program, although the International Atomic Energy Agency (IAEA) has never confirmed that claim. The head of the IAEA, Mohamed El Baradei mentioned many times in the news, said that his "gut feeling" was that Iran was seeking the ability to produce nuclear arms, if it desired, as an "insurance policy" against perceived threats either from outside or even from the inside through the democracy movement of the people of Iran.

This issue has become an international problem and the cause of fear and anxiety for the people of Iran, linked with the fear of possible attacks on nuclear facilities by the USA or Israel if the diplomatic talks, discussions, and meetings were are not successful. It is also necessary to mention that it looked as though the West could not understand the technique of dissimulation (*taghieh*) that Khomeini himself used and recommended to be used for Islam's cause to advance. This, as a technique, is referenced in chapter 14, a technique that encourages duality of purpose and action. As a result, all these talks and meetings with the West have not been successful in stopping Iran from pursuing the nuclear program, and always, the Iranian delegation can drag the talks out for years until probably the atom bomb would be made.

In the middle of April 2005, I had a call from Christine in response to my frequent invitation, that she was finally planning to visit us in the USA. This time, we decided to visit some place that neither one of us had seen in our life. By chance, we noticed that both of us had not seen Las Vegas, a most popular city and known as the entertainment capital of the world, or as the Sin City, where many people from around the world visit for any occasion. It looked as though we were among the few people who had not had any time or interest in visiting Las Vegas during our extensive travels around the world—maybe because neither one of us was interested in gambling. So during Christine's ten-day visit, we spent four days in Las Vegas, which surprised us with of the variety of unique entertainment and interesting sightseeing for everyone—and nothing to do with gambling. We stayed at the Mirage Hotel with its Volcano eruption show, visited the Conservatory at the Bellagio, and had dinner in the Paris hotel while watching the 220-foot-high fountains at the Bellagio hotel, which were orchestrated with music for public presentation. It was a unique experience. The show of circus alley and the magic show and the modern arts exhibition were also wonderful experiences. On our tour of Las Vegas, we visited again via imitation of practically all the interesting places in Europe and the world, such as Venice, but in a smaller yet beautiful scale. We enjoyed this tour by remembering the original places and their beauties. We thought Las Vegas was interesting and worthwhile to visit once. However, we did not think we would repeat this trip again. We returned from Las Vegas just in time for the celebration of my husband Sa'id's birthday. During this trip, Christine shared with me the good news that her daughter Anna was engaged and was preparing for her wedding. She was concerned because the groom, like Anna, had just graduated from Oxford, and he had been offered a job in Birmingham and Anna was offered a job in London, both as university professors but in different locations. As usual, we enjoyed having Christine with us. After she left, I had follow-up tests for my cancers, and since I had a good result, we became very busy for the preparation of Sa'id's home concerts—on May 1 for adults, and May 15 for children, young adults and adults. These home concerts had become an important event for him and his students, and this year, all his students played exceptionally well, and the parents were pleased. He was applauded many times and received thank-you notes and calls for the next days. Another year with two successful home concerts, which brought happiness and satisfaction to his students, their families, and to us.

---

1. Rhein Neckar Zeitung, Heidelberger Nachrichten, Nr.186, p. 5, Dienstag 13 August 1996.

2. Hemann Roehrs, Gesamelte Schriften, Band 11, Erinnerungen und Erfahrungen- Perspektiven fuer die Zukunft, Deutschen Studien Verlag, Weinheim 1997, pp. 541, 559, 518.

3. Details were provided in the special issue of the *Journal of Medical Care* devoted to these studies. See five articles in *Medical Care,* October, 199; Volume 34, Number 10 Supplement.

4. Alemi F. "Management matters: technology succeeds when management innovates," Front Health Serv Management, Fall 2000, 7(1):17-30.

5. Jean Archart- Treichel: *State's MH Inspector General; Watchdog, Detective, Psychiatrist, Psychiatric News,* American Psychiatry Association, May 2, 2003, Volume 38 Number 9, 2003.

6. See the interview with Mrs. Ansari

7. Vida Ghaffari, *Banned In Iran, Flourishes in D.C.* Iran Times, Vol. XXXVII, No.32. Friday, October 24,1997, and A. Lotfalian, *Dr.Sa'id Khadiri as Music Educator, Pianist and Composer,* Persian Heritage, vol.5 No. 20, 2000.

8. Azarsina, Mehdi. Two volume work on Karl Orff, written in Persian.

CHAPTER 19

An Ongoing Symphony
On the Road to Healing, Change,
Freedom, and Democracy
2005-2011

In the symphony of my life, the most—recent times have been an unfolding saga of personal healing, and unprecedented change for more freedom and democracy in both Iran and my adopted country, America. However, on all fronts, the roads have been fraught with many unpleasant and unexpected obstacles—just as the human body is prone to ravages and pestilence of diseases such as cancer, so it is with the nation's body politics.

Photo of the author taken during the final chapter of the book.

On the cancer healing front, I have kept myself informed of the latest promising cancer research results by attending workshops and support groups and by reading books and other available information media while faithfully following all the recommendations of my physician at Johns Hopkins and Fairfax Hospital. The sundry mammograms and blood tests, required by all cancer patients, are prone to generate an inordinate amount of anxiety and fear, before, during, and after the tests—which, in my case, were somewhat mitigated by writing this book.

Cancer drastically changed my life, and I had to delve deep within my soul to reach for the focus for a new life. Before, I was very active in work and kept a healthy balance between family life and relationships with my extended family and friends, but now, I was struggling to maintain these relationships. Hopefully, in the future, researchers can find ways that target only the cancer cells, but the current treatments and medication on cancer target healthy cells along with the cancer cells, and as a result, the oral medicine chemo Arimidex caused me to gain weight and left me afflicted with joint aches and sluggishness. My regular daily 1,200-calorie diet could no longer suit the changes of my body, and consequently, I became weak while also gaining weight. Most of my family members and friends could not comprehend or accept that I was not like before and I could not have my life as I used to. I therefore sometimes had to lecture them on the side effects of my cancer medication with the hope that they would understand my new situation. But they did not wish to hear about my cancer at all, and I had to struggle to keep up with understanding their expectations.

To continue the healing, I desperately needed to have a comprehensive and holistic plan to pull through and pass over this rough and jolting road. I have tried to keep myself well-informed on the latest studies in the physical and mental aspects of the healing process in order to design a plan for myself, as each individual's need is different. A prevalent theory states that the body's immune system consists of many types of cells carried by the blood to different parts of the body to keep cancer cells in check. If this theory is correct, then boosting one's immune system will help reduce the risk of cancer and perhaps cancer recurrence.[1] I therefore followed the theory to devise methods and means to boost my immune system. Cognizant of the fact that both physical and mental health were very important, I tried to write a plan for my exercise. I went through the list of all the physical injuries I had sustained in my life and collected the promising exercises (stretches, etc.) the physical therapists had recommended, and I included them in my plan of care. I then proceeded to start my daily life first by doing these exercises. For food and nutrition, I attended several workshops given as part of the comprehensive programs of the "Life with Cancer" offered by the Fairfax Hospital, read many insightful books, and met the dietician of the hospital for advice, and finally created a plan for healthy eating and having a reasonably active lifestyle. I learned that certain foods are good for fighting all types of cancers. These include whole grain cereals, beans, green tea, vegetables, fruits, nuts, and seeds. There are also several foods that should be avoided as much as possible, including all processed foods, refined carbohydrates, sugar, alcohol, red meats, and fried food. In my weekly programs, I have tried to include more of the recommended foods since some of their ingredients can activate the genes that protect us from cancer and turn off the genes that can promote the development of cancer. It seems likely that many of the plant foods that we eat are more important than the supplements we take, and the ongoing research is promising for the prevention of cancer in future.

Another factor that boosts our immune system is our efforts to bring about emotional healing. Again, fortunately, my education helped me in reducing emotional stress and avoiding a prolonged depression and anxiety, by staying emotionally connected both spiritually and socially I was better able to heal myself.

The United States Life Tables of 2005 indicate that for women, "the overall expectation of life at birth was 77.4 years."[2] With my intensive efforts, it looks like I will be meeting the overall average life expectancy, especially since my oncologist stopped my oral chemo medicine from Christmas 2009, and I officially became a cancer survivor. On that day, I was elated because I had finally conquered cancer and the bumpy road to healing because of, among other factors, the information and education I received through several health organizations and foundations. Education had come to my rescue yet again! Additionally, having special cancer insurance helped me financially afford all the costly recommendations for radiation and oral chemo for my cancer treatment. Based on my personal experience, it was prudent that as a middle-class American family we chose health insurance coverage carefully and, when feasible, obtained additional insurance to supplement the regular health insurance. With lucky foresight into the inevitable vagaries of ageing process, during my service with the State of Virginia, I had bought additional cancer, intensive care, and long-term care insurance to complement my regular health insurance should such needs arise. So far, the first two additional insurance supplements have helped me in the process of healing and gradually becoming a cancer survivor. I was pleased when my two surgeons released me, one after the other, to my oncologist and to my regular physician in 2007 and 2008 for follow-up only. Admittedly, the anxiety of the return of my two cancers has never left me. Their insidious gnawing at my tranquility, peace of mind, and happiness probably will remain for the rest of my life. However, the angst was mitigated by receiving the good news and invitation to attend the wonderful wedding of Anna, daughter of our old friends Christine and David Linton, which was to be held on the campus of the University of Oxford.

It was in the spring of 2006 that Sa'id and I received the beautiful invitation card for the wedding of Anna and Ben. At first, we were both happy and excited that together, we would be able to be a part of the wedding. We both love Anna like our daughter, Gita. Both were born on International Women's Day, March 8, but have a ten-year age difference. After a few days, Sa'id decided against travelling overseas because of his chronic back problems. However, he insisted that I attend the wedding on his behalf as well. He thought that, like his last trip to Europe, his back problems might recur during the wedding ceremony.

I arrived on July 27, a few days before the wedding. David was kind enough to meet me at Heathrow Airport and took me directly to Oxford and St. John's College, where they had made reserved bookings for the wedding guests near where the ceremony will be held. My suite was in a building for the handicapped graduate students, which, in summer, was available for those attending functions. It was very comfortable and near to all the wedding activities. On Saturday, July 29, at 1:30 p.m., Christine kindly collected me to join her in the car assigned for the mother of the bride. Then at 2:30 p.m., Anna Linton and Benjamin Noel Earle were married at Exeter College Chapel. It was a very interesting ceremony, following the tradition of the Anglican Church, which Anna belonged to. Afterward, there was the cake-cutting ceremony at St. Giles House, and we were served tea and wedding cake and then had our pictures taken in the beautiful gardens of the college. In the evening, there was a drinks reception at St. John's College followed by the dinner reception which was held again at St. John's College Hall. This is where the bride and groom had met for the first time while they were students, and now, after receiving their PhD degrees, they were celebrating their wedding along with their friends and relatives. What a beautiful and romantic location and ceremony! It is remarkable that Oxford offers this unique opportunity to its graduates to hold their wedding ceremony on the university campus during the summer holidays and use its housing for guest accommodations. I genuinely wish that other universities like my alma mater, Heidelberg, would follow this policy, which is both beneficial to the university for utilizing the vacant facilities (locations and dorms) and to the graduates, who, most likely, would enjoy their memorable wedding ceremony.

The author attending the wedding of Anna Linton and Benjamin Noel Earle at Oxford University.

While I was in Oxford, I met my dear friend Soheila and cousin Venus who were kind enough to come to Oxford to see me. After the wedding, I went to London with David and Christine where we stayed for a few days. Together, we also saw a Persian play in Hammersmith theater. I was scheduled to leave on August 11, which turned out to be the day of the bottle bomb scare!

The author meeting with her friend Soheila and Nazi in the beautiful gardens of David and Christine Linton in London.

In the morning of August 11, I was packing and getting ready to go to the airport. David suddenly called me from the breakfast table downstairs and said, "Simin, I am afraid you might not be able to fly today because Heathrow Airport had a terrorist bomb attempt and many flights are cancelled." I was so shocked from the news that, at first, I could not understand and believe his statement, and after he repeated, I rushed downstairs to the television for the breaking news. The news was real, and I also began to worry about my dear Christine and David who were planning to take me to the airport. The news indicated only a delay without mentioning a time we had to be at the airport. Usually, the travel time to the airport from South East of London takes almost two hours. We were anxious, on the road to the airport, we kept listening on the radio to find out more about the terrorist attack. We also heard that all the European flights were cancelled, but my United flight to the United States was still going ahead. Once there, I noticed that the most organized airport in the world had become chaotic. Every few minutes, there was a new announcement through the loudspeakers for the passengers. For the first time, they announced that nobody should hand-carry luggage to the plane. When I asked what I should do with my prescription drugs, they gave me a plastic bag to put them in. Also, the passengers were forbidden to take any liquid onto the plane, including any gels or lotions. Therefore, passengers had to check in their hand luggage and even their computers. Practically, everyone had only one plastic bag to carry the very essential items such as prescription drugs and passport or a small valise. Because nobody knew what was going on, the anxiety and fear was quite noticeable on people's faces, from the officers to the passengers. On the airport arrival/departure boards, most of the flights were cancelled, except for the transatlantic flights including my own to Washington Dulles Airport with an unknown departure time. I thanked David and Christine, said good-bye, and proceeded to passport control and security booth to wait for the announcement of the time of the flight for boarding. By this time, we already had a three-hour delay, but still nobody knew how many more hours we had to wait. An officer told the passengers that we had to sit and wait for the announcement of the flight departure time, which might be possibly more than ten hours. After having some drinks and snacks, while some passengers were still trying hard to call hotels near the airport without any success, after about fourteen hours of waiting, we heard some flight numbers were getting ready for boarding. When I heard about my own flight, I was happy that I finally could go home, all this while we still did not know what was going on. Over the next days, it became clear that on a transatlantic aircraft, there was a terrorist plot to detonate liquid explosives carried on board of at least ten planes travelling from the United Kingdom to the United States and Canada. Fortunately, the plot was discovered by the police in time and was foiled before it could be carried out, and as a result, unprecedented security measures, which I experienced, were immediately put in place at the airport. Since then nobody is allowed to carry any liquids to the plane. Once home, I was very happy and relieved after so many hours of delay and in a state of anxiety and fear. It dawned on me that from then on, air travel would become more and more difficult and tiresome, especially for older people.

More recently, events that have attracted my attention the most were those happening, for the first time, to the people of my two countries, America and Iran. These events were promising and exciting; they covered many surprises while ushering inspiration and hope for many around the globe. For the first time, in American history, a former first lady, Senator Hillary Clinton, became a presidential front runner of the Democratic Party. Also, for the first time in the history of America an African-American with a multicultural, multireligious background, and an exceptional orator, Senator Barrack Obama became another front runner of the Democratic Party, who, eventually defeated Senator Clinton and became the party candidate for the US presidency. The excitement of the election time increased when the nominee of the Republican Party, Senator John McCain, selected the governor of Alaska, Sarah Palin, as his running mate. This was the second time that a woman had become the nominee for the office of US vice president. In this exciting election, information technology and fund-raising via the Internet played an important role for the first time in the history of US elections. As a result, Obama, during the September of 2008 alone, raised a stunning 150 million dollars, 75 percent of which was raised through the Internet. However, another event that turned out to be quite discouraging suddenly shattered the lives of millions of people on a global scale. This was the economic news that Lehman Brothers, a major international investment bank, declared bankruptcy on September 15. This was followed by the Dow Jones dropping by five hundred points, and further downslides during the next few days. The news was shocking and disheartening to most people since their investments, retirement accounts, mortgages, and loans were directly and adversely affected, and a severe recession undermined their job security. The largest bailout in the US history was created in order to prevent another Great Depression. This economic crisis added to the excitement of the election, and with skillful speeches, Obama inspired and motivated the people to participate in the political process and the election. Finally, with slogans such as "Change" and "Yes We Can," Barack Hussein Obama was elected president of the United States, in the hope of bringing America out of economic recession and with the promise of a better life. This was the most exciting election I had experienced in my life; it showed that the education of the candidate played an important role. Obama was triumphant even with his limited executive experience. Finally, on November 4, 2008, change came to the country as Barack Obama, with a landslide victory over the Republican Candidate John McCain, became the first African American president in the US history.

Obama's administration immediately set out to tackle the recession aggressively to prevent an economic depression. The road to economic recovery has not been unlike my cancer treatment—bumpy and still continuing, in the hope that the devastation of the middle-class American families will slowly subside. So far, the most important change has been the Bill of Health Care Act, which promises, for the first time, that almost all Americans will have health care insurance coverage. Late Sunday, on March 21 in 2010, while we were customarily celebrating the Persian New Year (Nowruz) in our home, with our friends and families, the US House of Representatives, after almost a century of trying and a year of debate, finally passed the bill of the Patient Protection and Affordable Care Act amid cheers, thunderous applause, and standing ovations. On March 23, 2010, President Obama signed the measure, the Patient Protection and Affordable Care Act, during a festive and, at times, raucous ceremony in the East Room of the White House. He stated publicly at the signing that "the bill I'm signing will set in motion reforms that generations of Americans have fought for and marched for and hungered to see." This ceremony was held in the presence of nearly three hundred during which signature pens were passed as mementos to the lawmakers, aides, and a handful of others, including *Victoria_Reggie Kennedy*, the widow of the late Senator *Edward M. Kennedy*, who had made passing the health legislation his lifelong work. I, as an Iranian American, considered this bill a best Aidee (gift) for the people of America, if it passes the treacherous implementation process successfully.

During the Nowruz 2010 celebration, President Obama also sent, for the second year in a row, the following promising and public message to the Iranian people and the leader of Iran with the hope of opening a dialogue between Iran and the United States:

> Today, I want to extend my best wishes to all who are celebrating Nowruz in the United States and around the world. On this New Year's celebration, friends and family have a unique opportunity to reflect on the year gone by; to celebrate their time together; and to share in their hopes for the future.

> One year ago, I chose this occasion to speak directly to the people and leaders of the Islamic Republic of Iran, and to offer a new chapter of engagement on the basis of mutual interests and mutual respect. I did so with no illusions. For three decades, the United States and Iran have been alienated from one another. Iran's leaders have sought their own legitimacy through hostility to America. And we continue to have serious differences on many issues.

I said, last year, that the choice for a better future was in the hands of Iran's leaders. That remains true today. Together with the international community, the United States acknowledges your right to peaceful nuclear energy—we insist only that you adhere to the same responsibilities that apply to other nations. We are familiar with your grievances from the past—we have our own grievances as well, but we are prepared to move forward. We know what you're against; now tell us what you're for.

For reasons known only to them, the leaders of Iran have shown themselves unable to answer that question. You have refused good faith proposals from the international community. They have turned their backs on a pathway that would bring more opportunity to all Iranians, and allow a great civilization to take its rightful place in the community of nations. Faced with an extended hand, Iran's leaders have shown only a clenched fist.

Last June, the world watched with admiration, as Iranians sought to exercise their universal right to be heard. But tragically, the aspirations of the Iranian people were also met with a clenched fist, as people marching silently were beaten with batons; political prisoners were rounded up and abused; absurd and false accusations were leveled against the United States and the West; and people everywhere were horrified by the video of a young woman killed in the street.

The United States does not meddle in Iran's internal affairs. Our commitment—our responsibility—is to stand up for those rights that should be universal to all human beings. That includes the right to speak freely, to assemble without fear; the right to the equal administration of justice, and to express your views without facing retribution against you or your families.

I want the Iranian people to know what my country stands for. The United States believes in the dignity of every human being, and an international order that bends the arc of history in the direction of justice—a future where Iranians can exercise their rights, to participate fully in the global economy, and enrich the world through educational and cultural exchanges beyond Iran's borders. That is the future that we seek. That is what America is for.

That is why, even as we continue to have differences with the Iranian government, we will sustain our commitment to a more hopeful future for the Iranian people. For instance, by increasing opportunities for educational exchanges so that Iranian students can come to our colleges and universities and to our efforts to ensure that Iranians can have access to the software and Internet technology that will enable them to communicate with each other, and with the world without fear of censorship.

Finally, let me be clear: we are working with the international community to hold the Iranian government accountable because they refuse to live up to their international obligations. But our offer of comprehensive diplomatic contacts and dialogue stands. Indeed, over the course of the last year, it is the Iranian government that has chosen to isolate itself, and to choose a self-defeating focus on the past over a commitment to build a better future.

Last year, I quoted the words of the poet Saadi, who said: "The children of Adam are limbs to each other, having been created of one essence." I still believe that—I believe it with every fiber of my being. And even as we have differences, the Iranian government continues to have the choice to pursue a better future, and to meet its international responsibilities, while respecting the dignity and fundamental human rights of its own people.

Thank you, and Eid-e-Shoma Mobarak.

Prior to this message, for more than thirty years (from the Carter administration years through those of Reagan, Clinton, the Bushes and

Obama), Iran has been under intense scrutiny from the international community over its nuclear program. While Iran's intentions are unclear, its failure to declare all nuclear facilities and materials in a timely fashion has led to increased concerns that Iran intends to develop nuclear weapons. During each administration, especially Clinton's and Khatami's, with the latter's motto of "Dialogue Among Civilizations," there were several attempts made from United States and Iran for diplomatic talks between the two nations, but due to lack of mutual understanding of the cultural and language nuances, it was not successful. Besides, for the most part, the people of Iran were kept in a state of anxiety and fear of an imminent military attack by the United States or Israel on their nuclear facilities.

While political observers speculate about the risks of Iran developing nuclear weapons and the possibility of a US military attack on Iran, adequate attention has not been given to the actual situation of the ordinary Iranian citizens. Iranians live under very harsh and significant oppression by their government, including restrictions on their freedom of expression and repeated suppression of other basic democratic rights. Fortunately, we see clearly in the above-stated message of the US president to the Iranian government and the Iranian people a clear reference to their human rights and plight of the continuous severe repression by the government in Iran. From the inception of the dark revolution of 1979, most people of Iran from different walks of life and political persuasions gradually came to realize that the new regime of the Islamic Republic of Iran is neither Islamic, nor a republic, and definitely not Iranian. Khomeini himself was against any national identity. As a result, during the last thirty years, many ordinary people of Iran, even some of the ayatollahs, have parted company with the regime and its preapproved six presidents. The division between the Iranian regime and the people of Iran is underlined when the president of the United States and the heads of the Western countries routinely separate the people of Iran from their regime.

The palpable chasm between the people and the government, and their dismay with the regime played a pivotal role in Iran's last presidential election. Briefly after Khatami, the reformist president, stepped down on August 2, 2005, the next election led to the victory of the hard-liner mayor of Tehran, Mahmoud Ahmadinejad, in the second round of the presidential election even though he badly trailed his main opponent Ali Akbar Rafsanjani, a former president, in the first round. His victory in the second round was mainly due to his stated populist sentiments toward the poor and the active participation of the loyal supporters of the conservative Supreme Leader Khamenei. The losing candidates made a formal protest to the Guardian Council to claim irregularities at the polls, but the charges were dismissed without any investigations or comments. In addition to winning this election in a fog of doubt and irregularity, Ahmadinejad's performance and radical statements, such as his desire to "wipe out Israel from the map," or tangling religious beliefs with nuclear issues shifted and hardened Iran's foreign policy from reconciliation to confrontation with the international community, especially in connection with her nuclear enrichment program.

The confrontational policies of Ahmadinejad gradually increased the distance already separating the people and the government, as well as the distance between Iran and the Western countries. Inside Iran, because of incessant repression and oppression by the regime, several underground resistance movement groups were established and became active among workers, women, students, teachers, writers, ethnic and religious groups. This occured despite the draconian measures taken by the regime. These disparate groups, united by a set of common goals, have been waiting for the right opportunity to come out from underground and join together to fight for the freedom and democracy in Iran. Alas, their road ahead, like my own cancer treatment, is a bumpy one. However, there are hopeful signs along the road. One can notice that Iranian society, in general, and especially the younger generation, is undergoing major changes, mostly due to the progress in technology, which makes global information and communication almost instantly available, despite the suppression of the Iranian regime. The younger generation now wishes a gradual change to a civil society.[3]

In the last thirty year, I have been diligently following news from my native country, Iran, and especially its relationship with the West and the United States on a daily basis in the hope of finding a change for the better and a return to times bygone. Regarding Iran's relations with the West, Ahmadinejad rejects the stated position of his predecessor, President Khatami, who espoused nonconfrontational "Dialogue of Civilizations." He believes that there are no civilizations outside the purview of Islam, and instead, he speaks about the "Clash of Civilizations," both inside of Iran and in the world at large, and his ultimate dream is "to abolish the system of Capitalism." He also does not want Iran to become a member of the World Trade Organization, which he described as a club of global thieves.[4] With these extreme positions, it is no wonder that Ahmadinejad did not respond positively to Xavier Solana, the European Union Foreign Policy chief, who, after several meetings with the Iranian nuclear representative over the course of several years, came up with a package of eight incentives to open the door to a "new era of collaboration between Iran and the rest of the world, or to Obama's Nowruz [Persian New Year] message about opening a dialogue."[5]

In the course of the last presidential election in Iran, the people and the opposition groups, struggling for freedom inside the country, and the millions of Iranians in exile, through the marvel of various media, became better connected and were awaiting an opportunity to show their power and resolve to the repressive Islamic regime, and free the people through a regime change. However, the military-backed regime of Ahmadinejad was very careful not to give any opportunity to the opposition by having the highest number of the executions of the opposition per population in the world. In 2009, for the tenth presidential election, the people were given only a few days to declare their candidacy for the election.

On 20 May 2009, the Guardian Council officially rejected a large number of the registered nominees and approved only four candidates out of 476: Mir-Hossein Mousavi, the last prime minister of Iran; and Mehdi Karroubi, former speaker of the Majles, as the Reformist candidates; and Mahmoud Ahmadinejad, the incumbent; and Mohsen Rezaee, former commander of the Iranian Revolutionary Guard, as the Conservative candidates. After a few days of limited debates, Iran's tenth presidential election was held on June 12, 2009, with the incumbent, Ahmadinejad, running against his three challengers. Although all the votes were to be counted by hand and not electronically, the following morning, the Islamic Republic News Agency already announced that Ahmadinejad had won the election with 62 percent of the votes cast against the 34 percent cast for Mir-Hossein Mousavi. This quick announcement of the results shocked and surprised the people of Iran and the world. The people of Iran, the European Union, the United Kingdom, the United States, and most of the Western countries expressed concern over the irregularities during the voting process. Several analysts and journalists from the United States, Europe and other Western-based media voiced doubts about the veracity of the results. Several countries, Russia and

China among them, congratulated Ahmadinejad on his victory, while the people of Iran, who were hoping to express their opposition against the regime by casting their votes for the Reformists to bring about a political change, looked dumbfounded, especially when Mousavi issued the statement that "I'm warning that I won't surrender to this charade," and also added that 14 million unused ballots were missing. He urged his supporters and the people to fight the decision without committing any act of violence and displaying a green symbol. He also presented an official appeal to the Guardian Council. Although this time the Guardian Council ordered an investigation and a partial recounting, this formality did not change the results of the irregular election. Next, the people who were waiting for the opportunity to express their anger and frustration rushed into the streets, fighting for their votes, with the slogan Where Is My Vote?

Green was Mousavi's chosen color because he is a descendant of the Prophet Mohammad. However, gradually, even the people who did not agree with his ideology but were against the regime used the color green as a symbol of unity and hope for the future and for the change of regime. During this time, the world was witnessing the demonstrations of the people similar to the 1979 revolution that I had lived through in Iran, with the difference that this time I was experiencing it after thirty years and in America. I was living through this Green Movement in Fairfax, Virginia, in the spirit of a second revolution. However, this time, it looked more original and came out from deep inside of the people of Iran.

During the past thirty years, I have been in constant contact with many of my friends, relatives, colleagues, and former students from the National University of Iran and Shemiran College. Every day, I receive several e-mails and news items about Iran and its theocratic regime denying basic rights to its people. However, during that election, the news and my e-mails tripled, indicating a genuine revolutionary movement and striving for freedom and human rights. A blogger from Tehran on June 19, 2009, sums up very beautifully how the young generation, especially women, prodded by years of repression, discrimination, and oppression were thinking:

Tomorrow is a big day, maybe I'll get killed tomorrow!

I will participate in the demonstrations tomorrow. Maybe they will turn violent. Maybe I will be one of the people who are going to get killed. I'm listening to all my favorite music. I even want to dance to a few songs. I always wanted to have very narrow eyebrows. Yes, maybe I will go to the salon before I go tomorrow!

There are a few great movie scenes that I also have to see. I should drop by the library, too. It's worth to read the poems of Forough and Shamloo again. All family pictures have to be reviewed, too. I have to call my friends as well to say goodbye. All I have are two bookshelves which I told my family who should receive them.

I'm two units away from getting my bachelor's degree but who cares about that. My mind is very chaotic.

I wrote these random sentences for the next generation so they know we were not just emotional and under peer pressure. So they know that we did everything we could to create a better future for them. So they know that our ancestors surrendered to Arabs and Mongols but did not surrender to despotism. This note is dedicated to tomorrow's children.[6]

The next day, on June 20, 2009, several young people with similar ideology and belief were killed during peaceful demonstrations. One of the victims who was killed by a security officer drew great international attention. She was Neda Agha-Soltan, and her death was captured on video by a bystander and was broadcasted over the Internet, media, and news and was widely seen around the world. She became a rallying point for the Reformists and the Opposition. Her name, Neda, which means "voice" in Farsi, became synonymous with the "Voice of Iran" and the voice of people against the fraudulent election of Ahmadinejad and the Iranian regime. So in this way, the name Neda and the color green both became a unifying symbol of the change of regime. Hundreds more people may have died in Iran's post-election unrest than the authorities have admitted, amid allegations that the death toll has been obscured by hiding victims' bodies in secret morgues.

The investigation of the Guardian Council ended with partial recounting and Iran's Supreme Leader Khameini threw his support behind Ahmadinejad, and while raging protests were being held in front of the Parliament, his inauguration was held on 5 August 2009 in Tehran. However, despite the violent repression by the authorities, opponents of the regime are continuing their opposition through the Iranians in exile, and the international media make them noticed on the web and through campaigns for more freedom. Global protests and demonstrations in more than one hundred cities around the world called for the release of the thousands of people detained during the post-election unrest. Many groups, including the Human Rights Watch and Amnesty International, were backing a global day of action and supporting protests.

Photo taken at a Green Movement peace rally held in Washington DC. The rallies were held in Tehran and around the world to promote free elections. Protestors carried flags and pictures, including a picture of Neda who was killed in one of the demonstrations held in Tehran.

In the past few weeks, after the diplomatic attempts of President Obama proved unsuccessful, the UN Security Council for the fourth time imposed tougher sanctions in an attempt to force Iran to comply with the international demand over its nuclear programs. (Resolution 1929, June 9, 2010)

At this moment in time, the Green Movement is showing promise, and I am certain that with the world's support, the Iranian young generation, especially the women, who have suffered the most during the last thirty years, will be successful in bringing about the needed change and reform for a modern, democratic, and free Iran.

I end my book with a sincere hope that the industrialized countries, in their globalization quest, would think not only of their own economic advantages and gains, but temper their decisions with consideration for the rights of the ordinary citizens of the world and humanity at large, especially those living in countries in the Middle East and Africa, whose lands are rich in natural resources, but whose countries are not fully developed yet. I pray and hope that they always remember the poem displayed in the United Nations building by the great Persian poet Saadi:

> The children of Adam are the limbs of one body
> That share an origin in their creation
> When one limb passes its days in pain
> The other limbs cannot remain easy
> You who feel no pain at the suffering of others
> It is not fitting for you to be called human

With Human Rights of ordinary people protected, according to the American Pledge of Allegiance, "with liberty and justice for all," there will be no more need for violence and the never-ending wars on terror, and the people and countries of the world will be able to live together in peace and harmony. Humanity's grand symphony of life will then profusely blossom magically and melodiously, and this will compliment my very own symphony of life.

[1.] Julie K. Silver, After Cancer Treatment, The Johns Hopkins University Press, Baltimore, 2006, P.15.

[2.] United States Life Tables, 2005, National Vital Statistics Report, Volume 58, Number 10, March 2120. U.S. Department of Health and Human Services, CDC by Elizabeth Arias Ph. D; Brian l.Rostron, Ph.D.,and Betzaid Tejada-Vera, B.S.; Division of Statistics.

3. Azadeh Mooaveni, Lipstick Jihad, Public Affair, 2006, and Honeymoon in Tehran, Random House 2009.

4. Amir Taheri, The Persian Night, Encounter Books, 2008, p.291.

5. Sir Eldon Griffiths, Turbulent Iran: Recollections, Revelations and a Plan for Peace, Santa Anna, CA, Seven Locks Press, 2006, pp.236-7.

6. Payvand Iran News. From a blogger inside of Iran.

INDEX

I

J

K

Edwards Brothers Malloy
Thorofare, NJ USA
August 21, 2013